D0142160

HANDBOOK OF MEDICAL SOCIOLOGY

FOURTH EDITION

EDITED BY

Howard E. Freeman
University of California, Los Angeles

Sol Levine
Boston University
and
Henry J. Kaiser Family Foundation

PRENTICE HALL   *Englewood Cliffs, New Jersey 07632*

Library of Congress Cataloging-in-Publication Data

Handbook of medical sociology.
  Includes bibliographies and indexes.
  1. Social medicine.   I. Freeman, Howard E.
II. Levine, Sol, 1922– . [DNLM: 1. Social Medicine.
2. Sociology, Medical. WA 31 H236]
RA418.H29   1989   362.1   88–30744
ISBN 0–13–380305–8

Editorial/production supervision: Roseann McGrath Brooks
Cover design: Ben Santora
Manufacturing buyer: Peter Havens

Printed in the United States of America
10 9 8 7 6 5 4 3 2 1

ISBN 0-13-380305-8

Prentice-Hall International (UK) Limited, *London*
Prentice-Hall of Australia Pty. Limited, *Sydney*
Prentice-Hall Canada Inc., *Toronto*
Prentice-Hall Hispanoamericana, S.A., *Mexico*
Prentice-Hall of India Private Limited, *New Delhi*
Prentice-Hall of Japan, Inc., *Tokyo*
Simon & Schuster Asia Pte. Ltd., *Singapore*
Editora Prentice-Hall do Brasil, Ltda., *Rio de Janeiro*

Editing this fourth edition of the *Handbook*
has intensified our feelings of loss over the untimely death
of Leo G. Reeder;
we very much miss Leo's intellectual collaboration
and the fun of being with him.
It is only fitting that we dedicate this edition to
our longtime friend and colleague.

CONTENTS

PART **III**
THE ORGANIZATION OF HEALTH SERVICES

PART IV
USE OF HEALTH SERVICES

PART V
HEALTH CARE PROVIDERS

FOREWORD

Remembering painful experiences can be excruciating. The nervous system seems to become hyperalert. The immediate environment, sounds, smells, and sights are recalled with jarring suddenness that catches the breath and threatens to stop the heart. So it is with September 25, 1978. I remember so well dismissing my 9:00 class for their break, going to the secretary's office, and hearing a student say, "Did you hear about that plane crash in San Diego? It just happened." The icy fear that gripped me was like a sudden, physical blow. It was not until evening of that terrible day that we finally had confirmation of Leo's death.

"We are sorry to have to tell you that Leo G. Reeder was listed as a passenger on Flight 182 and there are no survivors."

Leo would have been the first to admonish us to get on with our work and his and not let what might have been impede our living life to the fullest, especially in the professional sphere. Indeed, enthusiasm was his hallmark. Not far behind was perseverance in the pursuit of cherished goals.

He graduated from the University of Chicago with a hard-won Ph.D., and his dedication to health-related matters in society soon became apparent. He is remembered as a pioneer in social epidemiology and the then-budding area of medical sociology. He was also the first sociologist to be interested in the epidemiology of coronary heart disease. He was an inspiration and role model to his many students and friends in these and other areas.

It was out of these professional concerns that he joined with his longtime friends and colleagues, Howard Freeman and Sol Levine, to produce the first edition of *Handbook of Medical Sociology*. These pioneers foresaw the tremendous growth and change that were soon to affect health and health care in society. They understood the importance of analysis and projection of current thought about these trends for the future.

From the initial conception of the first edition of this book, one principle has remained paramount: The book should bring together in one volume recent research and thinking which reflect, from a sociological perspective, current issues in the health care arena. Historical linkages are also traced so that the reader is made aware of the evolution of the major forces that have shaped perceptions and behavior in health, illness, health care utilization, and delivery. This is not a simple task. As noted above, the variety and complexity of issues in this field have increased significantly in contemporary society. It is precisely these features that make such an undertaking difficult, albeit rewarding. Over time, the content of this book has been modified as new findings appear. The present reorganization of the *Handbook* has facilitated a broad overview approach to these issues, together with an in-depth treatment of salient subtopics.

The editors have brought together contributors of international reputation from disciplines that are actively involved in the issues under discussion. The contributors' cogent descriptions and analyses of current conditions, together with their educated projections for the future, give much pause for thought. That responses to health and illness not only are personal but also are embedded deep within a sociopolitical context is underscored even more so in this edition than in previous editions.

This book is not meant to be an encyclopedic record of "What's What in Health Care Today." Rather, researchers and practitioners in the field have attempted to extract salient themes that are relevant to current medical sociological discourse and to examine them for the impact on individuals and society. In so doing, these authors have made this edition a valuable resource for students and professionals alike.

A good nursing colleague and mentor of mine, Rheba de Tornyay, distinguishes between "solid citizens" and "stars" in the professional world. It would be hard to put Leo G. Reeder in one or another of these categories, since both titles seem apt. So it is with this edition. He was looking forward to the *Handbook*'s revision and was cajoling his colleagues to revise. His persistence to take on a difficult task because he believed it needed to be done was often a motivating force for other busy professionals and friends.

I think he would have liked this edition: it is both stellar and solid, as he was. I am happy to have had the chance to remember him again through the continuation of his work.

Sharon J. Reeder, Ph.D., F.A.A.N.
School of Nursing
UCLA

CHAPTER

1

THE PRESENT STATUS
OF MEDICAL SOCIOLOGY

HOWARD E. FREEMAN
SOL LEVINE

When the first edition of this *Handbook* was published in 1963, the persistent theme of our contributors was the *potential* of the sociological enterprise for understanding the etiology, diagnosis, and treatment of diseases; the ways health care is provided and funded; the societal and communal commitments to the support of health activities; and, indeed, the very definitions of health and illness. By the time the second edition appeared in 1972 and, certainly by 1979, when the third edition was published, the promise of medical sociology was replaced by hard evidence as to its utility.

The remarkable growth of medical sociology can be explained by the commonplace observation that all scientific and intellectual endeavors are inherently linked to the social, ideological, and moral concerns of the times in which they take place, as well as to the social, structural, and technological developments that are transpiring during a particular period. In the quarter of a century since the first edition appeared, there have been truly important, far-reaching, and irreversible changes in all aspects of health care. The changes have dramatically increased the necessity of studying the sociological dimensions of the health sciences and medical care activities.

The list is long. Some of the most prominent developments are:

- an increased commitment to providing appropriate care to community members that has challenged conventional organizational arrangements for delivering health services and traditional ideas about individual and communal financial responsibilities for providing care;

- a changed demographic profile that has strained economic resources and directed increased attention to the ethical and value issues that surround the prolongation and termination of life;

1

- the rapid adoption of complex and costly technological innovations that have required calibrating the "benefits to costs" of providing care and the introduction of "quality of life" measures rather than simply biological survival in order to judge the value of health interventions;

- continually increasing specialization among practitioners, which has been accompanied by marked changes in the character of provider-patient relations, medical educational programs, and the definitions of appropriate roles of health practitioners; and

- spiraling costs of health services that have resulted in strenuous efforts at cost containment, major modifications in the ways health services are delivered and funded, and particularly the growth of pre-paid health care and the invasion of the health sector by for-profit organizations.

Each of these and other major changes in the health field raise issues that are distinctly sociological in their character. Some are concerns that have been present for a long period; others are more contemporary. But it is no wonder that this *Handbook* is markedly different in scope, content, and tone than its three previous editions!

THE CURRENT POSTURE
OF MEDICAL SOCIOLOGY

Medical sociology, as a specialty within the sociological discipline, began in the post–World War II period. To a large extent its initial growth was part of the burgeoning interest in graduate education in all of the social sciences and the efforts within the federal government to support social research in the health sector. Indeed, in many ways, support for social research in health, and for medical sociology in particular, was a means of providing training and research funds for the vitalization of the broader discipline of sociology.

It is incorrect, of course, to promote the image that the history of medical sociology began in the 1950s or is solely a U.S. phenomenon. Interest in the social aspects of

health had been present since the 18th century in a variety of disciplines and in a number of countries. Social medicine, social hygiene, and public health developed most notably in France, Germany, and the United Kingdom. Claus (1983) and Bloom (1986) remind us of the contributions of such figures as Rudolph Virchow, Solomon Naumann, Henry E. Sigerist, and Bernhard H. Stern. Nonetheless, social science in medicine, at least in the United States, is a relatively contemporary innovation.

THE GROWTH OF MEDICAL
SOCIOLOGY

In the immediate post–World War II period medical sociology displayed an apologetic tone. Within the discipline of sociology, it had to overcome the disdain and suspicion of colleagues who felt that it was solely an "applied" activity and lacked theoretical substance. Within medicine, then dominated by physicians for the most part unfamiliar with the knowledge base of sociology and conservative in professional and ideological outlook, there was limited appreciation of the potential contributions of medical sociology and some concern that it would "radicalize" health care.

Of course, from the start medical sociology had its supporters in both camps. The strong growth of medical sociology in the 1950s can be traced to the enthusiasm and farsightedness of a few sociologists who were intent on modernizing sociology. It can also be traced to restless innovators and change agents within medicine who saw the need for a strong social science input into basic medical research, patient care activities, public health, and psychiatry. Well-known sociologists who had made important contributions to the development of theory and research were able to provide support to the emerging specialty of medical sociology (e.g., Merton 1965; Parsons 1951). Established leaders in academic medicine, psychiatry, and public health (typically who had some experience collaborating with sociologists) were our advocates and opened seemingly tightly shut doors (e.g., Merton and Reader 1957; Hollingshead and Redlich 1958; Stanton and Schwartz 1954).

The history of the emergence of and legitimization of medical sociology is the subject of a recent monograph by Bloom (1986). A comprehensive review will not be attempted here; however, it is important to point out that not only were there key individuals whose contributions can be singled out but organizational efforts as well. In the 1950s, the Russell Sage Foundation, led by sociologist Donald Young, made a commitment to initiate and expand the role of the social sciences in professional education and chose health science schools as the first targets of opportunity. It devoted a significant proportion of its funds to the establishment of social science units within schools of medicine, public health, and nursing, almost all of which included sociologists.

At around the same time, the National Institute of Mental Health (NIMH) began social science training programs under the general rubric of psychiatric training programs (Freeman, Borgatta, and Siegel 1975). NIMH also began to support large-scale social research projects in sociology departments as well as in health science schools. This effort was fostered by the strategic presence within NIMH of a number of sociologists, including John Clausen and Melvin Kohn. NIMH's efforts stimulated interest in, and were the impetus for, the initiation of ambitious training and research grant programs by a number of National Institutes of Health.

These early scholarly and charismatic efforts of key individuals in sociology and medicine, together with the organizational innovations of government groups, produced a legacy that is still with us. Today, virtually every health science school in the United States and most of Western Europe includes a behavioral or social science unit, division, or department (almost always including sociologists).

Throughout this volume, the early contributions of medical sociologists are referenced, as are those of their medical colleagues who collaborated and utilized the results of social medical studies. Medical sociology rapidly shifted from being a field in which work was done by a few to a major specialty in the discipline. Medical sociologists who initially had difficulty finding positions in academic sociology departments and health science schools soon experienced surprising popularity. It became unnecessary to apologize for seeking and pursuing a career in medical sociology. Medical sociologists no longer were preoccupied with rationalizing and justifying their existence, both within sociology and within the health arena.

The growth of research, teaching, and consulting activities in the specialty is remarkable compared with the development of other areas of sociology, and the range and extent of research activities today is striking compared with the early 1950s. In a short review paper written three decades ago, Freeman and Reeder (1957) were able to examine and cite virtually every article on health written by one or more sociologists and published in sociology journals, as well as a fair sampling of similar papers that had appeared in medical journals. In contrast, it is clearly impossible today to encompass most of the relevant literature even in this relatively large volume.

Today sociologists are frequently found in administrative, consulting, and policy positions requiring knowledge of social surveys, organizational behavior, political dynamics, and social change. Further, as Freeman (1988) has noted, many graduates of schools of public health, schools of health services administration, and programs in management, public administration, and health policy are trained conceptually and methodologically in ways that are commonplace in sociology departments.

THE CHANGING SCOPE
OF MEDICAL SOCIOLOGY

In the 1950s and throughout the 1960s, the dominant activity of medical sociologists was to do research on and offer recommendations about how health providers could effectively alter patients' receptivity to advances in medical technology and therapeutic know-how. A major frustration for practitioners then (and now) was the failure of many persons in the community to take advantage of the presumed fruits of medical discoveries, technological developments, and the diagnostic and therapeutic knowledge gained from specialty education.

Failure of patients to seek out appropriate health care, to communicate fully and reliably symptoms and problems to their providers, to follow through on referrals, to comply with medical regimens, and to engage in appropriate preventive practices bewildered many practitioners and concerned those responsible for the medical education and postgraduate training of health providers. The saliency of this issue among health care providers was the basis for a wide range of studies by medical sociologists. Their findings often questioned assumptions made by physicians and other health providers about the motivations of patients, identified cultural and social structural impediments to effective use of the available technology of medicine and clinical acumen of physicians, and drew attention to the discrepancies between the interests of health care providers and the organizations with which they are associated and those of the patients they treat (Levine, Scotch, and Vlasak 1969).

During this period, an important teaching function of medical sociologists in health science schools was to sensitize physicians and other health professionals to features of their social and cultural backgrounds, personal socialization experiences, and educational careers, as well as to social structural characteristics of their provider organizations, that could impede the successful transmission of their technologies (Zola 1983). Over time, medical sociologists subjected medicine and different aspects of the health system to increasingly critical scrutiny in this regard. They challenged the assumptions of the biomedical model, questioned the overuse of complex and expensive technology, criticized the asymmetrical features of the doctor-patient relationship, and emphasized the importance of interpersonal, social, and economic considerations in efforts at health promotion and the healing of the sick (Mishler et al. 1981).

Even more, sociologists were at the forefront in documenting that medical decisions "do not emanate from a routine, scientific calculus but are made by people playing social roles, guided by social values, and located in particular social settings or contexts" (Levine 1987, p. 3). The distance that medicine and medical sociology have traveled is evident now in the emergence of quality of life as an overriding social dimension of judging health and illness, as well as a major criterion to evaluate health care in general and technological interventions in particular.

The 1950s also saw literally a revolution in the care of the mentally ill. In part it was a response to the inhuman physical and interpersonal environments of mental hospitals, in part to the widespread adoption of drug therapies, and in part to the influence of psychodynamic thinking and the beginnings of the social and community psychiatry movements. Sociologists were key players in the spate of activities that occurred in the decade or so that followed. Field studies of mental hospitals (e.g., Stanton and Schwartz 1954), studies of patients' and hospital staffs' role behavior and perspectives (e.g., Goffman 1961), social epidemiological studies (e.g., Hollingshead and Redlich 1958) and follow-up surveys of discharged patients (e.g., Freeman and Simmons 1977) represented an important fund of information that fed into a growing body of knowledge about deviant behavior and organizational relations.

Today, interest in the consequences of mental illness treatment persists. The aftermath of social psychiatric research and social action efforts during the late 1950s and 1960s was a movement to deinstitutionalize just about everyone. The populations of mental hospitals and facilities for the retarded and developmentally disabled were sharply reduced.

At the same time, community treatment became the vogue. Sociologists turned their attention to the study of the programs, organization, politics, and efficacy of community mental health centers, as well as to the actions of their advocates and opponents. Such work, commonplace in the 1970s, is still popular. In part this is because the success and support for community programs have not eventuated as their advocates anticipated. Also, social and economic conditions at the national and local levels did not emerge along the lines that optimistic advocates of planned social change had envisioned. Thus, problems of the homeless, in particular, and of the chronically mentally ill, in general, are now widespread interests of sociologists in the mental health area. Indeed, in many ways the conceptual and methodological approaches used in contemporary studies resemble those of two decades ago.

The 1960s and the decade that followed marked a period of emphasis on governmental programs to improve the lot of the poor. Although health care was originally given low priority, the Great Society programs, and those that followed and preceded them, were pressed to include health components (Freeman, Kiecolt, and Allen 1982). As a result, major efforts were undertaken to improve access to care, including the establishment of neighborhood, later called community, health centers, and of reorganized delivery systems in hospitals. Programs were also implemented to modify the interpersonal relations of professionals and patients in order to increase utilization and compliance. There also were attempts to increase the supply and to modify the distribution of physicians and other providers in order to relieve the shortages in rural areas and in inner cities.

The concern with the poor entailed a concern with ethnic and racial equality. Thus, this was a period in which efforts were made to increase the number of minority health science students and providers. The rationale for this was not only based on concerns for equality but on the belief that persons of minority background would be more effective in dealing with patients of their own ethnic backgrounds. Interest in providing access to care, in creating new types of health care organizational arrangements, and in expanding minority medical education flowered in the 1970s and continued in the 1980s, in part spurred on by the activities of the Robert Wood Johnson Foundation (Aiken, Blendon, Rogers, and Freeman 1980). In particular, the movement toward health maintenance organizations (HMOs) bloomed, and as a result of their expanded role, increased access to health services and patient care became a major research concern.

The concern with the poor, the implementation of government- and foundation-supported social programs in general, and health initiatives in particular, were accompanied by a need for hard information on the extent to which the efforts were successfully implemented, effective in their outcomes, and efficient from a benefit-to-cost standpoint. Although the assessment of social change efforts and social experiments has a long history, it was the spate of activities in connection with programs to reduce poverty and discrimination and to promote more equal access to and use of health and social services that led to the emergence of a new methodological field, generally referred to as "social program evaluation" or "evaluation research" (Rossi and Freeman 1985).

Sociologists in the health arena and in other social program areas have been key players in the program evaluation area. Many of the major health care initiatives have been evaluated by teams led or assisted by sociologists. Moreover, the impetus to improve access to and increase use of health services by the poor and other deprived groups to a large extent required modifying organizational, political, and geographical arrangements for the delivery of health services. Not only has the social, structural, and organizational character of many initiatives provided fertile research opportunities for sociologists, but it has also frequently involved them in more active "firing line" roles.

Indeed, the effort to improve health care for the poor and the otherwise disfranchised is one of the impetuses for medical sociologists to move into policy research, policy development, macroplanning, and managerial activities. At the same time, it has encouraged health professional schools to integrate the concepts, frames of reference and applied research approaches of sociology into their educational programs.

The 1980s have witnessed a shift in interest, further testifying to the validity of our opening observation about the linkage between the social contexts and the content of scientific and intellectual work. As there has been a shift to a more conservative ideological posture, there has been a dramatic change in emphasis from initiatives related to increased access to health services and interventions directed at improved health status to a concern with the costs of medical care. But cost-containment efforts have their sociological dimensions as well. Key initiatives to decelerate the increase in cost of health services require organizational modifications, redirected professional educational efforts, different criteria for the selection of health care providers, and new strategies for dealing with the political consequences of economic containment decisions. Consequently, although the policy issues have changed and the research questions are different, there is no diminution in opportunities for medical sociologists to contribute to work in the health arena and to accrue knowledge of general sociological interest. This has indeed proved the case, as some of the more

recent references in this *Handbook* will show.

Emphasis on the cost of care has brought with it increased interest in the quality of medical care. Efforts at cost containment that limit in one way or another the medical services provided almost automatically provoke concern with their impact on patient outcomes and future well-being. Thus, contemporary topics of sociological interest include studies of the health consequences of patients' membership in different forms of medical care arrangements, from solo practice to for-profit HMOs.

Concern with health care and the outcome of medical care is further intensified by the demographic trajectory of the United States and of most of the industrial world. The increase in the numbers of "frail elderly," the high activity levels and productivity of persons who even two decades ago would have been regarded as "old," and the availability of new technologies to extend life are conspicuous features of contemporary community life. These developments raise a number of important sociological questions concerning, for example, the motivations, satisfaction, and modes of coping of older people; the social networks of older people; the providers who care for older people; and the responses of political, religious, and other types of organizations to the needs of the elderly.

Indeed, the demographic dynamics, the economic considerations, and the continual technical advancements in medicine compel sociological attention to the issue of quality of life. Simply prolonging life in a biological sense may in many cases have little consequence. The key issue, which is a sociological matter, is how decisions—on the use of technology, on the allocation of economic resources for health care, and on the ways services are delivered—affect the quality of life.

This broad-brush examination of the past, present, and future of research opportunities germane to the interests of medical sociologists would be incomplete without at least a mention of the sociological ramifications of the Acquired Immune Deficiency Syndrome (AIDS) epidemic. No other single health problem in this century is likely to have comparable consequences for our social structure, for interpersonal relations, and for health resource allocation. Every aspect of the AIDS phenomenon has sociological import, from its etiology (Kaplan et al. 1987) to provider behavior and patient care (Lewis and Freeman 1987)—indeed to the possible resort to authoritarian means to identify and contain AIDS cases, the advent of massive discrimination against homosexuals and persons with "pre-AIDS" symptoms and test results, and restricted access to care and third-party insurance of high risk groups.

THE PLACE OF MEDICAL SOCIOLOGY IN THE DISCIPLINE

Earlier, we alluded to the difficulties medical sociologists had in making their way into the discipline during the specialty's fledgling period. Back then, in an effort to codify the activities of medical sociologists and to legitimize at least some of their efforts, Straus (1957) wrote a seminal paper in which he distinguished the sociology *of* medicine from sociology *in* medicine. The *of* and *in* connotations became status markers. Those involved in the sociology *of* medicine, for example, sociologists studying medical institutions and health occupations and professions, were regarded as being engaged in "appropriate" sociological pursuits, ones consistent with the interests and missions of the discipline. Persons involved in sociology *in* medicine were regarded as drones, simply handmaidens (sometimes other terms were used) to doctors. Sociology-*in*-medicine lackeys were held to be doing nonintellectual and nontheoretical work, which, even if very useful to persons in the health arena, was not considered sociology!

But now the distinction between sociology *in* medicine and sociology *of* medicine has become so blurred that it is irrelevant. In part this is because sociology as a discipline has moved at least somewhat closer to the firing line, and "applied" work has many more advocates in the discipline (Freeman and Rossi 1984). Also, some of what was construed as sociology *in* medicine has advanced the sociology *of* medicine and the overall discipline of sociology. Indeed, it is no longer clear that "better" or more "sociologically important work" is being conducted in traditional sociology departments than in health professional schools or health organizations.

Another difference between now and the 1950s is that the range of research questions that medical sociologists now address requires calling upon virtually the full conceptual repertoire and technical armamentarium of the discipline. Some work, for example, is undertaken that is based on ideas in political sociology and social psychology. Marxists and organizational analysts participate in sociomedical research investigations, and model builders, survey researchers, and ethnomethodologists can apply their crafts in the health area. In sum, medical sociology, in its breadth and diversity, provides exciting and stimulating intellectual opportunities for scholars with different conceptual and methodological perspectives.

THE CONGENIALITY OF THE MEDICAL ENVIRONMENT

The support for and continuing growth of activity in medical sociology today, as in the past decade or so, is only in part due to the encouragement of peers in the discipline and the place that medical sociologists have made for themselves in conventional sociology departments. It also is related to the continued utility of the work in the health arena and to the changes that have occurred in the outlook of persons with health science and medical careers.

Unlike in the past, when medical schools turned out mostly solo practitioners who were primarily concerned with their own patients and their own affluence, the health sector now consists of persons who range widely in interests, ideological bents, career trajectories, and social backgrounds. Almost all are exposed to social science instruction while medical students, if not as undergraduates. Many in health care have careers that require a social science perspective; this is the case, for example, of persons in public health, community psychiatry, medical care planning, management, and policymaking. Increasingly, physicians today see their role as much broader than providing individual patients with medical services that alleviate symptoms. Rather, there is growing awareness of the relevance of the social contexts of their patients, their interpersonal behavior and social networks, and their economic circumstances. These are essential factors that have to be taken into account in providing health care, in implementing programs of preventive health measures, in dealing with the persistent problems of substance abuse, and in understanding and approaching such emerging major sociomedical problems as teenage suicide, Alzheimer's disease, and AIDS (Levine and Lilienfeld 1986).

There are also important structural and organizational problems that demand the attention of sociologically trained persons. In several places in this chapter we have noted the changing sponsorship of medical care, which necessarily has ramifications for the economic and social positions and self-images of health providers. Contrast the solo practitioner of fifty years ago with the doctor-executive in today's for-profit health maintenance corporation. The "GP" literally practiced in private, and his or her diagnostic and therapeutic decisions were rarely scrutinized and the physician's medical errors rarely came to light. Indeed, the practitioner then had little more than the equipment that fit into his or her black bag and a relatively small number of pharma-

ceuticals to prescribe to patients. Consequently, while the practitioner then could hardly achieve the remarkable results that physicians often do today, the amount of harm they did also was constrained. Moreover, the physician's income was simply a result of having picked the right geographical location, possessing a pleasing bedside manner, and working enough hours. Today, his or her peer is much more likely to work for a salary, has a production quota to meet (and bonuses if met), is required to complete a variety of forms, supervises a technical and clerical staff that do much of what doctors used to do but at a cheaper wage, has his or her work audited by a quality of care committee and his or her demeanor rated by surveys of patients, and—if interested in more money or status in the organization—must practice less and administer and manage more.

Medical sociologists have observed various aspects of this shift in the profession of medicine, which Starr (1982) has called "the social transformation of American medicine." In part it is a rare instance of occupational "deprofessionalization" (Haug 1975). Others go so far as to designate it as a movement toward proletarianization (McKinlay 1982). Some of the debate is related to the long-term income and job prospects for physicians and other providers; another part is related to the implications for the recruitment and selection of medical, dental, and other health science students; another part is related to the implications for quality of care; and still other parts to the role and standing of physicians compared to other health providers (Freidson 1986). What is clear is that the organization of work in the health field provides fertile ground for research and is an area in which sociologists have unusual opportunity to work in policy, planning, and organizational roles.

Indeed, there is reason to believe that medical sociologists in particular and sociologists in general have not been active enough in meeting the research, policy, and planning needs of the health field. If there is any threat to the future flourishing of medical sociology, it is the partial validity of this claim.

COMPETITORS TO MEDICAL SOCIOLOGISTS

Earlier we noted the abatement of strain between medical sociologists and their more traditional peers in sociology departments, who in an earlier period were antagonistic to sociology *in* medicine activities. But even with comparatively full acceptance of medical sociology as a legitimate specialty in the discipline and the availability of graduate courses and research programs in most of our major universities, medical sociologists have not been able to maintain their "market share" of employment opportunities, research funds, nonacademic jobs, and consulting opportunities. In developing a case for the "success" of medical sociology, we also noted that many of the perspectives and methodological procedures of the sociologist have become mainstays in the training of planning, managerial, and applied researchers in a wide variety of professional schools in the health area.

Academic departments tend to be conservative on matters affecting them (Lipset 1982). Consequently, they have failed to anticipate and respond to the need for research analysts, evaluation specialists, and planners that was brought about by the rapid development of such federal programs as Medicare, Medicaid, and community mental health centers, as well as by the marked changes we have discussed in how health services are delivered at a local level. Professional schools tend to be much more entrepreneurial and pragmatic. Consequently, the majority of health services researchers, evaluation specialists, health planners, and organizational analysts produced over the last ten to twenty years have not been trained in sociology departments. Many who received their training in schools of public health, health care administration, and nursing have seized the opportunity to develop health services research, health policy, and similar programs to meet the demand. Other programs started *de novo* in schools of management, social planning, and public administration. Moreover, with the support of the federal government and such private foundations as the Robert Wood Johnson Foundation, a significant number of physicians and other clinically trained persons have learned much of the social research armamentarium and have undertaken sociomedical studies.

As these various schools and programs have developed, they have bred their own social researchers and theoretically oriented policy analysts who often are virtually indistinguishable from card-carrying sociologists—except that they do not identify themselves as members of the discipline, read or write for sociological journals, or have any stake in the future of the field. They have been joined by a few persons trained in sociology whose long tenure in professional schools and health care organizations have resulted in a change in identity.

These health service researchers are strong competition for medical sociologists. Given their more entrepreneurial work environments, compared to the academically based medical sociologist, they frequently are able to reorient their attention more rapidly to emerging research and policy issues, do their work in a more timely fashion, and are perceived by funding sources as doing more "relevant" research (Freeman 1988). At least in part, these differences explain, for example, why the health care research budget of the Rand Corporation is larger than the research grant funds administered by most, if not all, sociology departments throughout the country.

Serious competition to medical sociologists in the health care field has also emerged from medical economists. Because many policy-oriented questions are to a large extent initially defined or couched in economic terms or have a substantive economic aspect to them, medical economists often appear to possess the most appropriate intellectual repertoire. To health policy leaders, the methodologies and econometric techniques of medical economists seem very appropriate to the problems and issues raised in the health policy field. Economists have achieved unusual dominance in the health policy field. Finally, psychologists have moved into sociomedical research in relatively large numbers as well and, of course, have had a traditional toehold in social research on mental health and illness.

As partners in social research in the health field, we welcome the unique contributions of our sibling disciplines. As teachers and researchers, we are gratified with our success in sensitizing health professionals to our sociological perspectives and our research technologies. We also recognize that we are confronted with a challenge to continue to make distinctive and useful contributions to the health field. Considerable initiative is required on the part of the sociological discipline and sociologically trained health service researchers to continue to participate in the health field. We have unique competencies and perspectives in developing research questions, uncovering hidden value assumptions, and providing innovative methodological approaches. It also is necessary for medical sociologists to make some accommodations in their work style and in their relations with the health care sector.

It is difficult today to carry out various types of health care research unless one is attuned to the changes that are taking place in the health scene. If sociologists do not know what DRGs are, are not conversant with various types of capitation programs, or do not understand the current issues in the financing of postgraduate medical education, it is difficult for them to undertake sound organizational studies in the health field. Nor is it possible to carry out research without an understanding of the varying supply problems of different types of practitioners, the impacts of dif-

ferent types of technologies, and the roles of government and third-party insurance carriers in today's health care market. It has always been a maxim that one must understand the social context of research. It may well have special applicability today.

CONCLUDING COMMENT

This introduction to the fourth edition clearly is optimistic in its outlook. As the chapters that follow document, medical sociology has had three generations of remarkable research productivity, development of a wide range of conceptual outlooks, and significant broadening of topics examined from sociological perspectives.

In assigning areas for review to the contributors of each chapter, the editors delineated the material to be covered but encouraged authors to establish their own frameworks for organizing and addressing the material within their area of expertise. While there is some overlap in the material covered in different chapters, the diversity of work in medical sociology is evidenced by the minimal amount of redundancy in the contents of the volume. One innovation that distinguishes this edition from former ones was our advice to contributors to emphasize health policy issues as they proceeded to examine work within the boundaries of their chapters. While the attention paid to issues of health policy varies from chapter to chapter, overall we are pleased with this added feature of the volume.

A significant contribution of medical sociologists has been to question the importance of medical care and the diffusion of medical innovations in comparison with a more general "social program" approach to the problems of individual community members and the human condition. In some cases the "benefits to costs" argue against using medical interventions in comparison with changing social conditions and increasing the resources of individual community members. Another significant concern is the number of instances of the uncritical adoption of high technology when both limited efficacy and the risks of iatrogenic disease argue for the cautious application of this technology. Moreover, there are both individual and community conditions that can best be conceptualized as "social" rather than "medical," or at least situations in which the former should be emphasized.

Of course, it should be clear that the contributors are not therapeutic nihilists. They appreciate the value of thorough diagnostic procedures, the provision of appropriate health services, and the need to manage the course of illness effectively. At the same time, however, medical sociologists have a responsibility to alert various stakeholders, including those in governmental and other positions of influence, of the serious deficiencies in the ways services are provided from both a technical and a human standpoint, and to stress the need for major organizational and structural changes rather than the mere tinkering with the existing ways health care is provided.

Thus, medical sociologists have been properly responsive to the health care problems of the poor, minorities, and individuals otherwise disfranchised. They also have studied the special problems of the use of health services by the aged and the uninsured, as well as by vulnerable populations such as the homeless and the chronically mentally ill. In their research on the health professions and on the delivery of health services, medical sociologists have included the study of health providers, who are regarded as "marginal" by mainstream medical practitioners.

Along the same lines, medical sociologists have examined the bureaucratic barriers to health care for different segments of the population, the roles and influence of community organizations and interest groups, the lack of empowerment of patients, and the political and economic forces that shape the provision of and delivery of health services. Sociologists have been key players in evaluating various government and foundation initiatives and, less often than perhaps desirable, the consequences of these initiatives as well as of established programs targeted at persons and groups who have insufficient expertise to assess their utility and who lack social power. Most recently, medical sociologists have pressed for taking into account the consequences of medical programs and changes in medical practices on quality of life dimensions as well as on the more conventional indexes of morbidity, mortality, and patient satisfaction.

Medical sociologists in recent years have confronted the difficult questions of cost and quality of care, both in terms of medical care outcomes and the extent to which cost containment efforts have an impact on patients' psychological well-being and health status. New challenges in the organization and administration of health settings continue to emerge and require sociological study; these challenges include the shortage of nurses, the oversupply of physicians in a number of specialities, and the expanded influence of the for-profit sector.

In all these efforts, the grafting of a sociological perspective to the traditional and long-established biomedical and economic outlooks of the health field has been important, not only in challenging the status quo and questioning the ways providers work and health care organizations function, but also in broadening the education and influencing the professional socialization of health science students and fledgling providers and biomedical scientists. Indeed, research and development activities in the health field are shaped now, to a greater degree than ever before, by the ideas and views of sociologists and other social scientists.

Of course, it is obvious that sociologists are hardly monolithic in their sociological outlooks and their political orientations. The diversity of perspectives and ideological viewpoints among medical sociologists—ranging in outlook from social constructionist to Marxist, and varying in methodological approach from phenomenological to experimental—is a valued input into the health field. This is increasingly true today when both health researchers and medical providers are much more ecumenical in their views and much more questioning of the ways research and practice should be undertaken and the activities of health professionals organized.

We should conclude, however, by pointing out that the years ahead represent an even more challenging era for medical sociology. There is a need for more thorough conceptualization, more refined research methods, and more rigor in our empirical studies; and certainly we need to orient our antennae so that we are more quickly attuned to emerging health policy shifts and health care innovations. Nevertheless, the scope of medical sociology and the magnitude of its contributions happily are markedly greater than we ever would have predicted when we edited the first and even the subsequent editions of this *Handbook of Medical Sociology*.

REFERENCES

Aiken, Linda H., Robert J. Blendon, David E. Rogers, and Howard E. Freeman. 1980. Evaluating a Private Foundation's Health Program. *Evaluation and Program Planning* 3(April):119–129.

Bloom, Samuel W. 1986. Institutional Trends in Medical Sociology. *Journal of Health and Social Behavior* 27:265–276.

Bloom, Samuel W., and Robert N. Wilson. 1979. Patient-Practitioner Relationships, in H. Freeman, S. Levine, and L. G. Reeder, eds., *Handbook of Medical Sociology*, 3rd ed. Englewood Cliffs, N.J.: Prentice-Hall, pp. 295–296.

Claus, Lisbeth M. 1983. The Development of Medical Sociology in Europe. *Social Science and Medicine* 17(21):1591–1597.

Freeman, Howard E. 1988. Medical Sociology, in E. Borgatta and K. Cook, eds., *The Future of Sociology*. Beverly Hills: Sage Publications.

Freeman, Howard E., Edgar F. Borgatta, and Nathaniel H. Siegel. 1975. Remarks on the Changing Relationship between Government Support and Graduate Training, in N. J. Demerath, K. F. Schuessler, and O. Larsen, eds., *Social Policy and Sociology*. New York: Academic Press, pp. 297–305.

Freeman, Howard E., K. Jill Kiecolt, and Harris M. Allen, II. 1982. Community Health Centers: An Initiative of Enduring Utility. *Milbank Memorial Fund Quarterly* 60 (Spring):245–267.

Freeman, Howard E., and Leo G. Reeder. 1957. Medical Sociology: A Review of the Literature. *American Sociological Review* 22(1):73–81.

Freeman, Howard E., and Peter H. Rossi. 1984. Furthering the Applied Side of Sociology. *American Sociological Review* 4:571–580.

Freeman, Howard E., and Ozzie G. Simmons. 1977. Mental Patients in the Community: Family Settings and Performance Levels, in N. J. Smelser and W. T. Smelser, eds. *Personality and Social Systems*. New York: John Wiley, pp. 201–211.

Freidson, Eliot. 1986. The Medical Profession in Transition, in L. H. Aiken and D. Mechanic, eds., *Applications of Social Science to Clinical Medicine and Health Policy*. New Brunswick, N.J.: Rutgers University Press, pp. 63–79.

Goffman, Irving. 1961. *Asylums*. Garden City, New York: Anchor Books.

Haug, Marie R. 1975. The Deprofessionalization of Everyone? *Sociological Focus* 8:197–213.

Hollingshead, August B., and Frederick C. Redlich. 1958. *Social Class and Mental Illness: A Community Study*. New York: John Wiley.

Kaplan, Howard B., Robert J. Johnson, Carol A. Bailey, and William Simon. 1987. The Sociological Study of AIDS: A Critical Review of the Literature and Suggested Research Agenda. *Journal of Health and Social Behavior* 28 (2):140–158.

Levin, Lowell S., and Ellen L. Idler. 1981. *The Hidden Health Care System: Mediating Structures and Medicine*. Cambridge, Mass.: Ballinger.

Levine, Sol. 1987. The Changing Terrains in Medical Sociology: Emergent Concern with Quality of Life. *Journal of Health and Social Behavior* 28 (March):1–6.

Levine, Sol, and Abraham Lilienfeld, eds. 1986.

Epidemiology and Health Policy. New York: Tavistock Publications.

Levine, Sol, Norman A. Scotch, and George J. Vlasak. 1969. Unravelling Technology and Culture in Public Health." *American Journal of Public Health* 59:237–244.

Lewis, Charles E., Howard E. Freeman, and Christopher R. Corey. 1987. AIDS-Related Competencies of California's Primary Care Physicians. *American Journal of Public Health* 77(6):795–799.

Lipset, Seymour M. 1982. The Academic Mind at the Top: The Political Behavior and Values of Faculty Elite. *Public Opinion Quarterly* 46:143–168.

Merton, Robert K. 1965. *On the Shoulders of Giants.* New York: Harcourt, Brace and World.

Merton, Robert K., George G. Reader, and Patricia L. Kendall, eds. 1957. *The Student-Physician: Introductory Studies in the Sociology of Medical Education.* Cambridge, Mass.: Harvard University Press.

McKinlay, John B. 1982. Toward the Proletarianization of Physicians, in C. Derber, ed., *Professionals as Workers: Mental Labor in Advanced Capitalism.* Boston: G. K. Hall, pp. 37–62.

Mishler, Elliot G., Lorna R. AmaraSinghan, Stuart T. Hauser, Ramsay Liem, Samuel D. Os-

herson, and Nancy E. Waxler. 1981. *Social Contexts of Health, Illness and Patient Care.* Cambridge: Cambridge University Press.

Parsons, Talcott. 1951. Illness and the Role of the Physician: A Sociological Perspective. *American Journal of Orthopsychiatry* 21:452–460.

Stanton, Aalfred H., and Morris S. Schwartz. 1954. *The Mental Hospital.* New York: Basic Books.

Starr, Paul. 1982. *The Social Transformation of American Medicine.* New York: Basic Books.

Straus, Robert. 1957. The Nature and Status of Medical Sociology. *American Sociological Review* 22(2):200–204.

Wardwell, Walter I. 1972. Limited, Marginal, and Quasi-Practitioners, in H. Freeman, S. Levine, and L. G. Reeder, eds., *Handbook of Medical Sociology*, 2nd ed. Englewood Cliffs, N.J.: Prentice-Hall, pp. 250–273.

Zola, Irving K. 1972. Medicine as an Institution of Social Control. *Sociological Review* 20:487–504.

————. 1983. *Socio-Medical Inquiries: Recollections, Reflections, and Reconsiderations.* Philadelphia: Temple University Press.

CHAPTER 2

TRENDS IN DEATH AND DISEASE AND THE CONTRIBUTION OF MEDICAL MEASURES

JOHN B. MCKINLAY
SONJA M. MCKINLAY
ROBERT BEAGLEHOLE

INTRODUCTION

If the average person in the street were asked "Is the overall level of health of the American population improving?" he or she (in common with most medical care workers) would probably with no hesitation answer that it is. This answer may be based on personal experiences with disease and medical services, dramatic announcements in the media concerning some medical discovery, some new technique for treating a disease, or even a belief that the standard of living is generally higher today than, say, seventy-five years ago and that this must have some beneficial effect on health. Supposedly more knowledgeable medical workers might cite as "evidence" the presence of sophisticated biotechnology and health manpower. Several standard indices (e.g., life expectancy or infant mortality), which purportedly reflect an improvement in the nation's health, may also be selectively invoked.

This chapter has four aims:

- to review changes during the 20th century in U.S. mortality from infectious diseases and the three dominant chronic diseases (coronary heart disease, cancer, and stroke);
- to assess the contribution of a broad range of medical measures (e.g., chemotherapy, surgery, medical services) to overall improvements in mortality, where they have occurred;
- to consider complementary changes in morbidity;
- to assess whether, on the basis of available evidence and using a combined mortality and morbidity index, the overall health of the nation can be said to be improving.

Profound policy implications follow from our findings with respect to these issues. For if one subscribes to the view that we are slowly but surely eliminating one deadly disease after another (and that this is largely attributable to medical interventions), then there may be little commitment to social change, and even resistance to a reordering of social priorities. If X is getting better, or disappearing, primarily because of the presence of Y, then clearly Y should be left intact or preferably be expanded. Its demonstrable effectiveness justifies its presence. Alternatively, if it can be shown that there has been no overall improvement in the health of the population (and perhaps even some deterioration) despite the effort increasingly expended, then some commitment to social change and a reordering of priorities may ensue. For if X is showing no improvement, or is assuming unforeseen proportions because of, or despite the presence of, more and more of Y, then clearly the expansion and even the presence of Y—at least in its current form—can be reasonably questioned. In this case its demonstrable ineffectiveness justifies some reappraisal of its social utility and the wisdom of its expansion (Cochrane 1977; McKinlay 1980, 1979).

The following sections on the decline in mortality and contributions of medical care, recent trends in morbidity, and the measurement of a life free of disability address issues raised in this introduction. A final section discusses implications for current and future health policy.

THE DECLINE IN MORTALITY AND THE CONTRIBUTIONS OF MEDICAL CARE

The Twentieth-Century Decline in Infectious Diseases

Despite the fact that mortality rates for certain conditions, for selected age and sex categories, continue to fluctuate, or even increase, there has been a marked decline this century in overall mortality in the United States and most other countries. Between 1910 and 1984 there was a 41.3 percent decrease in overall crude mortality (*Statistical Abstract of the U.S.* 1976; NCHS 1986). Of the total fall in the standardized death rate this century, approximately 90 percent occurred prior to 1950, with a negligible rate of decline since (McKinlay and McKinlay 1977a, 1977b; NCHS 1986). Most of this decline is due to the virtual disappearance of the major infectious diseases, including typhoid, small pox, scarlet fever, measles, whooping cough, diphtheria, influenza, tuberculosis, pneumonia, acute digestive infections, and poliomyelitis.

Now to what phenomena or interventions can this modern decline in mortality be attributed? Who (if anyone), or what group, can claim to have been instrumental in effecting this reduction? Can anything be gleaned from an analysis of mortality experience to date that will inform health policy for the future? A major concern here is to estimate the contribution of specific medical measures to the decline or changes in mortality in the United States during the twentieth century.

McKinlay and McKinlay (1977a) examined the effect of major interventions, both chemotherapeutic and prophylactic, on the decline in the age- and sex-adjusted death rates in the United States, 1900–1973, for ten of the eleven major infectious diseases. Together, these diseases accounted for approximately 30 percent of all deaths at the turn of the century and nearly 40 percent of the total decline in the mortality rate in the next seventy-three years.

Only reductions in mortality from tuberculosis and pneumonia contributed substantially to the decline in total mortality between 1900 and 1973 (16.5 percent and 11.7 percent, respectively). The remaining eight conditions together accounted for less than 12 percent of the total decline over this period. Disregarding smallpox (for which the only effective measure had been introduced about 1800), only influenza, whooping cough, and poliomyelitis show what could be considered substantial declines of 25 percent or more after the date of medical intervention. However, even under the somewhat unrealistic assumption of a constant (linear) rate of decline in mortality after intervention, only whooping cough and poliomyelitis even approach the percentage that would have been expected. The remaining six conditions (tuberculosis, scarlet fever, pneumonia, diphtheria, measles, and typhoid) showed negligible declines in their mortality rates subsequent to the date of medical intervention. The seemingly quite large percentages for pneumonia and diphtheria must, of course, be viewed in the context of relatively early interventions—1935 and 1930.

Clearly, for tuberculosis, typhoid, measles, and scarlet fever, the medical measures considered were introduced at the point when the death rate for each of these diseases was already negligible. Any change in the rates of decline that occurred subsequent to the interventions could only be minute. Of the remaining five diseases (excluding smallpox with its negligible contribution), it is only for poliomyelitis that the medical measure produced any noticeable change in the trends. Given peaks in the death rate for 1930 and 1950 (and possibly for 1910), a comparable peak could have been expected in 1970. Instead, the death rate dropped to the point of disappearance after 1950 and has remained negligible. The four other diseases (pneumonia, influenza, whooping cough, and diphtheria) exhibit relatively smooth mortality trends, which are unaffected by the medical measures, even though these were introduced relatively early, when the death rates were still notable. If it were assumed that the change for poliomyelitis alone was due to vaccines, then only about 1 percent of the decline following interventions for the diseases considered could be attributed to medical measures. Rather more conservatively, if we also attribute some of the subsequent fall in the death rates for pneumonia, influenza, whooping cough, and diphtheria to medical measures, then perhaps 3.5 percent of the fall in the overall death rate can be explained through medical interventions for the major infectious diseases considered here. Indeed, given that it is precisely for these diseases

that medicine claims most success in lowering mortality, 3.5 percent probably represents a reasonable upper-limit estimate of the total contribution of medical measures to the decline in infectious disease mortality in the United States since 1900 (McKinlay and McKinlay 1977a; see also McKeown 1976a, 1976b; Powles 1973).

The Emergence of Chronic Diseases

The dramatic reduction in infectious disease mortality that continued during the twentieth century has been offset by a rise in costly chronic diseases. To provide perspective and depth, this chapter deliberately focuses only on three dominant conditions: coronary heart disease, cancer, and stroke. These three diseases alone account for about two-thirds of the total U.S. mortality—34 percent, 23 percent, and 7 percent, respectively, in 1980 (NCHS 1985)—and consume the vast majority of available resources. Other less prevalent conditions, their history, social distribution, and treatment, are adequately discussed in a variety of introductory epidemiology and medical sociology textbooks and anthologies (Susser, Watson, and Hopper 1985; Aiken and Mechanic 1986; Levine and Lilienfeld 1987).

Although it is now generally conceded that medical interventions (as opposed to public health measures) contributed little to the decline in infectious disease mortality, any recent improvements with respect to these major chronic diseases are still erroneously attributed to specific medical interventions (e.g., prehospital resuscitation, coronary care units, coronary bypass surgery, and drug therapy for coronary heart disease; widespread surgery, drug therapy, and radiation therapies for cancer; antihypertensive drugs for stroke). Figure 1 (McKinlay and McKinlay 1977a) illustrates how the proportion of deaths contributed by infectious and chronic conditions changed in the United States since the beginning of the twentieth century. In 1900, about 40 percent of all deaths were ac-

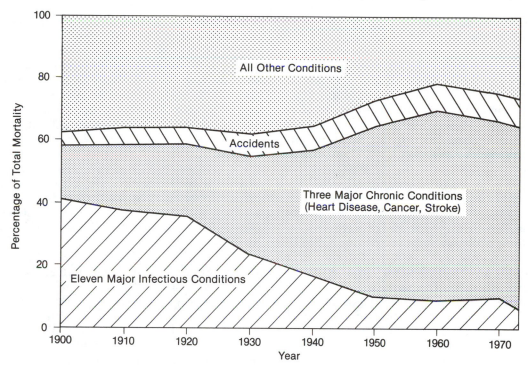

FIGURE 1   The Changing Contribution of Chronic and Infectious Conditions to U.S. Total Mortality (age- and sex-adjusted), 1900–1973. (*Source*: John B. McKinlay and Sonja M. McKinlay, 1977, The Questionable Effect of Medical Measures on the Decline of Mortality in the United States in the Twentieth Century, *Milbank Memorial Fund Quarterly* 55:405–428.)

counted for by eleven infectious diseases, 16 percent by three chronic conditions, 4 percent by accidents, and the remainder by all other causes. By the early 1970s, only 6 percent of all deaths were due to these eleven infectious diseases, 59 percent to the same three chronic conditions, 8 percent to accidents, and 27 percent to other causes.

Coronary heart disease (CHD) has an enormous impact on the health of the nation's population. As the dominant current cause of death, it is responsible for about 650,000 deaths, or approximately one-third of all deaths each year. It often develops in people during their most productive years. For men the chance of a first coronary attack before age 60 is one in five. The incidence of the disease is substantial beyond age 45 in men and beyond age 55 in women. Of those suffering a first attack, 30 percent die in the acute stages, and of those suffering a recurrent attack, 50 percent do not recover. Weinstein and Stason (1985) estimate that the annual economic burden of CHD in the United States, including both direct and indirect costs, is well in excess of $100 billion.

Cancer, the second leading cause of death, is responsible for over 20 percent of all deaths. It will claim an estimated 500,000 lives in 1987—just under one a minute. Over time it will strike three out of every four families, and three out of every ten individuals. Age-adjusted mortality rates for all cancers show a slow and steady increase since the 1950s. Indeed, cancer is the only major cause of death for which age-adjusted mortality rates are still increasing. Eighty percent of all cancers are believed to be caused by environmental factors. The total direct cost of medical care for cancer in 1983 was estimated to be $11 billion (American Cancer Society 1984), or about 7 percent of the total short-stay hospital expenditures in any one year (Mettlin 1984, quoted in Marshall and Graham 1986). The indirect cost of cancer (e.g., lost wages, lost workers, premature liquidation of assets) is much higher, amounting to well over $20 billion annually (Marshall and Graham 1986).

Stroke is the third leading cause of death in the United States, responsible for approximately 10 percent of all deaths each year. Death rates for stroke have been declining probably since the beginning of this century, although the rate of decline accelerated in the 1970s with the decline in CHD mortality. Despite this decline, stroke remains a major cause of death, at least in part because of the aging of the population. Stroke is associated with a high case fatality rate: Approximately 50 percent of people experiencing a stroke are dead within six months.

The Decline in Coronary Heart Disease Mortality and the Contribution of Medical Care

Since 1968, death rates from CHD have declined steadily in the United States. The age-adjusted death rate declined by around 40 percent in the twenty years since 1968 (Stern 1979; Gillum, Folsom, and Blackburn 1984; Kannel and Thom 1984; Stallones 1980; NHLBI 1984). As depicted in Figure 2, this decline has occurred in all age, sex, and race groups. In percentage terms, it has been greater in the younger age groups, began earlier in California, and has been slower in the Southeast (Wing 1984). Comparing rates of decline among insured men and men in general, it appears that the rate of decline was greater among the affluent (Metropolitan Life Insurance Company 1979), in parallel to similar social class gradients identified in the United Kingdom, where there is a national

health service (Marmot and McDowall 1986; Pocock et al. 1987, 1986).

The mortality declines in the United States are particularly impressive when viewed from an international perspective. Although similar declines to a lesser degree are occurring in several other industrial countries (including Japan, Israel, Australia, Finland, Belgium, Canada, New Zealand, Norway, and the Netherlands), there are also countries in which coronary heart disease death rates are still increasing (West Germany, Austria, France, Denmark, Ireland, and Eastern European countries) (Kannel and Thom 1984; Uemura and Pisa 1985).

The decline in CHD mortality in the United States is real and is not explained by changes in diagnostic, certification, or classification procedures. However, the precise causes of the decline remain unclear, at least in part because of the lack of concurrent information on trends in disease incidence and case fatality rates. Without this basic information, one cannot be certain whether the decline is due to the occurrence of fewer new events, or perhaps to increased survival of people with established disease. Internationally respected cardiovascular authorities, meeting in 1978 specifically to explain the decline, concluded that "primary prevention through changes in risk factors and fundamental and clinical research leading to better medical care probably have both contributed but do not fully explain the decline. . . ." (Havlik and Feinleib 1979).

At first sight, the decline in coronary heart disease mortality coincides with changes in both medical care for established coronary heart disease and with the treatment of coronary risk factors by pharmacological means (Levy and Moskowitz 1982; Kannel 1982). In theory, therefore, medical care could have directly reduced both coronary heart disease case fatality rates and the incidence rates. Considerable attention is devoted to CHD here because it remains the major killer in most countries and because it illustrates the complex-

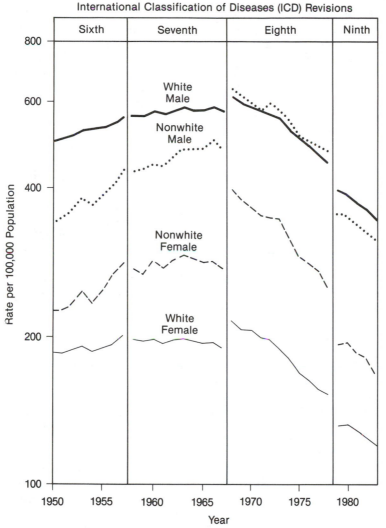

FIGURE 2 Age-adjusted U.S. Death Rates for Coronary Heart Disease by Race and Sex, Ages 35–74 Years, 1950–1983. *(Source:* National Center for Health Statistics, *Vital Statistics of the U.S.)*

ities involved in explaining the contribution of medical care to changes in chronic diseases.

Almost two-thirds of deaths from coronary heart disease are sudden and unexpected and occur outside hospitals, mostly as a result of acute arrhythmias (NHLBI 1984). It is reasonable to assume that a decline in sudden coronary death rates would contribute to the overall decline in CHD death rates. There is good evidence now, both from the United States and other countries, that the rate of out-of-hospital sudden deaths is declining dramatically (Elveback, Connolly, and Kurland 1981; Gillum et al. 1983; NHLBI 1984). However, trends in the *incidence* of acute myocardial infarction are not so clear, with conflicting trends by age, sex, and geographic location (Elveback, Connolly, and

Kurland 1981; Gillum et al. 1983). There is general agreement that there has been no widespread improvement in long-term survival after myocardial infarction (Goldberg et al. 1986; Weinblatt et al. 1982; Stewart et al. 1984; Martin, Hobbs, and Armstrong 1984; Aberg et al. 1984). However, recent analyses of Minnesota and Swedish data indicated improvement in long-term survival (Gomez-Marin et al. 1987; Aberg et al. 1984).

The decline of out-of-hospital deaths, particularly if it was restricted to people with no previous manifestation of coronary disease, would provide strong evidence for a central role of prevention in the overall decline in coronary heart disease mortality. The fact that short-term improvements in case fatality rates have occurred suggests a role for medical care in the acute phase, although it is not possible to exclude changing admission policies, referral rates, and diagnostic changes as important causal factors in this trend. If improvements in long-term survival are confirmed, this may indicate a role for medical care in the decline of coronary heart disease mortality rates or a change in the disease-host relationship.

Medical care could influence coronary heart disease mortality rates at several points in the natural history of the disease: (1) by reducing risk factor levels and, thus, the incidence of the disease (primary prevention); (2) by reducing pre-hospital mortality; (3) by reducing in-hospital mortality; and finally (4) by improving long-term prognosis after the development of overt clinical manifestations, angina pectoris, myocardial infarction, or chronic coronary disease. Each of these possibilities is considered below.

Two of the major risk factors for coronary heart disease—high blood pressure and high blood cholesterol—are amenable to pharmacological intervention. The benefits of treating high blood pressure with regard to coronary heart disease are still by no means clear. (This is in contrast to the unequivocal benefits demonstrated

for the treatment of stroke.) None of the nine randomized controlled trials completed to date have shown a statistically significant beneficial effect on the development of either fatal or nonfatal coronary heart disease, although several have demonstrated a favorable trend (McMahon et al. 1986). There are several possible explanations for this disappointing result. A likely explanation is the lack of statistical power of each of the trials considered individually. It is also possible that the treatment itself may be having an adverse effect by, for example, altering blood lipids or potassium levels.

Given this admittedly weak evidence that the treatment of hypertension may have a beneficial effect on coronary heart disease mortality, it is possible to assess this effect quantitatively by applying the estimated benefits from the trials to an estimate of the increase in the proportion of the population on treatment since the decline in coronary heart disease mortality began in 1968. Using this approach, Goldman and Cook (1984) estimated that in the period 1968–1976 approximately 8.7 percent of the decline in mortality could be attributed to the benefits from antihypertensive treatment. In Auckland, New Zealand, in the period 1974–1981 it was estimated that approximately 12 percent of the observed decline in coronary heart disease mortality could be attributed to antihypertensive treatment (Beaglehole 1986).

These analyses, in conjunction with the lack of long-term change in diastolic blood pressure in the population as a whole for the period 1960–1962 to 1976–1980 (Rowland and Roberts 1982), suggest that it is extremely unlikely that increased use of antihypertensive medication has had any significant effect on reducing coronary heart disease mortality rates.

Blood cholesterol is a powerful predictor of coronary heart disease, although there is continuing controversy concerning the effects of lowering blood cholesterol levels. There is now general consensus that lowering population cholesterol levels could have a considerable beneficial effect on population coronary disease mortality rates. However, the evidence for a decline in average levels since the early 1960s is far from conclusive and may be due to methodological differences. It is estimated that a decline of 5 mg per deciliter of serum cholesterol would result in about a 4.3 percent decline in coronary mortality among middle-aged men (Beaglehole et al. 1979). A larger effect of cholesterol reduction as a result of dietary change has been estimated for New Zealand for the period 1958–1981 (Jackson and Beaglehole 1987).

It is extremely unlikely that medication could have had any effect on population cholesterol levels, since evidence has only recently become available from randomized controlled trials concerning the efficacy of treatment (Brensike et al. 1984; Lipid Research Clinics Program 1984). Moreover, the indications for treatment until the recent Consensus Conference (NIH 1985) had been restricted to the small proportion of the population with extreme elevations of blood cholesterol. It is safe to conclude that for the period under consideration, the pharmacological management of hypercholesterolemia could have had only a negligible impact on coronary heart disease mortality rates. This may change in subsequent decades if the national education program launched in 1985 is effective.

Since approximately two-thirds of deaths from CHD occur outside hospitals, it is conceivable that the increase and improvements in the emergency management of acute myocardial infarction could have had an impact on overall mortality rates. However, Goldman and Cook (1984) have estimated that the basic techniques of pre-hospital resuscitation available in the period 1968–1976 could have accounted for no more than 4 percent of the decline in coronary heart disease mortality rates. There are, undoubtedly, parts of the country where more advanced techniques could be making a much larger contribution, but their distribution during the period under

consideration was limited. In 1979 only 20 percent of the emergency medical service regions in the country were in the "advanced life support" phase of a federally sponsored program designed to achieve complete regional coverage by 1982 (Stern 1979). In Auckland, New Zealand, where the entire population is covered with life support ambulances, it was estimated that pre-hospital resuscitation accounted for approximately 16 percent of the decline observed in coronary heart disease mortality between 1974 and 1981 (Beaglehole 1986).

To what extent has improvement in in-hospital management of CHD contributed to the documented long-term decline in CHD mortality in the United States? The introduction of coronary care units (CCU) in 1963 was one of the major developments in the management of acute myocardial infarction. Evidence on the effectiveness of CCUs comes largely from the unequivocal demonstration that in-hospital case fatality rates have declined since the pre-CCU era, and not from clinical trials (Killip 1979). However, it is unclear how much of this decline can be attributed to improvements in in-hospital management (except perhaps for left ventricular function [Killip 1979]) and how much to changes in admission policies. If, as seems likely, there has been a tendency to admit patients with less severe, or even nonexistent, coronary disease, case fatality rates will inevitably decline. Surprisingly, only about 50 percent of patients now admitted to coronary care units have a documented acute myocardial infarction.

The major contribution of CCUs to declining mortality appears to be through detection and treatment of potentially fatal arrhythmias. However, these arrhythmias are surprisingly rare: Only 5 percent of patients with acute myocardial infarction develop a potentially fatal arrhythmia in the coronary care unit, and their treatment within the coronary care unit is usually very successful. It has been estimated that only about 11 percent of the decline in coronary heart disease mortality in the United States in the period 1968–1976 can be attributed to the effects of coronary care units (Goldman and Cook 1984). In New Zealand a smaller estimate of benefit of approximately 5 percent was derived (Beaglehole 1986). No evidence was found in a nine-year study of all sixty-three acute care hospitals in the Boston area over the period 1973–1974 to 1978–1979 of any beneficial effect of the many new expensive interventions introduced during this time; hospital case fatality rates for acute myocardial infarction did not improve during this period (Goldman et al. 1982). Reviewing the accumulated evidence to date, Ostfeld (1986, p. 138) concludes:

after about 18 years of proliferation of CCUs, we have meager evidence except personal opinion that they are better than treatment elsewhere in the hospital or at home. The only controlled clinical trials that have been done show no value of CCUs over treatment at other sites. One analysis of data from a Canadian province likewise shows no benefits of CCUs. The Canadian data are particularly instructive because treatment in a CCU or regular hospital bed depended on where you lived and not on the presumed severity of the heart attack. One cannot, therefore, claim that CCUs perform as well as other treatment sites because they get the more severe cases.

Coronary artery bypass surgery has been performed increasingly in the United States since the mid-1960s, and its main indication remains the relief of symptoms. Only for left main stem and triple vessel disease has coronary artery bypass surgery been shown in randomized controlled trials to increase survival, although in some descriptive analytical studies, improved survival was found among other selected groups of high-risk patients (Detre et al. 1977; Takaro et al. 1982). The Veterans Administration Coronary Bypass Surgery Trial demonstrates no difference in survival by surgical or medical treatment after eleven years of follow-up, except for those at high risk of death (Veterans Administration Coronary Bypass Surgery Cooperative Study Group 1984; see also Braunwald 1983; Luchi et al. 1987). The major dif-

ficulty in assessing the benefits of coronary surgery is to determine the likely reduction in annual mortality that results from the surgery. Goldman and Cook (1984) assumed a range from 2.6 to 4.0 percent per year reduction and calculated that surgery could account for between 3.5 and 5.0 percent of the decline in mortality rates over the period. A similar estimate was derived independently in New Zealand for the period 1974–1981 (Beaglehole 1986).

The only medical treatment demonstrated to have unequivocal benefit in the period under consideration is the use of beta-blocking agents in post–myocardial infarction patients. However, this benefit was not conclusively shown until the Beta Blocker Heart Attack Trial was terminated early in October 1981 because of a significant reduction in total mortality. Similar reductions from beta blockers were demonstrated in Sweden and Norway (NHLBI 1984). Goldman and Cook (1984) have estimated that, in practice, beta-blocking agents could be responsible for about 10 percent of the overall decline in coronary heart disease mortality in the period 1968–1976. In New Zealand for the period 1974–1981 these agents were estimated to be responsible for only 2 percent of the decline in mortality, reflecting the rather low rate of use of beta-blocking agents in post-infarction patients in that country (Beaglehole 1986).

In summary, it is unlikely that the medical measures have had a major effect on population mortality data. The explanation for this perhaps surprising conclusion is that mortality rates for a large population are quite insensitive to the relatively small influences on small subsets of the population, such as post-infarction patients.

Trends in Cancer Mortality, the Failure of Treatments, and Continuing Neglect of Public Health Measures

Cancer is considered here because it remains the second leading cause of death in the United States. Of the top three killers, it is the only one that continues to show an increase, and therefore any beneficial contribution of medical measures cannot be considered in the same way. There is a lively debate between public health researchers, who argue that no overall improvement in cancer mortality has occurred in recent times, and government and American Cancer Society officials, who understandably argue that significant improvements have occurred. Although this debate cannot be resolved here, it is fair to say that the major investment in the "war on cancer" over the past decade or so, particularly in biotechnology and the search for a "magic bullet," has not yielded anything like the results that were promised. Without in any way suggesting a reduction in expenditures, one can reasonably question whether the national cancer effort is moving in the right direction—that is, whether the disproportionate investment in treatments or cures, as against public health measures, will hasten the hoped-for downturn in mortality now evident for CHD and stroke.

Cancer is, of course, not a simple entity. Each cancer site has its own characteristics and peculiarities. We shall briefly consider overall trends in cancer mortality and then examine the three leading cancers—lung, breast, and colorectal—which together represent over half of all cancer deaths. Despite the fact that incidence and survival data remain favored by National Cancer Institute officials (in contrast to other federal agencies), we elect not to use them because they are sensitive to major changes in detection rates and in the stage of disease at which detection occurs. The apparent increases in survival in several cancers may in fact be artifacts of increasingly early detection and may disappear when adjusted for disease severity, as pointed out by Bailar and Smith (1986a and 1986b). Rather we will report here on analyses completed by Bailar and Smith (1986a and 1986b), using mortality rates (age-standardized to 1980, the most recent census year) as the best overall measure of cancer trends in the general population.

The age-adjusted mortality rates for all forms of cancer for the period 1950–1982 are shown in Figure 3 (reproduced from Bailar and Smith, 1986a) by sex and race. In all groups combined there has been a slow increase over this period. Since these rates are standardized (weighted to account for age changes in the composition of the population over time), it *cannot* be argued that cancer rates are increasing because more and more people are surviving to be old, when the risk of cancer is highest. Mortality rates rose steadily throughout this period among white males; fell, slightly plateaued, and then rose again in white females; rose steadily among nonwhite males throughout this period; declined and then plateaued in nonwhite females. It is noteworthy that in no sex or race groups has there been a fall in mortality rates since 1980. It should be noted that all of these rates are *period* rates (as used in this chapter for all diseases discussed). With major environmental changes (including cigarette-smoking trends), site-specific cancer mortality rates may be subject to important cohort effects (see, for example, the recent analysis of Myers and Manton 1987). These cohort effects, however, only lessen and do not reverse the trends reported by Bailar and Smith (1986a and 1986b).

When the 1980 age-specific rates are compared with the correspondingly standardized 1950 rates, marked decreases in cancer mortality are apparent in all five age groups under age 50, although substantial increases have occurred in all age groups over 50 years. However, it should be noted that the majority of cancers occur in people over 50 years, and thus even impressive percentage declines in mortality rates in younger people are much less significant than even relatively smaller proportionate increases in older age. Perhaps an increase in mortality rates in the older age groups could be a reflection of improved diagnostic techniques that have evolved over the last quarter century. This seems unlikely, however, since the increase has occurred only in the very elderly and the increase has continued throughout the

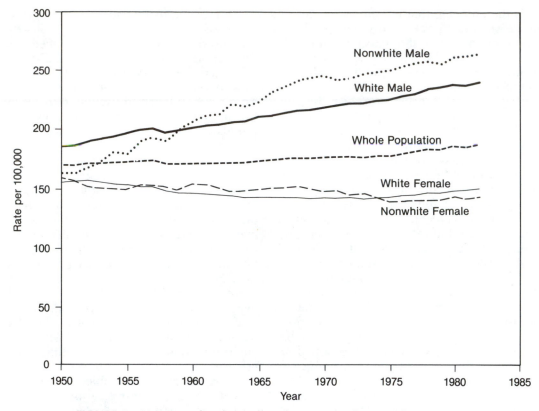

FIGURE 3   U.S. Mortality from All Malignant Neoplasms, 1950
through 1982, White Population and according to Race (white or
nonwhite) and Sex (Age-adjusted to the U.S. population of 1980).
(Source: J. C. Bailar and E. M. Smith, 1986, Progress against Cancer? Reprinted,
by permission of the *New England Journal of Medicine,* 314(19), p. 1227,
1986.)

1970s and early 1980s, during which time diagnostic techniques have not changed dramatically.

Mortality trends for the period 1950–1982 are shown in Figure 4 for lung, breast, and colorectal cancer. To preserve comparability across sites, the rates of each cancer are shown relative to the total population. There was a sharp and continuing rise in death rates from lung cancer throughout this period, although the rates in men are now stabilizing overall and even decreasing in younger men. The rates in women of all ages continue to increase, and lung cancer has now overtaken breast cancer as the leading cancer in women.

Eighty-five percent of all lung cancers are caused by cigarette smoking, a fact that was clearly spelled out in the 1950s and was generally agreed upon by medical authorities by 1960. There has been no change in mortality from breast cancer in women since 1950. Mortality from colorectal cancer has been declining slowly since at least the beginning of the period. The reasons for this improvement are not known, but may include better diagnostic procedures.

Reviewing incidence and survival trends for the period 1950–1982, Bailar and Smith (1986a) conclude that the trends for all cancers are upward for both white males and white females, and similarly

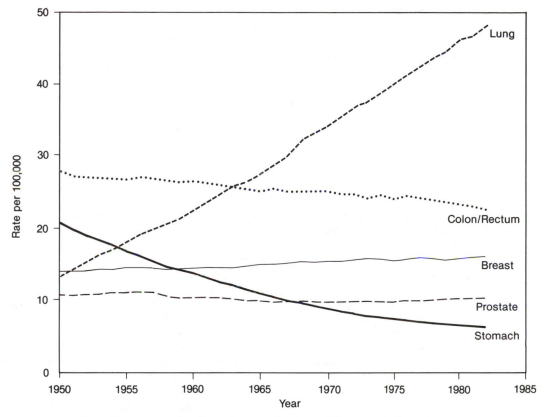

FIGURE 4 Mortality from Cancer of Selected Sites, 1950 through 1982, in the total U.S. Population (age-adjusted to the U.S. population of 1980). *(Source:* Bailar and Smith, 1986, Progress against Cancer? Reprinted, by permission of the *New England Journal of Medicine,* 314(19), p. 1228, 1986.)

there has been a slow rise in breast and colorectal cancer incidence rates. Although there have been some gains in absolute and relative five-year survival rates in the period 1973–1978 for some cancers, the gains are unimpressive, particularly when considered in light of the difficulties in interpreting such trends (Bailar and Smith, 1986a, 1986b). The difficulties are certainly of such a magnitude that it is inappropriate to use survival trends as a measure of progress in the efforts to control cancer.

The picture is not totally pessimistic, although perspective is necessary. No doubt medical measures in the form of cancer chemotherapy and radiation have been successful in treating rare forms of cancer, particularly in children and young adults (e.g., testicular cancer in young men, acute lymphocytic leukemia in children, and Hodgkin's disease, most often seen in young adults). But these highly publicized successes must be viewed in the context of the overall burden of cancer. On the basis of a careful review of available evidence, Marshall and Graham (1986) argue that "these success stories of cancer therapy—for cancer of the blood forming or lymphatic organs—comprise a relatively small portion of total incidence; in 1983 they involved only 8 percent of total cancer incidence" (p. 163).

It is worth speculating on the reasons for the failure of medical care to influence cancer mortality rates favorably. There have been successive (and overlapping) waves of enthusiasm for different approaches—from surgery and radiation therapy through chemotherapy, virology, immunology, and now molecular biology. McKinlay (1981) has described the way in which "promising reports" become institutionalized over time as "standard practice," only to be eventually discarded and even discredited as clinically ineffective. Today's research fad is the field of molecular biology. Believing that "we're ready for the next quantum jump in terms of being effective against cancer," Dr. Paul Marks (president and chief executive officer of Memorial Sloan-Kettering Cancer Center in New York) adds, "you have the feeling now that this research is making inroads toward the control and cure of the disease" (Boffey 1987). Convinced that "most of the answers to cancer lie down on the level of genes, in our understanding of how cells differentiate and divide," Marks has severely pruned programs in other areas, channeling a $335 million annual operating budget, a $325 million fund-raising drive, and a new thirteen-story Rockefeller Research Laboratory into this new area of research (Boffey 1987). It should be recalled that Marks's predecessor at Sloan-Kettering, Lewis Thomas, predicted "the end of cancer before the century is over." The optimism surrounding the latest research fad is evident in the National Cancer Institute's reported advances using immunotherapy against advanced tumors, particularly with the experimental substance interleukin-2. Commenting on two trials funded by the National Cancer Institute (Rosenberg et al. 1987; West et al. 1987)—in which 55 responses (9 complete, 33 partial, and 13 minor) are reported among 192 patients (of the 205 entered) treated with a variety of doses and schedules of interleukin-2 and lymphokine-activated killer (LAK) cells—Durant (1987)

suggests that "perhaps we are at the end of the beginning of the search for successful immunotherapy for cancer." Research in these fields has obviously been productive and has yielded a great deal of biochemical and physiologic information. Yet from a practical clinical viewpoint, little of direct benefit to cancer patients has yet emerged. The cost of these programs has, of course, been staggering.

The relative ineffectiveness of medical care with respect to cancer may be partially explained by the biologic nature of the disease. Once it has become clinically manifest, it often spreads well beyond its site of origin. Chemotherapeutic measures may seldom, if ever, be specific enough to kill every cancerous cell and yet spare the normal tissues, although recent developments with monoclonal antibodies (molecules that are genetically engineered to react with specific body cells) offer promise in this regard. Dr. Taylor-Papdimitrion at the Imperial Cancer Research Fund in London has reported the development of monoclonal antibodies that in laboratory tests can hit 95 percent of breast cancer cells without harming healthy tissues (Veitch 1987).

Only very peculiar (and rare) cancers have thus far responded to chemotherapy. For this reason, the programs of the last few decades, based as they have been on improving treatment, have generally failed. This failure is particularly ironic when it is considered that the cause of about 30 percent of all cancers has not only been well known for most of this period but is also readily amenable to prevention—cigarette smoking (Ravenholt 1985). Juxtaposing the contribution of medical care against public health activities (antismoking), Cairns (1985, p. 59) argues:

The waste of life is truly astonishing. Thanks to the cigarette, the U.S. now suffers a completely unnecessary additional 100,000 deaths per year from lung cancer. These numbers dwarf the 5,000 to 10,000 lives that are being saved by chemotherapy. So far the war against cancer is being lost because (to stay with the metaphor of war) we continue to tolerate the presence of a fifth column in our midst. The conquest of the commonest of all lethal cancers depends, therefore, on the will power of governments and not on the skill of physicians or the ingenuity of scientists.

Despite the known environmental and personal hygiene risk factors for the major cancers, there has been remarkably little effort in the primary prevention of cancer compared to similar efforts to prevent cardiovascular disease, although this appears to be changing. The focus on mass screening for specific cancers (cervical smears and mammography, for example) has been largely ineffective, as such programs tend to reach those at lowest risk. According to Dr. Vincent DeVita, director of the National Cancer Institute, adoption of a comprehensive cancer control program, *based on existing knowledge*, could cut the cancer death rate in half by the year 2000—saving around a quarter of a million lives annually! Such a program would involve a combination of cancer prevention, screening, and early detection and treatment. It also would require industry to increase health promotion in the workplace, the news media to disseminate information about cancer prevention and control more widely, voluntary organizations to offer more health education and screening programs at the local level, and health professional groups to reemphasize cancer control in training programs (Summers 1987). Such a program should be reinforced with economic disincentives to smoking. Summers (1987) estimates that the eight-cent increase in cigarette taxes legislated in 1982 caused two million adults to stop smoking and prevented 600,000 teenagers from starting. A further tax of 20 cents (on top of the 1982 increase) would avert more than half a million premature deaths among current adult smokers and reduce the federal budget deficit by around $5 billion.

The Decline in Mortality from Stroke and the Contribution of Antihypertensive Therapy

Stroke mortality rates in the United States have been declining since the beginning of the century (Whisnant 1984). Comparable declines have been observed in some other industrialized countries (Bonita and Beaglehole 1982; Haberman, Capildeo, and Rose 1982; Dobson et al. 1981; Levy and Moskowitz 1982), although exceptions have been noted (Uemura and Pisa 1985). During the period 1970–1980, the rate of decline in the United States and elsewhere accelerated, resulting in an overall mortality rate decline of 40 percent for people aged 35 to 74 years (Lenfant and Roccella 1984). The most plausible explanation for this is either a decrease in the incidence of stroke, improved rates of survival, or both. Although the evidence remains incomplete, the most plausible explanation is that the incidence has fallen (Bonita and Beaglehole 1986; Garraway, Whisnant, and Drury 1983).

Since hypertension is clearly the single most important risk factor for stroke (Roccella and Ward 1984; Dyken et al. 1984), the favorable trend observed since the early 1970s has been attributed to increased medical management with antihypertensive drugs (Soltero and Cooper 1980; Ostfeld 1986). This explanation for the decline in stroke mortality is strengthened by results from several randomized controlled therapeutic trials that demonstrate a major and consistent benefit of the treatment of hypertension for the prevention of both fatal and nonfatal stroke events (Amery et al. 1985; Medical Research Council Working Party 1985; Hypertension Detection and Follow-up Program 1982; Veterans Administration Cooperative Group 1970). Contemporaneous with this recent decline was the implementation of the national program to improve the detection, treatment, and control of hypertension through a wide range of educational and health promotion efforts (Roccella and Ward 1984).

Using data from two National Health and Nutrition Surveys (1970–1971; 1976–1980) and results from a pooled analysis of nine randomized trials of the treatment of hypertension, Bonita and Beaglehole (1987) estimate that 12 percent (95 percent confidence limit = 6 percent, 35 percent) of the observed decline in mortality from stroke in 1980 in people aged 35 to 74 years can be attributed to the extra six million people in treatment for hypertension in 1980 compared to 1970. In other words, at most one-sixth of the decline in stroke mortality in the period 1970–1980 can be attributed to improvements in hypertension control. An estimate based on the population attributable risk of hypertension for stroke mortality suggests that at most 38 percent of the decline could be explained by improvements in the medical management of hypertension. A separate analysis of the likely contribution of antihypertensive treatments to the decline in stroke mortality in New Zealand produced strikingly similar results (Bonita and Beaglehole 1986). In that country an acceleration of the decline in stroke mortality after 1972 also occurred, but in the absence of a coordinated national high blood pressure education program.

The medical management of hypertension appears then to be an unsatisfactory and quite limited explanation for the dramatic modern decline in stroke mortality. A satisfactory explanation will have to account for the reasons for the decline prior to the availability of the first antihypertensive drugs, the contribution of changes in other possible risk factors (e.g., the secular decline in the prevalence of smoking), and the reasons for the increase in stroke mortality in some industrialized countries over the same period that the decline occurred in the United States (Uemura and Pisa 1985). While still largely unexplained, data presently available suggest that the medical treatment of hypertension has contributed relatively little (between 12 and 25 percent)

to the decline in stroke mortality since 1970 (Bonita and Beaglehole 1987).

Some Limitations of Mortality Statistics

Mortality statistics have obvious limitations and, as has been observed, "measuring the impact of medicine only by its impact on mortality is insufficient in assessing the effects of medical advances" (Schneyer, Landefeld, and Sandifer 1981). Unfortunately, mortality statistics are often the only data that are accessible for the examination of time trends because comparable and complementary morbidity and disability data are not readily available.

It would be foolhardy indeed to dismiss all studies based on mortality measures simply because they are possibly beset with *known limitations*. Such data are preferable to those whose limitations are either unknown or, if known, cannot be estimated. Because of an overawareness of potential inaccuracies, there is a timorous tendency to disregard or devalue studies based on mortality evidence, even though there are innumerable examples of their fruitful use as a basis for planning and informed social action. Moreover, there is evidence that some of the known inaccuracies of mortality data tend to cancel each other out. Consequently, while mortality statistics may be unreliable for use in individual cases, when pooled for a country and employed in population studies, they can reveal important trends and generate fruitful hypotheses. Their use has already resulted in informed social action (for example, the use of geographical distributions of mortality in the field of environmental pollution).

In recent times, and mainly in Great Britain, it has been proposed that the effectiveness of medical treatment should be measured by mortality from specified diseases for which death is apparently avoidable given appropriate intervention (Charlton et al. 1983; Charlton, Lakhani, and Aristidou 1986; Bauer and Charlton 1986; Rutstein et al. 1976, 1980). It is claimed that such an outcome measures the effectiveness of medical treatment over a wide range of curative services (Charlton, Bauer, and Lakhani 1984) and may even indicate the impact of changes or differences in availability and access to medical care within individual countries (Charlton and Velez 1986). While sharing everyone's desire for valid and reliable indicators of the effectiveness of medical care, a group from Newcastle upon Tyne lament the absence of any direct analysis of the relation between medical care and avoidable mortality and argue that the proposal of Charlton and his colleagues has no theoretical basis (Carr-Hill, Hardman, and Russell 1987). They also identify three practical shortcomings: The coding of cause of death may not be sufficiently consistent, the choice of social indicators was arbitrary, and one of the main conclusions was based on superficial inspection rather than on rigorous statistical analysis. It should be added that the so-called "avoidable causes" make up only a small proportion of all causes.

Obviously, whatever limitations and risks may be associated with the use of mortality statistics, they apply equally to all studies that employ them—both those which attribute the decline in mortality to medical measures and those which argue the converse, or something else entirely. And, if such data constitute acceptable evidence in support of the expansion of high technology medical care, then it is not unreasonable, or illogical, to employ them in support of some opposing position. One difficulty is that, depending on one's point of view and the nature of the results, double standards of rigor seem to operate in the evaluation of different studies. Not surprisingly, those that challenge prevailing myths or beliefs concerning the effectiveness of medical care are subject to the most stringent methodological and statistical scrutiny, whereas supportive studies, which frequently employ the flimsiest impressionistic data and inappropriate techniques of analysis, receive general and uncritical acceptance. Some critics, while cautioning against the use of mortality statistics (often collected for other purposes) to assess the contribution of medical care to the decline in mortality, see no contradiction in using these same statistics in an attempt to demonstrate medicine's considerable, or likely, contribution!

RECENT TRENDS IN MORBIDITY

One dramatic method of indicating the insensitivity of mortality statistics as indicators of the health status of the population is to compare directly the major causes of mortality with several major causes of morbidity. In Table 1 the five leading causes of mortality are compared with the five leading chronic conditions causing limitation of activity, the major reasons for physician visits, and the main diagnoses for short-stay hospital discharges. It is clear from this comparison that only accident/injury (bodily impairment) and (chronic) respiratory disease are among the top five diagnoses for all three morbidity-related measures considered.

As a further indication of the divergence between the major causes of death and the major causes of ill health and disability in the general population, one can consider, for two of the three morbidity measures, the percent of all diagnoses contributed by the five major causes of death. Although these five major causes of death account for 76 percent of all mortality, they account for less than 50 percent of short-stay hospital discharges (43.7 percent for men, 27.1 percent for women) and about 34 percent of all physician visits.

Given the apparent inadequacies of mortality statistics, additional measures are required to develop a more complete description of the overall health status of the population. Probably the most direct measures of morbidity are those that measure the incidence or prevalence of specific diseases. The National Center for Health Statistics collects information on the occurrence of conditions in the National Health

TABLE 1 The Contribution of Five Primary Diagnoses to Mortality and Three Related Morbidity Measures, United States, 1980–1985

	Mortality[a] 1984				Limitation of Activity[b] 1985		Physician Visits[c] 1980		Short-Stay Hospital Discharges[d]			
Male	% Total	Female	% Total		Male	Female	Both Sexes	% Total	Male	% Total	Female	% Total
Heart disease	36.2	Heart disease	31.7		Chronic respiratory disease	Musculoskeletal system disorder	Acute upper respiratory infection	13.8	Digestive system diseases	13.5	Digestive system diseases	12.4
Malignant neoplasms	23.0	Malignant neoplasms	28.1		Heart disease	Bodily impairment (except paralysis)	Current injuries/poisonings	11.2	Heart disease	12.8	Genitourinary diseases	11.3
Accident/injury	7.4	Cerebrovascular disease	7.4		Musculoskeletal system disorder	Diseases of the circulatory system (except heart)	Musculoskeletal system disorder	9.6	Injury/poisoning	12.7	Respiratory system disease	9.3
Cerebrovascular disease	4.9	Accident/injury	4.7		Bodily impairment (except paralysis)	Heart disease	Diseases of the circulatory system (except heart)	8.8	Respiratory system disease	11.1	Heart disease	9. 2

	Chronic obstructive pulmonary disease (COPD)	Chronic obstructive pulmonary disease (COPD)	Diseases of the circulatory system (except heart)	Chronic respiratory disease	Chronic respiratory disease	Neoplasms	Injury/ poisoning
	4.0	3.0			7.4	7.1	8.6
Total contribution of five leading causes of mortality to each measure	75.5	74.9	Not calculable		27.4	43.7	27.1

aSource: National Center for Health Statistics, December 1986, *Health US, 1986*, DHHS Publication No. (PHS) 87-1232. These rates are age-adjusted.

bSource: National Center for Health Statistics, July 1986, Prevalence of Selected Chronic Conditions, US 1979–81, *Vital and Health Statistics*, Series 10, No. 155, DHHS Publication No. (PHS) 86–1583. These conditions are listed according to the number of persons limited in major activity because of them. However, as limitation can be caused by multiple concurrent conditions, these numbers cannot be meaningfully added or calculated as a percent of total limitations. Only a rank order is provided.

cSource: National Center for Health Statistics, June 1983. Physician Visits: Volume and Interval since Last Visit, US, 1980, *Health and Vital Statistics*, Series 10, No. 144, DHHS Publication No. (PHS) 83-1572. These data were not readily available by sex.

dSource: National Center for Health Statistics, March 1986, Utilization of Short-Stay Hospitals, US, 1984, Annual Summary, *Health and Vital Statistics*, Series 13, No. 84, DHHS Publication No. (PHS) 86–1745.

eFor physician visits, diseases of the circulatory system (primarily hypertension) are equated with cerebrovascular disease. Injury/poisonings are equated with accident/injury, and for hospital discharges, respiratory system diseases are equated with chronic obstructive pulmonary disease.

and Nutrition Examination Surveys (NHANES) through a checklist of chronic conditions as a part of the medical history component of the survey. However, variation in measurement techniques across various cycles of the surveys has limited the use of these data for the examination of secular trends in health status. Much of the identified increase in the prevalence of sixteen broad categories of chronic illness in the period 1960–1981 has been attributed to changes in the design of questionnaires, including longer condition lists with more specific diagnostic categories. The increase in the number of conditions about which the respondents are specifically asked has resulted in marked increases in the reporting of conditions that in the past had to be volunteered by the respondents (Wilson and Drury 1984). This use of longer lists may have, in fact, resulted in overreporting of conditions.

Other problems that have bedeviled this approach include changing diagnostic fashions, changing disease patterns, and measurement problems. This last problem is shown, for example, in the difficulties in interpreting secular trend data in blood pressure levels in the United States because of the lack of standardization of measurement technique over time and, in general, the absence of "gold standards" of measurement (a problem that remains even with such highly "standardized" techniques as the estimation of blood cholesterol).

Wilson and Drury further highlight the problems involved in the interpretation of trends in health status indicators. Although it is often claimed that the health of the nation is improving with few exceptions, it is difficult to document this improvement from the disease and disability statistics traditionally used to indicate health status at the national level:

Judgments that the health of Americans is improving are generally based on the recent declines in mortality, increased access to medical care, better maternal and child care, along with changes in health practices generally considered to have a favorable impact on health, such as reduced cigarette smoking, improved diet and increased exercise. Illness and disability time series, however, provide a more ambiguous data base for evaluating improvement in health status, because changes in health indicators do not always clearly reflect changes in the health phenomena they are purported to measure. (Wilson and Drury 1984, p. 85)

An alternative approach is to consider indirect measures of illness, such as days of restricted activity, workday loss, or the prevalence of some carefully defined type of disability. Because such measures can be uniformly defined and are not dependent on changing disease patterns for comparability, many of the major problems associated with assessing secular trends in disease prevalence are overcome. Not surprisingly, however, other difficulties may be introduced. For example, loss of workdays may be predominantly a function of benefit policies, changes in the type of work, morale on the job, and seasonal variations rather than of the presence of some medical condition, and thus may not be a reliable measure of morbidity.

Some approaches to morbidity measurement and their advantages and disadvantages are reviewed below.

Work Loss

Chirikos (1986) has addressed the question as to whether rapidly increasing prevalence rates of various functional disabilities or handicaps mean that the health status of the U.S. population is deteriorating and that there is, therefore, a corresponding need for new health-promoting interventions. He identifies five possible explanations for the increase in disability rates over the last thirty years: (1) It may reflect an increase in the prevalence of chronic disease, (2) it may reflect more frequent use of medical services and the encouragement that use gives to adopting a sick role, (3) it may stem from selective improvements in survivorship favoring individuals at high risk of disablement, (4) it may reflect economic opportunities to accommodate poor health or even adverse economic incentives to relinquish social role responsibilities arising from such programs, or (5) it may be an artifact of the manner in which the data are collected.

Chirikos examines trends in work disablement, that is, in persons reporting they are limited in the amount or kind of work they can do or are prevented from working altogether because of a health or physical condition. He concludes that work disability trends are real, with prevalence rates substantially higher in 1982 than they were twenty-five years earlier. Further, increasing disability rates do index deteriorating population health status because they are to a substantial extent accounted for by physical-sensory impairments and chronic disease conditions. The rising disability rates may be connected to concomitant reductions in age-adjusted mortality (discussed above). Although recent evidence suggests that, for example, heart disease incidence may be decreasing, this major cause of mortality is not apparently falling rapidly enough to offset disability prevalence rates that continue to rise. Finally, socioeconomic factors also influence disability, with perhaps one-third of the historical rise in prevalence stemming from economic changes.

Restricted Activity Days

Data from the National Health Interview Survey indicate that the number of bed days per person per year due to illness is slightly higher now than twenty years ago, but the trend has not been one of a consistent increase. Even though there have been no consistent trends in disability days, there have been marked increases among the poor in the average number of restricted activity and bed days (a subset of restricted activity days). At the same time there have been no such changes reported among higher income groups. It has been suggested (Wilson and Drury 1984) that the number of disability days may be a poor indicator of changes in health status

since it may reflect only trends in health utilization and a consequent increase in doctor-prescribed rest days. The implication is that, in the absence of a visit to a doctor, the individual would be less likely to restrict activity.

Limitation of Activity

During the past twenty-five years there has been a marked increase in the proportion of the population with long-term limitation of activity because of chronic illness. The rate for children under 17 years of age doubled between 1960 and 1979. Among adults the trends vary considerably by age and sex groups. The most striking change occurred between 1960–1961 and 1979, when the proportion of middle-aged males with activity limitations doubled from 4.4 to 10.8 percent. At least part of this increase has been attributed to the increase in disability benefit payments during the late 1960s and early 1970s, thus permitting earlier retirement on disability (Wilson and Drury 1984).

The Impact of Increasing Medical and Disability Benefits

It is thought that people are likely to classify themselves as disabled in some way if there is adequate compensation for any loss of earning power. Without recourse to direct empirical evidence, one could infer that such an effect would be most apparent in the male work force, a large sector of which either is unionized or otherwise has access to disability benefits. In contrast, a smaller effect would be expected among women in the labor force, who tend to be nonunionized and work in the competitive sector with minimal fringe benefits (O'Connor 1973). A negligible effect would be found in children and women not in the work force, as these groups are least likely to benefit economically from being classified as disabled.

These conjectures were investigated by McKinlay and McKinlay (1977b), who considered only the proportion unable to carry out, or limited in, major activity (hereafter just called "limited in major activity") within age, sex, and activity status groups. Limitation in other than major activity was excluded here because of changes in the method of collecting this information, which markedly affected the estimates as noted above (Wilder 1974; Gleeson 1972). Table 2 presents the estimated population and proportion limited in major activity by activity status, sex, and age. Usual activity is divided into two categories here—those *usually working*, aged 17 years and over only, and those *usually engaged in some other activity*, including all ages. There is a slight discrepancy in age groups for 1959–1960, when the "other" category was divided at age 15, not 17. (This accounts for the somewhat smaller population in the under-17 age group for all other usual activities, 1959–1960, and a compensating increase in population for the 17–44 age group.) A third classification (*currently working*), which is not exclusive of the two usual activity classifications but overlaps considerably with "usually working," is also included. It may be noted that for all years, substantially more women were currently working than considered themselves usually in the work force, indicating either temporary employment of women not regularly in the labor force or perhaps a tendency for women to classify themselves as homemakers, regardless of employment status. Differences in numbers currently and usually working are negligible for men, although in the same direction as for women, except for 1975, when slightly fewer men were currently working than usually did so.

When the proportion limited in activity was considered for these three classifications, men were more likely to be disabled than women in all categories, even among those under 17 years of age. (This difference remained when those limited in other than major activity were included in the estimates.) A second important finding is that women, regardless of activity status,

became increasingly disabled over the fifteen-year period considered—with an annual rate of increase between 2 and 3 percent for those 17 years and older. For those under 17 years (of both sexes) the disability rate, although low, more than doubled between 1959 and 1975, with the most rapid increase occurring after 1966. For men currently or usually working, the increase in activity limitation was negligible, but for those aged 17–44 not usually working there was more than a 50 percent increase. The decrease in limitation for the forty-five years and over group, not usually working, may be due to several factors, but it is notable that for the 45–64 age group (not shown in Table 2 because of variability in data availability over the period), there was a marked decline in absolute numbers usually working (particularly between 1971 and 1975) and a compensating increase in numbers not working. This shift out of the labor force clearly involved men not limited in major activity, given the apparent decrease in the proportion so disabled in this group (in the presence of a continuing rise in the actual number disabled).

These findings seem to confirm the conjectures made concerning the effect of benefits. It could be inferred that men have been affected by the increase in benefits, as the proportion disabled has not increased among those in the labor force but only among those in the younger age groups who are not working. Removal of the disabled from the work force because of increasingly available compensation would seem to be a reasonable explanation for this phenomenon. This inference is reinforced by the absence of such a shift among women, who have much more limited access to such benefits. It is possible that the higher rates of limitation in men are at least partly due to the rise in benefits, but given the marked increases in limitation among women and children (those under 17 years) it is reasonable to conclude that there has been a comparable real increase in disability in men. As an illustration, for women not working in the

TABLE 2 Percentage Limited in or Unable to Carry out Major Activity by Age, Sex, and Activity Status, United States, 1959–1975

Activity Status	Year	Male						Female					
		<17[a]		17–44		45+		<17		17–44		45+	
		Population[b]	%	Population	%	Population	%	Population	%	Population	%	Population	%
Usually working	1959–1960			25.0	4.1	17.6	10.6			11.0	3.2	7.6	7.0
	1966			26.0	4.4	18.7	11.4			11.9	2.8	9.1	6.2
	1971			30.0	4.0	19.4	11.0			15.3	3.6	10.5	8.5
	1975			31.1	4.4	18.9	11.6			18.8	4.3	10.6	9.7
Usually not working	1959–1960	28.3	1.0	7.5	6.8	6.4	55.7	27.2	0.7	24.6	4.4	19.2	22.3
	1966	34.0	0.9	6.0	9.6	7.6	58.7	32.8	0.8	23.6	4.8	20.9	24.2
	1971	33.9	1.6	7.7	9.1	8.6	56.7	32.7	1.3	23.7	5.1	22.0	27.6
	1975	31.6	2.1	8.8	10.6	10.4	54.5	30.4	1.6	23.9	6.5	24.4	31.8
Currently working	1959–1960			—	—	—	—			—	—	—	—
	1966			28.3	4.4	18.9	12.4			15.4	2.9	10.5	6.8
	1971			31.4	4.4	19.7	12.1			20.0	3.3	12.0	9.2
	1975			31.8	4.2	18.2	11.8			21.8	3.7	11.3	9.9

[a] In 1959–1960, the youngest group was defined as <15 and the next age group was 15–44.
[b] Population is given in millions.
Source: National Center for Health Statistics, Health Interview Survey, 1959–60, 1966, 1971, 1975, unpublished data.

age group 17–44 years, there was a 48 percent increase in limitation over the fifteen years considered, compared to a 56 percent increase among men in the same category. Thus, if we can assume a comparable rate of increase in disability, then only about one-sixth of the increase in this group of men would be attributable to the effect of benefits.

THE MEASUREMENT OF A LIFE FREE OF DISABILITY

If we conclude that there has been a real increase in disability, the next logical step is to combine this information meaningfully with mortality data to provide some more sensitive summary indicator of the health of the general population. Sullivan (1971) proposed a useful index of mortality and morbidity that consists of the calculation of a *life expectancy (L.E.) free of disability*. This is accomplished simply by multiplying the probability of survival by the estimated conditional probability of remaining free of disability (assuming survival). The resulting probability of survival free of disability is then used (instead of simply the probability of survival) to calculate an expected life span in the usual way. The resulting average is of life free of disability, which can then be compared with the overall life expectancy.

The conditional probabilities of remaining free of disability were calculated as follows, given the measurement problems outlined above. Because long-term or permanent disability is more closely measured by limitation in activity owing to chronic conditions than by restricted activity days, the proportion of the population either limited in, or unable to carry out, a major activity, or residing in a nursing home, was estimated for 1964, 1974, and 1985. Because this measure included only the more severely limited and because this limitation was due to a chronic condition, it seemed reasonable to assume that this limitation

persisted throughout the year. The proportion so calculated, therefore, could be considered as an estimate of the probability that a person alive at the beginning of the year would be so disabled during the year.

The resulting life expectancies for 1964, 1974, and 1985 are presented in Table 3. From the far right-hand columns of the table, it is clear that although overall life expectancy has increased over the two decades, most of this increase was in years of disability. For example, in 1964 a man reaching the age of 45 could expect to live nearly twenty more years free of disability and a further 7.2 years disabled. In 1985 a man of the same age had about the same number of years to live free of disability, but nearly ten years to live disabled. In other words, the gain of 2.8 years in overall life expectancy was almost entirely offset by a 2.5 increase in years of disability for men aged 45 years. The same argument applies for other age and sex categories, except for those over 65 years, who appear to have experienced small gains in expected life free of disability. Gruenberg (1977, p. 3) has argued that "the net effect of successful technological innovations used in disease control has been to raise the prevalence of certain diseases and disabilities by prolonging their average duration . . . the net contribution of our success has actually been to worsen the people's health." (See also Verbrugge 1984.)

The changes in L.E. free of disability demonstrated in Table 3 are consistent with changes in activity limitation already noted in Table 2. The major decreases in average life free of disability have been in the younger age groups (less than 45 years) for both sexes. The gain in years free of disability for those reaching 65 years is also consistent with improvements noted in older age groups in Table 2.

It is noteworthy that almost all of the changes in L.E. free of disability in Table 3 were observed since 1974, although small consistent changes were observed in the same directions in the prior decade.

TABLE 3 Trend in Total Life Expectancy (T.L.E.) and Life Expectancy Free of Disability (L.E.F.D.) for Various Ages, Male and Female, United States, 1964–1985

	Age	1964 T.L.E.	1964 L.E.F.D.	1974 T.L.E.	1974 L.E.F.D.	1985 T.L.E.	1985 L.E.F.D.	Increase in T.L.E.	Increase in L.E.F.D.
Male	0	66.8	59.2	68.1	59.2	71.2	51.9	4.4	−7.3
	45	27.1	19.9	27.8	19.8	29.9	20.2	2.8	0.3
	65	12.8	6.6	13.4	7.2	14.6	10.5	1.8	3.9
Female	0	73.7	65.5	75.8	65.3	78.2	57.9	4.5	−7.6
	45	32.5	25.0	33.9	24.6	35.5	23.8	3.0	−1.2
	65	16.2	10.2	17.5	10.7	18.6	13.4	2.4	3.2

Sources: U.S. Bureau of the Census, *Mortality Statistics*, part II, 1964. Washington, D.C.: U.S. Government Printing Office.

U.S. Bureau of the Census, *Vital Statistics*, 1974; unpublished data.

National Center for Health Statistics, Health Interview Survey, 1964, unpublished data.

C. S. Wilder (1976), Table 1.

National Center for Health Statistics, Nursing Home Survey, 1974, unpublished data.

Nelson (1967).

National Center for Health Statistics, *Vital Statistics of the US, 1984: Life Tables*: vol. 11, Section 6. DHHS Pub. No. (PHS) 87–1104. March 1987.

National Center for Health Statistics. Health Interview Survey, 1985, unpublished data.

National Center for Health Statistics. Nursing Home Survey, 1985, unpublished data.

These summary measures that combine morbidity and mortality data are, of course, not without methodological problems. Nursing home data are only available for those over 65 years, and it is assumed that residence in a nursing home occurs because the individual is unable to function in a non-institutional setting on a long-term basis. The extent to which younger people are confined to nursing homes is not well described by any national data sets. Moreover it is not clear that all nursing home admissions are for chronic functional limitations.

The startling recent increase in years of disability occurring at younger ages in both men and women has no obvious explanation but may at least partially result from real changes in disease patterns. For example, in 1984, for the first time, death from chronic obstructive pulmonary disease overtook influenza and pneumonia as the fifth major cause of mortality (NCHS 1985). In the last decade the equivalent category of diseases replaced digestive system diseases as the fifth group of conditions underlying physician visits and became the third major category of diagnoses for hospital discharges among women, when it had not previously been among the leading five discharge diagnoses for women (see sources for Table 1). Musculoskeletal system disorders and bodily impairments have also become more prominent in the last decade for both sexes as causes of activity limitation, replacing heart and circulatory system diseases. Asthma and other chronic lung conditions, as well as bodily impairment, may differentially affect younger age groups.

Finally, the apparent gains in L.E. free of disability for those over 65, in contrast with the losses evident for those under 45 in particular, may reflect real differences in disease patterns, and therefore health, between two very distinct generations—survivors of the pre–World War II cohort and the postwar "baby boom" cohort.

DISCUSSION

Returning to the central question posed in the introduction, it is not clear from the discussion and data presented here that the overall health of the American population is improving. On the contrary, evidence is presented that it may in fact be deteriorating in some measurable ways, despite decreases in most major causes of death.

Before proceeding to consider some of the implications of this general conclusion, let us summarize some of the findings presented with respect to the four goals posed in the introduction.

First, it is clear that mortality has declined in the United States this century, initially from rapid declines in infectious diseases and more recently from marked declines in coronary heart disease and stroke. At the same time, death rates from cancer, the second major cause of death, continue to increase.

Second, it is equally evident that a broad range of medical measures have had, and still have, relatively little impact on these declines. Primary medical prevention, such as vaccination, had some impact on poliomyelitis mortality, which was barely measurable in the overall decline of infectious diseases mortality. Secondary prevention through medication for high blood pressure and hypercholesterolemia has had commensurately small effects on coronary heart disease and stroke mortality. Medical interventions for cancer have had negligible or no effects on survival, and such medical interventions as coronary care units and coronary artery bypass surgery have had insignificant effects on cardiovascular deaths. The role of environmental and personal risk factors for major causes of death remains dominant, although the effects of *changes* in these primary factors on mortality have yet to be clearly assessed.

In other words, the recent decline in chronic disease mortality may, like the earlier decline in deaths from infectious diseases, be due primarily to environmental or personal hygiene changes rather than to traditionally defined medical interventions. Certainly, available evidence points in that direction.

Third, available morbidity data indicate that morbidity changes do not necessarily parallel mortality changes. Despite obvious methodological problems, it is also evident from data presented that morbidity, however measured, is not declining in a manner congruent with declines in mortality and may, in fact, be increasing for some subgroups.

Finally, a combined measure of morbidity and mortality—life expectancy free of disability—is presented which illustrates how some of these conflicting data could be meaningfully summarized. The implications of changes in this measure is that the gains in life expectancy may be largely (and increasingly) at the expense of health and, therefore, of the quality of life, if one assumes that health is a primary component of any measure of quality of life. For example, although medical care may not be a major factor in the decline of coronary heart disease mortality as demonstrated earlier, it may be an important factor in increasing survival, largely in the presence of disability. The importance of developing summary measures that include morbidity as well as mortality information (such as case-fatality rates or life expectancies free of disability) is obvious, if changing mortality trends are to be adequately explained. The implication that medical care may in fact be prolonging a life of less than optimal quality is certainly worthy of further investigation.

We have argued that medical measures and the presence of medical services were not primarily responsible for the modern decline in mortality in the United States and elsewhere. The question now remains, If they were not primarily responsible for it, then how is it to be explained? An adequate answer to this question would obviously require a more substantial research effort than that reported here, but is likely to be along the lines suggested by McKeown (1976a, 1976b) and those advanced above. We hope that continued discussion of the apparent modest contribution of medical care will serve as a catalyst for such research, incorporating adequate data and appropriate methods of analysis, in an effort to arrive at a more complete alternative explanation based on environmental or public health factors.

For many public health scholars, the underlying theme presented above—that medical care has contributed little to the modern decline in mortality and therefore to any improvement in health—is somewhat passé. There are, however, influential students of public health who continue to attribute far more to medical measures than the facts available warrant. Others continue to pay lip service to the importance of public health measures, while contradictorily supporting the perpetual expansion of more, but largely ineffective, medical services. In the context of the present fiscal crisis and limited resources, in which increased investments in medical care reduce support for public health initiatives, this may even be a disservice to the field.

We remain perplexed by at least the following: (1) the fact that the public health argument continues to be denounced by some influential figures as heretical, deliberately iconoclastic, or "just wrong"; (2) the spirited attempt made by some policy experts, usually in the name of humanism, to shore up and amplify the modest contribution of medical measures; (3) the disregard of decades of controversy in an attempt to broaden the scope of medical care so as to encompass and subsume the contribution of public health and other changes; (4) the lingering methodological quibbles over data and their presentation (e.g., logarithmic transformation versus arithmetic plot), as if their resolution would affect the explanation; (5) the fact that over the past decade at least there has been no significant reallocation of finite resources away from traditional curative care to public health; and (6) the fact that there has been little change in the content of medical training that would suggest acceptance, or even appreciation, of the modest contribution of specific medical measures as against public health contributions to the modern decline in mortality. On the basis of data presented by Cooper and Rice (1976) on the costs of broad categories of illness in the United States, Terris (1980) has estimated that an effective public health program could, by a conservative estimate, save annually 600,000 lives, 6 million person years of life, and $5 billion in medical costs.

To what extent has the reported wide appreciation of the contribution of public health measures been incorporated in national health policy? Is there any evidence that approaches to current problems are informed by lessons from the past?

Current policy with respect to the newly emerging infectious disease AIDS is very instructive in this regard. WHO estimates there may be 50 to 100 million persons infected with the virus of AIDS worldwide, 3 million of whom are sick with the disease. In the United States alone, more than 24,500 cases have been recorded, and between 1 and 1.5 million people are probably infected with the virus. With cases doubling annually, a tenfold increase is expected over the next five years, with 25 to 50 percent of those now infected progressing to AIDS. This means that by 1991 there will be 270,000 cases of AIDS in the United States alone—74,400 developing within that year. By that time, 179,000 will have died, 54,000 in 1991 alone (Silver 1987). Approximately $450 million was spent in the United States on AIDS research in 1987, and a further $500 million on treatment, primarily through the Medicaid programs of health care for the poor. This total of about $1 billion is up from only $8 million five years ago. Projections indicate that five years from now the federal government will be spending about $20 billion a year, primarily on treating the growing number of patients with AIDS. As in the past, progress against this modern scourge lies in public health measures (protection of the blood supply, reproductive education in schools, the use of condoms, community health interventions directed at IV drug abusers), *not* in the development of expensive and probably ineffective "magic bullets."

Viewing the current national effort against AIDS in its entirety, one can reasonably question whether the contribution of public health measures to improvements in a nation's health is really comprehended to the extent often claimed. Calling AIDS "Public Health Enemy Number 1," President Reagan, in the administration's first detailed policy statement on AIDS (presumably prepared by federal health officials), told a meeting of physicians that abstaining from sexual relations is the best way to prevent the disease (Boffey 1987). Public advertising of condoms is discouraged, and parents oppose the introduction of reproductive education in schools. Even public health figures, while acknowledging the contribution of public health measures to earlier diseases, view the search for a magic bullet (either a vaccine or a drug therapy) as the most promising approach to this new infectious epidemic.

In our view, the late-twentieth-century approach to the AIDS pandemic belies the claim that the arguments discussed above are passé and indicate instead that we still have a long way to go.

REFERENCES

Aberg, A., R. Bergstrand, S. Johanson, et al. 1984. Declining Trend in Mortality after Myocardial Infarction. *British Heart Journal* 51:346–351.

American Cancer Society. 1984. *Cancer Facts and Figures*. New York: The Society.

Amery, A., P. Brixho, D. Clement, et al. 1985.

Mortality and Morbidity Results from the European Working Party on High Blood Pressure in the Elderly Trial. *Lancet* 1:1349–1354.

Bailar, J. C., and E. M. Smith. 1986a. Progress against Cancer? *New England Journal of Medicine* 314(19):1226–1332.

———. 1986b. Progress against Cancer? *New England Journal of Medicine* 315:968.

Bauer, R. L., and J. R. H. Charlton. 1986. Area Variation in Mortality from Diseases Amenable to Medical Intervention: The Contribution of Differences in Morbidity. *International Journal of Epidemiology* 15:408–412.

Beaglehole, Robert. 1986. Medical Management and the Decline in Mortality from Coronary Heart Disease. *British Medical Journal* 292:33–35.

Beaglehole, Robert, Ruth Bonita, R. Jackson, A. Stewart, N. Sharpe, and G. E. Fraser. 1984. Trends in Coronary Heart Disease Event Rates in New Zealand. *American Journal of Epidemiology* 120:225–235.

Beaglehole, Robert, D. R. Hay, F. H. Foster, and D. N. Sharpe. 1981. Trends in Coronary Heart Disease Mortality and Associated Risk Factors in New Zealand. *New Zealand Medical Journal* 93:371–375.

Beaglehole, Robert, and R. T. Jackson. 1985. Coronary Heart Disease Mortality, Morbidity and Risk Factor Trends in New Zealand. *Cardiology* 72:29–34.

Beaglehole, Robert, John Larosa, Gerardo Heiss, et al. 1979. Secular Changes in Blood Cholesterol and Their Contribution to the Decline in Coronary Mortality, in R. Havlik and M. Feinleib, eds., *Proceedings of the Conference on the Decline in Coronary Heart Disease Mortality*. Washington, D.C.: Public Health Service, NIH Publication No. 79–610.

Boffey, Philip. 1987. Dr. Marks' Crusade: Shaking up Sloan-Kettering for a New Assault on Cancer. *The New York Times Magazine* April 26, 1987.

Bonita, Ruth, and Robert Beaglehole. 1982. Trends in Cerebrovascular Disease Mortality in New Zealand. *New Zealand Medical Journal* 95:411–414.

———. 1986. Does Treatment of Hypertension Explain the Decline in Mortality from Stroke? *British Medical Journal* 292:191–192.

———. 1987. The Increased Treatment of Hypertension Does Not Explain the Decline in Stroke Mortality in the United States, 1970–1980. Unpublished paper.

Braunwald, E. 1983. Effects of Coronary Artery Bypass Grafting on Survival. *New England Journal of Medicine* 309:1181–1184.

Brensike, J. F., R. I. Levy, S. F. Kelsey, et al. 1984. Effects of Therapy with Cholestyramine on Progression of Coronary Arteriosclerosis: Results of the NHLBI Type II Coronary Intervention Study. *Circulation* 69:313–324.

Cairns, John. 1985. The Treatment of Diseases and the War against Cancer. *Scientific American* 253:51–59.

Carr-Hill, Roy A., Geoffrey F. Hardman, and Ian T. Russell. 1987. Variations in Avoidable Mortality and Variations in Health Care Resources. *Lancet* i:789–791.

Charlton, J. R. H., R. Bauer, and A. Lakhani. 1984. Outcome Measures for District and Regional Health Care Planners. *Community Medicine* 6:306–315.

Charlton, J. R. H., R. M. Hartley, R. Silver, and W. W. Holland. 1983. Geographical Variation in Mortality from Conditions Amenable to Medical Intervention in England and Wales. *Lancet* i:691–696.

Charlton, J. R. H., A. Lakhani, and M. Aristidou. 1986. How Have Avoidable Death Indices for England and Wales Changed? 1974–78 compared with 1979–83. *Community Medicine* 8:304–314.

Charlton, J. R. H., and R. Velez. 1986. Some International Comparisons of Mortality Amenable to Medical Intervention. *British Medical Journal* 292:295–301.

Chirikos, Thomas N. 1986. Accounting for the Historical Rise in Work-Disability Prevalence. *Milbank Memorial Fund Quarterly* 64:271–301.

Cochrane, A. L. 1972. *Effectiveness and Efficiency: Random Reflections on the Health Service*. London: Nuffield Provincial Hospitals Trust.

Cooper, B. S., and Dorothy P. Rice. 1976. The Economic Cost of Illness Revisited. *Social Security Bulletin* 39:21–36.

Detre, K., M. L. Murphy, H. N. Hultgren, J. Thomsen, T. Takaro et al. 1977. Treatment of Chronic Stable Angina: A Preliminary Report of Survival Data of the Randomized Veterans Administration Cooperative Study.

New England Journal of Medicine 297:621–627.

Dobson, A. J., R. W. Gibberd, D. J. Wheeler, and S. R. Leeder. 1981. Age Specific Trends in Mortality from Ischaemic Heart Disease and Cerebrovascular Disease in Australia. *American Journal of Epidemiology* 113:404–412.

Durant, John R. 1987. Immunotherapy of Cancer: The End of the Beginning? *The New England Journal of Medicine* 316:939–940.

Dyken, M. L., P. A. Wolf, H. J. M. Barnett, J. J. Bergan, W. K. Kass, W. B. Kannel, L. Kuller, J. F. Kurtzke, and T. M. Sundt. 1984. A Statement for Physicians by the Subcommittee on Risk Factors and Stroke of the Stroke Council. *Stroke* 15:1105–1111.

Elveback, Lila R., D. C. Connolly, and L. T. Kurland. 1981. Coronary Heart Disease in Residents of Rochester, Minnesota: II. Mortality, Incidence, and Survivorship, 1950–1975. *Mayo Clinical Proceedings* 56:665–672.

Garraway, W. M., J. G. Whisnant, and I. Drury. 1983. The Continuing Decline in the Incidence of Stroke. *Mayo Clinical Proceedings* 58:520–523.

Gillum, R. F., M. R. Folsom, and H. Blackburn. 1984. Decline in Coronary Heart Disease Mortality: Old Questions and New Facts. *American Journal of Medicine* 76:1055–1065.

Gillum, Richard F., Aaron Folsom, Russell V. Luepker, David R. Jacobs, Jr., Thomas E. Kottke, Orlando Gomez-Marin, Ronald J. Prineas, Henry L. Taylor, and Henry Blackburn. 1983. Sudden Death and Acute Myocardial Infarction in a Metropolitan Area 1970–1980. *New England Journal of Medicine* 309:1353–1358.

Gleeson, G. A. 1972. Interviewing Methods in the Health Interview Survey. *Vital and Health Statistics*, Series 2, No. 48. DHEW Publication No. (HSM) 72–1048, National Center for Health Statistics.

Goldberg, R. J., J. M. Gore, J. S. Alpert, and J. E. Dalen. 1986. Recent Changes in Attack and Survival Rates of Acute Myocardial Infarction (1975 through 1981): The Worcester Heart Attack Study. *Journal of the American Medical Association* 255:2774–2779.

Goldman, Lee, and E. Francis Cook. 1984. The Decline in Ischemic Heart Disease Mortality Rates: An Analysis of the Comparative Effects of Medical Interventions and Changes in Lifestyle. *Annals of Internal Medicine* 101:825–835.

Goldman, Lee, E. Francis Cook, B. Hashimoto, P. Stone, J. Muller, and A. Loscalzo. 1982. Evidence that Hospital Care for Acute Myocardial Infarction Has Not Contributed to the Decline in Coronary Mortality between 1973–1974 and 1978–1979. *Circulation* 65:936–942.

Gomez-Marin, Orlando, Aaron R. Folsom, Thomas E. Kottke, Shu-Cher H. Wu, David R. Jacobs, Jr., Richard F. Gillum, Stanley A. Edlavitch, and Henry Blackburn. 1987. Improvement in Long-Term Survival among Patients Hospitalized with Acute Myocardial Infarction, 1970 to 1980: the Minnesota Heart Survey. *New England Journal of Medicine* 316:1353–1359.

Gruenberg, Ernest M. 1977. The Failures of Success. *Milbank Memorial Fund Quarterly* 55:3–24.

Haberman, S., R. Capildeo, and F. C. Rose. 1982. Diverging Trends in Cerebrovascular Disease and Ischaemic Heart Disease Mortality. *Stroke* 13:582–589.

Hill, J. D., J. R. Hampton, and J. R. A. Mitchell. 1978. A Randomized Trial of Home-versus-Hospital Management for Patients with Suspected Myocardial Infarction. *Lancet* 1:837–841.

Hypertension Detection and Follow-up Program Cooperative Research Group. 1982. Five-year Findings of the Hypertension Detection and Follow-up Program: III. Reduction in Stroke Incidence among Persons with High Blood Pressure. *Journal of the American Medical Association* 247:633–638.

Jackson, R. T., and R. Beaglehole. 1987. Dietary Fat, Serum Cholesterol, Cigarette Smoking and the Decline in Coronary Heart Disease Mortality in New Zealand. *International Journal of Epidemiology.* In press.

Kannel, William B. 1982. Meaning of the Downward Trend in Cardiovascular Mortality. *Journal of the American Medical Association* 247:877–880.

Kannel, William B., and T. J. Thom. 1984. Declining Cardiovascular Mortality. *Circulation* 70:331–336.

Killip, Thomas. 1979. Impact of Coronary Care on Mortality from Ischemic Heart Disease, in R. Havlik and M. Feinleib, eds., *Proceedings of the Conference on the Decline in Coronary Heart*

Disease Mortality. NIH Publication No. 79–610, Public Health Service.

Lenfant, C., and E. J. Roccella. 1984. Trends in Hypertension Control in the United States. *Chest* 86:459–462.

Levine, Sol, Jack Feldman, and Jack Elinson. 1981. Does Medical Care Do Any Good? In D. Mechanic, ed., *The Handbook of Health Care and the Health Professions*. New York: Free Press.

Levy, R. I., and J. Moskowitz. 1982. Cardiovascular Research: Decade of Progress, a Decade of Promise. *Science* 217:121–129.

Lipid Research Clinics Program. 1984. The Lipid Research Clinics Coronary Primary Prevention Trial Results: I. Reduction in Incidence of Coronary Heart Disease. *Journal of American Medical Association* 251:351–364.

Luchi, Robert J., Stewart M. Scott, Robert H. Deupree, and the Principal Investigators and Their Associates of Veterans Administration Cooperative Study No. 28. 1987. Comparison of Medical and Surgical Treatment for Unstable Angina Pectoris: Results of a Veterans Administration Cooperative Study. *New England Journal of Medicine* 316:977–984.

Marmot, M. G., and M. E. McDowall. 1986. Mortality, Decline and Widening Social Inequalities. *Lancet* 2:274–276.

Marshall, James, and Saxon Graham. 1986. Cancer, in L. Aiken and D. Mechanic, eds., *Applications of Social Science to Clinical Medicine and Health Policy*. New Brunswick, N.J.: Rutgers University Press.

Martin, C. A., M. S. T. Hobbs, and B. K. Armstrong. 1984. The Fall in Mortality from Ischemic Heart Disease in Australia: Has Survival after Myocardial Infarction Improved? *Australian and New Zealand Journal of Medicine* 14:435–438.

Mather, H. G. et al. 1971. Acute Myocardial Infarction: Home and Hospital Treatment. *British Medical Journal* 3:334–338.

———. 1976. A Comparison between Home and Hospital Care for Patients. *British Medical Journal* 1:925–929.

McKeown, Thomas. 1976a. *The Modern Rise of Population*. London: Edward Arnold.

———. 1976b. *The Role of Medicine: Dream, Mirage or Nemesis*. London: Nuffield Provincial Hospitals Trust.

McKinlay, John. 1979. Epidemiological and Political Determinants of Social Politics Regarding the Public Health. *Social Science and Medicine* 13:541–558.

———. 1980. Evaluating Medical Technology in the Context of a Fiscal Crisis: The Case of New Zealand. *Milbank Memorial Fund Quarterly* 58:217–267.

———. 1981. From "Promising Report" to "Standard Procedure": Seven Stages in the Career of a Medical Innovation. *Milbank Memorial Fund Quarterly* 59, no. 3: 374–411.

McKinlay, John B., and Sonja M. McKinlay. 1977a. The Questionable Effect of Medical Measures on the Decline of Mortality in the United States in the Twentieth Century. *Milbank Memorial Fund Quarterly* 55:405–428.

———. 1977b. A Refutation of the Thesis that the Health of the Nation Is Improving. Unpublished manuscript, Boston University.

McMahon, S. W., J. A. Cutler, C. D. Furberg, and G. H. Payne. 1986. The Effects of Drug Treatment for Hypertension on Morbidity and Mortality from Cardiovascular Disease: A Review of Randomized Controlled Trials. *Prog Card Dis* 29(Supp.):99–148.

McMahon, S. W., J. A. Cutler, J. D. Neaton, C. D. Furberg, J. D. Cohen, L. H. Kuller, and J. Stamler. 1986. For the Multiple Risk Factor Intervention Trial Research Group: Relationship of Blood Pressure to Coronary and Stroke Morbidity and Mortality in Clinical Trials and Epidemiologic Studies. *Journal of Hypertension* 4 (Supp. 6):514–517.

Medical Research Council Working Party. 1985. MRC Trial of Treatment of Mild Hypertension: Principal Results. *British Medical Journal* 291:97–104.

Metropolitan Life Insurance Company. 1979. *Statistical Bulletin* 60:2.

Morris, A. L., V. Nernberg, N. P. Roos, P. Henteloff, and L. Roos. 1983. Acute Myocardial Infarction: Survey of Urban and Rural Hospitals Mortality. *American Heart Journal* 105:44.

Morris, N. M., J. R. Udry, and C. L. Chase. 1975. Shifting Age-Parity Distribution of Births and the Decrease in Infant Mortality. *American Journal of Public Health* 65:359–362.

Multiple Risk Factor Intervention Trial. 1982. Risk Factor Changes and Mortality Results. *Journal of the American Medical Association* 248:1465.

National Center for Health Statistics (NCHS). 1973. Plan and Operation of the First National Health and Nutrition Examination Survey, 1970–73. *Vital and Health Statistics,* Series 1:10a. DHEW Publication No. (PHS) 78.

———. 1981. Plan and Operation of the Second National Health and Nutrition Examination Survey: United States 1976–80. *Vital and Health Statistics*, Series 1:15. DHEW Publication No. (PHS) 81.

———. 1985. Health Interview Survey. Unpublished data.

National Heart, Lung and Blood Institute (NHLBI). 1984. *Heart and Vascular Diseases: Tenth Report of the Director, NHLBI Ten-Year Review and Five-Year Plan.* NIH Publication No. 84–2357, Department of Health and Human Services.

National Institutes of Health (NIH). 1985. Concensus Development Conference Statement: Lowering Blood Cholesterol to Prevent Heart Disease. *Journal of the American Medical Association* 253:2080–2086.

O'Connor, J. 1973. *The Fiscal Crisis of the State.* New York: Saint Martin's Press.

Ostfeld, Adrian M. 1986. Cardiovascular Disease, in L. H. Aiken and D. Mechanic, eds., *Applications of Social Science to Clinical Medicine and Health Policy.* New Brunswick, N.J.: Rutgers University Press.

Pocock, S. J., D. G. Cook, A. G. Shaper, A. N. Phillips, and M. Walker. 1987. Social Class Differences in Ischaemic Heart Disease in British Men. *Lancet* July 25, 1987.

Powles, John. 1973. On the Limitations of Modern Medicine. *Science, Medicine and Man* 1:1–30.

Ravenholt, R. T. 1985. Tobacco's Impact on Twentieth-Century U.S. Mortality Patterns. *American Journal of Preventive Medicine* 1:4–17.

Roccella, E. J., and G. W. Ward. 1984. The National High Blood Pressure Education Program: A Description of Its Utility as a Generic Program mode. *Health Education Quarterly* 11:225–242.

Rosenberg, Steven A., Michael T. Lotze, Linda M. Muul, Alfred E. Chang, Fred P. Avis, Susan Leitman, W. Marston Linehan, Cary N. Robertson, Roberta E. Lee, Joshua T. Rubin, Claudia A. Seipp, Colleen G. Simpson, and Donald E. White. 1987. A Progress Report on the Treatment of 157 Patients with Advanced Cancer Using Lymphokine-activated Killer Cells and Interleukin-2 or High-Dose Interleukin-2 Alone. *New England Journal of Medicine* 316:889–897.

Rowland, Michael, and Jean Roberts. 1982. Blood Pressure Levels and Hypertension in Persons Ages 6–74 Years: United States, 1976–80. *Advancedata,* no. 84.

Rutstein, David D., William Berenberg, Thomas C. Chalmers, Charles G. Child III, Alfred P. Fishman, and Edward B. Perrin. 1976. Measuring the Quality of Medical Care. *New England Journal of Medicine* 294:582–588.

———. 1980. Measuring the Quality of Medical Care: Second Revision of Tables of Indexes. *New England Journal of Medicine* 302:1146.

Schneyer, S., J. S. Landefeld, and F. S. Sandifer. 1981. Biomedical Research and Illness: 1900–1979. *Milbank Memorial Fund Quarterly* 59 (Winter):44–58.

Silver, George. 1987. New Scourge: Old Challenge. *Lancet* ii:93.

Soltero, I., and R. Cooper. 1980. Improved Hypertension Control and Decline in Cardiovascular Mortality. *Comprehensive Therapy* 6:60–64.

Stallones, R. A. 1980. The Rise and Fall of Ischaemic Heart Disease. *Scientific American* 243:53–59.

Starfield, Barbara. 1985. Motherhood and Apple Pie: The Effectiveness of Medical Care for Children. *Milbank Memorial Fund Quarterly* 63:523–546.

Statistical Abstract of the U.S. 1975. Washington, D.C: U.S. Government Printing Office.

Stern, Michael P. 1979. The Recent Decline in Ischemic Heart Disease Mortality. *Annals of Internal Medicine* 91:630–640.

Stewart, A. W., R. Beaglehole, G. E. Fraser, and D. N. Sharpe. 1984. Trends in Survival after Myocardial Infarction in New Zealand, 1974–1981. *Lancet* 2:444–446.

Sullivan, D. F. 1971. A Single Index of Mortality and Morbidity. *HSMHA Health Reports* 86:347–354.

Summers, Lawrence H. 1987. A Couple of Good Taxes. *The Boston Sunday Globe* January 18, 1987.

Susser, M., W. Watson, and K. Hopper. 1986. *Sociology in Medicine.* New York: Oxford University Press.

Takaro, T., H. Hultgren, K. Detre, and W. Pe-duzzi. 1982. The VA Cooperative Study of Stable Angina: Current Status. *Circulation* 65(II):60–67.

Terris, Milton. 1980. Epidemiology as a Guide to Health Policy. *Annual Review of Public Health* 1:323–344.

Uemura, K., and Z. Pisa. 1985. Recent Trends in Cardiovascular Disease Mortality in 27 In-dustrialized Countries. *World Health Statistical Quarterly* 38:142–156.

Veitch, Andrew. 1987. Scientists Home in on Cancer Weapon. *The Manchester Guardian* April 26, 1987.

Verbrugge, Lois M. 1984. Longer Life but Worsening Health? Trends in Health and Mortality of Middle-aged and Older Women. *Milbank Memorial Fund Quarterly* 62, no. 3:475–519.

Veterans Administration Cooperative Group on Antihypertensive Agents. 1970. Effect of Treatment on Morbidity in Hypertension: II. Results of Patients with Diastolic Blood Pres-sure Averaging 90 through 114 mmHg. *Jour-nal of the American Medical Association* 213:1143–1152.

Veterans Administration Coronary Bypass Sur-gery Cooperative Study Group. 1984. Eleven-year Survival in the Veterans Admin-istration Randomized Trial of Coronary By-pass Surgery for Stable Angina. *New England Journal of Medicine* 311:1333–1339.

Weinblatt, E., J. D. Goldberg, W. Ruberman, C. W. Frank, M. A. Monk, and B. S. Chaudhary.

1982. Mortality after First Myocardial Infarc-tion: Search for a Secular Trend. *Journal of the American Medical Association* 247:1576–1581.

Weinstein, Milton C., and William B. Stason. 1985. Cost-Effectiveness of Interventions to Prevent or Treat Coronary Heart Disease. *American Review of Public Health* 6:41–63.

West, William H., Kurt W. Tauer, John R. Yanelli, Gailen D. Marshall, Douglas W. Orr, Gary B. Thurman, and Robert K. Oldham. 1987. Constant-Infusion Recombinant Inter-leukin-2 in Adoptive Immunotherapy of Ad-vanced Cancer. *New England Journal of Medi-cine* 316:898–905.

Whisnant, J. P. 1984. The Decline of Stroke. *Stroke* 15:160–168.

Wilder, C. S. 1974. Limitation of Activity and Mobility due to Chronic Conditions, United States, 1972. *Vital and Health Statistics,* Series 10, No. 96. DHEW Pub. No. (HSM) 75–1523, National Center for Health Statistics.

Wilson, R. W., and T. F. Drury. 1984. Interpret-ing Trends in Illness and Disability: Health Statistics and Health Status. *Annual Review of Public Health* 5:83–106.

Wing, S. 1984. The Role of Medicine in the Decline of Hypertension Related Mortality. *International Journal of Health Services* 14:649–666.

Wright, N. H. 1972. Some Estimates of the Po-tential Reductions in the United States Mor-tality Rate by Family Planning. *American Journal of Public Health* 62:1130–1134.

CHAPTER
3

HEALTH, DISEASE, AND THE SOCIAL STRUCTURE

HOWARD B. KAPLAN

OVERVIEW

Studies on the relationship between social structure and health or disease states are highly variable, depending on the aspects of the social structure they focus upon. The major elements of the social structure that investigators seek to relate to health and illness, both cross-sectionally and longitudinally, are social identities (positions or statuses), social relationships, and the more inclusive sociocultural system.

Social Identities

Numerous investigations examine the direct or indirect effects on health of socioeconomic characteristics, age, gender, religion, race, ethnicity, marital status, occupation, and a wide range of other structural characteristics. Underlying this work is the proposition that social positions evoke differential responses and prescribe differential behaviors within a group or community. For example, the differential valuation of age groups, such as infants, young people, and the aged, have implications for the amount and kinds of health care that are made available to individuals, and the role behavior associated with age results in greater or lesser exposure to pathogenic environmental circumstances and vulnerability to disease.

Social Relationships

Other investigations consider the influence of participation in social networks and the nature of the social relationships upon health status. The ways social relationships are structured depends on the individuals' particular social statuses and those of persons with whom they are interacting. The behaviors of individuals and their responses to the actions of others in such social contexts as marriage, friendship, parenthood, and work group affect the likelihood of exposure to health-promoting and health-threatening circumstances, vulnerability to disease, and the course of illnesses.

Sociocultural System

Relationships between the social structure and health frequently focus upon the characteristics of the social system, such as the rate of social change, the nature of consensual values, or health-relevant behavior patterns. Consensual values about health and cost containment influence decisions about the provision of health care facilities. The values that the society places upon science, technology, and equity influence arrangements for health care. Evaluative orientations toward prevention as opposed to cure, the stigmata associated with particular physical and psychological conditions, efficiency versus individualization, competition versus standardization, also affect responses to health-relevant conditions. Prevalent patterns relating to exercise, diet, alcohol and tobacco consumption, and sleep have more or less direct effects upon morbidity and mortality.

The differentiation between broad sociocultural context, social identities, and social relationships is blurred. Nevertheless, they are a heuristic means for organizing the relevant literature.

SOCIAL STRUCTURE, HEALTH, AND DISEASE: MEDIATING FACTORS

Generally, aspects of the social structure are believed to reflect or influence three categories of variables that, in turn, influence health or disease. First, social-structural factors are related to exposure to health-promoting or pathogenic circumstances. Second, these factors affect the ability of the individual to resist pathological outcomes of exposure to such factors. Third, they determine access to health care. In turn, the pathogenic circum-

stances, vulnerability characteristics, and access to health care determine the onset and course of disease.

Health-Promoting and Pathogenic Circumstances

Position in the social structure influences a person's health status by inducing him or her to behave in ways that either promote or threaten health status (eating, exercise, smoking patterns) and by exposing the person to social and physical environments that vary in the degree to which they are threats to psychological and physical health, for example, noise, chemical pollutants, social rejection, and risks of accidental injury.

The consequences of the person's behavior for his or her own health may be more or less consciously intended; an individual may behave without awareness of the relevance of the behavior for his or her health or may recognize that his or her anticipated behavior has consequences for health status.

As Berkman (1985, p. 258) observes,

individuals in a network frequently feel constrained to behave like other network members. Thus, people who have ties with people who smoke cigarettes, drink alcohol, are physically active, or maintain certain dietary practices may follow the pattern set forth by their group simply to maintain their group identity. . . . Therefore, groups or networks have the potential to be either health promoting or not, and this may influence the health status of individuals.

The health-threatening or health-enhancing aspects of the physical and social environment may be intrinsically or instrumentally relevant to health status. Thus, chemical pollution may represent an intrinsic risk to psychological health but, at the same time, is instrumental in leading to other intrinsically health-threatening conditions. The psychological distress that accompanies social rejection has an impact on the immune system and leads to maladaptive, intrinsically health-threatening responses. Immune-deficiency states render the individual vulnerable to disease that he or she would otherwise be able to ward off (Guillemin, Cohn, and Melnechuk 1985). In addition, any of a number of maladaptive responses to stress—such as alcohol abuse, smoking, drug abuse, suicidal behavior, and risk taking (Kaplan 1983, 1986)—increase the risk of illness or injury. The end result is the observation of linkages between stress and health (Cooper 1983; Elliott and Eisdorfer 1982).

Vulnerability

The environmental circumstances and personal behaviors that are shaped by social structural arrangements impact on individuals' vulnerability to adverse effects: For example, exposure to certain disease-causing organisms would not result in the full-blown disease if the person was not vulnerable to the adverse effects. Thus, poor, undernourished children may die from diarrhea, whereas better-fed ones are minimally affected.

Numerous indicators of vulnerability to disease have been posited, including psychological attitudes, physical hardiness, immunologic competence, genetic dispositions, and social networks. With regard to psychological attitudes, the notion of hardiness—a tendency to resist illness—has been introduced. In a prospective study over a five-year period, Kobasa, Maddi, and Kahn (1982) observed that hardiness (commitment, control, response to challenge) is associated with resistance to illness, particularly under increasingly stressful circumstances. Similar ideas are suggested by Antonovsky (1984). The resources that permit an individual to resist a disease have in common that they provide life experiences characterized by such features as consistency and participation in decision making. Such life experiences are provided by, for example, membership in the affluent class, living in a stable society, having a clear religious stance, and having social supports (Antonovsky 1984).

Health Care Activities and Resources

Another category of variables that are interpreted as mediating relationships between the social structure and health status are activities and resources that limit or reverse morbid processes. Thus, Berkman (1985, pp. 257–258) states that the relationship between social networks and health status may be mediated first, through the provision of advice, services, and access to social contacts. Individuals with particular network ties simply get superior health care, which in turn influences their physical health. Second is the direct provision of aid, services, and tangible or economic assistance to individuals. Some networks take better care of their members than others—independent of professional medical services—and this influences a member's health status.

SOCIAL IDENTITIES

Morbidity and mortality rates, in general and for particular diseases, and changes in these rates, have been associated with a variety of social identities, particularly of gender, socioeconomic status, occupation, minority status, and age. With regard to gender, the risk of death is higher for males than females for all leading causes of death and at all ages (Verbrugge 1985; Nathanson 1984). For example, males have more deaths from injuries than females. By the time a male reaches young adulthood he has nearly four times the risk of death from a nonintentional injury than does a female (Rivara 1984). Moreover, while men have fewer health problems, those they have tend to be more serious; particularly between ages 17 and 44, men are more likely to suffer injuries, long-term impairment, and such life-threatening chronic diseases as emphysema, athersclerosis, and coronary heart disease (Verbrugge 1985; Wingard 1984; Waldron 1983).

Women tend to have greater morbidity from both acute conditions (conditions of the respiratory and digestive system, infectious-parasitic diseases, injuries at older ages) and nonfatal chronic diseases (e.g., chronic bronchitis, sinusitis, arthritis, hemorrhoids, hypertensive disease) and short-term disabilities (even exclusive of reproductive conditions). This is reflected in restricted activities for health problems (Verbrugge 1985; Hing, Kovar, and Rice 1983; Wingard 1984). Particularly in the middle and older ages, women also report more long-term disabilities as a result of chronic health problems; these disabilities are reflected in limitations in shopping, going to church, and engaging in recreation (Verbrugge 1985). Rates for anorexia nervosa are higher in adolescent and young adult women (Johnson 1982). Rates for depression also have been found to be higher for women (Weissman and Klerman 1977; Al-Issa 1982). With regard to changes in gender differentials, there are indications that the American population may be shifting toward greater equality in mortality for the sexes (Verbrugge 1985).

Socioeconomic status has strong associations with morbidity rates. Age-adjusted rates of chronic illness indicate that the prevalence and severity of chronic disease is associated with socioeconomic status, with more impoverished individuals experiencing greater prevalence and severity (Newacheck et al. 1980; Egbuono and Starfield 1982; Dutton 1986). For example, socioeconomic status, as reflected in education and family income, varies inversely with systolic and diastolic blood pressures (Herd and Weiss 1984; Patel 1984). Children living in impoverished conditions have been noted to have higher injury rates (MacKay et al. 1979). In addition, social class differences have been observed with regard to rates of mental illness, whether the rates have been expressed in terms of treatment statistics or observation in the general population (Dohrenwend et al. 1980). In particular, Brown and Harris (1978) found that psychiatric disorder was more prevalent among working-class than middle-class women.

Differences in mortality and morbidity

rates also have been noted by employment status and occupation, although it is problematic as to whether or not the relationships are accounted for solely by the socioeconomic implications of these variables. Employment tends to be associated with good health (Haw 1982; Haynes and Feinleib 1980; Verbrugge and Madans 1985). A study of civil servants in London (Marmot, Shipley, and Rose 1984) reported an association between mortality rates and lower grades of employment for major causes of death. More particularly, Marmot and associates (1978) reported a relationship between employment grade and coronary heart disease mortality. Men in the lowest socioeconomic grade had between three and four times the coronary heart disease mortality, as well as higher levels of blood pressure, than the administrators that make up the highest employment grade.

The association of race with mortality and morbidity rates also may reflect, at least in part, effects of differential socioeconomic status. Nonwhites have higher mortality rates than whites in virtually all age groups (U.S. Congress 1984; NCHS 1982). Regarding cause of death, whereas only 6 percent of the deaths of white subjects in the 15–19 year old population are caused by homicide, nearly 26 percent of the deaths among black adolescents in this age group is attributed to homicide. The severity and prevalence of certain infectious diseases have also been reported to be greater among minority children (U.S. House of Representatives 1979). Among adults in the United States, blood pressures are consistently higher in blacks than in whites, regardless of age and gender (Harlan 1984; Herd and Weiss 1984).

Marital status is associated with better health for both sexes (Verbrugge 1985). Married subjects have lower mortality and morbidity rates than widowed subjects of comparable age and sex (Stroebe et al. 1982) and display fewer health difficulties than divorced individuals (Bloom, Asher, and White 1978; Verbrugge 1979).

Age has been associated with differential mortality and morbidity rates. The number of deaths from nonintentional injuries increases throughout childhood. The highest rates are in the late teenage–young adulthood years (Rivara 1984). Adolescents and young adults (age 15–24) currently have a higher death rate than they did some twenty years ago (Green and Horton 1982). School-age children are most susceptible to streptococcal infections, followed by 2 to 5 year olds. (Meyer and Haggerty 1985). Adults are the next highest, and infants under 2 years of age the lowest with regards to rates of acquisition. However, once the infectious agents have colonized, the chance of an individual becoming ill does not vary much among the different age groups.

Frequently, interaction effects among social identities are observed. Gender-related differences in morbidity are sometimes contingent on social grouping. Thus, black men have coronary heart disease rates similar to those of white men, whereas black women have much higher coronary heart disease rates than white women (Gillum and Gillum 1984). The significance of marital status for mortality appears to be greater for men than for women. Helsing, Szklo, and Comstock (1981) reported from a ten-year retrospective cohort study that widowerhood carried an increased mortality rate among men, an increased rate was not found among widows. This effect remained after controlling for age, education, age at first marriage, cigarette smoking, church attendance, and economic status. The relationship between parental status and health is contingent upon the performance of other social roles as well. Thus, Verbrugge (1985, p. 169) summarizes: "Non-married women who work and also have children have poorer health than their peers without children; the children make no health difference for employed married women." Finally, it is noted that changes in, as well as differentiation by, social identities are related to morbidity and mortality rates. For example, changes in

marital status (divorce and widowhood), occupational status, and residence have been associated with cardiovascular disease (Kasl and Cobb 1980; Jacobs and Ostfeld 1977; Syme, Hyman, and Enterline 1964).

Mediating Variables

Relationships such as those described above are accounted for in terms of (1) differential exposure to pathogenic or salutary circumstances, (2) variability in susceptibility or vulnerability to disease, and (3) variable access to health care resources.

Pathogenic circumstances. The roles associated with specific identities and the symbolic significance of these identities to others affect the likelihood of engagement in health-threatening or health-promoting behaviors.

Among the explanations for male-female differences in childhood injury rates is the differential role definitions imposed by parents. Parents expect male children to interact with their environment in a physically challenging manner, even though boys are no more skilled than girls in motor development. As Rivara (1984, p. 1011) observes, "the type of injuries that reflect the most marked sex differences are contusions, abrasions, lacerations, fractures, and concussions. These are exactly the types of injuries that result from the more physically active and aggressive style of the male." Greater exposure to some risk factors increases the likelihood of some injuries. Thus, males in all age groups had higher rates for bicycle-related injuries than females because they used them more frequently or for more hours (Rivara 1984). However, for other types of injuries, gender related differences are not accounted for by differential exposure to risk. Thus, although boys between the ages of 5 and 8 had higher rates of pedestrian injuries than girls in the same age group, the higher injury rates were not due to increased exposure to risk. Males and females had equal exposure to risk as measured by the number of roads crossed in the course of the day and the traffic density on these roads (Rivara 1984).

In the past, the masculine role has been associated with a number of other health-threatening behaviors as well, including greater lifetime use of tobacco, alcohol, and risk-related patterns of driving (Verbrugge 1985). However, changes in some aspects of these roles have occurred, in particular with regard to alcohol use, tobacco use, and sexual activity (Gordon and McAlister 1982; Marshall and Graham 1986).

Although there appears to be no overall gender-related advantage with regard to engaging in preventive health behaviors, gender-related differences in terms of preventive activities have been noted. Women are more likely to use vitamins, brush their teeth, and get preventive physical checkups, whereas men are more likely to engage in strenuous exercise and get chest X-rays (Verbrugge 1985; Mechanic and Cleary 1980).

Certain of the health-relevant effects of gender may be less direct and accounted for by consequences of prescribed gender-related roles. Conventional wisdom would have it that gender-related adult roles influence the risk of injury and illness. However, there is little comparative research regarding health risks in gender-related activities (Verbrugge 1985). But the roles that women are required to play may place them at greater risk of psychological distress (Gove 1985; Marcus, Seeman, and Telesky 1985), whether due to the social devaluation of the homemaker status or the excess demands placed on women by virtue of multiple roles (Verbrugge 1985).

Socioeconomic status also influences socialization of individuals with regard to health-related practices and exposure to social and physical environments that are pathogenic or health enhancing. The Alameda County study (Berkman and Breslow 1983) reports favorable health practices to be associated with higher socioeconomic

levels, and membership in higher socioeconomic groupings is associated with performing such preventive health behaviors as good nutrition habits, medical checkups, use of seat belts, and immunizations (Langlie 1977). Individuals of low socioeconomic status are more likely to engage in practices that induce ill health, and they are less likely to engage in practices that forestall illness-inducing conditions. They tend to use cigarettes and alcohol and to engage in dietary and exercise patterns that have been related to specific disease entities (Ostfeld 1986). Social status may have indirect effects: Status influences the likelihood that both parents are present in the household to exercise effective supervision over the children, thus restricting opportunity for engaging in early sexual activity (Zelnik, Kantner, and Ford 1981) that has adverse health-related effects for both the adolescent and any offspring that may result from precocious sexual activity. The life-style factors associated with poverty have direct or indirect implications for health status. Living in areas where chemical industries are common may affect rates of cancer, dermatological disorders, and respiratory diseases; living in poverty-stricken neighborhoods increases the likelihood of physical injury from accidents or crime and the likelihood of contracting communicable diseases as a result of crowded living arrangements or infestation with rats and other vermin (Dutton 1986).

The higher rates of injury observed among children in low-income families (Westfelt 1982) has been accounted for in part by the explanation that the nature of the risk factor encountered by these children requires an inordinately high level of performance to avoid such injuries. Examples are space heaters, open fireplaces, faulty wiring, firetrap tenements, and play areas with high traffic density. Lower socioeconomic status also increases the likelihood of exposure to a variety of stress-inducing circumstances, including noise (Starfield 1984), crowding (Gove, Hughes, and Galle 1979), and such self-devaluing circumstances as unemployment (Scholzmann and Verba 1978) or the recognition of having a disvalued social identity and concomitant self-derogating attitude (Lindheim and Syme 1983).

Socioeconomic status is associated with the nature of the occupations in which individuals engage as well as employment status. Certain occupations carry with them great physical risk, and others affect morbidity via the psychological stress associated with the position. X-ray technicians are more likely to be exposed to radiation injury, football players are more likely to be exposed to knee injuries, and construction workers are more likely to be exposed to head injuries (Rivara 1984). Likewise, workers in specific industries have differential risks for being exposed to carcinogenic substances (Marshall and Graham 1986).

Stress, in itself, may increase the likelihood of psychological or somatic disorders. In addition, stress may affect the person's willingness to participate in activities that may have positive health-promotional value. Such activities include weight loss programs, exercise classes, and other activities that are facilitated by stress-free circumstances. House and Cottington (1986) cite a number of prospective studies that suggest an association between job pressure and changes in health status. In a particularly interesting study (Kittel, Kornitzer, and Dramaix 1980), the incidence of coronary heart disease was appreciably higher among the employees of a private bank that was characterized by greater organizational change and competition than among employees of a public bank that was not undergoing such organizational change and where the employees did not appear to be susceptible to extreme occupational pressures.

Patel (1984) has reviewed a number of studies indicating that occupations requiring constant vigilance or extreme responsibility may adversely affect blood pressure. There is a higher prevalence and increased

incidence of hypertension occurring at a younger age in air traffic controllers, as compared to second-class airmen (Cobb and Rose 1973). Among controllers, those working at high-traffic density towers had a higher incidence than those at low-traffic density towers. An excessive incidence of hypertension was noted among workers at the central telephone exchange in the Soviet Union (Miasnikov 1961). Morris and associates (1966) reported higher levels of blood pressure and more ischemic heart disease in London bus drivers than in conductors.

Unemployment status is associated with a variety of adverse health-related outcomes that are interpretable as concomitants or maladaptive responses to psychosocial stress. Kasl and Cobb (1980) observed that the blood pressure of blue-collar workers tended to rise after a plant shutdown and remained higher during the period of unemployment. Dutton (1986) cites findings of relationships between unemployment and child abuse and between unemployment and suicide, homicide, and mental problems.

Adverse health effects associated with race-differentiated statuses, insofar as race is correlated with socioeconomic status, also tend to be mediated by differential exposure to pathogenic circumstances. Thus, behavior patterns associated with good health are less likely to be observed among blacks (Berkman and Breslow 1983). Black children are more likely to suffer from nutritional deficiencies (DHEW 1979; Rice and Danchik 1979). Differences in birth weight between white and black infants are observed even after controlling for such socioeconomic factors as maternal education (McCormick 1986).

Not all of the consequences of disadvantaged social identities are adverse. In the face of stress-inducing circumstances, sometimes otherwise socially disadvantaged persons will call forth competencies; thus, black adolescents are more likely to return to school following the birth of children than white ones, presumably because they continue to live with their families and have child caretakers (Mott and Maxwell 1981).

Pathogenic behaviors and experiences associated with age-differentiated identities may mediate observed relationships between age and morbidity and mortality rates. Role definitions associated with adolescence and their environments may pose severe risks to the adolescent's health status (Jessor 1984). Role definitions associated with adolescent maturation may involve experimentation—access to which is provided by their peer groups—with drug use, precocious sexual activity, risk taking, and changes in diet. Alcohol and drug use, alone or in combination with driving, increase the risks of life-threatening accidents. Further, adolescents may be at particular peril with regard to risks to health because they are subject to a wide variety of psychosocial stressors that create a disparity between their perception of the demands made on them and their ability to meet those demands. Ways in which they cope with these stressors may have adverse consequences for health. Consistent with these generalizations are observations that 70 percent of all deaths between the ages of 12 and 17 are due to accidents or violence. The leading cause of death is motor vehicle accidents, followed by other accidents, then by suicide, and then homicide (Green and Horton 1982). Half of the motor vehicle deaths among teens and young adults are related to alcohol use (Rivara 1984). Some pathogenic correlates of adolescence show some evidence of changing in a more favorable direction. For example, teenage smoking has decreased significantly among boys of all age categories and among girls aged 12 through 16 (Green and Horton 1982).

Correlates of older age have both pathogenic and health-protective consequences. Numerous potentially stressful circumstances accompany the aging process, including retirement, children leaving home,

death of a spouse, perceptions of increasing weakness of oneself or of one's loved ones, and the expectation of an abbreviated future (Achte, Malassu, and Saarenheimo 1986). Other correlates relate to role behaviors associated with blood pressure. In industrial societies, blood pressure increases are associated with increases in age; however, in certain primitive societies, blood pressure does not increase with age. The explanation may be that body weight does not increase with age in primitive populations that do not show an increase in blood pressure (Herd and Weiss 1984). On the other hand, older people are more likely to engage in such direct risk-preventive health behavior as safe driving and pedestrian behavior, personal hygiene practices, and abstention from smoking (Langlie 1977).

One of the most significant of social identities having an impact on subsequent health status is that of "patient" status itself. Wortman and Conway (1985) cite numerous studies indicating that the adoption of the social identity of "patient" evokes changed expectations and responses to the individual possessing the identity. Breast cancer patients report changing treatment, misunderstanding by others, and avoidance or fear reactions on the part of others in their social network after learning of the cancer diagnosis (Peters-Golden 1982). Among hemodialysis patients, the subjects reported feelings of increased alienation and estrangement associated with deterioration in the quality of social interaction (O'Brien 1980). The patient may evoke expressions of anger and resentment for any of a number of reasons, including the recognition on the part of others that the illness is disrupting their own lives (Dunkel-Schetter and Wortman 1982). On the other hand, the patient identity places the individual in a network of potentially helpful resources in which medical care and advice may ameliorate the patient's condition. Not inconsequential is the physician's potential as a provider of social support or as a source of stress in the patient-physician relationship (Bloom 1981).

Vulnerability. The observed associations between social identities and health status are believed to be mediated in part by features of social statuses that influence the vulnerability to disease. With regard to gender, while women experience a number of risks to health, they experience decreased vulnerability in some respects. Women tend to have larger and more intimate social supports than men (Verbrugge 1985; Fischer and Oliker 1983; Berkman and Syme 1979), and social support networks tend to be positively associated with health (Berkman 1984; Broadhead et al. 1983). Further, insofar as women have a significantly greater tendency to care for themselves and to access medical care over a longer period of time, their resistance to new diseases may be enhanced (Verbrugge 1985). This may be changing along with changes in sexual equality in the work place. As Solomon (1981, p. 177) suggests,

We might expect that, if the social roles of women shift in the context of the women's liberation movement and social evolution, the incidence of rheumatoid arthritis in women might drop, just as the incidence of peptic ulcer and hypertension in women with executive positions appears to have risen.

Vulnerability to disease may be reflected in such factors as absence of a supportive social network that might assuage the pathogenic effects of stressful circumstances. Thus, Berkman and Syme (1979) report that lower-income individuals are less likely to show evidence of social supports and that the absence of ties to family and community was associated with higher age-adjusted relative risk. Loss of work role has been related to subsequent increases in depression, a relationship that is mediated by the effects of loss of work role on economic strain, sense of mastery, and self-esteem (Pearlin et al. 1981), circumstances that are

thought to influence susceptibility to other diseases.

With regard to marital status, the changes in role definitions associated with such events as bereavement appear to have consequences for the capacity of the individual to resist disease or, conversely, to remain vulnerable to disease. Bartrop and associates (1977) reported decreased immune responsiveness in certain measures among twenty-six recently widowed women. Controls and bereaved subjects differed in immune responsiveness at both two and six weeks, with the responsiveness among the bereaved being lower. The influence of marital relationships upon constraining subjective distress and, possibly, other adverse health-related effects perhaps is accounted for by the greater availability of resources for coping with stress in the context of the marital relationship. Kessler and Essex (1982) and Thoits (1982) report data suggesting that married individuals might have experienced even higher levels of distress than the unmarried were it not for the resources for adapting to stress that are associated with marriage.

The effect of bereavement on mortality is conditional upon the gender and age of the survivor. Apparently bereavement events increase the risk of death for men but not for women in the first year following bereavement (Osterweis, Solomon, and Green 1984). The death of a spouse may constitute a greater interruption of resources for the male, thus rendering the husband more vulnerable to other stresses and diseases. The loss of a wife may constitute a particular loss of resources with regard to health care to the extent that the female role is one that is concerned with facilitating access to health care. The occurrence of widowhood at older ages carries with it lower risk of adverse health consequences than the occurrence of widowhood at younger ages (Kraus and Lilienfeld 1959; Morgan 1976). The more benign outcomes for the widowed at older ages may be accounted for by the availability of other widows who are able to provide support and empathy (Morgan 1976).

Aging is associated with reduced levels of social support (Stephens, Blau, and Oser 1978), a fact that has important implications for health status. In recent years investigators have attended to psychophysiological effects of social isolation and mental understimulation in elderly people, with specific emphasis upon elderly institutionalized people who lack social support and are characterized by an external locus of control. In one study, decreased urinary excretion of free cortisol has been reported following an intervention aimed at improving controllability for institutionalized elderly. In another controlled prospective study, psychoendocrine effects of social isolation and measures to counteract it were evaluated in a group of some sixty elderly institutionalized persons. Sampling and psychosocial evaluation were performed immediately before and after six months of a social activation program. Significant effects of the intervention were demonstrated, including improvement in a low indicator of overall blood glucose in the experimental group and not in the controlled group (Arnetz 1986).

Access to health care resources. The observed relationships between social identities and health status are believed to be mediated by differential access to health care resources. With respect to gender, on the basis of an extensive review of the literature, Verbrugge (1985, pp. 172–173) states:

> For *major* problems such as life threatening chronic diseases and severe acute conditions, women and men are similar in willingness and ability to take initial health actions. But women do take more extensive care for episodes (for example, more drugs or more kinds of actions) and more protracted care (such as more bed days per episode or earlier job retirement) for such problems. For *minor* health problems such as non-fatal chronic conditions and mild acute

ones, women have stronger predispositions to take both initial and continued care.

Differences in risk of contracting diseases according to socioeconomic status are not completely explained by differences in exposure to noxious circumstances. Also intervening may be such factors as lack of adequate health care. Apparently, when controlling for medical need, lower-income people have less access to quality care than upper-income people (Davis, Gold, and Makuc 1981; Kleinman, Gold, and Makuc 1981). Lower-income women are less likely to receive prenatal care (Aday, Anderson, and Fleming 1980), and their children are less likely to receive physical examinations (NCHS 1977). The poor are also less likely to receive such preventive services as Pap smears, breast exams, childhood immunizations, and dental care (Dutton 1986). Further, physicians act differently toward patients who are their socioeconomic-status equals than toward other patients with regard to the amount and nature of information and advice that is given (Waitzkin 1984).

Part of the variability in adequacy of medical care accounted for by socioeconomic differentials is due to the economic and other barriers that have to be overcome by the poor in order to achieve medical care. Expenditures for medical care constitute a greater proportion of total income for the poor (Dutton 1986; Barer, Evans, and Stoddart 1979).

The relationship between race and health status is accounted for in part by differences in preventive health care. Shapiro and his associates (1982) reported that screening for breast cancer eliminated the differences in five-year survival rate that were observed between white and nonwhite women. In the group of women that was not screened, nonwhite women with breast cancer had a poorer five-year survival rate than white women. However, no such racial differences were observed among white and nonwhite women who had been screened for breast cancer. Regarding coronary heart disease, the black-to-white mortality ratios are much greater (particularly in younger age groups) than would be expected on the basis of differences in hypertension prevalence. The disproportionate mortality rate for blacks probably reflects inadequate hypertension detection and treatment (Gillum and Gillum 1984).

Correlates of age-differentiated statuses influence utilization and availability of appropriate health resources. Woods and Birren (1984) cite several studies suggesting that older individuals are less likely to seek help that would improve their mental or physical health status. Older patients often seek medical help much later in the course of illness than do younger people—a tendency that reduces the opportunity for effective treatment. Older people are also less likely to participate in such health-promoting behavior as exercise. The negative attitude toward exercise as a health maintenance activity may be accounted for by the tendency of older people to underestimate their physical capabilities, to overestimate the conditioning value of the little exercise that they do get, and to exaggerate the danger that physical exertion may pose to their health. Further, older people may be embarrassed by the "age-inappropriate" behavior of exercising (Woods and Birren 1984).

For the most part, the preceding review has decomposed the observed relationships between particular social identities and health status in terms of intervening exposure to pathogenic circumstances, vulnerability, and access to health care resources. However, the effects of changes in social identities upon health status are mediated by similar processes. Changes in social identities (that is, loss, addition, or redefinition of roles associated with particular identities) are implicit in a number of life events, such as bereavement and retirement. Thus, bereavement "is associated with increased mortality (especially for men) for a variety of causes, with reduced

immunocompetence, with higher levels of psychophysiological symptoms, with greater distress, and with higher rates of health care utilization" (Kasl 1986, pp. 367–368).

SOCIAL RELATIONSHIPS

Participation in social relationships and circumstantial changes that promote or disrupt social relationships have been correlated with health status. A growing literature suggests that social support is positively related to longer and healthier lives (Berkman 1984; Berkman and Syme 1979; Broadhead et al. 1983). Social isolation has been observed to be associated with a broad range of diseases as well as with poor risk of recovery from disease (Cassel 1976; Ruberman et al. 1984). Berkman and Syme (1979) reported greater age-adjusted relative risk for socially isolated individuals after taking into account earlier health status, health care, health-relevant personal activities, and socioeconomic status. More particularly, marital relationships have been related to lower rates of mortality (House, Robins, and Metzner, 1982; Berkman and Syme 1979).

Generally, intervention in which social support is provided facilitates recovery from health problems (Wortman and Conway 1985; Broadhead et al. 1983; Wallston et al. 1983; Mumford, Schlesinger, and Glass 1982). Interpersonal support appears to be associated with hastened recovery from heart attacks (Gruen 1975) and the reduction of physical health complications of childbirth (Sosa et al. 1980). Conversely, the disruption of normally supportive social relationships is associated with adverse consequences for health status. A composite scale assessing childhood stability, stability of marriage and job, plans for the future, and recent significant loss predicted diagnosis of benign or malignant disease 73 percent of the time (Horne and Pickard 1979).

Mediating Variables

The literature suggests that associations between social relationships and health status are mediated by the effects of social relationships upon pathogenic circumstances, vulnerability, and access to health care resources.

Pathogenic circumstances. The roles played by the subject and complementary others in the context of social (including parent-child, marital, and peer) relationships affect the probability of exposure to pathogenic or health-enhancing experiences. In the context of the parent-child relationship, the adult's behavior has important implications for the health status of the child. Particularly in early years, the very nature of the dependency status of the child requires that much of the health outcomes of the child at that point in life and later be influenced by parental behavior (Roberts, Maddux, and Wright 1984). The behavior of the parent often has unintended consequences for the health of the child. For example, unsafe driving habits, alcohol use during pregnancy (Sokol, Miller, and Read 1980), and smoking during pregnancy may have adverse consequences for the health of the child. Much of the socialization regarding health-related behavior is not purposive but rather occurs through parental modeling processes, as in the transmission of alcohol and tobacco use patterns (Gordon and McAlister 1982; Evans and Raines 1982). Other behaviors by the adult, however, can purposely affect the child's health status. This is the case when the parent removes health hazards from the home, supervises the play of children, provides car safety seats, acquires immunization and health checkups for the child, and teaches the child good health habits.

Whether parent-child relationships will have benign or maleficent outcomes for the health of the child depends on a number of social, psychological, and biological characteristics of the parent. Childbearing at the age of 35 or older increases the risk of low birth weight, neonatal mortality, and congenital malformation (Shapiro et al. 1980). Where the mother is ignorant of proper health behavior, the child may suffer poor nutrition, illness, and accidents. Where the mother has few resources, the child is at great risk for failing to learn expected skills, including those measured by cognitive tests (Hardy 1982). Parents with strong needs for achievement and mastery of their environment may stimulate their children into precocious interaction with injury-related aspects of the environment (Waller and Klein 1973; Rivara 1984). That infants of teenage parents appear to have a higher risk of injury (McCormick, Shapiro, and Starfield 1980) may be accounted for by the failure of the parents to supervise the children's play in effective ways. Consistent with this hypothesis, Rivara (1984) cites a number of studies reporting relationships between childhood injuries and mother-child separation, single-parent families, and relatively loose parental supervision.

The parent-child relationship has implications for the health status of the parent as well. The roles played by women within the family, which include greater responsibility for child care, increase the risk of exposure to infectious diseases that are transmitted by children. Consistent with this hypothesis is the greater risk of common respiratory infections that have been observed among women in longitudinal studies of family illness (Verbrugge 1985).

With regard to marital relationships, Ostfeld (1986) cites findings that indicate an interaction between Type A behavior (time urgency, competitiveness, etc.) and wife's educational and employment status. The effect of Type A behavior on coronary heart disease was greater in men whose wives had some college education and worked outside the home (Eaker, Haynes, and Feinleib 1983). Ostfeld speculates that the process may involve psychological stress in the home and feelings of insecurity and self-doubt among the husbands.

Peer relationships exercise strong influences upon health-related behaviors. With regard to smoking behavior, Evans and Raines (1982, p. 115) observe that "comprehensive reviews of the literature ... conclude consistently that pressures from peers, particularly best friends or close friends, ... are important influences on the adolescent's decision to smoke."

Vulnerability. Participation in social relationships influences vulnerability to disease insofar as the relationships are the source of social support and the settings within which persons have variable success in meeting what are perceived as legitimate demands on them made by others. Social support has been related to resistance to disease in the face of life stress in a number of studies (LaRocco, House, and French 1981). Individuals who feel unable to meet role-related demands within social relationships are presumed to experience stress and, thereby, render themselves more vulnerable to infectious diseases. At the West Point Military Academy, Kasl and his associates (1979) screened entering cadets for the presence of Epstein-Barr virus antibody to infectious mononucleosis (IM). Those with the antibody were eliminated from the study, and the remaining cadets were followed for one of three possible outcomes: becoming infected and contracting IM, becoming infected and not contracting IM, and not becoming infected. Those students who in the course of their stay at the academy contracted IM appeared to be at greater risk for failing to conform to internalized role-related expectations insofar as they had a high level of motivation to succeed but had poor academic performance.

The mediating influence of vulnerability in the observed relationship between social relationships and health status has been suggested for a number of different relational contexts (including parent-child, marital, and occupation-related). Boyce (1985) cites a number of studies suggesting that destruction of the parent-child rela-

tionship by divorce has adverse psychological, behavioral, psychosomatic, and other biological consequences for the child (Jellinek and Slovik 1981; Kalter 1977; Offord et al. 1979; Boyce et al. 1977; and Heisel et al. 1973). The significance of divorce may be related to disruption of the family routine. Where family routine remains relatively stable during the divorce proceedings, children of divorced parents do not experience the same degree of disruption and distress as those who experience an upset of daily routine (Wallerstein 1977; Felner, Farber, and Primavera 1980).

More generally, the absence of family routine and the presence of life change are associated with vulnerability to illness. For example, in a prospective one-year study of fifty-eight preschool children, the severity of respiratory illness was strongly related to the combined influence of major life change and the degree of family routinization (Boyce et al. 1977; Boyce 1981). These results are compatible with the hypothesis that processes such as disorganization and disruption of family routine increase vulnerability to adverse health consequences. It is problematic, however, as to whether or not these processes are mediated by biological mechanisms whereby immunologic functions are disrupted by the stress related to disruption of routine. Such mediation is suggested, nevertheless, by observations that diabetes, an immune-related disorder, has been observed to be associated with parental loss and severe family disturbance (Stein and Charles 1971; Plaut and Friedman 1981).

With regard to marital relationships, in an analysis of five-year angina incidence rates, an interaction was observed between wives' love and support and anxiety. Under conditions of low anxiety, wives' love and support were not associated with angina. However, when anxiety was high, men who did not have the support and love of their wives were 1.8 times as likely to develop angina during the follow-up period as those with support (Goldbourt, Medalie, and Neufeld 1975). Marital relationships are also relevant to vulnerability insofar as hereditary predispositions such as inherited weaknesses in certain body organs or tissues that increase susceptibility to disease are influenced by socially prescribed and proscribed mating patterns.

Kasl and Wells (1985) cite a number of studies suggesting that the presence or absence of benign interpersonal relationships on the job and occupation-related stress have implications for physiological responses. Thus, shift workers with a stable network of co-workers had appreciably lower levels of cholesterol than those whose co-workers were changing (Cassel 1963). That such physiological responses may influence health status is consistent with observations that the absence of perceived social support by co-workers or superiors has been related to severe disease. Among men who perceived lack of appreciation and felt hurt by co-workers and superiors, a higher incidence of angina pectoris was observed (Medalie et al. 1973). Female clerical workers who reported having a nonsupportive supervisor had a higher incidence of coronary heart disease than other working women and housewives (Haynes and Feinlieb 1980).

Access to health care resources. Social relationships influence the readiness of individuals to seek health care, referral to resources, the provision of resources (money, transportation) that enable access to appropriate health care, and conformity to the expectations of the health care providers. The complementary roles in the relationship that an individual plays vary over time. Parents are initially responsible for providing health care to the children, but later in the life cycle roles may be reversed, with the children becoming responsible for providing health care resources to their elderly parents (Schulz and Rau 1985).

Social relationships influence physical health status among those who are recovering from illnesses by fostering adherence to medical regimens. Kirscht, Kirscht, and Rosenstock (1981), evaluating intervention involving a home support person and phone calls and home visits by a nurse, observed increased adherence to hypertensive medication regimens associated with the support intervention.

SOCIOCULTURAL SYSTEM

The inclusive culture that structures the lives of a population has implications for the health status of the individual. Some prescribed and proscribed normative patterns exclusively relate to the health status of individuals, whereas other patterns may not be recognized as being relevant for health status but nevertheless have implications for the current and changing health status of the population. As Levine and Sorenson (1984, p. 222) observe:

Culture embraces values, beliefs, and judgements about what is good, what is desirable, and how people should behave. Culture defines standards of morality, beauty, taste, and health. Societies vary in their perceptions of what constitutes health and their prescription for achieving and maintaining health and for combating illness. A culture will prescribe which foods to eat and which to avoid in order to be healthy, and many have varying prescriptions for men and for women, for puberty, for pregnancy, and for old age. In sum, the values, practices and beliefs held by the members of the society affect the health status and behavior and influence the effectiveness and efficiency of professional health promotion efforts.

A number of socioculturally defined patterns have been reported to be associated with health status. For example, the results of a 1965 survey of a representative sample of 6,928 American adults indicated that seven specific health practices were highly correlated with the physical health of these individuals: sleeping seven or eight hours daily, eating breakfast almost every day, never or rarely eating between meals, currently being at or near prescribed height-adjusted weight, never smoking cigarettes, moderate or no use of alcohol, and regular physical activity (Belloc and Breslow 1972). A follow-up 9½ years later indicated that men who followed all seven health practices had a mortality rate only 28 percent of that of the men who followed three practices or less. For women who followed all seven practices, the mortality rate was 43 percent of that of the women who followed three practices or less (Breslow and Enstrom 1980).

Mediating Variables

The correlations between characteristics of the inclusive sociocultural system and health status of the population have been interpreted in terms of the exposure to pathogenic circumstances, vulnerability, and access to health care resources that are reflected in or caused by the sociocultural system and, in turn, influence health status.

Pathogenic circumstances. Broad sociocultural patterns and changes in these patterns expose the population to noxious factors that increase the risk of disease. Thus, at the same time that coronary heart disease appears to be on the downturn in the United States and on the upswing in the Soviet Union, parallel changes in behavior patterns that appear to constitute risk factors for coronary heart disease have been observed. In the United States, male cigarette smoking has declined, and changes in dietary patterns have resulted in the reduced intake of sources of saturated fat. At the same time, in the USSR, tobacco consumption and the intake of foods high in saturated fat and cholesterol have been increasing (Ostfeld 1986). Other sociocultural characteristics constitute or influence threats to good health. Such culturally prescribed patterns as alcohol use, use of lethal weapons, and motor vehicle use influence the probability of violent death in a population (Rivara 1984). When radical cultural changes disrupt a familiar environment with a new set of demands for which the person is not traditionally prepared, the emotional strain of continuous behavioral adjustment is reflected in rising blood pressure (Patel 1984, p. 847).

Vulnerability. Patterns of behavior related to diet, sleep patterns, substance abuse, and other behaviors not only contribute to specific modes of disorder and reflect certain disease states, but also influence the organism's ability to ward off diseases. Such patterns have been associated with the organism's immunocompetence (Palmblad 1981). Vulnerability is also affected by the induction of psychosocial stress (a factor associated with lower levels of immunocompetence) and the loss of social supports that might assuage the stresses that are concomitants of the rapid change that characterizes some sociocultural systems. As Patel (1984, p. 849) observes:

In industrialized societies with fast-advancing technology, rapid changes in the environment are likely. With an increase in the complexity of tasks, a comparable increase in vigilance and job responsibility is unavoidable. Rising unemployment and inflation put extra demands on individuals to gain more education and more technical skills to compete for these jobs. With explosion in travel and communication, there is increase in social mobility. People move away from friends and relations and from familiar surroundings and cultures to unknown locations with strange cultures and differing social strata. All these factors are likely to put people under stress.

Access to health care resources. The provision and form of health care resources are influenced by the consensually held values that characterize the inclusive sociocultural system. The general respect that Americans have for technological development is reflected in particular in their expectation of continuing improvement in medical technology (Blendon and Altman 1984). However, the heroic measures undertaken to preserve life that are made possible by scientific and technological developments are applied only to the extent that they are congruent with the frequently competing values placed upon human life in general, the human life of categories of individuals such as infants, and the alternate uses to which the required scarce resources might be put. Fox (1986, p. 18) notes the evaluative significance of the neonatal intensive care unit because of its association with "the powerful cultural meaning with which our society endows birth, babies, and parenthood."

POLICY IMPLICATIONS

The literature that we have reviewed provides a number of observations and speculations that have implications for the formulation of policies toward the goal of enhancing the health status of the population. For example, risk taking is associated with a variety of adverse health-related outcomes. Adolescent experimentation with risk-taking behavior implies inexperience with such behavior. The lack of experience with these behaviors leads to a greater probability of misjudgment about consequences and adverse outcomes. As Petersen (1982, p. 69) observes, "If experience is the key factor, then the appropriate focus of intervention for adolescents is to give them the information, skills, and practice necessary to behave more wisely, in a manner consistent with their values and needs."

In another vein, Kiesler (1985, p. 350) comments on the public policy implications of the buffering hypothesis (the hypothesis that social support acts as a buffer to reduce the potentially negative effects of stress and perhaps other negative environmental events):

If the buffering hypothesis were a valid representation of reality, then very useful public policy could be built. We could identify wide varieties of stress in the environment currently having negative effects which society as a whole would wish to reduce. We could apply reliable

methods of enhancing the social support of these groups at risk, thereby reducing the consequent negative effects, enhancing public satisfaction, and reducing public cost. . . .

To consider such public policies, policymakers should be able to: (1) identify reliably those varieties of stress consistently producing negative effects for subpopulations that could be described in detail and inexpensively identified; (2) describe methods of enhancing social supports that are reasonably inexpensive and can easily be applied to very large populations at risk (e.g., new mothers, the widowed, or the unemployed); and (3) state precisely what the ameliorative effects are, the proportion of the population at risk they will be observed in, the relative cost-effectiveness of the policy, and the risks of negative unintended consequences of the policy.

However, Kiesler goes on to state that the current state of the scientific literature does not invite confidence about meeting such requirements.

That the findings reviewed in this chapter have implications for policymaking in the health field is clear. Nevertheless, the nature of the implications may be stated only imprecisely. Before specific policy determinations could be made, it would be necessary to understand not only that social structure and process are related to health outcomes, but more fully how social structure and process influence such outcomes. Do social-structural variables influence the probabilities of being exposed to health-impairing experiences, or influence the reduction of health-promoting/illness-preventing activities? Do social-structural variables influence the vulnerability of individuals to morbid outcomes of exposure to such influences? Do structural and process variables affect access to resources and facilities that forestall exacerbation of morbid processes?

When these questions are answered more precisely and when the social-structural and process variables are clearly delineated, we may begin to plan interventions that will forestall the onset or ameliorate the course of morbid processes. Until that time, we must work toward a fuller understanding of the relationships between sociocultural structures and processes on the one hand, and the course and management of illness on the other.

ACKNOWLEDGMENTS

This report was facilitated by a Research Scientist Award (KO5 DA 00105) and Research Grants (RO1 DA 02497, RO1 DA 04310) to the author from the National Institute on Drug Abuse.

REFERENCES

Achte, Kalle, Pirjo-Leena Malassu, and Marja Saarenheimo. 1986. Old Age and Stress, in K. Achte and A. Pakaslahti, eds., *Stress and Psychosomatics*. Proceedings of a symposium sponsored by the Signe and Ane Gyllenberg Foundation, September 19–20, 1985. *Psychiatria Fennica Supplementum* 1986. Hanasaari, Espoo, Finland, pp. 87–95.

Aday, Luann, Ronald M. Andersen, and Gretchen Fleming. 1980. *Health Care in the U.S.: Equitable for Whom?* Beverly Hills: Sage Publications.

Al-Issa, Ihsan. 1982. Gender and Adult Psychopathology, in Ihsan Al-Issa, ed., *Gender and Psychopathology*. New York: Academic Press, pp. 84–103.

Antonovsky, Aaron. 1984. The Sense of Coherence as a Determinant of Health, in J. D. Matarazzo, Sharlene M. Weiss, J. Alan Herd, N. E. Miller, and Stephen M. Weiss, eds., *Behavioral Health: A Handbook of Health Enhancement and Disease Prevention*. New York: John Wiley, pp. 114–129.

Arnetz, Bengt B. 1986. Psychoendocrine Studies of Social Isolation of Elderly People, in K. Achte and A. Pakaslahti, eds., *Stress and Psychosomatics*. Proceedings of a symposium sponsored by the Signe and Ane Gyllenberg Foundation, September 19–20, 1985. Psychiatria Fennica Supplementum 1986. Hanasaari, Espoo, Finland, pp. 79–85.

Barer, Morris L., Robert G. Evans, and Glen L. Stoddart. 1979. *Controlling Health Care Costs by Direct Charges to Patients: Snare or Delusions?* Toronto: Ontario Economic Council.

Bartrop, R. W., E. Luckhurst, L. Lazarus, L. G. Kiloh, and R. Penny. 1977. Depressed Lymphocyte Function after Bereavement. *Lancet* I:834–836.

Belloc, Nedra B., and Lester Breslow. 1972. Relationship of Physical Health Status and Health Practices. *Preventive Medicine* I:409–421.

Berkman, Lisa F. 1984. Assessing the Physical Health Effects of Social Networks and Social Support, in L. Breslow, J. E. Fielding, and L. B. Lave, eds., *Annual Review of Public Health*, vol. 5. Palo Alto, Calif.: Annual Reviews, pp. 413–432.

Berkman, Lisa F. 1985. The Relationship of Social Networks and Social Support to Morbidity and Mortality, in S. Cohen and S. L. Syme, eds., *Social Support and Health*. Orlando, Fla.: Academic Press, pp. 241–262.

Berkman, Lisa F. and Lester Breslow. 1983. *Health and Ways of Living*. New York: Oxford University Press.

Berkman, Lisa F., and S. Leonard Syme. 1979. Social Networks, Host Resistance, and Mortality: A Nine-Year Follow-up Study of Alameda County Residents. *American Journal of Epidemiology* 109:186–204.

Blendon, Robert J., and Drew E. Altman. 1984. Public Attitudes about Health Care Costs: A Lesson in National Schizophrenia. *New England Journal of Medicine* 311:613–616.

Bloom, Bernard, L., Shirley J. Asher, and Stephen W. White. 1978. Marital Disruption as a Stressor: A Review and Analysis. *Psychological Bulletin* 85:867–894.

Bloom, Joan. 1981. Cancer-Care Providers and the Medical Care System: Facilitators or Inhibitors of Patient Coping Responses, in P. Ahmed, ed., *Living And Dying With Cancer*. New York: Elsevier North Holland, pp. 253–272.

Boyce, W. Thomas. 1981. Interaction between Social Variables in Stress Research. *Journal of Health and Social Behavior* 22:194–195.

———. 1985. Social Support, Family Relations, and Children, in S. Cohen and S. Syme, eds., *Social Support and Health*. Orlando, Fla.: Academic Press, pp. 151–173.

Boyce, W. Thomas, Eric W. Jensen, John C. Cassel, Albert M. Collier, Allen H. Smith, and Craig T. Ramey. 1977. Influence of Life Events and Family Routines on Childhood Respiratory Tract Illness. *Pediatrics* 60:609–615.

Breslow, Lester, and James E. Enstrom. 1980. Persistence of Health Habits and Their Relationship to Mortality. *Preventive Medicine* 9:469–483.

Broadhead, W. Eugene, Berton H. Kaplan, Sherman A. James, Edward H. Wagner, Victor J. Schoenback, Roger Grimson, Siegfried Heyden, Gosta Tibblin, and Stephen H. Gehlback. 1983. The Epidemiologic Evidence for a Relationship between Social Support and Health. *American Journal of Epidemiology* 117:521–537.

Brown, George W., and Tirril O. Harris. 1978. *Social Origins of Depression: A Study of Psychiatric Disorder in Women*. London: Tavistock Publications; New York: Free Press.

Cassel, John C. 1963. The Use of Medical Records: Opportunity for Epidemiologic Studies. *Journal of Occupational Medicine* 5:185–190.

———. 1976. The Contribution of the Social Environment to Host Resistance. *American Journal of Epidemiology* 104:107–123.

Cobb, Sidney, and Robert M. Rose. 1973. Hypertension, Peptic Ulcer and Diabetes in Air Traffic Controllers. *Journal of the American Medical Association* 224:489–492.

Cooper, Cary, ed. 1983. *Stress Research*. New York: John Wiley.

Davis, Karen, Marsha Gold, and Diane Makuc. 1981. Access to Health Care for the Poor: Does the Gap Remain? In Lester Breslow, ed., *Annual Review of Public Health*, vol. 2. Palo Alto, Calif.: Annual Reviews, pp. 150–182.

Dohrenwend, Bruce P., Barbara Snell Dohrenwend, Marilyn Schwartz Gould, Bruce Link, Richard Neugebauer, and Robin Wunsch-Hitzig. 1980. *Mental Illness in the United States*. New York: Praeger.

Dunkel-Schetter, Christine, and Camille B. Wortman. 1982. The Interpersonal Dynamics of Cancer: Problems in Social Relationships and Their Impact on the Patient, in H. S. Friedman and M. Robin DiMatteo, eds., *Interpersonal Issues in Health Care*. New York: Academic Press, pp. 69–100.

Dutton, Diana B. 1986. Social Class, Health, and Illness, in L. H. Aiken and D. Mechanic, eds., *Applications of Social Science to Clinical Medicine and Health Policy*. New Brunswick, N.J.: Rutgers University Press, pp. 31–62.

Eaker, Elaine D., Suzanne G. Haynes, and Manning Feinleib. 1983. Spouse Behavior and Coronary Heart Disease in Men: Prospective Results from the Framingham Heart Study II: Modification of Risk in Type A Husbands according to the Social and Psychological Status of Their Wives. *American Journal of Epidemiology* 118:23–41.

Egbuonu, Lisa, and Barbara Starfield. 1982. Child Health Social Status. *Pediatrics* 69:550–557.

Elliott, Glen R. and Carl Eisdorfer, eds. 1982. *Stress and Human Health*. New York: Springer-Verlag.

Evans, Richard I., and Bettye E. Raines. 1982. Control and Prevention of Smoking in Adolescents: A Psychosocial Perspective, in T. J. Coates, A. C. Peterson, and C. Perry, eds., *Promoting Adolescent Health: A Dialog on Research and Practice*. New York: Academic Press, pp. 101–136.

Felner, Robert D., Stephanie S. Farber, and Judith Primavera. 1980. Children of Divorce, Stressful Life Events, and Transitions: A Framework for Preventive Efforts, in R. H. Price, R. F. Ketterer, B. C. Bader, and John Monahan, eds., *Prevention in Mental Health: Research, Policy, and Practice*. London: Sage, pp. 81–108.

Fischer, Claude S., and Stacey J. Oliker. 1983. A Research Note on Friendship, Gender, and the Life Cycle. *Social Forces* 62:124–133.

Fox, Renee C. 1986. Medicine, Science, and Technology, in L. H. Aiken and D. Mechanic, eds., *Applications of Social Science to Clinical Medicine and Health Policy*. New Brunswick, N.J.: Rutgers University Press, pp. 13–30.

Gillum, Richard P., and Brenda S. Gillum. 1984. Potential for Control and Prevention of Essential Hypertension in the Black Community, in J. D. Matarazzo, Sharlene M. Weiss, J. Alan Herd, N. E. Miller, and Stephen M. Weiss, eds., *Behavioral Health: A Handbook of Health Enhancement and Disease Prevention*. New York: John Wiley, pp. 825–835.

Goldbourt, Uri, Jack Medalie, and Henry N. Neufeld. 1975. Clinical Myocardial Infarction over a Five Year Period. III. A Multivariate Analysis of Incidence, the Israel Ischemic Heart Disease Study. *Journal of Chronic Disease* 28:217–237.

Gordon, Nancy P. and Alfred L. McAlister. 1982. Adolescent Drinking: Issues and Research, in T. J. Coates, A. C. Peterson, and C. Perry, eds., *Promoting Adolescent Health: A Dia-*

log on Research and Practice. New York: Academic Press, pp. 201–223.

Gove, Walter R. 1985. Gender Differences in Mental and Physical Illness: The Effects of Fixed Roles and Nurturant Roles. *Social Science and Medicine* 19:77–84.

Gove, Walter R., Michael Hughes, and Omer R. Galle. 1979. Overcrowding in the Home: An Empirical Investigation of Its Possible Pathological Consequences. *American Sociological Review* 44:59–80.

Green, Lawrence W., and Denise Horton. 1982. Adolescent Health: Issues and Challenges, in T. J. Coates, A. C. Peterson, and C. Perry, eds., *Promoting Adolescent Health: A Dialog on Research and Practice*. New York: Academic Press, pp. 23–43.

Gruen, Walter. 1975. Effects of Brief Psychotherapy during the Hospitalization Period on the Recovery Process in Heart Attacks. *Journal of Consulting and Clinical Psychology* 43:223–232.

Guillemin, Roger, Melvin Cohn, and Theodore Melnechuk, eds. 1985. *Neural Modulation of Immunity*. New York: Raven Press.

Hardy, Janet B. 1982. Adolescents as Parents: Possible Long-Range Implications, in T. J. Coates, A. C. Peterson, and C. Perry, eds., *Promoting Adolescent Health: A Dialog on Research and Practice*. New York: Academic Press, pp. 255–267.

Harlan, William R. 1984. Rationale for Intervention on Blood Pressure in Childhood and Adolescence, in J. D. Matarazzo, Sharlene M. Weiss, J. Alan Herd, N. E. Miller, and Stephen M. Weiss, eds., *Behavioral Health: A Handbook of Health Enhancement and Disease Prevention*. New York: John Wiley, pp. 806–824.

Haw, Mary Ann. 1982. Women, Work and Stress: A Review and Agenda for the Future. *Journal of Health and Social Behavior* 23:132–144.

Haynes, Suzanne G., and Manning Feinleib. 1980. Women, Work and Coronary Heart Disease: Prospective Findings from the Framingham Heart Study. *American Journal of Public Health* 70:133–141.

Heisel, J. Stephen, Scott Ream, Raymond Raitz, Michael Rappaport, and R. Dean Coddington. 1973. The Significance of Life Events as Contributing Factors in the Diseases of Children. III. A Study of Pediatric Patients. *Journal of Pediatrics* 83:119–123.

Helsing, Knud J., Moyses Szklo, and George Comstock. 1981. Factors Associated with Mortality after Widowhood. *American Journal of Public Health* 71:802–809.

Herd, J. Alan, and Stephen M. Weiss. 1984. Overview of Hypertension: Its Treatment and Prevention, in J. D. Matarazzo, Sharlene M. Weiss, J. Alan Herd, N. E. Miller, and Stephen M. Weiss, eds., *Behavioral Health: A Handbook of Health Enhancement and Disease Prevention*. New York: John Wiley, pp. 789–805.

Hing, Esther, Mary Grace Kovar, and Dorothy P. Rice. 1983. Sex Differences in Health and Use of Medical Care: United States, 1979. *Vital and Health Statistics*, Series 3, No. 24. DHHS Publication No. PHS. 83–1408. National Center for Health Statistics.

Horne, R. L., and R. S. Picard. 1979. Psychosocial Risk Factors for Lung Cancer. *Psychosomatic Medicine* 41:503–514.

House, James S., and Eric M. Cottington. 1986. Health and the Workplace, in L. A. Aiken and D. Mechanic, eds., *Applications of Social Science to Clinical Medicine and Health Policy*. New Brunswick, N.J.: Rutgers University Press, pp. 392–416.

House, James S., Cynthia Robbins, and Helen Low Metzner. 1982. The Association of Social Relationships and Activities with Mortality: Prospective Evidence from the Tecumseh Community Health Study. *American Journal of Epidemiology* 116:123–140.

Jacobs, Selby, and Adrian M. Ostfeld. 1977. An Epidemiological Review of the Mortality of Bereavement. *Psychosomatic Medicine* 39:241.

Jellinek, Michael S., and Lois S. Slovik. 1981. Divorce: Impact on Children. *New England Journal of Medicine* 305:557–560.

Jessor, Richard. 1984. Adolescent Development and Behavioral Health, in J. D. Matarazzo, Sharlene M. Weiss, J. Alan Herd, N. E. Miller, and Stephen M. Weiss, eds., *Behavioral Health: A Handbook of Health Enhancement and Disease Prevention*. New York: John Wiley, pp. 69–90.

Johnson, Craig. 1982. Anorexia Nervosa and Bulimia, in T. J. Coates, A. C. Peterson, and C. Perry, eds., *Promoting Adolescent Health: A Dialog on Research and Practice*. New York: Academic Press, pp. 397–443.

Kalter, Niel. 1977. Children of Divorce in an Outpatient Psychiatric Population. *American Journal of Orthopsychiatry* 47:40–51.

Kaplan, Howard B. 1983. Psychological Distress in Sociological Context: Toward A General Theory of Psychosocial Stress, in H. B. Kaplan, ed., *Psychosocial Stress: Trends in Theory and Research.* New York: Academic Press, pp. 195–264.

———. 1986. *Social Psychology of Self-Referent Behavior.* New York: Plenum Press.

Kasl, Stanislav V. 1986. The Detection and Modification of Psychosocial and Behavioral Risk Factors, in L. H. Aiken and D. Mechanic, eds., *Application of Social Science to Clinical Medicine and Health Policy.* New Brunswick, N.J.: Rutgers University Press, pp. 359–381.

Kasl, Stanislav V., and Sidney Cobb. 1980. The Experience of Losing a Job: Some Effects on Cardiovascular Functioning. *Psychotherapy and Psychosomatics* 34:88.

Kasl, Stanislav V., Alfred S. Evans, and James C. Niederman. 1979. Psychosocial Risk Factors in the Development of Infectious Mononucleosis. *Psychosomatic Medicine* 41:445–466.

Kasl, Stanislav V., and James A. Wells. 1985. Social Support and Health in the Middle Years: Work and the Family, in S. Cohen and S. L. Syme, eds., *Social Support and Health.* Orlando, Fla.: Academic Press, pp. 175–198.

Kessler, Ronald, and Marilyn Essex. 1982. Marital Status and Depression: The Importance of Coping Resources. *Social Forces* 61:485–507.

Kiesler, Charles A. 1985. Policy Implications of Research on Social Support and Health, in S. Cohen and S. L. Syme, eds., *Social Support and Health.* Orlando, Fla.: Academic Press, pp. 347–364.

Kirscht, John P., Jennifer L. Kirscht, and Irwin M. Rosenstock. 1981. A Test of Interventions to Increase Adherence to Hypertensive Medical Regimens. *Health Education Quarterly* 8:261–272.

Kittel, F., M. Kornitzer, and M. Dramaix. 1980. Coronary Heart Disease and Job Stress in Two Cohorts of Bank Clerks. *Psychotherapy and Psychosomatics* 34:110–123.

Kleinman, Joel C., Marsha Gold, and Diane Makuc. 1981. Use of Ambulatory Medical Care by the Poor: Another Look at Equity. *Medical Care* 19:1011–1029.

Kobasa, Suzanne C., Salvatore R. Maddi, and Stephen Kahn. 1982. Hardiness and Health: A Prospective Study. *Journal of Personality and Social Psychology* 42:168–177.

Kraus, Arthur S. and Abraham N. Lilienfeld. 1959. Some Epidemiologic Aspects of the High Mortality Rate in the Young Widowed Group. *Journal of Chronic Diseases* 10:207–217.

Langlie, Jean K. 1977. Social Network, Health Beliefs, and Preventive Health Behavior. *Journal of Health and Social Behavior* 18:244–260.

LaRocco, James M., James S. House, and John R. P. French, Jr. 1981. Social Support, Occupational Stress and Health. *Journal of Health and Social Behavior* 21:202–218.

Levine, Sol, and James R. Sorenson. 1984. Social and Cultural Factors in Health Promotion, in J. D. Matarazzo, Sharlene M. Weiss, J. Alan Herd, N. E. Miller, and Stephen M. Weiss, eds., *Behavioral Health: A Handbook of Health Enhancement and Disease Prevention.* New York: John Wiley, pp. 222–229.

Lindheim, Roslyn, and S. Leonard Syme. 1983. Environments, People and Health, in L. Breslow, ed., *Annual Review of Public Health,* vol. 4. Palo Alto, Calif.: Annual Reviews, pp. 335–359.

MacKay, Annette, Judith Halpern, Elizabeth McLoughlin, John Locke, and John A. Crawford. 1979. A Comparison of Age-Specific Burn Injury Rates in Five Massachusetts Communities. *American Journal of Public Health* 69:1149–1150.

Marcus, Alfred C., Teresa E. Seeman, and Carol W. Telesky. 1985. Comment on Gove, 1985. *Social Science and Medicine* 19:84–88.

Marmot, Michael G., Geoffrey Rose, M. J. Shipley, and P. J. S. Hamilton. 1978. Employment Grade and Coronary Heart Disease in British Civil Servants. *Journal of Epidemiology and Community Health* 32:244–249.

Marmot, Michael G., M. J. Shipley, and Geoffrey Rose. 1984. Inequalities in Death: Specific Explanations of a General Pattern? *Lancet* 1:1003–1006.

Marshall, James, and Saxon Graham. 1986. Cancer, in L. H. Aiken and D. Mechanic, eds., *Applications of Social Science to Clinical Medicine and Health Policy.* New Brunswick, N.J.: Rutgers University Press, pp. 157–174.

McCormick, Marie C. 1986. Implications of Recent Changes in Infant Mortality, in L. H. Aiken and D. Mechanic, eds., *Applications of Social Science to Clinical Medicine and Health Policy*. New Brunswick, N.J.: Rutgers University Press, pp. 282–306.

McCormick, Marie C., Sam Shapiro, and Barbara H. Starfield. 1980. Rehospitalization in the First Year of Life for High-Risk Survivors. *Pediatrics* 66:991–999.

Mechanic, David, and Paul D. Cleary. 1980. Factors Associated with the Maintenance of Positive Health Behavior. *Preventive Medicine* 9:805–814.

Medalie, Jack H., Mitchell Snyder, J. J. Groen, Henry N. Neufeld, Uri Goldbourt, and Egon Riss. 1973. Angina Pectoris among 10,000 Men: 5 Year Incidence and Univariate Analysis. *The American Journal of Medicine* 55:583–594. .

Meyer, Roger J., and Robert J. Haggerty. 1985. Streptococcal Infections in Families, in S. Locke, R. Adler, H. Besedovsky, N. Hall, G. Solomon, and T. Strom, eds., *Foundations in Psychoneuroimmunology*. New York: Aldine, pp. 307–317.

Miasnikov, A. L. 1961. The Significance of Disturbance of Higher Nervous Activity in the Pathogenesis of Hypertensive Disease, in J. H. Cort, V. Fencl, Z. Hejl, and J. Zirda, eds., *WHO/Czechoslovak Cardiology Society Symposium on the Pathogenesis of Essential Hypertension*. Prague: State Medical Publishing Co., pp. 153–162.

Morgan, Leslie A. 1976. A Re-examination of Widowhood and Morale. *Journal of Gerontology* 31:687–695.

Morris, J. N., Aubrey Kagan, D. C. Pattison, M. J. Gardner, and P. A. B. Raffle. 1966. Incidence and Prediction of Ischaemic-Heart Disease in London Busmen. *Lancet* 2:553–559.

Mott, Frank L., and Nan L. Maxwell. 1981. School-age Mothers, 1968 and 1979. *Family Planning Perspectives* 16:287–292.

Mumford, Emily, H. J. Schlesinger, and G. V. Glass. 1982. The Effects of Psychological Intervention on Recovery from Surgery and Heart Attacks: An Analysis of the Literature. *American Journal of Public Health* 72:141–151.

Nathanson, Constance A. 1984. Sex differences in mortality, in R. H. Turner and J. F. Short, eds., *Annual Review of Sociology*, vol. 10. Palo Alto, Calif.: Annual Reviews, pp. 191–213.

National Center for Health Statistics (NCHS). 1977. *Use of Selected Medical Procedures Associated with Preventive Care, United States, 1973*. Series 10, No. 110. Public Health Service.

———. 1982. *Annual Summary of Births, Deaths, Marriages, and Divorces: United States, 1981*. Monthly vital statistics report. Vol. 30, No. 13. Public Health Service.

Newacheck, Paul W., Lewis H. Butler, Aileen K. Harper, Dyan L. Piontkowski, and Patricia E. Franks. 1980. Income and Illness. *Medical Care* 17:1165–1176.

O'Brien, Mary Elizabeth. 1980. Effective Social Environment and Hemodialysis Adaptation: A Panel Analysis. *Journal of Health and Social Behavior* 21:360–370.

Offord, David R., Nola Abrams, Nancy Allen, and Mary Poushinsky. 1979. Broken Homes, Parental Psychiatric Illness, and Female Delinquency. *American Journal of Orthopsychiatry* 49:252–264.

Osterweis, Marian, Fredric Solomon, and Morris Green, eds. 1984. *Bereavement Reactions, Consequences, and Care*. Washington, D.C.: National Academy Press.

Ostfeld, Adrian M. 1986. Cardiovascular Disease, in L. H. Aiken and D. Mechanic, eds., *Applications of Social Science to Clinical Medicine and Health Policy*. New Brunswick, N.J.: Rutgers University Press, pp. 129–156.

Palmblad, Jan. 1981. Stress and Immunologic Competence: Studies in Man, in R. Ader, ed., *Psychoneuroimmunology*. Orlando, Fla.: Academic Press, pp. 229–257.

Patel, Chandra. 1984. A Relaxation-Centered Behavioral Package for Reducing Hypertension, in J. D. Matarazzo, Sharlene M. Weiss, J. Alan Herd, N. E. Miller, and Stephen M. Weiss, eds., *Behavioral Health: A Handbook for Health Enhancement and Disease Prevention*. New York: John Wiley, pp. 846–861.

Pearlin, Leonard I., Morton A. Lieberman, Elizabeth G. Menaghan, and Joseph T. Nullan. 1981. The Stress Process. *Journal of Health and Social Behavior* 22:337–356.

Peters-Golden, Holly. 1982. Breast Cancer: Varied Perceptions of Social Support in the Illness Experience. *Social Science and Medicine* 16:483–491.

Peterson, Anne C. 1982. Developmental Issues in Adolescent Health, in T. J. Coates, A. C. Peterson, and C. Perry, eds., *Promoting Adoles-*

cent Health: A Dialog on Research and Practice. New York: Academic Press, pp. 61–71.

Plaut, S. Michael, and Stanford B. Friedman. 1981. Psychosocial Factors in Infectious Disease, in R. Ader, ed., *Psychoneuroimmunology.* Orlando, Fla.: Academic Press, pp. 3–30.

Rice, Dorothy, and Kathleen Danchik. 1979. Changing Needs of Children: Disease, Disability, and Access to Care. Paper presented at Institute of Medicine Annual Meetings. Washington, D.C.

Rivara, Frederick P. 1984. Epidemiology of Childhood Injuries, in J. D. Matarazzo, Sharlene M. Weiss, J. Alan Herd, N. E. Miller, and Stephen M. Weiss, eds., *Behavioral Health: A Handbook of Health Enhancement and Disease Prevention.* New York: John Wiley, pp. 1003–1020.

Roberts, Michael C., James E. Maddux, and Logan Wright. 1984. Developmental Perspectives in Behavioral Health, in J. D. Matarazzo, Sharlene M. Weiss, J. Alan Herd, N. E. Miller, and Stephen M. Weiss, eds., *Behavioral Health: A Handbook of Health Enhancement and Disease Prevention.* New York: John Wiley, pp. 56–68.

Ruberman, William, Eve Weinblatt, Judith D. Goldberg, and Banvir S. Chaudhary. 1984. Psychosocial Influences on Mortality after Myocardial Infarction. *New England Journal of Medicine* 311:552–559.

Scholzman, Kay L. and Sidney Verba. 1978. The New Unemployment: Does It Hurt? *Public Policy* 26:333–358.

Schulz, Richard, and Marie T. Rau. 1985. Social Support through the Life Course, in S. Cohen and S. L. Syme, eds., *Social Support and Health.* Orlando, Fla.: Academic Press, pp. 129–149.

Shapiro, Sam, Marie C. McCormick, Barbara H. Starfield, J. P. Krischer, and D. Bross. 1980. Relevance of Correlates of Infant Deaths for Significant Morbidity at 1 Year of Age. *American Journal of Obstetrics and Gynecology* 136:363–373.

Shapiro, Sam, Wanda Venet, Philip Strax, Louis Venet, and Ruth Roeser. 1982. Prospects for Eliminating Racial Differences in Breast Cancer Survival Rates. *American Journal of Public Health* 72:1142–1145.

Shepard, J. M. 1977. Technology, Alienation, and Job Satisfaction, in R. H. Turner, ed., *Annual Review of Sociology,* vol. 3. Palo Alto, Calif.: Annual Reviews, pp. 1–21.

Sokol, Robert J., Sheldon I. Miller, and George Reed. 1980. Alcohol Abuse during Pregnancy: An Epidemiologic Study. *Alcoholism: Clinical and Experimental Research* 4:135–145.

Solomon, George F. 1981. Emotional and Personality Factors in the Onset and Course of Autoimmune Disease, Particularly Rheumatoid Arthritis, in R. Ader, ed., *Psychoneuroimmunology.* Orlando, Fla.: Academic Press, pp. 159–182.

Sosa, Robert, John Kennell, Marshall Klaus, Steven Robertson, and Juan Urrutia. 1980. The Effect of a Supportive Companion on Perinatal Problems, Length of Labor, and Mother-Infant Interaction. *New England Journal of Medicine* 303:597–600.

Starfield, Barbara. 1984. Social Factors in Child Health, in M. Green and R. J. Haggerty, eds., *Ambulatory Pediatrics III.* Philadelphia: W. B. Saunders, pp. 12–18.

Stein, Stefan P., and Edward Charles. 1971. Emotional Factors in Juvenile Diabetes Mellitus: A Study of Early Life Experiences of Adolescent Diabetics. *American Journal of Psychiatry* 128:56–60.

Stephens, Ronald, Zena S. Blau, and George T. Oser. 1978. Aging, Social Support Systems, and Social Policy. *Journal of Gerontological Social Work* 1:33–45.

Stroebe, Wolfgang, Margaret S. Stroebe, Kenneth J. Gergen, and Mary Gergen. 1982. The Effects of Bereavement on Mortality: A Social Psychological Analysis, in J. R. Eiser, ed., *Social Psychology and Behavioral Medicine.* New York: John Wiley, pp. 527–560.

Syme, S. Leonard, Merton M. Hyman, and Philip E. Enterline. 1964. Some Social and Cultural Factors Associated with the Occurrence of Coronary Heart Disease. *Journal of Chronic Disease* 17:277.

Thoits, Peggy. 1982. Life Stress, Social Support, and Psychological Vulnerability: Epidemiological Considerations. *Journal of Community Psychology* 10:341–363.

U.S. Congress. House Committee on Interstate and Foreign Commerce. 1979. *Child Health Assurance Act of 1979*, Report No. 96-568. Washington, D.C.: U. S. Government Printing Office.

———. Committee on Interstate and Foreign

Commerce. Subcommittee on Oversight. *Infant Mortality Rates: Failure to Close the Black-White Gap.* 98th Cong., 2d sess. Series no. 98-131. Washington, D.C.: U. S. Government Printing Office.

U.S. Department of Health, Education, and Welfare (DHEW). Public Health Service. 1979. *Dietary Intake Source Data: U. S., 1971–74.* DHEW Publication No. (PHS)79-1221.

Verbrugge, Lois M. 1979. Marital Status and Health. *Journal of Marriage and the Family* 41:267–285.

———. 1985. Gender and Health: An Update on Hypotheses and Evidence. *Journal of Health and Social Behavior* 26:156–182.

Verbrugge, Lois M., and Jennifer H. Madans. 1985. Social Roles and Health Trends of American Women. *Milbank Memorial Fund Quarterly* 63:691–735 (fall).

Waitzkin, Howard. 1984. Doctor-Patient Communication: Clinical Implications of Social Scientific Research. *Journal of the American Medical Association* 252:2441–2446.

Waldron, Ingrid. 1983. Sex Differences in Illness Incidence, Prognosis and Mortality: Issues and Evidence. *Social Science and Medicine* 17:1107–1123.

Waller, Julian A., and David Klein. 1973. Society, Energy, and Injury: Inevitable Triad? In F. T. Falkner and S. H. Knutti, eds., *Research Directions toward the Reduction of Injury in the Young and the Old.* DHEW Publication No. (NIH)73-124. National Institute of Child Health and Human Development, pp. 1–37.

Wallerstein, Judith S. 1977. Responses of the Preschool Child to Divorce: Those Who Cope, in M. F. McMillan and S. Henao, eds., *Child psychiatry: Treatment and research.* New York: Brunner-Mazel, pp. 269–292.

Wallston, Barbara Strudler, Sheryle Witcher Alagna, Brenda McEvoy DeVellis, and Robert F. DeVellis. 1983. Social Support and Physical Health. *Health Psychology* 2:367–391.

Weissman, Myrna M., and Gerald L. Klerman. 1977. Sex Differences and the Epidemiology of Depression. *Archives of General Psychiatry* 34:98–111.

Westfelt, J. N. 1982. Environmental Factors in Childhood Accidents. *Acta Paediatrica Scandinavica, Supplement.* 291:1–75.

Wingard, Deborah L. 1984. The Sex Differential in Morbidity, Mortality, and Lifestyle, in L. Breslow, J. L. Fielding, and L. Lave, eds., *Annual Review of Public Health*, vol. 5. Palo Alto, Calif.: Annual Reviews, pp. 443–458.

Woods, Anita M., and James E. Birren. 1984. Late Adulthood and Aging, in J. D. Matarazzo, Sharlene M. Weiss, J. Alan Herd, N. E. Miller, and Stephen M. Weiss, eds., *Behavioral Health: A Handbook of Health Enhancement and Disease Prevention.* New York: John Wiley, pp. 91–113.

Wortman, Camille B., and Terry L. Conway. 1985. The Role of Social Support in Adaptation and Recovery from Physical Illness, S. Cohen and S. L. Syme, eds., *Social Support and Health.* Orlando, Fla.: Academic Press, pp. 281–302.

Zelnik, Melvin, John F. Kantner, and Kathleen Ford. 1981. *Sex and Pregnancy in Adolescence.* Sage Library of Social Research, no. 133. Beverly Hills: Sage Publications.

4

SOCIAL AND PSYCHOLOGICAL FACTORS IN HEALTH AND ILLNESS

RONALD C. KESSLER
CAMILLE B. WORTMAN

Over the past decade, research on social and psychological influences on health and illness has focused on stress and the factors that modify its influence. The first section of this chapter examines attempts to conceptualize and measure stress and to estimate its impact on health. The second section focuses on three kinds of vulnerability factors thought to influence individual reactivity to stress: social support, coping strategies, and personality.

This selective focus, necessary due to constraints of space, neglects many of the social factors in health and illness that have traditionally been of greatest concern to medical sociologists—factors such as social class, sex, race, and urbanicity. It is important to note, though, that current work on the links between these social factors and health is largely based on the stress perspective. Investigators are examining group differences in such vulnerability factors as social support and coping strategies.

They are also assessing the extent to which such factors can account for group differences in health. A review of recent research attempting to interpret the effects of class, sex, and race in this way can be found in Kessler, Price, and Wortman (1985).

THE EFFECTS OF STRESS ON HEALTH

There is debate over the meaning of the term "stress." Some researchers define it as an objective feature of the environment. Others define it as an interaction between environment demands and individual coping resources. Still others define it as an appraisal of the implications of environmental demands. (See Dohrenwend and Dohrenwend 1974, for a discussion of these different perspectives.) For our purposes in this chapter, "stress" will be defined as a feature of the environment that, under certain circumstances, can affect the health of people exposed to it.

Three types of experimental literatures provide indirect information about the effects of stress on humans. One involves the physiological effects of stress on animals. Shuttle-avoidance experiments with mice, for example, document a variety of immune system responses that increase susceptibility to such experimentally induced infections as herpes simplex, poliomyelitis, Coxsackie B, and polyoma virus (Turkham Brady, and Harris 1982).

A second type of experimental evidence comes from laboratory studies in which humans are exposed to mild forms of stress. Research of this sort has shown, for example, that experimentally induced stress affects corticosteroid levels in humans (Plaut and Friedman 1981). Although these effects are too small to significantly impair health, it is plausible that more serious stresses would have much greater effects. This could be important because corticosteroids play a part in the onset of diabetes, peptic ulcers, and hypertension (Miller 1980).

Human stress exposure experiments have also provided information about psychological mediators of stress-reactivity, including situational cues and individual difference variables that modify the appraisal of stress and, in this way, influence the physiological effects of these situations (Lazarus and Launier 1978).

Finally, field experiments have been conducted among people exposed to serious stresses like job loss or widowhood (Price et al. 1980). These experiments manipulate some of the presumed intervening variables in the stress-illness relationship to study the protective influences of resistance resources. Although not designed to evaluate the effects of stress directly, these studies document the range within which an association between stress and illness can be modified.

Despite their importance, all of these experimental paradigms are limited in the evidence they provide about the effects of major stresses on man. The intervention experiments provide the most direct evidence that stressful life experiences can impair health. As most interventions are multifaceted, however, they fail to elucidate the mechanisms through which stress may influence health. As a result, most sociological research on stress has used nonexperimental methods to detect intervening links between stress and health.

Three varieties of nonexperimental stress research are considered below. The first focuses on life event inventories, the second on particular life crises, and the third on chronic stress situations.

Research on Aggregate Life Events

Numerous studies have shown that people often report some stressful event shortly before the onset of illness. Such research usually employs general population samples, in which respondents are asked about the recent occurrence of many different life events. Measures of health outcomes are usually based on self-reports. In case-control studies, patients are administered a life event inventory and asked to report on the events that occurred shortly before illness onset. Their reports are compared to those of healthy control respondents. Associations between illness and retrospective life event reports have been found for coronary heart disease (Wells 1985), some types of cancer (Sklar and Anisman 1981), several kinds of autoimmune disease (Solomon 1981), diabetes (Kimball 1971), mononucleosis (Roark 1971), self-reports of miscellaneous somatic complaints (Petrich and Holmes 1977), and symptoms of psychiatric disorders (Thoits 1983). Although less research has been done on the relationship between life events and course of illness, the evidence suggests that life events are somewhat more important in predicting recurrence and exacerbation than initial onset.

There are a number of methodological problems that suggest caution in interpreting the influence of life events on illness.

One is that some of the events may be results of ill health rather than causes. Being fired from a job, for example, might result from a prior mental health problem. Failure to adjust for this self-selection leads to upward bias in research on the health-damaging effects of unemployment (Kessler, Turner, and House 1987).

Another methodological problem is that poor health might be associated with better recall of recent stressful events, which would bias estimates of life event effects. Recent research by cognitive psychologists suggests that this kind of bias could occur in studies of mental health outcomes because depressed mood increases recall of depressing events (Blaney 1986). There is also evidence that such bias may occur among the physically ill, with illness increasing the number of negative events that are recalled (Schroeder and Costa 1984).

There is general agreement that contextual information is critical for a full appreciation of life event effects, but there is controversy about how best to obtain this information. Some researchers advocate asking respondents to rate the stressfulness of events that occurred to them (Sarason, Johnson, and Siegel 1978). Others advocate a complex scheme where an interviewer presents information about the objective circumstances under which events occurred to a panel of raters, who then score the events on a variety of contextual dimensions (Brown and Harris 1978).

Neither of these approaches is ideal. When respondents' ratings of perceived stress are used to measure context, the health of the respondents at the time of reporting can influence their judgments and thereby bias estimates of life event effects on these same measures of health. The panel rating scheme avoids one part of this problem by elaborating several different dimensions of the objective context that might be consequential for health. However, reliance on information about context provided by the respondent may contribute to the same distortion as the subjective rating procedure (Tennant 1983). Some researchers are experimenting with new approaches to obtain objective information, such as using the spouse as an informant (e.g., Stone and Neale 1984). Others have maintained that confounding between stress and appraisal is inevitable because these variables are fused together in nature (Lazarus et al. 1985).

Research on Life Crises

There is a long history of research on how people react to specific life crises such as bereavement, chronic illness, or rape. In the past, these studies were conducted by mental health professionals who sought to develop understandings that would guide clinical practice. This research consisted mostly of relatively small, descriptive studies focused on how people react emotionally to major crises and how such reactions change over time.

Taken together, the literature on reactions to life crises demonstrates that a substantial minority of people do not recover emotionally with the passage of time (Silver and Wortman 1980). The evidence for serious physical health effects is less readily available, because the small samples make it difficult to estimate rates of clinically significant illness reliably. Data are available for a few specific crises, though, including bereavement, retirement, and job loss (Kasl 1984). The evidence regarding bereavement shows that death of a spouse leads to increased mortality risk, reduced immunocompetence, and increased morbidity for a variety of physical and psychological disorders (Osterweis, Solomon, and Green 1984). The evidence on retirement documents no adverse aggregate health effects (Ekerdt, Bosse, and Goldie 1983). The evidence regarding the effects of job loss is mixed. Aggregate data suggest that mortality for several different causes increases as the unemployment rate increases, while individual-level studies find less persuasive evidence for effects of unemployment on the physical or mental health of people who experience it (Dooley and Catalano 1986).

As life events researchers become more interested in reactions to specific life crises, more sophisticated research is likely to appear. This will allow the selection of more carefully matched comparison groups, which, in turn, will lead to more accurate estimates of life event effects. There are a number of ways in which the methods developed by life events researchers can profitably be applied to studies of life crises. One area of probable development will be the comparative analysis of different life crises. There have been few serious attempts to administer parallel measures to people who experienced different events or to abstract from the evidence about different events to develop a more general understanding of how the predictors of adjustment vary from one stress situation to another. However, enough research is now in progress on specific crises that a comparative analysis will soon be feasible and is likely to be enlightening.

Research on Chronic Stress

People with chronic health problems commonly report that they have a long history of stress in one or more of their major life roles. An obvious question is whether these chronic stresses cause the illnesses. The most finely developed literature that addresses this question deals with job stress. Several different approaches have been adopted. One is to compare aggregate mortality and morbidity profiles of different occupations that are comparable in all known risk factors other than job stress. This approach has yielded striking evidence that indirectly implicates job stress in worker health (Kasl 1978).

Other investigators have used a multivariate approach to study the effects of job characteristics. The most persuasive of these investigations are based on longitudinal designs in which job demands are used to predict subsequent changes in health. These studies provide compelling evidence

that job pressures and conflicts can initiate and exacerbate coronary heart disease, peptic ulcers, diabetes, and psychological distress (Cobb and Rose 1973; Kasl 1978; House and Cottington 1984).

Longitudinal research on other kinds of chronic stresses exists but is less well developed than work on job stress. Illustrative results include the findings that academic pressure among students is associated with subsequent onset of infectious mononucleosis (Kasl, Evans, and Niederman 1979) and that chronic tension in a prison population is associated with subsequent onset of upper respiratory infection (McClelland, Alexander, and Marks 1982).

The mechanisms of action involved in these effects are unknown, but it is clear that host resistence is involved. This is shown in experimental research that documents that people with chronic role stresses are more likely than others to develop an acute upper respiratory infection when randomly exposed to a nasal spray containing viral material rather than a neutral solution (Jackson et al. 1960). Health habits such as dietary behavior or sleep patterns could be involved here, but systematic research to delineate potential influences of this sort remains to be done.

There are numerous methodological difficulties in research on the effects of chronic stress. The health problems and chronic stresses have typically been present for such a long time that it is difficult to separate cause and effect. The task of making a causal imputation is even more difficult because one cannot assume that stress exposure occurred for reasons that were random with respect to the respondent's prior health. The possibilities of dealing with these problems are too complex to consider here, but are discussed by Kasl (1978) and Kessler (1986).

Another difficulty is that chronic stress measures are based largely on subjective reports. This is particularly true in studies of interpersonal stresses, but it also occurs in studies of job stress. In the latter, it is almost always found that subjective reports about chronic stress are more strongly related than more objective measures to illness outcomes. This could reflect selective perception owing to illness or an intervening influence of appraisal. A challenge for future research is to develop more systematic ways to distinguish these possibilities.

VULNERABILITY FACTORS

Most people who are exposed to stressful life experiences do not develop health problems. The major thrust of current research on stress and health consequently involves the identification of factors that may explain differences in stress responsiveness. Several types of factors have been examined, including biogenic constitution and various aspects of personality. Intellectual capacities such as cognitive flexibility and effective problem-solving skills have also been considered, as have such interpersonal skills as social competence and communication ability. Financial assets, coping strategies, and social support are also among the resources that have been examined.

Research on vulnerability factors represents an important new direction in work on the relationship between psychosocial variables and health. Because full consideration is beyond the scope of this chapter, the following discussion is focused on three classes of variables that have generated intense interest over the past few years: social support, coping strategies, and personality.

Social Support

The term "social support" has been widely used to refer to the mechanisms by which interpersonal relationships presumably protect people from the deleterious effects of stress. Interest in these mechanisms was triggered by a series of influential papers published in the mid-1970s (Caplan 1974; Cassel 1976; Cobb 1976), which reviewed literature demonstrating associations between illness and such factors as marital status, geographic mobility, and social disintegration. They argued that a theme present in all of these associations is the absence of adequate social ties or supports or the disruption of social networks. Although highly inferential in their arguments, these early reviews generated great interest in the possibility that social support can protect health.

In recent years, this initial enthusiasm has been replaced by a more critical examination of the issues (Cohen and Syme 1985). Researchers have become increasingly sensitive to the methodological problems in the early research, and a new generation of studies has begun. Some of these new studies examine the relationship between life stress, social support, and health in normal population surveys or in case-control studies. Others examine the part played by social support in adjustment to particular life crises. Finally, a number of recent studies involve the experimental manipulation of support. Each of these is considered below.

General population studies. One line of investigation has examined the effects of network characteristics and social support on subsequent mortality and morbidity in prospective surveys of the general population. The most influential study of this sort showed that a number of network and support indicators (marriage, contact with family and friends, church membership, other group affiliations) were associated with reduced mortality risk over a nine-year follow-up period in a large sample of respondents living in Alameda County, California (Berkman and Syme 1979). Subsequent reports by Blazer (1982) and by House, Robbins, and Metzner (1982) showed similar results in other longitudinal community surveys. Reed et al. (1983) failed to find any such association, though, in an analysis of Japanese-Americans living in Hawaii.

All of these reports were based on secondary analyses, and none of them contained a comprehensive set of social support measures. Therefore, even though they provide strong evidence for the claim that social support is consequential for longevity, they do not allow us either to estimate the full extent of this influence or to study the precise components of support that promote longevity.

Similar longitudinal studies have studied the association between support and onset of physical illness. The most rigorous of these focus on coronary heart disease. Despite broad consistency in finding some indicator of support associated with reduced morbidity risk, there are numerous inconsistencies in these studies. In some, support is associated with subsequent disease incidence but not prevalence, while in others, the only significant predictions are associated with prevalence. The effects are limited to blue-collar women in one study, while they are found only among men in others. The kinds of support indicators that are most important vary from one study to the next. Clearly, results of this sort do not help specify the ways support may be important for health (See Berkman 1985 for a review).

While research on the relationship between support and physical illness has focused on direct effects, research on support and psychiatric disorder has concentrated on stress-buffering effects. In an influential program of research, Brown and Harris (1978) showed that the impact of life events on depression is reduced among people who have an intimate, confiding relationship with a friend or relative. In the largest of the studies conducted by Brown's group, nearly 40 percent of the stressed women without a confidant became depressed compared with only 4 percent of those with access to a confidant. This result has subsequently been replicated in several community surveys and case-control studies (See Cohen and Wills 1985 for a review).

Although these studies provide suggestive evidence, methodological problems make the results difficult to interpret. The most serious of these is that personal predisposition to become depressed might account for the presumed buffering effect. A group of investigators from Australia has shown that trait neuroticism disrupts close supportive relationships and that this personality characteristic is also associated with the exacerbation of stress effects. When neuroticism was statistically controlled in their analyses, the buffering effect of social support was explained away (Henderson, Burne, and Duncan-Jones 1981). There are methodological problems that prompt us to be cautious in concluding too much from this single study, but it calls into question a simple interpretation of support buffering effects. Other personality factors may also be implicated. New studies designed to investigate this possibility are currently under way.

Studies of specific life crises. In the past decade, numerous studies have been conducted to assess the impact of social support on adjustment to specific life crises such as widowhood (Vachon et al. 1982), unemployment (Gore 1978), and criminal victimization (Burgess and Holstrom 1979). Almost all of these studies have been concerned with mental health outcomes. Most of these studies find support shortly after the crisis to be a significant predictor of subsequent emotional adjustment. Moreover, these studies provide information about the importance of particular kinds of supportive ties for particular problems. For example, it has been found that when one of the coping tasks is to obtain new information or adopt a new role, low-density networks can promote adjustment more effectively than high-density networks (Hirsch 1979).

Life crisis studies also provide an opportunity to examine social support in relation to other aspects of the stress process—such as cognitions, feelings about the self, and coping strategies—and thus help clarify the mechanisms through which support may protect mental health in high-stress situations. Unfortunately, the life crisis studies carried out to date have not realized their potential in these ways. Most of these investigations have simply attempted to show that support is associated with subsequent adjustment without linking support to other variables that might help elucidate causal processes. For progress to be made, the advantages of this research design will have to be more fully exploited in the future.

Experimental support interventions. Most experimental support interventions have been designed and implemented in hospital settings and examine the impact of support on such outcomes as preoperative anxiety, recovery from surgery, or compliance with medical regimens (see Levy 1983, and Mumford, Schlesinger, and Glass 1982, for reviews). There have also been several support interventions to facilitate coping with life crises such as widowhood, rape, job loss, and life-threatening illness (see Leavy 1983 for a review).

These interventions operationalize support in many different ways, although all involve both emotional and informational interactions with support providers. Most have been provided by health care professionals and have been modest in scope. They have generally involved limited resources and a small number of sessions. Nonetheless, in the vast majority of cases, these manipulations have been effective in promoting both emotional adjustment and physical recovery. Unfortunately, the interventions carried out so far have not been designed to illuminate the mechanisms through which these influences occur. Furthermore, as most of these interventions have been multifaceted, it is impossible to determine which aspects of support are most effective (see DiMatteo and Hays 1981, and Wortman and Conway 1985, for reviews).

Future directions in research on social support. Taken as a whole, the evidence reviewed above leaves little doubt that something about support is consequential for both physical and mental health. A clearer understanding of these influences will require research advances in several directions. One of these involves further specification of components and characteristics of support, including the differential effects of support depending on who provides it.

A related issue involves the effects of negative social interactions. In the few studies that have compared positive and negative elements of social interaction, the negative have uniformly been more strongly related to illness outcomes (e.g., Rook 1984). We need to know more about the relative importance of positive and negative components as stress buffers and risk factors.

We also need more finely specified experimental support interventions to determine precisely which aspects of support affect particular illness outcomes. Research is also needed to trace out the intervening—presumably psychophysiological—mechanisms between support and illness.

Coping Processes

It is becoming increasingly clear that social support influences health by increasing coping effectiveness—by changing the ways people under stress appraise their situations and respond in an effort to master, tolerate, or reduce the demands imposed by stress (Gore 1985). The analysis of support, then, is a subarea of the analysis of coping processes. Unfortunately, this larger area is not yet well developed. This is true, in part, because the task of describing and analyzing the effectiveness of many different coping strategies is an enormous undertaking. The task is made even more difficult by the fact that the efficacy of particular coping strategies depends on the situation and on the individual (Meichenbaum, Turk, and Burstein 1975).

Considerable progress has been made in describing the most common strategies people use in particular stress situations (see Cohen and Lazarus 1979, and Silver and Wortman 1980, for reviews). However, our knowledge about the importance of coping for health is inadequate. As in research on social support, the methods used to document coping effects have included general population surveys, investigations of coping with particular life crises, and experimental interventions. Each of these is considered below.

General population studies. The relationship between coping and stress-reactivity has been studied in only a handful of general population studies (e.g., Andrews et al. 1981; Cronkite and Moos 1984). Two approaches have been taken. One asks respondents to describe, in general, how they cope with stressful experiences and then relates these responses to a variety of health outcomes. The other asks respondents to nominate the most stressful event that occurred to them recently and to indicate how they coped with that particular event. Both types of research interpret self-reports about coping strategies as if they caused the illness outcomes, despite the clear possibilities of selective recall, reciprocal causation, and joint determination by unmeasured variables.

Descriptive information from these studies demonstrates that most people in most stress situations employ a combination of coping strategies, some aimed at changing the situation and others aimed at controlling the individual's emotional response to the situation. Interindividual differences mainly reflect variations in the emphasis on problem- and emotion-focused strategies and in the specific strategies used to achieve each of these aims (Folkman and Lazarus 1980).

Research based on information about general coping strategies shows that people who report a vigilant coping style generally have better physical and emotional health outcomes than those who report avoidant styles (Mullen and Suls 1982). It is important to note, though, that denial and other strategies of focusing attention away from

the stress and one's reaction to it can promote good adjustment in situations where the individual is powerless (Lazarus 1983). Evidence for the importance of any particular coping strategy (as opposed to broad coping patterns) is inconsistent. It has been argued that in those cases where specific strategies predict subsequent illness onset, the results might be attributed to an underlying personality profile rather than to the strategies themselves (Miller et al. 1985). Recent empirical evidence lends some support to this notion (McCrae and Costa 1986).

Studies that ask respondents to describe how they coped with a particular stressful experience have been less successful in documenting consistent coping effects. This is probably due to the fact that variability in the situations is so great that the importance of coping is overwhelmed by the importance of stress variability.

Studies of specific life crises. Studies of reactions to specific life crises make it possible to compare the reactions of different people to the same life event. The vast majority of these studies have focused on physical health problems or major surgery (see Cohen and Lazarus 1979, and Moos 1977, for reviews). Most have examined the effects of coping on emotional adjustment, although some have also examined whether coping influences subsequent physical recovery (e.g., Taylor 1983).

These studies show fairly consistent evidence for the effectiveness of the following strategies (Hamburg and Hamburg 1980): (1) regulation of emotional reaction by a gradual transition from an initial period of denial or avoidance to a later period of vigilance; (2) creation of expectations about the future that include delineation of manageable tasks and intermediate goals; (3) rehearsal of emotional reactions and behavioral responses in a safe situation, followed by testing the same strategies in relevant situations; (4) information seeking from multiple sources and appraisal of coping strategies for adequacy; (5) commitment to a course of action on the basis of provisional testing; and (6) creation of contingency plans and strategies to buffer the effects of coping failure or setbacks.

No single coping strategy has been found that, by itself, is associated with good adjustment to a variety of major stresses. This is probably true because the effectiveness of coping efforts depends on a deeper level of coping, which can be realized in a number of ways (Ray 1982). There are many strategies, for example, that might be effective in distracting a person from the threatening nature of the situation, and it is possible that the use of *any* strategy of this sort is more important than whether a *particular* strategy is used. It might also be that an understanding of coping process and sequence is required to document significant influences of particular strategies (Lazarus and Launier 1978), or that the full importance of coping can only be uncovered by considering particular strategies in the context of broader patterns of coping responses (Menaghan 1983). The difficult measurement, design, and analysis problems created by these possibilities have yet to be tackled by coping researchers.

Experimental coping interventions. Given the lack of basic knowledge about the effectiveness of particular coping strategies, it is not surprising that experimental interventions to enhance coping effectiveness have not been widely attempted. The interventions that do exist focus on medical problems like management of pain (Turk, Meichenbaum, and Genest 1983) and preparation for various kinds of surgical procedures (Leventhal and Everhart 1979).

Several of these experiments report that teaching coping skills is more effective than merely providing information in promoting physical recovery among surgery patients (Langer, Janis, and Wolfer 1975). The effectiveness of coping skills training, furthermore, is enhanced when the intervention also attempts to alter maladaptive cognitions that can interfere with adaptive coping (Turk 1979).

The interventions conducted up to now have their main effects by using information as a kind of warning to "inoculate" people against a forthcoming stress (like a surgical procedure). This preparatory information seems to help the individual anticipate the stress, rehearse emotional reactions and coping responses, and develop some sense of control. Coping skills training is important because it provides the tools with which this anticipatory work is carried out (Hamburg, Elliot, and Parron 1982).

It is not clear that this is the only way in which coping interventions can enhance adjustment to stress. Nor is it clear that the procedures developed so far are equally effective for different populations and different stress situations. A challenge for future research is to develop parallel bodies of basic research and interventions across a range of stress situations and populations at risk.

Future directions in research on coping. The enormous complexity of coping efforts and the failure of general population studies to find consistencies in coping across situations suggest that progress in our understanding of coping is most likely to occur in focused analyses of particular stress situations. General population studies are likely to remain useful if they focus on coping with particular prototypic situations (Pearlin and Schooler 1978).

Research is also needed to determine more clearly what it is that people are coping with when they cope with life crises. Naturalistic studies have documented that crisis situations are usually made up of a number of components, each of which constitutes a separate coping challenge (Moos and Tsu 1977; Pearlin et al. 1981). Our understanding of coping will be advanced if we can distinguish the challenge(s) within the larger stress situation and determine whether particular coping strategies are more effective in dealing with particular challenges.

Finally, we need to develop more detailed procedures to describe the dynamics of coping processes. It is important to consider how the situation is initially appraised and how this appraisal changes over time, what coping strategies are used first, whether these strategies are appropriate under the circumstances, and whether people are able to alter or modify these strategies depending on the situation and their broader repertoire of coping skills (Kessler, Price, and Wortman 1985). These kinds of issues call for more fine-grained data collection techniques than have been used in previous studies (Stone and Neale 1982), as well as for theoretically grounded experimental interventions aimed at testing specific hypotheses about coping effectiveness (Kessler 1986).

Personality

At the same time that some researchers have been focusing on coping strategies, others have been concerned with more stable individual resources for managing stress. Among the most important of these are personality characteristics. Some of the personality characteristics that have been studied are actually stable clusters of coping dispositions (Kobasa, Maddi, and Kahn 1982; Rosenbaum 1984), whereas others are conceptualized as important largely because they influence the choice of coping strategies (Wheaton 1982). Some personality characteristics are thought to be important because they tap the individual's vulnerability to stress. Neuroticism (Henderson, Burne, and Duncan-Jones 1981), for example, is thought to modify the impact of stress because neurotic people are inherently more fragile emotionally. Other characteristics are thought to be important because they influence primary appraisal. The personality characteristic of interpersonal dependency is an example; it is thought to magnify the impact of interpersonal loss on health because dependent people appraise loss as particularly threatening (Hirschfeld et al. 1976).

A large number of personality charac-teristics, self feelings, and orientations to life that might be relevant to stress modification have been identified in the literature. Many attempts have been made to classify personality into core domains (see McCrae, Costa, and Busch 1986 for a review). There have also been attempts to specify the central personality characteristics that account for the effects of more global constructs such as the Type A behavior pattern (Matthews 1985). As noted earlier, there has also been considerable interest in determining whether any stable personality characteristics explain the putative effects of social support.

Pathogenic personalities. One line of research involves the hypothesis that particular personalities predispose people to particular illnesses. Examples include research on a cancer-prone personality, an arthritis-prone personality, and a personality type that predisposes to cardiovascular disease.

Cancer. Research on a cancer-prone personality began with a number of clinical reports pointing to an observed association between severe emotional loss and subsequent onset of cancer. More systematic epidemiologic studies verified this association in case-control designs and refined the argument into a two-part perspective: that cancer patients tend to have experienced a serious emotional loss and to have a premorbid personality, which makes them prone to feelings of helplessness and hopelessness in the face of such a loss. Coping strategies were implicated indirectly, by suggesting that people with a cancer-prone personality used excessive denial and repression of emotions (see Scurry and Levin 1978–79 for a review).

There have been only a handful of truly prospective studies in which personality characteristics were assessed prior to the onset of cancer, yet they have been surprisingly consistent with the personality hypothesis. A study of Veterans Administration patients who were administered the MMPI (Dattore, Shontz, and Coyne 1980) found clear evidence of greater repression of negative emotion among men who subsequently developed cancer. Grossarth-Maticek (1980) reported evidence of the same pattern based on a community sample of respondents in Yugoslavia who were administered a personality inventory at baseline and then followed prospectively for ten years.

Research has also been done on the personality predictors of survival among people who have cancer. Prospective studies find evidence that helplessness/hopelessness in the face of initial diagnosis is associated with poor prognosis after controlling for objective predictors (e.g., Greer, Morris, and Pettingale 1979). One recent study suggested that personality is not a predictor of survival, though, among patients with advanced cancer (Cassileth et al. 1985).

The major speculation about these influences is that personality affects the immune system, thereby changing host resistance to malignant transformation of cells. Evidence consistent with this view includes the documentation of higher incidence of cancer in individuals with prior immunologic deficiencies (Gatti and Good 1971) and evidence of an association between personality and immune competence (Jemmott and Locke 1984; Heisel et al. 1986). No research to date, though, has presented data documenting an intervening influence of immunocompetence on the relationship between personality and cancer incidence or course.

Arthritis. Research on an arthritis-prone personality has much the same history as work on personality and cancer. Unlike the latter, however, there have not been prospective studies to document whether premorbid personality predicts onset of arthritis. Instead, a series of studies have been carried out to examine the personality characteristics of people with early symptoms of arthritis and have shown that their personality profiles do not differ from those in the general population. On

the basis of this finding, it has been argued that the personality characteristics found to characterize people with advanced arthritis are probably results of the illness rather than causes (see Anderson et al. 1985, for a review). It is important to note, though, that there have not been prospective studies to determine whether personality predicts course of illness. Rheumatoid arthritis is an autoimmune disease; from what we know about the relationship between personality and immunity it is entirely plausible that evidence of a distinct personality among advanced cases of arthritis could reflect an influence of personality on the course of the disorder.

Coronary heart disease. Numerous poorly controlled studies show that coronary heart disease and hypertension occur more frequently to people who are neurotic or characterologically depressed. However, prospective studies show that personality changes on these dimensions follow rather than proceed diagnosis for heart disease, and this seems to explain the cross-sectional evidence. At the same time, there is some evidence to suggest that helplessness/hopelessness is a predictor of survival of a heart attack (Siegel 1985).

There is considerable research showing that a coronary-prone behavior pattern called Type A is a risk factor for coronary disease. Type A is seen as the interaction between a set of personality predispositions and situations that elicit responses of extreme competitiveness, hostility, and a sense of time urgency. Prospective studies have documented that this pattern is associated both with onset of coronary heart disease and with recurrence. Furthermore, an ongoing prospective intervention experiment has shown that recurrence rates in men who had previous myocardial infarctions is significantly lower in an intervention group designed to alter the Type A pattern (see Matthews 1985 for a review).

Some recent prospective studies have failed to find Type A to be a significant risk factor. Matthews (1985) suggests that the controlling style of Type A people is likely to make them particularly likely to engage in the health-promoting behaviors that have been widely publicized over the past decade and might account for the failure to find an effect of Type A on coronary heart disease risk in these recent studies.

At the same time, considerable work is going on to unpack the complex conceptualization and measurement of Type A behavior. It is not clear, at present, whether hostility or an overcontrolling interpersonal style or some other personality characteristic represents the core component of the Type A pattern that is consequential for health (Matthews 1982). As Kasl (1984) notes, it is likely that advancement here will require more careful analysis of explicit interactions between personality characteristics and the specific kinds of environmental situations that provoke Type A responses.

Other illness outcomes. Parallel literatures exist on the personality determinants of asthma, ulcerative colitis, and a wide range of autoimmune diseases (e.g., Stout and Bloom 1986). There is also fairly consistent evidence that low scores on the ego strength scale of the MMPI are positively associated with susceptibility to experimentally exposed viral material and with hypersensitivity to a variety of vaccines (See Jemmott and Locke 1984, for a review).

All of these investigations share a core set of methodological problems. The personality variables are often measured inadequately. Samples are often unrepresentative and poorly matched. Attempts to control for exogenous correlates are minimal. Prospective designs are rare. It is difficult to discount the possibility that results reflect an influence of illness on personality rather than vice versa. In those cases where it appears that personality is influential, it is unclear whether this is true because personality is associated with health behaviors (smoking, physical activity, etc.) or because personality has some more direct physiologic effect on host resistance.

Given the available evidence, it is likely that the influences of personality on course of illness are at least as great as on incidence. The logistics of studying personality determinants of illness course are considerably easier than those involved in studying initial onset. Furthermore, the potential value of such studies for intervention is greater than for studies of incidence. It is somewhat surprising, then, that there has been much less research on the personality determinants on course of illness than incidence.

Personality and stress-reactivity. Most research on pathogenic personalities is based on the hypothesis that particular personality characteristics interact with stressful life experiences to decrease host resistance to illness. Early laboratory studies documented that an interaction of this sort exists between experimentally induced mild stresses and personality in predicting a variety of physiological outcomes (see Ursin 1980 for a review). Unfortunately, subsequent research on the effects of major stress has not attempted to replicate this kind of analysis. Data are available to study the relationship between personality and stress-reactivity in the numerous studies that have examined the effects of psychosocial factors on susceptibility to infectious disease (see Jemmott and Locke 1984, for a review), but this kind of specification has not been estimated.

Data from general population surveys that examine mental health outcomes or self-reports of overall physical health are consistent with the hypothesis that personality influences stress-reactivity. Kobasa, Maddi, and Kahn (1982), for example, documented that a variety of personality characteristics assessed at baseline modified the relationship between subsequent stress and self-reported physical illness. Personality characteristics associated with resistance to stress included a belief that one can control his or her environment, openness to novel experience, and a predisposition to appraise potentially stressful situations as challenges rather than threats.

Kobasa and her colleagues have hypothesized the existence of a "hardy" personality constituted by high scores on the three personality dimensions investigated in the above research. However, several other attempts to replicate the results of their investigation by other researchers have failed to show that hardiness protects against stress (see Cohen and Edwards 1987, for a review). Consistent evidence exists that the belief in personal control is a resistance resource (Fisher 1984; Lefcourt 1985), though, and it is likely that this is the main dimension of the hardy personality that is consistently important for health.

There have also been a number of successful experimental interventions to enhance feelings of control. These studies demonstrate convincingly that perceptions of control can be changed and that these changes are consequential for health. Perhaps the most dramatic demonstrations of this sort have been control-enhancing interventions among residents of nursing homes that led to significant increases in longevity (see Rodin 1986 for a review).

The stress-buffering effects of other personality factors have not been as extensively examined, but there is nonetheless replicated evidence for the importance of self-esteem, introspectiveness, alienation, and neuroticism (Henderson, Burne, and Duncan-Jones 1981; Cohen and Edwards 1987).

Future directions in research on personality. Longitudinal research is needed to determine clearly whether personality is related to particular illness outcomes, including separate investigations of onset and illness course. Everything we know about psychophysiological influences on health and illness suggests that personality effects, to the extent they exist, are potentiated by stress. This means that further work is needed to trace out the ways in which stress exposure combines with particular personality characteristics to decrease host resistance to illness. As the preceding review shows, we currently lack so much as a clear description of the interactive influences of personality and stress in predicting most kinds of illness. It is likely that such investigations will find two main pathways: personality influences on appraisal of situations as stressful and personality influences on ways of coping. While it is unlikely that interventions aimed at modifying fundamental personality characteristics will be successful, attempts to manipulate appraisals or to channel coping efforts are feasible. Efforts to link personality characteristics to these intervention targets could be important in at least two ways. First, they could help to pinpoint stable person characteristics that are risk factors for particular kinds of cognitive and coping reactions which can be intervention targets. Second, they could help determine the range within which interventions are feasible.

ACKNOWLEDGMENTS

Work on this chapter was supported by a Research Scientist Development Award (K01 MH00507) to the senior author from the National Institute of Mental Health. We would like to thank Howard Freeman, James House, Jill Joseph, Philip Leaf, Sol Levine, Jane McLeod, and Elaine Wethington for help in preparing the chapter.

REFERENCES

Anderson, Karen O., Laurence A. Bradley, Larry D. Young, Lisa K. McDaniel, and Christopher M. Wise. 1985. Rheumatoid Arthritis: Review of Psychological Factors Related to Etiology, Effects, and Treatment. *Psychological Bulletin* 98:358–387.

Andrews, Gavin, Christopher Tennant, Daphne M. Hewson, and George E. Vaillant. 1981. Life Event Stress, Social Support, Coping Style, and Risk of Psychological Impairment. *Journal of Nervous and Mental Disease* 166: 307–316.

Berkman, Lisa F. 1985. The Relationship of Social Networks and Social Support to Morbidity and Mortality, in S. Cohen and S. L.

Syme, eds., *Social Support and Health*. New York: Academic Press, pp. 241–262.

Berkman, Lisa, and S. Leonard Syme. 1979. Social Networks, Host Resistance, and Mortality: A Nine-year Follow-up Study of Alameda County Residents. *American Journal of Epidemiology* 109:186–204.

Blaney, Paul H. 1986. Affect and Memory: A Review. *Psychological Bulletin* 99:229–246.

Blazer, Dan G. 1982. Social Support and Mortality in an Elderly Community Population. *American Journal of Epidemiology* 115:684–694.

Brown, George W., and Tirril O. Harris. 1978. *Social Origins of Depression: A Study of Psychiatric Disorder in Women*. New York: Free Press.

Burgess, Ann W., and Lynda L. Holmstrom. 1979. Adaptive Strategies and Recovery from Rape. *American Journal of Psychiatry* 136:1278–1282.

Caplan, Gerald. 1974. *Support Systems and Community Mental Health*. New York: Behavioral Publications.

Cassel, John. 1976. The Contribution of the Social Environment to Host Resistance. *American Journal of Epidemiology* 104:107–123.

Cassileth, Barrie R., Edward J. Lusk, David S. Miller, Lorraine L. Brown, and Clifford Miller. 1985. Psychosocial Correlates of Survival in Advanced Malignant Disease? *New England Journal of Medicine* 312:1551–1555.

Cobb, Sidney. 1976. Social Support as a Moderator of Life Stress. *Psychosomatic Medicine* 38:300–314.

Cobb, Sidney, and Robert M. Rose. 1973. Hypertension, Peptic Ulcer, and Diabetes in Air Traffic Controllers. *Journal of the American Medical Association* 224:489–492.

Cohen, Frances, and Richard S. Lazarus. 1979. Coping With the Stresses of Illness, in G. C. Stone, F. Cohen, and N. E. Adler, eds., *Health Psychology*. San Francisco: Jossey-Bass, pp. 217–254.

Cohen, Sheldon, and Jeffrey R. Edwards. 1987. Personality Characteristics as Moderators of the Relationship Between Stress and Disorder, in R. W. J. Neufeld, ed., *Advances in the Investigation of Psychological Stress*. New York: John Wiley.

Cohen, Sheldon and S. Leonard Syme, eds. 1985. *Social Support and Health*. New York: Academic Press.

Cohen, Sheldon, and Thomas A. Wills. 1985. Stress, Social Support, and the Buffering Hypothesis. *Psychological Bulletin* 98:310–357.

Cronkite, Ruth C., and Rudolf H. Moos. 1984. The Role of Predisposing and Moderating Factors in the Stress-Illness Relationship. *Journal of Health and Social Behavior* 25:372–393.

Dattore, Patrick J., Franklin C. Shontz, and Lolafaye Coyne. 1980. Premorbid Personality Differentiation of Cancer and Noncancer Groups: A Test of the Hypothesis of Cancer Proneness. *Journal of Consulting and Clinical Psychology* 48:388–394.

DiMatteo, M. Robin, and Ron Hays. 1981. Social Support and Serious Illness, in B. Gottlieb, ed., *Social Networks and Social Support*. Beverly Hills: Sage Publications, pp. 117–48.

Dohrenwend, Barbara S., and Bruce P. Dohrenwend. 1974. A Brief Historical Introduction to Research on Stressful Life Events, in B. S. Dohrenwend and B. P. Dohrenwend, eds., *Stressful Life Events: Their Nature and Effects*. New York: Wiley-Interscience, pp. 1–5.

Dooley, David, and Ralph Catalano. 1986. Do Economic Variables Generate Psychological Problems? Different Methods, Different Answers, in A. J. MacFadyen and H. W. MacFadyen, eds., *Economic Psychology: Intersections in Theory and Application*. Amsterdam: North-Holland Publishing.

Ekerdt, David T., Raymond Bosse, and Charlotte Goldie. 1983. The Effect of Retirement on Somatic Complaints. *Journal of Psychosomatic Research* 27:61–67.

Fisher, S. 1984. *Stress and the Perception of Control*. London: Erlbaum.

Folkman, Susan, and Richard S. Lazarus. 1980. An Analysis of Coping in a Middle-Aged Community Sample. *Journal of Health and Social Behavior* 21:219–239.

Gatti, Richard A., and Robert A. Good. 1971. Occurrence of Malignancy in Immunodeficiency Diseases. *Cancer* 28:89–98.

Gore, Susan. 1978. The Effect of Social Support in Moderating the Health Consequences of Unemployment. *Journal of Health and Social Behavior* 19:157–165.

———. 1985. Social Support and Styles of Coping With Stress, in S. Cohen and S. L. Syme, eds., *Social Support and Health*. New York: Academic Press, pp. 263–278.

Greer, S., T. Morris, and K. W. Pettingale. 1979. Psychological Response to Breast Cancer: Effect on Outcome. *Lancet* 2:785–787.

Grossarth-Maticek, Ronald. 1980. Psychosocial Predictors of Cancer and Internal Diseases. *Psychotherapy and Psychosomatics* 33:122–128.

Hamburg, David A., Glen R. Elliott, and Delores L. Parron. 1982. Stress, Coping, and Health, in D. Hamburg, G. R. Elliott and D. L. Parron, eds., *Health and Behavior: Frontiers of Research in the Biobehavioral Sciences*, Washington, D.C.: National Academic Press, pp. 63–87.

Hamburg, David, and Beatrix Hamburg. 1980. A Lifespan Perspective on Adaptation and Health, in B. Kaplan and M. Ibrahim, eds., *Family and Health: Epidemiological Approach*, vol. 2. Chapel Hill, N.C.: University of North Carolina Press.

Heisel, J. Stephen, Steven E. Locke, Linda J. Kraus, and R. Michael Williams. 1986. Natural Killer Cell Activity and MMPI Scores of a Cohort of College Students. *The American Journal of Psychiatry* 143:1382–1386.

Henderson, Scott, D. G. Burne, and Paul Duncan-Jones. 1981. *Neurosis and the Social Environment.* New York: Academic Press.

Hirsch, Barton J. 1979. Social Networks and the Coping Process, in B. Gottlieb, ed., *Social Networks and Social Support.* Beverly Hills: Sage Publications.

Hirschfeld, Robert M. A., Gerald Klerman, P. Chodoff, Sheldon Korchin, and J. Barrett. 1976. Dependency—Self-Esteem—Clinical Depression. *Journal of the American Academy of Psychoanalysis* 4:373–388.

House, James S., and Eric M. Cottington. 1984. Health and the Workplace, in L. H. Aiken and D. Mechanic, eds., *Applications of Social Science to Clinical Medicine and Health Policy.* New Brunswick, N.J.: Rutgers University Press, pp. 382–415.

House, James, Cynthia Robbins, and Helen Metzner. 1982. The Association of Social Relationships and Activities with Mortality: Prospective Evidence from the Tecumseh Community Health Study. *American Journal of Epidemiology* 116:123–140.

Jackson, George G., Harry F. Dowling, Truman O. Anderson, Louise Riff, Jack Saporta, and Marvin Turck. 1960. Susceptibility and Immunity to Common Upper Respiratory Viral Infections—the Common Cold. *Annals of Internal Medicine* 53:719–738.

Jemmott, John B., III, and Steven E. Locke. 1984. Psychosocial Factors, Immune Mediation, and Human Susceptibility to Infectious Disease: How Much Do We Know? *Psychological Bulletin* 95:78–108.

Kasl, Stanislav V. 1978. Epidemiological Contributions to the Study of Work Stress, in C. Cooper and R. Payne, eds., *Stress at Work.* New York: John Wiley, pp. 3–48.

———. 1984. Stress and Health. *Annual Review of Public Health* 5:319–341.

Kasl, Stanislav V., A. S. Evans, and J. C. Niederman. 1979. Psychosocial Risk Factors in the Development of Infectious Mononucleosis. *Psychosomatic Medicine* 41:445–466.

Kessler, Ronald C. 1986. The Interplay of Research Design Strategies and Data Analysis Procedures in Evaluating the Effects of Stress on Health, in S. V. Kasl and C. L. Cooper, eds., *Stress and Health: Issues in Research Methodology.* London: John Wiley, pp. 113–140.

Kessler, Ronald C., Richard H. Price, and Camille B. Wortman. 1985. Social Factors in Psychopathology: Stress, Social Support, and Coping Processes. *Annual Review of Psychology* 36:531–572.

Kessler, Ronald C., Blake Turner, and James S. House. 1987. Intervening Processes in the Relationship between Job Loss and Psychological Distress *Psychological Medicine* 17:949–961.

Kimball, Chase Patterson. 1971. Emotional and Psychosocial Aspects of Diabetes Mellitus. *Medical Clinics of North America* 55:1007–1018.

Kobasa, Suzanne C., Salvatore R. Maddi, and Stephen Kahn. 1982. Hardiness and Health: A Prospective Study. *Journal of Personality and Social Psychology* 42:168–177.

Langer, Ellen J., Irving L. Janis, and John A. Wolfer. 1975. Reduction of Psychological Stress in Surgical Patients. *Journal of Experimental Social Psychology* 11:155–165.

Lazarus, Richard S. 1983. Costs and Benefits of Denial, in S. Breznitz, ed., *The Denial of Stress.* New York: International Press, pp. 1–30.

Lazarus, Richard S., Anita Delongis, Susan Folkman, and Randy Gruen. 1985. Stress and Adaptational Outcomes: The Problem of

Confounding Measures. *American Psychologist* 40:770–779.

Lazarus, Richard S., and Raymond Launier. 1978. Stress-Related Transactions between Person and Environment, in L. A. Pervin and M. Lewis, eds., *Perspectives in Interactional Psychology*, New York: Plenum Press, pp. 287–327.

Leavy, R. L. 1983. Social Support and Psychological Disorder: A Review. *Journal of Community Psychology.* 11:3–21.

Lefcourt, Herbert M. 1985. Intimacy, Social Support, and Locus of Control as Moderators of Stress, in I. G. Sarason and B. K. Sarason, eds., *Social Support: Theory, Research and Application.* The Hague: Martinus Nijhoff, pp. 155–171.

Leventhal, Howard, and D. Everhart. 1979. Emotion, Pain and Physical Illness, in C. Izard, ed., *Emotions and Psychopathology.* New York: Plenum Press, pp. 263–299.

Levy, R. L. 1983. Social Support and Compliance: A Selective Review and Critique of Treatment Integrity and Outcome Measurement. *Social Science Medicine* 17:1329–1338.

Matthews, Karen A. 1982. Psychological Perspectives on the Type A Behavior Pattern. *Psychological Bulletin* 91:293–323.

Matthews, Karen A. 1985. Assessment of Type A Behavior, Anger, and Hostility in Epidemiological Studies of Cardiovascular Disease, in A. Ostfeld and E. D. Eaker, eds., *Measuring Psychosocial Variables in Epidemiologic Studies of Cardiovascular Disease: Proceedings of a Workshop.* Washington, D.C.: U.S. Department of Health and Human Services, pp. 153–184.

McClelland, David, Charles Alexander, and Emilie Marks. 1982. The Need for Power, Stress, Immune Function, and Illness among Male Prisoners. *Journal of Abnormal Psychology* 91:61–70.

McCrae, Robert R., and Paul T. Costa, Jr. 1986. Personality, Coping, and Coping Effectiveness in an Adult Sample. *Journal of Personality* 54:385–405.

McCrae, Robert R., Paul T. Costa, Jr., and Catherine M. Busch. 1986. Evaluating Comprehensiveness in Personality Systems: The California Q-Set and the Five-Factor Model. *Journal of Personality* 54:430–446.

Meichenbaum, Donald H., Dennis C. Turk, and Sam Burstein. 1975. The Nature of Coping With Stress, in I. G. Sarason and C. D. Spielberger, eds., *Stress and Anxiety,* vol. 2. Washington, D.C.: Hemisphere Publishers, pp. 337–360.

Menaghan, Elizabeth G. 1983. Individual Coping Efforts: Moderators of the Relationship Between Life Stress and Mental Health Outcomes, in Howard B. Kaplan, ed., *Psychosocial Stress: Trends in Theory and Research.* New York: Academic Press, pp. 157–191.

Miller, Neal E. 1980. A Perspective on the Effects of Stress and Coping on Disease and Health, in S. Levine and H. Ursin, eds., *Coping and Health.* New York: Plenum Press, pp. 323–354.

Miller, Patrick, Paul G. Surtees, Norman B. Kreitman, J. G. Ingham, and S. P. Sashidharan. 1985. Maladaptive Coping in Reactions to Stress: A Study of Illness Inception. *Journal of Nervous and Mental Disease* 173:707–716.

Moos, Rudolf H., ed. 1977. *Coping with Physical Illness.* New York: Plenum Press.

Moos, Rudolf H., and Vivian Tsu. 1977. The Crisis of Physical Illness: An Overview, in R. H. Moos, ed., *Coping with Physical Illness,* New York: Plenum Press, pp. 3–21.

Mullen, Brian, and Jerry Suls. 1982. The Effectiveness of Attention and Rejection as Coping Styles: A Meta-Analysis of Temporal Differences. *Journal of Psychosomatic Research* 26:43–49.

Mumford, E., H. J. Schlesinger, and G. V. Glass. 1982. The Effects of Psychological Intervention on Recovery from Surgery and Heart Attacks: An Analysis of the Literature. *American Journal of Public Health* 72:141–151.

Osterweis, Marian, Fredric Solomon, and Morris Green, eds. 1984. *Bereavement, Reactions, Consequences, and Care.* Washington, D.C.: National Academy Press.

Pearlin, Leonard I., Morton A. Lieberman, Elizabeth G. Menaghan, and Joseph T. Mullen. 1981. The Stress Process. *Journal of Health and Social Behavior* 22:337–356.

Pearlin, Leonard I., and Carmi Schooler. 1978. The Structure of Coping. *Journal of Health and Social Behavior* 19:2–21.

Petrich, John, and Thomas H. Holmes. 1977. Life Change and Onset of Illness. *Medical Clinics of North America* 61:825–838.

Plaut, S. Michael, and Stanford B. Friedman. 1981. Psychosocial Factors in Infectious Disease, in R. Ader, ed., *Psychoneuroimmunology.* New York: Academic Press, pp. 3–30.

Price, Richard H., Richard F. Ketterer, Barbara C. Bader, and John Monahan, eds. 1980. *Prevention in Community Mental Health: Research, Policy and Practice.* Beverly Hills: Sage Publications.

Ray, Colette. 1982. The Surgical Patient: Psychological Stress and Coping Resources, in R. Eiser, ed., *Social Psychology and Behavioral Medicine.* New York: John Wiley, pp. 483–508.

Reed, Dwayne, Daniel McGee, Katsihiko Yano, and Manning Feinleib. 1983. Social Networks and Coronary Heart Disease among Japanese Men in Hawaii. *American Journal of Epidemiology* 117:384–396.

Roark, Glenn E. 1971. Psychosomatic Factors in the Epidemiology of Infectious Mononucleosis. *Psychosomatics* 12:402–411.

Rodin, Judith. 1986. Aging and Health: Effects of the Sense of Control. *Science* 233:1271–1276.

Rook, Karen S. 1984. The Negative Side of Social Interaction: Impact on Psychological Well-Being. *Journal of Personality and Social Psychology*, 46:1097–1108.

Rosenbaum, M. 1984. A Model for Research on Self-Regulation: Reducing the Schism Between Behaviorism and General Psychology, in I. M. Evans, ed., *Paradigmatic Behavior Therapy: Critical Perspectives on Applied Social Behaviorism.* New York: Springer, pp. 18–42.

Sarason, Irwin G., James H. Johnson, and Judith M. Siegel. 1978. Assessing the Impact of Life Changes: Development of the Life Experiences Survey. *Journal of Consulting and Clinical Psychology* 46:932–946.

Schroeder, David H., and Paul T. Costa. 1984. Influence of Life Event Stress on Physical Illness: Substantive Effects or Methodological Flaws? *Journal of Personality and Social Psychology* 46:853–863.

Scurry, Murphy T., and Ellen M. Levin. 1978–1979. Psychosocial Factors Related to the Incidence of Cancer. *International Journal of Psychiatry in Medicine* 9:159–177.

Siegel, Judith M. 1985. Personality and Cardiovascular Disease: Prior Research and Future Directions, in A. M. Ostfeld and E. D. Eaker, eds., *Measuring Psychosocial Variables in Epidemiologic Studies of Cardiovascular Disease: Proceedings of a Workshop.* Washington, D.C.: U.S.

Department of Health and Human Services, pp. 315–344.

Silver, Roxane L., and Camille B. Wortman. 1980. Coping with Undesirable Life Events, in J. Garber and M. E. P. Seligman, eds., *Human Helplessness.* New York: Academic Press, pp. 279–375.

Sklar, Lawrence S., and Hymie Anisman. 1981. Stress and Cancer. *Psychological Bulletin* 89:369–406.

Solomon, George F. 1981. Emotional and Personality Factors in the Onset and Course of Autoimmune Disease, Particularly Rheumatoid Arthritis, in R. Ader, ed., *Psychoneuroimmunology.* New York: Academic Press, pp. 159–182.

Stone, Arthur A., and John M. Neale. 1982. Development of a Methodology for Assessing Daily Experiences, in A. Baum and J. Singer, eds., *Advances in Environmental Psychology*, Vol. 4: Environment and Health. New York: Erlbaum, pp. 49–89.

Stout, Christopher W., and Larry J. Bloom. 1986. Genital Herpes and Personality. *Journal of Human Stress* 12:119–124.

Taylor, Shelley E. 1983. Adjustment to Threatening Events: A Theory of Cognitive Adaptation. *American Psychologist* 38:1161–1173.

Tennant, Christopher. 1983. Life Events and Psychological Morbidity: The Evidence from Prospective Studies. *Psychological Medicine* 3:483–486.

Thoits, Peggy A. 1983. Dimensions of Life Events That Influence Psychological Distress: An Evaluation and Synthesis of the Literature, in H. B. Kaplan, ed., *Psychosocial Stress: Trends in Theory and Research.* New York: Academic Press, pp. 33–103.

Turk, Dennis C. 1979. Factors Influencing the Adaptive Process with Chronic Illness, in I. G. Sarason and C. D. Spielberger, eds., *Stress and Anxiety*, vol 6. Washington, D.C.: Hemisphere Publishing, pp. 291–311.

Turk, Dennis, C., Donald Meichenbaum, and Myles Genest. 1983. *Pain and Behavioral Medicine: A Cognitive Behavioral Perspective.* New York: Guilford Press.

Turkham, Jaylan S., Joseph V. Brady, and Alan H. Harris. 1982. Animal Studies of Stressful Interactions: A Behavioral-Physiological Overview, in L. Goldberger and S. Breznitz, eds., *Handbook of Stress: Theoretical and Clini-*

cal Aspects. New York: Free Press, pp. 153–182.

Ursin, Holger. 1980. Personality, Activation and Somatic Health: A New Psychosomatic Theory, in S. Levine and H. Ursin, eds., *Coping and Health*. New York: Plenum Press, pp. 259–280.

Vachon, Mary L. S., Joy Rogers, W. Alan L. Lyall, Wilhelm J. Lancee, Adrienne R. Sheldon, and Stanley J. J. Freeman. 1982. Predictors and Correlates of Adaptation to Conjugal Bereavement. *American Journal of Psychiatry* 139:998–1002.

Wells, James A. 1985. Chronic Life Situations and Life Change Events, in A. M. Ostfeld and E. A. Eaker, eds., *Measuring Psychosocial Variable in Epidemiologic Studies of Cardiovascular Disease*. Washington, D.C.: U.S. Department of Health and Human Services, pp. 105–128.

Wheaton, Blair. 1982. A Comparison of the Moderating Effects of Personal Coping Resources on the Impact of Exposure to Stress in Two Communities. *Journal of Community Psychology* 10:293–311.

Wortman, Camille B., and Terry L. Conway. 1985. The Role of Social Support in Adaptation and Recovery from Physical Illness, in S. Cohen and S. L. Syme, eds., *Social Support and Health*. New York: Academic Press, pp. 281–302.

CHAPTER
5

ECOLOGICAL FACTORS IN ILLNESS AND DISEASE

RALPH CATALANO

Chapters in handbooks such as this are typically descriptions of recent advances and controversies in fields defined by scholars and practitioners who share substantive interests. I do not believe that such a chapter could be written for the health-related literature often described as "ecological." The reason is that the term is typically applied *post hoc* to any literature concerned with the geographic distribution of health-related phenomena rather than to work that addresses questions that arise from ecological theory. There has, in fact, been little health-related work in recent years that explicitly draws from ecological principles.

This chapter is an attempt to renew interest in ecological explanations of health-related phenomena. I believe that concepts drawn from human ecology can be meshed with other insights from sociology to suggest new and parsimonious explanations of spatial and temporal variation in diagnosed illness.

A MODEL OF THE RISK OF BEING DIAGNOSED AS ILL

An explanation of why the incidence of labeled illness varies from community to community or over time in one community should start with an understanding of the individual risk of being labeled "ill." A sociological perspective implies that this risk is a function of two factors. The first is the probability that the individual will exhibit physical or behavioral characteristics included in one or more symptom syndromes. The second is the probability that the individual in question will exhibit these symptoms before an audience with low tolerance for his or her deviance. This proposition can be symbolically represented as:

$$D_i^s = S_i^s T_i \qquad (1)$$

where

D_i^s = probability that individual i will be diagnosed with syndrome s,

S_i^s = probability that individual i will exhibit symptoms from syndrome s,

T_i = probability that individual i will have an audience with low tolerance for his or her deviance.

The likelihood of exhibiting symptoms can, in turn, be understood as a function of two additional factors. The first is exposure to hazards that are necessary, but often insufficient, to elicit symptoms. Such hazards can be intuitively separated into three groups. The first includes microorganisms associated with infectious illnesses. The second is comprised of toxins that cause noninfectious illness. The third includes safety hazards that can result in trauma if not dealt with successfully.

The second factor affecting the likelihood of exhibiting symptoms is the ability of the exposed person to resist the hazard or to respond to it in ways that do not include symptoms of disorder. Substituting these further specifications in Equation 1 leads to the following equation:

$$D_i^s = E_i^s (1 - R_i^s)T_i \qquad (2)$$

where

E_i^s = probability that individual i will be exposed to the environmental hazard that is necessary but not always sufficient to elicit symptoms of syndrome s,

R_i^s = probability that individual i will be able to adapt without symptoms to the hazard to which he or she is exposed.

Each of the factors in Equation 2 needs to be elaborated to an additional level of specificity to offer an ecological explanation of being diagnosed ill. Exposure can be divided into two additional terms. The first is virulence, or strength of the hazard. Various strains of microorganisms, for example, are believed to be more or less likely to elicit symptoms from a population

that is relatively stable in its ability to resist. The second is extent of exposure measured in time exposed or amount of the hazard contacted or ingested.

Resistance can be further specified as a function of the genetically determined potential to cope with hazards and how much of that potential is realized or available at a given time. The population is, for example, normally distributed in its ability to resist infectious microorganisms. This ability is the "net" capacity remaining from our genetic potential after interaction with the environment. Interaction with the environment allows us to realize our potential by producing antibodies through immunizations or earlier exposures (Dubos 1955). Our immune systems, however, appear to age and respond less effectively as the number of demands upon them accumulate over a lifetime (Selye 1956). The ability to physiologically cope with exposures to noninfectious toxins is also believed to be normally distributed in a community for the same reasons (Fabro 1979; Gardner 1979). Resisting safety hazards implies a combination of manual dexterity and caution that may seem to be responses of a different type than those used to deal with infectious and noninfectious toxins (Forbes 1972). All, however, are physiological responses and, as such, are products of genetically determined potential realized or reduced by experience.

An important literature has suggested that the ability to resist hazards of all kinds is rooted in a single mechanism that can be depleted by acute exposures and only partially replenished (Selye 1952; 1956). The implications of this suggestion include the possibility that resisting one type of acute or chronic hazard can reduce the ability to cope with subsequent exposures to hazards of any type.

Audience tolerance can be understood as a function of the relative power of the audience and the observed as well as the interest of the audience in having the observed labeled as ill. A husband or wife who fears for the well-being of a family, for example, can be very effective in having a spouse accept or reject the label of "ill" depending on the effect of the label on the family (Freeman and Simmons 1963; Wylan and Mintz 1976). The interests of an employer, likewise, can be very influential in determining whether or not an employee accepts or seeks the label "ill" when he or she exhibits symptoms (Trice and Beyer 1984).

Substituting these further elaborations into Equation 2 yields the following equation:

$$D_i^s = V_i^s A_i^s P_i I_i^s [1 - G_i^s (F_i - C_i)] \qquad (3)$$

where

V_i^s = probability that individual i will be exposed to an environmental hazard (for syndrome s) that has high virulence,

A_i^s = probability that individual i will ingest, internalize or contact a sufficient amount of the hazard to require an adaptation,

P_i = probability that individual i will have an audience with the power to affect his or her acceptance of diagnosis,

I_i^s = probability that individual i will have an audience with an interest in individual i being diagnosed as ill with syndrome s,

G_i^s = probability that individual i will have been genetically endowed with a high potential (compared to the remainder of the population) to adapt without symptoms to an exposure,

F_i = probability that individual i has realized his or her genetic capacity to resist through previous experience,

C_i = probability that individual i has had sufficient chronic and recent exposures to hazards of any type to temporarily deplete whatever proportion of G_i^s he would otherwise realize.

It is my contention that ecological processes affect all the terms in the above equation and therefore are potentially important to understanding the probability of being diagnosed ill. Building the case for this contention requires that I be more specific as to what is meant by ecological processes.

AN OVERVIEW OF ECOLOGICAL CONCEPTS

There is an old and well-documented controversy in sociology over the prudence of borrowing methods and assumptions from ecology to explain the behavior of human populations (Gettys 1939). Much of this controversy stems from the failure of the early human ecologists to appreciate fully the role of culture in mediating the human response to environmental constraints and opportunities (Alihan 1938; Mukerjee 1968). There is, however, general agreement that the human ecologists made a considerable contribution to our understanding of the processes that affect the spatial distribution of phenomena of interest to sociologists. A concern for spatial distributions, in fact, became so strongly associated with human ecology that any work concerned with geographic arrays was referred to as ecological whether or not ecological theory (or any theory) was invoked by the author (Lander 1954). This attribution has led contemporary sociologists to overlook the propositions that originally led the human ecologists to an interest in spatial arrays. These propositions have implications for medical sociology that go beyond predicting the geographic distribution of health-related phenomena. I suggest that these principles can be combined with the above formulas to offer testable explanations of why the incidence of health and behavioral problems varies over time in geographically defined populations as well as across such populations at any point in time.

The human ecologists believed that the rules that govern the production and distribution of goods and services determine the size, socioeconomic and demographic composition, and spatial distribution of human communities (Park 1925). They posited that the rules of the competitive market created a concern for efficiency in that the individual or firm that produced the most product per unit of cost would be the most rewarded. They drew an analogy between the market's reward of efficiency and natural selection in the nonhuman ecosystem. The spatial and trophic (i.e., food chain) organization that emerged from the efficient use of abiotic resources in the ecosystem was assumed to be analogous to the spatial array of land uses and the division of labor in the city and its suburbs.

Borrowing from contemporary economics (Gras 1922; Weber 1968), the ecologists believed that each manufactured product had a location, or isobar of locations, at which it could be made most efficiently. This location was where costs of assembling raw materials, labor, and energy and of shipping finished products to market were minimized. Firms that made this product had to be at this location, or along the isobar, if they were to be successful in the market because locating elsewhere meant that a firm could always be undersold by competitors located at the optimum locations.

The ecologists asserted that communities arise at sites that are optimal for one or another industry. These industries are termed "basic," because they formed the base upon which a local economy was built (McKenzie 1925). Other firms and businesses spring up to serve the basic industry and its employees, thereby creating a local economy that is a mix of basic and service industries. The number of persons that could be supported by this economy supposedly depended on how many dollars were brought into the local area by the basic industries. The larger and more diverse the economic base, of a community, the more people with different skills it could support. Fewer people and fewer skills would be needed in communities with narrower and smaller bases.

The size and mix of the economic base also controlled the intensity of the competition for land in the community. The larger and more diverse the base, the more competitors there would be for the most accessible locations. The ecologists likened this competition to a regularly repeated auction in which all those interested in land bid against each other. The auction supposedly led to the assignment of bidders to the location at which no other user could make more profit because each bidder eventually found the location that was the best compromise between cost and access. The pattern of land uses under this condition was efficient from a market perspective and was analogous to the climax organization of niches that emerges in stable ecosystems when the amount of biomass per unit of available energy is maximized. The ecologists further speculated that the complex set of economic and social interdependencies that emerge in human communities were analogous to the trophic organizations or food chains that can be traced in nonhuman ecosystems.

The analogy between the human community and the nonhuman ecosystem inevitably led to the proposition that the dynamics of change in the two systems were similar and that ecological theory could be used to understand and predict changes in the size, composition, spatial distribution and behavior of human communities (McKenzie 1925). Principal among these theories was the proposition that the relationship between the abiotic elements (e.g., sunlight, moisture, soil composition, topography) of the ecosystem and the size, diversity, and spatial distribution of the biomass was homeostatic. If the abiotic elements changed slowly through gradual geologic processes, the biomass reached its climax size, diversity, and spatial distribution and remained relatively stable. Typical arrays of biomass could, therefore, be associated with types of abiotic elements, and ecosystems could be organized into a taxonomy that reflected this relationship (e.g., riparian ecosystems, chapparal ecosystems).

Sufficient observation of ecosystems allowed ecologists to develop models for predicting changes in biomass that would be necessitated by changes in abiotic elements. These models included changes in the spatial and trophic organizations and therefore inevitably dealt with the behavior of animals in the food chain. The behavior of these species was predictable as long as the abiotic elements changed slowly or cyclically. Rapid change in the abiotic elements, however, made behavior difficult to predict without observing many such perturbations of similar ecosystems. The hard work of ecology was to systematically accumulate the observational data that would allow discovery of the underlying laws that governed the adaptation of biomass to changes in abiotic elements.

The human ecologists believed that the abiotic elements of the human community included all those that the ecologists had identified for nonhuman ecosystems. These elements, however, were believed to be overshadowed by the economic base of the community for sheer effect on the size, diversity, and spatial organization of the human community. The object of human ecology, therefore, was to infer the laws that governed the relationship between types of economic bases and the size, diversity, spatial distribution, and behavior of the populations supported by those bases.

The analogy drawn by the human ecologists led to several important hypotheses (McKenzie 1925). Many of these were concerned with spatial arrays of populations and land uses. Migration of human populations, for example, was hypothesized to be a function of the differences among communities in their ratio of basic to nonbasic employees. Regions that had too few service workers given the size of the economic base were likely to pay higher wage rates than regions in which the ratio of

service workers to basic employees was greater. Risk-taking workers from the latter would inevitably be attracted to the former. Migration was the homeostatic mechanism that brought the system (governed by market rules) back to equilibrium. Migration could, therefore, be predicted if one understood the geometry of industry location.

Hypotheses regarding the intracommunity array of activities were frequently offered by the early ecologists and, as noted above, became the work for which they were best known. The auction for land inevitably created predictable patterns of land values that segregated people by income and job and often, therefore, by culture and demographics. The concentric zone model that Burgess (1925) inferred from Chicago was so powerful a demonstration of this segregation that similar mapping projects were repeated in many communities and controversy inevitably arose over the meaning of the observed pattern and its variants for sociology (Firey 1945; Quinn 1940).

All but forgotten amid the spatial hypotheses were several others that should be of interest to medical sociologists. These other hypotheses had to do with the implications of shifts in the economic base for the risk being judged deviant. The early ecologists, Park and McKenzie in particular, had been much influenced by the work of Simmel (Wolfe 1950) and Thomas and Znaniecki (1920) on the effect of urbanization on human behavior. A common theme in their work was that persons who migrated from rural to urban areas had to adapt not only to new physical environments but also to new modes of moral and practical reasoning. Although most migrants successfully made the transition, there was a period of learning during which they were at risk of exhibiting behavior that settled members of the receptor community would judge unexpected or unpredicted from environmental cues.

The ecologists generalized these observations into the proposition that any person changing physical or social environments would be at risk of exhibiting behavior different from that which would be exhibited given longer experience in the environment. Such persons were, therefore, at relatively high risk of being judged deviant by those who were settled in the environment. How great a risk depended on how fast a learner the individual was. Learning was the process of interacting with the environment to discover which behaviors were most efficient at eliciting that which the individual desired. "Culture" would come to include the expectation of the response most persons in the community found efficient. Unexpected responses would be viewed as deviance that suggested either an indifference or hostility toward the dominant culture or a defect in the individual that precluded understanding the lessons of experience.

The principal contribution of the human ecologists to the arguments I hope to make is the meshing of the notion of risky transitions with the model of community dynamics implied by the ecosystem analogy. The ecologists contended that communities with economic bases that were expanding, contracting, or shifting in structure (i.e., changing the mix of industries represented) would exhibit higher rates of deviance than communities with stable economic bases (McKenzie 1925, p. 71). The rate of deviance exhibited in a community would, moreover, vary longitudinally with the stability of its economic base. The reason for this relationship is that changes in the economic base of a community require the entire population to change its social or physical environments to some degree. These changes require individuals to learn the most efficient strategies for dealing with their new circumstances. The risk of exhibiting a strategy that deviates from cultural expectations depends on how great a change the individual experiences and on how fast he or she learns.

Another important effect of changes in the economic base for understanding deviance was only hinted at by the early human ecologists (Dunham 1937) but has received more attention in recent years (Catalano, Rook, and Dooley 1986). Tolerance for deviance may vary over time in a community and across communities at any given time owing to the "overstaffing" phenomenon (Wicker 1979). It has been noted that organizations with too few persons to fill all essential roles will be much more tolerant of the peculiarities of individuals that would bar them from holding roles in organizations with more participants per role. Tolerance of deviance, therefore, may vary with the status of the labor market. If there are surplus laborers, those with any manifestations of deviance that may affect productivity are less likely to find, and are more likely to be dismissed from, employment. Challenges to this type of discrimination inevitably lead to management's explanation that the person in question is deviant in some way related to work performance, and the individual is so labeled.

Labor shortages, on the other hand, lead employers to keep workers who are less than optimally productive and to hire persons who may be suspected of deviance that affects productivity. The alternative is to search for a less risky employee and to pay him or her more than other employers who are similarly searching. The cost of searching plus the relatively high wage may be greater than the value added by the more productive worker. The effect may be that the label of deviant is less likely to be applied in times of expansion of the economic base.

The "landscape" of the human ecologist, therefore, was one of enormous spatial and social change. The change was fueled by new technology, rules, or tastes that caused the costs of production and distribution of goods and services to shift. These shifts were reflected in changes in the relative attractiveness of communities for capital investment. The shifts in capital investment, in turn, perturbed the geographic balance between population and economic opportunity, triggering migrations from stagnant or stable to growing economies. The communities whose bases were shifting experienced the spatial and organizational adaptations that follow from changes in the size and mix of the local economy. The complex interdependencies of organizations transmitted the changes in wider and wider circles throughout the social and physical structure of affected communities. Individuals changed their physical and social environments, or those environments changed around them. Old behaviors were repeated when they were no longer appropriate. New behaviors were attempted out of the suspicion or knowledge that the old were no longer appropriate. A subset of the population could not or did not learn fast enough that their responses were inappropriate. The willingness of institutions to tolerate deviant responses was affected. The result was that communities predictably differed from each other and from their own histories in the rate of diagnosed deviance.

DIAGNOSED ILLNESS IN ECOLOGICAL CONTEXT

The understanding of community formation and change that I have attributed to human ecology offers testable propositions concerning spatial and temporal variation in the factors that affect the risk of being diagnosed ill. The following is list of several of these propositions.

1. *The mix of infectious microorganisms to which a community is exposed is, in part, a function of the economic base that supports it.* It has been empirically demonstrated that the spread of virulent microorganisms is predictable from understanding the economic relationships among communities (May 1958; Pyle 1968). This relationship governs the flow of goods and people from place to place and, therefore, affects the timing and spatial array of the transmission of microorganism from population to population.

2. *The noninfectious toxins to which a community is exposed are predictable from its natural setting and economic base.* Many of the noninfectious toxins to which a population will be exposed are products of the interaction among climate, topography, and industrial processes (McMullen 1967; Ozolins 1966; Welson and Stevens 1970). Each of these interactants is among the abiotic elements of the human community, and understanding them allows prediction of the temporal and geographic array of job-specific and ambient toxins. Knowing the economic base of a community allows prediction of the local industrial processes. Each of these processes creates an idiosyncratic mix of work-place toxins that, in turn, yield job-specific illnesses. A predictable geographic pattern of job-related illnesses that reflects the geometry of industrial location therefore emerges in industrialized countries.

Toxins in the ambient environment can also be anticipated from understanding abiotic elements of a community. Research has suggested that the composition of air pollution measured over cities, for example, can be predicted from the local economic mix (Welson and Stevens 1970). The same is certainly true of water pollution, given the close connection between industrial discharge and local water quality.

3. *The safety hazards to which a community is exposed can be predicted from its economic base and natural setting.* Safety hazards can be separated into work-place, residential, and ambient exposures. Each industrial process poses its own mix of safety hazards and therefore yields its peculiar signature of disabling accidents. Knowing the economic base of a community allows the prediction of the industrial mix and, in turn, of the work-related safety hazards peculiar to a community. Expanding employment, moreover, has been reported to be associated with increased rates of work-related injuries (Catalano 1979; Kossoris 1938; Smith 1972).

Residential accidents are a function of the interaction of occupant characteristics, particularly age, and housing age and style. Old, multiple-level houses (especially those that predate the uniform building code and its emphasis on safety) occupied by the elderly will, for example, yield injuries that are different in frequency and type than new, single-level homes that house families. Where these house-style and occupant-type combinations are likely to be found in a metropolitan area is predictable from the auction for land and the resulting pattern of land uses described originally by Burgess (1925) and updated and elaborated by several generations of sociologists and geographers (Berry and Horton 1970). The proportion that each combination represents of the total households in a given metropolitan area can, moreover, be estimated from the economic history of the area. Building technologies and safety codes have histories of greater and lesser use. Matching these histories with that of the economic growth of a given community should suggest which housing types dominate in the community.

Ambient safety hazards, such as the risk of automobile accidents, are a function of the physical characteristics of communities, such as weather, density, and array of land uses (which affects how auto-dependent a population is). All these are predictable from the natural settings and economic histories of communities. The density of traffic, moreover, is at least in part a function of the longitudinal variation in the local economy. Expanding economies increase the job-related use of roads and other public facilities and may affect the incidence of auto accidents and related injuries (Wagenaar 1984).

4. *The distribution of resistance in a community can be affected by the abiotic elements.* If the model of resistance that is described briefly above is accurate, abiotic factors can potentially affect the cross-sectional and longitudinal variation in resistance in communities. The genetic characteristics of a community can be understood, at least in part, as a function of when its economic base ex-

panded most quickly. Migration to that community is likely to have been greatest at that time (Kosa 1956; Thomas and Znaniecki 1920). Communities with relatively weak economic bases at that time are, obversely, likely to have lost population. The climatic and physical characteristics of a community may also repel or attract migrants who may seek or avoid environments similar to those they left. If the contracting communities are dominated by a genetically related population, expanding communities are likely to gain a large population with those genetic characteristics. Sickle cell anemia, for example, is more common among blacks than expected by chance. The migration of blacks has clearly been affected by ecological processes. The geographic distribution of sickle cell anemia, therefore, can be understood as determined, at least in part, by ecological processes.

The distribution in a community of the ability to resist health and safety hazards may vary over time with the status of the economic base. The proposition that all coping mechanisms are rooted in a common source that is at least temporarily depleted by acute exposures implies that individuals coping with several hazards are less likely to deal successfully with any than when coping with fewer (Selye 1956). This understanding of coping mechanisms has given rise to the considerable literature on the role of "stressful life events" in the etiology of health and behavioral problems (Dohrenwend and Dohrenwend 1974). These events are presumed to require cognitive and behavioral adaptations that draw from the basic coping capacity. Because they draw from this capacity, they can supposedly increase the risk that a stressed individual will fail to deal asymptomatically with other acute or chronic stressors. These other stressors can include infectious and noninfectious toxins as well as safety hazards.

The ecologists' contention that shifts in the economic base imply that the population will have to adapt to new physical and organization environments connects ecological theory to the stressful life events research (Cassell and Tyroler 1961; Catalano 1979; Hinkle 1974). Among the life experiences that research has found to be associated with subsequent increases in symptoms are those that are intuitively and empirically related to the economy. The loss of income through any means (job loss in particular) and its sequelae have been reported to be associated with increased symptoms of, and seeking help for, behavioral disorder, as well as with physiological illness serious enough to disrupt normal functioning (Catalano and Dooley 1983; Catalano et al. 1985; Dooley and Catalano 1984a). These events have been reported, as expected, to be more common during periods of economic change, including shifts in the economic base (Catalano and Dooley 1979; Dooley and Catalano 1984b). These stressors have also been related to the subsequent experience of other stressors (e.g., familial strife or changing job or residence) that are not as intuitively linked to the economy (Catalano, Dooley, Rook 1987).

Stressful life events, whether or not related to the economy, are not hazards in the sense of the exposures referred to by the V_i^s term in Equation 3. This is true because the stressful events are not risk factors peculiar to any syndrome and must, therefore, act on the resistance term, or C_i in Equation 3.

5. *Tolerance for disorder will be related to employment opportunities and, therefore, to the economic base.* To be diagnosed ill, particularly behaviorally ill, implies that the individual is deviant because he or she is too symptomatic to exhibit the societally desired or expected response to physical or social stimuli (Sontag 1978; Goffman 1963). There is considerable literature in sociology that demonstrates that the label "deviant," in any of its particular forms (e.g., "criminal", "insane"), is not uniformly applied to all who exhibit the same undesirable or unexpected behavior (Sarbin 1969; Scheff 1975). Tolerance, or the willingness

to label, apparently varies with other situational phenomena of interest to sociology (Nunn, Crockett, and Williams 1978). Recent research has suggested that, as the early ecologists implied, the ratio of supply and demand for labor affects interest in labeling deviance and the relative power of audiences and observed. It has been reported that perceived job security is inversely related to seeking help for behavioral disorder and that this relationship survives controlling for symptoms of disorder (Catalano, Rook, Dooley 1986). Perceived job security is, moreover, related to objective measures of employment opportunities in the industry in which respondents were employed.

IMPLICATIONS OF AN ECOLOGICAL CONTEXT FOR EMPIRICAL RESEARCH

The above propositions imply that additional terms measuring the abiotic elements (i.e., the physical environment and ratio of basic to service jobs) of the community in which the individual resides should be added to Equation 3. Estimating the equation by alternatively adding one type of variable (e.g., the abiotic elements) as a control for the other (e.g., individual-level variables measuring exposure, resistance, and audience tolerance) in a sample drawn from many communities could lead to either of two outcomes if ecological theories are correct. The first is that the abiotic elements would not be significant when controlling for the other factors and, vice versa, that the others would not be significant when controlling for the abiotic elements. This outcome would imply that the two groups of variables measure the same underlying construct or that one group causes all the variability in the other so that controlling for one precludes finding an effect of the other. Given that one group of variables is person based and that the other characterizes a physical environment and an economy, it is doubtful that the two would measure the same latent construct. It is, moreover, unlikely that the person-level variables of exposure, resistance, and tolerance determine the physical environment in which a community is located or the ratio of basic to service jobs. One would, therefore, be left with the explanation that the physical environment and economic factors drive the person-level variables.

The second, and more likely, outcome if ecological theory were correct is that the effect of the individual-level variables on the likelihood of diagnosis would be reduced but remain significant when the abiotic elements were added to the equation. An initially significant effect of the abiotic elements, however, would be reduced to an insignificant level when the individual-level variables were added. The implications of this finding would be that the abiotic elements have an effect but the effect is realized entirely through the individual-level variables of exposure, resistance, and audience tolerance. The finding would further imply that the variability in the individual-level variables was, in part, due to the differences among communities in abiotic elements.

Ecological theory would be rejected if no association were found between the abiotic elements and the likelihood of being diagnosed. The remaining computationally possible outcome is to find an effect of the abiotic elements that is not reduced by controlling for the individual-level variables. Given, however, that all explanations of the diagnosis of illness assume either the presence of symptoms or an audience with a strong interest in applying the label "ill" to a person regardless of symptoms, an effect of abiotic elements that is not reduced by controlling for the individual-level variables would defy explanation.

IMPLICATIONS FOR POLICY AND PRACTICE

The theory and research alluded to above have implications for policy regarding both the prevention of illness and the provision of health services. Prevention can be thought of as either proactive or reactive (Catalano and Dooley 1980). Proactive prevention reduces illness by controlling exposure to hazards. An example of proactive prevention is the control of vectors, such as mosquitoes or rodents, that carry infectious toxins to humans. Other examples include the design of work environments to preclude or reduce exposure to noninfectious toxins or to dangerous machinery. Machinery and consumer goods can also be designed to reduce their dangerousness.

A less intuitive form of proactive prevention that is suggested by an ecological perspective is the reduction of stressful life events that are inflicted on a community through economic policy made at the national and local level. Nearly all the industrial democracies have recently devised policies to increase the productivity of their economies in the hope of controlling inflation and raising the real standard of living. Many of these policies are intended to accelerate the movement of investment away from labor-intensive and toward capital-intensive industries. Typical of such policies were the accelerated depreciation schedules of recent years that had the intended effect of shortening the economic life of fixed capital and thereby encouraging the construction and equipping of new manufacturing and business properties. These new facilities, however, were often not in the same communities or regions as those that were being depreciated on the accelerated schedules. Terms such as the Rust Belt began to appear in the popular press to describe those areas whose economic bases were contracting as a result of the new policies.

It has been argued that policies such as the accelerated depreciation schedule demonstrate that the cost-benefit analyses that supposedly precede the choice of public policies have not sufficiently anticipated, or have undervalued, the adverse health effects of many options (Brenner 1976; Dooley and Catalano 1977; Iglehart 1985; Luft 1978; Mundinger 1985). If these arguments are compelling and the health and behavioral effects of policies are more fully accounted or more heavily weighted, it is possible that economic policy will increasingly become a means to proactive prevention. This is true because fewer communities would suffer sharp decline and the undesirable life events associated with such decline. If the model that posits that all adaptations draw from a single source were correct, a reduction in such stressors would lower the incidence of illnesses otherwise manifested via depleted resistance. Lowered likelihood of sharply declining communities would also reduce the loss of tolerance that may follow when economic bases contract and reduce job security.

The advent of economic policy as proactive prevention presumes that the cost-benefit analyses alluded to above are changed. The problem of failing to anticipate the health or behavioral cost of policy options may be a technical one in that the analysts did not understand the connection between shifts in economic base and the incidence of illness. The literature described above has, however, made a strong case for such effects and estimated risk ratios for the health and behavioral effects of the adverse life experiences likely to follow from economic policy (Catalano and Dooley 1983; Dooley and Catalano 1984b). The fact that the literature exists and is largely, although not entirely, ignored in policymaking suggests that the problem is as much one of political values as of ignorance. It appears that in the current political climate expected gains in productivity are more highly valued than reducing illness among populations in declining areas. Ecological theory cannot, of course, change the values of elected officials or of the electorate. It can, however, be used to help inform people of the distributional effects of the policy choices.

The states and local jurisdictions have traditionally influenced private investment in communities through strengthening or relaxing land use, building, and public health codes. The exercise of this power

has only recently been guided by the type of cost-benefit logic that supposedly shapes decision making at the federal level. It is possible, therefore, that "social impact assessment" will become increasingly widespread and that ecological assumptions will guide much of the work (Catalano 1984; Catalano and Monahan 1975; Finsterbusch and Wolf 1977). The actual effect of such assessments, however, depends on the values of the persons who eventually make the policy choices.

Proactive prevention in the form of intentional attempts to mitigate the stressors that flow from economic processes can be initiated by the private sector. Indeed a considerable literature has arisen concerned with "social auditing" (Dilley and Weygandt 1973; Estes 1976)—the attempt to make the beneficial and adverse effects of corporate decisions count in the assessment of the performance of managers. Social auditing is usually done by allowing managers the discretion to incur a minimal level of inefficiency in the name of corporate responsibility. Stockholders make the conscious decision to not count the cost of such programs against management so that socially responsible managers do not appear to be less competent than those expected to serve only the literal "bottom line." While social auditing could constrain the private sector from inflicting economic stress on communities, it requires stockholders to accept lower short-term returns on their investment. Such acceptance is unlikely in the age of corporate takeovers stoked by the claim that management has not been aggressive enough in controlling costs. Social auditing cannot be successful until the government creates economic incentives for socially responsible behavior. Government policies to this effect are not likely given the current political values of the country and the fear of making domestic industry less competitive with that of nations with lower "social overhead."

Reactive prevention is the attempt to increase the individual's ability to resist or cope with hazards that cannot be avoided. Immunization, for example, allows the individual to adapt without symptoms to exposures to infectious agents that cannot be cost-effectively removed from the environment. Recent attempts have been made to develop behavioral immunizations that enhance the ability of the individual to cope with stressors (Jaremko 1979; Meichenbaum and Jaremko 1983). This added coping skill supposedly reduces the risk of exhibiting illnesses peculiar to specific hazards as well as those that are believed to be manifestations of the adaptation process itself.

Reactive prevention of all kinds requires that the population at risk be identified and motivated to seek inoculation. This is particularly true of stress inoculation because the intervention is cognitive and the effect often short-lived. The method, therefore, works best with populations who know they are likely to be acutely stressed in the near future. The ecological literature described above provides a heuristic for locating populations at risk of economic stress in geographic as well as organizational space. Regional science has developed several methods for predicting which regions and industries are likely to be affected by various types of changes in public or private economic policies (Isard 1976). Knowing, for example, that a new industrial process or product is likely to make an old one obsolete can be combined with ecological principles to predict which communities are likely to be stressed. This type of prediction allows the use of labor unions, churches, and other local organizations as sponsors for stress inoculation programs.

It is not very likely that prevention of either kind will become so common or effective that the need for treating the acutely ill will be reduced on an absolute scale. The emphasis on cost containment for health care is, moreover, likely to increase. There will, therefore, be growing interest in finding ways to anticipate where and when scarce health-service resources will be needed. Current "needs assessments" for health services tend to depend on such cross-sectional data as demographic and socioeconomic profiles of catchment areas. An understanding of ecological theory and research should add a dynamic quality to these studies that could lead to better predictions of where and when funds and facilities are needed.

SUMMARY

Ecological theory has much to offer contemporary sociologists interested in the variation of diagnosed illness across communities and over time. The contribution is primarily in the form of a heuristic that integrates research from several fields to predict the spatial and temporal array of diagnosed illness. This contribution has been overlooked in recent years because of the mistaken belief that human ecology is useful only in understanding geographic distributions.

The above overview of ecological principles has stressed their implications for understanding illness. Space limitations preclude discussion of other implications, such as those for the spatial and temporal distribution of physicians and medical facilities. The hope is, however, that the above limited discussion will rekindle the interest of medical sociologists in a rich intellectual tradition concerned with the effects of social processes on health.

REFERENCES

Alihan, Milla. 1938. *Social Ecology*. New York: Columbia University Press.

Berry, Brian, and Frank Horton. 1970. *Geographic Perspective on Urban Systems*. Englewood Cliffs, N.J.: Prentice-Hall.

Brenner, M. Harvey. 1976. *Estimating the Social Costs of Economic Policy: Implications for Mental and Physical Health, and Criminal Aggression*. Report to the Congressional Research Service of the Library of Congress Joint Economic Committee of Congress. Washington, D.C.: U.S. Government Printing Office.

Burgess, Ernest. 1925. The Growth of the City: An Introduction to a Research Project, in R. Park and E. Burgess, eds., *The City*. Chicago: University of Chicago Press, pp. 47–62.

Cassell, John, and H. Tyroler. 1961. Epidemiological Studies of Culture Change, I: Health Status and Recency of Industrialization. *Archives of Environmental Health* 3:31–38.

Catalano, Ralph. 1979a. *Health, Behavior and the Community: An Ecological Perspective*. New York: Pergamon Press.

———. 1979b. Health Costs of Economic Expansion: The Case of Manufacturing Accidents. *American Journal of Public Health* 69:789–794.

———. 1984. Urban Planning, Public Health, and the Human Cost of Economic Change. *Journal of Planning Education and Research* 3:110–117.

Catalano, Ralph, and David Dooley. 1979. "The Economy as Stressor: A Sectoral Analysis." *Review of Social Economy* 37:175–187.

———. 1980. Economic Change in Primary Prevention, in R. Price, R. Ketterer, B. Bader, and J. Monahan, eds., *Prevention in Mental Health: Research, Policy and Practice*, vol. 1. Beverly Hills: Sage Publications, pp. 21–40.

———. 1983. The Health Effects and Economic Instability: A Test of the Economic Stress Hypothesis. *Journal of Health and Social Behavior* 24:46–60.

Catalano, Ralph, David Dooley, and Robert Jackson. 1985. Economic Antecedents of Help Seeking: A Reformulation of the Time-Series Tests. *Journal of Health and Social Behavior* 26:141–152.

Catalano, Ralph, David Dooley, and Karen Rook. 1987. A Test of Reciprocal Risk Between Undesirable Economic and Noneconomic Life Events. *American Journal of Community Psychology* 15:633–651.

Catalano, Ralph, and John Monahan. 1975. The Community Psychologist as Social Planner: Designing Optimum Environments. *American Journal of Community Psychology* 3:327–334.

Catalano, Ralph, Karen Rook, and David Dooley. 1986. Labor Markets and Help-Seeking: A Test of the Employment Security Hypothesis. *Journal of Health and Social Behavior* 27:277–287.

Dilley, S. C., and J. J. Weygandt. 1973. Measuring Social Responsibility: An Empirical Test. *Journal of Accountancy* 136:62–70.

Dohrenwend, Barbara, and Bruce Dohrenwend. 1974. *Stressful Life Events: Their Nature and Effects*. New York: John Wiley.

Dooley, David, and Ralph Catalano. 1977. Money and Mental Disorder: Toward Behavioral Cost Accounting for Primary Prevention. *American Journal of Community Psychology* 5:217–227.

———. 1984a. Why the Economy Predicts Help Seeking: A Test of Competing Explanations. *Journal of Health and Social Behavior* 25:160–175.

———. 1984b. The Epidemiology of Economic Stress. *American Journal of Community Psychology* 12:387–409.

Dubos, Rene. 1955. Second Thoughts on the Germ Theory. *Scientific American* 192:31–35.

Dunham, H. Warren. 1937. The Ecology of the Functional Psychoses in Chicago. *The American Sociological Review* 2:467–479.

Estes, R. 1976. *Corporate Social Accounting*. New York: John Wiley.

Fabro, Sergio. 1979. Introductory Remarks: Session on Developmental Factors Affecting Pollutant Toxicity. *Environmental Health Perspectives* 29:5–6.

Finsterbusch, Kurt, and C. P. Wolf. 1977. *Methodology of Social Impact Assessment*. New York: McGraw-Hill.

Firey, Walter. 1945. Sentiment and Symbolism as Ecological Variables. *The American Sociological Review* 10:140–148.

Forbes, T. W. 1972. *Human Factors in Highway Traffic Research*. New York: John Wiley.

Freeman, Howard, and Ozzie G. Simmons. 1963. *The Mental Patient Comes Home*. New York: John Wiley.

Gardner, Donald. 1979. Introductory Remarks: Session of Genetic Factors Affecting Pollutant Toxicity. *Environmental Health Perspectives* 29:45–48.

Gettys, Warner. 1939. Human Ecology and Social Theory. *Social Forces* 18:469–476.

Goffman, Erving. 1963. *Stigma*. Englewood Cliffs, N.J.: Prentice-Hall.

Gras, Norman. 1922. *An Introduction to Economic History*. New York: Harper and Brothers.

Hinkle, Lawrence. 1974. The Effects of Exposure to Culture Change, Social Changes, and

Changes in Interpersonal Relationships on Health, in B. Dohrenwend and B. Dohrenwend, eds., *Stressful Life Events: Their Nature and Effects*. New York: John Wiley, pp. 9–44.

Iglehard, John. 1985. Medical Care of the Poor—A Growing Problem. *Health Policy Report* 313:59–63.

Isard, Walter. 1976. *Introduction to Regional Science*. Englewood Cliffs, N.J.: Prentice-Hall.

Jaremko, Matt. 1979. A Component Analysis of Stress Innoculation: Review and Prospectus. *Cognitive Therapy and Research* 3:35–48.

Kosa, John. 1956. Hungarian Immigrants in North America: Their Residential Mobility and Ecology. *Canadian Journal of Economics and Political Science* 22:358–370.

Kossoris, M. 1938. Industrial Injuries and the Business Cycle. *Monthly Labor Review* March:579–594.

Lander, B. 1954. *Toward an Understanding of Juvenile Delinquency*. New York: Columbia University Press.

Luft, Harold. 1978. *Poverty and Health: Economic Causes and Consequences of Health Problems*. Cambridge, Mass.: Ballinger.

May, J. 1958. *The Ecology of Human Diseases*. New York: M.D. Publications.

McKenzie, Roderick. 1925. The Ecological Approach to the Study of the Human Community, in R. Park and E. Burgess, eds., *The City*. Chicago: University of Chicago Press, pp. 63–79.

McMullen, T. 1967. *Air Quality and Community Characteristics*. Paper presented at the Annual Meeting of the Air Pollution Control Association, Cleveland.

Meichenbaum, Donald, and Matt Jaremko. 1983. *Stress Reduction and Prevention*. New York: Plenum Press.

Mundinger, Mary O'Neil. 1985. Health Services Funding Cuts and the Declining Health of the Poor. *New England Journal of Medicine*, July 4: 44–47.

Murkerjee, Radhakamal. 1968. *Man and His Habitation: A Study in Social Ecology*. Bombay: Populat Prakoshan.

Nunn, Clyde, Harry J. Crockett, and J. Alan Williams. 1978. *Tolerance for Non-Conformity*. San Francisco: Jossey-Bass.

Ozolins, Guntis. 1966. *A Rapid Survey Technique for Estimating Community Air Pollution Emissions*. Cincinnati: U.S. Department of Health, Education and Welfare.

Park, Robert. 1925. The City: Suggestions for the Investigation of Human Behavior in the Urban Environment, in R. Park and E. Burgess, eds., *The City*. Chicago: University of Chicago Press, pp. 1–46.

Pyle, Gerald. 1968. Some Examples of Urban-Medical Geography. M.A. thesis, University of Chicago.

Quinn, James A. 1940. Burgess Zonal Hypothesis and Its Critics. *American Sociological Review* 5:210–218.

Sarbin, Theodore. 1969. Schizophrenic Thinking: A Role Theoretical Analysis. *Journal of Personality* 37:190–206.

Scheff, Thomas. 1945. *Labeling Madness*. Englewood Cliffs, N.J.: Prentice Hall.

Selye, Hans. 1956. *The Stress of Life*. New York: McGraw-Hill.

———. 1952. *The Story of the Adaptation Process*. Montreal: Acta, Inc.

Smith, R. 1972. Intemporal Changes in Work Injury Rates. *IRRA Proceedings*. New York: Industrial Relations Research Association, pp. 167–174.

Sontag, Susan. 1978. *Illness as Metaphor*. New York: Farrar, Straus and Giroux.

Thomas, William, and Florian Znaniecki. 1920. *The Polish Peasant in Europe and America*. New York: Knopf.

Trice, Harrison, and Janice Beyer. 1984. Work-Related Outcomes of the Constructive-Confrontation Strategy in a Job-Based Alcoholism Program. *Journal of Studies on Alcohol* 45:393–404.

Wagenaar, Alexander. 1984. Effects of Macroeconomic Conditions on the Incidence of Motor Vehicle Accidents. *Accident Analysis and Prevention*. 16:191–205.

Weber, Adna. 1968. *Theory of Industrial Location*. Chicago: University of Chicago Press.

Welson, John, and Benjamin Stevens. 1970. *Air Quality and its Relationship to Economic Meteorological and Other Structural Characteristics of Urban Areas in the United States*. Philadelphia: Regional Science Research Institute.

Wicker, Allen W. 1979. *An Introduction to Ecological Psychology*. Belmont, Calif.: Wadsworth.

Wolf, Stewart, John Bruhn, and Helen Goodall. 1978. *Occupational Health as Human Ecology.* Springfield, Ill.: Charles C Thomas.

Wolfe, Kurt. 1950. *The Sociology of Geog Simmel.* Glencoe, Ill.: Free Press.

Wylan, L., and N. L. Mintz. 1976. Ethnic Differences in Family Attitudes toward Psychiatric Manifestations with Implications for Treatment Programmes. *International Journal of Social Psychiatry* 22:86–95.

6

THE EPIDEMIOLOGY
OF MENTAL DISORDERS

BRUCE G. LINK
BRUCE P. DOHRENWEND

Epidemiology is generally defined as the study of the occurrence (incidence and prevalence), distribution, and determinants of states of health in a population (e.g., McMahon and Pugh 1960; Mausner and Bahn 1974). The ultimate goals of epidemiology are to contribute to our understanding of the etiology of these states and to their control. Like sociology, epidemiology can be distinguished from clinical studies of individuals by its emphasis on populations. It can be distinguished from sociology per se by its concern with states of health as opposed to other characteristics of populations such as the class structure or degree of integration (*cf.* Susser 1968). It shares an emphasis on health states with the sociological subspecialty of medical sociology. However, the epidemiologist often studies genetic, biological, or physical environmental factors in addition to the social factors that are the prime emphasis of medical sociologists working in this area.

Within the framework of these general distinctions, the epidemiology of mental disorders investigates the kinds of health and behavior problems that are described, for example, in the *Diagnostic and Statistical Manual of Mental Disorders* of the American Psychiatric Association (1952, 1968, 1980). Our purpose is to review studies that have investigated the occurrence and distribution of mental disorders. In doing so, we seek to specify why medical sociologists are likely to be interested in these studies and how their expertise can contribute to furthering knowledge in this area.

With very few exceptions, the epidemiological studies of mental disorders report prevalence rates for adults in community populations. These rates usually refer to the presence of disorders regardless of their time of onset and duration. Additionally, they refer to current cases of disorder whether or not the individuals involved have been in treatment with members of the mental health professions. For this reason, they have come to be known as true prevalence studies as opposed to studies of treated prevalence.

The focus on community populations in true prevalence studies raises difficult and yet very interesting issues concerning the definition of mental disorder. Most of the mental disorders are defined in terms of constellations or syndromes of symptoms. While there is considerable consensus about some of the symptoms of some disorders, conceptions of particular disorders often vary with the social contexts in which theorists, clinicians, and researchers are embedded. For example, exposure to long-term, mainly chronic inpatients in mental hospitals can lead to a different, more pessimistic, conception of the nature and course of schizophrenia than if one follows a cohort of patients diagnosed as schizophrenic through their careers (Cohen and Cohen 1984; Harding and Strauss 1985; Harding, Zubin, and Strauss 1987). Moreover, when clinical experience has been extended beyond both hospital and outpatient clinics to include samples of nonpatients, as in Selective Service screening and combat during World War II, not only have the boundaries of particular disorders widened but new disorders have been added to psychiatric nomenclatures. With respect to the World War II experience, Raines, writing in the foreword to the 1952 *Diagnostic and Statistical Manual of Mental Disorders* of the American Psychiatric Association, observed that psychiatrists found themselves "operating within the limits of a nomenclature not designed for 90% of the cases handled" (American Psychiatric Association 1952, p. vi). It is thus a broader, more varied, and more complex terrain that one encounters when the concern is with the general population.

It is no wonder, then, that the epidemiological investigators whose studies we will review have tended to differ in their methods of research and in their conceptions of the nature of various mental disorders. Such differences have led to great variations in the prevalence they report, with some studies finding overall rates of 50 percent and more and others reporting rates of under 1 percent (Dohrenwend and Dohrenwend 1974a). Nevertheless, most of the investigators present their findings in terms of similar broad nosological distinctions. Thus, many of them provide data on at least some of the following major types of mental disorders: schizophrenia involving behaviors that come closest to the lay person's stereotype of what is insane or crazy; affective psychoses including unipolar and bipolar or manic depressive psychosis; neuroses, whose hallmark is extreme anxiety and the panic, rituals, and phobias that can accompany it; and personality disorders, especially those that manifest themselves in antisocial behavior and that include problems in the abuse of alcohol and drugs. Moreover, there appears to be considerable agreement among the epidemiological investigators as to the nature of these vividly contrasting symptom complexes or syndromes despite sharp differences in where the investigators draw the boundaries among the different types and between all types and "normality." The reason for inferring such agreement is that, despite the differences in concepts and methods, there are, as we will see, strong consistencies from study to study in relationships between various types of mental disorder and such variables as gender, social class, and rural-urban location (Dohrenwend and Dohrenwend 1974a, 1974b). It is difficult to see how such consistent relationships can occur unless cores of common meaning are being tapped.

TWO GENERATIONS OF EPIDEMIOLOGICAL STUDIES OF MENTAL DISORDERS

Since the turn of the century, and continuing until at least 1980, when the American Psychiatric Association published its new and markedly different third edition of the *Diagnostic and Statistical Manual of Mental Disorders* (DSM-III) (American Psychiatric

Association 1980), there have been what one of us has described (Dohrenwend 1983) as two generations of epidemiological studies of mental disorders (Dohrenwend and Dohrenwend 1982). The first generation consists of sixteen studies, all of which took place before World War II; the second generation consists of the more than sixty studies that were conducted for the most part after the war (Dohrenwend and Dohrenwend 1974a, p. 425; Dohrenwend, Dohrenwend, et al. 1980). The third generation has just begun to make an appearance in the last few years. To date the results come in the form of a descriptive epidemiology of major disorders with diagnoses made via DSM-III criteria in what are called the Epidemiological Catchment Area (ECA) studies (Robins et al. 1984; Myers et al. 1984).

Our purpose will be to review the findings from the first two generations of epidemiological studies and the descriptive epidemiology arising from the more recent ECA studies in order to identify the problems and research issues they pose. We then will discern directions for future research that could lead to markedly increased understanding of etiology and opportunities for control. In keeping with the more general focus of this volume, we will emphasize the policy implications of the issues we discuss as we proceed. Specifically, we will mention four areas that Klerman (1987) has suggested should be influenced by epidemiological findings: (1) service delivery, (2) manpower and human resources, (3) research and scientific investigation, and (4) prevention.

The First Generation of Studies

In 1855, Edward Jarvis, a Massachusetts physician and epidemiologist, submitted a report of what was probably the most complete and influential attempt to investigate the true prevalence of mental disorder conducted in the nineteenth century (Jarvis [1855] 1971). Almost half a century before the beginning of the Kraepelinian era in psychiatry, Jarvis's main nosological distinc-

tion was between "insanity" and "idiocy." Jarvis was well aware of the inadequacy of treated rates for estimating either the amount or the distribution of disorder in communities; he had, in fact, published a classic study showing that such rates varied inversely with geographic distance from treatment facilities (Jarvis 1850). As a result, he conducted a survey of general practitioners, supplemented by reports of other key informants. These informant reports were checked against the records of mental hospitals and other official agencies, and the resulting data analyzed according to such demographic variables as gender, place of birth, and economic status.

Like Jarvis, the first generation of epidemiological investigators tended to rely on key informants and agency records to supply the information that would enable them to identify cases in the sixteen community studies conducted prior to World War II (Dohrenwend and Dohrenwend 1974a, p. 425). Such procedures are, of course, likely to underestimate untreated cases of disorders that are characterized mainly by subjective distress that would be more likely revealed in direct interviews or self-report questionnaires (e.g., Cawte 1972).

Direct interviews with all subjects were used in only six first generation studies. Even in the interview studies, where rates tended to be higher than in studies using key informants and agency records, the median for all types of disorders was only 3.6 percent compared to a median of close to 20 percent in second-generation interview studies that were conducted after World War II (Dohrenwend and Dohrenwend 1974a, p. 425). The difference is a dramatic illustration of the effect of the change in nomenclatures following World War II on the rates of mental disorders counted in communities.

The Second Generation of Studies

Unlike the first generation of studies, most of the investigators in the second-generation studies relied on direct interviews (Dohrenwend and Dohrenwend 1974a, p. 425). Only rarely were the interviews supplemented by data from key informants and official records, although such information is extremely useful for identifying or confirming some types of psychopathology such as substance abuse and antisocial behavior (e.g., Leighton et al. 1963; Mazer 1974). Two different types of interview were used.

First, in most of the European and Asian research, a single psychiatrist or a small team headed by a psychiatrist personally interviewed community residents and recorded diagnostic judgments on the basis of these interviews. As a rule, the interview procedures were not made explicit in this type of approach (e.g., Bash 1967; Hagnell 1966; Kato 1969; Lin 1953).

In the second type, by contrast, standard and explicit data-collection procedures were used. Although the interviews were done sometimes by psychiatrists and clinical psychologists and sometimes by lay interviewers, in all instances case identification depended on psychiatrists' evaluations of protocols compiled from the interview responses and, sometimes, from ancillary data from key informants, official records, and interviewers' observations (e.g., Leighton et al. 1963). The Midtown study and the Stirling County study (Srole et al. 1962; Leighton et al. 1963) pioneered this approach.

This approach is economical when, as in the Midtown and Stirling County studies, lay interviewers rather than clinicians are used to collect the data to be evaluated. More important, the written protocols that form the basis of the evaluation can be edited to remove direct clues to social and cultural background factors such as social class that could bias the clinical judgments (*cf.* Phillips and Draguns 1971). On the other hand, the procedure has a distinct disadvantage since it makes a difference whether the clinicians actually see the individuals; clinicians tend to be overimpressed by pathology when working from written records alone (Bluehler 1966; Dohrenwend, Egri, and Mendelsohn 1971; Gott-

heil, Kramer, and Hurwich 1966; Shader, Ebert, and Harmatz 1971). The questions of what information is required to make an informal clinical judgment and what information is likely to bias such judgment are two horns of a dilemma that has received considerably less attention than it deserves (e.g., Dohrenwend, Egri, and Mendelsohn 1971).

Even more economical than having clinicians evaluate data collected by lay interviewers is dispensing with clinical judgments altogether. Respondents are presented with a standardized set of questions that have fixed alternative response categories with preassigned weights associated with them. Because such measures are easy to administer, a number of the investigators in the second generation of studies employed them (e.g., Meile 1972; Phillips 1966). Unfortunately, however, their decisions to use these measures were based on considerations of practicality and cost rather than evidence for validity.

The objective measure used most often is a twenty-two-item screening instrument developed by the Midtown study researchers on a purely actuarial basis to provide an approximation of their Mental Health Rating of psychiatric impairment (Langner 1962). A similar although less widely used measure, consisting of twenty Health Opinion Survey questions, was developed by the Stirling County study researchers as well (Macmillan 1957). More recently developed are the Center for Epidemiological Studies Depression scale (CES-D) (Radloff 1977), the General Well Being Scale (GWB) (Dupuy 1972), and the ninety-item Symptom Checklist 90 (SCL-90) (Derogatis 1977). Each of these scales or variations on them has enjoyed wide usage in recent years.

Proponents of such measures are impressed that these instruments have been shown to be reliable, to relate consistently to a host of demographic variables, and to discriminate between nonpatients and psychiatric patients. Their critics worry about their lack of face validity as a representative sample of the range and variety of symptoms described in diagnostic manuals, their tendency to over-represent distress in some groups, the possibility that the more physiological items among them may be confounded with physical illness, and their susceptibility to response styles (e.g., see Crandell and Dohrenwend 1967; B. S. Dohrenwend 1973; Dohrenwend and Crandell 1970; Phillips and Clancy 1972; Phillips and Segal 1969; Thoits 1981).

We have found that these brief screening scales have an extremely high correlation with each other (Link and Dohrenwend 1980a, 1980b) and with measures of self-esteem, helplessness-hopelessness, dread, anxiety, sadness, and confused thinking (Dohrenwend, Shrout, et al. 1980). These latter components are major facets of what Jerome Frank (1973) has called "demoralization." In Frank's theoretical formulation, as well as in relevant research that we have reviewed with regard to the screening scales (Dohrenwend, et al. 1979), this type of nonspecific psychological distress is likely to occur in response to a variety of predicaments: severe physical illnesses, especially those that are chronic; a buildup of recent stressful life events; attempts to cope with psychotic symptoms; and lower social class origin. It is similar to physical temperature in that when it is elevated you know that something is wrong but not what is wrong. Thus, while these measures of nonspecific distress or "demoralization" are interesting in their own right, they do not directly measure the various types of diagnosable mental disorder.

The Epidemiological Catchment Area Studies

The Epidemiological Catchment Area (ECA) studies had their origin in a 1977 presidential commission of experts in the field. The commission was asked to determine the amount of mental disorder, the extent to which those afflicted were underserved, and which groups were most affected by such underservice. Because of the wide variability in reported rates of mental disorder in the first- and second-

generation studies, the originators of the ECA studies concluded that the questions posed to the president's commission could not be answered with existing data. A large-scale study was required that used up-to-date, standardized, diagnostic procedures in a variety of communities across the United States. This led to the establishment of five research settings, with research teams located at major universities in Baltimore, Durham, Los Angeles, New Haven, and Saint Louis. All used the same survey research instrument—the Diagnostic Interview Schedule (DIS) (Robins et al. 1981). The descriptive epidemiology from three sites—Baltimore, Hew Haven, and Saint Louis—have been published (Myers et al. 1984; Robins et al. 1984), as have results of the reliability of the DIS (Anthony et al. 1985, Helzer et al. 1985). We will discuss these findings shortly.

LEGACY FROM PREVIOUS STUDIES FOR FUTURE EPIDEMIOLOGICAL RESEARCH

The legacy from the epidemiological studies described above comes in five parts: (1) a host of methodological problems centering on how to conceptualize and measure mental disorders in communities, (2) a set of results bearing on questions about cultural similarities and differences, (3) data relevant to estimating the amount of various types of mental disorder in communities, (4) findings on their distribution, and (5) findings on the likelihood that "true" cases receive treatment. Let us describe the five parts of the legacy before going on to some of the main issues they raise.

Methodological Problems

As mentioned earlier, the different concepts and methods used in the first- and second-generation studies led to rates that ranged widely. There is no way to account for the variability in terms of substantive differences in the persons and places studied. Rather, methodological differences tended to produce great variability in rates in both the first- and second-generation of studies (Dohrenwend and Dohrenwend 1974a).

It would be fortunate for future research if, in retrospect, we could simply pick out the study or studies that used the best concepts and measurement strategies. Unfortunately, the first- and second-generation studies gave little attention to providing evidence for the validity of their methods that would permit us to make choices among them on a rational basis (Dohrenwend and Dohrenwend 1969, 1974a). Thus, one legacy of the first- and second-generation studies are a host of problems in the area of case identification and diagnosis.

Nor has the more recent ECA study ended controversy about these thorny issues. Studies comparing diagnoses using the Diagnostic Interview Schedule (DIS) to diagnoses using a semistructured, clinician-administered interview in unselected community populations have recorded extremely poor levels of agreement (Anthony et al. 1985; Shrout, Spitzer, and Fleiss 1987). These studies show that two methods, designed to achieve the same goal, identified very different people as having the disorders of interest to psychiatric epidemiologists. Of course, error in either instrument will hurt the level of agreement achieved, so it is not possible to identify the superior method in the absence of further research. However, B. P. Dohrenwend and his colleagues (Dohrenwend and Dohrenwend 1981; Dohrenwend and Shrout 1981) have pointed out that there are two traditions for dealing with measurement error, the clinical and the psychometric. The clinical tradition relies on expert judgement in the context of semistructured interviews that allow detailed, in-depth probing to determine the presence or absence of symptomatology. The psychometric tradition, in contrast, standardizes questions and response formats, and uses multiple questions—re-

peated tests—to deal with problems of measurement error. Dohrenwend and colleagues argue for "multi-stage procedures" that explicitly draw on both traditions to arrive at a final diagnosis (Dohrenwend 1983; Dohrenwend and Dohrenwend 1981; Shrout, Skodol, and Dohrenwend 1986). Such multistage procedures are, they argue, the best way to deal with the uncertainty that has prevailed, and apparently continues to prevail, in the ECA studies, in the area of case identification and diagnosis.

Cultural Similarities and Differences in Rates of Disorder

Ideally, the first- and second-generation studies would tell us something about whether rates differ by cultural context. However, as we have mentioned, the methodological differences between studies are far too great to allow direct comparisons. Still, there are studies that reflect on this question in an interesting and important way.

One of the most significant was conducted in the 1950s by Eaton and Weil (1955). They studied the Hutterites, an ethnic enclave that has been remarkably successful in preserving its traditions in the face of contact with mass society. Few Hutterites left their community, divorce was almost nonexistent, and there was no record of a Hutterite becoming a public charge. This extraordinarily stable society was highly effective in providing cradle-to-grave support for its members. Did it also protect them from developing psychopathology?

Eaton and Weil's expectation when the study was initiated was "that few cases of mental disorder would be found." (1955, p. 229) In fact, however, they arrived at a rate of psychosis that ranked the Hutterites as third highest in ten populations for which they computed age-sex adjusted rates—higher, for example, than the urban and far-from-affluent Eastern Health District of Baltimore. Given Eaton and Weil's initial expectation that mental illness would be very rare, it is difficult to argue with their conclusion that the "findings do not confirm the hypothesis that a simple and relatively uncomplicated way of life provides virtual immunity from mental disorders." (1955, p. 209)

Evidence from other studies is consistent with this conclusion. Leighton et al. (1963) used comparable methods in diverse cultural settings and found remarkably similar rates of disorder. In addition, Goldhammer and Marshall (1953) found no evidence to suggest that rates of functional psychosis were increasing as a consequence of rapid industrialization in Massachusetts between 1840 and 1940.

Evidence such as this suggests more consistency than contrast in rates of mental disorders across time and place. It would seem that the burden of proof is on those who would locate a symptom-free utopia in the real world. Nevertheless, there is strong evidence not so much for differences in overall amounts of disorder as for the relative predominance of different types of disorder.

Once again the Hutterite study provides a vivid example. Persistent antisocial behavior was close to being absent from this group. Only four Hutterites were diagnosed as having personality disorders, and only two of these involved antisocial behavior that posed persistent problems to the community. Moreover, Eaton and Weil found that cases of schizophrenia were relatively rare, far outnumbered by cases of manic depressive psychosis. Nor do the Hutterites appear to be an isolated instance of unusually low rates of schizophrenia. Murphy and Taumoepeau (1980) have reported evidence that rates of schizophrenia are probably also unusually low in the Kingdom of Tonga in the South Pacific.

Taken together, such findings suggest that different cultural settings may not differ sharply in aggregated amounts of mental disorders, but they do appear to differ in rates of different types of mental disorder. What accounts for differences in rates

of types of disorders is crucial since the populations of such communities and groups can differ in genes as well as environment.

AMOUNTS OF VARIOUS TYPES OF MENTAL DISORDER IN COMMUNITIES

Despite methodological problems stemming from lack of consensus about how to conceptualize and measure mental disorders, it is possible to get a very rough estimate of the extent of psychopathology in communities by looking at the aggregated results of past first- and second-generation epidemiological studies. Dohrenwend, Dohrenwend, et al. (1980) undertook this task using analyses of results from second generation studies which have tended to be based on the more inclusive nomenclatures introduced following World War II. The following estimates about the prevalence of disorder in children, among adults, and in the aged were the result.

The true prevalence of clinical maladaptation among schoolchildren in a representative sample of U.S. communities is unlikely to average less than 12 percent.

The true prevalence of functional psychiatric disorders in a sample of U.S. adults is estimated to be:

—Between 16 and 25 percent overall.
—Between 0.6 and 3.0 percent for schizophrenia.
—About 0.3 percent for affective psychosis.
—Between 8.0 and 15.0 percent for neurosis.
—About 7.0 percent for personality disorder.

The true prevalence of functional and organic mental disorder in the elderly (60+) is estimated to be:

—Between 18.0 and 24.5 percent overall.
—Between 3.5 and 5.5 percent for organic psychoses.
—About 3.5 percent for functional psychoses.
—Between 6.0 and 10.5 percent for neuroses.
—About 5.0 percent for personality disorders.

The true prevalence of "demoralization" or severe psychological distress is likely to be about 25 percent considering both those with a major mental disorder as well as those without a functional psychiatric disorder.

The ECA studies representing the first wave of the third generation of studies provide prevalence estimates that are remarkably similar to the estimates made by Dohrenwend, Dohrenwend, et al. (1980):

—Overall the six-month prevalence of a DIS/DSM-III disorder (excluding cognitive impairment for comparative purposes) ranged from 15.8 to 22.1 percent.
—Schizophrenia/schizophrenoform varied from .6 to 1.2 percent.
—Antisocial/substance abuse varied from 6.7 to 7.9 percent.

All of these figures are comparable to the Dohrenwend et al. (1980) estimates for disorders among adults. Some results from the ECA studies are not directly comparable to the Dohrenwend estimates since the DSM-III classification system did not maintain the psychotic/neurotic distinction that earlier studies used. For example:

—Rates of affective disorders varied from 4.6 to 6.5 percent.
—Rates of anxiety/somatoform varied from 6.6 to 14.9 percent.

DISTRIBUTION OF VARIOUS TYPES OF MENTAL DISORDER IN COMMUNITIES

When we examine the distribution of the mental disorders according to such important demographic variables as gender, social class, and urban-rural location, we find surprising consistencies. (Surprising, in view of the methodological problems involved in these studies and the very different definitions of mental disorder the investigators employed.) For the most part these consistencies are evident in the relatively low-rate, narrow-definition first-generation studies, the relatively high-rate,

more inclusive second-generation studies (Dohrenwend and Dohrenwend 1969, 1974a, 1974b, 1976, 1981), and the first reports of the third-generation ECA studies. We will review these consistent relationships by drawing on three main sources: the Dohrenwend and Dohrenwend review (1974) of first- and second-generation true prevalence studies, the Neugebauer, Dohrenwend, and Dohrenwend (1980) review of studies conducted from 1950 to the late 1970s in the United States and Western Europe, and the published results of the ECA studies (Robins et al. 1984; Myers et al. 1984).

Social Class/Socioeconomic Status

The most striking finding that Jarvis reported in his landmark epidemiological study in 1855 was that "the pauper class furnishes, in ratio of its numbers, sixty-four times as many cases of insanity as the independent class" ([1855] 1971, pp. 52–53). The association of mental disorders with social class is not limited to psychotic symptomatology or to particular times and places. Rather, it has proved remarkably persistent in the true prevalence studies conducted since the turn of the century, and holds for most of the important subtypes of mental disorder (Dohrenwend and Dohrenwend 1981).

The highest overall rates of mental disorder were in the lowest social class in twenty-eight out of the thirty-three studies. This relationship was strongest in the studies conducted in urban settings or mixed urban and rural settings (nineteen out of twenty studies, Dohrenwend and Dohrenwend 1974a).

When attention is restricted to studies conducted in the United States and Northern Europe since 1950, Neugebauer, Dohrenwend, and Dohrenwend's review (1980) shows seventeen of twenty studies with a higher rate in the lowest as opposed to the highest class. The average low to high class ratio across these studies is 2.59.

The ECA study found consistently higher lifetime prevalence rates of all disorders combined among those with less than a college education than among college graduates (the breakdown used in published accounts to date). This finding held across all three reporting sites (Baltimore, New Haven, Saint Louis) (Robins et al. 1984). The published report of six-month prevalence did not report rates by a social class indicator (Myers et al. 1984).

The inverse relationship with class was consistent for schizophrenia (five out of seven studies) in the Dohrenwend and Dohrenwend review (1974a). Further support for this finding is present in Eaton's (1985) review of incidence studies; fifteen out of seventeen studies showed higher incidence rates in the lowest social class. Moreover, the lifetime prevalence figures reported by the ECA study show that schizophrenia and schizophreniform disorders are two to five times more prevalent among noncollege graduates as opposed to graduates.

The inverse class relationship holds as well for personality disorders characterized mainly by antisocial behavior and substance abuse (eleven out of fourteen studies, Dohrenwend and Dohrenwend 1974a) (five out of six, Neugebauer, Dohrenwend, and Dohrenwend 1980). The ECA reports consistently higher lifetime prevalence rates for lower status persons across diagnoses of antisocial personality, alcohol abuse/dependence, and drug abuse dependence (eight of nine comparisons). The only exception is for drug abuse/dependence in the Baltimore site.

Two studies that provide relevant data (Brown and Harris 1978; Weissman and Myers 1978) indicate that the current prevalence of major depression as defined by Feighner criteria (Feighner et al. 1972) and Research Diagnostic Criteria (Spitzer, Endicott, and Robins 1978) is inversely related to social class, though perhaps only for women, who appear to show higher rates of depression than males (Weissman and Klerman 1977). In addition, Dohrenwend and colleagues' (1987) recent study in Israel shows the same inverse relationship for major depression as the previously mentioned studies. Note that these studies use criteria for affective disorder that are similar to those contained in the newly adopted third edition of the American Psychiatric Association DSM-III. The ECA study, which reports data for DSM-III, shows a similar pattern of significant social class effects for major depression. Rates in the lowest and the next to lowest social class groups are more

than one and a half times higher than the rate in the highest group (Holzer et al. 1986).

Finally, rates of the severe, nonspecific psychological distress or demoralization are consistently highest in the lowest social class (eight out of eight studies) (Link and Dohrenwend 1980a).

In summary, then, all of the major types of functional mental disorders and nonspecific psychological distress that have been investigated in epidemiological field studies, possibly excepting bipolar affective disorder (by contrast with unipolar affective disorder or major depression), appear to show an inverse relationship with social class in either males or females or in both sexes. These class relationships are especially strong in urban settings.

Gender

Most true prevalence studies provided data on mental disorders according to gender—though often not for the various types of disorder. The firm facts that we have been able to extract can be summarized as follows.

There are no consistent gender differences in rates of functional psychoses in general (thirty-four studies, Dohrenwend and Dohrenwend 1974; nineteen studies, Neugebauer, Dohrenwend, and Dohrenwend 1980) or in relation to one of the two major subtypes—schizophrenia (twenty-six studies, Dohrenwend and Dohrenwend, 1974; eleven studies, Neugebauer, Dohrenwend, and Dohrenwend 1980). Here the ECA departs from the pattern. Each ECA site found females to have higher lifetime rates of schizophrenia/schizophreniform disorder (Robins et al. 1984), and two of three show the same result for six-month prevalence (Myers et al. 1984). Rates of the other main subtype, manic-depressive psychosis (as defined prior to DSM-III), are generally higher among women (eighteen out of twenty-four studies, Dohrenwend and Dohrenwend 1974). Neugebauer, Dohrenwend, and Dohrenwend's (1980) review of post–World War II studies reported rates of affective psychosis and found women to have higher rates in six, men in two, and no difference in three. The average female to male ratio was 2.96 in this category. The ECA shows no clear pattern for the DSM-III diagnosis of a manic episode that resembles but is by no means the same as the pre–DSM-III manic-depressive disorder (Myers et al. 1984; Robins et al. 1984).

Rates of neurosis are consistently higher for women regardless of time or place (twenty-eight out of thirty-two studies, Dohrenwend and Dohrenwend 1974). The Neugebauer, Dohrenwend, and Dohrenwend's review (1980) of recent U.S. and Northern European studies found the relationship to hold for all eighteen studies with an average female to male ratio of 2.86. The ECA studies used more recent DSM-III classification that does not make the neurotic psychotic distinction. However, for such disorders as dysthymia, panic, obsessive compulsive, social phobia, simple phobia, and agoraphobia, women had consistently higher rates across all sites for both six-month and lifetime diagnoses.

ECA rates of major depression deserve separate mention since they may have been diagnosed as either psychotic or neurotic depression in the pre–DSM-III era. Women were more likely than men to have this disorder across all three sites and for both lifetime and six-month prevalence.

By contrast, rates of personality disorder are consistently higher for men regardless of time or place (twenty-two out of twenty-six studies, Dohrenwend and Dohrenwend 1974; ten out of fourteen, Neugebauer, Dohrenwend, and Dohrenwend 1980). Neugebauer, Dohrenwend, and Dohrenwend (1980) report a female to male ratio of .66 for this category. The ECA studies are entirely consistent with these earlier studies in showing that men predominate at each site in both lifetime and six-month prevalence for drug abuse/dependence, alcohol abuse/dependence, and antisocial personality.

Rates of nonspecific distress or demoralization were higher in women in seven out of seven studies reviewed by Link and Dohrenwend (1980).

Rural versus Urban Settings

The differences in concepts and methods used in identifying cases in the first- and second-generation studies preclude meaningful comparisons of rate differ-ences across studies done in rural and urban settings by different investigators. Fortunately, however, at least eight investigators reported data for both a rural and an urban setting, with two reporting data for two settings each.

The overall rate of mental disorder is higher in urban areas for eight of ten comparisons. Although quite consistent, the differences are not large (Dohrenwend and Dohrenwend 1974). Rates for functional psychoses combined were higher in rural settings (five out of seven studies, Dohrenwend and Dohrenwend 1974), and this appears to be so for the manic-depressive subtype (three out of four studies, Dohrenwend and Dohrenwend, 1974) though not for schizophrenia (higher in the urban area in three out of five studies, Dohrenwend and Dohrenwend 1974).

Rates of neurosis were higher in urban settings (five out of six studies), as were rates of personality disorder (five out of six studies).

One site in the ECA study (Saint Louis) reported rates by urban-rural location. Overall rates were higher in the central-city areas predominantly because of higher rates of alcohol abuse/dependence, drug abuse/dependence, antisocial personality, and schizophrenia.

Evidence on the Distribution of Treatment

Both the Link and Dohrenwend (1980) review of the first- and second-generation true prevalence studies and the recent ECA studies (Shapiro et al. 1984) show that there are large proportions of persons with clinically significant psychopathology who are not in treatment with a mental health professional. In the Link and Dohrenwend review the median proportion of current cases who had ever been in treatment with a mental health professional (psychiatrist, psychologist, social worker) was 26.7 percent. For the seven studies that reported results for psychotic disorders, the median proportion in treatment was 59.7 percent; the proportion for schizophrenia was 83.3 percent across six studies. The ECA study reports figures on relatively recent treatment as opposed to the lifetime prevalence of treatment reported by Link and Dohrenwend. Interestingly, according to Shapiro et al.'s (1984) report of data from three sites, there is no diagnostic category (based on six-month prevalence) for which a majority have seen a mental health professional in the last six months. Schizophrenia, the most severe diagnosis, has the highest proportion currently in mental health treatment, but still the highest figure across the three sites only reaches 48.1 percent (Shapiro et al. 1984).

These studies suggest that the increasingly effective treatments mental health professionals are able to offer (Davis 1975, 1976; Smith, Glass, and Miller 1980) are not provided to large numbers of those with clinically significant psychopathology. However, the problem is more complex and troublesome than these basic figures suggest. For one thing, the true prevalence studies show that the lowest socioeconomic status groups have the highest rates of psychopathology but the lowest rates of treatment by mental health professionals (Link and Dohrenwend 1980). Moreover, if one examines the mental health status of those who report current treatment, one finds startling results. In the Midtown Manhattan study only 52.5 percent of those in treatment were "clinically impaired," according to that study's classification scheme. Furthermore, in the ECA study approximately one-third of those reporting treatment in the past six months had *no* diagnosable disorder during the same period, according to the Diagnostic Interview Schedule (DIS).

ISSUES RAISED BY THE TRUE PREVALENCE STUDIES

The issues raised by the true prevalence studies we have reviewed have implications in two broad areas that are likely to be of interest to medical sociologists. First, epidemiological studies raise issues about selection into treatment and whether the current distribution of mental health resources is optimal. In terms of policy these considerations are important because of their implications for manpower recruitment and training and for the organization of service delivery (Klerman 1987). Second, the sheer number of people estimated to be affected, coupled with the distribution of disorder by variables such as socioeconomic status and gender, suggest the importance of inquiries into the etiology of these disorders. These issues tend to have policy relevance for research and prevention (Klerman 1987).

Selection into Treatment

The true prevalence studies, it will be recalled, find that a majority of the clinically impaired go untreated while many current patients are free of an identifiable clinical disorder. If our policy goal is to deliver treatment to those with the most need (as defined by the presence of significant psychopathology), the evidence from these studies suggests that current delivery practices are far from optimal. This would not be so bad if the evidence on the effectiveness of treatment was equivocal. However, there is now mounting evidence that a variety of treatments are effective in controlling the symptomatology of many major disorders (Davis 1975, 1976; Liebowitz 1984; Smith, Glass, and Miller 1980). If advances continue to be made, and there is considerable reason to expect this, it will become increasingly important to understand the factors that influence the distribution of treatment. With this as background, we present a brief sketch of factors influencing selection into treatment.

The process of selection into treatment has been conceptualized as occurring in stages (Kadushin 1969; Goldberg and Huxley 1980; Kessler, Brown, and Broman 1981). We will review evidence concerning five aspects that influence selection into treatment: (1) the recognition that something is wrong, (2) the identification of a problem in mental health–mental illness terms, (3) the selection of a help source, (4) the behavior of "gatekeepers," and (5) the effects of barriers to care.

Recognition that something is wrong. Thoits (1985) has outlined a theory of "self-labeling," which provides a persuasive account of how people come to identify their feelings and behavior as problematic. She constructs her explanation using two facets of sociological theory: symbolic interactionism and the sociological study of the emotions (Hochschild 1979, 1983). Briefly, Thoits argues that people, learn "feeling rules" as part of socialization: that is, prescriptions about how one should feel, "You should feel ashamed of yourself," and proscriptions about how one should not feel, "It's time to stop grieving." Drawing on Mead (1934), she points out that people learn to apply these standards to themselves and thus to monitor themselves for signs of what she calls "emotional deviance." When people suspect that their feelings run counter to how one "should feel," they seek the opinions of others. Through such processes as "social support," the person is often persuaded that the feelings are a normal response to a situation, and thus self-labeling does not occur. However, if the nonnormative feelings persist and cannot be ameliorated by management efforts, the probability of self-labeling increases.

Identification in mental health/mental illness terms. Once emotional states are recognized as being nonnormative it still remains problematic as to whether these are conceptualized in mental health–mental illness terms. Hollingshead and Redlich (1958) drew attention to this phenomenon with the concept of "lay appraisal," which they considered to be the public counterpart of psychiatric diagnosis.

Two strands of social science research have investigated the public's tendency to identify the signs and symptoms of mental disorders as mental health problems. One such strand retrospectively studies the process by which close kin come to define deviant behavior as mental disorder. The pioneering study in this regard was conducted by Yarrow et al. (1955). They showed that wives went to considerable, sometimes extreme, lengths to avoid interpreting their husbands' behavior in a mental illness framework. For most of the wives studied, mental illness imputation was adopted only after other people (employers, the police) exerted extreme pressure. Perruci and Targ (1982) used a similar design to study how social network members respond to the initial signs of mental disorder. Almost thirty years after the Yarrow et al. studies, they found evidence of what they called a "medical-high resources network," whose members conceived of the origins of the deviant behavior in mental illness terms and sought the advice of physicians rapidly. Such a perspective was virtually absent among the wives that Yarrow et al. studied. Yet they still found many other networks whose members continued to respond to initial symptoms in a manner consistent with earlier descriptions.

A second approach to studying public identification was initiated by Star in the late 1950s. She developed what have come to be called the "Star Vignettes," six descriptions of persons exhibiting various types of mental disorder as they were conceptualized at the time. Although clinicians tended to agree that these descriptions were evidence of mental disorders, the respondents in Star's nationwide study did not. Only 75 percent indicated that the violent, severely disturbed "paranoid schizophrenic" described a person with some kind of mental illness. Far fewer, always less than 50 percent, indicated that the less extreme cases (simple schizophrenic, alcoholic, anxiety neurotic, juvenile character disorder, compulsive phobic) could be so described. Star concluded that for the public, mental illness was

a very threatening, fearful thing and not an idea to be entertained lightly about anyone. Emotionally, it represents to people loss of what they consider to be the distinctively human qualities of free will, and there is a kind of horror at dehumanization . . . mental illness is something that people want to keep as far from themselves as possible. (p. 6)

During the 1960s, however, a consistent body of evidence suggested that the public had increased its tendency to identify the Star vignettes as cases of mental disorder (Spiro, Siassi, and Crocetti 1973). Some viewed this with great enthusiasm since it seemed to suggest a positive turn in public attitudes—pessimistic conclusions like Star's needed to be amended to fit the recent evidence (Lemkau and Crocetti, 1962; Crocetti, Spiro, and Siassi 1974; but compare Phillips 1967). Still, across ten studies that Spiro, Siassi, and Crocetti (1973) reviewed either a large minority (more than 20 percent) or a majority of the respondents thought that all but the most severe "paranoid schizophrenic" case were not suffering from a mental disorder. Unfortunately, we have relatively little recent information of this sort, and the data that we have from earlier studies are based on the Star vignettes, which do not directly correspond to the current DSM-III classification system.

In addition to data on the overall tendency of the public to identify deviant behavior as mental disorder, there is evidence showing that the application of a mental illness label is socially patterned. Horwitz (1982) draws on an extensive review of the literature to support several propositions in this regard. Specifically, he proposes that males and persons in lower social positions are less likely than females and higher status persons to label themselves and others. These observations lead him to the more general conclusion that "an individual's location in social space predicts the probability that he or she will recognize and label mental illness." (Horwitz 1982, p. 83) If so, it is likely that certain population groups are overrepresented among those who do not identify mental disorder when it occurs to them or others close to them.

Selection of a help source. Once a problem has been identified as a mental health concern, the issue of which help source will be chosen remains. When Gurin Veroff, and Feld (1960) asked respondents in their 1957 nationwide survey who they contacted for help, they found that most people relied on the clergy (42 percent). General practice physicians were the next most frequently contacted (29 percent). Psychiatrists and psychologists were far behind (17 percent). Twenty years later, Kulka, Veroff, and Douvan (1981) conducted a very similar study. Although they found a substantial increase in the numbers of persons contacting mental health professionals, the clergy remained first on the list. The epidemiological catchment area studies provide information on the use of general practice physicians as well. They report data on two categories of caregivers—general medical doctors and specialty mental health resources. The percentage seeking treatment from general medical providers only varied from 41 percent (New Haven) to 63 percent (Saint Louis) across the three sites reported by Shapiro et al. (1984).

Gatekeepers. Since people often have their initial contact with a clergyman or a general medical doctor, these groups have been called "gatekeepers." They can influence the process of selection into treatment in two major ways. First, they may or may not interpret the behavior of the person who comes to see them in mental health terms; that is, they may not "identify" what mental health professionals would generally regard to be cases of mental disturbance. Second, they may decide to treat the patient themselves, rather than refer him or her to a mental health specialist.

There is more information about the gatekeeping behavior of general medical doctors than there is about that of clergymen (for exceptions to this generalization, see Dohrenwend 1969 and Larson 1968). Larson conducted a study using vignettes resembling Star's but focusing more on the types of problems clergy are likely to see. He demonstrated sharp disagreements between a sample of psychiatrists and a sample of the clergy. The disagreements came both in the interpretation of the severity of the described behavior and in how the cases should be dealt with. Specifically, the clergy thought that delusions and hallucinations involving religious content were far less likely to indicate a severe problem than did psychiatrists. At the same time, when the disorder described in the vignette contained descriptions of sexual behavior, the clergy thought it far more severe than did the psychiatrists. Moreover, the clergy were substantially more confident in their ability to deal with problems than the psychiatrists thought they should be. Clearly the two groups viewed mental health problems from a different frame of reference.

The literature on general medical doctors as gatekeepers is more extensive. Nunnally's study of general practice physicians (1961) demonstrated two facts that have been a central focus of research on selection into treatment ever since. First, was the sheer magnitude of mental health problems in doctors' general practice. When asked what proportion of the cases they saw were largely brought on by mental problems, the doctors' average response was 31 percent. Second, Nunnally noted considerable variability in the physicians' tendency to identify cases in this way, a fact highlighted later by Shepard et al. (1966) in their study of British physicians.

Perhaps the most programmatic research effort aimed at understanding the role of general practice physicians on pathways into treatment is that conducted by Goldberg and his colleagues (*cf.* Goldberg and Huxley 1980). Among other things, this work has been instrumental in uncovering a number of physician characteristics that predict the successful identification of psychopathology (Marks, Goldberg, and Hillier 1979), thereby suggesting possible interventions that might lead to more appropriate treatment. Critical in this regard is an experimental study conducted by Johnstone and Goldberg (1976) which shows that patients improve when physicians are aware of their mental health problems. Patients scoring high on a symp-

tom scale were randomly assigned to two conditions. In one, physicians were made aware of the patients responses; in the other no information was conveyed. Six months later the identified patients showed significantly greater improvement in their symptomatology than the unidentified patients. This finding underscores the importance of processes that influence a physician's tendency to identify the mental health problems of his or her patients.

Barriers in the help-seeking process. The evidence we have reported so far implicitly identifies a number of factors that decrease the probability of mental health help-seeking. In many cases these should not be considered "barriers," since they may be indicative of effective alternative ways of coping with emotional disturbances. We conceive of barriers as factors that directly or indirectly impede a person's ability to obtain treatment he or she might otherwise seek. Some such barriers are clear-cut and obvious. Jarvis (1850), for example, showed that treatment seeking was influenced by distance from a treatment facility. Other factors include cost, insurance coverage, and the flexibility of a person's work schedule. In addition to barriers like these, we will briefly discuss two others that are important to the sociological study of help seeking.

For many, entering mental health treatment means becoming a "mental patient." When people "imaginatively rehearse" their entry into this social position, they are likely to conjure up their expectations about how others,. as well as they themselves, will respond to it. In this regard, Link (1987) has shown that many people believe that mental patients will be devalued and discriminated against by others. This being so, it is easy to see why a person who fears rejection might strenuously avoid a line of action that would lead to mental health care. For such a person, treatment seeking carries with it a negative label and means that devaluation and discrimination will follow.

A second barrier has been thoroughly

examined by social scientists over the past three decades. It involves the preferences of service providers for certain types of patients (Link and Milkarek 1980; Schoefield 1964). In a particularly instructive study in this regard, Goldman and Mendelsohn (1969) gave psychiatrists, psychologists, and psychiatric social workers an adjective checklist and asked them to identify desirable patient characteristics. They reported that the preferred patient was "imaginative, sensitive, curious, well motivated, but anxious" and noted that "if anxiety were removed from the list of the 25 most descriptive adjectives, the preferred patient would appear to be an unusually productive and creative person" (p. 170). Schofield (1964) has termed such preferred patients YAVIS (Youthful, Attractive, Verbal, Intelligent, and Successful). Such preferences are likely to influence the kinds of clients that therapists select into their care when they have a choice. Certainly a number of studies have shown that when ability to pay is held constant, therapists tend to select patients who fit the profile of a preferred patient (Myers and Schaffer 1954; Gallagher, Levinson, and Erlich 1957; Brill and Storrow 1964; Link and Milcarek 1980). Moreover, this tendency seems to be firmly embedded in the reward system operating among therapists. Link (1983) used a vignette experiment to show that a sample of therapists evaluated a fictitious colleague more positively if he was described as treating desirable (YAVIS) patients as opposed to less desirable (Non-YAVIS) patients.

The tendency to seek preferred patients can cause barriers for less desirable patients in many ways. In addition to the possibility of being rejected outright, such patients may be subtly discouraged from returning to treatment. Moreover, by actively seeking the kinds of patients they prefer—for example, locating their offices where it is convenient for such patients—therapists simultaneously create conditions that make it difficult for non-YAVIS patients to find their way into treatment.

Conclusion. The true prevalence studies of mental disorder demonstrate that mental health treatment is not optimally distributed. Social scientists have made strong contributions to our ability to understand why this occurs by conceptualizing and empirically examining factors that influence treatment seeking and service delivery. Future contributions from social scientists working in this area should take at least two directions. First, factors influencing selection into treatment need to be investigated in the context of epidemiological studies of true prevalence—an extremely rare occurrence to date. It is critical to determine whether the concepts, theories, and findings that social scientists have generated can, in fact, explain why many in treatment are not clinically disordered and why many who are clinically disordered are not in treatment. Second, interventions should be designed and evaluated that are guided by current knowledge and that have as a goal a more rational distribution of treatment than currently exists.

Issues of Etiology

We know a great deal from the first and second generations of epidemiological studies about how various types of mental disorder are distributed according to such important variables as gender, social class, and rural-urban location. We have evidence that types of mental disorders vary with cultural and subcultural differences. Speculation about the implications of this information has raised important issues for further research on etiology.

Gender differences. Findings that males have higher rates of the acting-out types of personality disorder while women have higher rates of the types of disorder characterized by depression (Dohrenwend and Dohrenwend 1976) raise interesting questions. Males and females in all societies differ in their social roles and their biology. The persistent problems of interpreting behavioral differences between males and females center on questions of how to unconfound the biological and social factors involved in these differences so that the relative importance of the two sets of factors and the nature of their interaction can be evaluated. Progress is most likely to come first with the identification of significant and theoretically meaningful contrasts within, as well as between, sex roles over time and place; and second, with investigation of the implications of these contrasts for the types of psychopathology that consistently vary by gender. Changes in sex roles over time and the contrasts in these roles provided by different cultural settings offer opportunities to develop quasi experiments that will provide major clues to the etiological role of gender differences in psychopathology.

Social class differences. No issues in psychiatric epidemiology have proved more persistent or compelling than those raised by the differences in rates according to social class. Two competing explanations for these consistent relationships—the social causation versus the social selection hypotheses—have been debated in the literature for some time (Jarvis [1855] 1971; Faris and Dunham 1939; Myerson 1940; Kohn 1972; Mechanic 1972). The social causation explanation is that lower socioeconomic class status involves exposure to socioenvironmental risk factors that may contribute to the development of mental disorder (Dohrenwend and Dohrenwend 1969; Kohn 1972). In contrast, the social selection explanation states that the lower socioeconomic status of persons with mental disorders is a consequence of that disorder. According to the latter view, it is because of disabilities associated with disorder or personality characteristics related to developing a disorder that individuals who experience severe psychopathology either fail to rise with the rest of their cohort or actually drop down the social ladder if they previously came from higher social positions. In terms of etiology the social causation explanation suggests a prominent role

for class-linked environmental risk factors, whereas the social selection explanation denies the importance of these factors, pointing instead to genetically inherited dispositions or early exposures that are class constant.

Examples of Useful Strategies for Investigating the Role of Social Factors in Etiology

The consistent findings from the true prevalence studies on social class and gender, coupled with the fact that social scientists have documented vast differences in the social experiences of people differentially located according to these variables, suggests the importance and the possible yield of studies that try to explain these findings. We call for two sorts of study that we believe are particularly likely to be informative.

Studies seeking strategic contrasts. The first kind of study is one which locates strategic circumstances that allow a relatively clear-cut interpretation with respect to the importance of social factors as potential causes. The plausibility of genetic factors as contributing causes of major mental disorders was greatly enhanced by ingenious study designs that took advantage of naturally occurring circumstances. The twin, adoption, and cross-fostering designs maximized the interpretability of results with respect to the role of genes (see, e.g., Gottesman and Shields 1976; Wender et al. 1974). Those investigating social factors would do well to search for similarly useful natural-occurring circumstances for testing the importance of social factors. Consider, for example, how much we learned from the study of the Hutterites about the ability of a society to shield its members from mental disorder and, simultaneously, about its power to shape types of psychopathology. A random sample of the U.S. population would have been far less informative about these matters. Some recent examples will exemplify the type of study we have in mind.

In order to study the impact of different cultural situations on the patterning of psychopathology in women, Schwartz (1985) studied the right and left wings of the Orthodox Jewish community. The design held many factors constant (for example, sex, work status, immigration status) but built in a sharp contrast in the adherence to culturally prescribed feminine sex roles. The right wing strictly adhered to explicit—codified in writing—traditional feminine sex roles. The left wing, while accepting the same rules, allowed far more adaptation to newer secular values emphasizing the equality of women. As she expected, Schwartz found depression to be considerably more prevalent among the right-wing women she studied. Antisocial or acting-out behavior was not extensive in either group, but the left-wing women were much more likely to have engaged in drug and alcohol use than those from the right wing. The key to the significance of this study lies in its location of a culturally determined variation on sex role expectations among otherwise quite similar women. This fact renders the results more interpretable concerning the impact of social factors on psychopathology.

A second study exemplifying this approach was conducted by Kessler, House, and Turner (1987). They wished to determine the impact of unemployment on mental health but recognized that impaired persons might become unemployed partly because of their psychological difficulties. As a result, they included in their study of unemployed Michigan workers a series of questions investigating the circumstances that led to the unemployment. They were thereby able to distinguish between persons who may have played a part in bringing on their unemployment and those who were victimized by such factors as plant closings. Thus, when Kessler, House, and Turner found effects among those in the latter group, they could be more confident that they were due to social experiences associated with unemployment.

A third study is presently being conducted by Dohrenwend et al. (1987) in Israel. As Dohrenwend and Dohrenwend (1969) have noted, social stress and social selection hypotheses both make the same prediction about an inverse relationship between social class and various types of psychopathology. The problem is to find a set of circumstances in which the two contrasting theoretical orientations lead to different predictions. B.P. Dohrenwend has argued that the assimilation of ethnic groups into the class structures of relatively open-class urban societies can be viewed as a quasiexperiment that provides such an opportunity (Dohrenwend 1966; Dohrenwend and Dohrenwend 1969; Dohrenwend 1975; Dohrenwend and Dohrenwend 1981). The opportunity arises out of the contrast between ethnic status and class status and the relationship between the two.

The crucial point is that one's view of the contribution of ethnic status to the relationship between social class and various types of psychopathology differs greatly depending on whether one holds a social causation theory or a social selection theory to explain why class is inversely related to various types of psychopathology. The social causation theorist would see the greater downward social pressure stemming, for example, from prejudice and discrimination, producing an increment in environmental adversity and stress on members of disadvantaged ethnic groups over and above that stemming from class membership. Accordingly, if the rate of a particular type of psychopathology in a particular class is a function of the amount of adversity and stress induced by the social environment, as such a theorist would maintain, then one should expect to find higher rates of the psychopathology among persons from disadvantaged ethnic groups than among persons from advantaged ethnic groups in the same social class.

The social selection theorist, by contrast, would predict just the opposite. Such a theorist would expect that the rate of psychopathology in a given social class is a function of sorting and sifting processes whereby the healthy and able tend to rise to, or maintain, high status and the unhealthy and disabled drift down from high status or fail to rise out of low status. Since the downward social pressure is greater on members of disadvantaged ethnic groups, the social selection theorist would expect that many of the healthier members of the disadvantaged ethnic groups would be kept down in lower-class positions. This would thereby dilute the rate of disorder among lower-class members of disadvantaged ethnic groups, with only the very healthiest and most able members rising against great obstacles to higher-class positions. With less pressure to block them, the tendency of healthier members of more advantaged ethnic groups to rise would leave a residue of disabled among lower-class members. The more advantaged the ethnic group, the more purely homogeneous in the characteristic of disabling psychopathology would be its lower-class members, inflating the rate of disorder. Moreover, the more advantaged the ethnic group, the more individuals suffering from psychopathology it would support at higher-class levels. Thus, social selection should function to give a higher rate of psychopathology among members of advantaged ethnic groups than among members of disadvantaged ethnic groups from the same social class. With this reasoning as rationale, Dohrenwend et al. (1987) have mounted a study in Israel, where the conditions are ideal to test these predictions.

Studies that seek to identify mechanisms. A second kind of study that can help elucidate the role of social factors in the etiology of mental disorders are ones that propose to "explain" the social class and gender findings by identifying the intervening variables that account for these associations. These variables can either be consistent with social selection or social causation explanations. Key is the fact that those who would explain class and gender differences in social selection terms would propose different intervening processes than those who explain them from a social

causation perspective. The success or failure of hypotheses about the mechanisms each group identifies will reflect on the plausibility of the more global selection causation issue. If intervening variables consistent with one explanation are more successful than those associated with the other, we would tend to interpret the observed class and gender associations in terms of the more successful explanation.

Consider by way of illustration a recent research project on the relationship between social class and schizophrenia that attempted to identify a mechanism consistent with a social causation explanation. Studies of the social mobility of schizophrenic patients show that social selection processes play a role in producing the consistent finding of the highest rate of this disorder in the lowest social class (*cf.* Eaton 1980; Eaton and Lasry 1978; Goldberg and Morrison 1963; Turner 1968). The studies are convincing in this regard because the occupations of first-admission schizophrenic patients are lower in social standing than one would expect given their class origins. These results leave room for argument, however, as to whether the social selection processes are strong enough to rule out an important role for environmental factors associated with social class (Dohrenwend and Dohrenwend 1969, pp. 41–48; Eaton 1980; Kohn 1972; Mechanic 1972; Turner 1968). In this regard, Link, Dohrenwend and Skodol (1986) presented evidence that suggested a possible role for class-linked stress despite the clear findings of downward mobility presented in earlier studies. First, they noted that people who develop schizophrenia attain a level of education that is comparable to similar people who do not develop it. This means that the downward mobility occurs between the time a person completes education and the time of the occupation held at first admission—a period of several years for many who develop the disorder. Link, Dohrenwend, and Skodol (1986) then examined an important event that occurs during this period—the acquisition of a first full-time occupation held for six months or more. In a study of schizophrenic episode cases and community well controls, they found no evidence to suggest that the schizophrenic cases were downwardly mobile into these first jobs. This finding tends to rule out selection explanations that might attribute occupational exposures in these jobs to downward movement in socioeconomic status. Given this, it was of particular interest that Link, Dohrenwend, and Skodol found that schizophrenic cases were more likely than well controls to hold blue-collar jobs that entailed noisome conditions—noise, hazards, extreme heat, extreme cold, fumes and excessive humidity. Such jobs, it should be noted, indicate exposure to intense stimulation, and research has shown that individuals who develop schizophrenia are susceptible to overstimulation of various kinds (Leff and Vaughn 1985, pp. 195–208). It is possible, therefore, that vulnerable individuals find jobs with noisome features particularly stressful in such a way as to contribute to the onset of the disorder and to a downward trajectory in the occupational sphere.

The strategy of investigating explanatory links can be applied to the gender issue as well. Rosenfield (in press), for example, has investigated women's exposure to role-related "demands" and their access to control over these demands in attempting to explain their higher rates of depressive symptoms. Lennon's recent work (1987) provides another example. She notes that powerful sociocultural forces sift and sort men and women into very different occupations. Once located in these occupational destinations, the incumbents of these positions are exposed to very different daily conditons of work. Lennon asks whether these differing conditions explain why women experience more psychological distress whereas men drink alcohol excessively. Tests of social mechanisms can also challenge their plausibility. Thoits (1987) investigated women's exposure and reaction to various types of life events. She found that neither perceptions of control

or exposure to events could explain gender differences in distress. In this case, a test of a possible mechanism was not supported, thereby indicating that the field should search for other explanatory mechanisms. Together, tests such as these will reflect on the plausibility of social factors as potential causes of mental disorder.

Etiology and policy. The two types of study we have outlined as ways of contributing to knowledge about etiology should have direct bearing on policy as well. Both types of study seek to explain why we observe consistent relationships between such factors as gender and class and various types of psychopathology. Determining the kinds of sociocultural factors that produce variation in rates of psychopathology and tracing the mechanisms through which such factors may operate can provide useful clues for the development of effective intervention strategies and can increase the public's awareness of events and situations that influence their lives.

Perhaps the strongest example of a program of social research leading to successful interventions in the area of the mental disorders is the series of studies that have investigated "expressed emotion" among family members diagnosed with schizophrenia. This research started with a broad epidemiological finding about the nature of the "living arrangement" patients experience when discharged from a hospital (Brown, Carstairs, and Topping 1958; Brown 1959). Patients who returned to parents or wives did not fare as well as those who returned to lodgings or to brothers and sisters. With this as a start, Brown and his colleagues set upon a course of studies that sought to determine why this might be so. As a result of careful observation of families, they set upon the notion of "expressed emotion" and developed ratings for it (Brown, Birley, and Wing 1972). Subsequent studies isolated the two most important aspects of expressed emotion, criticism, and overinvolvement, and showed that schizophrenic cases who returned to families rated high on these measures were far more likely to relapse than those who returned to families low on these dimensions (Leff and Vaughn 1985). Finally, as a consequence of these intriguing results, intervention programs were developed that sought to modify the family context. Evaluations of these interventions have shown remarkable success in reducing the probability of relapse in schizophrenia (e.g., Falloon et al. 1982; Leff et al. 1982).

While the foregoing example is particularly clear in showing a direct line to interventions that have had profoundly positive effects, it would be wrong to conclude that research findings that do not show such clear lines of influence have been ineffectual. Rather, as Mechanic and Aiken have emphasized in the context of health policy in general, "perhaps the most significant contribution of the social sciences has been the many ways in which their research has affected how intelligent lay persons, as well as decision makers in varying settings, conceive of and conceptualize their worlds. These mind-sets have powerful influences on how issues are conceptualized and managed." (Mechanic and Aiken 1986, p. 5).

Social research in the area of the mental disorders is no exception. Knowing that the events in one's life, the situations one encounters, or the background social conditions one experiences are connected to one's emotional well-being can be of considerable benefit—support may be sought from others, inappropriate self-defeating attempts to cope can be modified, or one can join people in similar circumstances and take action designed to modify environmental conditions. Just the simple fact of understanding these connections can make one feel less alone and alienated. And, of course, a person suffering from a mental disorder can benefit from others' awareness of these issues as well. Rather than distribute pink sheets, employers might provide troubled workers with benefits offered through employee assistance plans, to cite just one possibility. In all of these ways and many more, social sci-

ence information influences the social fabric and the polices that emerge from it.

CONCLUSION

Our review of true prevalence studies of the epidemiology of the mental disorders documents associations between sociocultural factors and the major mental disorders. It also provides evidence concerning the less-than-optimal distribution of treatment to the cases identified in these studies. These findings pose intriguing research questions about the delivery of services and the etiology of disorder. Medical sociologists have already contributed greatly to understanding these issues. However, although progress has been made, the fundamental problems posed by these studies have not been solved. We hope that our emphasis on them will spur a sustained effort in this area. Specifically, future research should use the consistent findings from the true prevalence studies as a starting point so that answers to the problems they raise can be systematically addressed and, we hope, answered.

REFERENCES

American Psychiatric Association. 1952. *Diagnostic and Statistical Manual of Mental Disorders*, 1st edition. Washington, D.C.: APA.

———. 1968. *Diagnostic and Statistical Manual of Mental Disorders*. 2nd edition. Washington, D.C.: APA.

———. 1980. *Diagnostic and Statistical Manual of Mental Disorders*. 3rd edition. Washington, D.C.: APA.

Anthony, James, Marshall Folstein, Alan J. Romananoski, Michael R. Von Korff, Gerald R. Nestadt, Raman Chahal, Alan Merchant, Hendricks Brown, Sam Shapiro, Morton Kramer, and Ernest Gruenberg. 1985. Comparison of the Lay Diagnostic Interview Schedule and a Standardized Psychiatric Diagnosis. *Archives of General Psychiatry* 42:667–675.

Bash, K. W. 1975. Untersuchungen Ueber die

Epidemiologie Neuropsychiatrischer Erkrankungen Unter der Landbevoelkerung der Provinz Fars, Iran. *Aktuelle Fragen der Psychiatrie Neurologie* 5:162.

Brill, N., and H. A. Storrow. 1964. Social Class and Psychiatric Treatment, in F. Reissman, J. Cohen, and A. Pearl, eds., *Mental Health of the Poor*. New York: Free Press, pp. 68–75.

Brown, George W. 1959. Experiences of Discharged Chronic Mental Hospital Patients in Various Types of Living Groups. *Millbank Memorial Fund Quarterly* 37:105–131.

Brown, George W., J. L. T. Birley, and J. K. Wing. 1972. Influence of Family Life on the Course of Schizophrenic Disorders: A Replication. *British Journal of Psychiatry* 121:241–258.

Brown, George W., G. M. Carstairs, and G. Topping. 1958. Post Hospital Adjustment of Chronic Mental Patients. *Lancet* ii:685–689.

Brown, George W., and Tirril Harris. 1978. *Social Origins of Depression*. New York: Free Press.

Buehler, J. A. 1966. Two Experiments in Psychiatric Interrater Reliability. *Journal of Health and Social Behavior* 7:192–202.

Cawte, J. 1972. *Cruel, Poor and Brutal Nations*. Honolulu: University of Hawaii Press.

Cohen, Patricia, and Jacob Cohen. 1984. The Clinician's Illusion. *Archives of General Psychiatry* 41:1178–1182.

Crandell, Dewitt L., and Bruce P. Dohrenwend. 1967. Some Relations among Psychiatric Symptoms, Organic Illness, and Social Class. *American Journal of Psychiatry* 123:1527–1538.

Crocetti, Guido, Herzl Spiro, and Irad Siassi. 1974. *Contemporary Attitudes Towards Mental Illness*. Pittsburgh: University of Pittsburgh Press.

Davis, John M. 1975. Overview: Maintenance Therapy in Psychiatry: I. Schizophrenia. *American Journal of Psychiatry* 132:1237–1245.

———. 1976. Overview: Maintenance Therapy in Psychiatry: II. Affective Disorders. *American Journal of Psychiatry* 133:1–13.

Derogatis, Leonard R. 1977. *SCL-90: Administration, Scoring and Procedures Manual for the Revised Version*. Baltimore: Clinical Psychometrics Research Unit, Johns Hopkins School of Medicine.

Dohrenwend, Barbara S. 1973. Social Status and Stressful Life Events. *Journal of Personality and Social Psychology* 28:225–235.

Dohrenwend, Bruce P. 1966. Social Status and Psychological Disorder: An Issue of Substance and an Issue of Method. *American Sociological Review* 31:14–35.

———. 1969. The Attitudes of Local Leaders Toward Behavioral Disorder, in L. C. Kolb, V. W. Bernard, and B. P. Dohrenwend, eds., *Urban Challenges to Psychiatry*. New York: Little, Brown, pp. 63–90.

———. 1975. Sociocultural and Social-Psychological Factors in the Genesis of Mental Disorders. *Journal of Health and Social Behavior* 16:365–392.

———. 1983. The Epidemiology of Mental Disorder, in D. Mechanic, ed., *Handbook of Health, Health Care, and the Health Professions*. New York: Free Press, pp. 157–194.

Dohrenwend, Bruce P., and DeWitt Crandel. 1970. Psychiatric Symptoms in Community Clinic, and Mental Hospital Groups. *American Journal of Psychiatry* 126:1611–1621.

Dohrenwend, Bruce P., and Barbara S. Dohrenwend. 1969. *Social Status and Psychological Disorder: A Causal Inquiry*. New York: John Wiley.

———. 1974a. Social and Cultural Influences on Psychopathology. *Annual Review of Psychology* 25:417–452.

———. 1974b. Psychiatric Disorders in Urban Settings, in S. Arieta and G. Caplan, eds., *American Handbook of Psychiatry*, vol. 2.: *Child and Adolescent Psychiatry Sociocultural and Community Psychiatry*, 2nd ed. New York: Basic Books.

———. 1976. Sex Differences and Psychiatric Disorders. *American Journal of Sociology* 81:1447–1454.

———. 1981. Socioenvironmental Factors, Stress, and Psychopathology—Part I: Quasi-Experimental Evidence on the Social Causation–Social Selection Issue Posed by Class Differences. *American Journal of Community Psychology* 9:146–159.

———. 1982. Perspectives on the Past and Future of Psychiatric Epidemiology. *American Journal of Public Health* 72:1271–1279.

Dohrenwend, Bruce P., Barbara S. Dohrenwend, M. Schwartz Gould, Bruce G. Link, Richard Neugebauer, and Robin Wunsch-Hitzig. 1980. *Mental Illness in the United States: Epidemiological Estimates*. New York: Praeger.

Dohrenwend, Bruce P., and Gladys Egri. 1981. Recent Stressful Life Events and Episodes of Schizophrenia. *Schizophrenia Bulletin* 7:12–23.

Dohrenwend, Bruce P., Gladys Egri, and Frederick Mendelsohn. 1971. Psychiatric Disorder in General Populations: A Study of the Problem of Clinical Judgement. *American Journal of Psychiatry* 127:1304–1312.

Dohrenwend, Bruce P., Patrick E. Shrout, Gladys Egri, and Frederick S. Mendelsohn. 1980. Nonspecific Psychological Distress and Other Dimensions of Psychopathology: Measures for Use in the General Population. *Archives of General Psychiatry* 37:1229–1236.

Dohrenwend, Bruce P., Itzhak Levav, Patrick E. Shrout, Bruce G. Link, Andrew E. Skodol, and John L. Martin. 1987. Life Stress and Psychopathology: Progress on Research Begun with Barbara Snell Dohrenwend. *American Journal of Community Psychology* 15:677–715.

Dohrenwend, Bruce P., Lois Oksenberg, Patrick E. Shrout, Barbara S. Dohrenwend, and Diane Cook. 1979. What Brief Psychiatric Screening Scales Measure, in *Health Survey Research Methods: Third Biennial Research Conference.* DHHS Publication No. (PHS) 81-3268. National Center for Health Services Research, U.S. Department of Health and Human Services.

Dohrenwend, Bruce P., and Patrick E. Shrout. 1981. Toward the Development of a Two-Stage Procedure for Case Identification and Classification in Psychiatric Epidemiology, in R. G. Simmons, ed., *Research in Community and Mental Health*, vol. 2. Greenwich, Conn.: JAI Press.

Dohrenwend, Bruce P., Patrick E. Shrout, Bruce G. Link, John Martin, and Andrew E. Skodol. 1986. Overview and Initial Results from a Risk-Factor Study of Depression and Schizophrenia, in J. E. Barret and R. M. Rose, eds., *Mental Disorders in the Community*. New York: Guilford Press, pp. 184–215.

Dupuy, Harold. 1972. The Psychological Section of the Current Health and Nutrition Examination Survey. *Proceedings of the Public Health Conference on Records and Statistics Joint Meeting with the National Conference on Mental Health Statistics.* Rockville, Md.: U.S. Department of Health Education and Welfare, Public Health Service, Health Resources Administration, National Center of Health Statistics.

Eaton, J. W., and R. J. Weill 1955. *Culture and Mental Disorders*. Glencoe, Ill.: Free Press.

Eaton, William W. 1974. Residence, Social Class, and Schizophrenia. *Journal of Health and Social Behavior* 15:289–299.

———. 1980. A Formal Theory of Selection for Schizophrenia. *American Journal of Sociology* 86:149–158.

———. 1985. Epidemiology of Schizophrenia. *Epidemiologic Reviews* 7:105–126.

Eaton, William W., and J. C. Lasry. 1978. Mental Health and Occupational Mobility in a Group of Immigrants. *Social Science and Medicine* 12:53–58.

Falloon, Ian. R. H., J. L. Boyd, C. W. McGill, J. Razani, H. B. Moss, and A. Gilderman. 1982. Family Management in the Prevention of Exacerbations of Schizophrenia: A Controlled Study. *New England Journal of Medicine* 306:1437–1440.

Faris, Robert E. L., and H. W. Dunham. 1939. *Mental Disorders in Urban Areas: An Ecological Study of Schizophrenia and Other Psychoses.* Chicago: Chicago University Press.

Feighner, J. P., E. Robins, S. B. Guze, R. A. Woodruff, G. Winokur, and R. Munoz. 1972. Diagnostic Criteria for Use in Psychiatric Research. *Archives of General Psychiatry* 26:57–63.

Frank, Jerome D. 1973. *Persuasion and Healing.* Baltimore: Johns Hopkins University Press.

Gallagher, Eugene B., Daniel. J. Levinson, and I. Erlich. 1957. Some Sociopsychological Characteristics of Patients and Their Relevance for Psychiatric Treatment, in M. Greenblatt, D. Levinson, and R. H. Williams, eds., *The Patient and the Mental Hospital.* Glencoe, Ill: Free Press, pp. 357–379.

Goldberg, D., and P. Huxley. 1980. *Mental Illness in the Community: The Pathway to Psychiatric Care.* London and New York: Tavistock Publications.

Goldberg, E. M., and S. L. Morrison. 1963. Schizophrenia and Social Class. *British Journal of Psychiatry* 109:785–802.

Goldhamer, H., and A. W. Marshall. 1953. *Psychoses and Civilization.* New York: Free Press.

Goldman, R. K., and G. A. Mendelsohn. 1969. Psychotherapeutic Change and Social Adjustment: A Report of a National Survey of Psychotherapists. *Journal of Abnormal Psychology* 74:164–172.

Gottesman, Irving I., and James Shield. 1976. A Critical Review of Recent Adoption, Twin, and Family Studies of Schizophrenia: Behavioral Genetics Perspectives. *Schizophrenia Bulletin* 2:360–398.

Gottheil, E., M. Kramer, and M. S. Hurwich. 1966. Intake Procedures and Psychiatric Decisions. *Comprehensive Psychiatry* 7:207–215.

Gurin, G., J. Veroff, and S. Feld. 1960. *Americans View Their Mental Health*. New York: Basic Books.

Hagnell, O. 1966. *A Prospective Study of the Incidence of Mental Disorder*. Stockholm: Svenska Bokforlaget Norstedts-Bonniers.

Harding, Courtenay, and John Strauss. 1985. The Course of Schizophrenia: An Evolving Concept, in M. Alpert, ed., *Controversies in Schizophrenia*. New York: The Guilford Press.

Harding, Courtenay, Joseph Zubin, and John S. Strauss. 1987. Chronicity in Schizophrenia: Fact, Partial Fact, or Artifact? *Hospital and Community Psychiatry* 38:477–486.

Helzer, John E., Lee N. Robins, Larry T. McEvoy, Edward L. Spitznagel, Roger K. Stoltzman, Anne Farmer, and Ian Brockington. 1985. A Comparison of Clinical and Diagnostic Interview Schedule Diagnoses: Physician Reexamination of Lay-Interviewed Cases in the General Population. *Archives of General Psychiatry* 42:657–666.

Hochschild, Arlie R. 1979. Emotion Work, Feeling Rules, and Social Structure. *American Journal of Sociology* 85:551–575.

———. 1983. *The Managed Heart: The Commercialization of Human Feeling*. Berkeley: University of California Press.

Hollingshead, August B., and Frederick C. Redlich. 1958. *Social Class and Mental Illness*. New York: John Wiley.

Holzer, C. E., B. Shea, J. Swanson, P. Leaf, J. Myers, L. George, M. Weissman, and P. Bednarski. 1986. The Increased Risk for Specific Psychiatric Disorders among Persons of Low Socioeconomic Status. *American Journal of Social Psychiatry* 6:259–271.

Horwitz, Allan. 1982. *The Social Control of Mental Illness*. New York: Academic Press.

Jarvis, Edward. 1850. The Influence of Distance from and Proximity to an Insane Hospital on Its Use by Any People. *Boston Medical and Surgical Journal* 42:209–222.

———. [1855] 1971. *Insanity and Idiocy in Massachusetts: Report of the Commission on Lunacy*. Cambridge, Mass.: Harvard University Press.

Johnstone, A., and David Goldberg. 1976. Psychiatric Screening in General Practice. *Lancet* i:605–608.

Kadushin, Charles. 1969. *Why People Go to Psychiatrists*. New York: Atherton.

Kato, M. 1969. Psychiatric Epidemiological Surveys in Japan: The Problem of Case Finding, in W. Caudill and T. Lin, eds., *Mental Health Research in Asia and the Pacific*. Honolulu: East-West Center Press, pp. 92–104.

Kessler, Ronald C., Roger L. Brown, and Clifford L. Broman. 1981. Sex Differences in Psychiatric Help-Seeking: Evidence from Four Large Scale Surveys. *Journal of Health and Social Behavior* 22:49–64.

Kessler, Ronald C., James S. House, and J. Blake Turner. 1987. Unemployment and Health in a Community Sample. *Journal of Health and Social Behavior* 28:51–59.

Klerman, Gerald L. 1987. Psychiatric Epidemiology and Mental Health Policy, pp. 227–264, in S. Levine and A. Lilienfeld, eds., *Epidemiology and Health Policy*. New York: Tavistock Publications, pp. 227–264.

Kohn, Melvin L. 1972. Class, Family, and Schizophrenia: A Reformulation. *Social Forces* 50:295–304.

Kulka, Richard A., Joseph Veroff, and Elizabeth Douvan. 1981. *Mental Health in America: Patterns of Help Seeking from 1957 to 1976*. New York: Basic Books.

Langner, Thomas S. 1962. A Twenty-two Item Screening Score of Psychiatric Symptoms Indicating Impairment. *Journal of Health and Human Behavior* 3:269–276.

Larson, Richard. 1969. The Clergyman's Role in the Therapeutic Process: Disagreement Between Clergymen and Psychiatrists. *Psychiatry* 31:250–263.

Leff, J. P., L. Kuipers, R. Berkowitz, R. Eberlein-Vries, and D. Sturgeon. 1982. A Controlled Trial of Social Intervention in the Families of Schizophrenic Patients. *British Journal of Psychiatry* 141:121–134.

Leff, Julian, and Christine Vaughn. 1985. *Expressed Emotion in Families*. New York: Guilford Press.

Leighton, D. C., J. S. Harding, D. B. Macklin, A. M. Macmillan, and A. H. Leighton. 1963. *The Character of Danger*. New York. Basic Books.

Lemkau, Paul, and Guido M. Crocetti. 1962. An

Urban Population's Opinion and Knowledge about Mental Illness. *American Journal of Psychiatry* 118:692–700.

Lennon, Mary Clare. 1987. Sex Differences in Distress: The Impact of Gender and Work Roles. *Journal of Health and Social Behavior* 28:290–305.

Liebowitz, Michael. 1984. The Efficacy of Antidepressants in Anxiety Disorder, in L. Grinspoon, ed., *Psychiatry Update*, vol. 3. Washington, D.C.: American Psychiatric Association Press.

Lin, T. 1953. A Study of the Incidence of Mental Disorder in Chinese and Other Cultures. *Psychiatry* 16:313–336.

Link, Bruce. 1982. Mental Patient Status, Work and Income: An Examination of the Effects of a Psychiatric Label. *American Sociological Review* 47:202–215.

———. 1983. The Reward System of Psychotherapy: Implications for Inequities in Service Delivery. *Journal of Health and Social Behavior* 24:61–69.

———. 1987. Understanding Labeling Effects in the Area of Mental Disorders: An Assessment of the Effects of Expectations of Rejection. *American Sociological Review* 52:96–112.

Link, Bruce, and Bruce P. Dohrenwend. 1980a. Formulation of Hypotheses about the Ratio of Untreated Cases in the True Prevalence Studies of Functional Psychiatric Disorders in Adults in the United States, in B. P. Dohrenwend et al., eds., *Mental Illness in the United States, op. cit.*, pp. 133–149.

———. 1980b. Formulation of Hypotheses about the True Prevalence of Demoralization in the United States, in B. P. Dohrenwend et al., eds., *Mental Illness in the United States, op. cit.*, pp. 114–132.

Link, Bruce G., Bruce P. Dohrenwend, and Andrew E. Skodol. 1986. Socio-Economic Status and Schizophrenia: Noisome Occupational Characteristics as a Risk Factor. *American Sociological Review* 51:242–258.

Link, Bruce G., and Barry Milcarek. 1980. Selection Factors in the Dispensation of Therapy: The Matthew Effect in the Allocation of Mental Health Resources. *Journal of Health and Social Behavior* 21:279–290.

MacMahon, B., and T. F. Pugh. 1960. *Epidemiologic Methods*. Boston: Little, Brown.

Macmillan, A. M. 1957. The Health Opinion Survey: Technique for Estimating Prevalence of Psychoneurotic and Related Types of Disorder in Communities. *Psychological Reports* 3:325–329.

Marks, J. N., D. P. Goldberg, and V. F. Hillier. 1979. Determinants of the Ability of General Practitioners to Detect Psychiatric Illness. *Psychological Medicine* 9:337–353.

Mausner, Judith S., and Anita K. Bahn. 1974. *Epidemiology: An Introductory Text*. Philadelphia: W. B. Saunders.

Mazer, M. 1974. People in a Predicament: A Study in Psychiatric and Psychosocial Epidemiology. *Social Psychiatry* 9:85–90.

Mead, George Herbert. 1934. *Mind, Self and Society*. Chicago: University of Chicago Press.

Mechanic, D. 1972. Social Class and Schizophrenia: Some Requirements for a Plausible Theory of Social Influence. *Social Forces* 50:305–309.

Mechanic, David, and Linda H. Aiken. 1986. Social Science, Medicine, and Health Policy, in L. H. Aiken and D. Mechanic, eds., *Applications of Social Science to Clinical Medicine and Health Policy*. New Brunswick, N.J.: Rutgers University Press, pp. 1–12.

Murphy, H. B. M., and B. M. Taumoepeau. 1980. Traditionalism and Mental Health in the South Pacific: A Reexamination of an Old Hypothesis. *Psychological Medicine* 10:471–482.

Myers, Jerome K., and L. Schaffer. 1954. Social Stratification and Psychiatric Practice: A Study of an Outpatient Clinic. *American Sociological Review* 19:307–310.

Myers, Jerome K., Myrna M. Weissman, Gary L. Tischler, Charles E. Holzer, Philip J. Leaf, Helen Orvaschel, James C. Anthony, Jeffrey H. Boyd, Jack D. Burke, Morton Kramer, and Roger Stoltzman. 1984. Six-Month Prevalence of Psychiatric Disorders in Three Communities. *Archives of General Psychiatry* 41:959–976.

Myerson, Abraham. 1940. Review of Mental Disorder in Urban Areas: An Ecological Study of Schizophrenia and Other Psychoses. *American Journal of Psychiatry* 96:995–997.

Neugebauer, Richard, Bruce P. Dohrenwend, and Barbara Dohrenwend. 1980. Formulation of Hypotheses about the True Prevalence of Functional Psychiatric Disorders among Adults in the United States, B. P.

Dohrenwend et al., *Mental Illness in the United States*, op. cit., pp. 45–94.

Nunnally, Jum. 1961. *Popular Conceptions of Health: Their Development and Change*. New York: Holt, Rinehart and Winston.

Perrucci, Robert, and Dena B. Targ. 1982. Network Structure and Reactions to Primary Deviance of Mental Patients. *Journal of Health and Social Behavior* 23:2–17.

Phillips, Derek L. 1966. The "True Prevalence" of Mental Illness in a New England State. *Community Mental Health Journal* 2:35–40.

———. 1967. Identification of Mental Illness: Its Consequences for Rejection. *Community Mental Health Journal* 3:262–266.

Phillips, Derek L., and K. J. Clancy. 1972. Some Effects of "Social Desirability" in Survey Studies. *American Journal of Sociology* 77:921–940.

Phillips Derek L., and J. G. Draguns. 1971. Classification of the Behavior Disorders. *Annual Review of Psychology* 22:447–482.

Phillips, Derek L., and B. E. Segal. 1969. Sexual Status and Psychiatric Symptoms. *American Sociological Review* 34:58–72.

Radloff, Lenore S. 1977. The CES-D Scale: A Self-Report Depression Scale for Research in the General Population. *Applied Psychological Measurement* 1:385–401.

Robins, Lee N., John E. Helzer, R. Crougham, and K. S. Ratcliff. 1981. National Institute of Mental Health Diagnostic Interview Schedule: Its History, Characteristics, and Validity. *Archives of General Psychiatry* 38:381–389.

Robins, Lee N., John E. Helzer, Myrna M. Weissman, Helen Orvaschel, Ernest Gruenberg, Jack Burke, and Darrel A. Regier. 1984. Life Prevalence of Specific Psychiatric Disorders in Three Sites. *Archives of General Psychiatry* 41:949–958.

Rosenfield, Sarah. In press. The Effects of Women's Employment: Personal Control and Sex Differences in Mental Health. *Journal of Health and Social Behavior*.

Schofield, William. 1964. *The Purchase of Friendship*. Englewood Cliffs, N.J.: Prentice-Hall.

Schwartz, Sharon. 1985. A Society unto Themselves: A Theoretical and Empirical Examination of Women's Proclivity for Depressive Disorders. Ph.D. diss., Columbia University.

Shader, R. I., M. H. Ebert, and J. S. Harmatz. 1971. Langner's Psychiatric Impairment

Scale: A Short Screening Device. *American Journal of Psychiatry* 128:596–601.

Shapiro, Sam, Elizabeth Skinner, Larry Kessler, Michael Von Korff, Pearl German, Gary Tischler, Philip Leaf, Lee Benham, Linda Cottler, and Darrell Regier. 1984. Utilization of Health and Mental Health Services: Three Epidemiologic Catchment Area Sites. *Archives of General Psychiatry* 41:971–978.

Shepard, M., B. Cooper, A. C. Brown, and G. W. Kalton. 1966. *Psychiatric Illness in General Practice*. London: Oxford University Press.

Shrout, Patrick E., Andrew E. Skodol, and Bruce P. Dohrenwend. 1986. A Two-Stage Approach for Case Identification and Diagnosis: First Stage Instruments, in J. E. Barret and R. M. Rose, eds., *Mental Disorders in the Community*. New York: Guilford Press, pp. 286–300.

Shrout, Patrick E., Robert L. Spitzer, and Joseph L. Fleiss. 1987. Quantification of Agreement in Psychiatric Diagnosis Revisited. *Archives of General Psychiatry* 44:172–178.

Smith, Mary L., Gene Glass, and Thomas Miller. 1980. *The Benefits of Psychotherapy*. Baltimore: Johns Hopkins University Press.

Spiro, Herzl, Irad Siassi, and Guido Crocetti. 1973. Ability of the Public to Recognize Mental Illness: An Issue of Substance and an Issue of Meaning. *Social Psychiatry* 8:32–36.

Spitzer, R. L., J. Endicott, and E. Robins. 1978. Research Diagnostic Criteria: Rationale and Reliability. *Archives of General Psychiatry* 35:773–782.

Srole, L., Thomas S. Langner, S. T. Michael, M. K. Opler, and T. A. C. Rennie. 1962. *Mental Health in the Metropolis*. New York: McGraw-Hill.

Star, Shirley. 1955. The Public's Ideas About Mental Illness. Chicago: University of Chicago. Mimeo.

Susser, Mervin W. 1968. *Community Psychiatry: Epidemiologic and Social Themes*. New York: Random House.

Thoits, Peggy A. 1981. Undesirable Life Events and Psychophysiological Distress: A Problem of Operational Confounding. *American Sociological Review* 46:97–109.

———. 1985. Self-labeling Processes in Mental Illness: The Role of Emotional Deviance. *American Journal of Sociology* 91:221–249.

———. 1987. Gender and Marital Status Differences in Control and Distress: Common Stress versus Unique Stress Explanations. *Journal of Health and Social Behavior* 28:7–22.

Turner, R. Jay. 1968. Social Mobility and Schizophrenia. *Journal of Health and Social Behavior* 9:194–203.

Turner, R. Jay, and M. O. Wagenfeld. 1967. Occupational Mobility and Schizophrenia: An Assessment of the Social Causation and Social Selection Hypotheses. *American Sociological Review* 32:104–113.

Weissman, Myrna M., and Gerald L. Klerman. 1977. Sex Differences and the Epidemiology of Depression. *Archives of General Psychiatry* 34:98–111.

Weissman, Myrna M., and Jerome K. Myers. 1978. Affective Disorders in a U.S. Urban Community: The Use of Research Diagnostic Criteria in an Epidemiological Survey. *Archives of General Psychiatry* 35:1304–1311.

Wender, Paul, David Rosenthal, Seymour Kety, Fini Schulsinger, and Joseph Welner. 1974. Crossfostering: A Research Strategy for Clarifying the Role of Genetic and Experiential Factors in the Etiology of Schizophrenia. *Archives of General Psychiatry* 30:121–128.

Yarrow, Marian Radke, Charlotte Green Schwartz, Harriet S. Murphy, and Leila Calhoun Deasy. 1955. The Psychological Meaning of Mental Illness in the Family. *Journal of Social Issues* 11:12–24.

CHAPTER
7

SOCIAL RESPONSES TO SUBSTANCE ABUSE

DIANA CHAPMAN WALSH

Throughout recorded history, humans have sought and found ways to alter their consciousness. On the individual level, this seems an intrapsychic, hence quintessentially private act. But who uses which mood-altering substances to what end and with what effect varies through time, across space, and between demographic subgroups. Social patterns like these invite social explanations. Empirical investigations of the use of specific drugs seek to compare users to nonusers; define important subpopulations and risk factors; establish temporal and other patterns of use, including age at initiation; differentiate experimental from chronic use; and map out progressive stages in a typical user's career, to the extent that one exists. This research tends to be grounded in theories about processes that carry some individuals from the "primary deviance" implied in first violating a social norm, through stigmatization and social isolation, to the more enduring

and limiting "secondary deviance" of a marginal subgroup (Lemert 1972).

On the social level, different societies vary widely in their response to these behaviors, and in the ways they constrain and limit the choices individuals can make, infuse those choices with meaning, and burden them with consequence. Most apparent for individuals are the consequences that operate through the law. Although the dichotomy between legal and illegal drugs crucially shapes both individual and social responses to their use, a substance's legal status is itself a social construction, surrounded and propped up by mythology about properties it may have (Gusfield 1963, 1981).

For example, although heroin and other opiates are closely regulated in the United States today, opium derivatives were freely and widely available in an astounding array of elixers and nostrums sold by American hucksters in the 1800s. Coffee and tobacco, now legally available, have at other times been considered threatening and debauching. As recently as 1927, cigarettes were illegal in parts of the United States; indeed, smoking cigarettes carried greater stigma in nineteenth-century America than did the use of opium. Although the relative cultural position of those two substances has completely reversed, the pendulum is beginning to swing back now on cigarettes; a fifty-year pattern of ambivalent and diffident regulation of tobacco products in the United States is yielding to new strictures at the federal, state, and municipal levels of government and in the private sector (Walsh and Gordon 1986). At the same time, a substance like marijuana or hashish can be a benign social lubricant in one society, a sanctified adjunct to religious ceremony in a second, and a dangerous illegal drug in a third (Clausen 1961, p. 299). And two opiate products, pharmacologically much the same, are viewed and managed orthogonally: one (heroin) as a menace to society, the other (morphine) as a miracle of medicine (Conrad and Schneider 1980, p. 110).

Psychoactive substances become "problems"—and their use blends into "abuse"—when prevailing sentiment views them as portending some kind of harm: physical, emotional, economic, or social damage to the user or to others. Understanding social factors in the use and abuse of psychoactive substances therefore requires a perspective on the harm they putatively can do: causing illness and injury, disrupting families and places of work, undermining morality and the economic and social order. Notions of the kind of harm a particular substance can do—how serious, destabilizing, and pervasive it is, who bears the responsibility and who suffers the consequence—also influence its placement within jurisdictional boundaries separating broad institutions of social control, particularly, in modern societies, the criminal justice and medical care systems.

The impact of legal categories is immediately manifest in the predictable fact that the most commonly used drugs are the licit ones, alcohol first, then nicotine (in cigarettes). Marijuana is the most frequently tried (and the least stigmatized) of the illicit drugs, followed by cocaine, other illicit drugs, then heroin. For purposes of discussion, we can array drug users along a crude gradient to reflect the social acceptability of their "drug of choice," recognizing, as we do so, how ephemeral, arbitrary and in some ways misleading these designations are, especially as multidrug use becomes more pronounced. We examine alcohol, marijuana, cocaine, and heroin, in that order, leaving other illicit substances, prescription drugs, and cigarettes largely outside our scope, except as they help to illuminate the general themes and sociologically informed lessons for policy with which the chapter concludes.

ALCOHOL USE
AND ALCOHOLISM

An appreciation of social factors entwined with alcohol use and control begins with recognition of the manifold functions drinking serves (Gusfield 1963, Makela et al. 1981). Alcohol can be a thirst-quenching beverage, a nutrient, a medicine, and a psychoactive drug believed capable of catalyzing such wide-ranging and inconsistent effects as euphoria, depression, stimulation, sedation, aggression, sociability, "disinhibition," and relaxation. Often these effects are shaped by the vagaries on any drinking occasion of the drinker's particular expectations of what they will be. Alcohol functions, too, as a commodity in modern industrial economies and a significant source of tax receipts and advertising revenues. Although relatively minor in overall national economies, the alcohol trade is nevertheless important to numerous vested interests (Makela et al. 1981). Also, drinking is a symbol of sophistication, social status, group identity, and commitment to a whole style of life (Gusfield 1963). The versatility of alcohol both explains and ordains its ubiquity; among substances ever used to titrate mood and perception, alcohol stands out as "the one that has probably been used by more of the earth's peoples in more places and times" than any other (Chambers, Inciardi, and Siegal 1975, p. 93). An omnibus invitation to leisure and conviviality in modern American society, alcohol is also the proximal cause of a treatable illness officially so designated by the medical and psychiatric professions and the putative underlying cause of death, disease, disability, dysfunction, and dissatisfaction.

Periodic reports to Congress by the National Institute on Alcohol Abuse and Alcoholism (NIAAA) summarize current research on alcohol and health. The 1983 report indicated that overall per capita consumption of alcoholic beverages increased steadily after World War II, accelerated in the early 1960s, and continues to rise, but less steeply. The 1981 estimated consumption rate of 2.77 gallons a year (or 1 ounce a day) of absolute alcohol per person aged 14 and older represented a 37 percent and 7 percent increase over 1961 and 1971, respectively (DHHS 1983). Since 1981, annual consumption has been slowly declining (by 4 percent between 1980 and 1984), but not yet to the levels recorded in the early 1970s (Arnold 1987).

Variations (by beverage, region, demographic group, type of drinker, drinking context, and so on) have remained fairly stable over the past decade, although wine and beer have grown in relative popularity and distilled spirits have declined. Beer accounts for about half of all alcohol consumed, and wine about one-seventh. The adult American population divides roughly into thirds: (1) "abstainers," who drink no alcoholic beverages; (2) "light drinkers," who report on average consuming at most three drinks a week; and (3) "moderate" and "heavy" drinkers, the former (about 25 percent of the population) who drink up to two drinks a day, the latter (roughly 9 percent of adults) who consume two to ten or more drinks daily (DHHS 1983).

Among subgroups, men drink more than women (three men drink heavily for every woman who does, and twice as many women as men say they abstain); drinking declines with age (faster for men than for women); and abstinence is slightly more common among lower than higher income and educational groups, among blacks, especially black women, and in southern regions of the country (DHHS 1983). Recorded per capita sales vary widely from state to state, from a high in 1984 of 5.35 gallons in the District of Columbia to a low in Utah of 1.53 gallons (Arnold 1987). Extensive subgroup analyses are tenuous in national surveys, owing to sample size limitations, but the influence of social factors is evident, even at this aggregate level, in the sensitivity of drinking to gender, age, income, and location.

Evidence that American youth are beginning to drink at earlier ages has recently aroused concern (Arnold 1987), and data are accumulating on the medical, social, and economic costs of problems related to alcohol use—deaths; hospital admissions; accidents on the highways, in aviation, at work, in recreation, and at home; absenteeism from work and school; and other disruptions of the social order as well as personal and family life. Overall, it is estimated that alcohol use may be a factor in 10 percent of all deaths in the United States, roughly 200,000 a year, and may annually cost the nation well over $100 billion in lost productivity, medical costs, and other social responses (DHHS 1983). However, aggregate statistics like these must always be recognized for what they are: extrapolations, using rather crude assumptions, from small-scale studies of widely varying internal validity and of limited generalizability.

Ethnic and religious variations in drinking patterns and problems have fascinated generations of social scientists (Bales 1945; Ullman 1958; Blacker 1966), whose observations influenced policy for a time in the perhaps naive hope that safer drinking norms could somehow be transplanted to cultures beset by alcohol-related problems (Beauchamp 1980, pp. 41–48). Some traditions (those, for example, of Jews, Italians, and Chinese-Americans) were believed to inculcate healthier drinking practices (by integrating alcohol more ritualistically into mealtimes and ceremonial occasions), whereas others seemed fraught with trouble. The Finns are known for their "utilitarian" drinking, with intoxication being the object (Bales 1945), and for what we would consider a "macho" attitude. In Finland "it is manly and prestigious to drink a great deal whenever one drinks." (Makela, Osterberg, and Sulkunen 1981) The French pay for their love of wine with one of the world's highest death rates from liver cirrhosis. Drinking among American Indians has been a long-recognized problem, although the social response has been characterized as inadequate (May 1986).

Scholarly attention is now turning to alcohol-related experiences of other special populations hitherto overlooked: "impaired physicians," adolescents and younger children, minorities, and women. Combining feminism and social epidemiology, writers on women and alcohol are building provocative theories about the symbolic and political functions of drinking in the context of changing sex roles. For example, an acceleration of concern about a "new epidemic" of women's drinking, starting in the 1970s, was demonstrated to be strangely at odds with the facts. Subsequent analysis interpreted the concern as a very belated response to "changes that took place almost a half century before," when the fragile alcoholism movement, post-prohibition, minimized the extent of women's drinking to avoid a social backlash by the temperance forces that had only just been cast aside (Fillmore 1986, p. 74). Now politically secure and seeking additional legitimacy and financial support, the alcoholism movement is well served by enlarging its boundaries around an expanding population "at need." Similar vested interests are served by mounting attention to unresolved conflicts said to haunt adult children of alcoholics and to treatment of the alcoholic's entire family system, members of which are sometimes termed "co-alcoholics."

Elasticity in the boundaries around the alcohol problem has inspired sociological inquiry into how deviant behavior becomes medicalized (Conrad and Schneider 1980), how definitions of a social problem evolve to justify transfers in its "ownership" (Gusfield 1963), and how these collective definitions constrain public debate and the formulation of rational policy (Beauchamp 1980). Changes in the "governing ideas" (Moore and Gerstein 1981) concerning alcohol have accompanied major shifts in policy, most remarkably the enactment of prohibition in 1919 and its repeal fourteen years later.

Over the years, three primary alcohol ideologies have waxed and waned: (1) a moral focus on alcohol and its abuse as punishable evils; (2) a medical orientation toward alcoholism, defined as a treatable disease; and (3) the beginnings of a public health perspective that blends elements of the first two in a more inclusive model comprising a "host" (the drinker), an "agent" (the intoxicating drink), and environments (physical and social) within which the agent can act upon the host to produce harm (Walsh and Hingson 1987).

Inebriation as Moral Failing: The Punishment Paradigm

Moralistic attitudes about alcohol dominated during the colonial and revolutionary eras. Drinking was generally heavy, but when it exceeded bounds of propriety, it was subject to sanctions by the church, the period's dominant institution of social control. Because the Puritan doctrine of free will viewed intoxication as an exercise of choice indicative of a moral failing, civil penalties, sometimes severe ones, were applied too (Aaron and Musto 1981, p. 132).

At the close of the eighteenth century, this punitive orientation was being challenged by an inchoate conception of habitual drunkenness as a disease. This became a cornerstone of the temperance movement, which led a successful drive for total prohibition. Despite an overall reduction of alcohol consumption by one-third to one-half in the prohibition years (Clark 1976, p. 164), the "noble experiment" was abandoned as an ignoble failure because it had stimulated the rapid growth of organized crime. This, of course, was true, but the rise and fall of prohibition involved issues deeper than the objective amount of drinking or the costs of organized crime. Gusfield (1963) portrays the temperance movement as a "cultural struggle of the traditional rural Protestant society against the developing urban and industrial social system." (Gusfield 1963, p. 7) The crusade was more symbolic than material, in Gusfield's view, because it was at heart "a struggle to assert the public dominance of old middle-class values," self-control, industriousness, the delay of gratification, and temperance or sobriety.

The repeal of the Eighteenth Amendment, the vehicle establishing prohibition, therefore augured a decline in middle-class values. But it also signaled the irreversibility of cultural and economic trends, including the opening of a new consumer era (Moore and Gerstein 1981). To restore alcohol as a legal, popular, and marketable product, drunken conduct had to be explained without prejudice to the substance itself. Alcohol needed an "alibi" and found it in what Beauchamp (1980) terms a "kinds-of-people" explanation, segregating normal or "social" drinking from the "alcoholic" drinking that only some people developed. Social concern was thus deflected from the producers and their harmful product to a small minority of "susceptible" consumers who would need to abstain entirely while the alcohol trade could flourish.

Alcoholism as a Treatable Disease

Designating alcoholism a disease also buffered the drinker from blame and admitted the logical possibility of treatment. Advocates of the disease model began campaigning in the 1930s for optimism about cure and for the creation of therapeutic programs. Alcoholics Anonymous (AA) was founded in 1935 and recruited a loyal membership of "recovering alcoholics" determined to promote the image of alcoholism as a tractable disease and the alcoholic a sick person worthy of help.

Over the next fifty years a great variety of treatment strategies came into vogue, in mental facilities, psychiatric clinics, acute general hospitals, welfare and social agencies, prisons, and halfway houses. Programs were under the aegis of psychiatrists and other physicians, psychologists, social workers, nurses, and lay counselors, many themselves former alcoholics engaged in helping others as prescribed by the "twelfth step" of AA. The treatment industry prospered as growing acceptance of the disease model of alcoholism facilitated increased third-party payment and as the service sector of the welfare state expanded generally (Christie 1981). Even before the ballooning market attracted proprietary investment in for-profit treatment facilities, interprofessional rivalries and institutional chauvinism had created a fragmented and forbidding patchwork of treatment options. Referrals from one to another were virtually unheard of, and philosophies and treatment goals were incommensurable and discordant. Some treated alcoholism as a medical disease; others as a psychological syndrome, a social problem, or a spiritual affliction. Goals ranged from total abstinence to "controlled drinking" (an intensely controversial topic) to physical or psychological healing, or improved social functioning (Glaser, Greenberg, and Barret 1978).

Then, in the 1980s, the favorable conditions began to erode. The oil crisis weakened the world economy, and governments moved to dismantle the welfare state. Doubts began to surface about how much could reasonably be expected from a further escalation of treatment strategies. Although the intricate differences among treatments made comparisons difficult, the weight of evidence from controlled research consistently suggested that the more intensive, expensive, high-technology approaches produced results in no way superior to far simpler interventions (Saxe 1983). What remains to be sorted out is which treatments are themselves insufficiently efficacious to show a measurable effect and in which instances uncertainties about outcome could be resolved with improvements in research design. Few studies accrue sizable enough samples to explore interaction effects, and few follow their subjects over the extended periods of time a chronic condition like alcoholism warrants.

Available evidence does suggest that some treatment is preferable to none, at least for those who find their way to organized programs. Longitudinal studies of the natural history of alcoholism indicate that many give up drinking, and motivation is evidently the *sine qua non* (Vaillant 1983); alcoholics are said to have a 10 percent to 30 percent chance of recovering on their own, without benefit of formal intervention (Slaby 1985). This phenomenon of "spontaneous recovery" means that outcome studies without adequate control groups (established preferably through randomization) can grossly overstate the success of treatments. The same natural history studies suggest that preventing relapse is the crux of the challenge clinicians face (Vaillant 1983).

That challenge arises, however, only after a diagnosis has been made, a much more arbitrary and elusive judgment than is generally recognized. At one time or another, nearly all of us have had occasion seriously to worry whether someone we know might "be an alcoholic," a term we had previously used automatically, without much critical thought. If we probe the question more deeply, we finally have to conclude that there exists no unambiguous or fully satisfactory diagnostic indicator.

Diagnoses of alcoholism alternatively focus upon: (1) the psychological meaning of alcohol to the drinker (does the drinker exhibit a life-style anchored in alcohol as a coping device?); (2) some social sequellae of "excessive" drinking (has alcohol disrupted the drinker's functioning within the family, in school, or at work, or has it provoked skirmishes with the law?); (3) physical effects of chronic heavy drinking (is there evidence of liver disease, cognitive impairment, or physical "dependence" manifested in withdrawal symptoms when alcohol intake is reduced?); (4) self-attribution of drinking problems (does the drinker believe he or she may have a problem, or do others say so?); all against a backdrop of (5) the quantity, variability, and frequency of drinking, and the extent to which it seems to be characterized by loss of control.

Many diagnostic inventories and scales tapping one or more of these dimensions of alcohol use have been developed, tested, and applied in clinical settings and in research. The experts' unwillingness to settle on one betrays shortcomings of them all, as well as a general lack of consensus in what has facetiously been called a dogma-eat-dogma field. However, agreement is fairly widespread now that "the difference between an alcoholic and a 'normal' heavy drinker is quantitative not qualitative, depending on the frequency of intoxication and the degree to which that intoxication interferes with role performance" (Robins 1980, p. 195). Social role, a sociological construct, is the essential common denominator in clinical, theoretical, and commonsensical notions of alcoholism.

Estimates suggest that perhaps a quarter of patients seeking primary medical care may have some background of alcohol abuse, mostly undetected. Primary physicians commonly underestimate the prevalence of problem drinking in their practices and hesitate to discuss alcohol with patients who know their own drinking is out of hand (Hingson, Mangione, et al. 1982). Programs of "intervention" in clinical settings, at work sites, in schools, and within families have been designed to enhance the chances of early detection, to confront problem drinkers with evidence of harm wrought by their drinking, and to coax them into treatment. These strategies assume that alcoholism is a disease of denial and that alcoholics have to "hit rock bottom" before they can give up drinking. Intervention programs seek to "raise the bottom," by persuading people close to the alcoholic (physicians, co-workers, job supervisors, union stewards, teachers, family, or friends) that they are inadvertent "enablers" of the disease, which will progress until they present the drinker with compelling evidence that his or her drinking has become literally intolerable. Empirical data to support these premises are scarce, as are valid demonstrations that intervention programs work. Adequate evaluative studies still remain to be done.

A Public Health Perspective on Drinking Problems

As doubts were surfacing about the efficacy of alcoholism interventions and treatments, another type of governing image started to unfold. It began in 1975, when a World Health Organization expert committee led by Scandinavians issued an influential report redefining the alcohol problem in public health terms (Bruun et al. 1975). These scholars highlighted the need for policies designed to reduce overall consumption of alcohol, theorizing that rates of associated problems would in turn decline. Large-scale surveys of alcohol use were challenging the prevailing assumption that the alcohol problem was concentrated in a small group of alcoholics. Instead, a wide range of drinking-related problems were being found throughout the general population of occasional and episodic drinkers. Shifting attention from "problem drinkers" to "drinking problems" revealed that although the heaviest drinkers incur the greatest risk of developing problems, their numbers are proportionately so few that the problems cluster in the group of less heavy drinkers. The heaviest drinkers (who drink five or more drinks a day) constitute some 5 percent of the total population and account for about one-fourth of

all drunken days and less than half of reported problems (illnesses; accidents; difficulties with friends, spouses, employers, and the police).

To some degree, the new public health paradigm, because it mobilizes the law, reinforces the criminalization of certain alcohol-related practices, such as "driving under the influence" or serving alcohol to an inebriated patron or guest or to a minor. It does depart from the old legal approach that penalized inebriation per se, but punitive impulses have never entirely disappeared. In the years during which the medical approach to alcoholism was rising to ascendency, laws against public drunkenness remained on the books. Ethnographic studies have documented the gratuitous and patently unfair processing of skid row alcoholics by a judicial system that was coercive, capricious, and much overburdened; the average trial time, one study found, was 30 to 45 seconds (Wiseman 1970). A series of contradictory Supreme Court decisions in the late 1960s stimulated Congress to enact a 1970 federal law abolishing the crime of public drunkenness and recommending treatment instead.

That same year Congress passed the act that established NIAAA to promote and coordinate federal alcohol policy, initiatives, and research. NIAAA early aligned itself with the established alcoholism forces and adopted the disease perspective, placing a strong emphasis on treatment programs and on education for responsible drinking. More recently, NIAAA, too, has begun to recast its thinking in public health terms and is seeking to harness the law, market incentives, and persuasive strategies in a broad-gauge campaign to prevent "high risk drinking," defined as any drinking (however unusual for the individual) that could lead to accidents (on the highways, on the job, and in recreation), criminal behavior, family violence, suicide, absenteeism from work or from school, and other social and economic costs (DHHS 1983; Moore and Gerstein 1981). Except in the realm of highway fatalities, the empirical links between these social problems and alcohol are tenuous at best (DHHS 1983), and even where drunk driving is concerned the "facts" are socially produced (Gusfield 1981).

Nevertheless, the public health philosophy holds that the most efficient and effective interventions are not the individually oriented programs of education and clinical treatment, but impersonal or technological approaches that demand no ongoing cooperation and motivation. For example, studies have been done to show that elevating alcohol prices does reduce both consumption and problems (liver cirrhosis and accident rates) and that specific laws (such as those raising the permissible drinking age or punishing drunken drivers) can be effective for a time, if circumstances are right (Cook 1981; Cook and Tauchen 1984; Ross 1982). To date, most drunk driving campaigns have emphasized educationally and behaviorally oriented strategies: high visibility law enforcement coupled with publicity to heighten consciousness of the risk of being arrested; swifter and more severe punishment; education and rehabilitation of offenders. A classic public health approach would lay its emphasis on more technological solutions, for example, improving the crashworthiness of vehicles, equipping vehicles with passive restraints for occupants, and engineering safer highways (Baker, Teret, and Daub 1987).

As elements of public health thinking seem gradually to be taking hold, the legal and medical metaphors remain powerful. Alcoholics continue to be viewed as sick people deserving help, while organizations like Mothers Against Drunk Driving (MADD) foster an increasingly intolerant and moralistic posture toward those who drive drunk or engage in other practices felt to endanger innocent people or involve public expense. Subtle transfers over time in the ownership of the alcohol problem— back and forth among religious authorities, law enforcement agencies, medical professionals, public health officials, and special interest groups—alter the social mechanisms and the institutional arrangements used to regulate drinking and the alcohol trade, as well as the ideologies on which the legitimacy of the regulation rests.

MARIJUANA

One of the things that recommends the study of substance use and abuse is the window it opens into the dynamics of social change. Marijuana is a case in point. In a span of less than two decades, marijuana smoking has been transformed from a largely secluded act by a few slum dwellers and jazz musicians to an institutionalized social practice among conspicuous and widening segments of American adolescents and young adults (Jessor 1979). In those age groups now, a majority has had some experience with marijuana. Although more likely to have tried alcohol than marijuana, high school seniors are more commonly regular marijuana smokers than regular drinkers (Bachman, Johnston, and O'Malley 1981). Fifty-one percent of a representative sample of American high school seniors graduating in the class of 1979 had used marijuana; of those, about half had used it in the previous month (Kandel 1980, p. 241). Some fifty to sixty million Americans, nearly one in four, report having tried marijuana, and twenty million use it once or more a month (President's Commission on Organized Crime 1986, p. 48).

The spread of a behavior like marijuana smoking has a spiraling quality because belonging to a social network of users is one of the strongest predictors of initial use. As the substance's popularity increases, so does the probability that any one adolescent will know others who use it. The social climate becomes more favorable, and the behavior diffuses to younger groups (Jessor 1979). But some adolescents resist these pressures, and therefore much empirical research on marijuana attempts to unravel the psychological and social factors separating users from nonusers. Since rates of marijuana use seem to peak in late adolescence, these studies have adopted a developmental framework to characterize young people's marijuana use (Kandel 1980, p. 257).

In search of predictors of the onset of drug use during adolescence, researchers have examined three classes of variables: (1) sociodemographic attributes (which contribute little to an understanding of marijuana initiation now that its use is so widely diffused) (Jessor 1979); (2) intrapersonal characteristics, such as nonconformist attitudes, rebelliousness, alienation, and low self-esteem; and (3) interpersonal factors, notably the influence of peers, a consistent finding that harks back to an early classic study of marijuana use (Becker 1953). Virtually all investigators have found that "beliefs and values favorable to the use of marijuana and association with marijuana-using peers [are] the strongest predictors of adolescent initiation into marijuana use" (Kandel 1980, p. 273). The influence of peer or friendship relationships operates through several mechanisms: "providing access to and availability of marijuana, models for using it and social support for such use" (Jessor 1979, p. 341).

Interest in this passage into marijuana use harbors and illuminates theoretical questions about normal adolescent development, deviance, and socialization (Kandel 1980). Also, the interest has emanated from a pragmatic concern that marijuana may be a "gateway" into other illicit drug use and eventual abuse. Many studies have shown marijuana to be a precursor of other drug taking, necessary although not sufficient, because only some marijuana smokers ever go on to the use of "harder" drugs. Recent evidence has begun to suggest that those most likely to make this progression are the youngest or most precocious experimenters with marijuana, those who try the drug earlier in life than their peers (Kandel and Logan 1984). Although there is a kernel of truth behind the gateway drug fear, it assigns a causal role to marijuana not supported by the facts: Many pass through the gate and never proceed to other drugs; the recent secular rise in marijuana use has not fueled similar increases in the use of other drugs; marijuana and other drug use doubtlessly can be traced back to common antecedents; and if experimentation with alcohol typically predates marijuana, why not label alcohol the gateway drug (Jessor 1979)?

In part owing to the fear that marijuana smoking may be a first step down a slippery slope, social policy has been quite repressive and, indeed, is viewed by many as the apotheosis of heavy-handed government. Marijuana was generally available in nineteenth- and twentieth-century America, principally for medicinal purposes, although the records show occasional recreational use as well. It came into somewhat wider use during the 1920s as a substitute for alcohol in the dry prohibition years. After the repeal of prohibition, marijuana might have faded away, except that the government kept it before the public in a clumsy propaganda campaign launched to root it out. The campaign achieved its overt goal: By 1937 most states and the federal government had enacted tough antimarijuana statutes. Penalties were severe, often no less so than for heroin possession and use, and over the years (as marijuana use continued to spread) became progressively more stringent. But the attempts to cut off supplies seemed merely to raise prices and the profits available on the black market, thereby stimulating trafficking (Brecher 1972). Meanwhile, the antiwar and antiestablishment protests of the 1960s and 1970s engendered a dramatic rise in marijuana use, together with mounting pressure to relax or rescind the restrictive laws.

Advocates of decriminalization argue (so far, largely fruitlessly) that restrictive policies have done more harm than good by increasing access to illicit marijuana of variable quality, by promoting disrespect for the law, and by blocking educational and preventive programs that could foster moderate and responsible use (Brecher

1972). Further, they assert that marijuana, and indeed any drug, should be judged "on its merits," with an eye toward the individual and social harm it demonstrably can do but without the hysteria or overreaction (Brecher 1973) typified in the 1936 film *Reefer Madness.* By 1972 a national commission was pronouncing marijuana completely benign, but studies conducted since then have raised concerns about long-term risks to health at least as serious as those associated with cigarette use (President's Commission on Organized Crime 1986, p. 56). A causal relationship between marijuana and delinquency or criminal behavior has been much discussed but never established; when an association is observed, the delinquency appears to antedate the drug involvement, not to follow from it. The same can perhaps be said of the assertion that marijuana use erodes ambition and motivation, although this relationship is complex (Jessor 1979). One study has correlated frequent marijuana use (at least twenty times a month) with absenteeism and poor performance in school (President's Commission on Organized Crime 1986, p. 59). There was a time when it seemed plausible that as marijuana use diffused more widely through the American population, it would eventually be destigmatized and decriminalized and function much as alcohol does. The more marijuana resembles cigarettes in its health effects, and the more cigarettes decline in favor, the more unlikely that scenario becomes.

COCAINE

Social policy has often seemed to accentuate rather than mute the marijuana "epidemic" and related problems. The more recent upsurge in cocaine use is likewise being propelled by the unintended consequences of a social overreaction. First, toward the end of the 1960s, the federal government began successfully to control amphetamine production and sale, where-upon, as a substitute, contraband cocaine began to appear in increasing quantities, chiefly from Latin American sources (Brecher 1972). Then, in the early 1980s, the Reagan administration declared a "war" on drug trafficking and began to interdict at the nation's borders sizable quantities of marijuana and cocaine. Domestic production of marijuana was stepped up to compensate for the confiscated imports, and it became easier and more lucrative to smuggle cocaine because it is more compact (thus easier to hide) than marijuana and is sold at a higher markup (so if part of a shipment is lost, the remainder still yields handsome profits) (Lieber 1986).

By 1985 a research monograph from the National Institute on Drug Abuse was calling cocaine "a major threat" to the public health (Kozel and Adams 1985, p. v). A year later the mass media were filled with alarmist stories about what President Reagan was calling the nation's "number one problem." The cocaine-related deaths of several young athletes and other public figures had captured public attention. Congress began jockeying with the White House for leadership in the "war on drugs" during the summer and early fall of 1986, an election year. In October 1986 the president signed into law an omnibus drug bill. The bill allocated money for education, research, and treatment; restructured the federal drug bureaucracy; and strengthened enforcement, although not to the unprecedented degree envisaged by drafts of the bill. Large corporations and the federal government began screening job applicants for drug traces in urine or blood samples, and even in a few cases to conduct unannounced drug tests of randomly selected employees. Civil libertarians were increasingly concerned that the excessive public reaction to cocaine might do much more damage than was being caused by the substance itself (Wisotsky 1983).

Behind the strong social reaction were three principal observations about cocaine, its use, and its effects. First, cocaine, the "champagne of uppers" during the 1970s, a glamour drug associated in the public mind with the rich and famous, was suddenly seeming to be much more dangerous than had generally been appreciated. A central nervous system stimulant said to produce exquisitely euphoric effects, cocaine is a powerful drug that produces a variety of harmful acute and chronic health effects. Its insidiousness depends, as with all drugs, on how it is taken, in what dose, over what period of time, in combination with what other drugs, and by whom. Debate over whether tolerance develops and creates a withdrawal syndrome has been rendered moot by certainty that cocaine is intensely reinforcing and "unquestionably addicting" (Wesson and Smith 1985, p. 200). Moreover, cocaine has resulted in hundreds of sudden, unpredictable deaths, including the high-visibility deaths of several celebrities. Yet, despite all the media attention, high school seniors in the class of 1983 were less impressed by the danger of exposure to the drug than were seniors six years before; 33 percent in 1983, as against 36 percent in 1977, saw "great risk" in using cocaine once or twice (O'Malley, Johnston, and Bachman 1985).

Second, cocaine was perceived to have penetrated wide strata of American society, affecting middle America, students, and workers on the job. An estimated twenty-five million Americans say they have tried cocaine, and five to six million report use at least once a month. Of the latter group, it is estimated that about half are addicted (President's Commission on Organized Crime 1986, p. 16). Use is correlated with higher educational attainment, employment in the managerial ranks, and, to a slight degree, higher income groups. On the other hand, the data fail to support the image of cocaine use as the exclusive province of the very rich. Nearly as wide a cross-section of Americans use cocaine as use marijuana. Cocaine users are more like users of other drugs than they are unique; in fact, one of their most striking characteristics is their use of other drugs, especially alcohol and marijuana, often concurrently with cocaine (Clayton 1985).

Third, it was felt that the epidemic was spreading rapidly, as prices for cocaine dropped and concentrations intensified. Between 1974 and 1982 the number of Americans who had tried cocaine increased by a factor of four, from 5.4 million to 21.6 million. Since 1979 there has been evidence that use may be moderating: The number of current users (reporting use in the previous thirty days) remained constant between 1979 and 1982, and a plateau was observed in use among some youth cohorts (Adams and Kozel 1985). However, if supplies continue to expand and prices to drop without effective communication of the risks of cocaine use, this leveling off may be transitory. An epidemiologist estimated conservatively in 1986 that half a million Americans are "seriously at risk for exhibiting negative consequences from their abuse of cocaine, and many many more are at risk for continuation of use or progression to abuse" (Clayton 1985, p. 32). Cocaine is now being called potentially "the most dangerous drug in recent history" (Kozel and Adams 1985, p. 221).

Social reactions over the years to the use of other substances should alert us to the possibility that the health effects of cocaine are less than the full story. One other facet is the worry that American industry is no longer competitive enough in world markets and the related fear that drug use is sapping the productivity of the nation's work force.

HEROIN

The designation "most dangerous drug" was long monopolized by heroin, a relatively little-used substance linked in the public mind with social disorganization, psychopathology, brutal violence, organized crime, and now with the frightening AIDS epidemic. These stereotypes do have some limited basis in fact. Although the least widely used of the illicit drugs, heroin is reportedly associated with the largest number of deaths (1,046 in 1984) and emergency room visits (10,901 in 1984), in part because of "the ease with which a user can overdose" (President's Commission on Organized Crime 1986, p. 41). But many of the problems associated with heroin reflect the influence of prevailing social policies toward heroin more than features of the substance itself (Brecher 1972).

Named originally for "heroic" qualities it was believed to have, heroin was synthesized in the 1870s and introduced in 1898 by a respected German pharmaceutical house. An opiate derived from morphine, and three times more potent than the parent drug, it was considered nonaddictive and was much heralded as a preferable substitute for morphine until, after just five years on the market, its addictive potential was clearly established. "Stripped of its medical respectability, heroin became defined as a drug with no redeeming value, a view which remains prominent today" (Conrad and Schneider 1980, p. 121).

Sentiment against the opium trade, grounded chiefly in prejudice against Chinese-American immigrants, was generalized during the early twentieth century into ever-tighter government control of commerce in narcotics of all kinds. The 1913 Harrison Act established federal government oversight of physicians' management of narcotic addiction, but in a decade's time this medical approach had been converted by "moral entrepreneurs" into complete prohibition of narcotic use and criminalization of addicts (Conrad and Schneider 1980).

By 1924 heroin manufacture was completely banned, drug addicts had become a wholly new category of criminals, and a social problem had been created where none had existed before (Goode 1972). As these forces drove heroin trading into the hands of organized crime and addiction into the ranks of the young lower-class black male, a punitive orientation became increasingly fashionable.

In keeping with these trends, much of early sociological writing on illicit drug use took a social problems perspective. Heroin became a focus for exploring the addiction process, deviance careers, and the addict as a social type, produced by a particular environment and living out a patterned social role. Emphasis was placed on the drug subculture, which had norms and values of its own, distinctive status symbols, even a special argot. Drug abuse was seen in structural terms, as a symptom of deeper pathology and an expression of alienation and anomie (Clausen 1961). More recently, social psychological concepts have come to the fore, and research has emphasized strategies for treating and preventing drug problems.

After methadone maintenance appeared in the 1960s as a viable treatment strategy, activists made sporadic efforts to redefine the addict as ill and to mobilize resources for care. Then, studies of Vietnam veterans returning from the war (Robins 1974) provided the first opportunity to trace the natural history of heroin use in a more heterogeneous (more "normal") population than just those addicts found in treatment. This research both kindled optimism toward the possibility of cure and shook complacent prejudice about the heroin addict as an unregenerate social outcast. Nevertheless, the punitive images—and public policy to match—have been powerfully resistant to change (Conrad and Schneider 1980).

CROSSCUTTING THEMES AND CONCLUSIONS

Even this distilled and cursory review of propelling and restraining forces in substance "abuse" makes abundantly clear how pronounced a place social factors occupy, not only in the use of drugs but also in policies defining and controlling abuse. On the individual level, studies consistently show that users of one kind of substance (cigarettes or marijuana, for example) are statistically more likely to be or become users of another. The strongest predictor of cocaine use is prior use of marijuana, which also has been shown a harbinger of future heroin use (Clayton 1985). Policies have often been based on the erroneous assumption that such associations are necessarily causal. But learning how risk factors cluster in bundles has led to the thesis that there is an identifiable "risk syndrome" among young people, a mosaic of risk-taking practices, such as early use of alcohol and drugs, precocious sex, careless driving, and such other "unconventional behavior" as delinquency and unsatisfactory academic performance. These findings lay the groundwork for efforts to profile antecedent risk factors (Perry and Jessor 1985).

Sociologists have known for a very long time that social problems like drug addiction find sustenance in subcultures whose norms and values clash with those of the larger society. Yet, some people belonging to subordinate or marginal social groups resist the lure of drugs, and some drug addicts, for example, addicted physicians and other health care workers, stay in conventional society. That leaves still to be explained the "career" of a regular drug user, which has been characterized as a social learning process, with three identifiable stages: (1) being exposed to the drug, (2) being taught how to use it, and (3) becoming physiologically or psychologically addicted, partly as a result of internalizing the reinforcing values, norms, and self-conceptions of a drug-using subculture (Becker 1953). "One chooses one's gods by choosing one's playmates" (Berger 1963), and circumstances often conspire to limit the choice of playmates. Still, even in the most alienated of subgroups only some people take up regular drug use. Which playmates one chooses is the important influence. For prevention policy, efficiencies can theoretically be gained by identifying high-risk populations and targeting resources to them. But the social sorting processes and symbolic functions attached to any drug tend to isolate its regular users from mainstream society, making them easy targets for opprobrium, prejudice, and neglect. In the turbulent 1960s, when President Nixon declared drug abuse "public enemy number one," drugs were standing in as a symbol for the protestors who were the real enemy (Conrad and Schneider 1980, p. 136).

The shape of a given drug policy speaks far more eloquently to the relative status of its users and distributors and to the cultural and economic position it occupies in a particular historical period than to any inherent or necessary health consequences of use and abuse. Cigarettes have been clearly implicated in extensive disability and death; yet they remain legal while users of marijuana, which seems roughly comparable in the hazards it entails, can be jailed for mere possession of the drug, and heroin users are converted into a criminal underclass. Tobacco products arrived on the market and established their social acceptability (and their economic and political power base) in a hospitable climate; marijuana came into wide use during a period of social protest; and it was heroin's misfortune to make its social debut at a time when repressive attitudes toward drugs were holding sway. Now, in a health-conscious culture, as the numbers of smokers decline in response to overwhelmingly strong evidence of hazard and mounting social pressure, they become a minority toward which the nonsmoking majority grows stridently less tolerant. What effects this will have remain to be seen.

We do know that the story of substance abuse policy is riddled with unintended consequences, something sociologists have come to expect (Merton 1968). Brecher documents and laments "the many ways in which laws, policies, and propaganda campaigns serve to encourage a shift from less dangerous to more dangerous drugs" (1972, p. 93), and framers of smoking policy seem stymied at every turn by perverse negative consequences of the best-intentioned efforts to shield the public from harm to health (Walsh and Gordon 1986). Anticipate the unintended is a basic precept sociology can offer policy.

A second guiding precept is to question the premises. Gusfield's writings demonstrate how we delude ourselves into thinking that we want unalloyed fact as a guide to action and then design our studies to pursue some causal chains and ignore others. Smoking research is rife with examples: investigations ascribing lost work time to smoking "rituals" (such as lighting and handling cigarettes), without attention to the possibility that nicotine-dependent workers can concentrate better when they have a cigarette, or to the time-wasting rituals of joggers and other health addicts. The resolute pursuit of evidence of harm to nonsmokers from "second-hand" or "sidestream" smoke (DHHS 1986) belongs in the same category, as does the rush to ascribe to the "fetal alcohol syndrome" a newly discovered class of birth defects that now seems to be associated with a number of maternal habits during pregnancy, not alcohol alone (Hingson et al. 1982). Although we think we have found a neutral utilitarian principle that justifies government intervention when one individual's behavior harms an "innocent" other (Mill 1871), we must recognize how biased we can be in accumulating scientific evidence to substantiate that case (MacIntyre 1977).

In the end, the questions to guide policy must probe to underlying values. What kind of society do we want to forge? What weight will we accord alternative desiderata—health conservation, public order, and individual self-determination? How, through it all, will we strike a tenable balance between the competing dystopias Fuchs (1974) aptly described: the "jungle" of unfettered individualism that abrogates security and order, or the "zoo" of lockstep collectivity that denies individual autonomy and self-actualization? Substance abuse provides fertile ground for sorting those issues out, while sociology supplies fundamental concepts for approaching the inquiry with an open and critical mind.

ACKNOWLEDGMENTS

Support from the Commonwealth Fund, the National Institute on Alcohol Abuse and Alcoholism, the Pew Memorial Trust, and the General Electric Foundation is gratefully acknowledged. I also acknowledge intellectual debts to the authors of the substance abuse chapter in the previous edition of the *Handbook of Medical Sociology*, especially Ralph W. Hingson whose thinking on the alcohol problem has strongly influenced my own. Susan Silbey and Sol Levine provided helpful critiques of an early draft.

REFERENCES

Aaron, Paul, and David Musto. 1981. Temperance and Prohibition in America: A Historical Overview, in Mark H. Moore and Dean R. Gerstein, eds., *Alcohol and Public Policy: Beyond the Shadow of Prohibition*. Washington, D.C.: National Academy Press, pp. 127–181.

Adams, Edgar, and Nicholas J. Kozel. 1985. Cocaine Use in America, in their *Cocaine Use in America: Epidemiologic and Clinical Perspectives*. NIDA Research Monograph 61. Rockville, Md.: National Institute on Drug Abuse, pp. 1–8.

Arnold, Charles B., ed. 1987. Alcohol Use in the United States. *Metropolitan Life Statistical Bulletin* 68(1):20–25.

Backman, Jerald G., Lloyd D. Johnston, and Patrick O'Malley. 1981. Smoking, Drinking, and Drug Use among American High School Students. *American Journal of Public Health* 71(1):59–69.

Baker, Susan, P., Stephen P. Teret, and Erich M. Daub. 1987. Injuries, in Sol Levine and Abraham M. Lilienfeld, eds., *Epidemiology and Health Policy*. New York: Tavistock Publications, pp.177–206.

Bales, Robert F. 1945. Cultural Differences in Rates of Alcoholism. *Quarterly Journal of Studies on Alcohol* 6:480–499.

Beauchamp, Dan E. 1980. *Beyond Alcoholism*. Philadelphia: Temple University Press.

Becker, Howard S. 1953. *Outsiders: Studies in the Sociology of Deviance*. New York: Free Press.

Berger, Peter. 1963. *Invitation to Sociology*. New York: Anchor.

Blacker, Edward. 1966. Sociocultural Factors in Alcoholism. *International Clinical Psychiatry* 3(2):51–80.

Brecker, Edward M. 1972. *Licit and Illicit Drugs*. Mount Vernon, N.Y.: Consumers' Union.

Bruun, Kettil, Griffith Edwards, Martti Lumio, Klaus Makela, Lynn Pan, Robert E. Popham, Robin Room, Wolfgang Schmidt, Ole-Jorgen Skog, Pekka Sulkunen, and Esa Osterberg. 1975. *Alcohol Control Policies in Public Health Perspective*. New Brunswick, N.J.: Rutgers Center for Alcohol Studies.

Chambers, Carl D., James A. Inciardi, and Harvey A. Siegal. 1975. *Chemical Coping*. New York: Spectrum Publications.

Christie, Nils. 1981. Foreword, in K. Makela et al., eds., *Alcohol, Society and the State: A Comparative Study of Alcohol Control*. Toronto: Addiction Research Foundation, pp. xii–xvii.

Clark, Norman H., 1976. *Deliver Us from Evil: An Interpretation of American Prohibition*. New York: Norton, pp. 8–34.

Clausen, John A. 1961. Drug Addiction, in Robert K. Merton and Robert A. Nisbet, eds., *Contemporary Social Problems*. New York: Harcourt, Brace and World, pp. 181–221.

Clayton, Richard R. 1985. Cocaine Use in the United States: In a Blizzard or Just Being Snowed? In Nicholas J. Kozel and Edgar H. Adams, *Cocaine Use in America: Epidemiologic and Clinical Perspectives*. NIDA Research Monograph 61. Rockville, Md.: National Institute on Drug Abuse, pp. 8–34.

Conrad, Peter, and Joseph W. Schneider. 1980. *Deviance and Medicalization*. St. Louis: Mosby.

Cook, Philip J. 1981. The Effect of Liquor Taxes on Drinking, Cirrhosis, and Auto Accidents, in Mark H. Moore and Dean R. Gerstein, eds., *Alcohol and Public Policy: Beyond the Shadow of Prohibition*. Washington, D.C.: National Academy Press, pp. 255–285.

Cook, Philip J., and George Tauchen. 1984. The Effect of Minimum Drinking Age Legislation on Youthful Auto Fatalities, 1970–1977. *Journal of Legal Studies* (January):169–190.

Fillmore, Kaye Middleton. 1986. Issues in the Changing Drinking Patterns among Women in the Last Century, in *Women and Alcohol: Health-Related Issues*. Rockville, Md.: National Institute on Alcohol Abuse and Alcoholism, pp. 69–77.

Fuchs, Victor R. 1974. *Who Shall Live?* New York: Basic Books.

Glaser, Frederick B., Stephanie W. Greenberg, and Morris Barret. 1978. *A Systems Approach to Alcohol Treatment*. Toronto: Addiction Research Foundation.

Goode, Erich. 1972. *Drugs in American Society*. New York: Knopf.

Gusfield, Joseph R. 1963. *Symbolic Crusade: Status Politics and the American Temperance Movement*. Westport, Conn.: Greenwood Press.

———. 1981. *The Culture of Public Problems: Drinking-Driving and the Symbolic Order*. Chicago: University of Chicago Press.

Hingson, Ralph W., Joel Alpert, Nancy Day, Elizabeth Dooling, Herbert Kayne, Suzette Morelock, Edgar Oppenheimer, and Barry Zuckerman. 1982. Effects of Maternal Drinking and Marijuana on Fetal Growth and Development. *Pediatrics* 70(4):539–546.

Hingson, Ralph, Tom Mangione, Allan Meyers, and Norman Scotch. 1982. Seeking Help for Drinking Problems: A Study in the Boston Metropolitan Area. *Journal of Studies on Alcohol* 43(3):273–288.

Jessor, Richard, 1979. Marihuana: A Review of Recent Psychosocial Research, in Robert I. DuPont, Avram Goldstein, John O'Donnell, (eds.), *Handbook on Drug Abuse*. Rockville, Md.: National Institute on Drug Abuse, pp. 337–56.

Kandel, Denise. 1980. Drug and Drinking Behavior among Youth. *Annual Review of Sociology* 6:235–285.

Kandel, Denise, and John A. Logan. 1984. Patterns of Drug Use from Adolescence to Young Adulthood: I. Periods of Risk for Initiation, Continued Use, and Discontinuation. *American Journal of Public Health* 74(7):660–667.

Kozel, Nicholas J., and Edgar H. Adams. 1985. *Cocaine Use in America: Epidemiologic and Clinical Perspectives*. NIDA Research Monograph 61. Rockville, Md.: National Institute on Drug Abuse.

Lemert, Edwin M. 1972. *Human Deviance, Social Problems, and Social Control*. Englewood Cliffs, N.J.: Prentice-Hall.

Lieber, James. 1986. Coping with Cocaine. *The Atlantic*, January:39–48.

MacIntyre, Alasdair. 1977. Utilitarianism and Cost Benefit Analysis, in Kenneth Sayre, ed., *Values in the Electrical Power Industry*. Notre Dame, Indiana: University of Notre Dame Press, pp. 217–237.

Makela, Klaus, Esa Osterberg, and Pekka Sulkunen. 1981. Drink in Finland: Increasing Alcohol Availability in a Monopoly State, in Eric Single, Patricia Morgan and Jan de Lint, eds., *Alcohol, Society, and the State: The Social History of Control Policies in Seven Countries.* Toronto: Addiction Research Foundation, pp. 31–61.

Makela, Klaus, Robin Room, Eric Single, Pekka Sulkunen, and Brendan Walsh, eds., 1981. *Alcohol, Society and the State: A Comparative Study of Alcohol Control.* Toronto: Addiction Research Foundation.

May, Philip A. 1986. Alcohol and Drug Misuse Prevention Programs for American Indians: Need and Opportunities. *Journal of Studies on Alcohol* 47(3):187–195.

Merton, Robert K. 1968. *Social Theory and Social Structure.* New York: Free Press.

Mill, John Stuart. [1871] 1977. Utilitarianism, in Stanley Joel Reiser, Arthur J. Dyck, and William J. Curran, eds., *Ethics in Medicine.* Cambridge, Mass.: MIT Press, pp. 79–87.

Moore, Mark H., and Dean R. Gerstein. 1981. *Alcohol and Public Policy: Beyond the Shadow of Prohibition.* Washington, D.C.: National Academy Press.

O'Malley, Patrick M., Lloyd D. Johnston, and Jerald G. Bachman. 1985. Cocaine Use Among American Adolescents and Young Adults, in Nicholas J. Kozel and Edgar H. Adams, *Cocaine Use in America: Epidemiologic and Clinical Perspectives.* NIDA Research Monograph 61. Rockville, Md.: National Institute on Drug Abuse, pp. 50–75.

Perry, Cheryl, and Richard H. Jessor. 1985. The Concept of Health Promotion and the Prevention of Adolescent Drug Use. *Health Education Quarterly* 12:169–184.

President's Commission on Organized Crime. 1986. *America's Habit: Drug Abuse, Drug Trafficking, and Organized Crime.* Report to the President and Attorney General. Washington, D.C.: U.S. Government Printing Office.

Robins, Lee N., 1974. *The Vietnam User Returns.* Final Report. Special Action Office. Monograph Series A., No 2. Washington, D.C.: U.S. Government Printing Office.

Robins, Lee N. 1980. Alcoholism and Labeling Theory, in David Mechanic, ed., *Readings in Medical Sociology.* New York: Free Press, pp. 188–198.

Ross, H. Laurence. 1982. *Deterring the Drinking Driver.* Lexington, Mass.: Lexington Books.

Saxe, Leonard. 1983. *The Effectiveness and Costs of Alcoholism Treatment.* Health Technology Case Study 22. Washington, D.C.: Office of Technology Assessment.

Slaby, Andrew E. 1985. Foreword, in Mark A. Schuckit, ed., *Alcohol Patterns and Problems.* New Brunswick, N.J.: Rutgers University Press, pp. xi–xv.

Ullman, A. D. 1958. Sociocultural Backgrounds of Alcoholism, *Annals of the American Academy of Political and Social Science* 351:48–54.

United States Department of Health and Human Services (DHHS). 1983. *Fifth Special Report to the U.S. Congress on Alcohol and Health.* Rockville, Md.: National Institute on Alcohol Abuse and Alcoholism.

———. 1987. *The Health Consequences of Involuntary Smoking.* A Report of the Surgeon General. Rockville, Md.: Office of Smoking and Health.

Vaillant, George E. 1983. *The Natural History of Alcoholism.* Cambridge, Mass.: Harvard University Press.

Walsh, Diana Chapman, and Nancy P. Gordon. 1986. Legal Approaches to Smoking Deterrence. *Annual Review of Public Health* 7:127–149.

Walsh, Diana Chapman, and Ralph W. Hingson. 1987. Epidemiology and Alcohol Policy, in Sol Levine and Abraham M. Lilienfeld, eds., *Epidemiology and Health Policy.* Tavistock Publications, pp. 265–291.

Wesson, Donald, and David E. Smith. 1985. Cocaine: Treatment Perspectives, in Nicholas J. Kozel and Edgar H. Adams, *Cocaine Use in America: Epidemiologic and Clinical Perspectives.* NIDA Research Monograph 61. Rockville, Md.: National Institute on Drug Abuse, pp. 193–203.

Wiseman, Jacqueline P. 1970. *Stations of the Lost.* Chicago: University of Chicago Press.

Wisotsky, Steven. 1983. Exposing the War on Cocaine: The Futility and Destructiveness of Prohibition. *Wisconsin Law Review* 6:1305–1426.

CHAPTER
8

TRENDS IN THE ORGANIZATION OF HEALTH SERVICES

RONALD M. ANDERSEN
ROSS M. MULLNER

This chapter examines the "organization" of health services from both a micro and a macro perspective. It describes major organizations that make up the U.S. health services system and the relationships among them, and it discusses trends in their size, form, and function.

The micro perspective will document the extent to which the delivery of health services is becoming more a group and less of an individual process. The group process requires more rules to coordinate people, capital, and technology in the delivery of services. It requires more "organization" in the micro sense. Many different micro organization forms are required to meet the various demands for health care in the United States.

From the macro perspective, these various organizations must also be coordinated. This combination of organizations directed toward maintaining or improving the health of the population is commonly referred to as the health services system.

Health care organizations can be classified according to the functions they perform in contributing to the achievement of the goals of the health services system. We will assume these are necessary functions in any health services system. What changes with time and place are the type of people and organizations that perform these functions. Table 1 summarizes these necessary functions of providing direct service and support and the types of organizations that fulfill them. Service organizations are defined as those that directly treat populations to maintain or improve health. Supportive and ancillary organizations are defined as those organizations that provide inputs required to maintain service organizations.

All of these functions of service and support were necessarily performed in the

TABLE 1 Functions, Definitions, and Major Categories of Health Care Organizations

Function	Definition	Categories
I. Direct service	Directly treating populations to maintain or improve health	1. Individual patient based 2. Community based
II. Supportive and ancillary	Supply or maintain service organizations	1. Finance 2. Suppliers 3. Regulation 4. Representation 5. Research 6. Consulting

past as well. The difference is the new organizational forms emerging to perform these functions today and tomorrow. As we shall see, the trend is toward larger and more complex organizations.

The rapidity of change in health care organizations can be better understood in the context of an increasingly dynamic environment represented by demography, technology, methods of finance, and societal norms. The health care system must respond to an aging population, increasingly complex chronic conditions (e.g., Alzheimer's disease), and menacing new acute diseases (e.g., acquired immune deficiency syndrome [AIDS]). Health care organizations are continually adjusting to rapid technological development and attendant needs for new personnel, facilities, and capital. Health care providers are being required to deal with payment systems that can be increasingly characterized as competitive, prospective, and restrictive. Finally, society's views of the ways health care organizations should and do function may be characterized as less trusting and more demanding. Further, while governmental and other sources of funding the care of the medically indigent decline, societal expectations remain that health care organizations will somehow provide needed services to all citizens regardless of their ability to pay.

Because this volatile environment stimulates organizational change and even de-

mands it if health care organizations are to survive, let alone thrive, we believe an open systems perspective (Thompson 1967) emphasizing the importance of the environment and its interaction with the organization is most useful for examining organization trends in health services (Shortell and Kaluzny 1987). In part, organization response will be "rational" as the organization seeks to modify itself, its environment, or both to achieve its ends. We also feel "natural" selection is useful in understanding that certain organization forms will emerge, survive, and thrive because they are best suited to deal with changing environmental conditions, while other forms are destined to have major problems no matter how skillful their managerial strategy might be (Hannan and Freeman 1984; Alexander, Kaluzny, and Middleton 1986).

Trends in service and supportive organizations will be described according to time periods, size, and number of organizations and organization type. Time periods include pre–Medicare and Medicaid (after World War II to 1964), emphasizing quality of care and facility development; post–Medicare and Medicaid (1965 to the late 1970s), emphasizing access to care; and the cost-containment era (from the late 1970s to the present). We label the type of organizations as traditional, transitional, and emergent. The traditional health care organizations were dominant in the pre–Medicare era. Transitional organizations are generally modifications of traditional forms. Although they may have been observed in the pre-Medicare era, their significant growth started largely in the post-Medicare era. The emergent organizations are usually more radical departures from the traditional organization forms. Their important growth is largely in the cost-containment era, and continued growth is projected for many of them in the future. In the final section of this chapter we will consider likely future trends that will affect health care organizations.

DIRECT SERVICES ORGANIZATIONS

Health care organizations providing services can be oriented toward individual patients or can be community based. The latter historically focused on provision of a sanitary environment, including pure air, water, and food; control of communicable disease through mass immunization; and preventive health services. Primary organizations for providing community or public health services are the state and local health departments, which number over 3,000. In recent years much of the work of local health departments has been toward direct patient service. Over one-half of the funds allocated to local health departments in 1982 were for personal health services, including maternal and child health, communicable diseases, crippled children, and mental health services. About 10 percent was allocated to environmental services (Shortell and Kaluzny 1987).

Organizations that provide individual patient services make up most of the health care delivery system. They can be divided into those that emphasize primary, acute, and long-term care. Primary care services are mostly ambulatory. They are directed toward prevention, health maintenance, and disease detection. Acute care is aimed at curing the ill or injured patient. It includes the most sophisticated medical technology, which is generally provided to inpatients in general acute care hospitals. Long-term care is aimed at chronically ill and disabled patients. It seeks to return the patient to a former or higher level of functioning. When rehabilitation is unrealistic, custodial and palliative services are provided.

Table 2 classifies individual patient care organizations according to the kind of care they are most likely to provide, as well as by organizational type and time period when the organization became a significant

TABLE 2 Individual Patient Care Organizations by Type and Time Period

	Time Period		
Type	*Traditional (World War II–1964)*	*Transitional (1965–late 1970s)*	*Emergent (late 1970s–present)*
Primary care organizations (ambulatory services)	Physician solo, partnership, group practices Hospital outpatient department Clinic/emergency room	HMO group HMO staff Community Health Center	Emergi centers Urgi centers PPOs; HMO-IPAs HMO-network Sponsored primary care centers
Acute care organizations (acute hospital services)	Single-nonprofit hospital Single proprietary hospital Public and religious hospital systems	Affiliations Corporate investor-owned multihospital systems Hospital shared services	Vertically integrate multihospital systems High technology diagnostic centers
Long-term care organizations (rehabilitation, nurturing, and palliative services)	Nursing home Extended care Personal care Rehabilitation services	Home care Hospice care	Adult day care

TABLE 3   Number and Percent of Physicians in Group Practices, United States, 1969, 1975, 1980, and 1984

Year	Number of Physicians	Percent of Total
1969	40,093	17.6
1975	66,842	23.5
1980	88,290	26.2
1984	125,135	28.4

Source: American Medical Association, 1971, 1976, 1982, 1985, *Medical Groups in the United States*, Chicago: The Association.

force in the health services system. This classification scheme is far from exact but is rather of "the more or less" variety. It is intended to aid the reader in visualizing the organizational dynamics of the health services system and provide a framework for the following discussion.

Primary Care Organizations

Physicians traditionally practiced by themselves or in partnership with another doctor. However, a number of forces are associated with movement toward larger partnerships and other forms of group practice. These include the large capital investment needed to start a practice, rapid growth of medical knowledge and technology requiring increased cooperation among physicians, and an expanding physician supply resulting in more competition among physicians for patients.

Table 3 shows how the proportion of physicians practicing in group settings increased in recent years to reach 28 percent in 1984. While there is little doubt about the movement toward larger and more complex forms of physician practice, the number of physicians that results in a substantive change in the nature of the practice from solo to group is debated. Table 3 uses the American Medical Association definition of group practice, which is three or more physicians sharing facilities and ancillary personnel with a formal agreement for the distribution of revenues from the practice. Another point of view represented by Friedson is that "a minimum of five full-time physicians—not all of them

providing primary care—would seem to be of analytical significance" (Friedson 1979, p. 302). According to this latter perspective, 45.2 percent of the private practice physicians were in group practices in 1984 (AMA 1985).

Hospital-sponsored ambulatory care is a traditional alternative source to physicians in private practice for primary care. Table 4 shows changes in visits to these facilities through 1985. Emergency department visits, which grew rapidly in the 1960s and 1970s, have leveled off in recent years. In contrast, visits to organized outpatient departments have continued to grow substantially. Visits for ambulatory surgery, while still a relatively small proportion of all visits to hospital facilities, show by far the largest rate of growth as they more than doubled between 1980 and 1985. This trend reflects new technology that allows procedures that formerly required inpatient admissions to be performed on an outpatient basis and efforts by the hospitals to cut costs and compete with emergent organizational types also performing surgery on an outpatient basis.

The most important transitional organizational form of ambulatory care is the health maintenance organization (HMO). The key features of an HMO are prepayment for a specified period of time, which guarantees enrollees service at little or no payment at the time of service and comprehensive coverage of a range of inpatient and outpatient services.

HMOs existed long before the post-Medicare era (well-known ones include Kaiser Permanente in northern California,

TABLE 4   Trends in Total and Type of Visits to Hospital-Sponsored Ambulatory Care Facilities, United States, 1965, 1975, 1980–1985

Year	Total Number of Outpatient Visits (in thousands)						
1965	125,793						
1975	254,844						
1980	262,951						
1985	282,140						

Type of Visits* (in thousands)	1980	1981	1982	1983	1984	1985	Percent Change, 1980–1985
Ambulatory surgery	3,207	3,715	4,275	4,987	5,827	6,086	112.2
Emergency department	82,293	81,107	79,659	79,190	78,762	81,623	− 0.1
Clinic	40,150	39,003	40,462	42,940	41,150	40,556	− 0.1
Organized outpatient department	217,794	220,896	223,377	229,557	232,831	242,377	11.3

*The totals for types of visits exceed the total outpatient visits above for the same years because the types are not mutually exclusive and probably include some visits to facilities not included in the total outpatient count.

Source: American Hospital Association, 1986, *Hospital Statistics 1986*. Chicago: The Association; American Hospital Association, 1986, Hospital-Sponsored Ambulatory Care Utilization Trends, 1980–1985, *Outreach* 7(2):35.

Health Insurance Plan in New York, and Ross Loos in Los Angeles), but the significant growth in enrollment, which has made the prepayment plans a national force, has occurred in the post-Medicare and cost-containment eras. Growth has been stimulated by federal government support, the popularity of first-dollar coverage among consumers, and, most importantly, by the belief on the part of third-party payers that prepayment can be a cost-containment mechanism.

Table 5 shows the growth in the number of HMO plans and enrollment from 1970 to 1985. By 1985 there were 480 plans, insuring 21 million people. Currently, about 9 percent of the population are enrolled in HMOs, with the proportion much higher in some areas such as Minneapolis–

St. Paul (50 percent) and the metropolitan areas of California.

There are a number of different types of HMOs. The "classic" forms include the staff and group models. Forms that have emerged more recently include the independent practice association (IPA) and the network model. These models differ from each other in the way physicians are organized and reimbursed.

Physicians are salaried employees of the HMO in the staff model. Groups of physicians contract with the HMO and determine their own internal method of reimbursement in the group model. Generally, physicians in the staff model practice in larger and more organized settings than in the group model.

Although we have identified the IPA as

TABLE 5   Number of HMO plans and enrollees: United States, 1970, 1975, 1980, and 1985

Year	Number of HMO Plans	Number of Enrollees (in millions)
1970	26	2.9
1975	166	5.8
1980	236	9.1
1985	480	21.0

Source: InterStudy, 1986, personal communication with Ms. Laura Pitts, Excelsior, Minn., 1986.

TABLE 6   Number and percent of HMO Enrollees by HMO model type: United States, 1984 and 1985

Model Type	1984		1985	
	Number (in millions)	Percent	Number (in millions)	Percent
IPA	7.8	41	9.7	46
Network	3.6	19	4.6	22
Group	4.3	23	3.8	18
Staff	3.2	17	2.9	14
Total	18.9	100	21.0	100

Source: InterStudy, 1986, personal communication with Ms. Laura Pitts, Excelsior, Minn.

an emergent form, medical foundations, which are forerunners of the rapidly expanding IPAs of today, have existed on the West Coast for some decades. In the IPA, private practitioners working out of their own offices contract with the HMO to provide physician services at negotiated fees and usually bear some financial risk if the fees exceed the budget of the HMO. The IPA benefits the patient who wishes to maintain an established relationship with a physician in a private practice setting and allows the physician more autonomy and the possibility of practicing in a less bureaucraticized environment.

The network model is based on contracts between the HMO and a number (or network) of multispecialty group practice clinics that provide care on a prepaid basis to a defined group of enrollees.

Table 6 shows the numbers of persons enrolled in each type of HMO and recent growth patterns between 1984 and 1985. The emergent HMOs (IPA and network) grew at substantial rates during this period and together accounted for 68 percent of all HMO enrollees in 1985. In contrast, transitional forms (group and staff) actually had a net loss of members between 1984 and 1985 and had only one-third of HMO members in 1985.

Another transitional organizational form of ambulatory care is the Community Health Center (CHC). A successor to the Neighborhood Health Centers Program established by the Office of Economic Opportunity in the 1960s, this federally sponsored program is designed to provide primary care services to communities and individuals with limited access to care because other providers are not available or they lack the means to pay for services. The CHC is then a safety net to catch people who "fall through the cracks" of other public and private programs, including the unemployed, uninsured, migrant workers, minorities, and the poor. CHCs are staffed by full-time salaried physicians and provide a wide range of preventive and curative services.

Table 7 shows that the number of CHC projects grew consistently from 157 in 1974 to 872 in 1982 and then declined to 590 in 1985. Similarly, the number of CHC users increased from 1.2 million in 1974 to 6 million in 1982 and then declined to 4.9 million in 1985. Federal appropriations during the entire period from 1974 to 1985 appeared to increase, using current dollars, but adjustment for inflation shows appropriations considerably less at the end of the period than at the beginning.

The era of cost constraint not only limited federal appropriations but also brought pressures on the CHCs to increase project collections from other payers. Table 7 shows that revenues from other payers increased from 17.4 percent of the total in 1974 to 52 percent in 1985. In 1985 the largest of these other payers included Medicaid (14 percent of total revenues), state and local contributions (13 percent), and patient fees (10 percent).

Emergent forms of ambulatory care or-

TABLE 7   Number of Community Health Centers, Number of Users, Federal Appropriations, and Percent of Other Sources of Revenues, United States, 1974, 1978, 1980, 1982, 1984, and 1985

Category	1974	1978	1980	1982	1984	1985
Number of centers	157	591	872	872	590	590
Number of users (in millions)	1.2	3.0	4.2	6.0	4.9	4.9
Federal appropriations (current dollars in millions)	$197	$247	$320	$281	$351	$383
Federal appropriations (constant 1974 dollars in millions)	$197	$169	$181	$128	$139	$130
Percentage of Revenues from First and Third Parties						
Medicare	NA	2.3	2.5	4.9	4.7	5.0
Medicaid	NA	12.4	13.3	15.6	14.6	14.0
Title XX	NA	0.3	0.3	0.5	0.5	1.0
Private insurance	NA	6.5	7.0	NA	NA	NA
Other third party	NA	3.2	3.4	7.0	6.7	7.0
Patient fees	NA	12.5	13.5	11.4	10.0	10.0
State/local	NA	NA	NA	15.9	15.4	13.0
Total	17.4	37.2	40.0	55.3	52.0	52.0

Source: L. A. Aday and R. Andersen, 1981, Equity of Access to Medical Care: A Conceptual and Empirical Overview, *Medical Care* 19 (Supp.):22; Health Care Finance Administration, Department of Health and Human Services, 1987, Personal communication with Mr. Michael Millman, Baltimore, Md.

ganizations in addition to the newer forms of HMOs include Preferred Provider Organizations (PPOs) and freestanding surgical and ambulatory care centers. PPOs are private physicians, hospitals, and other providers who contract with large employers and insurance companies to provide services to insured persons. The providers are paid fee for service but discount their prices by some percent of their usual charges (20 percent is a typical discount).

PPO arrangements are most often found in highly competitive areas; physicians join PPOs to maintain and increase their patient base. Insured persons have an incentive to go to the PPOs: If they go to other providers they will not be fully insured and will be required to pay a larger proportion (up to $2,000 or more) out-of-pocket. Table 8 shows that the number of PPOs in the country grew from only 5 in 1981 to 371 in 1986.

Table 9 illustrates that freestanding centers also grew rapidly in the 1980s. "Freestanding" means that the centers are not on the hospital campus and traditionally are not owned or sponsored by hospitals. These centers grew as competitive options to private doctors and hospitals. They were more likely than private doctors to have

TABLE 8 Number of PPOs and Number of Persons with the Option Available to them, United States, 1981–1986

Year	Number of PPOs	Number of Persons with Option Available to Them (in millions)
1981	5	—
1982	42	—
1983	73	—
1984	143	—
1985	325	5.5
1986	371	17.1

Source: American Association of Preferred Provider Organizations, 1986, Personal communication with Mr. Mark Abe, Alexandria, Va.

convenient evening and weekend hours. They were usually less expensive than hospitals because they emphasized ambulatory surgery rather than requiring an inpatient admission for surgery. Other ambulatory visits were also less expensive than visits to emergency rooms and hospital outpatient clinics because the freestanding centers had simpler facilities and equipment and lower overhead costs.

Table 9 shows that the number of freestanding outpatient surgery centers almost doubled from 1983 to 1985. In 1985, 459 "surgicenters" performed some 783,864 procedures. Freestanding ambulatory care centers show similar rapid expansion (Table 9). The number increased from 600 in 1982 to an estimated 3,000 in 1985.

There is evidence that hospitals are responding to these competitive pressures from emerging ambulatory care organizations. A recent study of the starting date and ownership of 212 ambulatory care centers suggests that the ambulatory care market is evolving from one dominated by physician ownership to one dominated by hospital and nonphysician ownership (Table 10). Thus, among centers opening four or more years ago, 36 percent were owned by physician corporations, compared to 20 percent that were hospital affiliated. In contrast, among those opening in 1986, 15 percent were opened by physicians, compared to 30 percent by hospitals.

Hospital interest in ambulatory centers is in keeping with efforts to "vertically inte-

TABLE 9 Number of freestanding ambulatory care centers and freestanding outpatient surgery centers, United States, 1982–1985

Year	Number of Freestanding Ambulatory Care Centers	Number of Freestanding Outpatient Surgery Centers
1982	600	—
1983	1,200	236
1984	2,300	330
1985	3,000*	459

*Projected

Source: National Association of Ambulatory Care Centers, 1986, personal communication with Ms. Ann Stafstrom, Dallas; SMG Marketing Group, Inc., 1986, personal communication with Mr. John Henderson, Chicago.

TABLE 10 Ownership of Ambulatory Care Centers by Months in Operation, United States, 1986 (in percent)

	Months in Operation				
Ownership	*1–12*	*13–23*	*24–35*	*36–47*	*48 +*
Physician corporation	15.1	33.4	26.4	32.2	36.0
Nonphysician corporation	27.3	20.8	21.0	25.0	18.0
Hospital affiliated	30.4	18.7	23.7	10.7	20.0
Professional association	12.1	14.6	13.1	14.3	16.0
Single physician	15.1	12.5	15.8	17.8	10.0
Total	100.0	100.0	100.0	100.0	100.0

Source: Joyce Riffer, 1986, Hospitals Becoming Driving Force in ACC Market, *Hospitals* 60(23):67. Reprinted by permission from *Hospitals*, Volume 60, No. 23, December 5, 1986, copyright, 1986, American Hospital Publishing, Inc.

grate" services to develop feeder systems to bring in admissions. Further, the ambulatory care centers seem to be evolving from concern primarily with emergency care to focus on more comprehensive primary care practice.

Acute Care Organizations

The hospital is the prime acute health care organization and traditionally has been the focal point of the entire health care system. Since before the pre-Medicare era, it has been a source of community pride and the distributional center for the wonders of medical science and technology. In the post-Medicare era it has benefited from a cost-based reimbursement system.

In all of the eras it has consumed the largest proportion of the health-care dollar, and the price increases for its services have consistently outstripped increases of the general consumer price index. Because of its salience and expense, it has been the object of the major and most stringent efforts to control health care expenses in the cost-containment era and is likely to remain so in the future.

Table 11 shows the major trends in all hospitals from 1946 through 1985. The total number increased through the mid-1970s but has declined in recent years to a total of 6,872 in 1985. The total number of beds began to decline earlier, peaking in the mid-1960s at about 1.7 million and declining thereafter to about 1.3 million in

TABLE 11 Trends among all Hospitals, United States, 1946, 1955, 1965, 1975, 1980, and 1985

Year	Hospitals	Beds (in thousands)	Admissions (in thousands)	Average daily census (in thousands)	Occupancy (percent)	Full-time employed Personnel (in thousands)
1946	6,125	1,436	15,675	1,142	79.5	830
1955	6,956	1,604	21,073	1,363	85.0	1,301
1965	7,123	1,704	28,812	1,403	82.3	1,952
1975	7,156	1,466	36,157	1,125	76.7	3,023
1980	6,965	1,365	38,892	1,060	77.7	3,492
1985	6,872	1,318	36,304	910	69.0	3,625

Source: American Hospital Association, 1986, *Hospital Statistics 1986*, Chicago: The Association.

1985. Total number of admissions continued to increase throughout the period, but the rate of increase slowed in the last decade. There was a total of 36.3 million admissions in 1985. In recent years both occupancy rates and average length of stay have declined. In contrast, number of employed personnel has continued to rise, as has the average number of personnel per patient day.

Traditional organizational forms of hospitals include: solo nongovernment not-for-profit hospitals, solo proprietary (for-profit) hospitals, state or local government-owned public hospitals, and regional hospital systems often under religious ownership. For-profit hospitals and hospital systems might be thought of today as transitional or emergent organization forms, but some types of them existed tra-

ditionally. The modal proprietary hospital in the pre-Medicare era was a solo hospital of modest size often owned by physicians. Also, systems of hospitals owned by Catholic religious orders have been a significant part of the community hospital picture for many years.

Table 12 shows trends in hospital characteristics according to ownership. Nongovernmental not-for-profit hospitals make up the bulk of general hospitals (58 percent) and hospital beds (71 percent). Growth in the numbers of these hospitals has declined from a high point in the 1960s. As smaller hospitals close or consolidate, average size of these hospitals grows. Their trends in beds, admissions, average daily census, and personnel are similar to those for all general hospitals since they dominate the scene.

TABLE 12 Trends among Nongovernment Not-for-Profit, Investor-Owned, State and Local Government Short-term General and Other Special Hospitals, United States, 1946, 1955, 1965, 1975, 1980, and 1985

Year	Hospital	Beds (in thousands)	Admission (in thousands)	Average Daily Census (in thousands)	Occupancy (percent)	Full-Time Employed Personnel (in thousands)
Nongovernment Not-for-Profit						
1946	2,584	301	9,554	231	76.7	362
1955	3,097	389	13,875	285	73.0	597
1965	3,426	515	19,001	401	77.8	1,011
1975	3,364	659	23,735	510	77.4	1,714
1980	3,339	693	25,576	542	78.2	2,087
1985	3,364	708	24,188	476	67.2	2,217
Investor-Owned (For-Profit)						
1946	1,076	39	1,408	25	64.1	35
1955	1,020	37	1,459	22	59.5	41
1965	857	47	1,844	32	68.6	70
1975	775	73	2,646	48	65.9	139
1980	730	87	3,165	57	65.2	189
1985	805	104	3,242	54	52.1	221
State and Local Government						
1946	785	133	2,694	84	63.2	108
1955	1,120	142	3,766	100	70.4	188
1965	1,453	179	5,617	131	72.8	306
1975	1,840	215	7,138	150	69.7	546
1980	1,835	212	7,458	150	70.7	602
1985	1,616	191	6,071	120	62.8	565

Source: American Hospital Association, 1986, *Hospital Statistics 1986*, Chicago: The Association.

While investor-owned hospitals are receiving much publicity, they still account for only 14 percent of the hospitals and 10 percent of the beds (Table 12). They have, however, been the growth segment of the industry in the last decade, particularly according to number of beds (42 percent growth) and admissions (18 percent growth). Investor-owned hospitals differ from the nongovernmental not-for-profits by their smaller average size (129 beds vs. 210 beds), lower average occupancy rate (51 percent vs. 67 percent), and fewer personnel per occupied bed (4.1 vs. 4.7).

State and local government hospitals have been the declining segment of general hospital care in the last decade. These hospitals have traditionally been a major source of care for the poor and still in 1985 accounted for 18 percent of all admissions to nonfederal short-term general hospitals. However, in the last decade the number of state and local government hospitals declined by 12 percent, and the number of admissions to them dropped by 15 percent (Table 12).

The transitional organization forms for acute care services are generally the result of joint actions, mergers, or consolidations on the part of hospitals. They represent efforts by hospitals to ensure their viability or at least survival. They are intended to achieve economies of scale, improve ability to raise capital, increase political power, and increase access to technology and managerial expertise.

These transitional forms range along a continuum according to the degree individual organizations are integrated with and subject to a parent or corporate body or maintain their own organizational autonomy. From the least to most integrated are shared service organizations, consortia, contract-managed multisystem units, and multisystem units that are owned, leased, or sponsored.

Shared-service organizations are separate legal entities established by two or more hospitals to allow the joint or cooperative use of administrative, clinical, or service functions. Table 13 shows that of 144 shared-service organizations identified in the United States, three-quarters were established since 1970. The majority of general hospitals apparently have one or more shared-service contracts. In 1985 the most common contract was for medical/surgical supply purchasing (3,647 contracts, Fine 1986). Other common joint purchasing agreements include those for medical equipment, laboratory supplies, office equipment, furniture, nonmedical equipment, pharmaceuticals, X-ray film, educational services, and microcomputers.

Consortia are alliances in which individual hospitals voluntarily give up certain

TABLE 13 Year Hospital-Shared Services Organizations and Consortia Were Founded, United States, 1950–1984

Year	Shared Services Organizations		Consortia	
	Number	*Percent*	*Number*	*Percent*
Before 1950	5	3.5	1	1.5
1950–1957	2	1.4	1	1.5
1960–1969	28	19.4	3	4.5
1970–1979	91	63.2	51	76.1
1980–1984	18	12.5	11	16.4
Total	144	100.0	67	100.0

Source: American Hospital Association, 1984, *Directory of Shared Services Organizations and Consortia of Health Care Institutions*, Chicago: The Association.

rights to the consortia with expectations of gaining advantages in purchases, management, and capital accumulation. The largest and best known of the consortia includes the Voluntary Hospitals of America (VHA), with 571 hospitals and more than 157,000 beds. Consortia such as VHA whose members span two or more states are defined as multistate alliances by the American Hospital Association (1986). Table 13 shows there were sixty-seven consortia in 1984, with three-quarters of them formed in the 1970s.

The most integrated forms of multi-institutional arrangements are the multihospital systems. One form is contract management in which the managing organization has responsibility for the general day-to-day management of the hospital and reports directly to the board of trustees or owners of the managed organization. The board, however, retains total legal responsibility and ownership of the facility's assets and liabilities. The most organized form of multihospital system is one in which the umbrella or managing organization actually owns, leases, or sponsors the hospital. In this case the managing organization not only manages the hospital but assumes legal responsibility and control of the facility's assets and liabilities.

Table 14 shows that multihospital systems grew from 59 in 1950 to 267 in 1980. The number actually declined to 249 in 1985, with mergers of systems and buy outs of one system by another accounting

for the decrease. Over 2,000 hospitals—more than one-third of all short-term hospitals—are in multihospital systems. Although the number of systems declined between 1980 and 1985, the number of hospitals and the number of beds in systems continued to grow during that period.

About 75 percent of the hospitals in multihospital systems are owned, leased, or sponsored. The remainder are contract managed. Contract management is a more recent form, first coming on the scene in the 1970s. While the opportunity for large profits is limited for the management company, the company is not at risk for the hospital's risks and liabilities. Contract management also gives the managing company a trial period to train personnel and determine if it wishes to purchase the managed hospital. Contract management is most common for state and local government hospitals: In 1984, 18 percent were contract managed, compared to 11 percent of the nongovernment not-for-profit and 6 percent of the investor-owned hospitals (American Hospital Association 1984).

Table 15 shows that while investor-owned multihospital systems are largest according to the number of hospitals in the systems (842), Catholic systems are, on average, considerably larger than those of any other system. Other non-profit systems including both state and local, and nongovernmental systems account for about one-quarter of both hospitals and beds in systems. Non-Catholic church systems have

TABLE 14 Trends in Multihospital Systems, United States, 1950, 1960, 1970, and 1985

| Year | Number of Multihospital Systems | Number of Hospitals in Multihospital Systems | | | Percent of all U.S. Hospitals |
		Owned, Leased, or Sponsored	Contact Managed	Total	
1950	59	261	0	261	4.5
1960	76	331	3	334	6.2
1970	123	578	14	592	10.1
1980	267	1,400	397	1,797	30.4
1985	249	1,564	486	2,050	35.4

Source: American Hospital Association, 1985, *Data Book on Multihospital Systems 1980–1985*, Chicago: The Association.

TABLE 15   Hospitals and Beds in Multihospital Systems by Type of System, United States, 1985

| | Hospitals | | | Beds | | |
Type of System	Number	Percent of all Systems	Percent of all Community Hospitals	Number (in thousands)	Percent of all Systems	Percent of all Community Hospitals
Catholic Church	519	25	9	139	37	14
Other church	160	8	3	29	8	3
Other non-profit	517	25	9	98	26	10
Investor-owned	854	42	15	112	29	11
All systems	2,050	100	36	378	100	38

Source: American Hospital Association, 1985, *Data Book on Multihospital Systems 1980–1985*, Chicago: The Association.

about 8 percent of hospitals and beds in systems. All systems account for 37 percent of community hospital beds. Catholic system hospitals account for the largest proportion of all hospital beds (14 percent), followed by investor-owned (11 percent), other non-profit (10 percent), and other church (3 percent).

Table 16 provides a picture of the ten largest multihospital systems in the country in 1985. They accounted for about one-third of all multihospital system hospitals and beds. Four of the top five were investor-owned systems. This group was dominated by Hospital Corporation of America (HCA), which accounted for 17 percent of system hospitals and 13 percent of system beds. Humana was ranked sec-

TABLE 16   Ten Largest Multiple Hospital Systems by Type of System, Number of Hospitals and Number of Beds, United States, 1985

Rank	Name	Type	Hospitals	All System Hospital Beds		Percent of all System Beds
				Percent	Number	
1	Hospital Corporation of America	Investor owned	351	17.1	48,622	12.9
2	Humana	Investor owned	81	4.0	15,498	4.1
3	American Medical International	Investor owned	93	4.5	12,767	3.4
4	New York City Health & Hospital Corp.	Government, not-for-profit	12	0.6	9,368	2.5
5	National Medical Enterprises	Investor owned	64	3.1	9,301	2.5
6	Mercy Health Services (formerly, Systems of Mercy Health Corporation)	Church-Catholic	23	1.1	5,883	1.6
7	Kaiser Foundation Hospitals	Private	27	1.3	5,668	1.5
8	SCH Health Care System (formerly, Sisters of Charity Health Care System, Sisters of Charity of the Incarnate Word)	Church-Catholic	15	0.7	5,371	1.4
9	Daughter of Charity–St. Vincent De Paul	Church-Catholic	11	0.5	4,305	1.1
10	Sister of Mercy of the Union (St. Louis)	Church-Catholic	13	0.6	4,064	1.1
	Total of top ten hospitals	—	690	33.7	120,847	32.0

Source: American Hospital Association, 1985, *Data Book on Multihospital Systems 1980–1985*, Chicago: The Association.

ond but accounted for only 4 percent of both hospitals and beds. The only system in the top five that was not investor owned is the publically owned New York City system, which owned 2.5 percent of the system beds in its twelve hospitals. It had by far the largest hospitals of the major systems, with an average size of 781 beds.

Four of the second five largest multihospital systems are Catholic systems (Table 16). Only the Kaiser Foundation Hospitals (in seventh place) is non-Catholic in this group. This second-tier group is considerably smaller than the top five, with the largest (Mercy Health Services) having over 3,400 beds fewer than the fifth-ranked National Medical Enterprises. However, the Catholic systems have, on average, considerably larger hospitals (317 beds) than the "big four" investor-owned systems (146 beds).

One emergent organizational type that must be mentioned when we consider health care organizations providing acute care services are the vertically integrated health care systems. Vertical integration refers to the linkage of organizations at different stages in the "production process." Organizations can vertically integrate "backward" with other organizations that supply inputs they use in producing their own products. They can also vertically integrate "forward" with organizations that utilize their output or products in producing other goods or services. In the case of hospitals, backward integration might be with ambulatory care organizations, suppliers of medical equipment and pharmaceuticals, or third-party payers who insure the patients admitted to the hospital. Forward integration for the hospital might be with extended care facilities, nursing homes, or organizations providing home care or rehabilitation services—all providing services relevant to patients being discharged from the hospital.

Hospitals engage in vertical integration to ensure adequate inpatient referrals, to extend their inpatient referral base, to secure the allegiance of their medical staffs, to develop new revenue centers to support their inpatient operations or increase profits, and to provide more coordinated and comprehensive service for their patients.

While the rate of horizontal integration of hospitals has slowed considerably of late, vertical integration is proceeding at a rapid pace. Recent activities of the largest investor-owned multihospital systems to link with HMOs, PPOs, and insurance companies illustrate the vertical integration movement (Federation of American Hospitals 1985). For example, Humana and Mutual Benefit Life Insurance Company of Newark, New Jersey, and Kansas City, Missouri, have formed a cooperative marketing arrangement in which Humana's group health care insurance is combined with Mutual's established life and disability insurance and distributed through traditional insurance agents. Hospital Corporation of America acquired three HMOs; planned expansion of PriMed—a PPO in which its employees are encouraged to use HCA facilities; and purchased New Century Life Insurance Company. American Medical International acquired Fidelity Interstate Life Insurance Company and established a joint venture with George Washington University to run its HMO, which was established in 1972. Finally, National Medical Enterprises acquired Assured Investors Life Assurance Company of San Francisco.

Vertical integration is proceeding apace in the not-for-profit as well as in the investor-owned sector. Examples of expansion through vertical integration by hospitals generally include their increasing involvement in ambulatory surgery (Table 4), ambulatory care centers (Table 10), and home health agencies (Table 18). Although there are numerous logical reasons and presumptions as to why hospitals should engage in both horizontal and vertical integration, the evidence as to their success in achieving financial and organizational goals for the hospital is fragmentary and mixed (Center for Health Administration Studies 1987).

TABLE 17 Trends in the Total Number of Nursing Homes and Beds, United States, 1967, 1971, 1976, 1982, and 1986

Year	Number of Nursing Homes	Number of Nursing Home Beds
1967	10,636	584,052
1971	12,871	917,707
1976	13,417	1,174,092
1982	13,326	1,356,050
1986	14,250	1,470,000

Source: National Center for Health Statistics, *Inpatient Health Facilities as Reported from the 1967, 1971, and 1976 MFI Surveys*, 1972 Series 14, No. 4, 1–6; 1974, Series 14, No. 12, 2–5; and 1980, Series 14, No. 23, 2–6. The 1986 data were obtained from Mr. Al Sirocco of the National Center for Health Statistics, Hyattsville, Md., 1987.

Long-Term Care Organizations

Long-term care organizations have expanded greatly in size and function in recent years. The increased demand for services to manage chronic disease and to provide rehabilitative, palliative, and custodial support results from a number of factors. Included among these are the aging population, people living longer with chronic problems who require medical and nonmedical services, inability or unwillingness of relatives to provide nursing services to the aged and chronically ill, and increased third party payment for such services, especially through Medicaid.

The nursing home is the major long-term care organization. Table 17 shows the growth in nursing homes and nursing home beds from 1967 through 1986. Both the number of homes and beds increased steadily during this period. The number of nursing homes increased from 10,636 in 1967 to 14,250 in 1986, an increase of 34 percent. The number of nursing home beds grew even more rapidly from 584,052 to almost 1.5 million, an increase of 152 percent. These changes indicate that the average nursing home has increased in size from 55 beds in 1967 to 103 beds in 1986.

A transitional care organization that increased greatly in number from 1967 through 1986 was the home health agency. Table 18 presents the number of home health agencies by type. The total number of home health agencies increased from 1,753 to approximately 6,000. The greatest growth occurred among proprietary and hospital-based agencies. In 1967, for example, there were no proprietary agencies; in 1986 they numbered 1,904. There were 133 hospital-based agencies in 1967; in 1986 the number had risen to 1,362. This growth reflects an increased demand for custodial and nursing services in the home. The demand is fueled by a number of forces, including the trend to discharge inpatients sooner from hospitals, when nursing assistance is still required, and increasing efforts to maintain the chronically ill and frail elderly in the home rather than institutionalize them in nursing and custodial care homes.

Hospices—dedicated to making the process of dying more humane and comfortable—represent a newer transitional form of long-term care. Table 19 illustrates the rapid growth of these organizations. The table shows that in 1974 there was only one hospice in the United States. In

TABLE 18 Trends among Home Health Agencies, United States, 1967, 1977, 1982, and 1986

Year	Total	Visiting Nurse Association	County Agencies	Rehabilitation Facility Based	Hospital Based	Skilled Nursing Facility Based	Proprietary	Private Not-for-Profit	Other
1967	1,753	549	939	0	133	0	0	0	132
1977	2,496	503	1,242	0	281	0	81	309	80
1982	3,415	520	1,232	13	481	20	471	587	91
1986	5,963	502	1,179	16	1,362	116	1,904	820	64

Source: National Association for Home Care, 1986, personal communication with Robert Hoyer, Washington, D.C.

TABLE 19 Trends among Hospices, United States, 1974, 1978, 1980, 1984, and 1986

Year	Hospices	Estimated Number of Patients
1974	1	—
1978	75	—
1980	450	—
1984	1,345	100,000
1986	1,568	140,000

Source: National Hospice Organization, 1987, personal communication with Mr. Jay Mahoney, Arlington, Va.

1986, however, the number increased to 1,568. In that year approximately 140,000 individuals received services at a hospice.

Adult day care, an emergent long-term care organization that has experienced rapid growth in very recent time, represents another alternative approach to nursing homes and hospitals in the treatment of chronically impaired individuals. Although lacking a standard definition, adult day care generally provides supervision and activities during the day to persons who return to their own homes in the evening. Adult day care has expanded rapidly over the last several years. For example, in 1971 there were only 3 adult day care programs in the country; by 1978 there were nearly 300 programs; and by 1985 there were over 1,200 programs (Harder, Gornick, Burt 1986).

SUPPORTIVE AND ANCILLARY ORGANIZATIONS

Organizations that provide supportive and ancillary services to the direct providers of medical care can also be classified according to time period and type of major activity provided in the health services system. Table 20 classifies individual supportive and ancillary health services organizations into six categories (finance, supply, regulation, representation, research, and consulting), as well as by the time period when specific organizations became a significant force in the health services system. It also provides examples of each type of organization.

Table 21 presents the frequency of organizations by the six categories of supportive and ancillary health services organizations. In total, there were over 12,000 organizations providing supportive services (Kruzas, Gill, and Backus 1985). The table also illustrates the large number of organizations in each of the six categories.

Finance

Table 22 shows the health expenditures in billions of (current) dollars for the period 1950 through 1984. It illustrates the dynamic growth of resources allocated to health care. In 1950 the nation was only spending $12.7 billion on health care. In contrast, by 1984 the country was spending $387.4 billion.

Although private expenditures for health care have always been greater than the public sector, Table 22 shows the large increase in the federal portion of health care expenditures. Specifically, with the passage of the Medicare and Medicaid Programs (1965), the federal portion of health care expenditures increased greatly. By 1970, for example, the federal government had spent $10.0 billion on these two programs, and by 1984 the amount had grown to $101.1 billion.

Table 23 presents the number of persons with private health insurance coverage in the United States for the years 1950 through 1983. Specifically, it shows the number of persons with hospital and surgical insurance coverage with Blue Cross–Blue Shield, commercial insurance companies, and independent insurance plans.

In 1950, Blue Cross–Blue Shield had the largest number of persons (38.8 million) enrolled in hospital insurance plans; commercial insurance had the second largest number (36.9 million); and independent insurance plans had the least (4.4 million). By 1983, commercial insurance had the largest number (110.8 million) of

TABLE 20 Supportive and Ancillary Health Organizations by Type and Time Period

	Time Period		
	---	---	---
Type	*Traditional* *(World War II–1964)*	*Transitional* *(1965–late 1970s)*	*Emergent* *(late 1970s–Present)*
Finance	Local government Private insurance Blue Cross–Blue Shield Charity	Federal government Prepayment	Employees Self-insurance Coalitions
Suppliers	Pharmaceuticals, equipment, and technology firms Medical Schools and allied health schools	Group purchasing firms	Corporate conglomerates
Regulation	Local government Joint Commission on the Accreditation of Hospitals	Federal government Regional medical programs Comprehensive health planning Health systems agencies Professional service review organizations	Professional review organizations
Representation	American Medical Association American Hospital Association American College of Healthcare Executives	Federation of America Health Systems	American Association of Preferred Provider Organizations National Hospice Organization
Research	Medical Schools and research hospitals Private corporations National Institutes of Health	Health services research centers	Multidisciplinary clinical institutes or centers University/management partnerships
Consulting	Departments of provider organizations	Independent organizations	University/management consulting collaboration

enrollees for hospital insurance; Blue Cross—Blue Shield was second (79.6 million); and independent insurance plans were last (57.7 million).

In terms of surgical insurance coverage, for the entire period, commercial insurance companies always had the largest number of enrollees, followed by Blue Cross–Blue Shield and independent insurance plans.

An important new organizational form in the financial area is the health care coalition. Health care coalitions are voluntary organizations that occur in a variety of forms; they are initiated or sponsored by one or more special interest groups—particularly employers—in a community. Their purpose is to implement programs to restrain the rate of increase in health care expenditures.

Since the first health care coalitions were formed in the late 1970s, these organizations have greatly expanded in number, membership, and scope of activities. They now exist in virtually every major metropolitan city in the country. They have expanded at such a rapid rate that they have been described as one of the fastest growing and most visible manifestations of the quest by employers to become wiser buyers of health care.

Table 24 demonstrates the growth of health care coalitions during the 1980s. Before 1980 there were only 13 coalitions in the nation; by 1985 the number had grown to 154.

TABLE 21 Type and Number of Supportive and Ancillary Health Services Organizations, United States, 1985

Type of Organization	Number
Finance	
Federal grants and domestic assistance programs	207
Blue Cross–Blue Shield Plans	113
Health insurance companies	702
Dental care plans	49
Suppliers	
Medical and allied health schools	2,249
Pharmaceutical companies	536
Regulation	
State government agencies	1,154
Federal government agencies	183
Representation	
National and international associations	2,917
State and regional associations	1,655
Research	
Research centers and institutes	1,535
Foundations and grant-awarding organizations	810
Consulting	
Consultants and consulting organizations	619
Total	12,729

Source: A. Kruzas, K. Gill, and K. Backus, eds., 1985, *Medical and Health Information Directory*, Detroit: Gale Research Co.

TABLE 22 Trends in Health Expenditures (in billions of dollars), United States, 1950, 1960, 1970, 1980, and 1984

Category	1950	1960	1970	1980	1984
All health expenditures	12.7	26.9	75.0	248.0	387.4
Expenditures for personal health care	10.9	23.7	65.4	219.1	341.8
Private	8.5	18.5	42.9	132.4	202.5
Public	2.4	5.2	22.4	86.7	135.4
Federal component of public	1.1	2.2	14.5	62.5	101.1
Medicare and Medicaid component of federal	NA	NA	10.0	49.5	82.8
Other health expenditures	1.8	3.2	9.6	28.8	45.6

Source: Levit, K., H. Lazenby, D. Waldo, and L. Davidoff, 1987, National Health Expenditures, *Health Care Financing Review* 7(1):1–35; Health Care Finance Administration, Department of Health and Human Services, 1987, personal communication with Mr. Michael Millman, Baltimore, Md.

TABLE 23   Trends in the Number of Persons (in thousands) with Private Health Insurance for Hospital and Surgical Care, United States, 1950, 1960, 1970, 1980, and 1983

Year	Blue Cross–Blue Shield		Commercial Insurance Companies		Independent Plans	
	Hospital	Surgical	Hospital	Surgical	Hospital	Surgical
1950	38,822	19,690	36,955	33,428	4,445	3,760
1960	58,050	50,281	69,226	65,093	5,994	7,336
1970	75,055	66,042	89,688	85,661	8,131	10,532
1980	86,721	73,626	107,313	100,999	33,152	36,885
1983	79,600	66,100	110,839	102,331	57,700	61,800

Source: Health Insurance Association of America, 1985, *Source Book on Health Insurance Data 1984–1985*. Washington, D.C.: The Association.

Suppliers

A large number of organizations are necessary to produce the goods and services the health care providers need. A host of pharmaceutical companies supply health care organizations with drugs and vaccines. Medical equipment and technology firms supply hospital beds and surgical and laboratory equipment. Table 21, presented earlier, gives the reader a rough idea of the number of organizations involved in supplying the nation's health care system. The table indicates there were 536 pharmaceutical companies and 2,249 medical and allied health schools in the country in 1985.

Regulation

Health care providers are controlled by a large number of regulatory organiza-tions. Hospitals, for example, must obtain a state license to operate. They must also have either accreditation from the Joint Commission on the Accreditation of Healthcare Organizations (JCAHO) or federal accreditation in order to receive federal health funds. Further, if a hospital wants to expand, remodel, or purchase new equipment, it must, in many states, submit a request to a state agency for Certificate of Need (CON) review and possible approval. Peer Review Organizations (PROs), another important type of regulatory agency under contract to the Health Care Financing Administration, monitor use and quality of care of Medicare patients. Table 21 presents the number of state and federal organizations involved in the regulation of the health care system. In 1985 there were 1,154 state government agencies and 183 federal agencies involved in such activities.

TABLE 24   Year of Establishment of Operational Health Care Coalitions, United States, 1986

Year of Establishment	Number of Coalitions	Percent	Cumulative Percent
Before 1980	13	8.4	8.4
1980	9	5.8	14.2
1981	20	13.0	27.2
1982	51	33.2	60.4
1983	38	24.7	85.1
1984	16	10.4	95.5
1985	7	4.5	100.0
Total	154	100.0	—

Source: American Hospital Association, 1986, personal communication with Mr. Reid Stanton, Office of Health Coalitions and Private Sector Initiatives, American Hospital Association, Chicago.

Representation

Health care organizations are represented by a large number of professional and trade organizations. Some of the largest of these organizations are the American Medical Association, American Hospital Association, American College of Surgeons, American College of Healthcare Executives, Association of American Medical Colleges, Federation of American Health Systems, and Healthcare Financial Management Association. Many of these organizations serve as lobbying organizations for their membership. Table 21 shows the number of representation organizations in the nation in 1985. There were almost 3,000 (2,917) national and international associations and 1,655 state and regional associations.

Research

After World War II, large amounts of funds were spent on medical research. The National Institutes of Health gave increasing dollars to medical schools, research institutes, and hospitals for research purposes. Also, many large foundations started to provide research funds to support projects in the health field. Such foundations as the Ford, Kellogg, and Robert Wood Johnson foundations provided generous funding for various health research projects. Table 21 shows that in 1985 there were 1,535 medical and health research centers and institutes in the United States; there were also 810 foundations and grant-awarding organizations.

Consulting

As health care organizations expanded and became involved in complex activities, a host of consulting organizations arose. Many of the "big eight" accounting firms developed specific divisions to deal with health care organizations, and a large number of smaller consulting firms were established to conduct various types of health

TABLE 25 Characteristics of Health Care Management Consultant/Auditor Firms, United States, 1983 and 1985

Characteristics	1983	1985	Percent Change
Number of firms	151	171	13.2
Number of consultants	3,202	4,452	39.0
Number of hospital clients	7,451	11,511	54.5
Number of consulting engagements	11,269	16,013	42.1
Average revenue per engagement	$25,289	$26,829	6.1
Total estimated revenue	$284,978,000	$429,618,900	50.8

Source: Surveys of hospital management consultants/auditors, in Donald E. L. Johnson, Hospitals Shell out $285 Million to 151 Consulting Firms in 1983, *Modern Healthcare*, Aug. 15, 1984, pp. 97–126; in Kari E. Super, Healthcare Consultants Expect to Upgrade Level of Expert, *Modern Healthcare*, Sept. 12, 1986, pp. 70–112.

related activities. Table 21 indicates that in 1985 there were 619 health and medical consultants and consulting organizations.

Table 25 shows some of the specific characteristics of a national sample of health care management consulting/auditor firms for 1983 and 1985. During this time, the number of firms increased from 151 to 171 (an increase of 13 percent). The estimated total revenues increased even more, from approximately $285 million to $430 million (an increase of 50.8 percent).

THE FUTURE

In this chapter we have tried to document the dynamic nature of health care organizations as they have expanded and changed through various eras of our health services system. Most likely, this momentum will lead to additional change. We will close by suggesting two interrelated developments likely to have a major impact on health care organizations at least to the turn of the century. First, a new competitive "modified consumer's market" for health care services is emerging. In this evolving market, "organizations" (intermediate consumers or purchasers of services including employers, the government, private insurers, and health care management) will increasingly have a say about care for a patient. In many cases, these organizations will make choices that may differ from those the patient might make for himself or herself with full knowledge. Further, in this new market an increasing number of care givers will have financial incentives to limit services or will be committed to follow organization rules and protocols rather than to prescribe a regimen dictated by the special needs of the patient. It may be that only the well-to-do will be able to buy out of this modified consumer's market to escape queues, attain exactly the services and specialists they would like, and have access to all of the most expensive technology medical science has to offer.

Second, we appear to be entering into a new era that is concentrating on the relationship between the cost and the quality of health services. This new cost-quality era will be marked by a continued interest in cost containment as well as by vigorous efforts to measure the quality of care in order to judge the value of services received and the real efficiency of health care organizations and programs. Further, this era will likely witness renewed efforts to provide access to some medical care for all people regardless of ability to pay. However, the appropriate level of this care will be hotly debated, and it will become clearer which services society is and is not willing to pay for.

REFERENCES

Aday, L. A., and R. Andersen. 1981. Equity of Access to Medical Care: A Conceptual and Empirical Overview. *Medical Care* 19 (Supp.): 22, 24.

Alexander, Jeffrey A, A. D Kaluzny, and S. Middleton. 1986. Organizational Growth, Survival and Death in the U.S. Health Care Industry: A Population Ecology Perspective. *Social Science and Medicine* 22:303–308.

American Association of Preferred Provider Organizations. 1986. Personal communication with Mr. Mark Abe, Alexandria, Va.

American Hospital Association. 1984. *Directory of Shared Services Organizations and Consortia of Health Care Institutions.* Chicago: The Association.

———. 1985. *Data Book on Multihospital Systems 1980–1985.* Chicago: The Association.

———. 1986a. *Directory of Multihospital Systems, Multistate Alliances and Networks.* Chicago: The Association.

———. 1986b. Hospital-Sponsored Ambulatory Care Utilization Trends, 1980–1985. *Outreach* 7 (2):3.

———. 1986c. *Hospital Statistics 1986.* Chicago: The Association.

———. 1986d. Personal communication with Mr. Reid Stanton, Office of Health Coalitions and Private Sector Initiatives, American Hospital Association, Chicago.

American Medical Association. 1971. *Medical Groups in the United States, 1969*. Chicago: The Association.

———. 1976. *Medical Groups in the United States, 1975*. Chicago: The Association.

———. 1982. *Medical Groups in the United States, 1980*. Chicago: The Association.

———. 1985. *Medical Groups in the United States, 1984*. Chicago: The Association.

Center for Health Administration Studies. 1987. Does Diversification Make Health Care Organizations Healthier? The 29th Annual George Bugbee Symposium on Hospital Affairs, University of Chicago.

Federation of American Hospitals. 1985. *1986 Directory Investor-owned Hospitals and Hospital Management Companies*. Little Rock, Ark.: FHH Review.

Fine, Jennifer. 1986. Group Purchasing Spurs Growth of Shared Service Organizations. *Modern Healthcare* 16(18):65.

Freidson, Eliot. 1979. The Organization of Medical Practice, in Howard E. Freeman and Sol Levine, eds., *Handbook of Medical Sociology*. Englewood Cliffs, N.J.: Prentice-Hall, pp. 297–307.

Hannan, Micheal T., and John Freeman. 1984. Structural Inertia and Organizational Change. *American Sociological Review* 49:149–164.

Harder, W. Paul, Janet C. Gornick, and Martha R. Burt. 1986. Adult Daycare: Substitute or Supplement? *The Milbank Memorial Fund Quarterly* 64(3):414–441.

Health Care Finance Administration. Department of Health and Human Services. 1985.

———. 1987. Personal communication with Mr. Michael Millman, Baltimore, Md.

Health Insurance Association of America. 1985. *Source Book on Health Insurance Data 1984–1985*. Washington, D.C.: The Association.

InterStudy. 1986. Personal communication with Ms. Laura Pitts, Excelsior, Minn.

Johnson, Donald E. L. 1984. Hospitals Shell out $285 Million to 151 Consulting Firms in 1983. *Modern Healthcare* August 15 (16):97–126.

Kruzas, A., K. Gill, and K. Backus, eds. 1985. *Medical and Health Information Directory*. Detroit: Gale Research Co.

Levit, K., H. Lazenoy, D. Waldo, and L. Davidoff. 1985. National Health Expenditures, 1984. *Health Care Financing Review* 7(1):1–35.

National Association for Home Care. 1986. Personal communication with Mr. Robert Hoyer, Washington, D.C.

National Association of Ambulatory Care Centers. 1986. Personal communication with Ms. Ann Stafstrom, Dallas.

National Center for Health Statistics (NCHS). 1972. *Inpatient Health Facilities as Reported from the 1967 MFI Survey*, Series 14, No. 4, 1–6.

———. 1974. *Inpatient Health Facilities as Reported from the 1971 MFI Survey*, Series 14, No. 12, 2–5.

———. 1980. *Inpatient Health Facilities as Reported from the 1976 MFI Survey*, Series 14, No. 23, 2–6.

———. 1985. Advanced Data From Vital and Health Statistics, Number 111, 2.

———. 1987. Personal communication with Mr. Al Sirrocco of the National Center for Health Statistics, Hyattsville, Md.

National Hospice Organization. 1987. Personal communication with Mr. Jay Mahoney, Arlington, Va.

National Institute on Adult Day Care. 1986. Personal communication with Ms. Betty Ransom, Washington, D.C.

Riffer, Joyce. 1986. Hospitals Becoming Driving Force in ACC Market. *Hospitals* 60(23):67.

Shortell, Stephen M., and Arnold D. Kaluzny, eds. 1987. Organization Theory and Health Care Management, in Stephen M. Shortell, Arnold Kaluzny, eds., *Health Care Management*. New York: John Wiley.

SMG Marketing Group, Inc. 1986. Personal communication with Mr. John Henderson, Chicago.

Super, Kari E. 1986. Healthcare Consultants Expect to Upgrade Level of Expertise. *Modern Healthcare* 16(19):70–112.

Thompson, James D. 1967. *Organizations in Action*. New York: McGraw-Hill.

CHAPTER
9

ACCESS TO HEALTH CARE AND USE OF MEDICAL CARE SERVICES

DAVID MECHANIC
LINDA H. AIKEN

The social programs of the 1960s reflected a strong commitment to the value, widely shared by Americans, that access to medical care should be available to all and should not be rationed by income, race, or region (Lewis, Fein, and Mechanic 1976). This objective was substantially accomplished by the introduction of Medicare and Medicaid in 1966 and a variety of health programs for infants, mothers, children, and other categorical populations. These programs dramatically improved access to physician services, modified long-established trends favoring the affluent in physician and hospital utilization, and were accompanied by dramatic improvement in a variety of indicators of health status (Mechanic 1978). Although the poor had made enormous advances in access, studies still suggested underutilization relative to existing patterns of morbidity and need for

medical intervention (Robert Wood Johnson Foundation 1983). Some of the advances in health could be linked specifically to access to efficacious technology—for example, regionalized intensive neonatal care in lowering infant mortality (McCormick 1986)—but the links between increased access and improved health are complex and are yet to be explicated fully.

In the past several years, shifts in the economy, efforts at cost containment both in government programs and in the private sector, and conservative political philosophies have resulted in more stringent eligibility criteria for government assistance and have significantly increased cost sharing in the private sector. Medicaid, which covered more than three-fifths of those in and near poverty in 1975, now covers less than one-half of this population. It is now estimated that thirty-seven million people have no insurance coverage of any kind, and providing unreimbursed care increasingly places great pressures on public hospitals and on many nonprofit hospitals that

---

This chapter is adapted from David Mechanic, *Mental Health and Social Policy*, 3rd. ed., © 1989. Reprinted by permission of Prentice-Hall, Inc., Englewood Cliffs, New Jersey.

serve poverty populations. There is increasing indication that gains in access to care achieved between 1966 and 1975 are being eroded and that failure to provide necessary care is resulting in health decrements (Lurie et al. 1984; Blendon et al. 1986).

In this chapter, we examine data and research on access and use of health services. Our intent is not only to provide a portrait of the distribution of services and the factors that influence health care delivery but also to examine how gaps in access may affect health outcomes. Since the aggregate national data can only provide circumstantial evidence, whenever possible we examine key studies that speak to these issues. In addressing inequalities and special problems in access, we find it more informative to explore a few issues with greater specificity than to attempt to address the large array of disease areas. Thus, we plan to illustrate many of our key points by examining in detail such areas as the growing crisis of the uninsured, the health problems of the homeless, the special problems of the chronically mentally ill, and black-white differences in cancer, and nursing home residence.

THE CONCEPT OF ACCESS: DEFINITIONS AND ASSUMPTIONS

The health services system is highly complex and differentiated, but most studies of access focus on whether individuals report a regular source of medical care that is available to them when needed, whether they have seen a physician in the past twelve months, and, if so, how many times. Because comparable questions on physician visits have been asked on surveys for more than two decades, it is possible to examine patterns of physician access over a relatively long time. Prior to the new health initiatives of the 1960s better physician access was associated with higher socioeconomic status. With the implementation of health programs for the poor in the 1960s,

the trend was reversed, with highest utilization among the poor. In 1982, for example, the poor averaged 5.9 physician visits per year in comparison to a national average of 5. Similarly, during this period, hospital admissions increased among the poor and decreased among the nonpoor, resulting in a much more adequate distribution of hospital services relative to need (Aiken and Blendon 1986). A major redistribution of hospital care to the nonwhite population also took place. Although there is evidence that the extent of redistribution is still too little, given patterns of morbidity by socioeconomic status and ethnicity (Freeman et al. 1987), the country has experienced a dramatic transformation in the delivery of services.

In studying physician access it was assumed that if individuals could make contact with a physician, the source of primary care would be sufficiently linked to medical facilities and specialized practitioners to allow appropriate referral depending on the problem. Thus, much less emphasis has been given to access to specialized facilities and services, to the content of care, or to the management of complex episodes of illness among varying groups in the population.

There are reasons to doubt the adequacy of general physician accessibility as a measure of access to complex episodes of care and specialized services. How the physician appraises the patient, decides about the services needed, and makes referrals depends not only on linkage to the larger system of specialized services (Lewis, Fein, and Mechanic 1976) but also on the attitudes and resources of the patient, the physician's needs, and the payment context (Eisenberg 1986). The ability of the physician to link the patient with needed services also depends on an established relationship with the patient and continuity of care, but the data persistently show that the poor are more likely than other groups to receive services from clinics and emergency rooms characterized by little continuity and high levels of impersonality (Department of Health and Human Services 1985a). Knowing that a patient can identify a regular source of care and has seen a doctor in the past year fails to tell us whether early and appropriate diagnosis has occurred, whether care is suitable for the problem, or whether, for example, specialized cancer, mental health, or nursing home services are available at the times they are needed. As the issue of the quality of services returns to the nation's agenda, it will be essential to examine access more deeply and to assess the adequacy of fit between patients' needs and the services available to them.

MODELS OF PHYSICIAN UTILIZATION

In the past couple of decades there have been a large number of multivariate studies of physician utilization (Mechanic 1978, 1979a, 1979b). A conceptual approach developed by Andersen and his co-workers commonly guides analysis (Andersen, Kravits, and Anderson 1975; Andersen and Aday 1978), and utilization is viewed within the model as a product of predisposing (e.g., age, sex, education, health beliefs), enabling (e.g., family resources such as income, level of health insurance, accessibility of medical care), and need measures. Typically, the model explains only a modest amount of variation, and most of the variance explained is accounted for by the illness measures in the model (Mechanic 1979b). These analyses lead to the conclusion that illness almost exclusively accounts for utilization differences, a judgment very much at variance with many studies in medical sociology that find large psychosocial and organizational variations.

Among the factors accounting for the discrepancies between the large multivariate models and other studies are the interpretation of "illness" measures, differences (and varying degrees of specificity) in measurement and data aggregation, and major contrasts in theoretical conceptions of the behavioral processes affecting utilization

(Roghmann and Haggerty 1975; Gortmaker, Eckenrode, and Gore 1982; Verbrugge and Harel 1983; Antonovsky 1972). Discussion of these problems in detail will take us too far afield from our concerns here (for an explication of these points, see Mechanic 1979b). However, by reviewing the Rand Health Experiment, an outstanding example of health services research, and some of its major findings, we can illustrate weaknesses typical of many of the large cross-sectional utilization surveys and also set the stage for much that will follow.

THE RAND HEALTH EXPERIMENT

A puzzling aspect of many of the large-scale multivariate studies of physician utilization is the underestimation of the importance of such enabling variables as insurance. A common problem with these studies, however, is the very limited and crude measures used. Asking a person a simple question, for example, as to whether they have insurance, and simply distinguishing between no insurance, basic coverage, and major medical as these studies tend to do fails to provide the information essential for prediction. Studies also often fail to clearly ascertain if respondents are covered by public programs such as Medicaid. Physician visits will depend on the specific configuration of co-insurance, deductibles, and other limits on coverage, and the failure to obtain this necessary data erodes the credibility of many of the multivariate studies in the literature.

Consider, in contrast, the results of the Rand Health Experiment. This study, carried out between 1974 and 1982, randomized 6,970 respondents into insurance plans with varying co-insurance requirements and, in one setting, an HMO (Group Health Insurance in Seattle). In some cases there were no co-insurance requirements (labeled the "free care" group), while in other cases families had to pay 25, 50 or 95 percent of their bills up to a $1,000 per year maximum. There were other variations (Newhouse 1974), but for our purposes what is most important is the different obligations families had to share in their costs of care. Most insurance programs in the United States have some cost sharing, and in recent years such requirements have increased substantially in employment-related health insurance plans (Hewitt Associates 1984). Deductibles and co-insurance also play an important role in Medicare, although the Rand group did not study the Medicare age group.

In contrast to many of the multivariate studies, physician use was demonstrated to respond substantially to insurance variations. Persons in the "free" plan (no co-insurance or deductibles) accrued expenditures of about 50 percent more for outpatient medical care than those with 95 percent co-insurance (Newhouse et al. 1981). Visits in these contrasting groups varied from 5.5 to 3.5 visits per person each year. This effect was found in all subgroups studied.

There were many important observations in this very large study, but here we emphasize just a few that are particularly pertinent to our topic. Perhaps, most important, is that cost sharing had more deleterious effects on the poor sick than on the affluent. The Rand group studied a variety of health status indicators and in general found only modest effects of cost sharing on health (Brook et al. 1983). The most important effects were in blood pressure control, vision correction, and, in the case of children, the prevalence of anemia. These effects were primarily concentrated among poor persons who did better in the experimental conditions without cost sharing. Low-income individuals in the experiment who began the study in poor health showed the largest health improvements with free care. Similar advantages of limiting financial barriers to care were reported for the community health centers established for the poor by the Office of Equal Opportunity in the 1960s (Freeman, Kiecolt, and Allen 1982; Dutton 1986).

Many advocates of co-insurance favor it not only because it reduces the health program's overall costs, but also because they believe that such obligations encourage prudence among consumers and lead them to reduce the demands for service in trivial instances (Mechanic 1979a). While there has been no empirical basis for these claims, the absence of disconfirmation gave such advocates greater policy influence than justified. The Rand group found that cost sharing did not result in appropriately selective decision making. Financial barriers limited the use of care in instances where care was appropriate and efficacious, as well as in situations where it was unnecessary and ineffective. These effects were particularly marked in the case of low-income children who used substantially less care of the types judged efficacious by the research team. The probability of at least one episode of "highly effective care" for poor children in programs with co-insurance was only 56 percent of the level of use in the free care condition, while the comparable figure for nonpoor children was 85 percent (Lohr et al. 1986).

These data are particularly important because of persistent pressures to increase cost sharing in public and private health care programs. Those who are more affluent tend to have comprehensive insurance with the least cost-sharing requirements. Lower-income workers are more likely to have less complete coverage, but co-insurance in these populations is likely to result in barriers to access and appropriate use of care and to less positive health status. These problems are very much exacerbated for those in the population who have neither private nor public health insurance.

THE UNINSURED POPULATION

There is a common belief among the public that the Medicaid program constitutes a health safety net for those who become poor. However, while the number of poor persons has increased markedly in the 1980s (a 27 percent increase in the number of Americans living at or below the poverty level between 1979 and 1984), the Medicaid program has failed to adapt to changing economic circumstances. In the average state in 1975, Medicaid eligibility covered about 71 percent of the poor, but by 1986 the threshold had dropped to 48 percent, a one-third decrease (Curtis 1986). The thresholds, and cutbacks, were also distributed unevenly by state. Some states regressed enormously, decreasing coverage of the poor, for example, by 63 percent in Arkansas, 60 percent in Missouri, 59 percent in Tennessee, and 65 percent in Puerto Rico. Many states showing large decreases were already in a disadvantageous situation. The consequence is that in some states less than one-quarter of the poor are eligible for Medicaid protection. Even in such generous states as New York, about one-third of the poor are ineligible for Medicaid, including some 300,000 children (Vladeck 1986).

The numbers of uninsured fluctuate and estimates vary (Bazzoli 1986), but it is commonly believed that between 1978 and 1984 the uninsured population increased by more than a third, from approximately twenty-eight to thirty-seven million. Contrary to the common assumption, most of the uninsured are in households with a wage earner, but many work in marginal jobs. Manufacturing jobs continue to decrease, and employment gains are primarily in the service sector and in small businesses, where many employers offer either no health insurance or programs that are prohibitively expensive.

The uninsured are a heterogeneous group who lack insurance for varying reasons. A substantial proportion are simply poor people who are excluded from Medicaid and whose marginal and low-paid employment makes health insurance relatively inaccessible. Approximately one-third of the uninsured are poor by federal poverty standards but are excluded from Medicaid (Swartz 1984). Medicaid eligibility is tied to eligibility requirements for welfare or disability. The nation's welfare system is primarily limited to single parents and their dependent children. Therefore, certain categories of poor people, particularly adult males, are not eligible for Medicaid unless they are disabled. Another third are within 200 percent of the poverty level, but limited incomes make purchase of health insurance difficult, particularly when it is not part of an employment benefit package. Still another category are unemployed workers and their families who lose their insurance when the primary wage earner loses employment. Federal law now requires employers to provide for continuation of benefits. The unemployed worker must pay for such coverage, and the expense is often more than these unemployed families can manage. Also among the uninsured are some whose medical conditions are sufficiently severe and so potentially costly that they are unable to purchase individual insurance at an affordable rate. Although an important idea of health insurance was to pool risk across large populations, more and more health plans are adopting risk-rating approaches that increase premiums for subgroups with greater need and sometimes deny insurance completely.

Some segments of the uninsured population have sufficient income to acquire health insurance but because of cost and alternative spending preferences choose to play the odds, given their age and health status, that they are unlikely to have large medical expenses. Young people just out of school often fail to acquire insurance, and some workers have insurance that covers themselves but not their dependents. Then, of course, there is a small group of people who are sufficiently affluent to pay all of the necessary costs out-of-pocket. From a social policy perspective, the subgroups of greatest concern are those families below or near the poverty line and workers with marginal incomes whose employers offer little or no health insurance benefits. A smaller but equally compelling group are those who because of their illnesses and disabilities cannot obtain health insurance at an affordable cost, despite the fact that they exemplify a group that needs such protection.

Those without insurance who become ill can obtain services from public clinics and hospitals; many nonprofit hospitals also provide considerable amounts of indigent care. But the burden is distributed very unevenly, and a small number of hospitals that cannot readily shift costs to other patients are put into financial jeopardy (Gray 1986). It is difficult to measure unreimbursed care accurately, but the levels of such care available seem to be declining as hospitals face greater financial constraints and as opportunities to shift costs diminish. Patients without health insurance who are sick must increasingly depend on public hospitals, although not-for-profit hospitals provide more uncompensated care than investor-owned hospitals (Gray 1986). There is great variation, however, as shown by the fact that in the early 1980s, one-third of hospitals expended less than 8 percent of their revenues on charity patients, patients who never paid, and those on Medicaid. In contrast, one-quarter of hospitals provided 60 percent of all such care (Hadley and Feder 1984). As more uninsured and underinsured patients are pushed to public hospitals, these institutions, traditionally serving the most needy and poorest subgroups in the population, face increasing economic difficulties. Caught in the vise of increasing numbers of poor and uninsured patients and constrained government budgets, they find it difficult to maintain an adequate standard of care.

There are no solutions to the overall problem of the uninsured outside a more equitable system of health insurance that ensures protection for the entire population. There are, however, remedies that can reduce the magnitude of the problem and lighten the burden of hospitals that take on disproportionate responsibility for indigent care. Some states have devised mechanisms to garner resources to care for this population (Mechanic 1986). In New Jersey, for example, the all-payor DRG system in place adjusts hospital payment in light of the magnitude of indigent care hospitals provide and requires all payors to share in this cost. Florida taxes net hospital revenues to accumulate resources for indigent care, and New York taxes insurance premiums for the same purpose. Although these devices to share costs are often innovative, they are too limited for the magnitude of the problem, which is a national one.

The federal government has made some small initial efforts, for example, the recent legislation that makes it somewhat less difficult for unemployed workers and workers' divorced wives to retain health insurance. In the face of a large federal deficit, however, the country seems reluctant to confront the financial requirements to address this issue. Evidence is accumulating that the uninsured use far fewer health services and their limited access to care is adversely affecting health (Blendon et al. 1986; Vladeck 1986; Bazzoli 1986). Neither the health safety net nor the incentives for employment-related insurance as they apply to many low-income workers are functioning well. The issue is of wide concern in the public and private sectors and is likely to be high on the health care agenda for several years. The uninsured are vulnerable, but the problem is seriously compounded among those who, in addition to other liabilities, lack adequate shelter. We now turn to a discussion of the special health needs and problems of the homeless population.

THE HEALTH CARE OF THE HOMELESS

There have always been homeless people in large urban areas in this country, but not since the years immediately following the Great Depression has homelessness been so visible (Bassuk 1984). Estimates of the number of homeless individuals in the United States have ranged from 350,000 to three million (HUD 1984; U.S. General Accounting Office 1985b). However, recent attempts to estimate systematically the size of the homeless population have led to estimates close to HUD's estimate of 350,000 (Rossi et al. 1987; Freeman and Hall 1986).

The determinants of homelessness are not well understood nor is there agreement on its permanence. The diminishing supply of low-cost housing in many cities is a contributing factor. In addition, general assistance payments and welfare stipends in most states have not kept pace with inflation, which in combination with rising housing costs has severely reduced the ability of low-income individuals and families to obtain housing. A third factor commonly believed to be associated with homelessness is physical and psychiatric disability. Thus, homeless people have a complex and interrelated array of problems and needs that are both medical and social in nature (Bassuk 1984; U.S. General Accounting Office 1985b).

In a recent study of the homeless in Chicago, more than one in three homeless people reported themselves in ill health, a rate twice as high as that found in general population surveys (Rossi and Wright 1987). More than one in four reported having a health problem that prevented their employment. Mental illness and psychiatric symptoms were major sources of disability. Almost one in four Chicago homeless reported having been in a mental hospital for stays of over forty-eight hours. Nearly half of the Chicago homeless exhibited levels of depression that suggested a need for clinical attention. Contacts with the criminal justice system, suggesting perhaps another kind of disability, were frequent. The cumulative incidence of these disabilities was very large, with 82 percent of the homeless either reporting ill health, having been in a mental hospital or detoxification unit, having received clinically high scores on psychiatric symptom scales, or having been sentenced by a court (Rossi et al. 1987).

The Robert Wood Johnson Foundation's nineteen-city Health Care for the Homeless Program provides the only large data set on the health problems of the homeless (Wright 1987), with data available at the time of this writing on 118,098 clinic encounters with 42,539 homeless people. The Health Care for the Homeless Program provides medical and social services to homeless persons without charge in clinics located in shelters, soup kitchens, and single room occupancy hotels. The demographic profile of patients cared for in these special clinics is similar to that found among the homeless nationally (Bassuk 1984; Freeman and Hall 1986; Rossi et al. 1987). About one-third were homeless women; approximately 40 percent had dependent children. Over half were nonwhites. The median age was 33 years. A tenth of all patients seen in the clinics were ages 15 and under.

The most frequent health problem of the homeless in the nineteen cities was alcohol abuse, followed by mental illness. Approximately 38 percent of the homeless had an alcohol-related problem, and one-third had serious psychiatric symptoms or a history of mental illness. These estimates are roughly similar to other studies of the homeless population (Lamb 1984; Bassuk, Rubin, and Lauriat 1984).

The most common physical health problems encountered in the clinics were acute disorders: specifically, upper respiratory infections, injuries, and skin ailments. Forty-one percent of clinic patients had a chronic physical disorder; the most prevalent were hypertension, gastrointestinal ailments, and peripheral vascular disease. One in six patients had an infectious or communicable disorder. Most of these were minor conditions, such as lice infestations, but pneumonia and other serious respiratory infections were observed in more than 3 percent, sexually transmitted infections in about 2 percent, and active tuberculosis in about 0.5 percent. In some cities, active tuberculosis rates among the homeless have been documented to be substantially in excess of the national average (Brickner et al. 1985).

About 15 percent of the homeless children seen in the clinics exhibited one or more chronic health problems (see Bassuk, Rubin, and Lauriat 1986, for another source of data on homeless children). About one-tenth of the female clients were pregnant, the highest pregnancy rates being for women 16 through 19 years old.

The homeless face major barriers in obtaining medical care despite their very high levels of need. Only a minority have medical insurance—Medicaid in most cases. The available evidence suggests that a substantial share of the homeless are eligible for general assistance or meet Social Security criteria for disability, thus entitling them to Medicaid, Supplemental Security Income (SSI), and subsidized housing. However, the actual number of homeless people who have these entitlements is much lower than would be expected. Recent legislation has removed some barriers to obtaining entitlements, such as the requirement of an address for receipt of monthly SSI payments. However, the process of applying for disability is a long and arduous one, and few homeless people have the persistence and the necessary help from others to follow the process through to its conclusion.

Serious illness among the homeless poses some unique problems. In many communities, access to inpatient care for serious medical problems may be easier to obtain for the homeless than ambulatory care, especially in communities with public general hospitals. However, average length of stay in hospitals has declined in recent years owing to cost-containment pressures. Many patients now leave the hospital in earlier stages of recovery than in years past. Most people have homes and someone to help; some, especially the dependent elderly, are transferred to nursing homes. But the homeless have no place to go upon hospital discharge except to shelters that provide little medical care. This problem only affects a relatively modest number of people now. However, as AIDS associated with drug use increases among the homeless, access to "respite," or recovery-type, services will be an important element of medical care services—an element that is almost nonexistent at this time.

Being poor without health insurance makes access to medical care difficult (Blendon et al. 1986). The homeless must rely, in large part, on charity care provided by public hospitals and clinics. However, many of the homeless fear or reject large institutions and, except in emergencies, will not go there for medical care. They also often lack transportation money to reach a centralized location. Additionally, the homeless are not perceived by health providers to be desirable clients. They often appear disheveled and sometimes display bizarre or unusual behavior. Often their problems are not those health providers like to manage, for example, alcoholism, mental illness, and drug abuse. Compliance with medical advice among this patient group is often low, which discourages health professionals. Thus, the barriers to access to appropriate health care for the homeless are numerous, multifaceted, and difficult to remedy.

ACCESS AND USE OF SERVICES AMONG THE SERIOUSLY MENTALLY ILL

Epidemiological studies of serious mental illness find an extraordinary amount of untreated disorder. Epidemiological estimates are sufficiently imprecise to allow argument about the magnitude of unmet need, but the effects are so large as to leave little doubt of significant barriers to access. These barriers exist because of the unavailability and poor organization of needed facilities and services, lack of insurance and economic deterrents, and attitudes and stigmata that inhibit defining certain types of problems as appropriate for medical care (Mechanic 1980). Our purposes here are limited to exploring barriers to care; mental illness issues are discussed in much more detail in Chapter 13.

The NIMH collaborative Epidemiological Catchment Area Program (ECA), a five-site epidemiological study of the adult population as well as persons in institutions, is an important source of data for estimating the prevalence of illness, use of services, and unmet need (Eaton and Kessler 1985). In analyzing ECA data from the Baltimore survey of the general population, Shapiro and his colleagues (1985) estimate the proportion of patients with different types of disorders who received a mental health service from either nonpsychiatric physicians or specialized mental health providers. In the aggregate, only 7 percent of the population who presented evidence of a recent emotional problem received a mental health service of any kind during the prior six months. Twenty-three percent of those studied were estimated to have had a disorder during the prior six months consistent with DSM-III psychiatric criteria, but only a minority received any kind of care. Although the implications may be arguable for such aggregate data, particularly disturbing was the fact that 45 percent of schizophrenics, 56 percent of those with affective disorders, and 62 percent of those with substance abuse problems and dependence received no care at all.

Leaf and his colleagues (1985), reporting on the data from New Haven, provide comparable results. Only half of those meeting DSM-III criteria for schizophrenia reported receiving any relevant service during the prior six months. Rates for other serious conditions showed even less utilization: depressive episode with grief (37 percent), alcohol or drug abuse or dependence (13 percent), manic episodes (25 percent), and phobias (22 percent). Some of these conditions, such as depression and phobias, are responsive to treatment, and appropriate management of schizophrenia can ameliorate symptoms and suffering and promote function. These grim data are consistent with many other studies showing major gaps between psychiatric need and appropriate access (see Chapter 13). Ap-

proximately half of the services that are provided for mental health problems are given in the general medical sector and are part of primary care. There is serious concern that general physicians are insufficiently trained in psychiatry and the use of neuroleptic drugs to provide appropriate care, particularly for those with the most serious disorders.

A major barrier to receiving appropriate services is the sparse coverage under health insurance plans for outpatient psychiatric care. Such benefits typically are limited in most private health insurance and in Medicare by high deductibles and co-insurance (typically 50 percent) and by stringent ceilings on total expenditures relative to other medical conditions. Despite the impressive growth in mental health coverage among employees in firms above a minimum size studied by the Level of Benefits Survey of the Bureau of Labor Statistics (Brady, Sharfstein, and Muszynski 1986), only 7 percent of employees studied had psychiatric outpatient benefits provided on the same basis as other medical services. The gap is even larger in Medicare and other public programs. Some states, for example, do not provide psychiatric coverage under their Medicaid programs.

Not only are cost-sharing features and service limits more characteristic of mental health than other medical services, but they also appear to inhibit outpatient services even more than in other areas (Frank and McGuire 1986). McGuire (1981), for example, in a study of use of psychotherapy among more than 4,000 patients, found that this service is particularly sensitive to insurance coverage, and the effects for lower-income persons were greater than for more affluent groups. McGuire's excellent study, however, focused on patients and, thus, pertains to volume of use and not to whether help would be sought.

The Rand study, discussed earlier, provides an opportunity to examine use of mental health services in the context of overall patterns of use. In early publications, the Rand researchers reported that cost sharing affected mental health service use in a way comparable to its effect on other services (Wells et al. 1982), but these results have been subject to considerable controversy. Ellis and McGuire (1984, 1986) suggested that the Rand researchers underestimated the mental health co-insurance effects because of a special design feature, the maximum dollar expenditure (MDE) level for a family. Once a family reached the MDE in a particular year, services at that point become free for the remainder of the period. The probability that families in programs with different co-insurance requirements reach the MDE at different rates may distort estimates of the size of the effects of cost sharing on mental health expenditures.

In an extension and reanalysis of the data, stimulated by the Ellis and McGuire (1984) observations, the Rand researchers concluded that outpatient mental health use is indeed more responsive to price than other types of medical care (Keeler et al. 1986). There was a fourfold variation between extreme co-insurance groups, and those with 50 percent co-insurance and no limits on cost sharing spent only two-fifths as much as those with free care. Co-insurance primarily affected the number of episodes of treatment, but once a person entered care the duration and intensity varied less. Since few patients seek specialized mental health care whatever their insurance levels, the per person cost in the study for such services was low. Other factors found to affect use included educational level and age (young adults used more), and there were also variations by site. Seattle and Massachusetts had more use than Dayton and South Carolina. The site effect is probably a product of the different availability of mental health providers in the sites and varying dispositions toward · mental health services in geographic areas that differ a great deal culturally.

A large literature supports the observation that mental health status, insurance, sociodemographic variations, attitudes, social networks, other social and cultural variables, and characteristics of the health care delivery system all affect the likelihood of a mental health contact. In New Haven the relative odds of a recent mental health contact of any kind were substantially greater among those who had a regular source of medical care (3.06), who were receptive to professionals (2.42), who were young adults (2.11), who used clinics (1.76), and who were white (1.95), unmarried (1.64), female (1.49) and had some college education (1.42) (Leaf et al. 1985). In Baltimore unmet need for mental health care was found to be most substantial among the elderly, among nonwhites, and among those with eight or fewer years of education (Shapiro et al. 1985). A number of behavioral models have been developed to account for the wide variety of social, cultural, and attitudinal factors that affect the use of mental health services (Mechanic 1975, 1980; Greenley, Mechanic, and Cleary 1987). Some of these factors affect help-seeking in general, while others help explain alternative choices among mental health providers (Greenley and Mechanic 1976; Greenley, Mechanic, and Cleary 1987).

These population studies convey only part of the access problem, because, as discussed in Chapter 13, the issue is not only access to a mental health service, but the availability of the spectrum of services essential for those most seriously ill who have substantial needs of many kinds, ranging from appropriate housing to medical and psychiatric assistance. Performance of the necessary functions of appropriate care for many highly disabled patients requires the financial, organizational, and clinical capacity to provide a wide array of necessary services or guarantee them through contract (Mechanic 1986). The mental health services system is in disarray and requires major restructuring (Mechanic 1987; Mechanic and Aiken 1987; Robert Wood Johnson Foundation, 1986; Aiken, Shore, and Somers 1986).

A NOTE ON PREPAID GROUP PRACTICE AND ACCESS TO CARE

This is not the context for a detailed review of the large and important literature on health maintenance organizations (HMOs) despite their growing influence in the larger health care arena (Mechanic 1986). Since the way health services are organized importantly affects access, costs, service mix, and health outcomes, differences in organization are highly pertinent to our concerns here. This brief review of some recent studies of the performance of prepaid practice is illustrative.

There is a large literature that supports the conclusion that prepaid group practice significantly reduces costs by limiting hospital admissions by as much as 40 percent and yields an overall cost savings of 20 to 30 percent (Luft 1981; Mechanic 1979a, 1986). These differences have been found to persist when controls for population characteristics, out-of-plan use, and other factors are considered as well. Yet these studies could not exclude the possibility of significant selection effects relating to the health status of enrollees who choose prepaid practice plans for their medical care needs. In the Rand study, however, families were randomized into a prepaid group practice in Seattle (Group Health Insurance). This provided an opportunity to examine the impact of this type of organization independent of selection effects.

Group Health was found to have 40 percent less admissions than the free care experimental group, although both populations faced no financial barriers to care. Overall, expenditures in Group Health were 28 percent less than in the free care group (Manning et al. 1984). A subsequent analysis of health status suggested that poor sick patients randomized into prepaid practice did less well than those assigned to the fee-for-service free care condition (Ware et al. 1986). These data are not fully convincing, but they are consistent with other studies that suggest that less edu-

cated patients have difficulties negotiating the bureaucratic barriers typical of organizational types of practice (Mechanic 1979a). Such barriers can be overcome through well-designed outreach efforts to enrollees at high risk.

The way organization and financing affect mix of services is illustrated by analyses of the use of mental health care in the fee-for-service free care condition as compared with prepaid practice. More enrollees of prepaid practice actually used mental health services, but they were provided much less intensively. Those in prepaid practice were more likely to receive mental health services from a general medical provider, and overall mental health expenditures were only one-third of the free care condition ($25 per year per enrollee versus $70). When prepaid enrollees saw a mental health provider, they had only one-third the number of mental health visits of the comparable fee-for-service free care group. Group Health relied more on social workers than on psychiatrists or psychologists and less on individual therapy than on group or family therapies (Manning, Wells, and Benjamin 1986; Manning and Wells 1986). These results are similar to those found in nonexperimental studies.

ACCESS TO MEDICAL CARE AND MINORITY HEALTH

The relative disadvantages of the poor on such indicators of health as infant mortality, longevity, the prevalence of serious disease, and disability and incapacity have been repeatedly documented. Children born in poverty are exposed to many more health risks than others, and throughout the life span poverty and poor health reinforce one another (Dutton 1986; Mechanic 1978; Brown 1986; Susser, Hopper, and Richman 1983; McCormick 1986; Furstenberg and Brooks-Gunn 1986; Robins 1983). In many instances, each of the major indicators of socioeconomic status—education, income, and occupation—independently affect health outcomes (Kitagawa and Hauser 1973; Mechanic 1978; Kessler 1982). The processes are complex, because these variables are related to almost every aspect of living, including material resources, attitudes and values, exposure to environmental risk, household structure and family life, childbearing, child-rearing processes, acquisition of coping skills, and the ability to obtain necessary and appropriate medical care and other types of assistance.

As noted earlier, the social programs of the 1960s did much to close gaps in access to care, but large gaps remain in access, particularly in relation to blacks and some other minority groups. Health status differentials are affected by life opportunities and conditions far more than by medical care. The poor and minorities have less life opportunities than others in the population. In many instances, race and ethnic factors compound the risks associated with limited income and education.

It is difficult to talk about minority status in general because minority groups vary substantially in background, resources, and life conditions. There are also very large intragroup differences, and it is foolish to aggregate, for example, persons of Hispanic background, since the differences among Cubans, Puerto Ricans, Mexicans, and South Americans may be greater than those between each of these groupings and other American ethnic groups or "nonethnics." Some minority groups have atrocious health experiences, whereas others are relatively advantaged and have superior health outcomes (e.g., Japanese Americans). Particularly large problems exist among blacks, native Americans, Puerto Ricans, and Mexican Americans, but because the blacks are the largest and best-studied minority, we shall focus on this group for illustrative purposes.

Being black in America is highly associated with disadvantaged socioeconomic status, and many if not most of the observed adverse health outcomes are attributable to socioeconomic influences (Haan and Ka-

plan 1985). Indeed, the association is sufficiently large so that many investigators and reviewers use being black as a proxy for disadvantaged economic status. Unfortunately, most studies fail to disaggregate income, educational, and occupational effects from effects of race and ethnicity, and thus it is difficult to ascertain how different aspects of the background and life conditions of minority groups affect health outcomes. Conclusions will also depend substantially on the specific health indicator at issue. In the case of blacks, for example, excess infant deaths or homicides cannot be explained solely on a socioeconomic basis, while in many other instances careful statistical controls for income, education, and occupation will completely explain the black-white variations.

Health effects associated with race beyond those explained by socioeconomic status may be due to differences in geographic residence, household structure, life-styles, preventive health practices, genetic vulnerabilities, and racism and other forms of discrimination. Few, if any, studies have samples of adequate size and measurements of sufficient variety to explore how these influences interact to bring about differences in access, utilization, and outcomes among groups. Since the influences will vary from one health dimension to another, we would require extraordinarily large samples of individuals with specific medical conditions. In order to improve national data on such minorities as Mexican Americans, Puerto Ricans, and Cuban Americans, the National Center for Health Statistics has carried out a large Hispanic version of the Health and Nutrition Examination Survey (DHHS 1985b). Unfortunately, in most instances we have to rely on aggregate descriptive statistics.

The Department of Health and Human Services (DHHS) has made a major effort to bring together existing data on black and minority health (Report of the Secretary's Task Force 1985). DHHS estimated that in the period 1979–1981, among blacks up to age 70, 58,942 of an annual

total of 138,635 deaths would not have occurred if blacks had the same age- and sex-
specific death rate as the nonminority
population, yielding an "excess death" ratio
of 42.5 percent. Six causes accounted for
four-fifths of these deaths: heart disease
and stroke (31 percent), homicide and accidents (19 percent), cancer (14 percent), infant mortality (11 percent), cirrhosis (4
percent), and diabetes (3 percent). The relative risks of mortality for blacks as compared with whites is particularly high for
homicide, cirrhosis, diabetes, infant mortality, and stroke. These causes of death all
have important behavioral components.

The possible areas of inquiry are too
complex to do more than provide some
brief illustrations of varying types of processes affecting access, use, and outcome.
Each disease or health condition may involve different biological aspects, risk factors, behavioral responses, and interactions
between the condition, behavior, and characteristics of the health care system. Although it is important to have a general
picture of overall access and how it can be
facilitated though improved public policy,
considerable specificity is necessary if we
are to target effectively our preventive and
curative efforts. To explicate these points
we choose two rather different areas: cancer survival rates by race and nursing
home utilization.

Black male cancer survival compared
with white males of comparable age was 40
percent less in the period 1979–1981; comparable excess risk among black women
was 20 percent. This difference resulted in
almost 9,000 excess cancer deaths per year
among blacks up to age 70. (DHHS 1985a,
p. 5). Cancer deaths by race are accounted
for by differences in the incidence of varying cancers and chances for survival among
cases. Blacks have higher cancer incidence
rates for most sites than any other major
American group (DHHS 1985a, p. 91). Excess incidence is particularly large for lung
cancer (among black males), for multiple
myeloma, and for cancer of the cervix,
esophagus, pancreas, and prostate gland.
In contrast, blacks have significantly lower
incidence of breast cancer. Overall, the excess incidence of cancers relative to non-
Hispanic whites is about 10 percent, but
blacks also have lower survival rates for
most cancer sites.

Compared with whites, blacks have less
chance of surviving cancer for five years,
38 percent versus 50 percent (National
Cancer Institute 1986, p. 7). Poorer survival is particularly characteristic in the
case of cancer of the rectum, larynx,
breast, corpus uteri, prostate, and bladder.
These are generally areas where five-year
survival rates are reasonably high, and
where early and effective medical intervention can probably make some difference.
Black five-year survival is much less dis-
crepant with white rates in those areas
where little medical progress has been
made: multiple myeloma and cancer of the
stomach, pancreas, and lung. These estimated differences between whites and nonwhites may be exaggerated because blacks
may come into care later than whites, and
staging in many instances is an uncertain
process. Thus, black survival may be underestimated. Reports of improved survival
in cancer similarly may be exaggerated owing to greater medical care access in recent
years and detection of cases that may not
have fatal consequences (Bailar and Smith
1986).

Much of the black-white differences are
attributable to socioeconomic factors. Such
factors affect exposure to risk. For example, blacks and nonblack men of low socioeconomic position smoke more, and black
men in the steel and rubber industries
work in jobs with the highest toxic and carcinogenic exposure (National Cancer Institute 1986, p. 8). Lower socioeconomic
status also affects nutrition, access to cancer screening and sophisticated cancer detection, ability to obtain state-of-the-art
treatment, and general health status.
Blacks may live in geographic areas with
less access to sophisticated cancer treat-

ment; it is instructive that in the Medicare program, poor persons residing in areas of lesser concentration of medical facilities seem less able to "cash in" on their Medicare entitlements (Davis 1975). Access to the best types of care, ensuring the most advanced treatment, requires more than simple physician access. It requires being linked into a well-integrated treatment system. But compared with whites, blacks are less likely to have a usual source of care and to see physicians in an office-based setting. They tend to use hospital outpatient departments or health clinics, which offer less continuity of care and where patients may see different doctors each time they visit.

There is much uncertainty in understanding cancer incidence and survival, and the data are inadequate for disentangling complex causal chains. But the evidence overwhelmingly suggests that part of the story of cancer survival relates to differential access to appropriate medical care.

NURSING HOME UTILIZATION

As the American population ages and as extensions of longevity increase the numbers of persons at very advanced ages, demand for nursing home beds increases (Suzman and Riley 1985). The proportion of persons reaching age 65 who attain age 85 increased from 23 percent in 1950 to 38 percent in 1983 (Siegel and Taeuber 1986, p. 90). Those who survive to very old ages have high prevalence of chronic disease and disability, have a relatively high rate of dependency in the performance of activities of everyday life, and are at increasing risk of nursing home admission. Using data for 1973–1974, the risk of women entering a nursing home at age 85 or over was 29 percent as compared with 7 percent among those age 75–84. Among men the comparable rates were 18 and 4 percent (Russell 1981).

As of 1980, there were approximately 1.4 million licensed nursing home beds in the United States (U.S. General Accounting Office 1985a); about 45 percent of all nursing home expenditures are now paid by Medicaid. The vast majority of patients in nursing homes are old and infirm and require assistance in many of the activities of daily care (NCHS 1979). As the demand for nursing home beds accelerates and as hospitals release patients earlier in efforts to contain costs, patient mix in nursing homes is characterized by increasing levels of dependency.

Since blacks are poorer, have more deprived housing situations, and have more illness and disability than whites, one would anticipate that rates of black admission to nursing homes would be at least similar to those of whites of comparable age. In fact, the black admission rate in the aggregate is about 50 percent less than the white rate for those over age 65 and less than half the white rate for those 85 and older (Institute of Medicine 1981).

Entry into a nursing home is typically a last resort, and the trigger is commonly the loss of a spouse or other significant supportive person or a major illness or accident that makes persons lacking substantial supports unable to care for themselves. Common problems leading to nursing home admission include urinary incontinence, loss of memory and disorientation, and confused wandering. The ability to contain these behaviors in the community depends on resources, household structure, and tolerance for the behaviors at issue. In examining black-white differences, data are not available to assess the relative importance of varying predictive factors. Elderly blacks are more likely than elderly whites to live in extended family structures, but it is not clear whether this is cause or effect or what role different values and household constellations might play in explaining these differences.

There are many factors that probably contribute to black-white differences. It is unlikely however that either differences in health or life expectancy are significant causes. Elderly blacks are probably sicker and more frail than comparable whites. More likely causes include the fact that blacks reside in states where nursing beds have been in short supply, and the dependence of blacks on Medicaid, which is a less attractive source of payment, limits access to many nursing homes. Many white and middle-class patients ultimately "spend down" their assets and eventually become eligible for Medicaid, but they initially enter nursing homes as private patients.

It is very difficult to prove, but the existing evidence makes a very strong case for discrimination against blacks in nursing home admission in some areas of the United States. In several states in the deep South the relative representation of white Medicaid patients in nursing homes greatly exceeds blacks. Nursing homes also tend to be relatively segregated in many areas, comparable to patterns of housing segregation that characterize many areas of the country.

After making an exhaustive effort to review the available data and to examine competing hypotheses, an Institute of Medicine study came to the following conclusion:

There is a strong likelihood that racial discrimination is an important factor in the admission of blacks into nursing homes, though how widespread a factor is not clear. The evidence . . . suggests a basis for focussing civil rights compliance review activities. (Institute of Medicine 1981, pp. 9–10)

Ironically, the nursing home sector developed largely in response to federal programs and depends heavily on government reimbursement. Although racial selectivity is intolerable under any circumstances, it is particularly offensive in this governmentally stimulated sector. Medicare played a significant role in desegregating the American hospital. Medicare and Medicaid could be a comparable influence in the nursing home.

CONCLUSION

In this chapter we have only touched lightly on the large and expanding literature on access to care and health status outcomes. The evidence overwhelmingly supports the conclusion that while access to medical care has improved dramatically in the past two decades, major gaps exist in bringing appropriate care to many millions of Americans in need. The crisis of the thirty-seven million uninsured, the plight of the homeless and neglected chronically mentally ill, and the needs in long-term care of a growing population of the oldest-old challenge the equity and effectiveness with which the country organizes and delivers health care services. Moreover, any serious scrutiny that explores beyond the surface shows major inequalities by socioeconomic status and disadvantaged minority status in access to our sophisticated subsystems of specialized care.

Many remedies are being debated, but politics and the federal budget deficit put major constraints on attacking these issues in forthright ways. In the short term, progress will depend on a sustained commitment by hospitals, professionals, government officials, and private industry to contribute to closing some of these gaps. But in the long term, these efforts cannot be successful outside a larger health care insurance framework that rededicates our society to the principle that medical care should be available in relation to need and not depend on race, income, or region.

REFERENCES

Aiken, L., and R. Blendon. 1986. Access to Medical Care: Trends and Early Warning Signs. *Internist* 27(2):7–10.

Aiken, L., M. Shore, and S. Somers. 1986. Private Foundations in Health Affairs: A Case Study of the Development of a National Initiative for the Chronically Mentally Ill. *American Psychologist* 41:1290–1295.

Andersen, R., and L. A. Aday. 1978. Access to

Medical Care in the U.S.: Realized and Potential. *Medical Care* 16:533–546.

Andersen, R., J. Kravits, and O. W. Anderson, eds. 1975. *Equity in Health Services: Empirical Analyses in Social Policy.* Cambridge, Mass.: Balinger.

Antonovsky, A. 1972. A Model to Explain Visits to the Doctor: With Specific Reference to the Case of Israel. *Journal of Health and Social Behavior* 13:466–454.

Bailar, J. C., III, and E. M. Smith. 1986. Progress against Cancer. *New England Journal of Medicine* 314:1226–1232.

Bassuk, E. 1984. The Homeless Problem. *Scientific American* 251:40–45.

Bassuk, E., L. Rubin, and A. S. Lauriat. 1984. Is Homelessness a Mental Health Problem? *American Journal of Psychiatry* 141:1546–1549.

———. 1986. Characteristics of Sheltered Homeless Families. *American Journal of Public Health* 76:1097–1101.

Bazzoli, G. J. 1986. Health Care for the Indigent: Overview of Critical Issues. *Health Services Research* 21:353–393.

Blendon, R., L. H. Aiken, H. E. Freeman, B. L. Kirkman-Liff, and J. W. Murphy. 1986. Uncompensated Care by Hospitals or Public Insurance for the Poor. *New England Journal of Medicine* 314:1160–1163.

Brady, J., S. S. Sharfstein, and I. L. Muszynski, Jr. 1986. Trends in Private Insurance Coverage for Mental Illness. *American Journal of Psychiatry* 143:1276–1279.

Brickner, P. W., L. K. Scharer, B. Conanan, A. Elvy, and M. Savarese. 1985. *Health Care of Homeless People.* New York: Springer.

Brook, R. B., J. E. Ware, Jr., W. H. Rogers, E. B. Keeler, A. R. Davies, C. A. Donald, G. A. Goldberg, K. N. Lohr, P. C. Masthay, and J. P. Newhouse. 1983. Does Free Care Improve Adults' Health? Results from a Randomized Controlled Trial. *New England Journal of Medicine* 309:1426–1432.

Brown, G. W. 1986. Mental Illness, in Linda H. Aiken and David Mechanic, eds., *Applications of Social Science to Clinical Medicine and Health Policy.* New Brunswick, N.J.: Rutgers University Press, pp. 175–203.

Curtis, R. 1986. The Role of State Governments in Assuring Access to Care. *Inquiry* 23:277–285.

Davis, K. 1975. Equal Treatment and Unequal

Benefits: The Medicare Program. *Milbank Memorial Fund Quarterly* 53:449–488.

Department of Health and Human Services (DHHS). 1985a. *Black and Minority Health, Report of the Secretary's Task Force.* Washington, D.C.: The Department.

———. 1985b. Plan and Operation of the Hispanic Health and Nutrition Examination Survey, 1982–84. *Vital and Health Statistics.* Series 1, No. 19. DHHS Pub. No. (PHS) 85–1321.

Dutton, D. B. 1986. Social Class, Health, and Illness, in Linda H. Aiken and David Mechanic, eds., *Applications of Social Science to Clinical Medicine and Health Policy.* New Brunswick, N.J.: Rutgers University Press, pp. 31–62.

Eaton, W. W., and L. G. Kessler, eds. 1985. *Epidemiologic Field Methods in Psychiatry: The NIMH Epidemiologic Catchment Area Program.* Orlando, Fla.: Academic Press.

Eisenberg, J. 1986. *Doctors' Decisions and the Cost of Medical Care.* Ann Arbor: Health Administration Press.

Ellis, R. P., and T. G. McGuire. 1984. Cost Sharing and Demand for Ambulatory Mental Health Services: Interpreting the Results of the Rand Health Insurance Study. Boston University, Department of Economics. Unpublished.

———. 1986. Cost Sharing and Patterns of Mental Health Care Utilization. *Journal of Human Resources* 21:359–379.

Frank, R. G., and T. G. McGuire. 1986. A Review of Studies of the Impact of Insurance on the Demand and Utilization of Specialty Mental Health Services. *Health Services Research* 21:241–265.

Freeman, H. E., R. J. Blendon, L. H. Aiken, S. Sudman, C. F. Mullinix, and C. R. Corey. 1987. Americans Report on Their Health Care. *Health Affairs* (Spring): 7–18.

Freeman, H. E., K. J. Kiecolt, and H. M. Allen III. 1982. Community Health Centers: An Initiative of Enduring Utility. *Milbank Memorial Fund Quarterly* 60:245–267.

Freeman, R. B., and B. Hall. 1986. Permanent Homelessness in America? Working Paper No. 2013. Cambridge, Mass.: National Bureau of Economic Research. Unpublished.

Furstenberg, F. F., Jr., and J. Brooks-Gunn. 1986. Teenage Childbearing: Causes, Consequences, and Remedies, in Linda H. Aiken and David Mechanic, eds., *Applications of Social Science to Clinical Medicine and Health Policy*. New Brunswick, N.J.: Rutgers University Press, pp. 307–334.

Gortmaker, S. L., J. Eckenrode, and S. Gore. 1982. Stress and the Utilization of Health Services. *Journal of Health and Social Behavior* 23:25–38.

Gray, B., ed. 1986. *For-Profit Enterprise in Health Care*, Report of the Committee on Implications for Profit Enterprise in Health Care, Institute of Medicine. Washington, D.C.: National Academy Press.

Greenley, J. R., and D. Mechanic. 1976. Social Selection in Seeking Help for Psychological Problems. *Journal of Health and Social Behavior* 17:249–262.

Greenley, J. R., D. Mechanic, and P. D. Cleary. 1987. Seeking Help for Psychological Problems: A Replication and Extension. *Medical Care* 25:1113–1128.

Haan, M. N., and G. Kaplan. 1985. The Contribution of Socioeconomic Position to Minority Health. *Black and Minority Health*. Rockville, Md: U.S. Department of Health and Human Services, pp. 69–103.

Hadley, J., and J. Feder. 1984. Troubled Hospitals: Poor Patients or Management? *Business and Health* 1:15–19.

Hewitt Associates. 1984. *Company Practices in Health Care Management*. Lincolnshire, Ill.

Institute of Medicine. 1981. *Report of a Study: Health Care in the Context of Civil Rights*. Washington, D.C.: National Academy Press.

Keeler, E. B., K. B. Wells, W. G. Manning, J. D. Rumpel, and J. M. Hanley. 1986. *The Demand for Episodes of Mental Health Services*. R-3432-NIMH. Santa Monica. Rand Corporation.

Kessler, R. 1982. A Disaggregation of the Relationship between Socioeconomic Status and Psychological Distress. *American Sociological Review* 47:752–764.

Kitagawa, E. W., and P. M. Hauser. 1973. *Differential Mortality in the United States: A Study in Socioeconomic Epidemiology*. Cambridge, Mass.: Harvard University Press.

Lamb, H. R. ed. 1984. *The Homeless Mentally Ill*. Washington, D.C.: American Psychiatric Association.

Leaf, P., M. M. Livingston, G. L. Tischler, M. M. Weissman, C. E. Holzer III, and J. E. Myers. 1985. Contact with Health Professionals for the Treatment of Psychiatric and Emotional Problems. *Medical Care* 23:1322–1337.

Lewis, C. E., R. Fein, and D. Mechanic. 1976. *A Right to Health: The Problem of Access to Primary Medical Care*. New York: Wiley-Interscience.

Lohr, K. N., R. H. Brook, C. J. Kamberg, G. A. Goldberg, A. Leibowitz, J. Keesey, D. Reboussin, and J. P. Newhouse. 1986. *Use of Medical Care in the Rand Health Insurance Experiment: Diagnosis- and Service-Specific Analyses in a Randomized Controlled Trial*. R-3469-HHS. Santa Monica: Rand Corporation.

Luft, H. 1981. *Health Maintenance Organizations: Dimensions of Performance*. New York: Wiley-Interscience.

Lurie, N., N. B. Ward, M. F. Shapiro, and R. H. Brook. 1984. Termination from Medi-Cal—Does It Affect Health? *New England Journal of Medicine* 311:480–484.

Manning, W. G., A. Leibowitz, G. A. Goldberg, W. H. Rogers, and J. P. Newhouse. 1984. A Controlled Trial of the Effect of a Prepaid Group Practice on Use of Services. *New England Journal of Medicine* 310:1505–1510.

Manning, W. G., and K. B. Wells. 1986. Preliminary Results of a Controlled Trial of the Effect of a Prepaid Group Practice on the Outpatient Use of Mental Health Services. *Journal of Human Resources* 21:293–320.

Manning, W. G., K. B. Wells, and B. Benjamin. 1986. *Use of Outpatient Mental Health Care: Trial of a Prepaid Group Practice Versus Fee-For-Service*. R-3277-NIMH. Santa Monica: Rand Corporation.

McCormick, M. 1986. Implications of Recent Changes in Infant Mortality, in Linda H. Aiken and David Mechanic, eds., *Applications of Social Science to Clinical Medicine and Health Policy*. New Brunswick, N.J.: Rutgers University Press, pp. 282–306.

McGuire, T. 1981. *Financing Psychotherapy: Costs, Effects, and Public Policy*. Cambridge, Mass.: Ballinger.

Mechanic, D. 1975. Sociocultural and Social-Psychological Factors Affecting Personal Responses to Psychological Disorder. *Journal of Health and Social Behavior* 16:393–404.

———. 1978. *Medical Sociology*, 2nd ed. New York: Free Press.

———. 1979a. *Future Issues in Health Care: Social Policy and the Rationing of Medical Services*. New York: Free Press.

———. 1979b. Correlates of Physician Utilization: Why Do Major Multivariate Studies of Physician Utilization Find Trivial Psychosocial and Organizational Effects? *Journal of Health and Social Behavior* 20:387–396.

———. 1980. *Mental Health and Social Policy*, 2nd ed. Englewood Cliffs, N.J.: Prentice-Hall.

———. 1986. Health Care for the Poor: Some Policy Alternatives. *Journal of Family Practice* 22:283–289.

———. 1987. Correcting Misconceptions in Mental Health Policy: Strategies for Improved Care of the Seriously Mentally Ill. *The Milbank Fund Quarterly* 65:203–230.

Mechanic, D., and L. H. Aiken. 1987. Improving the Care of Patients with Chronic Mental Illness. *New England Journal of Medicine* 317:1634–1638.

National Cancer Institute. 1986. Cancer Control Objectives for The Nation: 1985–2000. *NCI Monographs*, No. 2. Washington, D.C.: U.S. Government Printing Office.

National Center for Health Statistics (NCHS). 1979. *The National Nursing Home Survey, 1977 Summary for the United States*. Series 13, No. 43. DHEW Publication No. [PHS] 79-1794.

Newhouse, J. 1974. A Design for a Health Insurance Experiment. *Inquiry* 11:5–27.

Newhouse, J., W. G. Manning, C. N. Morris, L. L. Orr, N. Duan, E. B. Keeler, A. Leibowitz, K. H. Marquis, M. S. Marquis, C. E. Phelps, and R. H. Brook. 1981. Some Interim Results from a Controlled Trial of Cost Sharing in Health Insurance. *New England Journal of Medicine* 305:1501–1507.

Robert Wood Johnson Foundation. 1983. *Special Report: Updated Report on Access to Health Care for the American People*. Princeton, N.J.: The Foundation.

———. 1986. *Program for the Chronically Mentally Ill*. Princeton, N.J.: The Foundation.

Robins, L. 1983. Continuities and Discontinuities in the Psychiatric Disorders of Children, in David Mechanic, ed., *Handbook of Health, Health Care, and the Health Professions*, New York: Free Press, pp. 195–219.

Roghmann, K. J., and R. J. Haggerty. 1975. The Stress Model for Illness Behavior, in Robert J. Haggerty, Klaus J. Roghmann, and Ivan B. Pless, eds., *Child Health and the Community*. New York: Wiley-Interscience, pp. 142–156.

Rossi, P. H., and J. D. Wright. 1987. The Determinants of Homelessness. *Health Affairs* (Spring): 19–32.

Rossi, P. H., J. D. Wright, G. A. Fisher, and G. Willis. 1987. The Urban Homeless: Estimating Composition and Size. *Science*. 235:1336–1341.

Russell, L. 1981. An Aging Population and the Use of Medical Care. *Medical Care* 19:633–643.

Shapiro, S., E. Skinner, L. Kessler, M. Von. Korff, P. German, G. Tischler, P. Leaf, L. Benham, L. Cottler, and D. Regier. 1985. Utilization of Health and Mental Health Services: Three Epidemiological Catchment Area Sites. *Archives of General Psychiatry* 41:971–978.

Siegel, R., and C. M. Taeuber. 1986. Demographic Perspectives on the Long-Lived Society. *Daedalus* 115:77–117.

Susser, M., K. Hopper, and J. Richman. 1983. Society, Culture, and Health, in David Mechanic, ed., *Handbook of Health, Health Care, and the Health Professions*. New York: Free Press, pp. 23–49.

Suzman, R., and M. W. Riley. 1985. The Oldest-Old. *Milbank Memorial Fund Quarterly* 63 (special issue).

Swartz, K. 1984. The Changing Face of the Uninsured. Paper presented at the annual meeting of the Association for Health Service Researchers, Chicago.

U.S. Department of Housing and Urban Development (HUD). 1984. *A Report to the Secretary on the Homeless and Emergency Shelters*. Washington, D.C.: Office of Policy Development and Research.

U.S. General Accounting Office. 1985a. *Constraining National Health Care Expenditures: Achieving Quality Care at an Affordable Cost*. Washington, D.C.: General Accounting Office.

———. 1985b. *Homelessness: A Complex Problem and the Federal Response*. Washington, D.C.: General Accounting Office.

Verbrugge, L. M., and Y. Harel. 1983. Triggers of Symptoms and Health Care. Paper presented at the meetings of the American Sociological Association, Detroit.

Vladeck, B. 1986. The End of Health Insurance. *President's Letter*. New York: United Hospital Fund.

Ware, J. E., Jr., R. H. Brook, W. H. Rogers, E. B. Keeler, A. R. Davies, C. D. Sherbourne, G. A. Goldberg, P. Camp, and J. P. Newhouse. 1986. Comparison of Health Outcomes at a Health Maintenance Organization with Those of Fee-for-Service Care. *Lancet* 14:1017–1022.

Wells, K. B., W. G. Manning, Jr., N. Duan, J. E. Ware, Jr., and J. P. Newhouse. 1982. *Cost Sharing and the Demand for Ambulatory Mental Health Services*. CR-2960-HHS. Santa Monica: Rand Corporation.

Wright, J. D. 1987. The National Health Care for the Homeless Program: The first year. Amherst, Mass.: Social and Demographic Research Institute, University of Massachusetts. Unpublished report to the Robert Wood Johnson Foundation.

10

TECHNOLOGY IN MEDICINE: DEVELOPMENT, DIFFUSION, AND HEALTH POLICY

SUSAN E. BELL

INTRODUCTION

There are many ways to understand the "problem" of medical technology, and these understandings have changed over time. After World War II, for example, new technologies were perceived as desirable, and researchers investigated ways to hasten development and diffusion. Public policy was intended to encourage expansion and to strengthen medical research and medical care, particularly hospital services. In the mid-1960s, policy objectives shifted, to the equitable distribution of the supply and, by the 1970s, to control over costs. This "succession of objectives in medical policy—expansion, equity, cost containment—[parallels] the more general succession of concerns in postwar social policy" (Starr 1982, p. 338). The way in which medical technology is perceived as a problem mirrors the particular and practical concerns of investigators. In turn, these are influenced by broader cultural and social values (Gusfield 1981).

Today, it is commonly agreed that control of costs is one of two important problems to solve. National health expenditures rose from $4 billion in 1940 (4 percent of the GNP) to $387.4 billion in 1984 (10.6 percent of the GNP). Concomitantly, per capita expenditures have increased, from $30 in 1940 to $1,580 in 1984 (NCHS 1985, table 80). Although the role of medical technology in total expenditures is not clear, researchers at the Office of Technology Assessment estimate that it accounts for one-third to three-quarters of the costs of hospital care (Banta, Behney, and Willems, 1981).

The second and closely related problem is efficacy (Roth and Ruzek 1986): the extent to which medical technologies improve diagnoses (Fineberg 1979), reduce morbidity and mortality (Powles 1980), and improve the quality of life (Najman and

Levine 1981). These different criteria of efficacy may be incompatible and lead to conflicting policies (Aiken and Freeman 1980). For example, neonatal intensive care rescues newborn infants once considered hopeless (at costs up to $250,000), yet some of these infants "remain alive, in a reduced biological sense, but without the capacities this society most identifies with meaningful life: full consciousness, responsiveness to others, reflection, physical autonomy, and the capacity for affection" (Guillemin and Holmstrom 1986, p. 3).

Furthermore, practitioners consistently adopt new medical technologies before they are evaluated and continue to use them after evaluation indicates they are ineffective or unsafe. Promising reports in the mass media and medical journals typically launch the careers of medical technologies. More often than not, these reports are based on uncontrolled studies; not until the technologies are already in use do controlled trials begin (McKinlay 1982). Thus, repeatedly, technologies of questionable value diffuse rapidly, and usage persists long after they should be abandoned or modified (Greer 1988). As a consequence, many patients receive costly and inappropriate care.

Although cost and efficacy dominate current discussions, a sociological perspective emphasizes the contingent nature of the medical technology "problem" and associated policy "solutions." Although at any particular time, one version of the problem may be dominant, there are others that contest it.[1] The predominant version is constructed, presented, and sustained by the groups with authority; not all parties have equal authority to do this (Gusfield 1981). These multiple ways of perceiving and evaluating the problem of medical technology are linked to multiple policies for controlling it.

Most of the literature focuses on understanding problems associated with medical technology and determining effective policy solutions because researchers assume that the process of development and diffusion is unproblematic. Typically, development is described as a sequence of stages, initiated by scientific discoveries (Bell 1986). This version, championed by groups with authority, presents medicine as a scientifically neutral enterprise, that is, objective, rational, and value free. Science produces medical technology, and scientific thinking results in decisions to adopt and use it (Mishler 1981; Wright and Treacher 1982). The predominant version of the diffusion process is that it is controlled by physicians, who want to innovate, agree in their assessment of new technologies, and respond rationally to the availability of information (Budrys 1986; Greer 1984, 1986).

Although views of the technology problem have changed, those of the process of technology development and diffusion generally have not. A sociological perspective shows that there are alternative ways to understand development and diffusion. According to this perspective, the predominant explanation of the process is simplistic, because it assumes that development proceeds in an orderly sequence and that diffusion is controlled by physicians who innovate after learning about new technologies. A sociological approach considers how specific institutional and organizational contexts shape technology development and diffusion by guiding the interests, values, and paradigms of producers and users (Bell 1986; Budrys 1986; Greer 1986; Levine 1987). This approach describes a process that is disorderly and influenced by actors other than physicians. Elucidating this process is a prerequisite to setting effective policy, regardless of which problems are identified.

As with technology in general, even the meaning of medical technology has little consistency (Mayr 1976). There are numerous definitions of medical technology, and each has implications for understanding

---

[1]Other problems associated with medical technology are informed consent for participation in research, equal access, and social consequences. These are addressed by others (see, e.g., Apfel and Fisher 1984; Guillemin and Holmstrom 1986; Plough 1986; and Reiser 1978).

development and diffusion and for devising policy (Bell 1986). The most straightforward definition is that it "includes all elements of medical practice that are knowledge-based . . . the set of techniques, drugs, equipment, and procedures used by health care professionals in delivering medical care to individuals and the systems within which such care is delivered" (U.S. Congress 1976, p. 4). However, this definition is so general that it is useful only by way of reminding us that stethoscopes, intensive care units, coronary bypass surgery, Pap smears, and medical information systems are all technologies. As Nathanson and Morlock (1980, p. 328) observe, different types of medical technology "are associated with different sets of structural and normative conditions" and thus have different policy implications. Therefore, differences may be more significant than similarities for understanding and control. Various categorizations have been proposed; here I present the predominant one (for others, see Bell 1986; Rettig 1978; Rettig and Harman 1979).

Physician Lewis Thomas identifies three separate levels of medical technology, each so unlike the others as to seem an "altogether different undertaking" (Thomas 1971, p. 1367). Nontechnology, valued highly by physicians and patients, consists of caring, standing by, providing reassurance, and tiding patients over through diseases that are not understood, such as cancer, stroke, and rheumatoid arthritis. Halfway technology postpones death and alleviates the incapacitating effects of certain diseases. Exemplified by organ transplants and kidney dialysis, it is both "highly sophisticated and profoundly primitive" (Thomas 1971, p. 1367). Definitive technology ("real high technology"), such as antibiotics and immunization, results from a genuine understanding of disease mechanisms and enables the prevention or cure of bacterial infections and diseases like diptheria, syphilis, and tuberculosis. It is relatively inexpensive, simple, and easy to deliver. This differentiation leads Thomas to advocate the production of definitive

technologies and therefore to promote basic research, because it is the one source of this type of medical technology. When disease mechanisms are understood, halfway technology will no longer be needed, costs will decrease, and ethical dilemmas will no longer be posed (Thomas 1971).

To summarize, there are alternative ways of defining medical technology, describing its development and diffusion, and identifying problems associated with it. The predominance of one or another version depends on which groups are in positions of authority. In this chapter I consider conceptions of the development and diffusion of medical technology. I consider how sociologists and others have addressed two questions: How is medical technology brought into being? How is it diffused, that is, adopted and used? I then review policies that have been proposed and implemented, evaluating them in light of these questions. In each section, I consider multiple ways that development and diffusion can be conceived, contrasting them with typical conceptions. Throughout, I use one specific case for illustrative purposes, DES, and refer to other examples as needed to expand on the two questions.

DES

DES (diethylstilbestrol) is a drug that was synthesized in 1938 and used to treat various conditions associated with estrogen dysfunction, most notably menopausal symptoms and threatened miscarriage. It has had a profound impact on gynecology, endocrinology, obstetrics, and oncology (Bell 1986; Noller and Fish 1974). DES was the first estrogenic substance that was cheap to produce, easy to purify, and potent orally; hence, it was inexpensive and simple to use. In addition, the drug was not patented. DES "was welcomed for clinical trial with guarded hopefulness throughout the world" (Mazer, Israel, and Ravetz 1941, p. 675). By 1940, experts were "practically unanimous" in their evaluation of its estrogenic potency (Novak 1940, p. 594).

However, they seriously disagreed about its toxicity. Reports of the incidence of toxic reactions ranged widely from 5 to 80 percent (*Journal of the American Medical Association* 1939). Because of the medical controversy and potential for widespread use, a great deal of attention was turned to DES research within the medical community and in the Food and Drug Administration (FDA), the agency charged with enforcing federal regulations that required proof of safety for all new drugs. By 1941, most of the scientific and medical experts consulted by the FDA believed that DES was safe, and because so much evidence had amassed in its favor, the FDA approved DES for marketing in four conditions—treatment of menopause, senile vaginitis, juvenile gonorrheal vaginitis, and lactation suppression (Bell 1986).

Beginning in 1940, physicians prescribed DES to women for pregnancy complications, including threatened miscarriage. Although DES was originally recommended for pregnant women who had diabetes or other illnesses or who had had repeated miscarriages (Apfel and Fisher 1984), it was ultimately used even by "normally pregnant" women to help having "larger, healthier, or happier" babies (Ferguson 1953, p. 600).

The FDA banned the use of DES during pregnancy in 1971, when researchers discovered an association between prenatal exposure to DES and a rare form of vaginal cancer (clear cell adenocarcinoma) in DES daughters. The total number of DES daughters is estimated to be between 500,000 and two million (Apfel and Fisher 1984).

HOW IS MEDICAL TECHNOLOGY BROUGHT INTO BEING?

Stage Models of Development

Analyses of medical technology development are usually based on a sequential, or stage, model, which examines the different steps technology passes through from its initial conceptualization to its adoption and use by medicine. This framework of understanding the process has largely determined policy solutions. Given a stage framework, the logical solution is to control movement of technology within or between stages by slowing down progress from one stage to the next, rearranging the order of stages, or improving the work done in one or more stages of the sequence. Sociological studies of medical technology development show the limitations of the stage model, propose alternative ways of conceiving of technology development, and suggest why present policies are only partially successful.

The sequential model of development has been clearly described by the Office of Technology Assessment (U.S. Congress 1976, pp. 67–68):

First a background or conceptual basis is laid by theoretical research and the sum of previous experience. Then, basic empirical research provides a framework of knowledge about the mechanisms involved, discovers points in a natural process that are susceptible to technological intervention, and suggests strategies for technological development. Applied or mission-oriented research is then directed at applying this basic knowledge to a practical purpose and demonstrating the feasibility of the proposed technology. Once feasibility is demonstrated, engineers, entrepreneurs, and developers, usually in the private sector, can develop goal-oriented programs. Prototypes are built and problems of transferring the technology from the laboratory to the marketplace are faced. Once the manufactured item is ready, its effectiveness and efficiency can be assessed in a realistic way in industrial testing laboratories, in field tests, or in consultation with potential users. Finally, the technology is marketed and, if all goes well, it is adopted by the proper class of consumers, be they manufacturers or industries, public groups or institutions, or private individuals.

By picking out certain "facts" of technology development and creating a sequential order out of them, researchers can discern patterns. In 1976 the President's Biomedical Research Panel (1976) solicited retrospective studies of technology development, resulting in research that divided the process into stages for 132 advances in cardiovascular pulmonary medicine and surgery and 25 case histories of successful innovations. By fitting the process into stages, an unexpected pattern emerged: Laboratory discoveries were applied prematurely to medical care, before "clinical validation." Subsequent studies have confirmed these findings (McKinlay 1982; Silverman 1980).

The framework created by the stage model leads to specific types of policies, such as drug and device regulations to control the availability of new technologies, certificate-of-need laws to control adoption, and diagnosis-related groups to control use (all of these policies are discussed below). Thus, stage models offer a framework for understanding development and creating social policies. However, they are based on a number of assumptions about science and technology: that scientific knowledge is impervious to social forces and precedes technological development, that the process is discontinuous, and that the work of each stage is performed by distinct communities. Each of these assumptions has been addressed critically.

The sequential theory of the process of technology development is based on a "hierarchical" model of the relationship between science and technology: Scientific knowledge precedes technological development, both temporally and causally (Barnes and Edge 1982). Even though the Office of Technology Assessment (U.S. Congress 1976, p. 68) cautions that this sequence is a "sociological ideal rather than a realistic description," it continues to treat the sequence as the most accurate description of the process (Banta, Behney, and Willems 1981; Banta 1983, 1984; Ruby, Banta, and Burns 1985). Indeed, this view of the causal relationship between science and technology "is deeply embedded in the medical research community" (Maxwell 1986, p. 23).

The policy implied by a hierarchical relationship between science and technology is to give high priority to research in basic science because it will yield truly useful, inexpensive, and effective technologies (Thomas 1971, 1986). The federal government accepts the hierarchical model and is the primary supporter of basic biomedical research through the National Institutes of Health (NIH); the NIH also fund applied research when an "adequate fundamental science base exists" (President's Biomedical Research Panel 1976, p. 5). (In contrast, most industry investment is in applied research and development [Banta 1984].)

A number of scholars have pointed out that the hierarchical view of science and technology is simplistic. Price (1965) argues that technology and science have separate cumulating structures and a reciprocal relationship. Only in "special and traumatic cases" does technology flow from the research front of science or vice versa. For example, use of the iron lung [technology] to ventilate patients suffering from respiratory failure resulting from poliomyelitis unexpectedly "led to a greater understanding of respiratory physiology [basic science]" (Maxwell 1986, p. 22). A different relationship has been proposed by Barnes and Edge (1982, p. 152), who write that the relationship between them is symmetrical, and "nothing in the relationship itself favours one direction or causal connection over the opposite." They even go so far as to claim that "advocacy of the hierarchical model is in a steep decline and among those involved in the serious study of science and technology it may already be defunct" (Barnes and Edge 1982, p. 149). Technology and science interact in complex and unpredictable ways.

Related to the assumption of hierarchy is the notion that the development of medical technology, because it is based on scientific knowledge, is unaffected by social forces. The direction it takes results from successful transformation of basic knowledge into drugs, devices, procedures, or techniques that can be applied in medicine. In a discussion of technology generally, Winner (1980, p. 122) labels this viewpoint "naive technological determinism—the idea that technology is the sole result of an internal dynamic."

An examination of the development of DES shows how science is not impervious to social forces (Bell 1986). When sex endocrinologists (mostly biochemists) synthesized DES, their work was guided by the paradigm of biochemistry. However, they also wanted to find a cheap substitute for physicians to use in medical care. Their basic research was stimulated by a perceived clinical need. At the same time, they accepted the prevailing social view of the 1930s that sex differences and sexual and reproductive behavior were determined by hormones. They believed that their studies of estrogen function would enable them to understand the hormone's role in shaping emotions and behavior in females and thereby confirm the biological basis of sex differences. Sex endocrinologists were also interested in solidifying their professional position and proving that their work was "real science." As one of the biochemists— later knighted for his role in the synthesis of sex hormones (Apfel and Fisher 1984)— wrote:

It is difficult to call to mind any subject upon which more rubbish has been written than the sex hormones. This is largely the result of the general public's desire for the maintenance of youth and all that it implies, together with the successful exploitation of this trait by commercial firms." (Dodds 1934, p. 1318)

This scientist and others who synthesized DES and observed its estrogenic effects did not simply discover these facts; their interests and intellectual traditions led them to produce this particular substance and to highlight specific aspects of it, such as its potency and oral effectiveness.

The stage model also assumes that development ends before diffusion begins, that the process is discontinuous. This, too, has policy implications: Prevent premature diffusion and evaluate new technologies before they are diffused. One way to prevent premature diffusion is with new drug and device regulations. In the United States these regulations are enforced by the FDA. Until 1962 the FDA controlled drug safety and truth in labeling. In 1962 proof of efficacy was added to drug regulations, and in 1976 the FDA was given the same authority to regulate new devices (Lashoff 1981).

Research required by the FDA, and clinical research in general, involves setting methodological standards. However, these standards are contested. For example, there are many ways to interpret the meaning of "safety" and "efficacy" (Banta, Behney, and Willems 1981; Bell 1986; Davis 1984). Determining safety and efficacy, once they have been defined, is also a matter of dispute. Randomized controlled trials (RCTs)[2] are often promoted as the best method to determine safety and efficacy (McKinlay 1982; Silverman 1980), although they are resisted by clinicians (Apfel and Fisher 1984) and patients (Kramer 1987), especially in desperate situations. Furthermore, even RCTs often yield ambiguous results (Fineberg and Hiatt 1979). Thus, the research on which FDA decisions are made is inconsistent and often ambiguous.

The DES case reveals how diffusion can occur before development ends. It thereby illustrates weaknesses inherent in the stage model's assumption that development ends before diffusion begins, and in the policies associated with this assumption. With DES, diffusion began before development ended because of particular political and economic conditions that shaped relationships between drug companies, the FDA, and medical specialists (Bell 1986). In 1938, the same year that DES was synthesized, the U.S. Congress passed the Federal Food,

---

[2]If a new medical technology is being tested for efficacy using a RCT, subjects are randomly assigned to one of two groups. One group (the experiment) is treated with the new technology, and the other (the control) receives the established treatment, a placebo, or no treatment at all. The groups are expected to be similar in all ways except for treatment. After treatment, the two groups are compared to see if there is a statistically significant difference between the results of the experiment and control.

Drug and Cosmetic Act, which required that before new drugs could be sold, firms had to meet new standards. Each firm wishing to market a new drug was required, among other things, to show that animal and human research by scientific experts proved it was safe for use in the condition prescribed, recommended, or suggested in labeling. For each new product, each firm had to submit a new drug application to the FDA for review. These drug regulations permitted experts to gather evidence of safety by exempting all drugs from these requirements if they were used for investigational purposes only. Theoretically, this exemption prevented the use of unapproved drugs in clinical practice at the same time that it promoted their use in clinical research. Typically, though, "research" was often little more than a label to bring clinical practice into conformity with federal regulations (Bell 1986).

Most firms did not yet have their own research divisions and depended on physicians and scientists to conduct research for them (Bell 1986). To amass evidence of the safety of DES, drug companies, through detail men, exchanged money and supplies (free samples) for free labor power and information. Because most medical research was privately funded until World War II, this exchange was welcomed by the medical community. Giving free samples to physicians also helped firms to create a market for DES. In their publications, researchers indicated brand and dosages used, thereby giving free advertising to each company. These were significant benefits, since DES was not patented and almost one hundred firms were interested in marketing it. In these ways, the relationships between interested communities—drug companies, physicians, and the FDA—led to the diffusion of DES before development ended.

Aside from these problems, regulating the development of medical technologies from the perspective of a stage model suffers from an additional limitation. Medical technology evolves and undergoes constant modification (Fox and Swazey 1974). Devel-

opment, in other words, is continuous. The DES case illustrates this well (Bell 1986).

Even though medical specialists and the FDA reached a consensus that DES was safe if used to treat four conditions, there were already published reports of its effects in many other medical problems, such as amenorrhea, dysmenorrhea, and pregnancy complications. These were summarized in a 1941 review article (Morrell 1941). After DES was approved for marketing in 1941, physicians applied it in their clinical research and practice to these other conditions. DES continues to be prescribed for some conditions, although it is no longer considered safe and effective in others (Apfel and Fisher 1984). This expansion and contraction of uses cannot be explained merely by the discovery of new facts about DES. The changing contexts of the fact finders must also be taken into account. These contexts, in Gusfield's (1981, p. 20) words, enabled them to pick certain facts out of a pile and then scrub, polish, and highlight them, as well as to have the authority to legitimate these findings.

The DES example shows that diffusion and development are not separate sequential stages and, moreover, that development is shaped by the contexts in which investigators work. Although it may be possible, in retrospect, to describe the development of specific medical technologies using versions of the stage model, this vastly oversimplifies the process (Bell 1986; Jevons 1976). Thus, we need to rethink how and why new technologies are brought into being in order to judge the strengths and weaknesses of new drug and device regulations and other policies for controlling the development of new technologies.

Alternative Models of Technology Development

Two alternative views of medical technology development have been proposed by sociologists, both contesting the assumption that the work of each stage is performed by distinct communities. To the contrary, they emphasize the relationships between communities. One is a Marxist, or social determinist, view that "the very nature of capitalist production necessitates the continuing development of new products and sales in new markets" (Waitzkin 1979, p. 1260). Innovations are usually stimulated or initiated by industrial corporations seeking to expand by producing and selling new products. According to this view, the structure of the capitalist system determines the development of medical technology. This structure includes private corporations, academic medical centers, private philanthropies, the health labor force, and the state. Technological change serves their common interests. What matters "is not the technology itself, but the social or economic system in which it is embedded" (Winner 1980, p. 122). Since technological innovation is instigated by private corporations, the "compulsory restriction of profit in health care and eventual public ownership of medical industries" will contain costs and eliminate the production of ineffective new technologies (Waitzkin 1979, p. 1267; see also Waitzkin 1983). The solution to control of medical technology development lies in the curtailment of private profit, which would dramatically alter the relationships between these groups. The structure of the system must be revised in order to control medical technology.

The other viewpoint is "interactive" (Bell 1986). This model reveals complexities in the development process and, like the Marxist model, underscores the importance of interactions between communities. However, unlike the Marxist model, it proposes that the development of medical technology is shaped, but not determined, by economic and social forces. In contrast to Marxism, which leads to the conclusion that technology development can be explained by its social origins, and technological determinism, which "fails to look behind technical devices to see the social circumstances of their development" (Winner 1980, p. 122), the interactive model attends to both social origins and the characteristics of technologies themselves.

According to the interactive model, specific communities in particular political and economic circumstances produce new technologies. These communities have particular ways of seeing and solving problems, as well as distinctive interests that shape their practices. Each of these communities has its own internal dynamics as well as patterns of interaction with the others. Yet, these communities have different positions and levels of power within a broader political-economic context. This context organizes and structures their relationships. Although communities produce technology, their ideas and practices change in response to it over time (Bell 1986).

In the DES case, for instance, drug companies, medical specialists, the FDA, and research scientists brought a new medical technology into being. Their interactions were conditioned by New Deal politics, specifically, new drug regulations. In turn, the production of DES influenced their practices. For example, the availability of DES was one of the factors that led to the medicalization of menopause (Bell 1987).

Both the Marxist and interactive models show how difficult it is to discover points in the development process at which to intervene. Policy is, correspondingly, more difficult to construct because solutions are less dramatic and clear. Yet, they imply that there are many levels on which change can occur, thereby expanding the possibilities for policy intervention.

To summarize, sociological approaches to medical technology development reveal complexities in the relationships among science, technology, and society. According to these versions of the development process, there is not a straightforward, hierarchical connection between science and technology, nor is science separate from social values. Scientists are not merely discoverers of reality; they, along with other interested parties, construct reality. Reality, thus, is not firmly fixed but emerges continuously. As social context changes so do technologies, and vice versa. Finally, there is more than one way to understand the development process.

HOW DOES MEDICAL TECHNOLOGY DIFFUSE?

Diffusion is "the process by which an innovation [an object, practice, or idea that is new to an adopting unit] is communicated through certain channels over time among the members of a social system" (Rogers 1983, p. 5). Studies of diffusion examine the characteristics of early and late adopters; patterns of communication about new medical technologies; the "shape" of the diffusion process; the relationship between adoption, use, and abandonment of technologies; and the way characteristics of the innovation and the environment influence diffusion. A thorough introduction to this vast field of research can be found in Greer (1977, 1981), Kaluzny and Hernandez (1983), and Rogers (1983). As in the case of development, there is more than one way to understand the diffusion process. Alternative frameworks suggest alternative policies.

In addition to conceiving of medical technology development in stages, with development preceding diffusion, policymakers have identified physicians as the driving force behind the adoption and use of technology (Budrys 1986, Greer 1984, 1986). According to this view, physicians' desire to innovate and their ability to do so has caused the adoption and use of costly, often unproven, medical technologies. The policy that is consistent with this view of the process involves control of physician behavior at specific points. Sociological studies of diffusion explore the origins of this version of the process and its limitations and construct alternative explanations for the diffusion of medical technologies.

The typical version of diffusion may be summarized as follows: Physicians want to innovate. They respond to the availability of information about technologies by adopting, using, or abandoning them. They make all decisions in this regard, and they all agree (Budrys 1986; Greer 1984, 1986). According to this view, even when hospitals or other organizations adopt and use technologies, they do so in response to the desires of individual physicians. Specific policy solutions follow. One policy associated with this view is to inform physicians about technologies through continuing education programs and articles in medical journals. Unfortunately, this policy has not been successful (Anderson et al. 1986; Greer 1981).

A second type of policy involves the use of regulations to control the adoption of new medical technologies. In 1974, Congress passed the National Health Planning and Resources Development Act, which authorizes regional planning by local agencies to regulate the diffusion of expensive capital equipment and the number and scope of medical facilities. This legislation requires that each hospital or nursing home seek a certificate-of-need (CON) from a regional agency (Health Systems Agency) before it can purchase expensive new medical technology. Applications can be denied if the local agency determines that there is not sufficient need for the technology (Banta 1984; Lashoff 1981). A weakness in the CON program is that it does not cover private offices and clinics. This loophole has been used by hospitals to circumvent denial of their requests for new technologies (Banta and Russell 1981).

The diagnosis-related group system (DRG) is a third type of policy that attempts to control the use of hospital technologies. Until 1983 hospitals were guaranteed that Medicare would reimburse them for all costs. Under the new system, each hospital receives the same payment rate for patients with a given diagnosis, regardless of how long they stay or what type of care they need. The primary objective of the DRG system is to reduce the rate of increase in federal expenditures for care to elderly and disabled patients by providing a financial disincentive to overuse of hospital services. The system also is designed to promote more cost-conscious policies in the adoption and use of medical technologies. Davis, Anderson, and Steinberg (1984, p. 146) review the strengths and weaknesses of DRGs and conclude that although they provide a basis for a fair, rational allocation of resources, they bring the potential for a new set of problems: "underutilization of services, possible reductions in the quality of care, and the thwarting of technological development."

Alternative policies can be derived from different versions of the diffusion process. Sociologists specify the circumstances under which physicians do and do not want to innovate, respond to information, have decision-making power, and agree. By differentiating categories of physician, types of technology, and varieties of decision systems and environments, sociologists can reveal variations in the diffusion of new technologies. These systematic variations provide an alternative framework for thinking about policy.

To test the adequacy of the typical version of diffusion, I examine, first, how individual physicians adopted and used DES as a clinical tool and, second, how organizations, specifically hospitals, decide to adopt new medical technologies. The patterns of DES use in pregnancy demonstrate how physicians can diverge in their assessment of technologies and why they might not respond to the availability of information (i.e., be resistant to change). Paradoxically, individual physicians resist some changes at the same time they champion others. Regarding organizations, others have shown that different decision systems operate for different types of technology, with physicians' power varying accordingly. In organizations, physicians' interest in adopting new technologies depends on the type of technology and varies along the lines of specialty, type of practice, and relationship to the organization (Budrys 1986; Greer 1984, 1986; Nathanson and Morlock 1980).

Individual Physicians: Diffusion Models and Reality

Researchers have generally confirmed a standard pattern of adoption of technologies such as DES that are prescribed by individual physicians to individual patients[3] (see Greer 1977, 1981, 1988). Early adopters are professionally ambitious. They seek out information and innovate in order to increase their prestige and status among their colleagues (Becker 1970), but they use new technologies cautiously at first (Coleman, Katz, and Menzel 1966). Furthermore, they are integrated into collegial networks, in which they are central figures. They convince others in their network to adopt specific technologies. They are "cosmopolites," individuals who are oriented toward national groups, events, and information sources instead of their local communities, and they are younger, better educated, and more geographically mobile than later adopters (Coleman, Katz, and Menzel 1966).

Overall, their adoption behavior creates a pattern. Diffusion begins slowly, accelerating as those who adopt an innovation influence their colleagues to adopt it subsequently, and levels off after most individuals adopt it. This S-shaped curve occurs in two steps, first for the integrated physicians and then for the isolated ones (Coleman, Katz, and Menzel 1966). Variations in adoption occur, depending on characteristics of the medical technology (Becker 1970) and the illness (Warner 1975, 1977).

There is also diversity in the use of new and routine medical technologies (Greer 1981). Variation has been observed in use of a computerized hospital information system by physicians in a single private group practice (Anderson and Jay 1985), in rates of surgery for nine procedures in comparable hospital service areas in Maine and Vermont (Wennberg and Gittelsohn 1975), and in utilization of diagnostic tests for similar patients by physicians in different teaching hospitals and in a teaching hospital compared to a community hospital (Fineberg 1979). These variations suggest that physicians disagree about the appro-

---

[3]There has been no systematic study of the patterns of adoption of DES for use in pregnancy.

priate use of medical technologies, posing a challenge to the standard conception that physicians are unanimous in their assessment of medical technology. Understanding how and why their assessment varies can lead to policy alternatives.

Epidemiological data show variability in the use of DES (Gutterman 1983). Like other technologies, the distribution of DES-exposed births ranged from none in some hospitals to as much as 13 percent of female live births in others (Heinonen 1973; Nash et al. 1983). There were also differences in timing (from less than one week to nine months of exposure) and dosage (from less than 1 gram to more than 45 grams total) (Heinonen 1973). Most likely, these variations resulted from factors other than the characteristics of patient populations (Apfel and Fisher 1984; Sipe 1982).

The variations in use can be traced to characteristics of physicians, the innovation, and the social context. Collegial networks (Coleman, Katz, and Menzel 1966) were probably significant in the distribution of DES. Biochemist Olive Smith and her husband, obstetrician George Smith, were respected, Harvard-based researchers. The Smiths pioneered and championed the use of DES in pregnancy. Their advocacy of DES and their centrality in a network of physicians help to explain why DES was used more widely in the Boston area than elsewhere and often according to their protocol (although use varied even in Boston [Nash et al. 1983]). One of the Smiths' retired colleagues said at a specialty society meeting in 1953, "As a former Bostonian, I would be entirely lacking in civic loyalty if I had not used stilbestrol in my private practice" (Dieckmann et al. 1953, p. 1080).

Another explanation for these differences is disagreement among physicians, which has been endemic to the study of DES since its synthesis (Bell 1986, 1987). Physicians contested the effectiveness of DES in preventing miscarriage, indications for its use, proper timing and dosage, and

methodologies for its evaluation (Apfel and Fisher 1984). Even today, the link between prenatal exposure to DES and vaginal cancer is challenged on methodological grounds (McFarlane, Feinstein, and Horwitz 1986), and some physicians continue to express belief in the ability of DES to prevent miscarriage (for an example, see Apfel and Fisher 1984, pp. 112–113).

Disagreements such as these are common within medicine and are often distributed among particular categories of physician. Sociological studies show that physicians may divide along the lines of specialty, type, or location of practice. Budrys (1986), for example, argues that socialization in residencies leads different specialties to value some forms of treatment over others; see also McKinlay (1982), Millman (1976), and Light (1979) on this point. Each specialty has its own paradigm (Kuhn 1970), or way of seeing and solving problems. Kaufert and McKinlay (1985) demonstrate that even within specialties, researchers and clinicians can differ.

A policy response flows from these observations. If collegial networks and patterned ways of seeing and solving problems influence physicians' use of medical technologies, then one way to reach individual physicians is to identify networks and influential individuals in them and direct information toward these individuals (Anderson et al. 1986; Becker 1970; Greer 1988). Locating the particular category of physicians included in the network can be a means of understanding how they think (i.e., their paradigms) and therefore what kind of information is most likely to be absorbed and disseminated through the network.

Close study of DES use indicates a lack of correlation between available literature about its efficacy and physician behavior, challenging the view that they are linked. For example, in 1953, the results of two controlled studies indicated that DES is no more effective than a placebo in preventing miscarriage (Dieckmann et al. 1953; Ferguson 1953). Both sets of results were presented at specialty society meetings and subsequently published in the *American Journal of Obstetrics and Gynecology*. Yet, a retrospective review of hospital records indicates that perhaps 10,000 to 16,000 DES daughters were born each year between 1960 and 1970 (Heinonen 1973). The peak usage of DES at a Wisconsin clinic was in 1964, when 9 percent of all babies born were exposed to DES (Nash et al. 1983).

Greer (1981, 1988) suggests that one reason for the lack of correlation between the availability of information and diffusion is that physicians are suspicious of published studies, probably with good reason, since studies often contain serious methodological flaws and provide little help on transferring results to different settings or categories of patients. Physicians are not well trained in research methods either, making it difficult for them to interpret results (Lipton and Hershaft 1985).

The clinical mentality (Freidson 1970) may also account for why physicians did not change their behavior in response to controlled studies. DES was usually prescribed to pregnant women by clinicians in private practice—doctors oriented toward the practical solution of individual problems (Nash et al. 1983). Their work, according to Freidson (1970), is applied work, involving intervention irrespective of available knowledge and revolving around experiences with individual cases. These characteristics of everyday medical work encourage physicians to make treatment decisions based on firsthand clinical experience rather than scientifically verified knowledge. Physicians build up a world of clinical experiences, which is self-validating and which devalues scientific knowledge. They act on the basis of clinical experience, and if their acts seem "to get results, or at least no untoward results, [they are] resistant to changing [them] on the basis of statistical or abstract considerations" (Freidson 1970, p. 170). The clinical experiences of obstetricians, whose patients gave birth to healthy babies, continually validated their

belief that DES worked. The power of the clinical mentality is evidenced by some physicians who prescribed DES to pregnant women and still assert its efficacy (see Apfel and Fisher 1984, pp. 112–113). Physicians' suspicion of published results and clinical mentality suggest the need for face-to-face discussions about medical technologies, instead of communication through published reports.

The broader context may have been an additional factor in the continued use of DES. DES was one of many therapies used in the era following World War II, when science was recognized as a "national asset" and medicine was viewed as the "epitome" of progress without conflict (Starr 1982, p. 336). It was a wonder drug, an "example of daring, of tampering with nature and expecting to save and cure" (Apfel and Fisher 1984, p. 29). In this context, to withhold treatment with DES might have seemed "an act of cruelty rather than caution" (Apfel and Fisher 1984, p. 35). Pressure may have been exerted both by members of the medical community and by the public to continue to use DES in pregnancy.

The medicalization of reproduction may be another way the broader context influenced the use of DES after 1953. The experiences of women are particularly vulnerable to "medicalization," the process in which human experiences are defined as medical problems that medical personnel should treat (Conrad and Schneider 1980; Riessman 1983). By the 1950s, childbirth and pregnancy were medical affairs and focused more and more sharply on the fetus's condition as opposed to the woman's (Leavitt 1983; Oakley 1984; Silverman 1980). Prematurity was associated with low birth weight and infant mortality; medicine took on the task of preventing premature births and caring for premature babies in an effort to reduce infant mortality (McCormick 1986; Silverman 1980). DES was one of the medical solutions to prematurity. Thus, it is not surprising that although at first DES was prescribed only for a few, serious conditions, later it was prescribed for slight or no apparent problems (Apfel and Fisher 1984). Medicalizing pregnancy led to the expanded and continued use of DES.

Put simply, individual physicians make decisions about the use of medical technologies in the context of a broader culture; medical thinking is "parallel in some way with the structure of other intellectual products or of the society itself" (Wright and Treacher 1982, p. 11). Sociologists have explored how medicine both represents and contributes to American (or Western) culture (Bell 1987; Conrad and Schneider 1980; Wright and Treacher 1982). The biomedical model, the predominant model guiding medical work, is compatible with this culture (Mishler 1981). This model is presented and sustained by groups with authority—medical professionals, biomedical researchers, the drug industry, the state, academic medical centers, hospitals—in short, the medical establishment. It is reaffirmed by individual doctors and patients who, despite evidence to the contrary, believe that "industrial populations owe higher health standards to scientific medicine, that such medical technology as currently exists is largely effective in coping with the tasks it faces, and it offers great promise for the future" (Powles 1980, pp. 34–35). Medical decision making, in many respects, is inextricably bound up with broader cultural values. To change aspects of medical thinking is to challenge cultural beliefs more generally.

In sum, this brief discussion of DES shows that like development, the adoption and use of a medical technology by individual physicians is a complex process, shaped by many factors. It is marked by disputes about matters such as efficacy and safety, which are distributed among different categories of physician in different collegial networks. These disputes, in turn, explain variation in usage. Usage persists, despite evidence from controlled studies, for many reasons, including characteristics of physicians (suspicion of published results, poor understanding of research methods, the

clinical mentality), the innovation (a "wonder drug"), and the social context (medicalization).[4]

The use of DES in pregnancy provides strong counterevidence to standard views about consensus in medicine and the relationship between the availability of information and utilization of technologies. It illustrates the importance of looking at variations in use, and then for ways that usage might vary systematically. Systematic variations suggest ways to influence behavior—beyond exposing all to the same information in traditional sources—by influencing particular physicians.

Two other issues remain in the DES example: (1) the notion that physicians make the major decisions about adoption, use, and abandonment of new medical technologies and (2) the idea that they want to innovate. In fact, DES usage supports these views of the diffusion process. Physicians seized upon DES as a panacea and controlled its use (Apfel and Fisher 1984). To address these issues, I will examine the diffusion of new medical technologies in organizations.

Diffusion in Organizations

Today, medical technologies are primarily adopted by and used in organizations, usually hospitals (Russell 1978). Technologies account for one-third to three-quarters of the cost of hospital care, which in turn accounts for a high proportion of the cost of medical care in general (Banta, Behney, and Willems 1981; NCHS 1985).

Studies of diffusion generally assume that physicians have the power to make decisions in organizations because of their au-

---

4It is beyond the scope of this study to explore other factors that may account for variations in the use and abandonment of medical technologies by individual practitioners: financial incentives (reimbursement) activity by industry suppliers, consumer or patient preferences, patient reassurance, legal or regulatory requirements, and malpractice concerns (Banta 1984; Greer 1981; Ost and Antweiler 1986; Waitzkin 1979).

thority and their economic leverage, or "patient leverage" (Greer 1984). Their authority stems from "professional dominance," meaning that medicine supervises and gives orders to all other occupations in the division of labor and this hierarchy of authority is sanctioned by law (Freidson 1985). Professional dominance also functions at the level of the hospital because physicians control clinical decisions and have influence over hospital workers. Because of their medical authority, physicians also have power over hospital trustees and administrators (Greer 1984). Physicians have economic leverage as well. They control patient admissions, and a sufficient patient load is essential for the operation of hospitals (Greer and Zakhar 1979). Thus, professional dominance and economic leverage explain why physicians control the adoption and use of new technologies.

In her detailed study of technology adoption in twenty-five midwestern community hospitals, Greer (1984, 1986) offers a more complex model. She specifies different types of technology, physicians, hospital decision systems, and environments. This specification reveals that professional dominance and patient leverage explain some, but not all, of the dynamics of technology adoption. For example, Greer identifies four categories of physician. Professional dominance and patient leverage are greatest among two of them— community-based generalists and specialists. These categories concentrate on primary care in private offices. Of the two, only community specialists are knowledgeable about and interested in new technologies; the particular types of technology that they find interesting are "clinical tools"— technologies that are relatively inexpensive and minimally disruptive to other units in a hospital, since they are used by the community specialists on private patients. Examples are electronic fetal monitors, laser surgery, and phacoemulsification (a technique for cataract removal). When community specialists want hospitals to adopt new clinical tools, their requests are reviewed,

judged, and typically approved by their medical peers. They have the authority and economic leverage, as well as the knowledge, interest, and organizational experience, to persuade other physicians in the hospital hierarchy to purchase new clinical tools.

Greer finds that community-based generalists and specialists are not interested in changing the service offerings of a hospital by adopting technologies such as CAT scanners (computer axial tomography), which require hospital-based specialists for their operation (in this case, radiologists). They also have no interest in persuading hospitals to alter their "missions" and adopt whole new systems, such as neonatal intensive care units. Even if they had such an interest, they could not implement these goals, because different decision systems are brought into being for these types of technology. In addition, they cannot successfully resist adoption of these types of technology, which are championed by hospital-based specialists or administrators and brought into hospitals through fiscal-managerial decision-making systems. Despite their professional dominance and patient leverage, community generalists and specialists are not powerful in the adoption of some types of technology.

The evidence presented by Greer challenges the view that physicians control the adoption of new technologies. Different groups are powerful in different types of technology adoption using resources appropriate to different decision-making systems. (For other examples, see Budrys [1986] and Nathanson and Morlock [1980].)

Finally, the predominant version of diffusion portrays physicians as eager innovators. Their eagerness has variously been attributed to a desire to offer improved care, which they have been socialized to associate with innovation; quest for prestige, which is related to being up-to-date, scientific, and innovative; response to peer pressure from members of their collegial networks; fear of malpractice suits, which encourages a greater reliance on technologies to confirm diagnoses; lack of incentive to keep costs down because the technologies they adopt and use are reimbursed by third parties; and desire for personal financial gain. The role of these factors in innovation has been explored by numerous sociologists (Budrys 1986; Greer and Zakhar 1979; McKinlay 1982; Ost and Antweiler 1986; Waitzkin 1979). Organizational studies of technology adoption indicate that only some categories of physician champion new technologies. Hospital-based specialists, such as radiologists, who work under contract to hospitals and provide services to patients admitted by other physicians, desire new technologies to maintain state-of-the-art practices (Greer 1986; Ost and Antweiler 1986).

Just as individual physicians resist new technologies, so do physicians in organizational contexts. In a comparative study of twelve hospitals, Nathanson and Morlock (1980) find that obstetrical departments resist the adoption of new services (such as abortion care and adolescent pregnancy clinics) because their work activities are most affected by this type of technology. Greer (1986, p. 207) finds that community physicians - are "usually skeptical about medical innovations, cautious about the ability of local persons and institutions to successfully implement different procedures, and resistant to changes in hospital organization." Put simply, organizational studies specify the conditions under which physicians want to innovate and control the adoption of medical technologies. It is simplistic to assume that all physicians want to innovate, that they have the power to effect their decisions, and that they unanimously adopt and use all new technologies.

In sum, the diffusion process is marked by disputes reflecting variations in the characteristics of both physicians and technologies. The process is also marked by resistance, stemming from the clinical mentality and broader social context; resistance also occurs in patterned ways, along the lines of specialty, type of medical practice, and type of technology. Within hospitals, different categories of physicians draw on different resources to promote different technology types. They are joined in this effort by administrators, whose participation is reflective of hospital goals and environments.

CONCLUSION

The predominant versions of the development and diffusion of medical technology portray them as orderly and predictable processes. The regulatory framework of governmental policy assumes that development and diffusion occur in stages, controlled by specific actors (namely, physicians), who eagerly innovate. New drug and device regulations, certificate-of-need legislation, and diagnosis-related groups exemplify policies directed to the control of this version of the process. The sociological perspective suggests that the weaknesses in these policies may be connected to oversimplification. Regarding the adoption and use of hospital technologies, for example, the findings of recent studies imply that it is difficult, if not impossible, to construct universal policies. Different types of policies are appropriate for different types of technologies adopted and used in different hospital situations.

The version of medical technology development and diffusion I have presented emphasizes the extent to which they are complex processes, evolving over time and marked by uncertainty. They are shaped by values and structures at the broadest levels of society, as well as those in local environments. Relationships between and among institutions and organizations, having standard ways of thinking about problems, create the context in which decisions are made to pursue some research questions and to adopt and use specific types of technologies. More directly, the production of medical technologies is carried out by interacting groups of physicians, scientists, regulators, and industrialists. Decisions to adopt and use new medical technologies are made by different categories of physician or hospital administrators, who also interact.

The greater complexity of development and diffusion revealed by a sociological analysis has implications for policy. Here I sketch out but a few. First, the ability to construct policy alternatives depends on redistribution of the authority to define the problems and solutions and suggests that the process be opened up, that new participants be invited, and that they be empowered (Gusfield 1981). These participants could include lay citizens, professionals in fields unrelated to the medical technologies under consideration, and representatives of public interest groups (Dutton 1984). In the DES case, the public began to have a meaningful voice after prenatal exposure was linked to cancer in 1971 (Dutton 1984). DES-exposed persons formed a self-help group (DES Action), which became involved in the evaluation of risks and benefits associated with DES usage and helped to broaden the analysis so that it included quality of life concerns. DES Action also successfully lobbied at the national level for appointment of a DES Task Force, which recommended against the use of oral contraceptives and estrogens by DES mothers and daughters despite the lack of scientific evidence and opposition from medical experts: "Prudence" was the basis for this decision (Dutton 1984). Involvement by nonexperts helps to frame discussions in such a way that "soft" issues are more likely to be included.

A second approach to policy implied by my discussion relates to the evaluation and reevaluation of technologies and the uses to which they are put. "Technology assessment" is an evaluative strategy growing out of the perspective of a stage model that addresses some of the difficulties arising when technologies develop continuously (Fineberg and Hiatt 1979; Greer 1981). Technology assessment considers and explicates the broad effects on society, especially unintended, indirect, or delayed social effects that are "caused by the introduction of a new technology or by the extension of the use of an existing technology" (Banta and Sanes 1978, p. 248). Its goal is to "provide decision makers with information on policy alternatives, such as allocation of research and development funds, formulation of regulations, or development of new legislation" (Banta, Behney, and Willems 1981, p. 152). Long-term evaluation such as this could help to expose difficulties and suggest modifications in usage for specific technologies.

Two government programs currently use technology assessment to evaluate medical technologies. The first is the Office of Technology Assessment, which was established by Congress in 1972 and which has completed evaluations of thirty-seven technologies (U.S. Congress 1986). The second is the Consensus Development Program of the National Institutes of Health, which supports fifteen to twenty conferences each year to bring together practicing physicians, medical specialists, academic researchers and other experts to evaluate technologies and recommend appropriate uses of them (Banta 1982; Budrys 1986).[5]

A sociological perspective suggests that technology assessment begin by identifying collegial networks and their standard ways of seeing and solving problems and by studying network practices. This can help to map out how use of specific technologies varies geographically, categorically, and temporally; it can provide a means for comparing efficacy and safety in different settings over time. Findings could be communicated with network leaders to counter the clinical mentality and suspicion of published results that lead physicians to resist incorporating new medical knowledge (Greer 1988).

---

[5]There are a number of unresolved problems in technology assessment, including how to isolate the effects of specific technologies and extrapolate the results from one setting to another, how to determine costs and benefits, how to assess future events, and how to disseminate results (Banta and Sanes 1978; Budrys 1986; Fineberg and Hiatt 1979; Greer 1981).

Reevaluation of technology usage could also be conducted on a case-by-case basis and include more participants—parents, families, and patients themselves whenever possible. In their study of neonatal intensive care, Guillemin and Holmstrom (1986) recommend that if critically ill newborns are resuscitated, their status be reassessed after the crisis has passed. Likewise, when a long patient career is predicted, multiple points of reevaluation could be fixed (see Plough [1986] on this point regarding kidney dialysis).

Finally, development and diffusion are influenced by ideas and institutional arrangements at the broadest levels of society, where change occurs slowly, against great resistance. Nevertheless, the foregoing analysis suggests that attention be focused on how these contexts shape development and diffusion and begin to look for alternatives. As with the other proposals, alternatives are more likely to emerge if there are more participants, beyond the experts who currently define the problems and solutions. Put simply, there are no "quick fixes."

ACKNOWLEDGMENTS

The author thanks Ann Lennarson Greer, Craig McEwen, and Catherine Kohler Riessman for helping to clarify the points in this essay. Research assistance from Catherine Dempsey is gratefully acknowledged. Work on this chapter was supported by a grant from the Faculty Development Fund, Bowdoin College.

REFERENCES

Aiken, Linda H., and Howard E. Freeman. 1980. Medical Sociology and Science and Technology in Medicine, in P. T. Durbin, ed., *A Guide to the Culture of Science, Technology and Medicine*. New York: Free Press, pp. 527–580.

Apfel, Roberta J., and Susan M. Fisher. 1984. *To Do No Harm: DES and the Dilemmas of Modern Medicine*. New Haven: Yale University Press.

Anderson, James G., and Stephen J. Jay. 1985. Computers and Clinical Judgment: The Role of Physician Networks. *Social Science and Medicine* 20:969–979.

Anderson, James G., Stephen J. Jay, Harlan M. Schweer, and Marilyn M. Anderson. 1986. Physician Utilization of Computers in Medical Practice: Policy Implications Based on A Structural Model. *Social Science and Medicine* 23:259–267.

Banta, H. David. 1982. Technology: Review of Medical Technology Policies Shows Need, Opportunities for Changes. *Hospitals* 56:87–90.

———. 1983. Social Science Research on Medical Technology: Utility and Limitations. *Social Science and Medicine* 18:1363–1369.

———. 1984. Embracing or Rejecting Innovations: Clinical Diffusion of Health Care Technology, in S. Reiser and M. Anbar, eds., *The Machine at the Bedside*. New York: Cambridge University Press, pp. 65–92.

Banta, H. David, Clyde J. Behney, and Jane Sisk Willems. 1981. *Toward Rational Technology in Medicine: Considerations for Health Policy*. New York: Springer.

Banta, H. David, and Louise B. Russell. 1981. Policies toward Medical Technology: An International Review. *International Journal of Health Services* 11:631–652.

Banta, H. David, and Joshua R. Sanes. 1978. Assessing the Social Impacts of Medical Technologies. *Journal of Community Health* 3:245–258.

Barnes, Barry, and David Edge. 1982. The Interaction of Science and Technology, in B. Barnes and D. Edge, eds., *Science in Context*. Cambridge, Mass.: MIT Press, pp. 147–154.

Becker, Marshall H. 1970. Factors Affecting Diffusion of Innovations Among Health Professionals. *American Journal of Public Health* 60:294–304.

Bell, Susan E. 1986. A New Model of Medical Technology Development: A Case Study of DES, in J. Roth and S. Ruzek, eds., *Research in the Sociology of Health Care*, vol. 4. Greenwich, Conn.: JAI Press, pp. 1–32.

———. 1987. Changing Ideas: The Medicalization of Menopause. *Social Science and Medicine*. 24:535–542.

Budrys, Grace. 1986. Medical Technology Policy: Some Underlying Assumptions, in J.

Roth and S. Ruzek, eds., *Research in the Sociology of Health Care*, vol. 4. Greenwich, Conn.: JAI Press, pp. 147–183.

Coleman, James S., Elihu Katz, and Herbert Menzel. 1966. *Medical Innovation: A Diffusion Study*. New York: Bobbs-Merrill.

Conrad, Peter, and Joseph W. Schneider. 1980. *Deviance and Medicalization: From Badness to Sickness*. St. Louis: Mosby.

Davis, Karen, Gerard Anderson, and Earl Steinberg. 1984. Diagnosis Related Group Prospective Payment: Implications for Health Care and Medical Technology. *Health Policy* 4:139–147.

Davis, Philip W. 1984. An Incipient "Wonder Drug" Movement: DMSO and the Food and Drug Administration. *Social Problems* 32:197–212.

Dieckmann, W. J., M. E. Davis, L. M. Rynkiewicz, and R. E. Pottinger. 1953. Does the Administration of Diethylstilbestrol during Pregnancy Have Therapeutic Value? *American Journal of Obstetrics and Gynecology* 65:592–601.

Dodds, E. C. 1934. The Practical Outcome of Recent Research on Hormones. *Lancet* 227:1318–1320.

Dutton, Diana. 1984. The Impact of Public Participation in Biomedical Policy: Evidence from Four Case Studies, in J. C. Peterson, ed., *Citizen Participation in Science Policy*. Amherst, Mass.: University of Massachusetts Press, pp. 147–181.

Ferguson, James Henry. 1953. Effects of Stilbestrol Compared to Effect of a Placebo. *American Journal of Obstetrics and Gynecology* 65:592–601.

Fineberg, Harvey V. 1979. Clinical Chemistries: The High Cost of Low-cost Diagnostic Tests, in S. H. Altman and R. Blendon, eds., *Medical Technology: The Culprit Behind Health Care Costs?* DHEW Publication No. (PHS) 79-3216. Washington, D.C.: U.S. Government Printing Office, pp. 144–161.

Fineberg, Harvey V., and Howard H. Hiatt. 1979. Evaluation of Medical Practices: The Case for Technology Assessment. *New England Journal of Medicine* 301:1086–1091.

Fox, Renee C., and Judith P. Swazey. 1974. *The Courage to Fail: A Social View of Organ Transplants and Dialysis*. Chicago: University of Chicago Press.

Freidson, Eliot. 1970. *Profession of Medicine: A Study of the Sociology of Applied Knowledge*. New York: Harper and Row.

———. 1985. The Reorganization of the Medical Profession. *Medical Care Review* 42:11–35.

Greer, Ann Lennarson. 1977. Advances in the Study of Diffusion of Innovation in Health Care Organizations. *Milbank Memorial Fund Quarterly* 55:505–532.

———. 1981. Medical Technology: Assessment, Adoption, and Utilization. *Journal of Medical Systems* 5:129–145.

———. 1984. Medical Technology and Professional Dominance Theory. *Social Science and Medicine* 18:809–817.

———. 1986. Medical Conservatism and Technological Acquisitiveness: The Paradox of Hospital Technology Adoptions, in J. Roth and S. Ruzek, eds., *Research in The Sociology of Health Care*, vol. 4. Greenwich, Conn.: JAI Press, pp. 185–235.

———. 1988. The State of the Art vs. the State of the Science: The Diffusion of New Medical Technologies into Practice. *International Journal of Technology Assessment in Health Care* 4:5–26.

Greer, Ann Lennarson, and Arlene A. Zakhar. 1979. Patient Leverage Theory Proves to be False. *Hospitals* 53:98–106.

Guilleman, Jeanne, and Lynda Lytle Holmstrom. 1986. *Mixed Blessings: Intensive Care for Newborns*. New York: Oxford University Press.

Gusfield, Joseph R. 1981. *The Culture of Public Problems*. Chicago: University of Chicago Press.

Gutterman, Elane M. 1983. *The Psychological and Social Response to Toxic Exposures: The Case of Women Who Took DES*. Ph.D. diss., Columbia University.

Heinonen, Olli P. 1973. Diethylstilbestrol in Pregnancy: Frequency of Exposure and Usage Patterns. *Cancer* 31:573–577.

Jevons, F. R. 1976. The Interaction of Science and Technology Today, or, Is Science the Mother of Invention? *Technology and Culture* 17:729–738.

Journal of the American Medical Association. 1939. Estrogen Therapy—A Warning. 113:2323–2324.

Kaluzny, Arnold D., and S. Robert Hernandez. 1983. Organizational Change and Innovation, in S. M. Shortell and A. D. Kaluzny, eds., *Health Care Management: A Text in Organization Theory and Behavior.* New York: John Wiley, pp. 378–417.

Kaufert, Patricia M., and Sonja M. McKinlay. 1985. Estrogen Replacement Therapy: The Production of Medical Knowledge and Emergence of Policy, in E. Lewin and V. Olesen, eds., *Women, Health, and Healing.* New York: Tavistock Publications, pp. 113–138.

Kramer, Larry. 1987. The F.D.A.'s Callous Response to AIDS. *New York Times* March 23: A19.

Kuhn, Thomas. 1970. *The Structure of Scientific Revolutions,* 2nd ed. Chicago: University of Chicago Press.

Lashoff, Joyce C. 1981. Government Approaches to the Management of Medical Technology. *Bulletin of the New York Academy of Medicine* 57:36–44.

Leavitt, Judith Walzer. 1983. "Science" Enters the Birthing Room: Obstetrics in America since the Eighteenth Century. *Journal of American History* 70:281–304.

Levine, Sol. 1987. The Changing Terrains in Medical Sociology: Emergent Concern with Quality of Life. *Journal of Health and Social Behavior* 28:1–6.

Light, Donald. 1979. Uncertainty and Control in Professional Training. *Journal of Health and Social Behavior* 20:310–322.

Lipton, Jack P., and Alan M. Hershaft. 1985. On the Widespread Acceptance of Dubious Medical Findings. *Journal of Health and Social Behavior* 26:336–351.

Maxwell, James H. 1986. The Iron Lung: Halfway Technology or Necessary Step? *Millbank Quarterly* 64:3–29.

Mayr, Otto. 1976. The Science-Technology Relationship as a Historiographic Problem. *Technology and Culture* 17:663–672.

Mazer, Charles, S. Leon Israel, and Elkin Ravetz. 1941. The Synthetic Estrogen Stilbestrol: An Experimental and Clinical Evaluation. *Journal of the American Medical Association* 116:675–681.

McCormick, Marie C. 1986. Implications of Recent Changes in Infant Mortality, in L. H. Aiken and D. Mechanic, eds., *Applications of Social Science to Clinical Medicine and Health Policy.* New Brunswick, N.J.: Rutgers University Press, pp. 282–306.

McFarlane, Michael J., Alvin R. Feinstein, and Ralph I. Horowitz. 1986. Diethylstilbestrol and Clear Cell Vaginal Carcinoma: Reappraisal of the Epidemiologic Evidence. *American Journal of Medicine* 81:855–863.

McKinlay, John B. 1982. From "Promising Report" to "Standard Procedure": Seven Stages in the Career of a Medical Innovation, in J. B. McKinlay, ed., *Technology and the Future of Health Care.* Cambridge, Mass.: MIT Press, pp. 233–270.

Millman, Marcia. 1976. *The Unkindest Cut.* New York: William Morrow.

Mishler, Elliot G. 1981. Viewpoint, in E. G. Mishler, L. R. AmaraSingham, S. T. Hauser, R. Liem, S. D. Osherson, and N. E. Waxler, eds., *Social Contexts of Health, Illness, and Patient Care.* New York: Cambridge University Press, pp. 1–23.

Morrell, J. A. 1941. Stilbestrol: Summary of Some Clinical Reports on Stilbestrol. *Journal of Clinical Endocrinology* 1:419–423.

Najman, Jackob M., and Sol Levine. 1981. Evaluating the Impact of Medical Care and Technologies on the Quality of Life: A Review and Critique. *Social Science and Medicine* 15F:107–115.

Nash, Sally, Barbara C. Tilley, Leonard T. Kurland, Jerome Gundersen, Ann B. Barnes, Darwin LaBarthe, Pamela S. Donohew, and Linda Kovacs. 1983. Identifying and Tracing a Population at Risk: The DESAD Project Experience. *American Journal of Public Health* 73:253–259.

Nathanson, Constance A., and Laura L. Morlock. 1980. Control Structure, Values, and Innovation: A Comparative Study of Hospitals. *Journal of Health and Social Behavior* 21:315–333.

National Center for Health Statistics (NCHS). 1985. *Health, United States, 1985.* DHHS Publication No. (PHS) 86-1232, Public Health Service.

Noller, Kenneth L., and Charles S. Fish. 1974. Diethystilbestrol Usage: Its Interesting Past, Important Present, and Questionable Future. *Medical Clinics of North America* 58:793–810.

Novak, Emil. 1940. The Management of Menopause. *American Journal of Obstetrics and Gynecology* 40:589–595.

Oakley, Ann. 1984. *The Captured Womb: A History of the Medical Care of Pregnant Women.* New York: Basil Blackwell.

Ost, John, and Phillip Antweiler. 1986. The Social Impact of High Cost Medical Technology: Issues and Conflicts Surrounding the Decision to Adopt CAT Scanners, in J. Roth and S. Ruzek, eds., *Research in the Sociology of Health Care*, vol. 4. Greenwich, Conn.: JAI Press, pp. 33–92.

Plough, Alonzo L. 1986. *Borrowed Time: Artificial Organs and the Politics of Extended Lives*. Philadelphia: Temple University Press.

Powles, John. 1980. On the Limitations of Modern Medicine, in D. Mechanic, ed., *Readings in Medical Sociology*. New York: Free Press, pp. 18–44.

President's Biomedical Research Panel. 1976. *Report of the President's Biomedical Research Panel*. DHEW Publication No. (OS) 76-500. Washington, D.C.: U.S. Government Printing Office.

Price, Derek J. DeSolla. 1965. Is Technology Historically Independent of Science? A Study in Statistical Historiography. *Technology and Culture* 6:553–568.

Reiser, Stanley Joel. 1978. *Medicine and the Reign of Technology*. New York: Cambridge University Press.

Rettig, Richard A. 1978. Lessons Learned from the End-Stage Renal Disease Experience, in R. H. Egdahl and P. M. Gertman, eds., *Technology and the Quality of Health*. Germantown, Md.: Aspen Systems Corp., pp. 153–173.

Rettig, Richard A., and Alvin J. Harman. 1979. The Development of Medical Technology: A Policy Perspective, in *Medical Technology*. DHEW Publication No. (PHS) 79-3254, National Center for Health Services Research, pp. 82–91.

Riessman, Catherine Kohler. 1983. Women and Medicalization: A New Perspective. *Social Policy* 14:3–18.

Rogers, Everett. 1983. *Diffusion of Innovations*, 3rd ed. New York: Free Press.

Roth, Julius A., and Sheryl Burt Ruzek. 1986. Introduction, in J. Roth and S. Ruzek, eds., *Research in the Sociology of Health Care*, vol. 4. Greenwich, Conn.: JAI Press, pp. ix–xiv.

Ruby, Gloria, H. David Banta, and Anne Kesselman Burns. 1985. Medicare Coverage, Medicare Costs, and Medical Technology. *Journal of Health Politics, Policy and Law* 10:141–155.

Russell, Louise B. 1978. *Technology in Hospitals: Medical Advances and Their Diffusion*. New York: Brookings Institute.

Silverman, William A. 1980. *Retrolental Fibroplasia: A Modern Parable*. New York: Grune and Stratton.

Sipe, Patricia. 1982. The Wonder Drug We Should Wonder About. *Science for the People* 14:9–16, 30–33.

Starr, Paul. 1982. *The Social Transformation of American Medicine*. New York: Basic Books.

Thomas, Lewis. 1971. Notes of a Biology Watcher: The Technology of Medicine. *New England Journal of Medicine* 285:1366–1368.

———. 1986. Response to James H. Maxwell's Essay, "The Iron Lung." *Milbank Quarterly* 64:30–33.

U.S. Congress, Office of Technology Assessment. 1976. *Development of Medical Technology*. Washington, D.C.: U.S. Government Printing Office.

———. 1986. *Abstracts of Case Studies in the Health Technology Case Study Series*. OTA-P-225 (revised). Washington, D.C.: U.S. Government Printing Office.

Waitzkin, Howard A. 1979. A Marxian Interpretation of the Growth and Development of Coronary Care Technology. *American Journal of Public Health* 69:1260–1268.

———. 1983. *The Second Sickness: Contradictions of Capitalist Health Care*. New York: Free Press.

Warner, Kenneth E. 1975. A "Desperation-Reaction" Model of Medical Diffusion. *Health Services Research* 10:369–383.

———. 1977. Treatment Decision Making in Catastrophic Illness. *Medical Care* 15:19–33.

Wennberg, John E., and Alan Gittelsohn. 1975. Health Care Delivery in Maine I: Patterns of Use of Common Surgical Procedures. *Journal of the Maine Medical Association* 66:123–149.

Winner, Langdon. 1980. Do Artifacts have Politics? *Daedalus* 109:121–136.

Wright, Peter, and Andrew Treacher, eds. 1982. *The Problem of Medical Knowledge: Examining the Social Construction of Medicine*. Edinburgh: University of Edinburgh.

11

CARE AND TREATMENT
OF ACUTE ILLNESS

GORDON H. DeFRIESE
JO ANNE EARP

THE NATURE OF ACUTE ILLNESS

"Acute illness" is a general, but imprecise, term that usually refers to a condition of ill health characterized by the sudden onset of, or a sharp rise in, pain, discomfort, or inflammation suggesting the need for urgent attention. Acute conditions are generally ones with a short course which can usually be moderated or eliminated entirely through medical care of some type. Chronic diseases, which may or may not be potentially fatal, are those from which patients, even under the best of circumstances, are unable to recover fully and from which there is some residual disability.

Hornbrook (1983) makes a distinction between the "self-limiting" natural histories of some diseases or conditions and "non-self-limiting, acute" diseases. Self-limiting diseases are those from which patients can be expected to recover fully without any medical care or attention. Non-self-limiting, acute diseases are those for which medical care intervention is required to prevent more serious medical complications or even death.

Most of the illnesses we experience with greatest frequency are one of two types, acute self-limiting or acute non-self-limiting. The problem is one of distinguishing between the two and taking necessary and appropriate action when each occurs. Because it is not always possible, even for trained health care professionals, to be certain whether the signs and symptoms of ill health are indications of self-limiting, less-serious disease or whether medical care is needed, it is difficult to determine precisely to what extent measured levels of use of health care services, among individuals or among populations, are appropriate.

THE IMPORTANCE OF ACUTE ILLNESS CARE

Acute care services represent a sizable proportion of all medical care expenditures. It is Hornbrook's observation that "private preferences would value [the diagnosis and treatment of] acute disease relatively more than [for] other disease types . . . all other factors held constant, because treatment of this disease type provides relatively greater returns in the current time period" (Hornbrook, 1983). Clearly, no matter what our social philosophy may be, some bounds must be established within which acute medical care is provided. The way these bounds are set and implemented is a critical aspect of social policy for health.

The concept of the "acuity" of illness suggests a continuum of seriousness (or urgency) where discretion may or may not be operative. The higher the level of acuity of a given instance of ill health, the relatively lower is the level of discretion presumably associated with health services use. Hospital services are usually called for when acuity is high and discretion is at a minimal level. This is especially true when hospital services are accessed through an emergency room. Physician services accessed through conventional outpatient clinics and doctors' offices are generally considered to involve lower levels of acuity and more patient discretion with regard to use. Dental health services are examples of those for which discretion is usually high and acuity very low (Anderson and Andersen 1979, p. 373).

Because acute disease, when left untreated, has significant implications for the health and life course of the individual, it is socially important to make certain that those who experience acute illness are able to obtain necessary and appropriate treatment as soon as possible after the onset of symptoms. However, because it is impossible always to be completely certain that acute episodes of illness are, in fact, non-self-limiting, there is the possibility of excessive demand for services that might better be used to serve those truly in need. Moreover, because there are situations where clinical judgment with regard to the best or most appropriate course of action is equivocal, there is the potential for wide variability in physician response to the same set of presenting symptoms and complaints. For these reasons, social policy affecting the volume and type of acute medical care becomes an important aspect of any strategy for national health improvement.

As financial resources invested in personal health care services in the United States have exceeded 10 percent of the gross national product, considerable public policy debate has arisen over the affordability of the highest standards of personal health care for all citizens. Much of this debate has focused on how part of the cost of health care could be shifted to the client so that a greater incentive could be created among consumers of health care for more prudent use of these expensive services, presumably shifting some of the burden of illness management to self-care. At the same time, a wide variety of controls have been placed on the providers (hospitals and physicians) of health care to influence their decisions about ordering expensive diagnostic tests, recommending extensive therapeutic procedures, and admitting or discharging patients from hospitals and other health care facilities. Even as these and other national health policies have been debated, changes have occurred in the way in which acute health care services are organized, provided, and used.

In this chapter we first provide a discussion of changing patterns of use of acute care services. Next, we discuss some of the changing strategies for the provision of acute health care services and the likely consequences of these changes for people's access to, continuity of, and equity in obtaining health care. We conclude with an assessment of what these changes might mean for the average consumer of health care and the provider of acute care services in the future.

SELF-CARE AS A RESPONSE TO ILLNESS SYMPTOMS

When illness or its symptoms occur, individuals and their families respond in various ways. Self-care, those activities undertaken for promoting health, preventing disease, limiting the debilitating effects of illness when it occurs, or maintaining optimal functional status despite long-term health limitations, are usually steps taken without professional or formal health care involvement. It is estimated that more than 80 percent of patients visiting a primary care physician's office for acute medical care have already attempted to remedy the acute health problem through their own initiative or the assistance of close family members, friends, or neighbors (Williamson and Danaher 1978; White et al. 1967; Elliott-Binns 1973; Demers et al. 1980). The predominant form of medical self-care is self-medication, usually involving the taking of nonprescription drugs (Dunnell and Cartwright 1972; Dean 1986). A broad spectrum of formal curricula has made available to lay persons instruction in the physical diagnosis of illness conditions, the treatment of minor trauma, and the maintenance of health promotive life-style practices (DeFriese 1988).

Although the role that self-care plays in the diagnosis and management of self-limiting acute illness is significant, available research on this issue is not without controversy. Vickery (1986) argues that even a small decrease in the volume of self-care for minor illnesses and health complaints could lead to a substantial increase in the volume of visits to physicians' offices. Conversely, a small increase in the extent of self-care practice among laypersons could lead to substantial savings in the cost of formal medical care.

Of greatest policy significance is the question of whether self-care is a substitute for, supplement to, or a stimulator of extensive use of the formal health care system. Berg and LoGerfo (1980) conclude that adherence to the recommended algorithms for the self-care management of common illness symptoms recommended by a standard self-care text in common use in the United States would have caused an increase of 20 percent in the level of health services use among enrollees in a prepaid health care plan. Contradictory findings emerge from a randomized experimental trial of a formal self-care instructional program. Vickery (1983) reported a 17 percent reduction in physician visits overall and a 35 percent reduction in visits for minor illnesses among the intervention group exposed to a self-care curriculum. Similarly, Lorig et al. (1985) report on a self-care program in a worksite setting that was associated with substantial reductions in overall medical care expenditures among employees. Whether the reduction in the volume of use was, indeed, attributable to those individuals in the self-care group practicing self-care, and exactly how self-care operated to reduce medical expenditures, could not be determined from the design of the study.

Fleming et al. (1984), drawing on data from a nationwide cross-sectional survey on access to care, show that among those who report experiencing a "relatively severe episode of illness in the past year," self-care users (i.e., those who report either using a nonprescribed home treatment or seeking lay consultation about their health condition) had fewer visits to physicians' offices or days in hospital compared to non-self-care users. These findings, while suggestive of potentially large savings in health care expenditures as a result of self-care, clearly must be interpreted cautiously since they are subject to self-report and recall bias and are obtained from a cross-sectional survey. It is possible that individuals who make less use of formal health care providers for other reasons (e.g., dislike of medical personnel, fear, or inconvenience) are also more likely to use home remedies in the first place. Indeed, the decision to consult a formal health care provider for a particular instance of ill health has been found to be related to such factors as the availability and accessibility of health care resources, the personal experience of individuals with health care providers, and severity of symptoms (Dean 1986). Regardless of findings on the correlates of self-care practice or the differences between self-care users and nonusers, the major contribution of self-care as a response to illness symptoms and as a critical element of acute illness care must be acknowledged.

CHANGING PATTERNS OF USE OF ACUTE CARE SERVICES

As one reviews the literature on patterns of use of acute care services what is most striking is the relative consistency with which our understanding of these patterns of service use has been confirmed and reconfirmed by one study after another. We have known for many years that women are more likely than men to define illness symptoms as significant (Hibbard 1983–1984). As a result, women tend to practice self-care and to consult formal sources of health care more frequently than men (Nathanson 1977a). This remains a generalizable phenomenon, at least in Western societies, and certainly in the United States (Nathanson 1977b). Women also are more likely to report symptoms of psychological distress as reasons for seeking medical care, and women use more mental health services than men (Weissman and Klerman 1977; Russo and Sobel 1981; Moore 1980). There is some research to suggest that part of the differential in utilization of medical services between men and women is explained by health provider patterns and practices, as well as by differences in male-female perceptions and responses to symptoms and illness (Armitage, Schneiderman, and Bass 1979; Bernstein and Kane 1981).

Beyond these findings related to gender there are now a number of recent longitudinal studies of particular populations that underscore the consistency of certain patterns of health service use by particular groups. Building on the early work of Den-sen et al. (1959) conducted among the members of the Health Insurance Plan of Greater New York (HIP), recently published results of newer panel studies have shown that a small number of high-volume service users account for a disproportionate share of outpatient services provided, days of hospital care, and surgical procedures performed. Densen et al. (1959) found that 4 percent of HIP subscribers accounted for a quarter of all physician visits, while 12 percent of all subscribers accounted for half (50 percent) of all health care services provided by the plan. These findings have been reconfirmed by Roos and Shapiro (1981) among a population of elderly in Manitoba, by McCall and Wai (1983) among a population of elderly persons enrolled in the U.S. Medicare program, by McFarland et al. (1985) among enrollees of the Kaiser Permanente Northwest Region health care plan, and by Shapiro et al. (1986) among members of a prepaid health care plan in Sault Sainte Marie, Ontario.

What is even more important about these studies than their consistency with earlier findings is that they show that among specific groups of individuals there are distinctive patterns of health services use. That is, those who have ever demonstrated a pattern of high use will, as much as fifteen years later, demonstrate those same patterns of use. Likewise, those who have earlier been low-volume service users will demonstrate that same pattern a decade and a half later. Hence, it should not be concluded that a high rate of use over a single period of one or two years will, over time, evolve into a more moderate pattern of service use. Rather, it is likely that "once a high use consumer, always a high user."

Only recently has it been possible to make these types of temporally comparative observations. Only in the last ten years in the United States and Canada have there been a sufficient number of patients enrolled as defined populations in the same health care organization for the minimum number of consecutive years. With the advent of several large, multispecialty group medical practice organizations in North America in the 1950s and 1960s it became possible to establish several prospective data bases on which to apply this kind of analysis. In the past five years or so, findings from these data have begun to emerge. Although these types of practice arrangements are more numerous in the United Kingdom and certain other countries of Western Europe, the record systems in those countries have often been inadequate to support large-scale longitudinal research. When large prepaid practice organizations emerged in North America, it was deemed essential for their management that computer-based information systems be developed for keeping track of the volume and types of care provided to their insured populations. As a result, health services researchers and sociomedical scientists can now begin to learn important lessons about the way in which health and medical care services are used and by whom.

Another new development in the use of acute care services concerns the organizational arrangements through which these services are made available to consumers. After several decades of slow but steady growth in the number and variety of prepaid health care plans in the United States, there has been a rapid escalation in their number since the passage of relevant federal legislation in 1973. Through a panoply of federal loan guarantees, developmental program grants, and mandated eligibility for employees, U.S. governmental policy has encouraged the widespread development of health maintenance organizations (HMOs) of several varieties (Luft 1983). As a result, there has been a significant increase in the number of Americans enrolled in prepaid health care plans, with enrollment almost tripling in a little more than half a decade. In July 1980 it was estimated that there were 234 HMOs in the United States, with a combined enrollment of 9.03 million (Luft 1983). By June 1986, more than 23.6 million Americans were members of 595 HMO plans (Medical Benefits 1987).

There are several types of HMOs. These include the:

1. *Group model:* where the practice organization is the only (or major) source of care for HMO enrollees; its employees, however, serve others, including unaffiliated, fee-for-service clients.
2. *Staff model:* where the practice organization is essentially owned and operated by the HMO and serves *only* HMO enrollees.
3. *Network model:* where the practice organization is one of several medical groups affiliated with the HMO; its employees serve other clients as well as enrollees.
4. *Gatekeeper IPA model:* where the practice organization receives a "management fee" from the HMO for every enrollee who selects a member of its primary care staff as a regular physician.
5. *Traditional IPA model:* the predominant form of HMO in the mid-1980's, where the practice organization receives a fee from the HMO for each service it provides to an HMO member, but HMO enrollees are not obligated to select physicians in the organization as their regular physicians.

Of major importance to those doing acute care health services research on HMOs is an examination of their presumed effects on the total consumption of ambulatory and hospital services. Though it is expected that this form of health care plan will achieve certain cost efficiencies through the reduction of unnecessary discretionary services, not all acute care services provided by HMOs have decreased. In fact, most HMOs, regardless of type, report an increase in the total volume of ambulatory care office visits to their physicians. Presumably this increase is due to the extended coverage these types of medical care plans often provide now, as well as the recent switch to outpatient care for many procedures formerly thought to require inpatient service. However, explanations for the recent increase are not really clear at this time since HMO population use rates are usually compared to rates for groups without similar access to ambulatory care, and such a comparison is obviously not an adequate test of the HMO's impact on ambulatory care use. An HMO-enrolled population's use of ambulatory services should be compared, ideally, to the use of services by a population with similar sociodemographic characteristics *plus* comprehensive indemnity-type health insurance, including coverage of a similar range of ambulatory services. This type of comparison group is rarely possible to find in HMO research, however, and therefore HMOs' greatest financial advantage to prospective enrollees is rarely adequately evaluated.

With respect to an evaluation of the benefits of HMOs in the area of hospital inpatient services, the evidence of a positive effect is much more striking. In the majority of cases studied, HMOs have successfully demonstrated significant savings in overall hospital expenditures and admissions (Luft 1983). HMO emphasis on reducing discretionary, or optional, hospital admissions accounts for most of the reason for their success in reducing overall health care costs. HMOs have systematically set out to eliminate unnecessary and costly days in hospital. The end result is that the time patients actually spend in the hospital is reserved for those procedures that cannot be performed in any other setting. As a result, only the more acutely ill patients in HMO populations are hospitalized, and the in-patient case-mix profiles for HMO and non-HMO populations have begun to diverge (Dunn and Mitchell 1984; Manning et al. 1984; Welch 1985; McFarland et al. 1986).

Another important trend in acute care utilization concerns the length of a typical hospital stay. While there appears to be a downward spiral in length-of-stay (LOS) in this country, the explanation for this trend is not entirely clear. Using data from the Commission on Professional and Hospital Activities (CPHA) collected from 521 hospitals throughout the United States between 1971 and 1981, Sloan and Valvona (1986) have shown that substantial decreases in the length of hospital stays cannot be attributed to prospective rate setting or the influence of Professional Standards Review Organizations (PSROs—private organizations established contractually to review claims for reimbursement from hospitals and physicians under the Medicare and Medicaid programs). Neither has competition among hospitals proven to be an adequate explanation for the downward trend in LOS. Instead, Sloan and Valvona attribute at least part of the explanation to developments in surgical technology and other changes in patterns of medical practice (e.g., the way that patients are managed postoperatively or worked up prior to surgery out of hospital). This suggests that important local and regional differences in the way physicians make decisions about the care of their patients significantly affect the cost of that care; the impact of these decisions on the quality of care is a relatively unstudied area at this time.

In sum, the emphasis in acute health care services has shifted. Whereas in years gone by the focus for hospitals was on inpatient care and, especially, on keeping as high a rate of bed occupancy as possible so as to maximize the institution's revenues, there are now numerous pressures to reduce both rates of admission and length of hospital stay. These trends, together with the dramatic entrance of for-profit interests into an already crowded hospital market, have produced a climate of aggressive competition within the hospital industry. As inpatient services in high-cost, acute care beds have declined, hospitals have sought ways of diversifying their range of "products." Many have entered other health care markets, such as extended care, home health services, outpatient surgical care, and health promotion and wellness centers.

CHANGING STRATEGIES FOR THE PROVISION OF ACUTE HEALTH CARE SERVICES

There are at least three issues of significance to national health policy regarding acute health services:

1. Can we differentiate between necessary and unnecessary use of acute health care services?
2. Can we reduce or eliminate unnecessary use of acute care services?
3. Can we guarantee access to acute health care for those who actually need these services?

These questions should not be interpreted as pertaining solely to the health services utilization behavior of patients; they suggest important changes in the way health services are organized and provided by professionals and health care institutions as well. Because acute health care represents so large a portion of total national health expenditures, these questions are as crucial for policymakers to answer as they are for employer organizations who purchase health care services on behalf of their employees and dependents. The social and behavioral sciences have had, and must continue to play, an important role in answering questions such as these. In the sections that follow we discuss some of the current research directed to these questions.

Differentiating Necessary from Unnecessary Use

It is almost axiomatic in the field of health services research that the most important predictor of use of health care services is "need" for those services, measured by the extent of disability or self-reported symptoms of ill health. Yet there is a body of evidence which suggests that, for about a third of most populations, need is not the most important determinant of use (Maurana, Eichorn, and Lonquist 1981).

For a number of years it has been part of the conventional wisdom of health services research that a substantial proportion of all users of primary health care services were persons who merely needed reassurance that their symptoms and complaints had no basis in actual disease. The concept of "the worried well" has become a common part of our vocabulary (Garfield et al. 1976). The phrase is used most often by health services researchers to describe people whose specific health services needs are minimal in a given instance, but whose patterns of use over time may account for a significant volume of office visits and health care provider time. The finding among some of the larger panels of patients served by prepaid group practices that a relatively small number of patients actually use the majority of health care services (Shapiro et al. 1986; McFarland et al. 1985) has been interpreted as part of the worried well phenomenon. Whether this assumption is actually true has not yet been demonstrated. However, it has major implications for those interested in reducing the volume of services used by changing the behavior of certain population subgroups, because it has been shown that patterns of health services use are similar among family members of several generations, suggesting that parent-child modeling of health care use may be an actual phenomenon (Gorton et al. 1979).

Evidence from child health care research supports the suggestion that levels of use do not reflect only, or even primarily, actual need. Researchers at Johns Hopkins University have conducted several studies in recent years which have documented that (1) there is a persistent pattern of children's use of health care services over time (Starfield et al. 1979); (2) children with persistently high levels of use of health services are likely to contract a larger variety of concurrent morbidity than children with lower levels of use (Starfield et al. 1985); and (3) children with high levels of use are more likely than other children to have health problems of all types, both concurrent and over a subsequent two-year period (Diaz et al. 1986).

The subjects in these studies were enrolled in the Columbia Medical Plan, a prepaid group practice health maintenance organization in Maryland. The instruments used in that series of studies have considerable potential for measuring the extent of actual physical need for medical care in community studies, since school record and parent interview data were coupled with physical examinations of each child by a physician's assistant. In the Diaz et al. study it was found that the 34 percent of children who were classified as "high users" of health care services

comprised 100 percent of the children with more than 1 hospitalization, 86 percent of those with very low mental health scores, 86 percent of those with very low general health scores, 85 percent of those with large numbers of different types of morbidities in the past, 65 percent of those with at least 1 hospitalization, 62 percent of those with abnormal physical exams, 60 percent of those taking medications in the most recent 48 hours, 59 percent of those with very low social health scores, 56 percent of those whose maximum disability was severe or moderate, and 53 percent and 56 percent of those with very high absence rates in the previous 2 years, respectively. (Diaz et al. 1986, p. 854)

While studies examining the patterns of health services utilization experience of adults have raised the issue of the appropriateness of use, few of these studies have actually been able to determine to what extent the persistently high utilizers consist of separate groups of (1) the chronically ill; (2) persons highly susceptible to frequent minor illness or accidents; or (3) persons who suffer from certain psychosocial problems, including dependency. When such studies rely primarily on secondary data, it is almost impossible to determine differences in rates of service use among these

three categories of patients with respect to the prevalence or acuity of certain conditions since the groups and conditions are intercorrelated and therefore confounded when examined retrospectively.

One study, conducted among 1,401 adults continuously enrolled in the Kaiser-Permanente Northwest Region health care plan, was able to explore more deeply the reasons for persistently high rates of health service use. It found that those who made more visits for chronic health conditions also had higher levels of psychological distress, especially depression (McFarland et al. 1985). While that study and others like it can raise questions about whether psychiatric interventions designed to reduce emotional distress might lead to subsequent reductions in overall levels of personal health care use, they cannot disentangle the pattern of associations between chronic illness and psychological distress in relation to health services use. Without prospective, inception cohort studies we cannot begin to get a handle on whether depression and other distress symptoms are antecedents or products of chronic illness, or whether they are only concomitant symptoms of chronic illness. What *is* well known as a result of these studies is that those who consistently report fair to poor subjective health status also report more physical and mental symptoms of illness and are consistently high volume users of many, if not most, health care services.

The distinctive characteristic these studies share is their emphasis on patient-level behavior as the frame of reference for the explanation of patterns of acute care health services utilization. Another perspective rapidly gaining supporters because of its policy significance shifts the analytical focus from the patient to the system of care within which the patient is served. Research in this new direction, sometimes called "small area analysis," emphasizes patterns of care for specific health care conditions (or specific surgical procedures) within defined geographic areas. Numerous studies in this tradition have documented a pattern of considerable variation by geographic area in the use of medical and surgical procedures for patients who have essentially the same diagnosis (Wennberg and Gittleson 1973, 1982; Roos et al. 1986; Salber et al. 1976; Wennberg 1985; Wennberg, Barnes, and Zubkoff 1982; Chassin et al. 1986). For example, Wennberg, Barnes, and Zubkoff (1982) demonstrated a wide range in the rates of tonsillectomy and adenoidectomy, hysterectomy, and prostatectomy, as well as a somewhat smaller variation in rates of inguinal hernia repair, among hospital service areas in Rhode Island, Maine, and Vermont. With the exception of inguinal hernias, where the diagnosis is relatively straightforward and the condition almost always treated by surgical repair, the extent of variation among counties is marked. For the other three conditions, variations in patient demand for the surgical procedure exist, as do differences among physicians with respect to the ability to diagnose whether the condition is present and how necessary or effective surgery is to correct it. Tonsillectomy, for example, has been a controversial surgical procedure for more than twenty years. As in the case of circumcision, tonsillectomy has been described as a form of "ritualistic surgery" (Bolande 1969).

Many hypotheses have been advanced to account for these "area" variations. While most researchers conclude that nuances in local practice convention strongly influence the way in which patients with a given diagnosis (or set of symptoms) are typically managed by physicians (Wennberg, Barnes, and Zubkoff 1982; Wennberg 1985), others argue that the dramatic differences in the frequency of use of hospital care and diagnostic or surgical procedures for particular conditions have much to do with the density of physician supply in relation to population. The latter refers to the so-called "supply-created demand" phenomenon. Dramatic differences in the rates of both surgical procedures and hospital admissions for medical conditions have been found to be highly correlated with the presence of physician specialists with a clinical interest in these procedures or conditions. Furthermore, people living in communities with high ratios of surgeons-to-population are far more likely to have surgery than people in communities where the ratio of surgeons-to-population is lower (Bunker 1970; Roos L.L., 1983).

Considerable research on small-area practice variations has dealt with the extent to which physicians disagree about the appropriateness, or value, of medical and surgical diagnostic procedures or therapies for specific illness conditions. Most of this research has focused on hospitalized patients and is based on the premise that clinical disagreements arise primarily because physicians are not equally aware, or convinced, of the existence of detailed evidence about the circumstances under which diagnostic or therapeutic procedures are and are not efficacious. Research testing the validity of these competing explanations (i.e., whether it is a deficiency in knowledge or a problem of attitudes and beliefs) is less frequent. The descriptive studies can be divided into two groups: those that ask whether diagnostic or therapeutic procedures performed for given patients necessitated that those patients be admitted to a hospital at all, and those that question the clinical appropriateness of particular procedures in light of patients' medical conditions. One theoretical explanation often given for the variation in physicians' prescription of medical and surgical procedures is that physicians are uncertain about the efficacy of specific therapies or the accuracy of specific diagnostic procedures, hence they vary in their tendency to use these approaches in similar clinical situations (Park et al. 1986).

Wennberg (1977) has argued that the degree of clinical uncertainty associated with common medical and surgical conditions could be reduced through educational programs designed to inform physicians about the efficacy and possible effectiveness of these procedures. In a discussion of variability in the rates of tonsillectomies, Wennberg offered the following observations:

The standard and historically correct defense against the claim of unnecessary surgery is professional uncertainty: physicians do not know which level of use of a procedure is "appropriate" and, hence, geographic variations are inevitable. But this defense, while explaining the past, cannot justify the future. For one thing, the dollar costs of uncertainty are too great: tonsillectomies undertaken at the low rate in Maine incur a per capita expenditure of 85 cents; those at the high rate, $4.55. Projected nationally, the low-rate strategy costs less than $200 million; the high-rate strategy costs nearly $1 billion. But the costs, of course, are not only in dollars. In Vermont (1969 to 1973) and Maine (1973), three postoperative deaths occurred following tonsillectomy. For so costly a procedure, ambiguity concerning its value will likely become increasingly intolerable. (Wennberg, 1977, p. 952)

In an effort to study the appropriateness of care phenomenon, Gertman and Restuccia (1981) developed an objective, criteria-based procedure for determining the degree of appropriateness of hospital days of care. Previous studies of this outcome had relied on the subjective judgments of reviewers of medical records. In those studies, while inter-rater agreement on the percentage of all cases considered "appropriate" was relatively high, the percentage of specific cases where the rater's judgments were in agreement was relatively low. Thus, Gertman and Restuccia set out to develop a simple procedure to judge, as objectively as possible, the appropriateness of a given number of hospital days for groups of patients without reference to the specific diagnosis of those patients. In their initial study, only patients admitted to adult medicine, surgery, and gynecology services were studied. The instrument they developed is called the Appropriateness Evaluation Protocol (AEP). It incorporated twenty-seven objective criteria (e.g., procedure performed in operating room *that day*; respiratory therapy needed thrice or more *that day*; inability to void *that*

day) into three categories: (1) use of medical services, (2) use of nursing/life support services, and (3) patient condition factors. If *any one* of the twenty-seven criteria was met, the hospital day was deemed "appropriate"; if none was met, the day was considered "inappropriate" at an acute hospital level of care.

Siu et al. (1986), using the AEP in the Health Insurance Experiment conducted by the Rand Corporation between 1974 and 1982, found that 23 percent of admissions to hospitals were inappropriate by AEP criteria, and an additional 17 percent might have been avoided had ambulatory surgery services been available or used. Using this conservative index of "appropriate care," about a third of all hospital days were judged to be unnecessary. Even more interesting, perhaps, is the fact that those areas with the highest levels of hospital use did not necessarily have the highest levels of inappropriate care.

In the Rand Health Insurance Experiment, which took place between November 1974 and January 1982, 7,700 persons residing in six geographic areas of the country were enrolled in one of three types of experimental health insurance plans: plans in which all care was free; plans with cost sharing for all services; and plans with cost sharing for outpatient services only. All patients received their medical care from fee-for-service providers of their choice. When the appropriateness of hospital care was analyzed by type of health insurance plan, no significant differences among these types of plans was found (Lohr et al. 1986). However, the use of services was reduced both for those health care conditions where medical interventions are considered highly effective (e.g., treatment for vaginitis and pharyngitis), as well as for those treatments that are considered somewhat less effective (e.g., therapies for acute upper respiratory infection). Cost sharing had only minimal adverse effects on general health status.

The fact that cost sharing tended to reduce the number of "appropriate" hospital days also was seen as a potential drawback of such plans when these were used to control health care costs. Yet, cost-sharing plans also seemed to reduce the frequency of "inappropriate" admissions and hospital days as well. A beneficial side effect associated with the reduction in both appropriate and inappropriate hospital visits was presumed to be the lowered risk of iatrogenic illnesses that might otherwise have occurred during these visits.

In another study using appropriateness criteria to gauge the effect of clinical uncertainty on medical practice variations, researchers at UCLA and Rand studied six surgical procedures whose rates varied widely in different geographic areas of the United States. In order to develop quantitative indices of appropriateness associated with each procedure (coronary angiography, coronary artery bypass graft surgery, cholecystectomy, diagnostic upper gastrointestinal endoscopy, colonoscopy, and carotid endarterectomy), systematic literature reviews were done of the many clinical indications for each procedure. Because a lack of consensus exists about those indications for which a given surgical procedure should be performed (even when laboratory and pathology reports verify that a condition exists for which the procedure is normally considered a relevant therapy), it was assumed that there would be a range of viewpoints among clinicians with regard to the appropriateness of surgery for most indications. For example, ultrasonography and oral cholecystography are the major diagnostic modalities for identifying patients with gallstones. These tests, in combination with other tests of gallbladder function, are capable of diagnosing the presence of gallstones in 99 percent of patients who have them. But surgery to remove the gallbladder (cholecystectomy), particularly for patients without persistent symptoms (e.g., belching or fatty food intolerance), is a matter about which there is considerable clinical disagreement.

The Rand/UCLA researchers developed lists of all known clinical indications for each of these six surgical procedures and submitted them to panels of clinicians with expertise in the six procedures. The expert panels were asked to rate each clinical indication as a justification for surgery (along a nine-point scale) according to whether they considered it to be "extremely inappropriate" (a score of 1), "equivocal—neither clearly appropriate nor clearly inappropriate" (a score of 5), or "extremely appropriate" (a score of 9). In each of six geographic areas of the country approximately 500 hospital charts were selected randomly. Using the expert panel's ratings of appropriateness to code the data in these charts, the association between clinical uncertainty and practice variation in the volume of procedures performed was assessed. It was found that even among physicians with expertise in a given disease area, considerable disagreement about the value of surgical procedures, when these were studied by clinical indicators, existed. It was therefore hypothesized that clinical uncertainty, and not solely patient preferences, explained at least some of the geographic variation in medical practice. This, in fact, turned out not to be the case. Results from the study indicate that patterns of variations in medical practices do not correlate with inappropriateness of care. Geographic areas with high rates of selected procedures do not have higher proportions of inappropriate procedures than geographic areas with low rates (Chassin et al. 1987).

The studies reviewed in this section tend to focus on the system and providers of care as the explanatory variables in medical care utilization, and this orientation has been referred to as "medical care epidemiology" (Wennberg, Barnes, and Zubkoff 1982). These studies are significant developments in sociomedical science because they redirect our attention from explanations at the level of the individual patient as consumer of health and medical care services to the structural and economic forces that constrain or channel patient behavior once formal health care is sought.

Reducing or Eliminating Unnecessary Use

Since the care provided in hospitals accounts for the majority of health care expenditures, efforts to control or reduce the extent of unnecessary use of services have focused mostly on inpatient care. The most widely known and effective of these approaches has been the federal government's effort to introduce prospective pricing of health care services (PPS) as part of Medicare and Medicaid programs serving the elderly and the poor, respectively. Prospective pricing has meant that providers of health care to Medicare and Medicaid beneficiaries must agree to provide all in-hospital medical and surgical care for a patient with a given diagnosis for a fixed price. This price is determined on the basis of the average cost of hospital (but *not* physician) care for all patients with a similar diagnosis treated in similar size and type hospitals throughout the country. Once patients are admitted to a hospital they are assigned to a Diagnosis-Related Group (DRG) classification for which a predetermined fee has been established. This fee includes a consideration of basic hospital room charges, laboratory and radiology charges, operating room fees, and the costs of ancillary services associated with the care of "normal" (i.e., uncomplicated) patients with a given diagnosis.

The pros and cons of the prospective pricing of American hospital care have been thoroughly discussed elsewhere (Worthman and Cretin 1986). Suffice it to say here that the system is based on statistical average cost experiences of patients within 467 diagnostic categories that represent the compression of many thousands of separate diagnostic entities. It is assumed that for any third-party payer, the "average" of all patients within a diagnostic grouping will balance out over time (i.e., in some cases, the insurance company or the federal government will pay more than the hospital stay actually costs, while in other cases the payer will be charged less). But for the individual who pays for his or her

own care out-of-pocket, without insurance, the disparity between the actual hospital charges and the DRG value could be enormous. Hence, exemption from DRG billing has been required in some cases to deal with this artifact of the PPS system.

Since the federal government (through Medicare, the federal share of the Medicaid program, the health care programs for federal employees and their dependents, and the Veterans Administration health care system) accounts for over 40 percent of all health care expenditures in this country, the implications of prospective pricing of hospital services for the American health care industry are enormous. Not only have these federal programs adopted the prospective pricing method of paying hospitals, but several private third-party payers have followed suit, and efforts are underway to apply this same prospective pricing approach to the services provided by physicians and other health care professionals (Arnett et al. 1985).

The impact of prospective pricing on hospitals can be visually illustrated by the data summarized in Figure 1. These data, which are drawn from the 1984 statistical volume published by the American Hospital Association, clearly show a marked decline in the rate of admissions and the rate of hospital days per 1,000 persons per year beginning around 1980. These declines are associated with a similar decline in average length of hospital stay which began in the early 1970s (Donabedian et al. 1986, p. 69).

Prospective pricing also influences the cost of health care in American hospitals through the feedback of cost-related information to physicians. Many hospitals have now begun to collect detailed data on specific services and costs associated with particular types of patients served in their facilities. These data can be inexpensively summarized for the benefit of the hospitals' physicians; in this way each physician can be made aware of the cost profile of his or her own patient care in relation to that provided by other physicians in the same hospital. This kind of "induced regression to the mean" is presumed to have an im-

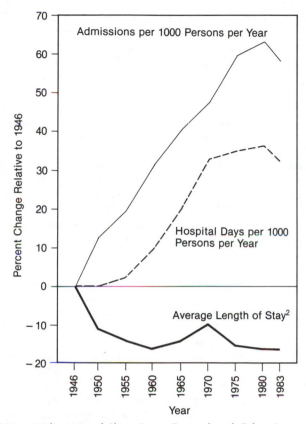

FIGURE 1 Utilization of Short-Term General and Other Special Hospitals,[1] USA, Selected Years, 1946–1983. (*Source:* Reproduced by permission from *Medical Care Chartbook*, 8th ed., A. Donabedien, Solomon J. Axelrod, Leon Wyszewianski, and Richard L. Lichtenstein, Ann Arbor: Health Administration Press, 1986, chart C-25, p. 69.)

[1]A short-term hospital is one in which the average length of stay (ALOS) is fewer than thirty days or in which more than 50 percent of all patients are admitted to units in which the ALOS is less than thirty days.
[2]Data on ALOS prior to 1970 include short-term psychiatric and TB hospital figures. After 1970, those hospital figures are excluded from ALOS calculations.

pact on the practice patterns of physicians while adding increased pressure on the care delivery system to lower the use of inappropriate services and acute medical care facilities (Worthman and Cretin 1986). More research evaluating this simple experiment with social comparisons is sorely needed.

Prospective pricing of hospital care has disproportionately affected the elderly population, who have traditionally been the highest users of hospital care, and especially the frail elderly, who are at highest risk of readmission. In a sense, a positive side effect of prospective pricing has been an increased interest in, or emphasis on, continuity of care. Most hospitals have begun intensive efforts to plan for the discharge of frail elderly and other dependent patients at the outset of their hospital stay. This can involve complicated negotiations with social service agencies and home care services to ensure that, after hospitalization, adequate home-based or extended facility care is available to monitor both compliance with medical regimens and maintenance of functional activities of daily living.

Continuity of care beyond the hospital stay, including care required in ambulatory settings and in the home environment, means that hospitals have become increasingly concerned about the pre-hospital admission planning of patient care, in addition to concerns for the earlier and more effective post-hospital management of patients. Indeed it has become important to hospitals to assess carefully the care needed *prior* to admission of *all* their patients, not just of the elderly. Since most hospital admissions are "elective" (i.e., there is no urgent reason for the admission to occur on a particular day), admission scheduling can take into account the availability of beds and competing demands for space and technological services. The object is to admit all patients for as short a time as possible, perform whatever acute care services are required, and discharge the patient to home care or some other level of service. The traditional hospital has become more of a "technology application center" and not the comprehensive health care facility of days gone by.

Partly as a result of the changes described above, programs for academic health professionals' training, once almost exclusively based in hospitals, are finding the contemporary hospital less attractive as a training site. The complex processes associated with clinical diagnosis are tending to take place more and more often outside the hospital in ambulatory settings. Unless the object is to train young physicians or nurses in the performance of specific diagnostic techniques or surgical procedures, or in the postoperative care of patients, the hospital is no longer the most important setting for educating health professionals (Foreman 1986).

Another widely adopted strategy for reducing unnecessary health care services, especially for elective surgery, are presurgical screening programs (or surgical second-opinion programs). These programs are usually sponsored by those who must pay for surgical care, such as insurance plans, corporations, or governmental agencies, and are often described by these organizations as efforts to better inform the consumer of health care services about their options with respect to health problems they may encounter. Although many of these programs are voluntary on the part of patients, in many health insurance plans second opinions are required before the insurance plan will pay for the performance of certain types of surgery. Those procedures for which second opinions are most often required are those for which physician discretion and clinical uncertainty are greatest (e.g., cholecystectomy, hysterectomy, removal of cataracts, tonsillectomy, adenoidectomy, disc surgery, varicose vein excision and ligation).

The potential for significant cost savings constitutes one of the main reasons for requiring second opinions prior to surgery. There is an implicit assumption in mandatory second opinion programs that a sufficient number of physicians are recommending unnecessary surgical procedures to warrant the expenditure of additional funds for the duplication of diagnostic effort. There also seems to be an assumption that the accuracy of the physicians recommending *against* surgery is better than of those physicians recommending surgery in the first instance. Few, if any, second opinion plans have been evaluated for the impact that delay or cancellation of surgery has had on the escalation of disease or an increase in secondary illness, pain, or other symptoms. No study has been done that tests the assumption that the definitive surgical "cure" exists, or that surgery foregone could have effectively dealt with a patient's problem (Reiter 1985).

The available evidence regarding the impact of surgical second opinion programs on health care costs and acute care utilization is inconclusive. There are two types of effects usually attributed to these programs. The first, and easier to measure, is the "direct effect." This is defined as the difference between the total number of persons who seek a second opinion when surgery is initially recommended and the number of persons who, after receiving the second opinion, actually have the surgery performed. The second, and more difficult effect to measure, is the so-called "sentinel effect" (McCarthy and Finkel 1978). This is defined as the extent to which the surgical second-opinion program reduces the total number of surgical cases (or patients) actually recommended for surgery in the first place. The "sentinel effect" is usually estimated as the difference in the rates of surgery before a second-opinion program's initiation and afterward.

Selected findings from four major studies of the impact of surgical second opinion programs (Paris, Salsberg, and Berenson 1979; McCarthy and Finkel 1980, 1981; Gertman et al. 1980; Martin et al. 1982) include the following: first, most people (probably between 85 and 90 percent) who participate in a surgical second-opinion program have their initial surgical recommendation confirmed by the second consultant; second, those who seek a second opinion are much more likely to have received an initial opinion in favor of surgery; third, most of those who receive a contradictory opinion in the second consultation decide against surgery; fourth, most of those who obtain a confirmatory opinion in the second consultation go ahead with the procedure. Hence, it may be concluded that a confirming opinion in the second case may cause some people to have surgery that they might otherwise have foregone on the basis of a single recommendation.

Gertman and Manuel (1980) have argued that there are several deficiencies in studies of the impact of second opinions. One is that aggregating several reasons for "nonconfirmation" presumes that there is little clinical difference between a procedure "not recommended" (for a variety of reasons pertaining to a particular patient's health state and condition) and a procedure considered "unnecessary." Furthermore, Gertman and Manuel call attention to the fact that it is not clear whether physicians who offer a second opinion go through a diagnostic process comparable (in intensity or extensiveness) to that performed by physicians who offer the initial opinion. This question is especially relevant when the initial referral for surgical consultation comes from a primary care physician. While such a referral may be a recommendation for surgery, it also may be a recommendation that the patient seek the opinion of a surgically qualified physician. This distinction is usually not made when data are collected and coded from medical records.

Gertman and Manuel also raise the issue of whether surgical second-opinion programs may undermine patients' confidence in their regular physicians, possibly leading to confusion and unnecessary anxiety. Paris, Salsberg, and Berenson (1979) found that second-opinion physicians tended to offer more extensive advice and consultation to patients than could be adequately captured by a simple coding of either confirmation or nonconfirmation. Although these investigators reported that their study seemed initially to indicate a surgical nonconfirmation rate of about 25 percent, more detailed analysis of the actual recommendations of the second physician showed that a firm rejection of surgery occurred in only about 8 percent of cases. Thus, in two-thirds of apparently nonconfirmatory cases, physicians actually took a "wait and see" or "further testing" approach. In sum, the "direct effect" of second opinions on surgical utilization rates tends to be low (7–8 percent) across studies. However, substantial reductions in the overall number of procedures performed among the studied populations did occur, suggesting that these programs do have significant "sentinel effects" on the behavior of both physicians and patients. Finally, the effects on quality of life and outcomes other than rates of procedures have not been evaluated.

In addition to prospective pricing, pre-admission screening, early discharge planning, and surgical second opinions, there are two other principal methods for gaining some degree of control over the unnecessary use of health and medical care services. The first of these, consumer cost sharing, attempts to transfer some of the incentive for prudent health care decision making to the consumer through a system of financial disincentives for use. The second approach involves a variety of measures designed to put the health care provider at financial risk for the total cost associated with the health care utilization experience of a defined population of patients. This second approach includes efforts to organize health maintenance organizations of several types and the introduction of a "gatekeeper" role for primary care physicians.

The transfer of some responsibility for the cost of care to consumers tends to take one of two forms: *copayment or co-insurance,* when consumers agree to pay a specified percentage of insured expenses (usually between 20 and 25 percent), and *deductibles,* when consumers' health benefits do not take effect until their accumulated health expenditures exceed a specified amount (e.g., $50 or $100) within a year. Under most deductible plans, certain types of uses are excluded from the deductible arrangement (e.g., emergency use of services).

Studies of the effect of copayment options on the overall cost and levels of utilization of acute medical care have generally suffered from problems of study design. Most such studies tend to be "natural experiments," where the health care benefits of a single insured population change from one time period to another (Greene and Gunselman 1986; Roddy, Wallens, and Meyers 1986), instead of controlled trials in which persons or families are randomly assigned to different insurance plans for the purpose of study (Ginsburg and Manheim

1973). As a consequence, it is hard to disentangle the effects of co-insurance on usage rates from secular trends or other confounding factors. The Rand Corporation's National Health Insurance Experiment, described earlier, is a major exception to this analytical difficulty, but social experiments of this scale are rare. In that study, low-income persons enrolled in the cost-sharing plans were significantly less likely than those in the free plan to use either medical care for acute conditions or preventive health services. However, for the nonpoor, there were no differences in use of services between the plans (Lohr et al. 1986).

These findings have important public policy implications for they suggest that it is nearly impossible to achieve the goals of health care utilization controls through consumer economic disincentives on use and at the same time achieve a socially equitable and desirable allocation of health care resources (Ball and Roskamp 1986).

The movement toward prepaid health care, of which health maintenance organizations (HMOs) are the best-known example, represents an important attempt to gain some level of control over rising health care costs, while at the same time ensuring that the quality of care provided to persons enrolled in these plans remains high.

As a result of intense marketing by HMOs among certain populations they would prefer to serve, as well as a preference for this type of health care coverage by certain population groups (e.g., families with young children), there are sometimes charges of "selection bias" leveled against HMOs in those communities where these plans are in competition with other types of insurance plans. On the other hand, many people with long-standing relationships with their primary care providers are unwilling to consider a change to an HMO, no matter how great their need, the volume of service they anticipate, or how attractive the benefits, *if* their regular physician is not a member of the HMO in question. However, while HMOs are not for everyone, if the trend toward this kind of health care coverage continues, we can expect the volume of ambulatory care services in this country to increase dramatically, while the volume of inpatient care services may level off or even take a downward turn.

Critics point to HMO efforts to guard against "adverse selection," that is, the tendency of high-risk or unhealthy persons to select the HMO option more frequently than other persons because of the expected cost advantage. There are conflicting data on this point. The 1984 Louis Harris and Associates' survey of physicians, employers, and the general public's attitudes toward HMOs found that "there were few, if any, differences between the health status of HMO members and eligible nonmembers nationwide, whether in the incidence of chronic illness, in days spent in bed due to illness, or in health status" (Taylor and Kagay 1986). On the other hand, Buchanan and Cretin (1986) report that among 30,000 employees of a large aerospace corporation with an HMO option, the HMOs attracted a younger, lower-income population who made less use of health care services. Wilensky and Rossiter (1986) have interpreted the presence of apparent selection biases between HMOs and their non-HMO competitors in light of the "newness" of the prepaid plans on the health care scene. They argue that any new plan in a local health care market should attract a younger, lower-risk population since these groups have lower "transition costs" associated with the decision to switch regular sources of health and medical care. However, confounding between the preference for a new plan vs. the preference for a prepaid plan makes measurement of selection effects difficult.

Diehr et al. (1984) confirm the fact that "adverse" or "favorable" selection may be a difficult thing to interpret. In their study comparing a closed-panel HMO and a conventional Blue Cross/Blue Shield (BC/BS) plan, they found that the HMO had a rela-tively younger group of enrollees. However, age was not found to be related to the use of the HMO's services by its members. On the other hand, the BC/BS plan was selected by significantly older individuals and in this group age *did* turn out to have a significant effect on health services utilization. Furthermore, Diehr et al. (1984) also found that adverse selection with respect to *use* can be quite different than adverse selection effects with respect to *cost*. Plan members who used more services were not always using those with higher unit costs; increased rates of visits or number of hospital days were not always associated with the performance of expensive procedures.

Another means HMOs have used to control the use of unnecessary services (and therefore costs) is a reliance on primary health care providers as "gatekeepers" to health care (Somers 1983). Under such systems, the primary care physician responsible for the majority of the care provided to a specific patient is also responsible for authorizing and approving all nonprimary care provided to the patient, with the exception of emergency care. While the conventional orientation of primary care practitioners (in general internal medicine, pediatrics and family medicine) is to think of their role as including responsibility for *coordinating* the full spectrum of care required by their patients, until recently this has not meant administrative and financial control by primary care physicians of *all* medical care (Eisenberg 1985). In the gatekeeper model systems, the primary care physician not only guides the patient through the health care system, providing coordination to ensure the quality of care, but also controls all but emergency access to care to ensure nonduplication of services as well as a reduction in unnecessary use of services. The term "case manager" is sometimes applied to this role of the primary care physician.

The gatekeeper concept is not new. More than 85 percent of health maintenance organizations do not allow patients to refer themselves to the care of medical specialists without first being seen and evaluated by a primary care physician (Catlin, Bradbury, and Catlin 1983; Eisenberg 1985). The Medicaid program in many states uses the gatekeeper model to review and approve the use of services for Medicaid beneficiaries (Freund 1984; Hurley 1986). The innovative aspect of the recent use of the gatekeeper model is the linking of a capitation payment system to the case managerial approach by primary care providers. Since the primary care physician is paid a fixed sum to manage the total care of a panel of patients, to the extent that the aggregate health care utilization experience of that patient panel results in lower costs than the capitation amount, the primary care physician realizes a financial incentive to continue as an efficient case manager.

One widely known private gatekeeper model health care plan was the United Healthcare Corporation, organized by the SAFECO Life Insurance Company (Moore 1979; Richardson, Martin, Moore 1982). This plan used an IPA network model HMO; that is, primary care physicians shared a financial risk with the plan for the patients' total medical care cost. This was done by depositing in each physician's account at the outset of the plan's operation a certain amount of money (usually about a quarter of each patient's premium amount). The remainder of the premium was used by United Healthcare Corporation to pay for services other than those provided by the primary care physician. Hospitals and nonprimary care physicians, paid on a fee-for-service basis, were reimbursed by United Healthcare only upon the signature approval of the primary care physician. At the end of the fiscal year, any surplus premium income was shared equally by the primary care physicians participating in the plan (up to a limit of 10 percent of each physician's own fees). If there was a deficit, primary care physicians were expected to pay back part of the initial deposit in their account, also up to a maximum of 10 percent. All catastrophic medical care expenditures were excluded

from the risk-sharing arrangement (Eisenberg 1985). The 10 percent cap, plus other aspects of the arrangement, meant that physicians in the SAFECO plan had a very limited financial risk. The plan, which was implemented in four cities, did demonstrate that it was possible to reduce the overall volume of specialist physician use and total days of hospital care, although the rising costs of fee-for-service specialist care and hospital bed days eventually closed down the experiment.

Since SAFECO, the idea of the primary care physician as the gatekeeper of the health care system has been extended to other types of health care plans developed as alternatives to fee-for-service systems. So-called "preferred provider organizations" (PPOs) have used a variant of the gatekeeper model in their attempt to structure health care services around panels of providers, all of whom agree to assume patient care responsibility for groups of patients according to a predetermined fee schedule (Gabel et al. 1986). These newer variants of the gatekeeper concept of cost control have not yet been evaluated in terms of either their cost control objectives or their attempt to reduce the volume of specialty services.

One of the most important policy issues underlying all these approaches to the control of health services utilization and costs is the question, Whose agent is the physician? Whereas the physician has historically been viewed as the agent solely of the patient, acting to ensure the highest level of care possible when need arises, these new approaches to the organization of, and payment for, medical care significantly alter the role of the physician in relation to the patient. As principal allocators of health care resources, often under arrangements where their prospective income is directly affected by their diagnostic or treatment choices, physicians in acute medical care situations now must contend with a new, and much more complex, ethical context for clinical decision-making than they ever had to before (Cassel 1985).

Guaranteeing Access to Needed Services

As important as the elimination of unnecessary use of health care services is the effort to ensure that services are available to those who have a genuine need for them. Despite the relative affluence of the United States and the relatively ample supply of health care resources, there have always been specific subgroups of the population that experience considerable difficulty in gaining timely access to quality health care services. This is especially true for residents of small, remote rural communities and low-income residents of inner cities who have problems attracting adequate numbers of health care providers to their communities. Every major industrialized nation, no matter how affluent or how universal the extent of their health care coverage, has had to make special arrangements for ensuring access to basic health care services for these same populations (Madison and Combs 1981). Yet, in times of rapid cost escalation and apparent surpluses of health care practitioners, it is unlikely that public policies that emphasize equity of access will be paid significant attention. Since access-oriented policies always lead to increased health care expenditures, the period from 1980 until the present has seen few new initiatives designed to address access issues in the United States.

There are really two separate public policy issues related to access to health care. The first of these is referred to as *coverage*, or the percentage of a population in need who actually receives a given service. The second is *equity*, or the extent to which coverage is extended to all elements of the population, without discrimination or preference (Montoya-Aguilar and Marin-Lira 1986). Coverage is a much more easily understood concept and one more easily addressed through the instruments of public policy. Most public initiatives in this country designed to improve access to acute health care services have been designed to improve coverage rather than eq-

uity of services. The two issues are related, obviously, since special programs to bring those groups with the lowest levels of coverage up to the "average" level of other groups will presumably, in the long run, improve equity of access to care.

The predominant American approach of the past twenty years for guaranteeing coverage of, and equity of access to, acute health care services has been the effort to ensure that every person, regardless of social class, ethnicity, or place or residence, has a regular source of "primary medical care." This orientation has involved two principal dimensions. The first has been the effort to alter the balance between specialists and generalists in clinical medicine through improving the quality of primary care training programs for physicians and efforts to make primary care training and practice an attractive career option. The second dimension involves the design of new programs to encourage the development of organized clinical services, with primary care as their centerpiece, for the benefit of underserved populations.

In the mid-1960s concern about the significant gap in health care services that arose as a result of the push toward highly specialized post-graduate training resulted in the convening of a Citizens Commission on Graduate Medical Education, chaired by President Millis of Western Reserve University. In its 1966 report, the Millis Commission called for the training of a new type of physician, the so-called "primary physician, [who would] . . . serve as the primary medical resource and counselor to an individual or family." The role envisioned was much like that of the current gatekeeper model, but without the present emphasis on controlling unnecessary health services use. This report played a major role in the years that followed in the creation of the American Board of Family Practice and in the promulgation of federal legislation for the support of formal post-graduate training for family physicians, specialists in both general internal medicine and general pediatrics (Somers 1983)

Other commissions and reports in the years since the Millis Commission have underscored the need for a reconsideration of the role and importance of primary care as a basic component of American health care services. Among the most important of these was the 1978 report of the special task force on manpower needs for primary care convened by the Institute of Medicine (IOM) of the National Academy of Sciences (Institute of Medicine 1978; Scheffler et al. 1978). This report further emphasized the need for additional manpower in primary care practice and dealt extensively with the role and function of primary care in relation to specialist physicians. One of the main recommendations of that task force was that distinctions should be eliminated between specialists and generalists, as well as between physicians and nonphysician providers (e.g., nurse practitioners and physicians' assistants), with regard to rates of reimbursement for clinically similar procedures. The task force further recommended that specialists should receive differential rates of reimbursement *only* for care they provided upon referral, usually from a primary care physician.

These kinds of recommendations were intended to reduce the tendency for specialists, particularly in geographic areas in which there was a surplus of specialists, to attract to their practice patients for whom they were essentially providing continuing "primary care." These recommendations were further intended to increase the relative financial attractiveness of primary care in relation to specialty practice for young physicians considering primary versus specialty care as a career choice. The IOM report suggested that primary care physicians should be assigned a "managerial role" with respect to the totality of care needed by a given patient, a concept which evolved into the gatekeeper role.

The other significant contribution of the 1978 IOM task force report was its delineation of several dimensions or criteria on which primary health care services should be evaluated; these were viewed by some as a set of standards by which the adequacy of

primary care programs could be judged. The IOM task force identified six principal components of the "ideal" model of primary care: continuity, coordination, accessibility, availability, accountability, and efficiency. For each of these components, specific "indicators" were identified that could be used to assess the presence or absence of the criterion in the case of a specific primary health care setting.

Research and program evaluation over the past several years have greatly added to our understanding of the role played by, and the importance of, each of these various dimensions of primary care in producing desirable health outcomes (Greganti et al. 1982; Fletcher et al. 1981; Fletcher et al. 1983). Although space does not allow a comprehensive review of the vast literature in this area, we briefly summarize below the major findings on access to, and continuity of, medical—and particularly primary—care.

Various pronouncements over a number of years by prestigious commissions, as well as significant federal legislation to support the training of additional primary care practitioners, did lead to a substantial increase in the number of postgraduate trainees in these specialties. But between 1980 and 1986, the rate of growth of these training programs slowed, casting doubt on the prospect of making significant changes in the ratio of specialist-to-generalist physicians in the United States (Ricketts, DeFriese, and Wilson 1986). Furthermore, the desirable versus adverse consequences of specialists serving as primary care physicians have not been rigorously evaluated on all relevant dimensions: cost, performance, equity, accessibility, and continuity. There is even a considerable lack of consensus about whether primary care is actually in short supply at all. Aiken et al. (1979), using data from a nationwide study of the content of practice in twenty-four medical specialties, argue that the volume of "continuing care" provided by specialist physicians constitutes a "hidden system of primary care."

In an effort to ensure the availability of

primary health care services to under-served populations in rural areas and in the inner cities, considerable experimentation has taken place since the mid-1960s. There are presently a variety of both public and privately financed efforts to support the development of comprehensive primary health care clinics in previously unserved or underserved geographic areas. The best known of these initiatives are the "neighborhood health centers" (or comprehensive health centers) sponsored by the U. S. Department of Health and Human Services, first through the Office of Economic Opportunity and currently through the Health Resources and Services Administration of the U.S. Public Health Service. In most instances, these clinics were started through the local initiative of citizens in small rural communities or urban neighborhoods, often with outside technical assistance and support, in response to a solicitation from the federal government. Community organizations applying for these funds were required to demonstrate that a viable local organization had been identified to take responsibility for the planning, implementation, and operation of the proposed health care program, and to manage the federal start-up funds. Further, these local groups or organizations were required to make arrangements for hiring appropriate health professionals to staff these clinics, and to ensure that they provided a comprehensive range of primary health care services compatible with the needs of the defined target population. In some cases, there were specific requirements to be met with respect to the appointment and functions of a consumer-dominant board of directors. In the period 1968–1975, some estimates put the number of such clinics, started with both federal and private foundation funds, at more than 900 (Sheps and Bachar 1981).

In 1980 a national evaluation study, funded by the Robert Wood Johnson Foundation, attempted to evaluate the impact of these subsidized clinics on access to care, the stability of these programs over time, and their impact on health status indicators in the target communities (Sheps and Bachar 1981). Several important findings emerged from this four-year study. A variety of different types of sponsored primary care programs had been developed to meet the needs of small rural communities; most involved very simple organizations, often staffed on a daily basis by a nurse practitioner or physician's assistant, with back-up support from a nearby physician. The more comprehensive, and therefore complex, primary care clinics anticipated by federal program requirements developed in only a small number of communities. Most rural communities simply could not attract a sufficient number of health care providers to offer a comprehensive range of primary health care services. Few, if any, of these clinics were able to operate independently of subsidy by one or more outside sources of nonpatient care revenue (e.g., federal funds or private foundation grants), and almost all reported persistent problems with recruitment and retention of professional staff. Many, and especially the more comprehensive, health centers reported difficulties in their relationships with local professional groups and providers, although satisfaction with the medical care they provided the minority and poor populations they served was high. These subsidized rural primary care programs had a positive impact on their communities by making primary care more conveniently available. Furthermore, utilization of ambulatory care increased without a concomitant increase in the rate of hospitalization (Ricketts, Konrad, and Wagner 1983; Sheps et al. 1983; Ricketts et al. 1984; Bradham, McLaughlin, and Ricketts 1985).

During this same ten-year period, considerable effort was made to influence the number of health care professionals (particularly physicians, nurses, and dentists) who would consider entering professional practice in rural areas and the inner cities. The National Health Service Corps (NHSC), established in 1971 by Congress, was one such program designed to reduce the shortage of health personnel in these types of communities. Both volunteer recruitment and the provision of professional educational scholarships, with obligated service after training, were used to recruit NHSC professionals who were either federally salaried employees or commissioned officers in the U.S. Public Health Service. Their placement in applicant communities was carried out under a cooperative arrangement between the federal government and the local community or health care setting. While the NHSC provider was in residence, funds accumulated by the sponsoring local organization were shared between the local sponsor and the federal government by a predetermined formula. No patient was refused service by an NHSC provider because of inability to pay.

Before the NHSC was initiated and throughout the 1970s, when Corps placements of physicians in rural and inner city areas received widely publicized attention, there were fears among physicians in existing private practices adjacent to the NHSC practice sites that the subsidization of the NHSC medical care would constitute an economic threat to the private practitioners' financial viability. An evaluation of the impact of the NHSC program (Kehrer et al. 1982) demonstrated that this fear was unfounded. Instead, the subsidized NHSC practices tended to serve an entirely different, often previously underserved, population. The most important competitive threat to these existing private practices was the presence in the local area of "other private doctors," not the Corps-staffed clinics. In other words, the NHSC and private physicians already working in underserved areas were serving "segmented" markets; hence, the equity and coverage purposes of this social experiment seemed to be achievable side by side with traditional, fee-for-service, medical care.

Other findings of the Mathematica study (Kehrer et al. 1982) of the NHSC Program revealed that primary care practices subsidized through the placement of Corps personnel were less efficient than conventional private health care practices in the same areas. They had substantially lower clinical work loads per practitioner, recorded fewer office visits per week and fewer telephone consultations, and had fewer patients in the hospital. Therefore, it came as no surprise when this study revealed that access to NHSC physicians was easier than to similarly situated private physicians. NHSC physicians had shorter waiting times for patients, provided longer office visits, and charged lower fees. However, since almost all NHSC physicians were young, recently trained practitioners, it was impossible to disentangle provider inexperience from the organizational form of health care delivery in explaining the findings of less efficiency and greater access among NHSC physicians. If they had entered nonsubsidized practices in the same communities instead of accepting a Corps assignment, their profile and pattern of practice may have looked very similar to non-Corps physicians of the same age (Kehrer et al. 1982).

Among the many efforts to guarantee greater access to adequate primary health care in underserved areas were programs to train nurse practitioners (NPs) and physicians' assistants (PAs) to provide care traditionally provided only by physicians. In 1986 the Office of Technology Assessment of the U.S. Congress estimated that there were approximately 15,400 NPs and 16,000 PAs practicing in the United States (Brooks 1986). Although these practitioners were never envisioned as independent providers of primary health care, their mode of practice in some remote areas of rural America essentially put them in this position most of the time (Brooks et al. 1981). In most cases, however, where NPs or PAs staffed primary health care facilities, their legal basis for practice was closely tied to the supervision they received from a clearly designated physician who was required to cosign their clinical notes in patient charts, approve their prescription of drugs and laboratory tests, and observe them periodically in clinical care of patients.

As the national supply of physicians has rapidly increased in the period since 1975, and along with it the financial pressures of competition in medical care, the primary care role of the NP and PA has come under serious question. The federal Medicare program and most state Medicaid programs impose legal restrictions on the ability of these practitioners to bill patients for their services directly; all financial transactions they are involved in have to occur over a signature of the supervising physician. The major exception to this restriction occurs as a result of the Rural Health Clinic Services Act of 1977 (Public Law 95-210), which authorized the direct billing for services of NPs and PAs in certified rural health clinics serving designated underserved populations; in these areas NPs and PAs are backed up by local physicians but not directly supervised by them at all times. Hence, NPs and PAs have come to be viewed as employees of medical practice organizations and rarely, if ever, independent practitioners themselves. The stipulation enjoining these providers from direct billing, plus the fact that in the late 1980s there are far more physicians than many consider necessary to meet the general need for health care, portends continued restrictions for some time to come on the independent practice of medicine by these mid-level health personnel.

At the present time, another organizational phenomenon has emerged whose impact on access, equity, volume of care provided, and cost have yet to be fully evaluated. Health service "vendors" are providing what could be considered "primary health care services" for acute illnesses or conditions directly to consumers, with no expectation of, or requirement for, primary care provider coordination of that care. This often takes the form of twenty-four-hour emergency care for people without strong connections to a regular source of primary care or for persons who find their usual route of access to care blocked in a given instance. These "emergency centers," "emergicare centers," "urgicenters,"

"convenience clinics," or "jiffy clinics," as they have been variously called, presumably fill a vacuum in the health care system of a country whose people have become accustomed to having personal services provided quickly, with a standardized approach and uniformity of product (e.g., fast-food restaurants). In some communities, local hospitals have established these clinics in facilities off the hospital grounds, in easy reach of community residents who "need" acute medical care services "on the run." Such emergency centers are usually staffed either by nurse practitioners, who have close telecommunication supervision from physicians in the emergency room of the sponsoring hospital, or by primary care, "emergency medicine" physicians (Rice and Oltvedt 1980; Schaffer 1984). Sometimes private primary care physicians have established such practices independently of hospitals. Their target population is not necessarily economically disadvantaged, but rather a subgroup of the population that never established firm connections with a regular provider of health care. These practices, disparagingly referred to as "doc-in-the-box" clinics by some, have gone on, in some parts of the country, to develop affiliated, easily accessible, biomedical laboratory services open directly to the public (e.g., clinics to measure lipid cholesterol). Very little evaluation of any aspect of health care delivery provided by these "convenience clinics" has been undertaken.

Hospitals have also developed freestanding primary care group practices as joint ventures with members of the hospital's medical staff, with the hospital providing the physical facility for the practice and access to laboratory and other ancillary services. Special arrangements are made usually by the physician group for preferential use of the hospital when inpatient care is required. Part of the impetus for these developments was the realization that hospital emergency rooms and outpatient departments were the principal source of acute, primary care for many Americans. It was also thought that such organized group medical practices within hospitals, while emphasizing regular, primary care to defined patient populations, would strengthen the linkages among primary, secondary, and tertiary care providers. The Robert Wood Johnson Foundation sponsored a national series of fifty-four demonstration efforts of this type over the seven-year period from 1976 to 1983 (Shortell, Wickizer, and Wheeler 1984). The evaluation of this national demonstration indicated that not all practices of this type were completely financially viable or independent during the initial years of their operation. However, many hospitals sponsoring these initiatives seemed to benefit financially from them, especially the larger, better managed, and financially healthier hospitals with strong, supportive medical staffs.

A different type of organizational effort that hospitals and nursing homes have been experimenting with lately may be classified as "subacute" care (Lipson 1986). The focus of these ventures is on the transitional care needs of patients who no longer need the intensive services of inpatient hospital care but who can benefit from a level of care slightly more intense than skilled nursing home care or care provided in intermediate care facilities. The type of patients targeted by these subacute care facilities include AIDS patients, ventilator-dependent patients with chronic obstructive pulmonary disease or emphysema, quadriplegics, and a wide variety of patients with multiple medical problems too complicated for at-home care by families or by visiting nurses. In part, these facilities arose either as a result of the pressures hospitals faced for early release of Medicare and Medicaid patients under DRG constraints or as a way of generating additional revenue from underutilized, existing beds. In many communities there are extreme shortages of nursing home beds to which patients can be discharged when their hospital stay has exceeded the allowable number of days of care under DRG

ratings. This has meant a shift in acute care services from primary care to a focus on rehabilitation (Hospital Progress 1984).

ACUTE ILLNESS CARE: WHAT LIES AHEAD?

What do these changes mean for guaranteeing access to acute health care services for those in need? It is apparent from even a casual glance at the contemporary American health care scene that whereas there once was a rather simple array of choices for the average consumer of acute health care services, the medical care marketplace of today is filled with a multiplicity of options and opportunities for satisfaction, as well as possible displeasure, in meeting acute health care needs. Whereas the ideology of "good" medical care suggests the need for a regular source of primary medical care, usually a physician who can act as an agent in negotiating one's way through the maze of health services options in times of need, we now find that many Americans are using as their "regular" sources of primary health care a series of readily available, discrete service providers because they perceive these as being more convenient and accessible. Yet, most Americans continue to consider a single physician as "their doctor" (Aday, Fleming, and Andersen 1984). Furthermore, Americans are becoming more aware of, if not better educated about, health and medical care issues. Practically every publication of popular appeal has one or more articles on matters related to health and medical care. Cable television stations carry daily programs on a variety of health topics of interest to both health professionals and the lay public.

Perhaps as a result, the lay public in this country seems to be insisting more and more on the right to select, without restriction, from among any available medical or health care service that *they* define as relevant to their immediate health care needs. Contrary to the philosophical tenets of primary care, we are seeing health care services in this country "unbundled" and individually marketed to the lay public by the popular press, by physicians, by hospitals, and by third-party payers. This is happening at the same time that the public in large numbers are being encouraged by their employers and those who pay for health care to consider enrollment in HMOs, PPOs, and other forms of managed health care that embrace one of several versions of the so-called "gatekeeper" model. These two trends have quite different implications for the way in which acute health care services might be used in the future.

Physicians, too, are faced with several important transitions in their relationships with patients. The increasing pressure to market separate health care services directly to consumers (e.g., pharmaceutical supplies and drugs) has put physicians in an entrepreneurial, vested-interest position vis-à-vis those technologies and services with which they may be associated for economic reasons (Relman 1987). Moreover, pressures toward cost containment and encouragement of consumer affiliation with managed care plans have put physicians in the position of gatekeepers, acting to control access to the panoply of health care services available from a wide variety of sources. Physicians in such circumstances have changed from being *advocates* for their patients, to the principal *allocators* of resources for health care. As larger and larger segments of our population are enrolled in managed health care plans, the traditional patient-physician relationship will likely undergo further changes. Consumers' desire for immediate access to any and all health-related services will have to be accommodated by a medical profession that has traditionally valued a regular, continuous relationship with a single provider as the portal of access to the health care system. Physicians, themselves, mainly working as salaried employees of large medical care provider organizations, will find it more difficult to establish and maintain these continuing relations with patients.

If patients are simultaneously encouraged to be affiliated with organized health care programs, yet more and more services are readily available in an "unbundled" form, the burden of distinguishing between unnecessary and necessary use of acute care services clearly cannot be allowed to lie solely with either health care consumers or providers. To the extent that many of the unbundled services are not covered by conventional health insurance, consumers will have access only to those their personal incomes allow. As the availability of services is perceived to increase, yet the number or type of services actually able to be covered remains stable or decreases, expectations are likely to be unmet for direct and immediate access to any level of health care desired as the need arises. The gap between perceived availability and actual access may become more salient, and a better informed public more vocal in support of its demands for "health care rights." Meeting this type of demand for access to acute health care services will go beyond the reach of most programs designed to ensure equitable access and quality of care.

Within organized health care programs (e.g., HMOs, PPOs) clearly effective means of controlling the unnecessary use of health care services have been developed. Moreover, prospective payment systems have attempted to place much of the burden of demonstrating the necessity for care on the providers of these services. At the same time, the general phenomenon of wide variations in medical practice, as illuminated by recent advances in small area analysis, may have heightened professional sensitivity to questions about the appropriateness of medical and surgical care. More research evaluating this as well as other provider-specific outcomes is clearly needed. In the absence of evidence to substantiate the claim that there is a differential burden of illness in one community (or one hospital service area) as opposed to another, the extraordinary range of medical and surgical procedures per capita should be cause for a closer examination of the way in which clinical decisions are made in the course of patient care. Perhaps it is time to deemphasize behavioral science research on why patients use or do not use the services they do, as well as why types or groups of health care consumers differ from each other. Despite a rich social science tradition to substantiate the existence of psychosocial predispositions that mediate people's use of health care services, the predominant thrust in recent years has been the study of structural and organizational mechanisms in health care service delivery systems that *produce* (and possibly may be used to *reduce*) the variable and, at times, inflated rates of use reflected in aggregate health care statistics. Given the rapid rise in the total cost of health care services in our national economy, public policy interest in gaining fiscal control over this human services sector has understandably increased. Even small differences (i.e., on the order of 1 to 3 percent) in the rates of use of health care, extrapolated to the state or national level of policy application, could have tremendous financial implications for our system of care. For this reason, it is likely that future research into the sociology of acute health care will emphasize system and economic aspects of service delivery and pay relatively less attention to the sociopsychological aspects of health and illness behavior.

REFERENCES

Aday, LuAnn, Gretchen V. Fleming, and Ronald Andersen. 1984. *Access to Medical Care in the United States: Who Has It, Who Doesn't.* CHAS Research Series No. 32. Chicago: University of Chicago Center for Health Administration Studies.

Aiken, Linda H., Charles E. Lewis, John Craig, Robert C. Mendenhall, Robert J. Blendon, and David E. Rogers. 1979. The Contribution of Specialists to the Delivery of Primary Care: A New Perspective. *New England Journal of Medicine* 300:1363–1370.

Andersen, Ronald and Odin W. Anderson. 1979. Trends in the Use of Health Services, in Howard E. Freeman, Sol Levine and Leo G. Reeder, eds., *Handbook of Medical Sociology.* Englewood Cliffs, N.J.: Prentice-Hall, pp. 371–391.

Armitage, K. J., L. J. Schneiderman, and R. A. Bass. 1979. Response of Physicians to Medical Complaints in Men and Women. *Journal of the American Medical Association* 241:2186–2187.

Arnett, Ross H., Carol S. Cowell, Lawrence M. Davidoff, and Mark S. Freeland. 1985. Health Spending Trends in the 1980's: Adjusting to Financial Incentives. *Health Care Financing Review* 6:1–26.

Ball, Judy K., and Jeanette A. Roskamp. 1986. Foreword. Use of Medical Care in the Rand Health Insurance Experiment: Diagnosis and Service-Specific Analyses in a Randomized Controlled Trial. Special Supplement to *Medical Care* 24: unnumbered pages.

Berg, Alfred O., and James P. LoGerfo. 1980. Potential Impact of Self-Care Algorithms on the Number of Physician Visits. *New England Journal of Medicine* 300:535–537.

Bernstein, Barbara, and Robert Kane. 1981. Physicians' Attitudes toward Female Patients. *Medical Care* 19(6):600–608.

Bolande, R. P. 1969. Ritualistic Surgery: Circumcision and Tonsillectomy. *New England Journal of Medicine* 280–591.

Bradham, D. D., C. P. McLaughlin, and T. C. Ricketts. 1985. The Ability of Aggregate Data to Predict Self-Sufficiency Levels in Subsidized Primary Care Practice. *Journal of Rural Health* 1:56–58.

Brook, Robert H., and Kathleen N. Lohr. 1985. Efficacy, Effectiveness, Variations, and Quality: Boundary-Crossing Research. *Medical Care* 23(5):710–722.

Brook, Robert H., John E. Ware, William H. Rogers, Emmett B. Keeler, Allyson R. Davies, Cathy A. Donald, George A. Goldberg, Kathleen N. Lohr, Patricia C. Masthay, and Joseph P. Newhouse. 1983. Does Free Care Improve Adults' Health? Results from a Randomized Controlled Trial. *New England Journal of Medicine* 309:1426–1434.

Brooks, Edward F. 1986. *Nurse Practitioners. Physician Assistants, and Certified Nurse-Midwives: A Policy Analysis,* Health Technology Case

Study 37. Washington, D.C.: Office of Technology Assessment, U.S. Congress.

Brooks, Edward F., James D. Bernstein, Gordon H. DeFriese, and Robin M. Graham. 1981. New Health Practitioners in Rural Satellite Health Centers: The Past and Future. *Journal of Community Health* 6:246–256.

Buchanan, Joan L., and Shan Cretin. 1986. Risk Selection of Families Electing HMO Membership. *Medical Care* 24(1):39–51.

Bunker, John P. 1970. Surgical Manpower: A Comparison of Operations and Surgeons in the United States and in England and Wales. *New England Journal of Medicine* 282:135–144.

Cassel, Christine K. 1985. Doctors and Allocation Decisions: A New Role in the New Medicare. *Journal of Health Politics, Policy and Law* 10(5):549–564.

Catlin, Rita F., Robert C. Bradsbury, and Robin J. O. Catlin. 1983. Primary Care Gatekeepers in HMO's. *Journal of Family Practice* 17:673–678.

Chassin, M. R., Robert H. Brook, Rolla Edward Park, J. Keesey, Jacqueline Kosecoff, Katherine L. Kahn, Nancy J. Merrick, and David H. Solomon. 1986. Variations in the Use of Medical and Surgical Services by the Medicare Population. *New England Journal of Medicine* 314:285–290.

Chassin, Mark R., Jacquelin Kosecoff, R. E. Park, Constance M. Winslow, Katherine L. Kahn, Nancy J. Merrick, Joan Keesey, Arlene Fink, David H. Solomon, and Robert H. Brook. 1987. Does Inappropriate Use Explain Geographic Variations in the Use of Health Care Services? *Journal of The American Medical Association* 258:2533–2537.

Dean, Kathryn. 1981. Self-Care Responses to Illness: A Selected Review. *Social Science and Medicine* 15:673–687.

———. 1986. Lay Care in Illness. *Social Science and Medicine* 22(2):275–284.

DeFriese, Gordon H., Alison Woomert, Priscilla A. Guild, Allan B. Steckler, and Thomas R. Konrad. 1988. The Self-Care Movement in the United States: The Education of Laypersons as Self-Care Practitioners. *Social Science and Medicine*. In press.

Demers, R. Y., R. Altamore, H. Mustin, A. Kleinman, and D. Leonard. 1980. An Exploration of the Dimensions of Illness Behavior. *Journal of Family Practice* 11(7):1085–1092.

Densen, Paul H., Sam Shapiro, and M. Einhorn. 1959. Concerning High and Low Utilizers of Service in a Medical Care Plan and the Persistence of Utilization Levels over a Three-Year Period. *Milbank Memorial Fund Quarterly* 37:217.

Diaz, C., B. Starfield, N. Holtzman, E. D. Mellits, J. Hankin, K. Smalky, and P. Benson. 1986. Ill Health and Use of Medical Care. *Medical Care* 24(9):848–856.

Diehr, Paula. 1984. Small Area Statistics: Large Statistical Problems. *American Journal of Public Health* 74(4):313–314.

Diehr, Paula, Diane P. Martin, Kurt F. Price, Lindy J. Friedlander, William C. Richardson, and Donald C. Riedel. 1984. Use of Ambulatory Care Services in Three Provider Plans: Interactions between Patient Characteristics and Plans. *American Journal of Public Health* 74(1):47–51.

Donabedian, Avedis, Solomon J. Axelrod, Leon Wyszewianski, and Richard L. Lichtenstein. 1986. *Medical Care Chartbook*, 8th ed. Ann Arbor: Health Administration Press.

Dunn, James P., and John Mitchell. 1984. Health Care Experience among Employees prior to and after Enrollment in a Prepaid Health Insurance Plan (HMO). *Journal of Occupational Medicine* 26:86–90.

Dunnell, K., and Ann Cartwright. 1972. *Medicine Takers, Prescribers and Hoarders*. London: Routledge and Kegan Paul.

Eisenberg, John M. 1985. The Internist as Gatekeeper: Preparing the General Internist for a New Role. *Annals of Internal Medicine* 102(4):537–543.

Elliott-Binns, C. P. 1973. An Analysis of Lay Medicine. *Journal of the Royal College of General Practice* 23:255–264.

Finkel, Madelon L., Eugene G. McCarthy, and Hirsch S. Ruchlin. 1982. The Current Status of Surgical Second Opinion Programs. *Surgical Clinics of North America* 62(4):705–719.

Fleming, Gretchen V., Aida L. Giachello, Ronald M. Andersen, and Patricia Andrade. 1984. Self-care: Substitute, Supplement, or Stimulus for Formal Medical Care Services. *Medical Care* 22(10):950–966.

Fletcher, Robert H., Suzanne W. Fletcher, Jo Anne Earp, M. A. Greganti, and T. A. Littleton. 1981. Measuring the Attributes of Primary Care. *Clinical Research* 29:35.

Fletcher, Robert H., Michael S. O'Malley, Jo Anne Earp, T. A. Littleton, Suzanne W. Fletcher, M. A. Greganti, R. A. Davidson, and J. Taylor. 1983. Patients' Priorities for Medical Care. *Medical Care* 21:234–242.

Foreman, S. 1986. The Changing Medical Care System: Some Implications for Medical Education. *Journal of Medical Education* 61:11–21.

Freund, Deborah A. 1984. *Medicaid Reform: Four Studies of Care Management.* Washington, D.C.: American Enterprise Institute.

Gabel, Jon, Dan Ermann, Thomas Rice, and Gregory de Lissovoy. 1986. The Emergence and Future of PPOs. *Journal of Health Politics, Policy and Law* 11(2):305–322.

Garfield, S., M. Collen, R. Feldman, K. Soghikian, R. Richart, and J. Duncan. 1976. Evaluation of an Ambulatory Medical-Care Delivery System. *New England Journal of Medicine* 294:426.

Gertman, Paul M., and Barry Manuel. 1980. A Scientific Approach to Second Opinions: Editorial Comment. *Obstetrics and Gynecology* 56(4):411–412.

Gertman, Paul M., and Joseph D. Restuccia. 1981. The Appropriateness Evaluation Protocol: A Technique for Assessing Unnecessary Days of Hospital Care. *Medical Care* 19(8):855–871.

Gertman, Paul M., Debra A. Stackpole, Dana Kern Levenson, Barry M. Manuel, Robert J. Brennan, and Gary M. Janko. 1980. Second Opinions for Elective Surgery: The Mandatory Medicaid Program in Massachusetts. *New England Journal of Medicine* 302(21): 1169–1174.

Ginsburg, Paul B., and Larry M. Manheim. 1973. Insurance, Copayment, and Health Services Utilization: A Critical Review. *Journal of Economics and Business* 25:142–153.

Gorton, T. Ann, Donald L. Doerfler, Barbara S. Hulka, and Herman A. Tyroler. 1979. Intrafamilial Patterns of Illness Reports and Physician Visits in a Community Sample. *Journal of Health and Social Behavior* 20:37–44.

Greene, Sandra B., and Dan L. Gunselman. 1986. Cost Sharing and Its Effect on Hospital Utilization. *Medical Care* 24(8):711–720.

Greganti, M. A., Suzanne W. Fletcher, Robert H. Fletcher, Jo Anne Earp, and A. T. Hyde. 1982. Primary Health Care—Perspective of the Faculty of a Department of Medicine. *Archives of Internal Medicine* 142:325–329.

Hibbard, Judith H. 1983–1984. Sex Differences in Health and Illness Orientation. *International Quarterly of Community Health Education* 4(2):95–104.

Hornbrook, M. C. 1983. Allocative Medicine: Efficiency, Disease Severity, and the Payment Mechanism. *Annals of the American Academy of Political and Social Science* 468:12–29.

Hurley, Robert E. 1986. Status of Medicaid Competition Demonstrations. *Health Care Financing Review* 8:65–75.

Institute of Medicine. 1978. *A Manpower Policy for Primary Health Care.* Publication No. 78-02. Washington, D.C.: National Academy of Sciences.

Kehrer, Barbara H., Thomas W. Grannemann, Marilyn E. Manser, Mark V. Pauly, Ewe E. Reinhardt, Frank A. Sloan, and Judith Wooldridge. 1982. *Evaluation of the Effects of NHSC Physician Placements Upon Medical Care Delivery in Rural Areas.* Nontechnical Summary Report, Contract Number 240-79-0056, prepared for the Department of Health and Human Services.

Levin, Lowell S., and Ellen L. Idler. 1983. Self-Care in Health. *Annual Review of Public Health* 4:181–201.

Lipson, Debra J. 1986. State Regulation of Subacute Care: A 50-State Survey. *Focus On . . . Issue No. 12.* Washington, D.C.: Intergovernmental Health Policy Project.

Lohr, Kathleen N., Robert H. Brook, Caren J. Kamberg, George A. Goldberg, Arleen Leibowitz, Joan Keesey, David Reboussin, and Joseph P. Newhouse. 1986. Use of Medical Care in the Rand Health Insurance Experiment: Diagnosis- and Service-Specific Analyses in a Randomized Trial. Supplement to *Medical Care* September: S1–S87.

Lorig, Kate, R. Guy Kraines, Byron Wm. Brown, Jr., and Nancy Richardson. 1985. A Workplace Health Education Program That Reduces Outpatient Visits. *Medical Care* 23:1044–1054.

Luft, Harold S. 1983. Health Maintenance Organizations, in D. Mechanic, ed., *Handbook of Health, Health Care and the Health Professions,* New York: Free Press, p. 318–351.

Madison, Donald L., and C. D. Combs. 1981. Location Patterns of Recent Physician Settlers in Rural America. *Journal of Community Health* 6:267–274.

Manning, Willard G., Arleen Leibowitz, George

A. Goldberg, William H. Rogers, and Joseph P. Newhouse. 1984. A Controlled Trial of the Effect of a Prepaid Group Practice on Use of Services. *New England Journal of Medicine* 310:1505–1510.

Martin, Suzanne G., Michael Shwartz, Bernadette J. Whalen, Deborah D'Arpa, Greta M. Ljung, John H. Thorne, and Anne E. McKusick. 1982. Impact of a Mandatory Second Opinion Program on Medicaid Surgery Rates. *Medical Care* 20(1):21–45.

Maurana, C., R. Eichorn, and L. Lonnquist. 1981. *The Use of Health Services: Indices and Correlates. A Research Bibliography 1981*. Hyattsville, Md.: National Center for Health Services Research.

McCall, Nelda, and H. S. Wai. 1983. An Analysis of the Use of Medicare Services by the Continuously Enrolled Aged. *Medical Care* 21:567.

McCarthy, Eugene G., and Madelon L Finkel. 1980. Second Consultant Opinion for Elective Gynecologic Surgery. *Obstetrics and Gynecology* 56(4):403–410.

———. 1981. Second Consultant Opinion for Elective Orthopedic Surgery. *American Journal of Public Health* 71(11):1233–1236.

McFarland, Bentson H., Donald K. Freeborn, John P. Mullooly, and Clyde R. Pope. 1985. Utilization Patterns among Long-term Enrollees in a Prepaid Group Practice Health Maintenance Organization. *Medical Care* 23(11)1221–1233.

———. 1986. Utilization Patterns and Mortality of HMO Enrollees. *Medical Care* 24:200–208.

Medical Benefits. 1987. *A Mid-Year Report on HMO Growth: 1986 June Update*. Charlottesville, Va.: Kelly Communications, p. 6.

Montoya-Aguilar, C., and M. A. Marin-Lira. 1986. Intranational Equity in Coverage of Primary Health Care: Examples from Developing Countries. *World Health Statistics Quarterly* 39:336–344.

Moore, Emily C. 1980. Women and Health: United States 1980. Supplement to *Public Health Reports*. September–October.

Moore, Stephen H. 1979. Cost Containment through Risk-Sharing by Primary Care Physicians. *New England Journal of Medicine* 300:1359–1362.

Moore, Stephen H., Diane P. Martin, and William C. Richardson. 1983. Does the Primary-Care Gatekeeper Control the Costs of Health Care? *New England Journal of Medicine* 309(22): 1400–1404.

Nathanson, Constance A. 1977a. Sex Roles as Variables in Preventive Health Behavior. 3(2):142–155.

———. 1977b. Sex, Illness and Medical Care: A Review of Data, Theory and Method. *Social Science and Medicine* 11:13–25.

Paris, Martin, Edward Salsberg, and Louise Berenson. 1979. An Analysis of Nonconfirmation Rates: Experiences of a Surgical Second Opinion Program. *Journal of the American Medical Association* 242(22):2424–2427.

Park, Rolla Edward, Arlene Find, Robert H. Brook, Mark R. Chassin, Katherine L. Kahn, Nancy J. Merrick, Jacqueline Kosecoff, and David H. Solomon. 1986. Physician Ratings of Appropriate Indications for Six Medical and Surgical Procedures. *American Journal of Public Health* 76:766–772.

Reiter, David. 1985. The Divergent Second Opinion: Eventual Outcome of Physician-Changing. *Transactions of the Pennsylvania Academy of Ophthalmology and Otolaryngology* 37:231–234.

Relman, Arnold S. 1987. Doctors and the Dispensing of Drugs. *New England Journal of Medicine* 317:311–312.

Rice, James A., and Gregory T. Oltvedt. 1980. The Emergicare Center. *Journal of Ambulatory Care Management* 3(3):99–111.

Richardson William C., Diane P. Martin, and Stephen H. Moore. 1982. *Consumer Choice and Cost Containment: An Evaluation of SAFECO's United Healthcare Plan*, vol. 1. Publication No. PB-264-812. Springfield, Va: National Technical Information Service.

Ricketts, Thomas C., Gordon H. DeFriese, and Glenn Wilson. 1986. Trends in Family Practice Residency Training. *Health Affairs* 5(4):84–96.

Ricketts, T. C., P. A. Guild, C. G. Sheps, and E. H. Wagner. 1984. An Evaluation of Subsidized Rural Primary Care Programs: III. Stress and Survival, 1981–82. *American Journal of Public Health* 74:816–819.

Ricketts, T. C., T. R. Konrad, and E. H. Wagner. 1983. An Evaluation of Subsidized Rural Primary Care Programs: II. The Environmental Context. *American Journal of Public Health* 73:406–413.

Roddy, Pamela C., Jacqueline Wallen, and Samuel M. Meyers. 1986. Cost Sharing and Use of Health Services: The United Mine Workers of America Health Plan. *Medical Care* 24:873–876.

Roos, L. L., Jr. 1983. Supply, Workload and Utilization: A Population-Based Analysis of Surgery in Rural Manitoba. *American Journal of Public Health* 73:414–421.

Roos, Noralou P. 1984. Hysterectomy: Variations in Rates across Small Areas and across Physicians' Practices. *American Journal of Public Health* 74(4):327–335.

Roos, Noralou P., Gordon Flowerdew, Andre Wajda, and Robert B. Tate. 1986. Variations in Physicians' Hospitalization Practices: A Population-Based Study in Manitoba, Canada. *American Journal of Public Health* 76(1): 45–51.

Roos, N. P., and E. Shapiro. 1981. The Manitoba Longitudinal Study on Aging: Preliminary Findings on Health Care Utilization by the Elderly. *Medical Care* 21:644.

Ruchlin, Hirsch S., Madelon L. Finkel, and Eugene G. McCarthy. 1982. The Efficacy of Second-Opinion Consultation Programs: A Cost-Benefit Perspective. *Medical Care* 20(1): 3–20.

Russo, Nancy F., and Suzanne B. Sobel. 1981. Sex Differences in the Utilization of Mental Health Facilities. *Professional Psychology* 2(1): 7–19.

Rutkow, Ira M. 1982. The Determinants of Surgical Rates. *Health Services Research* 17(4): 379–385.

Salber, Eva J., Sandra B. Greene, Jacob J. Feldman, and G. Hunter. 1976. Access to Health Care in a Southern Rural Community. *Medical Care* 14:971–986.

Schaffer, Daniel J. 1984. A Survey of Washington State Freestanding Emergency Centers. *Annals of Emergency Medicine* 13:259–262.

Scheffler, Richard M., Neil Weisfeld, Gloria Ruby, and E. Harvey Estes, Jr. 1978. A Manpower Policy for Primary Health Care. *New England Journal of Medicine* 298:1058–1062.

Shapiro, Stanley H., Glenn Wilson, Fred Griffith, and Robert Oseasohn. 1986. Longterm Adult Use of Ambulatory Services Provided by Physicians in a Canadian Medical Care Plan. *Medical Care* 24(5):418–428.

Sheps, Cecil G., and Miriam Bachar. 1981. Rural Areas and Personal Health Services: Current Strategies. *American Journal of Public Health* 71(1):71–82.

Sheps, C. G., E. H. Wagner, W. R. Schonfeld, G. H. DeFriese, M. Bachar, E. F. Brooks, D. B. Gillings, P. A. Guild, T. R. Konrad, C. P. McLaughlin, T. C. Ricketts, C. Seipp, and J. S. Stein. 1983. An Evaluation of Subsidized Rural Primary Care Programs: I. A Typology of Practice Organizations. *American Journal of Public Health* 73:38–40.

Shortell, Stephen M., Thomas M. Wickizer, and John R. C. Wheeler. 1984. *Hospital-Physician Joint Ventures*. Ann Arbor: Health Administration Press.

Showstack, Jonathan A., Kenneth E. Rosenfeld, Deborah W. Garnick, Harold S. Luft, Ralph W. Schaffarzick, and Jinnet Fowles. 1987. Association of Volume with Outcome of Coronary Artery Bypass Graft Surgery. *Journal of the American Medical Association* 257(6):785–789.

Siu, Albert L., Frank A. Sonnenberg, Williard G. Manning, George A. Goldberg, Ellyn S. Bloomfield, Joseph P. Newhouse, and Robert H. Brook. 1986. Inappropriate Use of Hospitals in a Randomized Trial of Health Insurance Plans. *New England Journal of Medicine* 315(20):1259–1266.

Sloan, Frank A., and Joseph Valvona. 1986. Why Has Hospital Length of Stay Declined? An Evaluation of Alternative Theories. *Social Science and Medicine* 22(1):63–73.

Somers, Anne. 1983. And Who Shall Be the Gatekeeper? The Role of the Primary Physician in the Health Care Delivery System. *Inquiry* 20:301–313.

Starfield, Barbara, Janet Hankin, Donald Steinwachs, S. D. Horn, P. Benson, H. Katz, and A. Gabriel. 1985. Utilization and Morbidity: Random or Tandem. *Pediatrics* 75: 241.

Starfield, Barbara, B. Van den Berg, Donald Steinwachs, H. P. Katz, and S. D. Horn. 1979. Variations in Utilization of Health Services by Children. *Pediatrics* 63:633.

Taylor, Humphrey, and Michael Kagay. The HMO Report Card: A Closer Look. *Health Affairs*, Spring:81–89.

Vickery, Donald M. 1986. Medical Self-Care: A Review of the Concept and Program Models. *American Journal of Health Promotion* 1(1):23–28.

Vickery, Donald M., Howard Kalmer, Debra Lowry, Muriel Constantine, Elizabeth Wright, and Wendy Loren. 1983. Effect of a Self-Care Education Program on Medical Visits. *Journal of the American Medical Association* 250:2952–2956.

Weissman, Myrna M., and Gerald L. Klerman. 1977. Sex Differences and the Epidemiology of Depression. *Archives of General Psychiatry* 34:98–111.

Welch, W.P. 1985. Health Care Utilization in HMO's: Results of Two National Samples. *Journal of Health Economics* 4:293–308.

Wennberg, John E. 1977. Physician Uncertainty, Specialty Ideology, and a Second Opinion prior to Tonsillectomy. Commentary in *Pediatrics* 59(6):952.

———. 1985. On Patient Need, Equity, Supplier-Induced Demand and the Need to Assess the Outcome of Common Medical Practices. *Medical Care* 23:512–520.

Wennberg, John E., Benjamin A. Barnes, and Michael Zubkoff. 1982. Professional Uncertainty and the Problem of Supplier-Induced Demand. *Social Science and Medicine* 16:811–824.

Wennberg, John E., and A. Gittelsohn. 1973. Small Area Variations in Health Care Delivery. *Science* 182:1102–1108.

———. 1982. Variations in Medical Care among Small Areas. *Scientific American* 246:120–134.

White, K. L., A. Dragana, J. H. Pearson, A. R. Marby, and O. K. Sagen. 1967. International Comparison of Medical Care Utilization. *New England Journal of Medicine* 277(10):520.

Wilensky, Gail R., and Louis F. Rossiter. 1986. Patient Self-Selection in HMOs. *Health Affairs* Spring:66–80.

Williams, Sankey V., and John M. Eisenberg. 1986. A Controlled Trial to Decrease the Unnecessary Use of Diagnostic Tests. *Journal of General Internal Medicine* 1:8–13.

Worthman, Linda C., and Shan Cretin. 1986. *Review of the Literature on Diagnosis Related Groups.* N-2492-HCFA. Santa Monica: Rand Corporation.

CHAPTER 12

HEALTH CARE OF THE CHRONICALLY ILL

GEORGE L. MADDOX
THOMAS A. GLASS

INTRODUCTION

Health and health care are strategic intellectual sites for exploring the intersecting, complementary interests of health professionals and social scientists. Chronic illness and long-term care for the chronically ill provide particularly good illustrations of this point. Chronic illness and social responses to it also illustrate how the expertise required to analyze and discuss the relevant intellectual and public policy issues does not belong to any particular discipline. Demographers, epidemiologists, physicians, social scientists, and health care managers all make essential contributions to identifying and understanding key issues and options. One of the consequences of this multidimensionality is that we must spend a relatively large amount of time in this chapter explicating key concepts whose meanings have emerged in multidisciplinary contexts and which are often discussed in journals not routinely read by sociologists. We must also devote more attention than usual to identifying relevant data sources that have not until recently included information specifically focused on chronic illness and care.

Two themes will be apparent in this critical review of issues and evidence regarding health care for the chronically ill. First, we stress that sociocultural factors are particularly important in the etiology and development of chronic conditions and in both professional and organizational responses to these conditions. We will illustrate how the nonspecificity of chronic conditions ensures considerable uncertainty about the measurement of functional impairment and about the best type and location of appropriate care. Second, we stress the limits of rationality in finding optimum solutions for organizing care for the chronically ill that promise maximum access to high-quality care at economically and politically bearable cost. All organizational solutions proposed by health care planners will be suboptimal, we argue. Further, in a democratically organized society like the United States, which has strong ideological preferences for conceptualizing all goods and services, including health services, as economic goods, achieving any national consensus regarding long-term health care policy will be difficult. We are more likely to observe that the best that can be achieved is a national policy that maximizes options, encourages decentralization, and accepts heterogeneity in access, quality, and cost.

The emphasis in this chapter on chronic illness deliberately focuses on adults, because long-term care of older adults is a preoccupying national issue. Our choice is not meant to suggest that chronicity is not a factor in the health and quality of life of children and adolescents. In fact, given commonly accepted developmental theories, we recognize that the deleterious psychological impact of chronicity may be a particularly significant and long-lasting problem in children with chronic conditions (see, e.g., Hollingsworth 1983). There is also new evidence that chronicity in children may have a unique impact on families that has been underinvestigated (see, in particular, Hobbs, Perrin, and Ireys 1985). For an extensive and broad review of epidemiological and psychosocial evidence in the area of chronicity and children and adolescents, the interested reader is referred to the recent sourcebook by Hobbs and Perrin (1985).

The focus of this chapter is also deliberately on the United States. Systematic comparative analysis of chronic illness and care of the chronically ill in developed countries is not practical here. We do, however, direct the reader to several useful sources of information about chronic illness and care abroad. It is relevant to anticipate here that the patterns of chronic illness that are currently found in the United States are also observed in other developed countries. The organization and financing of long-term care observed in the United States, however, tend to be distinctive in their emphasis on individual responsibility for long-term care and for purchasing that care in the private sector.

SOCIOCULTURAL FACTORS IN CHRONIC ILLNESS AND THE ORGANIZATION AND FINANCING OF CARE

The Emergence of Chronic Illness and Care as Dominant Concerns

Beginning in the nineteenth century, the effects of societal investments in public health and sanitation and the improved availability of stable sources of food and medical care became evident. These factors triggered a demographic transition characterized by reduced infant mortality rates, increasing average life expectancy at birth, and age-specific increases in longevity in the later years. A predictable outcome of what has been called the "first revolution in public health" was the aging of populations in both developing and developed societies. A correlate of this demographic transition was, and is, an increased incidence and prevalence of chronic as compared with acute disease and illness (Maddox 1985a). In developed societies, the delay, amelioration, and care of chronic illness have become dominant concerns of health and welfare specialists.

Behavior and life-style as risk factors. The risk of both cardiovascular and neoplastic disease appears, for example, to be positively related to what have come to be called "behavior and life-style" factors such as inadequate exercise, poor stress management, cigarette smoking, and certain dietary practices. If behavior and life-style factors do, as they appear, have negative outcomes for health, then deliberate efforts in the promotion of healthy behavior and life-styles in the interest of preventing disease seem to be warranted. This conclusion, which has been described as the "second revolution in public health," was reached by major governmental reports in the 1970s in both Canada and the United States. The conclusion is made more dramatic by the assertions that over 50 percent of all health-related problems are derived from unhealthy behaviors and life-styles (see Maddox 1985a for a review of issues and publications). Some observers have expressed concern that a strong emphasis on personal responsibility for health and illness invites "blaming the victim." This is a possible but certainly not a necessary consequence of documenting the importance of psychosocial and cultural factors in the etiology of chronic diseases.

Relevance of an epidemiologic thought-style. Sociocultural context is critical to understanding chronic illness and care. The thought-style of epidemiologists, which is fundamentally holistic, systemic, interactive, and multidimensional, makes a distinctive contribution to an understanding of health and illness for precisely this reason. The classic trinity of epidemiology is *agent*, *environment*, and *host*. Historically, epidemiology maintained a relatively narrow view of these three components. Noxious agents were characteristically illustrated by germs and viruses; hosts were primarily illustrated by their involvement as vectors in the transmission of epidemic disease; and environment was characterized primarily in physical terms.

A radical and useful transformation has occurred in epidemiology in recent decades, a transformation stimulated by publications such as Jerome Morris's *Uses of Epidemiology* (1967). Morris suggested broadening the definition of noxious agents to include behavior and life-style factors; the definition of hosts to include persons perceived as complex organic and psychosocial systems that are more or less vulnerable to various challenges, including the challenges of the psychosocial environments that they have themselves created; and the definition of environments to include social as well as physical components. Noxious agents now include not only toxic substances but also the possible toxicity of such sociocultural contexts as poverty, social and occupational stress, ignorance, isolation, noise, and overcrowding. Morris extended the uses of epidemiology further to the study of societal responses to illness by making the provision and utilization of health care services proper domains for epidemiologic investigations. Out of such considerations the field of social epidemiology has emerged.

Those interested in the emergence of interest in and the rationale for social epidemiology will find adequate discussion of these issues in the chapters on chronic illness by Saxon Graham and colleagues in earlier editions of this *Handbook* (e.g., Graham and Reeder 1972). The concept of stress, traced to earlier work by the biologist Hans Selye, has become central in the thought-style of social epidemiology (see, e.g., Mechanic 1968, p. 296). Factors such as socioeconomic status, ethnicity, social support, and gender have been identified as etiological factors in illness and social responses to illness. In this review, we pursue two additional correlates of the emergence of chronic illness as the dominant expression of illness in contemporary society: (1) the challenges to the existing organization and financing of the care produced in a society in which care of the chronically ill becomes the central issue and (2) the fact that the dominant issue in care for the chronically ill is provision of long-term care for older adults.

Distinguishing Disease State and Functional Status

Chronicity. The distinction between acute and chronic illness focuses our attention on five key dimensions of illness: (1) An illness is likely to be regarded as chronic if it is relatively long in its typical *persistence* (e.g., three months is used by the National Center for Health Statistics). (2) Chronic illnesses are characterized by low *specificity*, that is, the absence of definitive etiology, natural course, and interventions. (3) Chronic conditions are distinctive in that their *course* is often self-sustaining rather than self-limiting as in many acute illnesses. Most chronic illnesses result from the cumulative effects of the interaction of relatively stable environmental factors with factors associated with the host. There is typically no single infectious assault on the system that can be corrected in short course. Rather, the conditions defeat the host system's ability to alter or limit its course. (4) Chronic conditions most often result from etiological factors with an endogenous *locus*. Whereas in most acute conditions, the primary etiological factor is outside of the organism (e.g., a bacteria, virus, or environmental threat), the primary etiological factors in chronic illness is in some manner associated with the constitution of the host. (5) Finally, chronic conditions often are characterized as having an ambiguous *identity*. The host usually can identify and label an acute illness. In the case of chronic conditions, symptoms may be intermittent, difficult to identify, or highly nonspecific. The host may be highly conscious of the condition (e.g., rheumatoid arthritis or stroke) or completely unaware of it (e.g., hypertension or neoplastic disease). For a related discussion, see Burish and Bradley (1983).

The nonspecificity of chronic disease. The concept of a continuum of specificity and nonspecificity of disease provides insight into the concept of chronicity (see, e.g., Marshall, Gregorio, and Walsh 1982). At one extreme, there are the diseases or conditions we tend to label *acute*, which characteristically are specific (childhood diseases of viral origin come to mind immediately as illustrations). At the other extreme are nonspecific diseases or conditions characterized by debatable etiologies, variable natural courses, and the absence of definitive, effective intervention (illustrations include substance abuse, obesity, and a variety of mental illnesses). Of intermediate specificity are the number one and number two sources of morbidity and mortality in developed countries—cardiovascular disease and neoplasms. These disease processes appear to have multiple etiologies and courses of development, as well as the relative absence of definitive therapeutic interventions across the full range of conditions observed.

Nonspecific conditions have organizational consequences because they generate debate about which professional groups have jurisdiction and particularly about whether they are properly assigned to medicine. These conditions also tend to evoke unique social movements and advocacy groups (e.g., Perrow 1965). Alcoholism, for example, long considered a morally reprehensible habit, was in the 1950s legislatively defined by the American Medical Association to be a disease. The intention was to have alcoholics qualify for health insurance coverage and hospital admission by defining their problem as a disease. For the same reason, advocates for Alzheimer's disease victims have favored classifying the disease not as a psychiatric but as a medical problem.

Human responses to pathological conditions. It is axiomatic in medical sociology that a particular diagnosis does not predict perfectly how an individual will perceive, present, describe, or experience symptomatology; whether, when, and how that individual will seek and utilize health care; and how compliant that person will be in a treatment setting (e.g., Svarstad 1986). Medically defined illness does not ensure that an individual will take the sick role or determine how that role will be played (Maddox 1972). Parsons was at least partially right in locating the sick role and the behavior of sick persons in social contexts in which such matters are likely to be defined normatively. He was also right in recognizing that, from a sociological perspective, sickness and related illness behavior are forms of social deviance.

Such observations as these, reinforced

by the experience of health practitioners, underlie the distinctions that have been promoted by the World Health Organization (WHO) among disease, impairment, disability, and handicap (WHO 1980).

Disease, Impairment, Disability, Handicap

In the terminology promoted by WHO, *disease* refers to a particular manifestation of pathology that may compromise a person's capacity for survival or the achievement and maintenance of well-being. *Impairment* designates the condition responsible for that compromise. *Disability* designates the limitations expressed by a person in meeting the expectations of significant others for role performance. The significant others may be clinicians judging performance by professional norms or social peers judging performance by social norms. Both types of norms tend to be derived from average performances of similar individuals in similar sociocultural settings performing similar tasks with these average expectations translated into normative statements. There is thus a large component of social expectations incorporated into definitions of *disability* and *handicap*. Disabled or handicapped persons therefore tend to view themselves and to be viewed by others differently in terms of how disabled or handicapped they are in various societal contexts.

The concept of handicap recognizes even more explicitly than disability the importance of social context and social expectations. A person is handicapped if personal and social resources are not available to meet existing social expectations; hence, the concept calls attention to variations in the relative advantages or disadvantages of persons in a population. For example, diseases of the eye such as glaucoma or a detached retina are impairments that tend to be disabling. The extent of handicap depends not only on the severity of the disease but also on how independent persons are expected to be, on the availability of

therapies designed to minimize severity (drugs), and the extent to which compensatory factors (prosthetics or Braille) are available to and are used by an individual.

The persistent association between lower socioeconomic status and both treated and untreated chronic impairment and disability has been repeatedly demonstrated in epidemiologic research (Syme and Berkman 1976). This demonstration illustrates that differential distribution of societal resources (e.g., income, education, social integration) constitutes a risk factor for disability and its appropriate treatment and for the degree of disability and handicap associated with any given impairment.

Personal Consequences of Chronic Conditions: Impaired Functioning and Dependency

Health planners and providers of services have a very specific reason for being interested in the consequences of disease on personal and social functioning rather than simply in the presence or absence of disease. A particular health condition potentially becomes a social problem when an impairment results in personal dependency (Shanas and Maddox 1985). Social resources tend to be mobilized not only when an individual's survival or physical well-being are at risk but also when an individual is unable to meet the basic requirements of self-care. These basic conditions are typically described by professional caregivers as "activities of daily living" (ADL) and "instrumental activities of daily living" (IADL). These designations include demonstrated or reported capacity for self-care, such as dressing, grooming, feeding, and toileting, as well as elemental instrumental tasks such as shopping, communication, ambulating, and financial management (Manton and Soldo 1985b; Maddox 1977, 1985b). We know that an individual's limited capacity for self-care may not be totally or even primarily explained by the presence or absence of disease, although disease is the single best predictor of the utilization of health care resources. An individual with a strong informal social support network may be able to compensate for disability by using available help from others (Blazer and Kaplan 1983; Minkler 1985). An individual with ample financial resources may purchase compensatory care from others to reduce the disabling and handicapping implications of disease. Chappel (1981) in an analysis of evidence from the Manitoba (Canada) Longitudinal Study of Aging argues that evidence of functional capacity is more useful to health care planners than evidence of disease in predicting service utilization.

Health promotion, disease prevention, self-care, and rehabilitation. As noted above, interest in health promotion and disease prevention received considerable stimulation in the 1970s as research on risk factors demonstrated the importance of learned and modifiable components of unhealthy behavior and life-style (Knowles 1977; Maddox 1985a). Interventions designed to promote healthy behavior and life-styles in the interest of preventing disease seemed warranted and were in fact widely proposed and implemented in the following decades.

One of the most distinctive characteristics of the "American view" of health is the extent to which illness and health care are perceived to be the responsibility of the individual. The extensive public health effort to educate the individual on the risk factors associated with chronic illness is a case in point (Maddox 1985a). Individuals are expected to reformulate their life-styles in the interest of improving health and reducing demand for health care. It is a curious irony that the American propensity to locate responsibility for treatment in individuals has been less pronounced in regard to self-care for chronic illness. For example, systematic research on self-care and its effects among the chronically ill is very rare (see, e.g., Vogel and Palmer 1983). There is a modest literature on patients' efforts at active management of the illness and self-

care (e.g., Holroyd and Creer 1986; Burish and Bradley 1983). However, much of this literature emphasizes either the prevention of chronic illness (e.g., pharmacological regimens in hypertension) or the moderation of symptoms in illnesses that are low in severity (e.g., diet control in diabetes). Overall, this apparent irony may be explained in the case of older adults by negative collective assumptions about the inevitable dependency and incapability of the elderly and chronically ill to care for themselves.

Health Care Systems

Chronic illnesses, because they are complex mixtures of biological and functional impairments, make special demands on the organization of health care, particularly on the types and coordination of care services required. In turn, this more complex organization increases management costs on top of the elevated cost associated with the longer periods of care required by chronically ill individuals.

Comparative studies of the organization and financing of health care in developed societies experiencing increasingly high rates of chronic illness provide lessons for managers and planners. First, health care systems in various developed countries have been organized and financed in a variety of ways. Second, all of the alternatives observed in the organization and financing of care seem to work tolerably well in their own social, political, and historical contexts. Third, all health care systems are suboptimal; that is, the superior efficiency and effectiveness of any system have not been demonstrated convincingly. And, fourth, simple transfer of attractive organizational features for one society to another without regard to historical and value differences is ordinarily neither practical nor feasible (e.g., Rodwin 1984). Thus, the search for an optimal system to deal with chronic illness is not likely to be rewarded, particularly in democratically organized societies that demand choice in the care offered and think of health care as an economic, not just a social, good that ought to be responsive to market forces (Anderson 1972).

Both theory and research evidence suggest that we should expect a variety of organizational responses to chronic disease. The biologist and systems theorist Ludwig von Bertalanffy (1968) argued persuasively that organizations are typically designed to function best in particular environmental contexts. As environmental demands change, the organizations most likely to be efficient and effective are likely to be different. Further, Bertalanffy argued, the effects of organizational leadership must be considered. Leaders operate in political contexts to define and advocate valued ends to be pursued. Feasibility of implementation involves an assessment of political acceptability. If societies are capable of defining different desirable end states to be achieved by the organization of health care, then different ways of organizing and financing of care are likely to be observed not because they are necessary but because they are preferred. In the United States there is a clear, current preference for highly technical care offered in hospitals by highly trained technicians, for fee-for-service payment, and for use of the private sector in developing strategies of care.

Anderson (1972) seconded Bertalanffy's conclusion regarding the suboptimality of all health care organizations and illustrated the improbability of optimal solutions in the trade-off of three basic variables that must be addressed by all care systems—access, quality, and cost. A change in any of these three parameters affects the other two. Increasing access to health care resources and increasing the quality of those services is likely to be achieved only at increased cost. Thus, a decision to increase or decrease access to care or to modify the quality of health care services tends to be primarily a political rather than a medical question.

The economist Enthoven (1980) has also made a persuasive case against the probability of optimal health care systems. Medicine, he argues, is not an exact science that

is able to diagnose and prescribe with certainty in a timely and demonstrably cost-effective way. Therefore, he proposes a comprehensive and coordinated system of care in which financially responsible providers offer services for a prepaid annual fee. Enthoven's proposal thus addresses indirectly some of the concerns mentioned most often by critics of the system in the United States, that is, a system highly fragmented and oriented to the provision of medical services for acute conditions in hospital settings.

Rodwin (1984) has made an additional point regarding health care planning. He stresses a distinction between the construction of technical solutions for providing health care and the actual implementation of planned solutions. Intellectually, one can plan systems of care that appear to satisfy demands for optimal comprehensiveness, access, quality, and cost but that, in experience, prove to be infeasible politically (see, e.g., Maddox 1971). Dozens of such technically sophisticated solutions to health care have been proposed in the United States. But the various proposed plans have not fared well because they are proposed for implementation in a sociopolitical context in which neither public nor professional consensus about the objectives of our health care system and about where responsibility lies for planning, organizing, and financing appropriate long-term care exists. Further, health care planning in the United States is extraordinarily decentralized, particularly in long-term care for the elderly who are chronically ill.

Long-term care. Long-term care of the chronically ill older adult will continue to preoccupy health care planners and policy analysts in the decades immediately ahead (Vogel and Palmer 1983). Basic demographic transformations have ensured a large and growing older adult population whose current risk for functional impairment and dependency is known to be high (Katz et al. 1983).

While the risk for chronic illness is not confined to older adults, the association between age and dependency is sufficiently high to justify concentration on long-term care for older adults. The nonadult population requiring long-term care is quite small when compared with the size of the older adult population, a fact reflected in the current policy debate (Vogel and Palmer 1983).

MAJOR DATA SOURCES AND PROFILES OF CHRONIC CONDITIONS

Orientation

Observers agree that a major characteristic of the changing patterns of health and illness in all contemporary industrial societies has been the increasingly dominant proportion of disease, illness, disability, and health care utilization related to chronic conditions. The modern triumph of long life for the average individual has as one of its concomitants high rates of chronic conditions (Maddox 1985a; Knowles 1977). Many common data sources familiar to medical sociologists do not make it easy for an inquirer to ask and answer simple questions about the distributions of acute and chronic conditions. Of most value in this respect are longitudinal data, not cross-sectional information. But the former are rare. The key sources of data are the studies and surveys of the National Center for Health Statistics (NCHS), the National Center for Health Services Research (NCHSR), and the Health Care and Financing Administration (HCFA). It is worth noting that much of the data pertaining to chronic illness and a good deal of the analysis of those data are found substantially and conspicuously outside of refereed journals in the social sciences.

Comprehensive Reviews of Issues and Evidence in Long-Term Care

Long-term care has become and promises to remain in the foreseeable future a central issue in health care organization and financing and hence a central issue in health policy. Four recent volumes provide comprehensive, complementary introductions to the background, current situation, relevant data, and policy issues in long-term care.

Long-Term Care: Perspectives from Research and Demonstration, edited by Vogel and Palmer (1983), provides a summary overview of evidence from projects supported by the HCFA. Several chapters summarize the demographics of population aging in the United States and argue that changes in age composition ensure high levels of dependency related to morbidity and disability. As the authors correctly note, the older (65+) population includes a large subset of very old (85+) with a high risk of dependency (see also Manton and Soldo 1985a, 1985b).

Vogel and Palmer document the extraordinary array of organizational responses to long-term care observed currently in the United States. Nursing homes receive substantial attention because currently there are, in this country, more beds in nursing homes than in acute care hospitals (NCHS 1987a). The 1985–1986 National Master Facility Inventory of NCHS identified 20,500 nursing homes and related care homes in the United States. These facilities offered 1,624,200 beds, most of which (1,121,500) were privately owned.

Under the rubric of long-term care, Vogel and Palmer include home care (home health/home help), special housing and transportation, adult day care, and domiciliary care. These alternative resources for long-term care of the chronically ill have not figured prominently in discussions of national policy regarding long-term care of the chronically ill. Medicare legislation, which remains a key feature of the political context in which health planning occurs in the United States, intentionally restricted the use of services not explicitly provided or approved by hospitals and physicians. Consequently, only a small fraction of nursing home care is purchased by Medicare. The purchase of such care is primarily from state-administered Medicaid funds, which are available only to persons who are considered indigent or from personal resources (see Harrington et al. 1985).

HCFA has made substantial and continual investment in documenting through research and demonstration the available community alternatives to the use of nursing homes, how and by whom they are used, and with what effect. In the final analysis the question on which HCFA has focused has been cost containment: Are there efficient and effective alternatives to nursing homes?

What Vogel and Palmer's *Long-Term Care* provides is not a definitive answer to this question of cost containment but evidence that the question is not likely to have a simple answer. The United States does not have a national consensus regarding the objectives of long-term care and tolerates and encourages enormous variations at state and local levels (see Meltzer, Farrow, and Richman 1981). Public policy, which concentrates on cost containment, has tended to be associated with strategies attempting to achieve economics through administrative regulation or coordination and more recently through competition in the marketplace.

Finally, Vogel & Palmer provide useful historical materials on the rise of the nursing home industry. This industry, as we see it in 1987, was largely generated by Medicaid legislation in the mid-1960s, which made it possible for states to pay for institutional long-term care, typically nursing home care, with federal support. Significantly and characteristically in the United States, the industry developed almost exclusively in the private sector but was heavily regulated by states and supported by both federal and state money (Harrington et al. 1985).

A second volume of interest is Meltzer, Farrow, and Richman, eds., *Policy Options in Long-Term Care* (1981), which summarizes thoughtful reflection on problems and evidence by a group of scholars at the University of Chicago. Although initially impressed by the continuing *ad hoc* quality

of the policy solutions proposed and tried in dealing with long-term care problems, they concluded that almost everything tried in long-term care works more or less well in one or another context. But nothing has worked distinctly well enough to suggest a national policy ensuring accessible long-term care of acceptable quality at an economically and politically affordable price.

The contributors to *Policy Options in Long-Term Care* are probably correct in concluding that the best explanation for the disconnected and discontinuous array of long-term care services we observe and the greatest impediment to developing a coherent national policy regarding long-term care is the absence of a consensual framework in the United States for making choices. In a democratic society in which policy analysts prefer rationally defined solutions for real world problems, the limits of rationality become most evident when a wide range of plausible solutions are evident, each promising a different trade-off among access to care, quality of care, and cost of care. There is no general consensus about acceptable standards of access, quality, and cost in the United States. Currently there is at least implicit consensus that financial responsibility for long-term care is primarily an individual responsibility. For the nonindigent adult individual at risk for morbidity leading toward dependence, long-term care remains the greatest risk for which a viable insurance strategy has not emerged.

The authors also perceive correctly that in the United States health is currently perceived primarily not as a social good but an economic good for which the individual is primarily responsible. One consequence of this expectation is that, as a nation, we have become very dependent on informal social support systems to supplement formal care of the chronically ill. The U.S. General Accounting Office provides a rather startling estimate: In the case of the very dependent elderly individuals living in the community, approximately 80 percent of the resources used in providing care comes from kin and friends, not public sources (Maddox 1985b, 1980). Consequently, Meltzer and colleagues note that a persistent concern in long-term care policy is that any proposed policy must not diminish informal support.

What one presumably is trying to achieve and maintain through long-term care policy in the United States, Meltzer and colleagues argue, is maximum feasible functional independence of chronically ill individuals in the least restrictive environment possible, without undermining existing informal supports. There is a lack of consensus about the nature and extent of public responsibility for such long-term care. We can conceive technically satisfactory solutions that we have been unable to implement politically. A key question that remains unanswered is, How shall *need* be determined? Meltzer and colleagues are attracted to a national income policy as the major potential contribution of the federal government to long-term care. There is little evidence, however, that such a policy is likely to be considered seriously, much less implemented.

Elizabeth Kutza in her chapter in *Policy Options in Long-Term Care* concentrates on "the puzzle of who should be served." The WHO definition of health-related needs ("comprehensive well being") is, as health economist Robert Evans (1985) has noted, a health economist's nightmare because there is no simple way to exclude any conceivable service as irrelevant to one's well-being. The makers of public policy must establish these criteria because the physician alone cannot. In a 1972 Social Security survey, Kutza notes, an estimated 11.2 million adults age 16 to 64 were considered functionally disabled; about a third were either homebound or institutionalized. About 3 percent of the total population were classified as "developmental disabled" (most "mildly" so) and 5 percent profoundly disabled. An estimated 1 percent were "mentally" retarded. About 25 percent of disability among adults is related to accidents. Mental illness at the time of the 1972 estimate was about as fluid as it is now—about 10 to 15 percent were classified as having some psychiatric difficulty (see Chapter 16 of this *Handbook*).

To ask, Who has what kinds of needs? is complex enough. An even more complex question is how to estimate the probability that needs will be translated into a demand for services even when services are provided. Kutza cites longitudinal evidence to suggest this translation of need into actual service demand may be as low as 9 percent.

Long-Term Care of the Elderly—Public Policy Issues, edited by Harrington et al. (1985), includes up-to-date discussions of the most significant current policy issues. Its emphasis on federal legislation on long-term care and the responses of states to that legislation is particularly valuable. Focus on states is necessary because Medicaid, which is the principal funding mechanism for longterm care services in nursing homes, is a federal-state arrangement in which states have considerable financial responsibility and administrative authority.

Harrington and colleagues document the heterogeneity of approaches to long-term care in the various states as each attempts to achieve effective and efficient care in economically and politically feasible ways. The authors conclude that the achievement of effective comprehensive long-term care policy faces formidable obstacles in the political and health care environment, which (1) has focused and continues to focus on biomedical acute care, (2) has decentralized responsibility and authority, (3) prefers a welfare approach to meeting needs, and (4) accepts a fragmented service system as inevitable. Medicare and Medicaid remain substantially medicalized in the sense that care to be provided is primarily either directly medical, under medical supervision, or certified by a physician.

Further, financial mechanisms continue to reinforce care that is offered in an institutional context. Development of noninstitutional or home-based care arrangements consequently is hindered. The overall effect is, as we have argued, inconsistent with an adequate understanding of the probable health care needs of chronically ill individuals. These needs are only partially medical, leading to an awkward fit between the chronic patient's needs and the health care system.

The decentralization to which Harrington and colleagues refer is the involvement of states in Medicaid administration and the historic national dependence in this country on states to develop and administer health services. Services for which states have responsibility have substantial nonmedical components related to income maintenance, home health and home help services, housing, and transportation. The fragmentation and lack of coordination among health and welfare services are legendary in the United States. Consequently, we do not have and typically do not even contemplate a national long-term care policy or an integrated system of care.

In the United States, we continue to think of health care generally as an economic good to be purchased rather than a social good to be societally ensured. We, therefore, spend a great deal of time and effort on determining eligibility for publicly supported services. The hallmark of entitlement to Medicaid, the principal source of publicly supported long-term care, remains the documentation of financial impoverishment. The "spend down" is a phenomenon worth noting as an illustration of current policy regarding long-term care. An individual seeking long-term care who is not initially entitled by poverty to receive Medicaid support may, as a result of personal payment for that care, "spend down" to become impoverished enough to be eligible for Medicaid. Cost control, Harrington and colleagues conclude, is the dominant concern in the trinity of interest to health policy analysts—cost, quality, access. And the Medicaid "spend down" illustrates a national long-term care policy that promises publicly supported care for indigents only.

The authors document particularly well why such an extraordinary variety of procedures for long-term care have been tried and why most may have some beneficial effect. But they also illustrate why few generalizations about optimally efficient, effective long-term care interventions to serve the chronically ill can be defended convincingly with evidence. The quasi-experiments in long-term care developed in the contexts of various states typically involve so many variables operating simultaneously that defensible generalizations remain scarce and very tenuous. And, in any case, the focus of the typical research studies or demonstrations tends to be on cost control, with minimum interest in documenting effects on quality and access.

Harrington and colleagues argue from evidence that the most clearly effective interventions in long-term care involve capped budgets, which do appear to have a beneficial economic effect. This is the sort of evidence that has been used to support the prospective payment strategy illustrated by the current use of diagnosis-related groups (DRGs) to pay for medical charges. Convincing evidence has not, however, been available to allay suspicions that DRGs have tended to reduce access to and the quality of care without achieving more than moderate reduction in total cost of care.

Finally, Rabin and Stockton's *Long-Term Care for the Elderly: A Factbook* (1987) is a timely and very useful source of basic background information on demographic, epidemiologic, organizational, and financial aspects of long-term care in the United States. As the references in Rabin and Stockton illustrate and as we have noted elsewhere in this chapter, data relevant to aging populations and to long-term care are typically being generated from very large-scale data banks not routinely used by many academic investigators; and these data are reported in commissioned papers and monographs not initially published in refereed sources. For these reasons, the academic readers of this chapter will find in the Rabin and Stockton factbook a thoughtful compilation of information about large-scale, national data sources on the demography and epidemiology of an aging population. As a supplemental source, readers with an interest in epidemiological evidence will find a chapter by White et al. (1986) useful.

Chapter Five in Rabin and Stockton's book summarizes recent data on health care utilization expenditures and pays particular attention to documenting the persistent high proportion of out-of-pocket personal financing of health care in the United States. The clear shift in recent decades toward federal financial participation, particularly in regard to care in nursing homes, is also documented. A good review of the high cost of care in the last year of life is provided, supplementing the evidence presented initially in Kovar's analysis (1986) of National Medical Care Expenditure Survey (NMCES) data.

Rabin and Stockton's factbook provides, in addition to a convenient history of the rise of nursing homes as the dominant organizational response to long-term care needs after the enactment of Medicare and Medicaid in 1965, a rare comprehensive review of the characteristics of persons who use home care services and of how these services are organized and financed are provided. A chapter is also devoted to reviewing the distinctive challenge of an aging veteran population. Two final chapters are directed to reviewing research and demonstration activities in long-term care and to international comparisons of long-term care utilization.

EMPIRICAL PROFILES OF CHRONIC ILLNESS AND CARE

Orientation

The concept of chronicity has been only modestly developed as an analytic concept. Having classified a condition as chronic by some minimal criteria (e.g., continuing for at least three months), we do not ordinarily find data that specify either actual length of time in a chronic condition or the severity of conditions as possible explanatory variables. Absence of such information has complicated assessment of the fairness of the current prepayment strategy used in Medicare reimbursement (Maddox and Manton 1987; Worthman and Cretin 1986). It is not enough to know that a treated individual is diagnosed as having one or another acute or chronic condition. How advanced and serious is the condition? What level of care is appropriate? In brief, then, we know that incidence and prevalence of chronic diseases increase with age or that, among persons 65 years of age and older, 80 percent have at least one chronic condition and frequently more than one. But such information is of limited usefulness for purposes of policy and planning without additional information about duration and seriousness.

The kind of conceptualization and the data required to inform us about the social as well as medical implications of chronic disease have been brought into focus by a debate among demographers and epidemiologists precipitated by a physician, James Fries, in a controversial article that appeared in the *New England Journal of Medicine* (1980). A balanced assessment of the issues, the arguments, and the evidence is found in a review article on geriatric epidemiology by White and colleagues (1986). Fries argued that there is a biologically programmed limit to longevity (he estimated 85 as likely) and that, as average longevity increases, it is possible if not probable that the onset of morbidity and of disabling morbid conditions can be delayed. Morbidity and disablement can be "compressed" so that capacity for years of relative independence and acceptable quality are not reduced as life expectancy lengthens. Fries's argument is illustrated in Figure 1. If morbidity and disablement are compressable, we would expect the three curves in the figure to become closer even as the mortality curve moves to the right of the figure.

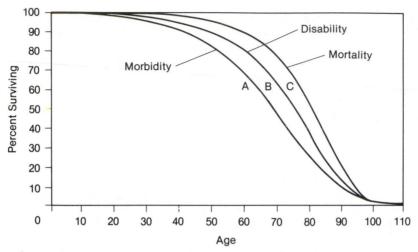

FIGURE 1   Hypothetical Mortality, Morbidity, and Disability Survival Curves for a Contemporary Aging Population. *(Source:* Adapted from World Health Organization, 1984, *The Uses of Epidemiology in the Study of the Elderly: Report of the WHO Scientific Group on the Epidemiology of Aging,* Geneva, p. 29.)

A focused debate (e.g., Manton 1982; Manton and Soldo, 1985b; White et al. 1986) generated by Fries's arguments has occasioned a review of evidence indicating that Fries is surely wrong in his optimistic estimate of age 85 as maximum average life expectancy. His second point, the possible delay in onset of disabling chronic disease, remains problematic.

The prevalence of chronic conditions. The most recent unpublished data on chronic conditions from the NCHS Health Interview Survey (HIS) illustrates a now familiar pattern of conditions and their relationship to age (Table 1). The most notable observation from these data is the inclusion of highly prevalent chronic conditions related to hearing and vision problems that are usually correctable with prosthetics. Prosthetics for neither condition, however, are currently reimbursable under Medicare. Heart disease, which leads all other conditions in generating demand for ser-

TABLE 1   Top Ten Chronic Conditions among Adults, 1984

Condition	Rate per 1000 by Age		
	17–44	*45–64*	*65 plus*
Arthritis	47.7	246.5	464.7
Hypertensive disease	54.2	243.7	378.6
Hearing impairments	43.8	142.9	283.8
Heart conditions	37.9	122.7	277.0
Chronic sinusitis	158.4	177.5	183.6
Visual impairments	27.4	55.2	136.6
Orthopedic impairments	90.5	117.5	128.2
Arteriosclerosis	0.5	21.3	97.0
Diabetes	8.6	56.9	83.4
Varicose veins	19.0	50.1	83.2

Source: From NCHS/HIS (unpublished), in B. Soldo and K. Manton, 1985, Health Status and Service Needs of the Oldest Old, *Milbank Memorial Fund Quarterly* 63(2):286–319.

vices among older adults, accounts for 10 percent of all doctor visits, 18 percent of all hospital and bed disability days, and 45 percent of all deaths. If one adds stroke and cancer to heart disease, these three conditions alone account for 20 percent of doctor visits, 40 percent of hospital days, 50 percent of bed disability days, and 75 percent of all deaths (Senate Special Committee on Aging 1985).

Prevalence of functional impairment. The concepts of activities of daily living (ADL) and instrumental activities of daily living (IADL) are now widely used in social survey and epidemiologic research to illustrate how chronic conditions are translated into increased risk for dependency. Table 2 illustrates typical data from NCHS/HIS on adults of various ages that specify the kinds of information about ADL (here "basic physical activities") and IADL (here "home management activities") and the distribution of functional incapacity by age. The increased risk of disability with age is apparent. It is worth noting, however, even at

advanced ages, that a majority of noninstitutionalized adults in NCHS surveys and other surveys are found to be functioning with relative independence (Maddox 1985b; Soldo and Manton 1985).

In addition to asking about capacity for self-care, NCHS/HIS also asks more general questions about activity limitation, such as, Are you limited by a chronic condition but not in a major activity? The risk of activity limitation and of limitation of major activity increase monotonically with age, from 5 percent among those under age 25 to 53 percent among those 75 and older. These findings are typical.

Katz et al. (1983) used a sample of adults in the state of Massachusetts to lay the groundwork for explicating the concept of compression of morbidity (see Figure 1). Among older adults whose age-specific average remaining years of life could be estimated from life tables, how many of those years were likely to be "active" and how many "impaired"? Table 3 reports their estimates based on probable risk for physical limitations suggested by

TABLE 2 Percentage Needing Help with Selected Basic Physical Activities and Home Management Activities, by Age Group, for the Civilian Noninstitutionalized Population, United States, 1979

	Age					
	18–44	*45–54*	*55–64*	*65–74*	*75–84*	*85+*
Basic Physical Activities						
Walking	0.4	0.9	1.9	3.9	8.4	26.0
Going outside	.3	.7	1.4	3.4	7.4	26.9
Bathing	.2	.4	1.1	2.0	5.1	17.3
Dressing	.2	.6	.9	1.4	3.3	11.7
Using the toilet	.1	.3	.6	1.2	2.8	10.5
Getting in or out of bed or chair	.1	.4	.6	.9	2.6	7.3
Eating	.1	.1	.3	.4	.8	3.8
Help needed with at least one activity	.5	1.3	2.9	5.3	11.4	34.8
Home Management Activities						
Shopping	.4	1.2	2.2	4.4	11.9	35.5
Household chores	.4	1.4	2.5	4.1	9.8	29.3
Handling money	.3	.5	.7	1.5	5.1	17.6
Meal preparation	.3	.8	1.5	2.5	6.5	22.5
Help needed with any home management activities	.6	1.8	3.2	5.7	14.2	39.9

Source: Data adapted from tables in NCHS, 1983, Physical and Home Management Activities, *Advancedata* 92, 2–3.

TABLE 3 Active Life Expectancy (Remaining Years of Independent ADL) among Noninstitutionalized Persons in Massachusetts, by Sex and Age, 1984

Age	Average Remaining Active Years		Average Remaining Life Expectancy		Average Remaining Impaired Years	
	Male	Female	Male	Female	Male	Female
65–69	9.3	10.6	13.1	19.5	3.8	8.9
70–74	8.2	8.0	11.9	15.9	3.7	7.9
75–79	6.5	7.1	9.6	13.2	3.1	6.1
80–84	4.8	4.8	7.4	9.8	2.6	5.0
85 plus	3.3	2.8	6.5	7.7	3.2	4.9

Source: Adapted from information appearing in *New England Journal of Medicine*, S. Katz, L. Branch, M. Branson, J. Papsiders, J. Beck, and D. Greer, 1983, Active Life Expectancy, *New England Journal of Medicine* 309:1218–1224.

longitudinal study on an elderly population. In every age category, the risk for impaired years in later adulthood is relatively high and increases with age. At age 85, for males the risk of activity or impairment for the 6.6 remaining years is about 50 percent. For females at age 85 the risk for impairment in the remaining 7.7 years is about 64 percent.

Manton and Soldo (1985a) review the gap in, and hence the need for, information required to resolve the issue posed by Figure 1. They note that Katz and colleagues, as well as investigators in Japan and Canada, are attempting to fill this gap. In every instance, however, we find that the evidence available is not adequate to permit a definitive resolution of Fries's "compression of morbidity" argument. The time series presented by Manton (1982) for the NCHS Health and Nutrition Examination Survey (HANES) and Health Examination Study (HES) suggest improvement in the health and functional capacity of the U.S. population in terms of such measures as cholesterol levels and hypertension. Manton (1982) concludes that nationally representative data on disability, activity restrictions, self-appraisal of health, and rates of long-term institutionalization at advanced ages, as well as selected clinical indicators, do not show marked deterioration in health status of individuals age 65 and older through the 1960s and 1970s despite significant increase in life expectancy at advanced ages. What remains bothersome about the evidence, then, is not indications of expansion of disabling morbidity as the population ages but failure to find clear evidence of compression of morbidity in the face of significantly increased numbers of disabled elderly individuals.

Rice (1985), former director of NCHS, has done extrapolations of what is implied by assuming the constancy of rates of disablement in a progressively aging population *if* compression of morbidity is *not* assumed (Table 4). For example, between 1980 and 2040, the size of the older population is projected to increase by slightly less than threefold (from 25,892,000 to 67,256,000). During the same period, Rice estimates proportionately higher numbers of persons with ADL impairment and related demands for care. The sheer absolute size of the estimated demand for services captures our attention. This is because the size of this demand has implications for the kinds of facilities and professional personnel that must be anticipated and the increased number and cost of facilities and services for the chronically ill. Estimating the cost of caring for chronically ill, vulnerable elderly persons is at the root of current cost-consciousness in all discussions of geriatric care. Specifically, this cost-consciousness has been expressed in public policy in the form of legislation instituting the system of prospective payment for care to control Medicare cost known as Diagnosis Related Groups (DRGs).

ILLUSTRATIVE POLICY ISSUES

A Prospective Payment System: Diagnosis-Related Groups

Worthman and Cretin (1986) have prepared for the Health Care Financing Administration a comprehensive review of the literature on diagnosis-related groups (DRGs) as a prospective payment strategy for medicare. This perceptive review notes that in a single stroke in 1983, Medicare's Prospective Payment System (PPS) completely overhauled hospital reimbursement of elderly inpatients while leaving the implications of this policy for long-term care largely implicit. Reimbursement for hospitalization is based primarily on the diagnosis-related group (one of 470 classifications related to the current International Classification of Diseases) into which a case falls, with final calculation of payment adjusted for a variety of factors affecting hospital cost (e.g., teaching activity, local wages, geographical location). Significantly, the Congress applied PPS only to hospital inpatients, not to residents of long-

TABLE 4   Size of the U.S. Population 65 and Older, 1980–2040, and Associated Health-Related Correlates

Characteristic and Year	Age 65 and Older	Age 75 and Older
Population		
(thousands)		
1980	25,892	10,265
2000	36,252	17,918
2020	52,653	22,560
2040	67,256	37,831
Persons with ADL*		
Limitations		
(thousands)		
1980	1,780	1,132
2000	2,775	1,991
2020	3,954	2,645
2040	5,920	4,632
Physician Visits		
(millions)		
1980	166	66
2000	231	115
2020	335	144
2040	428	241
Days of Hospital Care		
(millions)		
1980	105	56
2000	160	102
2020	225	130
2040	312	219
Nursing Home Residents		
(thousands)		
1980	1,315	1,088
2000	2,316	2,051
2020	3,129	2,695
2040	4,979	4,554
Personal Health		
Expenditures		
(in constant 1980		
$ billions)		
1980	64.5	
2000	90.3	N.A.
2020	131.2	
2040	167.5	

*Activities of Daily Living
Source: See D. Rice, in C. Harrington, R. Newcomer, C. Estes, and associates, 1985, *Long Term Care of the Elderly: Policy Issues*, Beverly Hills: Sage Publications.

term care facilities or to the calculation of physician fees (Maddox and Manton 1987).

The attention of readers is called to the Worthman and Cretin report for another reason anticipated earlier in this chapter, the issue of data availability. These authors use primarily evidence reported or published and interpreted *outside* journals and sources routinely read by medical sociologists who are not specialists in health care organization and financing. Worthman and Cretin are correct, we believe, in concluding that this special technical literature on DRGs is, on average, superior to and more timely than the evidence published in academic journals.

It does not follow that federal agencies ask all the right questions and provide definitive answers. Quite the contrary. Evidence for a definitive characterization of the cost-effectiveness or cost benefits of PPS/DRG and its effects on access to and quality of care still do not exist three years after that program's implementation. Hence, it can be demonstrated that, since the introduction of DRGs in 1983, average hospital stays have decreased slightly. But there is no definitive evidence regarding whether total system cost of Medicare or the quality of care of elderly inpatients have been decreased. A major concern among hospital managers is whether the DRG formula results in equitable payment as the mix of patients and of severity of disease processes within diagnostic categories vary, as invariably they would. While inequity is demonstrably a continuing risk (Maddox and Manton 1987), no definitive conclusion can be drawn about the probability of inequity for any particular hospital as the system determines winners and losers. Further, Worthman and Cretin conclude that no available single adjustment in the DRG formula for payment demonstrably ensures a more equitable payment scheme.

There has been a pronounced movement toward for-profit hospitals in the private sector, stimulating concern about the probability of reduced access and increased cost of geriatric inpatient care. The concern is legitimate, but the definitive evidence for reaching a conclusion has not been forthcoming. Similarly, anecdotal evidence of hospital stays that have been inappropriately shortened by DRG calculations in the interest of minimizing loss or maximizing gain has continued but without support from systematic evidence. In the United States, when thinking of doctors' visits, medications, and hospitalization, we tend to think of more as better. The possibility that exposure to a day in the hospital might increase risk for a patient rather than provide help is uncongenial. Hence, we tend to equate the loss of one hospital day as, by definition, a deprivation rather

than a reduction in risk of inappropriate treatment. In any case, the reduction in length of stay is real; average length of stay for Medicare patients was ten days in 1983, and eight days in 1986. The consequences of reduced length of hospital stays for the quality of care of older patients remain conjectural.

PPS/DRG has not demonstrably scored unambiguously well in beneficially affecting access and quality. Moreover, the effect on cost is not as clear as one might expect. Intuitively, Medicare cost should be reduced as average hospital stays among older adults are reduced. Yet, even if such a cost reduction were effective, the total federal system cost represented by Medicare and Medicaid expenditures would not necessarily be less. Savings represented by an average hospital stay by a day or two could easily be neutralized by increased utilization of nursing homes or community-based care (Maddox 1977). Medicare spent $79.9 billion dollars in 1986, up from $56.9 billion in 1983. Further, the Congressional Budget Office (Pear 1987) reported that in the first two full years under PPS/DRG rules for Medicare reimbursement, the average hospital experienced a profit (or surplus) of 17.6 percent in 1985 and 15.7 percent in 1986.

Community-Based Care

Discussions of long-term care have tended to focus on the high cost of hospitalization for Medicare patients; on the 1.6 million elderly persons in hospital-like long-term care facilities financed largely by Medicaid; and on the required medical certification of most care paid for by Medicare outside a hospital. Until very recently, an elderly Medicare recipient did not have access to community-based services or to a long-term care facility until after three days in the hospital and medical certification.

After the passage of the Older Americans Act in 1965, community-based services for older adults were enhanced by, among other things, such programs as senior centers, special transportation, meal services, and home help/home health services. In 1984 a relatively small proportion (22 percent) of community-dwelling older adults reported using any special service, and only 7 percent used more than one service (NCHS 1986b). More recently, rules of access to community care services financed by Medicare and Medicaid have been modified to increase access.

An argument has persisted for a decade (Maddox 1980, 1985b) that community-based services are an obviously cheaper and probably better way to care for disabled elderly. Research evidence used to reach this conclusion has been conceptually and methodologically flawed. The best evidence indicate that in a fragmented service system (1) any particular local program or demonstration may achieve reduced program cost without demonstrable reduction of total system cost and (2) cost-effectiveness of community care is very much a function of the severity of disability among the individuals served. Evidence indicates that for those chronically ill patients in the community who have the severest impairment, institutionalization is more economical, though not necessarily a more attractive solution from the standpoint of quality of care or quality of life. The most convincing argument for community-based care currently is not that it is more economical but that it responds to the preferences of many older patients and their informal caregivers (Maddox 1985b; see also Callender and LaVor 1975). Concerns about the high cost of institutional long-term care have expectedly increased interest in community-based care.

Since about 1970, there has been a long-term trend toward reduced average length of stay in nonfederal short-term hospitals in the United States. The average length of stay in 1985 for all inpatients was 6.5, compared with 7.7 days a decade ago. For patients served by Medicare, length of hospital stay has decreased on average from ten days in 1983 to eight days in 1986. Discharge rates in 1985 fell below 150 per 1000 of the civilian population for the first time since 1971. Average length of hospital stay for persons 65 and older varies by sex. For example, in 1985 average length of stay was 8.7 days; for males it was 8.4, and for females 9.0 (NCHS 1986c).

Reduction in average length of stays in hospital and reduction of restrictions on access to hospital care have had a significant effect on the use of Medicare funds for home health services, although expenditures for home health services account for only 2.4 percent of total Medicare expenditures. A "small" percent in a program such as Medicare, however, translates a 2.4 percent budget item in 1983 into almost $1.4 billion. This expenditure purchased an average of one home visit per enrollee and an average of 26.3 visits per user of home services (Leader 1986). As might be expected in a society that emphasizes private sector initiatives and institutional care, the most substantial rates of growth in community care services was found in the hospital-based and for-profit sectors. Although most states require a certificate of need (CON) to create a home health agency certifiable under Medicare, there are virtually no uniform requirements for training, supervision, or certification of home health aides nationwide. The United States clearly has not sorted out the role of community-based care in its national policy on long-term care (see, e.g., the review articles on community and home care by Kavesh 1986 and in Vogel and Palmer 1983).

In an article documenting relative lack of involvement of physicians in community-based care, Koren (1986) argues that noninstitutional care has placed increased emphasis on highly technical procedures that are neither controlled nor supervised by physicians. Consider, for example, the hospice movement for the terminally ill in the United States. Hospice in this country, in contrast to its English predecessor, was consciously developed primarily as a community-based, not institutionally based, service. Movements in both countries, however, minimized the use of medical technology. In England hospice was paid for as a service of the British National Health Service. In the United States hospice was financed totally in the private sector until recent legislation included this service as an option under Medicare. The hope that hospice would prove to be an organizationally flexible and cost-effective option under Medicare has apparently not been realized (Mor and Kidder 1985; Paradis and Cummings 1986). Furthermore, increased use of high technology services in community-based care will tend to increase cost.

The Channeling Project

In September 1980 the National Long Term Care Demonstration—known informally as the Channeling Project—was initiated to assess the effects of comprehensive case management of community care on cost containment in long-term care for needy, impaired elderly (DHHS 1986). The demonstration was designed to finance some direct services and to arrange for waiver of some financial restrictions on certain types of community care; but the demonstration did not include direct control over medical and nursing home care. Case management in the basic demonstration of how an existing service system might be effectively coordinated consisted in the Channeling Project of seven features: (1) outreach, (2) standard eligibility screening, (3) comprehensive assessment, (4) initial care planning, (5) service arrangement, (6) monitoring, and (7) periodic assessment. An alternative financial control model made it possible for health care managers in some demonstrations sites to expand the range of services offered, to offer services on the basis of need rather than eligibility, to pool resources for strategic allocation to particular services, and to require partial copayment by recipients in some cases. The five sites selected to test each model were operational in 1982 and continued fully operational through June 1984.

Over the life of the demonstration, 11,769 applicants were screened, and 9,890 were identified as eligible. Of these, 6,341 were randomly assigned to demonstration or control categories. Several data sources were used in the evaluation of the program's effects. In addition to telephone screening interviews, an extensive in-person survey was administered to both treatment and control groups at baseline and then at six, twelve, and (for half the sample) eighteen months. Contact was subsequently made by telephone with a subset of informal caregivers at six and twelve months. Service use and cost data were collected from Medicare, Medicaid, and channeling records, as well as from providers directly.

The Channeling Project's selection criteria did identify an extremely vulnerable group of older adults. Twenty-two percent were unable to perform any of five ADL activities, over 90 percent were IADL-impaired, and 53 percent were incontinent. There was evidence of cognitive impairment; one-third lived alone; and over half reported incomes of below $500 a month.

The demonstration, whose design was implemented essentially as planned, provided an evaluation of the effects of coordination of basic and slightly enriched services for older adults. These effects included the following:

1. Channeling increased formal community service use.
2. Neither type of demonstration (basic or financial model) reduced or had any major effects on the informal care being provided to participants.
3. In spite of identifying a group of elderly persons living in the community who were at high risk for institutionalization, the demonstration did not identify the subpopulation at highest risk nor did it reduce nursing home use.
4. The channeling interventions did not reduce the relatively heavy use of physicians and medical services among these high-risk older adults.
5. The cost of expanded case management and community services were not offset by reductions in nursing home and other costs.

6. In general, the demonstration increased client and informal caregiver confidence and satisfaction with life.
7. The demonstration did not significantly affect client functioning or risk of mortality.

The Channeling Project was an expensive demonstration and reconfirmation of several general observations repeatedly made about the organization of health care in the United States over many years (Maddox 1980). Manipulation of the system of formal care services does not appear ordinarily to reduce the availability of informal support. In the case of the Channeling Project, both the persons receiving care and their care givers responded positively to efforts to improve care for the elderly persons for whom they were responsible. The presumption that a large number of persons in nursing homes do not need to be there has persisted for a long time without the benefit of definitive evidence. Our own estimates based on data generated by Duke University and the U.S. General Accounting Office Older Americans Resources and Services Program (Maddox 1985b) suggest that the number of nursing home residents who might, on medical grounds, be treated more appropriately elsewhere may be 10 percent. On the other hand, in our estimation, possibly an equal percent of community-dwelling elderly may be so disabled as to benefit from nursing home placement.

In demonstrations like the Channeling Project, which emphasized comprehensive screening, it would be reasonable to assume, therefore, that some screening of community-dwelling residents would lead to a recommendation *for* rather than *against* institutionalization. In any case, the demonstrated failure of the well-conceived Channeling Project to reduce institutionalization and medical care usage illustrates how such projects may add to rather than reduce or moderate total system cost for the care of older populations. Research suggests that the most likely way in which total system cost can be reduced is through

a capped organizational budget covering inpatient, outpatient, and community care services (Enthoven 1980; Harrington et al. 1985; Maddox 1977, 1980; Evans 1985). In such cases the issue becomes one of suballocation of a specified total budget to these various services and the decentralization of health planning and delivery. Budget capping has technical merit as a cost-control strategy but is politically quite controversial, as illustrated by recent assessment of the merits of using health maintenance organizations to provide Medicare-financed care for older adults (Iglehart 1987).

Long-Term Care Financing

There is no mistaking that, as a matter of public policy in the United States, major responsibility for ensuring health care continues to reside with the individual. Medicare, which is insurance with public participation, nonetheless stresses personal payment of premiums and substantial copayment; it requires that, failing on one's ability to pay premiums or meet copayments, one must qualify as indigent under Medicaid. A surprisingly high proportion (about 25 percent overall, as high as 40 percent for minorities) of Americans are without personal health insurance, and the noninsured tend to be the poor and marginally employed who are at greatest risk for requiring long-term care.

But even the elderly, who as a subgroup have the greatest coverage with private and public resources such as Medicaid and Medicare, are not covered for health catastrophes that result in long hospital stays or, following hospitalization, require lengthy nursing care. As noted above, Medicare has limited coverage in terms of number of incidents and days of covered illness in a year and has no provision for long-term care in a nursing home or in the community not certifiable as following naturally from the event that initially required hospitalization (for a general review of Medicare provisions, implementation, and recommended changes, see Davis and Rowland 1986).

Former Secretary of the Department of Health and Human Services Bowen, who served during part of the Reagan administration, suggested adding a form of catastrophic insurance to Medicare. Bowen, himself a physician, recommended limiting the total out-of-pocket cost to an individual to about $2,000 for an additional Medicare premium of about $60 per year. Critics of this proposal were particularly harsh in pointing out initially that the medical catastrophes presumably covered would benefit a relatively few older individuals. Nonetheless, Congress passed legislation in 1987 to create Catastrophic Health Insurance. Premiums were expected to be added to current Medicare payments and to be income related, with higher-income individuals paying between $600 and $900 annually in addition to current Medicare premiums (*New York Times* 1987). Analysts argue about how many persons would benefit from catastrophic health insurance. In 1980, for example, about 12 percent of older adults living in the community had total health care charges of $3,000 or more. But the principal objection of critics of the proposed legislation is that the financing of long-term care is not addressed.

Nursing home insurance in the private sector has generated considerable interest but little action in the marketplace. Failure of insurance companies to expand into this market appears to reflect some uncertainty about the actuarial evidence of the age-specific risk of institutionalization. But there is apparently also uncertainty about the future cost of nursing home care. In 1985 averaging per diem cost for skilled nursing home care was $61, for intermediate care $48, and for residential care $30 (NCHS 1987a). Further, the conditions of eligibility to enter an institution and the willingness to purchase the insurance at an age at which an affordable premium could be written remain problematic. Immobilization in the marketplace has been the result.

Long-Term Care Financing Options

A group at the Brookings Institution under the leadership of economist Rivlin and sociologist Wiener has begun to report informally on a review of policy options for financing long-term care. This project's reports to date are very preliminary, unpublished, and hence subject to modification. The project's conceptualization of options and the modeling of the affects of various options, however, warrant at least a preliminary note in anticipation of a final report expected late in 1987.

The project joined with a private consulting organization to develop a "long-term care financing microsimulation model." This model was used to develop estimates of the impact of various options for financing long-term care. Simply described, the model simulates the effects of various financing options after assumptions are made regarding such factors as retirement income and assets, rates of disability and of remission from disability, admission rates to nursing homes or home care services, length of stay in nursing homes, and alternative public or private financing of services. Estimates of the probable total use and cost of long-term care services from 1986 to 2020 were generated.

One of the most interesting observations from the preliminary simulations comes from evaluation of the public policy option of doing nothing. In this case, assuming that nursing home beds increase with demand and annual inflation in cost in the long run is about 5.8 percent, total nursing home expenditures are estimated to increase by 197 percent from 1986–1990 to 2016–2020, and Medicaid expenditures by 227 percent. In addition, the total number of persons in nursing homes at any time during a year are estimated to increase by 76 percent.

The simulation of what one might expect from a preference for private long-term care insurance begins with assumptions like the following: Assume insurance to take effect after one hundred days (i.e., after Medicare eligibility is exhausted) and assume $30–$50 per day nursing home coverage with a maximum length of stay of six years. In 1986 persons up to age 81 would be eligible to purchase the insurance; after 1986, policies would have to be purchased by age 67 for persons not disabled at the time of purchase. A 1986 annual premium for a $50 a day indemnity policy for long-term care would range from about $607 at age 67 to $1,710 at age 81. The premium would continue to be paid by an individual if the premium were between 5 percent and 7 percent of the individual's annual income.

The simulation estimates that this option would result in insuring 45 percent of the population at age 67, with an average premium of $1,078. The effect on federal health care expenditures by 2016–2020 is probably that Medicaid cost for nursing homes would decrease by 6 percent, and out-of-pocket cost and asset reduction for individuals to pay for such care would decrease between 11 percent and 19 percent. Although the estimated 45 percent of 67-year-olds with long-term care insurance is a quantum jump from where we are at present in insuring long-term care financing, the proportion remaining uninsured is impressively high.

The model applied to other options estimates that resorting to various forms of "individual medical accounts" would cover in 2020 a disappointingly low 28 percent of the elderly population. Alternatively, a home equity conversion option has the effect in the simulation model of increasing the number of Medicaid patients in nursing homes by 4 percent and reducing self-payment of nursing home care by about 17 percent.

These illustrations from the Brookings project provide the flavor of this useful exercise in the evaluation of policy options for financing long-term care. The quality of the work suggested in the preliminary reports justifies the expectation of a significant contribution to public consideration of policy options when the final report is available.

CONCLUSIONS

It has been our intention to impress the reader with the extent to which achieving consensus about policy in the decades ahead will be difficult. The expected difficulty stems in large part from past and current failure to achieve a workable national consensus regarding a health care system we would like and also would be able to finance. Further, personal responsibility for health and health care continue to be the dominant theme in the nation's culture. It is clear that increased decentralization and heterogeneity of health planning have been accepted as an alternative to a coherent and unified national policy. It is also clear that as health planners and social scientists begin to address the growing needs of an aging population, the evidence available to answer major questions will continue to be limited and often problematic. Answers to the question of who needs care are hampered by the nature of many forms of chronic illness that are incompatible with standard accepted conceptions of morbidity as self-limiting, acute in onset, and specific in course and treatment. Rather, the reality of chronic illness in our society demands a response that conceptualizes illness as a problem with multiple causes and different courses affected by sociocultural factors. An alternative model of illness is required—one that is more holistic; that addresses the entire range of issues affected by chronic conditions; that is sensitive to social, psychological, and medical factors; and that places adequate attention on functioning and disability rather than on the presence or absence of disease. It remains to be seen, however, whether such a shift in conceptualization is within or beyond our collective limits of rationality.

REFERENCES

Anderson, Odin. 1972. *Health Care: Can There be Equity?* New York: John Wiley.

Bertalanffy, L. 1968. *General Systems Theory.* New York: Braziller.

Blazer, D., and B. Kaplan. 1983. Assessment of Social Support in an Elderly Community Population. *American Journal of Social Psychiatry* (3): 29–36.

Burish, T., and L. Bradley, eds. 1983. *Coping with Chronic Disease: Research and Applications.* New York: Academic Press.

Callender, M., and J. LaVor. 1975. *Home Health Care: Development, Problems and Potential.* Washington, D.C.: U.S. Department of Health, Education and Welfare.

Chappel, N. 1981. Measuring Functional Ability and Chronic Health Conditions among the Elderly. *Journal of Health and Social Behavior*, 22(1):90–102.

Davis, K., and D. Roland. 1986. *Medicare Policy: New Direction for Health and Long-Term Care.* Baltimore: Johns Hopkins Press.

Department of Health and Human Services (DHHS). 1986. *The Evaluation of The National Long Term Care Demonstration: Final Report.* Washington, D.C.: The Department.

Enthoven, Alain. 1980. *Health Plan.* Reading, Mass.: Addison-Wesley.

Evans, Robert. 1985. *Strained Mercy: The Economics of Canadian Health Care.* Toronto: Butterworths.

Fries, J. 1980. Aging, Natural Death, and the Compression of Morbidity. *New England Journal of Medicine* 303: 130–135.

Graham, S., and L. Reeder. 1972. Social Factors in the Chronic Illnesses, in H. Freeman, S. Levine, L. Reeder, eds. *Handbook of Medical Sociology*, 3rd ed. Englewood Cliffs, N.J.: Prentice-Hall, pp. 63–107.

Harrington, C., R. Newcomer, C. Estes, and associates. 1985. *Long Term Care of the Elderly: Policy Issues.* Beverly Hills: Sage Publications.

Hobbs, N., and J. Perrin, eds. 1985. *Issues in the Care of Children with Chronic Illness.* San Francisco: Jossey-Bass.

Hobbs, N., J. Perrin, and H. T. Ireys. 1985. *Chronically Ill Children and Their Families.* San Francisco: Jossey-Bass.

Hollingsworth, C. E. 1983. *Coping with Pediatric Illness.* New York: SP Medical and Scientific Books.

Holroyd, K., and T. Creer. 1986. *Self-Management of Chronic Disease: Sourcebook of Clinical Interventions and Research.* Orlando, Fla.: Academic Press.

Inglehart, J. K. 1987. Second Thoughts about HMOs for Medicare Patients. *New England Journal of Medicine* 316:1487–1492.

Katz, S., L. Branch, M. Branson, J. Papsiders, J. Beck, and D. Greer. 1983. Active Life Expectancy. *New England Journal of Medicine*, 309: 1218–1224.

Kavesh, W. 1986. Home Health Care, in C. Eisdorfer, ed., *Annual Review of Gerontology and Geriatrics*, vol. 6. New York: Springer, pp. 135–196.

Knowles, J. H. 1977. The Responsibility of the Individual, in J. H. Knowles, ed., *Doing Better and Feeling Worse.* New York: Norton.

Koren, M. J. 1986. Home Care—Who Cares? *New England Journal of Medicine* 314(14):917–920.

Kovar, M. G. 1986. Expenditures for Medical Care of Elderly People Living in the Community in 1980. *The Milbank Memorial Fund Quarterly* 64(1):100–132.

Leader, S. 1986. *Home Health Care Benefits under Medicare.* Washington, D.C.: Public Policy Institute, American Association of Retired Persons.

Maddox, G. L. 1971. Muddling through: Planning for Health Care in England. *Medical Care* 9:439–448.

———. 1972. Social Determinants of Health Behavior, in F. Hine, E. Pfeiffer, G. Maddox, P. Hein, and R. Friedel, eds., *Behavioral Science: A Selective View.* Little, Brown.

———. 1977. The Unrealized Potential of an Old Idea, in A. N. Exton-Smith and J. G. Evans, eds., *Care of the Elderly: Meeting the Challenge of Dependency.* London: Academic Press, pp. 147–160.

———. 1980. The Continuum of Care: Movement toward the Community, in E. W. Busse and D. G. Blazer, eds., *Handbook of Geriatric Psychiatry.* New York: Van Nostrand Reinhold, pp. 501–520.

———. 1985a. Modifying the Social Environment, in W. Holland, R. Detels, and G. Knox, eds., *Oxford Textbook of Public Health*, vol. 2. Oxford: Oxford University Press, pp. 19–31.

———. 1985b. An Information System for Planning and Evaluating Geriatric Care: The Duke Older Americans Resources and Services Program, in L. Burstein, H. E. Freeman, and P. Rossi, eds., *Collecting Evaluation Data: Problems and Solutions.* Beverly Hills: Sage Publications, pp. 247–262.

Maddox, G., and K. Manton. 1987. Limits of

Rationality in Reshaping Geriatric care. In C. Eisdorfer, ed., *Reshaping Health Care for the Elderly: Recommendations for National Policy.* Baltimore: Johns Hopkins University Press.

Manton, K. G. 1982. Changing Concepts of Morbidity and Mortality in the Elderly Population. *Milbank Memorial Fund Quarterly,* 60(2):183–224.

Manton, K., and B. Soldo. 1985a. *Long-Range Planning for the Elderly: An Integrated Policy Perspective.* Washington, D.C.: U.S. Senate Special Committee on Aging.

———. 1985b. Dynamics of Health Change in the Oldest Old. *Milbank Memorial Fund Quarterly,* 63(2):206–285.

Marshall, J., D. Gregorio, and D. Walsh. 1982. Sex Differences in Illness Behavior: Care Seeking among Cancer Patients. *Journal of Health and Social Behavior* 23:197–204.

Mechanic, D. 1968. *Medical Sociology: A Selective View.* New York: Free Press.

Meltzer, J., F. Farrow, and H. Richman. 1981. *Policy Options in Long Term Care.* Chicago: University of Chicago Press.

Minkler, M. 1985. Social Support and Health of the Elderly, in S. Cohen and L. Syme, eds., *Social Support and Health.* Orlando, Fla.: Academic Press, pp. 199–218.

Mor, V., and D. Kidder. 1985. Cost Savings in Hospice: Final Results of the National Hospice Study. *Health Services Research* 20:407–423.

Morris, J. N. 1967. *Uses of Epidemiology.* Edinburgh: E. & S. Livingstone.

National Center for Health Services Research. 1987. *Annotated Bibliography of the National Medical Care Expenditure Survey.* Washington, D.C.: Department of Health and Human Services.

National Center for Health Statistics (NCHS). 1983. Physical and Home Management Activities. *Advancedata* 92.

———. 1986a. Aging in the 80s: Preliminary Data from the Supplement to the Health Interview Survey, U.S. January-June 1984. *Advancedata* 115.

———. 1986b. Aging in the 80s, Age 65 and over—Use of Community Services. *Advancedata,* 124.

———. 1986c. 1985 Summary: National Hospital Discharge Survey. *Advancedata* 127.

———. 1987a. Nursing Home Characteristics: Preliminary Data from the 1985 National Nursing Home Study. *Advancedata* 131.

———. 1987b. Preliminary Data from the 1985 National Nursing Home Survey. Communication.

New York Times. 1987. Catastrophic Health Insurance, June 7, p. 10EY.

Paradis L. F., and S. B. Cummings. 1986. The Evolution of Hospice in America toward Organizational Homogeneity. *Journal of Health and Social Behavior* 27:370–386.

Pear, Robert. 1987. Hospital Profits Increase Under DRG Regulation. *New York Times.* March 29, p. 1.

Perrow, C. 1965. Hospitals: Technology, Structure, Goals, in J. March, ed., *Handbook of Organizations.* Chicago: Rand McNally.

Rabin, D. L., and P. Stockton. 1987. *Long-Term Care for the Elderly: A Factbook.* New York: Oxford University Press.

Rivlin, Alice. 1987. *Long Term Care Financing and Organization Project.* Washington, D.C.: The Brookings Institution.

Rodwin, Victor. 1984. *The Health Care Planning Predicament.* Berkeley: University of California Press.

Senate Special Committee on Aging. 1985. *Aging in America: Trends and Projections.* Washington, D.C.: U.S. Senate Special Committee on Aging and the American Association of Retired Persons.

Shanas, E., and G. Maddox. 1985. Health, Health Resources and the Utilization of Care, in R. Binstock and E. Shanas, eds., *Handbook of Aging and the Social Sciences.* New York: Van Nostrand Reinhold, pp. 697–726.

Soldo, B., and K. Manton. 1985. Health Status and Service Needs of the Oldest Old. *Milbank Memorial Fund Quarterly,* 63(2):286–319.

Svarstad, B. 1986. Patient-Practitioner Relationships and Compliance with Prescribed Medical Regimens, in L. Aiken and D. Mechanic, eds., *Applications of Social Science to Clinical Medicine and Health Policy.* New Brunswick, N.J.: Rutgers University Press, pp. 438–459.

Syme, S. L., and L. F. Berkman. 1976. Social Class, Susceptibility, and Sickness. *American Journal of Epidemiology,* 104:1–8.

Vogel, R. J., and H. C. Palmer, eds. 1983. *Long Term Care: Perspectives from Research and Demonstrations.* Washington, D.C.: Health Care Financing Administration, U.S. Department of Health and Human Services.

White, L. R., W. S. Cartwright, J. Cornoni-Huntley, and D. B. Brock. 1986. Epidemiology of Aging, in C. Eisdorfer, ed., *Annual Review of Gerontology and Geriatrics,* vol. 6. New York: Springer, pp. 215–311.

World Health Organization (WHO). 1980. *International Classification of Impairments, Disabilities, and Handicaps.* Geneva: The Organization.

———. 1984. *The Uses of Epidemiology in the Study of the Elderly: Report of the WHO Scientific Group on the Epidemiology of Aging.* Geneva: The Organization.

Worthman, L. G., and S. Cretin. 1986. *Review of the Literature on Diagnosis Related Groups.* Santa Monica: Rand Corporation.

CHAPTER
13

THE MANAGEMENT
OF MENTAL ILLNESS
Progress, Prospects,
and Policy Considerations

DAVID MECHANIC

The concept of mental health is used broadly to characterize disorders ranging from chronic psychoses that are highly disruptive and disabling to everyday problems in living involving stress, difficulties in coping, and issues of self-actualization. Mental health problems continue to be associated with greater stigma than many other health conditions, but the use of mental health services has become more acceptable and more prevalent. Public education and increased access to acceptable services have resulted in more people seeking care for psychological problems. The Institute for Social Research at the University of Michigan surveyed public views of mental illness in the U.S. population in 1957 and in 1976, using many of the same questions (Gurin, Veroff, and Feld 1960; Kulka,

Veroff, and Douvan 1979, 1981). The survey found that over the twenty-year period use of professional help for psychological problems increased from 14 to 26 percent, although the levels of well-being in the population were approximately the same. Despite these gains, however, recent surveys continue to show that many persons with serious psychiatric disorder are not in contact with mental health services of any kind (Shapiro et al. 1984; Leaf et al. 1985).

THE SPECIALIZED MENTAL HEALTH SECTOR: A BRIEF DESCRIPTION

Since the beginning of deinstitutionalization in the middle 1950s, the mental health sector has grown in size and in the variety of settings where mental health services are provided. In addition to the traditional state and county hospitals and psychiatric

This chapter is adapted from David Mechanic, *Mental Health and Social Policy*, 3rd ed. © 1989. Reprinted by permission of Prentice-Hall, Inc., Englewood Cliffs, New Jersey.

services of the Veterans Administration (VA), the system is now characterized by large numbers of psychiatric units in general hospitals, community mental health centers, and psychiatric clinics. There are increased numbers of private psychiatric hospitals and large numbers of clinic- and office-based psychiatrists, psychologists, social workers, and counselors who offer a wide range of services. Mental patients are now also commonly found in board and care facilities, nursing homes, and specialized residential settings. Clergy, self-help groups, and mental health organizations such as the Alliance for the Mentally Ill, a nationwide organization of families of the mentally ill, also play an important role. In short, the mental health system has become a highly differentiated and decentralized system of care.

The most serious episodes of mental illness typically lead to inpatient care, and this area of services has undergone a major transformation. State and county mental hospitals now constitute only about one-tenth of mental health facilities, although they still have more than half the beds (NIMH 1985). The community general hospital, with or without specialized psychiatric units, has become the dominant setting for acute inpatient treatment. Basically, there are two streams of inpatient care: one characterizing the acute psychiatric patient typically with insurance coverage; the other the chronically mentally ill who depend on public hospitals. Median length of stay in the state and county mental hospitals in 1980 was about double that of nonpublic general hospitals, reflecting in part the more difficult problems they treat.

In 1982 the equivalent of 390,000 full-time staff were employed in mental health organizations other than the Veterans Administration, approximately 303,000 involved in patient care positions. Registered nurses were the largest group with professional training (numbering 48,305), followed by social workers (34,439), psychologists (20,816), and psychiatrists (20,704). Between 1972 and 1982 the number of full-time staff decreased in state and county hospitals, but those involved in patient care actually increased (NIMH 1985, p. 22), reflecting the treatment-oriented roles that many of these hospitals have now assumed.

An important but relatively unnoticed change has been the growth of private psychiatric hospitals. Although the number of such hospitals only increased from 150 in 1970 to 211 in 1982, the number of admissions substantially increased from approximately 92,000 in 1969 to 162,000 in 1981. The development of private hospitals is reflected in growth of full-time staff between 1972 and 1982 from 21,504 to 38,125, encompassing a tripling of full-time patient care staff. Private hospitals serve affluent and better-insured individuals and are more likely than other hospitals to provide individual, family-couple, group, and activity therapies (NIMH 1985, p. 49).

The ambulatory mental health sector is more difficult to track since there are a wide variety of professionals providing services through offices, clinics, social agencies, and various other organizations. In 1982, there were almost 30,000 psychologists reporting that they provide mental health services, and this group is rapidly growing. A comparable number of psychiatrists provide services; the National Ambulatory Medical Care Survey estimated 15.8 million office visits to psychiatrists in 1980. The number of social workers and registered nurses is much larger, but most work in organizational settings and outpatient clinics, and relatively few are in independent office-based practice. The reimbursement system and the definition of which providers are eligible to receive payment set limits on the magnitude of ambulatory mental health utilization. There is potentially a very large number of service providers who are held in check by narrow definitions of which providers are eligible for reimbursement under varying insurance programs. Copayment requirements also deter many patients from seeking services from mental health professionals.

THE EPIDEMIOLOGICAL PICTURE

Epidemiological data on the incidence and prevalence of mental disorder are uncertain because of the absence of valid criteria for diagnosis in general surveys and the considerable subjectivity with which people respond to even the most carefully formulated survey questions. When patients consult physicians for mental health problems, the act of consultation itself serves as sufficient justification for a medical response, although many untreated patients with comparable or even more serious symptoms commonly do not seek treatment.

The introduction of the *Diagnostic and Statistical Manual—III* (DSM-III), with its careful specification of criteria for making varying psychiatric diagnoses, has contributed improved rigor to the diagnostic process. The incorporation of these criteria in an epidemiological instrument—the Diagnostic Interview Schedule (Robins et al. 1985, 1984)—provides a methodology for making diagnostic estimates consistent with psychiatric conceptualizations. Relevant data come from the National Institute of Mental Health–sponsored Epidemiological Catchment Area (ECA) project, a large population-based survey (Eaton and Kessler 1985). This collaborative study initially involved approximately 20,000 people, 18 years or older, in New Haven, Baltimore, and St. Louis, and was organized to provide estimates of disorder as defined by DSM-III. Although the survey reports both lifetime and six-month prevalence, the latter are emphasized since these data are less likely to be distorted by memory, respondent reconstructions of past events, and other method biases. Validity continues to be a critical and debated issue (Anthony et al. 1985; Robins 1985).

Total six-month prevalence of disorders as assessed by questions based on DSM-III criteria ranged from 15 to 23 percent depending on study site and sex (Myers et al. 1984). Phobias and major depression were the most common diagnoses for women, and alcohol abuse or dependence for men.

The above prevalence data exclude dysthymia (a persistent feeling of loss of interest and pleasure in most activities), which if included might contribute another 1 to 4 percent to total prevalence. Rates of disorder were lower in the age group over 45, with the exception of cognitive impairment, which is substantially higher in the elderly group. Six-month prevalence for schizophrenia varied in the three sites from 0.6 to 1.2 percent, major depressive disorder from 2.2 to 3.5 percent, alcohol abuse/dependence from 4.5 to 5.7 percent, manic episodes from 0.4 to 0.8 percent, and drug abuse and dependence from 1.8 to 2.2 percent. Although these are only a modest portion of all disorder, they constitute some of the most difficult and persistent challenges to the mental health services system.

These prevalence estimates must be viewed as relatively crude given the method artifacts and biases inevitable in such studies and the difficulty of establishing validity of diagnosis. But even if we assume relatively wide confidence levels, the ECA studies quite convincingly substantiate many other community studies documenting high levels of psychiatric disorder in general populations and associated limitations of function (Dohrenwend et al. 1980). This observation is not qualitatively different from epidemiological evidence documenting a high prevalence of various untreated medical disorders and symptoms. Contact with the medical care system is influenced by severity of symptoms and disability, illness behavior orientations, and factors characterizing the financing and organization of services (Mechanic 1978).

Approximately two-thirds of individuals in each ECA site who were assessed as having a recent DSM-III disorder, as measured by the Diagnostic Interview Schedule (DIS), made an ambulatory visit for health services of some kind during the previous six months (Shapiro et al. 1984), but, depending on site, this was only about 8–10 percent more than in the population as a whole. In contrast, average number of medical visits were considerably higher among those with a psychiatric diagnosis, as were inpatient admissions. Inpatient admissions for mental health reasons, however, explain most of the excess, and in one site (St. Louis), excluding mental health admissions results in a lower proportion of respondents with DSM-III diagnoses having hospital admissions than among those with no diagnosis. A majority of visits and admissions occur in the general medical sector, in contrast to psychiatric settings, with considerable variation among study sites.

Most important is that a majority of patients in almost all disorder categories received no care for a mental health problem during the six-month period under consideration. Such care-seeking is particularly low among persons with cognitive disorders and substance abuse or dependence. In contrast, about one-third of respondents who visit for a mental or emotional problem did not meet study criteria for a psychiatric diagnosis, illustrating again the importance of symptoms and their effects on social functioning, behavioral inclinations, and other types of illness behavior. More detailed data have been reported on help-seeking patterns for Baltimore (Shapiro et al. 1985) and New Haven (Leaf et al. 1985). In Baltimore, 62 percent of persons judged to have a DSM-III disorder in the prior six months did not receive any mental health services during that period from either physicians in general or the specialized mental health sector. Those diagnosed as schizophrenic were most likely to receive some care (55 percent), while the group least treated were those with severe cognitive impairment (25 percent). Receipt of care for a mental health problem was particularly low among the elderly and nonwhites.

In the New Haven sample, efforts were made to assess use of mental health services provided by a wider range of health professionals and clinics. Sixteen percent of the sample met criteria for a DSM-III disorder during the six months prior to interview, but most received no mental health services. In the sample overall, 6.7 per cent had a mental health service in the six-month period: 2.6 percent only from general physicians, 3.2 percent from the specialized psychiatric sector, and 0.9 percent from both (Leaf et al. 1985). Utilization was highest for schizophrenia, panic, antisocial behavior, and somatization, and lowest for alcohol or drug abuse or dependence.

Leaf and his colleagues used regression analysis to examine a variety of factors associated with having a mental health visit during the previous six months and number of such visits, controlling for DSM-III disorder. Among the factors limiting the likelihood of such visits were being male, under age 24 or over age 65, nonwhite, of lower educational status, and unmarried. Persons who lacked a regular source of care, who had less receptive attitudes to mental health professionals, and who faced barriers to access also were less likely to receive such care. If patients entered the specialized mental health system, they had many more mental health visits than persons treated solely by generalists (a mean of 15.6 for those exclusively treated by the specialty sector as compared with 2.1 for those treated by generalists).

It is difficult to correctly estimate help-seeking for emotional problems from the general medical sector. Survey questions related to such ambulatory visits will typically not identify patients who emphasize somatic aspects of psychiatric disorder in their presentations or patients who believe it inappropriate to present emotional symptoms as a basis for a medical visit. Cross-cultural studies indicate that patients select presenting symptoms they believe to be consistent with the help-seeking context (Cheung and Lau 1982). Patients visiting general physicians are likely to focus on the physical concomitants of distress and may be unwilling to discuss emotional problems or do so only when physicians give indications of interest in such symptoms (Ginsberg and Brown 1982).

The relationship between the presence of a DSM-III disorder and need requires careful examination. Assuming that the DIS provides reasonable approximations of true disorder, the fact that as many as 45 to 60 percent of schizophrenics, 55 to 75 percent of depressed patients, and the vast majority of phobic patients are out of contact with any mental health services for as much as six months prior to being assessed as having these disorders implies unfilled needs. Thus, one might expect that the majority of such patients could benefit from professional care. This assumption requires careful examination. In some instances of substance abuse, antisocial personality, and severe cognitive impairment among the elderly, for example, it remains unclear what benefits would derive from increased mental health intervention. Often, there is little that mental health professionals can do, and some patients have learned through experience with the mental health system that they get limited help. We need better data to define clearly which of these patients should be induced into care through public policy initiatives and what types of services they should receive. Even in the case of cognitive impairment among the elderly it is important to assess to what degree such impairment may be a function of depression and whether patients could be assisted in learning skills that help maintain functioning despite memory loss.

Assessing the issue of need and appropriate care requires information on the long-term course of treated and untreated DSM-III disorders as measured both clinically and by survey, particularly among subpopulations who choose not to seek care from the medical care system, or who do so but in the more narrow context of physical complaints. It is essential to distinguish between patients who present their complaints somatically because they perceive such presentations as appropriate to the context, but are receptive to explicit mental health interventions, and those who

are not. In the case of the former. there is some evidence suggesting that attention to mental health issues reduces the use of nonpsychiatric medical services (Jones and Vischi 1979; Smith, Monson, and Ray 1986). Patients with psychiatric morbidity and distress use more outpatient and inpatient care than others in the population (Mechanic, Cleary, and Greenley 1982). It remains uncertain whether savings in total expenditures are achieved when use of both general medical care and mental health services are taken into account (Borus et al. 1985). For those patients resistant to mental health treatment, physicians have little alternative but to treat them within a more narrow medical definition and provide whatever support and encouragement feasible.

Despite the inadequacy of definitions of need, the data identify a variety of barriers to care: (1) the unwillingness of many patients to define themselves as having a mental or emotional disorder, or to seek care for such a problem from a mental health professional; (2) perceived stigma associated with mental health services and the lack of support from significant others in using such services; (3) lack of access to appropriate care because of the absence of a regular source of medical care, inadequate insurance coverage for mental health services, or high levels of copayment in using such services; and (4) lack of knowledge or sophistication among physicians in recognizing mental health problems and making appropriate referrals, or attitudes among physicians that inhibit appropriate care and referral.

Primary care studies suggest that how physicians manage patients with mental health needs depends substantially on their attitudes, interests, and work load, as well as on financing mechanisms (Mechanic 1974, 1976; Goldberg and Huxley 1980; Shepherd, et al., 1966). Referral to specialized mental health settings, in turn, depends on the doctors' confidence and interest in managing the patient, attitudes toward mental health professionals, the patient's wishes and inclinations, and the overall structure of reimbursement as it affects both the doctor and patient.

LEVELS OF MENTAL HEALTH CARE

It is useful to separate, at least, three general populations of persons requiring mental health care. Of greatest public concern is the highly visible chronically mentally ill who suffer from significant impairments, constitute an important segment of the homeless, and are often upsetting and disruptive to the community (Mechanic 1985). These patients who typically now reside in community settings as a consequence of deinstitutionalization trends over the past thirty years constitute a population of immense medical and social need. They are primarily clients of public mental health, income maintenance, and social services programs, but they are often out of touch with the services they require. Many sporadically come into contact with the general medical sector, often through emergency rooms during times of psychiatric crisis or for general medical needs (Mechanic and Aiken 1987).

A second population, more commonly served by the general medical sector but often referred to psychiatric services, includes patients with acute episodes of depression and serious problems with alcohol and drugs. These patients constitute a majority of psychiatric inpatients in psychiatric units in general hospitals and psychiatric admissions in community hospitals without specialized psychiatric beds. They also account for a significant amount of care provided by office-based psychiatrists and psychologists and community mental health clinics. Most of these patients have some insurance coverage for inpatient care.

A third group consists of patients seen in conventional general medical settings who are treated primarily by general medi-

cal practitioners. On average, such patients are less severely disturbed than those treated within the specialized mental health sector, although there is much overlap.

CHRONIC MENTAL ILLNESS: A CHALLENGE TO PUBLIC POLICY

Chronic mental illness (CMI), affecting some 1.7 to 2.4 million people (Goldman, Gattozzi, and Taube 1981), depending on definition, is a problem of devastating dimensions and enormous public import. It wrecks individual lives, destroys families, and creates enormous tensions within the community (Freedman and Moran 1984). The CMI population is not one but many subgroups with different problems and varying levels of disability and need. They differ in the styles with which they express their illnesses, their conceptions of and cooperation with the mental health and social services systems, and their ties to kin and the community (Estroff 1981). They also consist of varying age cohorts who have been exposed to radically different psychiatric ideologies and modes of mental health care (Mechanic 1987).

Schizophrenia is the prototype of CMI, and much pessimism has been expressed about the intractability of this disorder. The epidemiological evidence, in contrast, indicates persuasively that this condition follows a fluctuating course and need not result in inevitable deterioration. Long-term studies show extraordinary variability in adaptation and levels of functioning, suggesting that these patients are not as unmanageable as many professionals and others have believed.

In a remarkable clinical study, carried out over twenty-seven years, Manfred Bleuler (1978) studied the course of disorder among 208 patients in Zurich in varying cohorts over two decades. He described the continuing adaptations among these patients who fluctuated between varying outcomes. Half to three-quarters of the schizophrenic patients achieved long-term recoveries, and only 10–20 percent become severe chronic schizophrenics. The estimate of recovery is conservative, since it only includes patients reaching an end state, and, as Bleuler notes, prognosis of all schizophrenia combined is better. Moreover, in some patients, even after 40 years of psychosis, marked changes still occur. Long-term studies carried out by Ciompi (1980) in Lausanne and by Huber, Gross, and Scheuttler (1979) in Bonn confirm Bleuler's conclusions on the variable, and often favorable, course of the schizophrenias.

In the American context, follow-up after an average of thirty-two years of a cohort of 269 chronic patients released from Vermont State Hospital revealed that one-half to two-thirds had significantly improved or recovered confirming European results (Harding et al. 1987a, 1987b). The patients studied had on average been totally disabled for ten years and had been continuously hospitalized for six years. Most were functioning adequately in the community in later life, although ten years after release many of these patients had uncertain adjustments and were socially isolated. Using records, the investigators rediagnosed patients, selecting out those 118 patients who met DSM-III criteria for schizophrenia at hospital admission in the mid-1950s. At follow-up, most were living in the community and needed little or no help in meeting basic needs. Two-fifths of patients of working age were employed in the prior year, a majority had few significant symptoms, and about three-quarters were assessed as leading "moderate to very full lives." The picture that emerges is one highly divergent with clinical assumptions and suggests that the image of inevitable deterioration that dominates the psychiatric literature may have been a self-fulfilling prophesy. Similar findings have been reported by Clausen, Pfeffer, and Huffine (1982). Tsuang, Woolson, and Fleming (1979) found in a thirty- to forty-year follow-up that although schizophrenics had

a less favorable course than patients with affective disorders, a significant number of schizophrenics had "good" outcomes.

Findings from studies converge in suggesting a complex and differentiated course of illness depending on social and environmental conditions. A good illustration is the International Pilot Study of Schizophrenia, which followed 1202 patients in nine countries (WHO 1979). At two-year follow-up, 27 percent of schizophrenics had a complete recovery after the initial episode, and 26 percent had several psychotic attacks with periods of complete or partial recovery. Five-year follow-up in a subsample of American patients was highly correlated with appraisals at two years (Strauss and Carpenter 1977). Most striking was the large variation between developed and developing countries, with proportions of patients showing complete recovery varying from 6 percent in Denmark to 58 percent in Nigeria. While patients in each country are not representative of the total population of schizophrenics in that nation, the findings are striking. These findings have now been replicated in a second international collaborative study using more adequate sampling techniques (Sartorius et al. 1986).

Waxler (1979) in a careful five-year follow-up study of schizophrenics in Sri Lanka found that 45 percent were symptom-free as measured by the Psychiatric Status Schedule developed by Spitzer and his colleagues. Fifty percent were rated by the psychiatrist as having adjusted normally, 58 percent were seen by their families as having normal social performance, and 42 percent had no impairment in the previous six months. Almost half of the patients, according to their families, had worked continuously over the previous five years. Even allowing for errors in measurement, this is an impressive outcome, and at variance with typical Western conceptions of the course of schizophrenia. Waxler, who carefully examined possible artifacts in her results, makes a persuasive case that her findings are indicative of important cultural differences and suggests a social labeling model as the best approach to understanding these differences.

Another alternative is that in rural contexts schizophrenics can more easily continue to play an economic role and can insulate themselves from interpersonal stresses and intense associations. In some cultural contexts, there may be strong mutual expectations within kinship structures that encourage efforts at functioning from the patient and more acceptance from the community (Kleinman and Mechanic 1979). Family members may be less critical of the patient, a factor associated with less exacerbation of symptomatology (Leff 1978). While some of the best outcome results have been noted in underdeveloped countries or in rural contexts in developed nations, good outcomes have also been reported from industrialized cities in Europe, suggesting a more complex process than can be explained by such gross comparisons alone. Predictors of long-term course have not been effectively identified, but continuing efforts in this area are necessary.

In the short term, expressed emotion seems to be an important prognostic factor. A growing body of research indicates that schizophrenic patients do less well in family environments characterized by negative emotional relationships and criticisms (Brown et al. 1962; Brown, Birley, and King 1972; Vaughn and Leff 1976; Leff 1978). While these effects are attenuated to a considerable degree when patients are maintained on neuroleptic medications, differences in outcome persist even among medicated patients. Patients who have less face-to-face contact with relatives are also less likely to relapse in families with high-expressed emotion (Vaughn and Leff 1976; Leff 1978).

The prognostic research on schizophrenia suggests that successful maintenance is a complex task involving a balance between maintaining a sufficient level of demand and activation to encourage motivation and functioning without excessive excitement or stimulation. If patients are left alone or isolate themselves, they often lapse into inactivity and withdrawal, and the negative features of the condition tend to become exaggerated (Wing 1978). Similarly, involving the patient too intensely in interpersonal relations or in highly stressful situations triggers vulnerabilities. The expressed emotions research also identifies an important role of medication in protecting the patient in situations of overinvolvement and criticism. Since expressed emotion as measured consists mostly of negative affect, it remains unclear to what extent intense positive affect has comparable effects. Since intense involvement commonly involves both positive and negative affect, it is reasonable to anticipate that schizophrenics are vulnerable to intense emotional relationships more generally, but this is yet to be convincingly demonstrated. Research in this area has important implications for public policy as it affects intervention programs.

Chronic Mental Illness and Public Policy

The above findings have been used in designing interventions for controlled clinical trials in studies in both England (Leff et al. 1982) and the United States (Falloon, Boyd, and McGill 1984; Falloon et al. 1985). In a controlled social intervention trial in London, schizophrenic patients having intense contact with relatives demonstrating high-expressed emotion were randomly assigned to either routine outpatient care or an intervention program for patients and their families emphasizing education about schizophrenia and the role of expressed emotion (Leff 1982). The intervention also included family sessions in the home and relatives' groups. All patients were maintained on psychotropic drugs. After nine months, half of the twenty-four control patients relapsed, but only 9 percent in the experimental group. There were no relapses in the 73 percent of the experimental families where the aims of the intervention were achieved.

A similar experimental trial was carried out in California. Family members of schizophrenics were taught about the condition and were instructed in problem-solving techniques, and efforts were made to reduce family tensions (Falloon, Boyd, and McGill 1984). Follow-up at nine months found that patients in families receiving such interventions had a much lower rate of exacerbations than those in a control group receiving clinic-based individual supportive care. Only one patient in the intervention group (6 percent) was judged to have a relapse, in contrast to eight (44 percent) in the control group (Falloon et al. 1982). A less systematic and intense follow-up after two years found that the reduction in exacerbations was maintained over the longer period (Falloon et al. 1985). Because of changes in procedures and modes of evaluation, the two-year data are less rigorous but generally consistent with earlier results.

Both of the intervention trials based on the expressed emotion research are family based, certainly an important context for the long-term care of schizophrenic patients. Many schizophrenic patients, however, live outside of family contexts and depend more completely on care available in community settings (Segal and Aviram 1978). Here, too, there have been studies that persuasively demonstrate the value of an aggressive, well-organized program of community care.

One important experiment in Wisconsin involved a training program in community living for chronic patients (Stein and Test 1980a, 1980b). This study compared an educational coping model with a progressive hospital care unit. An unselected group of patients referred for admission to a mental hospital was randomly assigned to experimental and control groups. The control group received good hospital treatment, linked with a progressive program of community aftercare services. The experimental group was assisted in developing an independent living situation in the community, given social support, and taught simple living skills such as budgeting, job seeking, and use of public transportation. Patients in both groups were evaluated at various intervals by independent researchers. The findings showed that it was possible for highly impaired patients to be cared for almost exclusively in the community. Compared with control patients, patients in the experimental group made a more adequate community adjustment as measured by higher earnings from work, involvement in more social activities, more contact with friends, and more satisfaction with their life situation. Experimental patients at follow-up had fewer symptoms than the controls. This experiment illustrated that a logically organized and aggressive community program can effectively manage even highly impaired patients in the community, with minimal use of hospitals, and that the provision of services yields high benefits relative to cost (Weisbrod, Test, and Stein 1980).

These studies represent some of the more persuasive among a much larger number of studies strongly supporting the value of community care as an alternative for hospital care (Kiesler 1982; Gudeman and Shore 1984; Kiesler and Sibulkin 1987; Stein and Test 1978). Programs for community care for chronic mental illness have not suffered from lack of innovation or evaluation. The major difficulty has been the lack of a public policy framework that facilitates the development of necessary organizational entities, that allows the essential service elements and funding to be brought together, that provides reimbursement for the many service components and mental health providers, and that contains incentives for balancing trade-offs between traditional medical and hospital services and a broader range of social services needed by chronic patients with large rehabilitative needs (Stein and Ganser 1983; Mechanic 1985; Talbott 1985). Good rehabilitation treats acute psychiatric episodes, ensures appropriate medication monitoring, maintains nutrition and health more generally, makes provision for shelter and reasonable levels of activity and participation, provides crisis support, and builds on patients' personal capacities through continuing educational efforts. To be effective, programs must be organized in relation to the longitudinal needs of the patient and must aggressively retain the patient in the care system (Davis, Pasamanick, and Dinitz 1974; Stein and Test 1980a, 1980b; Wing and Brown, 1970). Many of the needed care elements receive relatively limited funding relative to more conventional inpatient and outpatient medical and psychiatric services. To understand the current context, it is useful to retrace the deinstitutionalization process and how it affected sources and the directions of funding.

While individual states varied significantly in the timing and rates of deinstitutionalization (Gronfein 1985), a common reference point is 1955, when public mental hospitals reached their peak census and started on a downward course. In 1955, most psychotic patients were treated in public mental hospitals; there was relatively little coverage for such conditions in conventional insurance policies, and voluntary hospitals were not an important site of care. The reduction of inpatients in public hospitals began in 1955, with the widespread introduction of phenothiazines, which were helpful in blunting patients' most bizarre symptoms and gave professionals, administrators, family members, and the community more confidence that psychotic symptoms could be contained. It was not, however, until the middle 1960s that the reduction of inpatients in public hospitals proceeded apace.

There were many social factors that supported the release of large numbers of patients from public hospitals, including a more optimistic public influenced by the rhetoric of community psychiatry, a vital litigation movement on behalf of the civil liberties of the mentally ill (Ennis 1972; Miller 1976), and social science research and analysis demonstrating harmful consequences of involuntary commitment and long-term residence in custodial institutions (Mechanic 1980; Scull 1977). But the transformation of psychiatric care would have been impossible without the expansion of social programs in the middle 1960s, the most important of which were not directed at mental patients at all.

In the 1960s and 1970s, health insurance coverage for inpatient psychiatric care improved dramatically, providing incentives for general hospitals to provide significant amounts of acute care to patients covered by such insurance. While such insurance never equaled that characteristic of other health conditions, it was sufficient to induce hospitals into providing psychiatric care and, in many cases, to develop specialized psychiatric units within the general hospital. The implementation of Medicare and Medicaid in 1966 stimulated substantial growth in nursing home beds, and Medicaid financing for nursing home care provided an alternative site for caring for the growing numbers of elderly patients with dementias. Medicaid also provided reimbursement for nursing home care for younger chronic mental patients as well. Many other chronic patients previously unable to support themselves in the community or to maintain stable employment were now able to subsist in the community with the expansion of Social Security Disability Insurance (SSDI) and Supplemental Security Income (SSI), which provided benefits to the disabled. The magnitude and influence of benefits to the mentally ill in Medicaid, SSDI, and SSI dwarfed federal mental health categorical programs that have been the focus of most professional analysis during the past three decades.

The care of the chronically mentally ill has always been primarily a state responsibility (Grob 1983), and states in anticipating a growing burden of caring for the chronically mentally ill in institutional settings were major advocates for increased federal involvement in the post–World War II period (Mechanic 1980). Deinstitutionalization allowed transfer of some state obligations to the federal sector (Scull 1977).

and states used their massive mental health budgets to convert large custodial hospitals to more active treatment units as the public mental health system contracted from 560,000 patients in 1955 to approximately 125,000 in 1981. Communities in which hospitals were located, and hospital employees, became strong lobbies for maintaining state commitments to institutions. Thus, while average per capita cost and the ratio of employees to patients increased dramatically and brought many positive changes for patients within public mental hospitals, the amount of state funding for chronic patients who returned to the community, or who were now being treated there as an alternative to the traditional pattern, was relatively meager. As of 1981, two-thirds of state mental health expenditures went to mental hospitals, although these hospitals only took responsibility for a small proportion of all chronic mental patients (NIMH 1985). The irony is that we are now spending large sums to support the general subsistence of chronic patients in the community but have not developed appropriate service systems to maintain their levels of functioning or improve the quality of their lives. Many mental patients, desperately in need of service, are increasingly found in jails (Lamb 1982) or are homeless. During the 1960s and 1970s the largest federal mental health initiative was in developing community mental health centers throughout the nation, but despite the dominant rhetoric these institutions provided relatively little for those patients with the most severe mental impairments until very recently (Gronfein 1985). It appears obvious that funds should more substantially be concentrated where the patients are (Stein and Ganser 1983), but the political barriers are difficult to overcome.

With deinstitutionalization and the payment for nursing home care under the Medicaid program, large numbers of the mentally ill, particularly elderly demented patients, are maintained in nursing homes. Goldman, Feder, and Scanlon (1986) estimated the number of chronically mentally ill in nursing homes using the 1977 Nursing Home Survey, the latest such data available. In 1977, there were 72,396 nursing home patients with a chronic mental illness, 34,804 patients with both physical and mental illnesses, and 21,165 patients who were both senile and psychotic. The vast majority of nursing home patients were senile, and if all such patients are counted in the mental illness category, some 668,000 would meet the chronic mental illness definition. From a rehabilitation point of view, the most important groups are the chronically ill and those with both physical and mental illness, of whom 46 percent and 31 percent are less than 64 years of age. More than 5,500 of those with chronic mental illness are 45 years of age or less, and one-quarter of the total group need no help in activities of daily living. This is in sharp contrast to senile patients, most of whom require assistance in simple daily living activities. The chronic mental patients in nursing homes are more active than other patients and pose more behavioral problems, such as agitation and wandering.

As the shift to nursing homes occurred, there was little constructive examination of whether nursing homes truly provided better or even comparable care to the services available in mental hospitals, however deficient. Public mental hospitals were overcrowded, understaffed, and often highly regimented and impersonal. But they had mental health staff and varying programmatic mental health elements, at least for the more acute subgroups of their patient populations. In contrast, nursing homes typically have few or no medical or mental health professional staff, patients are commonly oversedated to ease management problems, and there are limited opportunities for activity (Stotsky 1970; Vladeck 1980; Linn et al. 1985). Comparable conditions describe many community sheltered housing alternatives for the mentally ill as well (Lamb 1979). Yet one fact we have learned well in chronic mental illness is that inactivity leads to additional disabilities not inherent in the underlying illness that can be limited by effective management (Wing 1978).

Concerns about quality of care played little role in this major transition to nursing homes as contrasted with the cost-shifting opportunities provided to state authorities. The motives for this shift were, of course, complex and were influenced by dominant mental health ideologies, the desire to improve acute care in mental hospitals, growing civil liberties litigation on behalf of the mentally ill, and ingenuity in garnering all available financial resources. As nursing home bed supply becomes more constrained in the future because of the press of growing numbers of disabled elderly, it will be increasingly difficult to place publicly supported chronic mental patients in even this inadequate housing alternative. Identifying and financing appropriate housing for the long-term mentally ill, consistent with rehabilitation needs, continues as one of the most pressing issues for the years ahead.

Among federal programs, Medicaid has become the single most important program affecting the mentally ill. Medicare, the federal program covering mostly acute illness for those over 65 and certain disabled beneficiaries, has limited mental health benefits and does not cover long-term care needs. In contrast, Medicaid is a major source of payment for a variety of mental health services among eligible persons, and the major government source of payment for long-term care. A major difficulty with Medicaid is the varying eligibility criteria and benefits in different jurisdictions. Although a large proportion of long-term chronic patients are eligible for Medicaid, only some poor people in need of acute psychiatric care receive it under this program because Medicaid covers less than half of those who are poor (Mechanic 1986). Small alterations in eligibility and benefits within the Medicaid program can have a very large impact on the mental health system (Frank and Lave 1985).

Most mental health professionals have directed their attention to relatively limited categorical mental health programs, such as those now funded under block grants to the states, while neglecting the generic medical care and welfare programs. But many crucial policy decisions that vastly affect the mentally ill (such as those relevant to Medicaid, Medicare, and SSDI) are made with other populations in mind and with no special sophistication about the special needs and problems of the mentally ill. The lack of such understanding was a significant factor contributing to the elimination of many chronic mental patients from the SSDI program in the early 1980s. A major responsibility of mental health professionals and advocacy groups is to educate and influence both policymakers and the general public concerning the needs of their constituencies. Policymakers are not indifferent to the mentally ill; they typically know little about them. The effectiveness of mental health advocacy pales in comparison to the efforts of other categorical disease groups, such as those concerned with cancer, heart disease, and Alzheimer's disease.

THE TREATMENT OF ACUTE PSYCHIATRIC ILLNESS

Millions of encounters occur each year for acute mental disorders and problems in living in general hospitals (with or without specialized psychiatric units), in private psychiatric hospitals, outpatient departments and emergency rooms, community mental health centers and social agencies, and in the offices of psychiatrists, psychologists, social workers, and other mental health professionals. While public attention in the past twenty years has been focused on deinstitutionalization, the specialized mental health sector has developed enormously, with dramatic increases in numbers of episodes treated in general hospitals and outpatient settings. Utilization has substantially increased as services have become more acceptable, as they are increasingly provided in the mainstream, and as public and private insurance plans cover more acute mental disorders.

Estimates of use of mental health services come from special studies such as those in the ECA program, from general surveys, or from national data sets on hospital and physician use. It was noted earlier that 6.7 percent of a New Haven sample reported receiving a mental health service in the prior six months, approximately half of which was in the specialized mental health sector. National data on use of short-stay hospitals come from the hospital discharge survey. In 1984 there were almost 1.7 million discharges from short-stay hospitals with a primary diagnosis of mental illness (Dennison 1985): 625,000 for psychoses, 392,000 for alcohol dependence, and 228,000 for neurotic and personality disorders (primarily involving depression). Rates of hospitalization were highest in the age groups 45 and over, and alcohol diagnoses were highest in the age group 45–64. Average length of stay for psychiatric diagnoses was 11.9 days. The predominant pattern, even for psychoses, is a relatively short hospital stay to stabilize the patient's condition. The average inpatient stay in such hospitals for psychotic disorders in 1984 was only fourteen days.

The distribution of inpatient admissions for mental disorder vary by type of hospital. State and county mental hospitals have the largest proportion of schizophrenic admissions and a high rate of alcohol-related admissions; these two areas account for three-fifths of all admissions. A similar situation characterizes V.A. hospitals, although they have fewer schizophrenics and more alcohol-related problems. In contrast, the community general hospital and private psychiatric hospitals have only about one-third such admissions and a much larger proportion of admissions for affective disorders: 31 percent in community hospitals and 43 percent in private psychiatric hospitals (NIMH 1985, p. 19). The public mental hospitals are clearly dealing with the tougher and more chronic problems.

Good estimates of ambulatory care for mental disorder are more difficult to obtain because of definitional problems, distortions in patient reports, and the wide array of possible providers. Perhaps the most careful estimates come from the National Medical Care Utilization and Expenditure Survey (NMCUES) for the year 1980 (Taube, Kessler, and Feuerberg 1984). This survey collects detailed information from respondents, which is then checked against insurance and other data. In the data that follow, a visit meets the criterion of a mental health visit if the respondent indicates this as the reason for the visit or has gone to a psychiatrist, psychologist, or psychiatric clinic. Using this relatively conservative definition, an estimated 9.6 million people, some 4.3 percent of the noninstitutionalized population, made such a visit in a one-year period. Including such nonspecific complaints as "nerves" would increase estimates of mental health utilization by as much as 50 percent (Taube, Kessler, and Feuerberg 1984). The NMCUES estimate is lower than the proportions reported for the three ECA sites (New Haven, Baltimore, and St. Louis), which varied from 6 to 7.1 percent of the population using a six-month recall period (Shapiro et al. 1984). Given inaccuracies in recall and other problems in comparability, it seems reasonable to estimate that approximately 5–10 percent of the population seek a mental health service during a year (Horgan 1985). The NMCUES found that psychiatrists and psychologists each had approximately one-quarter of all visits. Approximately 40 percent were to other providers in office settings, and about one-tenth occurred in mental health clinics, outpatient departments, and emergency rooms. The aggregate charges for mental health ambulatory services were estimated as $2.4 billion in 1980, approximately 10 percent of all mental health expenditures for that year. As with other types of health care utilization, 10 percent of those making a mental health visit (those with twenty-five visits or more per year) accounted for one-half of all ambulatory expenditures. Utilization was highest among women, whites, those in the age group 25–64, and individuals with thirteen or more years of schooling. Low-income persons used services most, but persons at both ends of the income spectrum were relatively high users.

Estimates of the number of mental health visits vary depending on the data source used. The NMCUES estimates 79 million visits in 1980, 25.5 million to psychiatrists. In contrast, the National Ambulatory Medical Care Survey (NAMCS), a study of office-based physicians, estimates 16.7 million visits to psychiatrists in their offices for the same year (Taube, Kessler, and Feuerberg 1984). These estimates, of course, exclude visits to psychiatrists in other than office settings, and thus the two figures are not comparable. The most important fact to remember, however, is the growing acceptability of the specialized mental health sector for dealing with common mental health problems and the increased importance of ambulatory mental health care, provided not only by psychiatrists but also by psychologists and other professionals. Despite the continuing reluctance of many people to seek mental health services, such services have come a long way in becoming integrated into the larger medical care system.

Although treatment of acute psychiatric disorder has shifted to acute general hospitals, we have little systematic knowledge of the content or quality of care provided. Hospitals with psychiatric units provide more of most types of care than hospitals without specialized beds, but aggregate data suggest that a remarkably large number of patients receive little specialized treatment and few psychosocial services. The hospital is used typically to stabilize patients medically during acute episodes, and the typical length of stay is limited. The dominant model is a traditional medical approach, yet we have little evidence that this offers the best management for such patients. We have no existing data that allow us to link up hospital episodes

with the ambulatory mental health care that often follows after discharge.

One consequence of increased insurance coverage is the separation of insured populations from the disadvantaged mentally ill into separate systems of care. Insured populations are increasingly integrated into the mainstream. Those lacking insurance, or groups who have exhausted whatever insurance coverage they have, are routed into the public sector. In 1980, for example, there was no payment for almost half of all admissions to state and county mental hospitals, and only about one-quarter of admissions involved either insurance or personal resources. In contrast, private psychiatric hospitals and nonpublic general hospitals, respectively, had only 1 and 2 percent of admissions without payment, and 67 percent and 51 percent were covered by private insurance or personal resources. Most of the remaining admissions were paid for by Medicare and Medicaid (NIMH 1985, p. 46). Outpatient services are available for those eligible for public programs, but many patients with substantial psychiatric need often have little access to care or the appropriate spectrum of services they require. Since many patients are reluctant to seek mental health services in any case, the additional barriers create major impediments to appropriate care.

Psychiatric coverage in health insurance programs has become more prevalent, but it continues to remain an area that is rationed more stringently than other services. The health arena is in ferment and subject to strong cost restraints. As more employment groups self-insure and as the trend toward increasing co-insurance and deductibles accelerates, mental health benefits are vulnerable to cutbacks. A countervailing tendency in some states is to require insurers to offer specified mental health coverage. Still other states do not mandate coverage but require insurers to offer it as an option. Such requirements for insurance plans to cover certain areas of care limit choice, but their rationale is that they induce persons to seek needed services, increase essential access, and provide necessary services that prevent other types of utilization (Frisman, McGuire, and Rosenbach 1985). Such mandates can have a major influence on access and the distribution of services depending on how eligible services and reimbursable providers are defined. Those who oppose mandates view them as involuntary taxes that increase overall health insurance premium payments. From a public policy point of view, however, there seems little justification in discriminating against patients with psychiatric disorders who have needs comparable to those with more traditional medical complaints. The differential coverage and public support for care for the mentally ill reflects the longstanding stigma associated with mental illness and serves to reinforce this stigma.

MENTAL ILLNESS AND GENERAL MEDICAL SETTINGS

The doctor of first contact in the case of most psychological morbidity is the primary care physician. Such physicians see many patients who suffer from significant psychological symptoms or diseases compounded by high levels of psychological distress. The ECA data indicated that mental health visits to general physicians constitute 41 to 63 percent of all mental health visits. These estimates may be low, because many patients with depression, anxiety, and serious psychosocial problems do not define their problems in mental health terms and primarily present somatic symptoms and nonspecific physical complaints when seeking care. Estimates vary widely on what proportion of all medical visits are motivated by psychological need, but almost everyone agrees that such consultations are highly prevalent. Such patients use extensive health care resources, but many physicians remain ambivalent and uncertain about appropriate treatment and referral, are commonly insecure about diagnosis and psychotropic medication, and

must cope with the somatization of psychological distress and the unacceptability of mental health diagnoses to many patients. Persons with psychiatric disorders may have a large range of alternative help-seeking options, but insurance reimbursement criteria, public attitudes, and many patients' unwillingness to view their distress and symptoms outside traditional medical concepts make the primary care physician the dominant mental health provider in the United States and other Western nations (Institute of Medicine 1979).

Referral to the specialized mental health sector depends on the seriousness of the disorder, attitudes toward psychiatry of the attending physician, the availability of insurance, and the physician's perception of the willingness of the patient to accept mental health treatment. Patients' cultural background and attitudes toward the use of psychological services are significant factors affecting referral (Mechanic 1978, 1980). Studies comparing independent standardized psychiatric assessment of primary care patients to how such patients were diagnosed and managed indicate that primary care physicians commonly do not recognize psychiatric symptoms and, even less frequently, make a mental health diagnosis or prescribe appropriate psychotropic medication for these patients. Also, the prevalence of such diagnoses from one physician to another is not related to accuracy as assessed independently (Goldberg and Huxley 1980). Accuracy appears to depend on the way the doctor interviews patients, personality, and academic ability; it does not appear related to self-assessment of psychological skills or experience.

Physicians often deal with patients they perceive as distressed by prescribing psychotropic drugs. Data from the NAMCS for 1980 and 1981 indicate that such drugs were prescribed by office-based physicians in 6 percent of all visits and in 10 percent of all visits in which a drug was prescribed (Koch 1983). The five most common diagnoses for using such drugs were neurotic disorders, essential hypertension, depression, schizophrenia, and affective psychosis. While psychiatrists were most likely to use such drugs (441 times per 1,000 visits), rates were also high in internal medicine (115 times per 1,000 visits) and general and family practice (84 times per 1,000 visits). Office-based physicians used 136 different psychotropic drugs that have different biological functions and varying types of side effects. There is a great deal of concern about the appropriate use of such drugs and allegations that primary care physicians often choose the wrong drugs in relation to the patient's symptomatology.

The response of the doctor to the patients' distress is affected by conceptions of etiology. To the extent that such common problems as depression and substance abuse are masked by the presentation of general physical complaints and are linked to unalterable life stresses, severe disappointments, or grave misfortunes, the physician realistically may not see himself or herself in a position to do very much beyond prescribing drugs to relieve symptoms. The patient's somatization may be adaptive as compared to intolerable alternatives, and it may be unproductive to undermine the patient's defenses when the patient is unwilling or unable to deal with the conditions of his or her life (Corney 1984). A cross-cultural example brings this issue sharply into focus.

In China, neurasthenia is a common diagnosis in psychiatric outpatient clinics, and perhaps the most common "psychiatric diagnosis" in general medical settings. Such patients typically complain of somatic complaints characteristic of depression in Western countries but usually do not report comparable affective disturbance. Kleinman notes that psychiatrists in China routinely view neurasthenia as a "disorder of brain function involving asthenia of cerebral cortical activity" (Kleinman 1982, 1986). In a project at the Hunan Medical College, Kleinman identified eighty-seven patients with this diagnosis who met DSM-III criteria for major depression and

treated them with antidepressants. At follow-up, while a majority appeared to show significant improvement in psychiatric symptoms, there was much less effect in decreasing help-seeking, maladaptive functioning, and social impairment. The patients remained skeptical of the value of the drug treatment.

Kleinman views neurasthenia as a bioculturally patterned illness experience, and he links it to extraordinary hardships in the lives of patients from which they could not escape given the harsh realities of the Chinese social system. The somatic discourse used by patients, and accepted by doctors, serves as a limited escape from involuntary and taxing life situations, and the illness idiom offers greater legitimacy than alternative escape routes. The issue is whether modifying the Chinese doctor's concept of the clinical problem serves any constructive purpose. To the extent that the patient needs the illness and neither the doctor nor the patient has the means to modify the harsh circumstances of the patient's life, the diagnosis and its underlying meanings may serve a useful purpose in providing a release, however limited, from restrictive and unalterable social conditions. The organic etiology attributed to the condition is culturally acceptable, while a diagnosis of depression or another emotional diagnosis is more suspect and more stigmatized. From one perspective, Chinese medical practice appears out-of-date; from another, it seems to fit the cultural and social conditions exceedingly well.

In Western societies, physicians have more influence than in China, and the societies offer more opportunities for life changes. Moreover, there is a strong element of psychologism and a widely shared view that it is desirable that people be in touch with themselves, a view that increasingly has affected conceptions of primary medical care and the orientation of physicians to patients with psychological distress. This trend, which some physicians intuitively if not openly resist, is as much the result of a psychological ideology as it is of an established foundation of empirical results. It is undoubtedly true that some patients experience relief of physical symptoms by acknowledging their feelings and sharing them with an empathic person. Specific forms of psychotherapy focused on interpersonal relations or cognitive orientations appear even more helpful. But it is also true that in many instances denial is an extraordinarily effective coping device and that excessive exploration of feelings and thoughts may increase negative affect and a sense of physical discomfort (Mechanic 1979). Psychologizing medical practice has its benefits but also its risks.

The primary care physician, better aware of psychiatric morbidity, however, can use such information constructively. The practitioner can communicate an interest and willingness to listen, a cue that many depressed patients feel is lacking and whose absence inhibits expression of their distress (Ginsberg and Brown 1982). Such information also alerts the physician to suicide and related risks and encourages greater supportiveness, vigilance, and referral when the physician is insecure. Knowledge of psychiatric syndromes and appropriate specific medication also allows more competent management. All of this can be accomplished without imposition of psychological interpretations, without undermining the patients' coping efforts, and without requiring the patient to adapt to an unacceptable definition of the problem. Through use of a skill highly dependent on cognitive and communication capacities, the primary care physician is in a strong position to relieve the patient's symptoms, offer meaningful support, and assist in strengthening coping capacities. With trust and patience, and communication of a willingness to listen, even recalcitrant patients shed some of their defenses and become more amenable to influence. Much of the potential of the doctor-patient relationship, even in an age of high technology, arises from the authority of the physician and the patients' faith (Frank 1974). These assets are extraordinarily powerful and a significant force if used prudently.

As physicians are more commonly organized in groups, and with the growing importance of HMOs and other organized arrangements, it becomes more practical for psychiatrists and other mental health professionals to provide support and effective backup for the primary care physician managing many patients with moderate psychiatric disorders (Coleman and Patrick 1978). The advantage is that the primary care physician has the security and help of more specialized personnel when it is needed, but can continue to manage patients with whom he or she has a relationship and who may not be receptive to direct mental health interventions. With the substantial increase in the number of physicians in coming decades and the increased emphasis on emotional and behavioral factors in medical school and residency training, physicians are likely to cooperate in providing such care more than in the past. It is likely that the primary care physician will remain a significant mental health provider for the vast majority of the population with nonpsychotic illness and that the majority of patients needing help identified in surveys may never be treated within the specialized mental health sector. Primary care physicians, better informed about psychiatric diagnosis and psychopharmacology and more aware of the dynamics of illness behavior and psychosocial processes, can be in an advantageous position for helpful intervention.

CONCLUSION

At present, much attention is focused on how the prospective reimbursement system under Medicare, using the diagnosis-related group (DRG) methodology, will be implemented in relationship to psychiatry. There is much concern on how it will affect the organization of psychiatric care and the content of care for varying types of psychiatric episodes. Studies of psychiatric DRGs indicate that they are extremely poor predictors of resource use (Taube, Lee, and

Forthofer 1984) and a universal system is likely to have perverse distributional effects (English et al. 1986). Acute care hospitals without specialized psychiatric units provide much less care per episode than those with such units. Plans for reimbursement under Medicare, or any other payment program, must take such differences in care into account. The data available suggest that hospitals without specialized units are primarily stabilizing the patient during crisis, but do relatively little active treatment. A reimbursement system that reinforces this pattern could be retrogressive.

Focusing on hospital payment, however important, as the core concern distorts the types of considerations that are essential for effective policy formulation in the mental health arena. As this chapter has illustrated, the arena is highly complex and greatly differentiated. It faces challenges at varying levels: financial, organizational, professional, and in relation to public opinion. Effective mental health practice requires careful intraorganizational relationships among sectors that are now highly fragmented. Rigorous evaluations are necessary in considering trade-offs between traditional medical and psychiatric services and the broad array of other human services that seriously disabled patients need.

The field also suffers from a confusion of priorities and appropriate balance in meeting varying demands. The most critical population to serve continues to be the chronically mentally ill, whose needs are poorly met by the competing systems of care that provide one or another component of specialized care. There is no greater challenge than that of putting systems into place that can resolve the duplication and inefficiencies of current services, that can direct resources in a more calculated and balanced way, and that can produce the blend of services that many demonstrations have found to be effective. The task is not easy but it is doable with appropriate modifications in financial and organizational arrangements.

In reviewing varying levels of care from the patient in primary medical settings to the homeless chronically mentally ill on the streets, the absence of a coherent, coordinated system should be evident. It is grandiose to think we can ever have a unitary system of mental health care, one that embraces everyone from the unhappily married to the young recalcitrant chronic patient. Dealing with the tough mental health problems is an especially taxing challenge, and the effort requires well-trained and highly specialized personnel. It should be possible, however, to organize care more coherently in relationship to populations and levels of need, to build a coordinated spectrum of needed services, to develop better approaches to case management and referral, and to focus responsibility and accountability more clearly (Mechanic 1982, 1985, 1987). A central problem is the numerous and confusing sources of funding and their complex and inconsistent eligibility criteria. These problems are not resolved easily or quickly, but significant progress can be made.

As with most human problems, many factors intervene between theory and practical reality. Unforeseen influences undermine the best of intentions. Medical sociologists interested in mental health policy can contribute a great deal in helping to define the structures that are most effective for varying types of needs, the forces that distort efforts and subvert objectives, and the essential elements for future viable systems. They can also contribute to tough but sympathetic evaluations of how human services perform and how they can be strengthened. And by asking and teaching about the "big issues," medical sociologists help sensitize and socialize future leaders who will manage mental health services in coming decades.

REFERENCES

Anthony, J. C., M. Folstein, A. J. Romanoski, M. R. VonKorff, G. R. Nestadt, R. Chahal, A. Merchant, C. H. Brown, S. Shapiro, M. Kramer, and E. M. Gruenberg. 1985. Comparison of the Lay Diagnostic Interview Schedule and a Standardized Psychiatric Diagnosis. *Archives of General Psychiatry* 42:667–675.

Bleuler, M. 1978. *The Schizophrenic Disorders: Long-Term Patient and Family Studies*, translated by S. M. Clemens. New Haven: Yale University Press.

Borus, J. F., M. C. Olendzki, L. Kessler, B. J. Burns, V. C. Brandt, C. A. Broverman, and P. R. Henderson. 1985. The "Offset Effect" of Mental Health Treatment on Ambulatory Medical Care Utilization and Charges. *Archives of General Psychiatry* 42:573–587.

Brown, G., J. L. T. Birley, and J. K. Wing. 1972. Influence of Family Life on the Course of Schizophrenic Disorders: A Replication. *British Journal of Psychiatry* 121:241–258.

Brown, G. W., E. M. Monck, G. M. Carstairs, and J. K. Wing. 1962. Influence of Family Life on the Course of Schizophrenic Illness. *British Journal of Preventive and Social Medicine* 16:55–58.

Cheung, F. M., and B. Lau. 1982. Situational Variations of Help-Seeking Behavior among Chinese Patients. *Comprehensive Psychiatry* 23:252–262.

Ciompi, L. 1980. Natural History of Schizophrenia in the Long Term. *British Journal of Psychiatry* 136:413–420.

Clausen, J. A., N. G. Pfeffer, and C. L. Huffine. 1982. Help-seeking in Severe Mental Illness, in D. Mechanic, ed., *Symptoms, Illness Behavior and Help-Seeking*. New Brunswick, N.J.: Rutgers University Press, pp. 135–155.

Coleman, J. V., and D. L. Patrick. 1978. Psychiatry and General Health Care. *American Journal of Public Health* 68:451–457.

Corney, R. H. 1984. The Effectiveness of Attached Social Workers in the Management of Depressed Female Patients in General Practice. *Psychological Medicine* Monograph Supplement 6.

Davis, A., B. Pasamanick, and S. Dinitz. 1974. *Schizophrenics in the New Custodial Community: Five Years After the Experiment.* Columbus, Ohio: Ohio State University.

Dennison, C. F. 1985. 1984 Summary: National Discharge Survey. *Vital and Health Statistics*, No. 112. DHHS Publication No. (PHS) 85-1250, National Center for Health Statistics.

Dohrenwend, B. P., B. S. Dohrenwend, M. S. Gould, B. Link, R. Neugebauer, and R. Wunsch-Hitzig. 1980. *Mental Illness in the United States: Epidemiological Estimates.* New York: Praeger.

Eaton, W. W., and L. G. Kessler, eds. 1985. *Epidemiologic Field Methods in Psychiatry: The NIMH Epidemiologic Catchment Area Program.* Orlando, Fla.: Academic Press.

English, J. T., S. S. Sharfstein, D. J. Scherl, B. Astrachan, and I. L. Muszynski. 1986. Diagnosis-related Groups and General Hospital Psychiatry: The APA Study. *American Journal of Psychiatry* 143:131–139.

Ennis, B. 1972. *Prisoners of Psychiatry: Mental Patients, Psychiatrists, and the Law.* New York: Harcourt Brace Jovanovich.

Estroff, S. 1981. *Making It Crazy: An Ethnography of Psychiatric Clients in an American Community.* Berkeley and Los Angeles: University of California Press.

Falloon, I. H. R., J. L. Boyd, and C. W. McGill. 1984. *Family Care of Schizophrenia.* New York: Guilford Press.

Falloon, I. H. R., J. L. Boyd, C. W. McGill, J. Razani, H. B. Moss, and A. M. Gilderman. 1982. Family Management in the Prevention of Exacerbations of Schizophrenia: A Controlled Study. *New England Journal of Medicine* 306:1437–1440.

Falloon, I. H. R., J. L. Boyd, C. W. McGill, M. Williamson, J. Razani, H. B. Moss, A. M. Gilderman, and G. M. Simpson. 1985. Family Management in the Prevention of Morbidity of Schizophrenia. *Archives of General Psychiatry* 42:887–897.

Frank, J. 1974. *Persuasion and Healing: A Comparative Study of Psychotherapy*, rev. ed. New York: Shocken Books.

Frank, R. G., and J. R. Lave. 1985. The Impact of Medicaid Benefit Design on Length of Hospital Stay and Patient Transfers. *Hospital and Community Psychiatry* 36:49–53.

Freedman, R. I., and A. Moran. 1984. Wanderers in a Promised Land: The Chronically Mentally Ill and Deinstitutionalization. *Medical Care Supplement* 22:12.

Frisman, L. K., T. G. McGuire, and M. L. Rosenbach. 1985. Costs of Mandates for Outpatient Mental Health Care in Private Health Insurance. *Archives of General Psychiatry* 42:558–561.

Ginsberg, S. M., and G. W. Brown. 1982. No Time for Depression: A Study of Help-Seeking among Mothers of Preschool Children, in D. Mechanic, ed., *Symptoms, Illness Behavior and Help-Seeking*. New Brunswick, N.J.: Rutgers University Press, pp. 87–114.

Goldberg, D., and P. Huxley. 1980. *Mental Illness*

in the Community: The Pathways to Psychiatric Care. New York: Tavistock Publications.

Goldman, H. H., J. Feder, and W. Scanlon. 1986. Chronic Mental Patients in Nursing Homes: Re-examining Data from the National Nursing Home Survey. *Hospital Community Psychiatry* 37:269–272.

Goldman, H. H., A. A. Gattozzi, and C. A. Taube. 1981. Defining and Counting the Chronically Mentally Ill. *Hospital and Community Psychiatry* 32:21–27.

Grob, G. N. 1983. *Mental Illness and American Society. 1875–1940*. Princeton: Princeton University Press.

Gronfein, W. 1985. Incentives and Intentions in Mental Health Policy: A Comparison of the Medicaid and Community Mental Health Programs. *Journal of Health and Social Behavior* 26:192–206.

Gudeman, J. E., and M. F. Shore. 1984. Beyond Deinstitutionalization: A New Class of Facilities for the Mentally Ill. *New England Journal of Medicine* 311:832–836.

Gurin, G., J. Veroff, and S. D. Feld. 1960. *Americans View Their Mental Health*. New York: Basic Books.

Harding, C. M., G. W. Brooks, T. Ashikaga, J. S. Strauss, and A. Breier. 1987a. The Vermont Longitudinal Study of Persons With Severe Mental Illness, I: Methodology, Study Sample, and Overall Status 32 Years Later. *American Journal of Psychiatry* 144:718–726.

———. 1987b. The Vermont Longitudinal Study of Persons With Severe Mental Illness, II: Long-Term Outcome of Subjects Who Retrospectively Met DSM-III Criteria for Schizophrenia. *American Journal of Psychiatry* 144:727–735.

Horgan, C. M. 1985. Specialty and General Ambulatory Mental Health Services: Comparison of Utilization and Expenditures. *Archives of General Psychiatry* 42:565–572.

Huber, G., G. Gross, and R. Scheuttler. 1979. *Schizophrenia*. Berlin: Springer.

Institute of Medicine. 1979. *Mental Health Services in General Health Care*. Washington, D.C.: National Academy of Sciences.

Jones, K. R., and T. Vischi. 1979. Impact of Alcohol, Drug Abuse, and Mental Health Treatment on Medical Care Utilization: A Review of the Research Literature. *Medical Care Supplement* 17:12.

Kiesler, C. A. 1982. Mental Hospitals and Alternative Care. *American Psychologist* 37:349–360.

Kiesler, C. A., and A. E. Sibulkin. 1983. Proportion of Inpatient Days for Mental Disorders: 1969–1978. *Hospital and Community Psychiatry* 34:606–611.

———. 1987. *Mental Hospitalization: Myths and Facts about a National Crisis*. Beverly Hills, Calif.: Sage Publications.

Kleinman, A. 1982. Neurasthenia and Depression: A Study of Somatization and Culture in China. *Culture, Medicine and Psychiatry* 2:117–190.

———. 1986. *Social Origins of Distress and Disease: Depression, Neurasthenia and Pain in Modern China*. New Haven: Yale University Press.

Kleinman, A., and D. Mechanic. 1979. Some Observations of Mental Illness and Its Treatment in the People's Republic of China. *Journal of Nervous and Mental Disease* 167:267–274.

Koch, H. 1983. Utilization of Psychotropic Drugs in Office-based Ambulatory Care. *National Ambulatory Medical Care Survey, 1980 and 1981*. Advanced Data, No 90. DHHS Publication No. (PHS) 851250, National Center for Health Statistics.

Kulka, R. A., J. Veroff, and E. Douvan. 1979. Social Class and the Use of Professional Help for Personal Problems: 1957 and 1976. *Journal of Health and Social Behavior* 20:2–17.

———. 1981. *Mental Health in America. Patterns of Help-Seeking from 1957 to 1976*. New York: Basic Books.

Lamb, H. R. 1979. The New Asylums in the Community. *Archives of General Psychiatry* 36:129–134.

Lamb, H. R., and R. W. Grant. 1982. The Mentally Ill in an Urban County Jail. *Archives of General Psychology* 39:17–22.

Leaf, P., M. Livingston, G. L. Tischler, M. W. Weissman, C. E. Holzer III, and J. Myers. 1985. Contact with Health Professionals for the Treatment of Psychiatric and Emotional Problems. *Medical Care* 23:1322–1337.

Leff, J. 1978. Social and Psychological Causes of Acute Attack, in J. Wing, ed., *Schizophrenia: Toward a New Synthesis*. New York: Grune and Stratton, pp. 139–165.

Leff, J., L. Kuipers, R. Berkowitz, R. Eberlein-Vries, and D. Sturgeon. 1982. A Controlled Trial of Social Intervention in the Families of Schizophrenic Patients. *British Journal of Psychiatry* 141:121–134.

Linn, M. W., L. Gurel, W. O. Williford, J. Overall, B. Gurland, P. Laughlin, and A. Barchies. 1985. Nursing Home Care as an Alternative to Psychiatric Hospitalization. *Archives of General Psychiatry* 42:544–551.

Mechanic, D. 1974. *Politics, Medicine, and Social Science.* New York: Wiley-Interscience.

———. 1976. *The Growth of Bureaucratic Medicine.* New York: Wiley-Interscience.

———. 1978. *Medical Sociology,* 2nd ed. New York: Free Press, pp. 249–289.

———. 1979. Development of Psychological Distress among Young Adults. *Archives of General Psychiatry* 36:1233–1239.

———. 1980. *Mental Health and Social Policy,* 2nd ed. Englewood Cliffs, N.J.: Prentice-Hall.

———. 1982. Nursing and Mental Health Care: Expanding Future Possibilities for Nursing Services, in L. Aiken, ed., *Nursing in the 1980's—Crises, Opportunities, Challenges.* Philadelphia: J. B. Lippincott, pp. 343–358.

———. 1985. Mental Health and Social Policy: Initiatives for the 1980's. *Health Affairs* 4:76–88.

———. 1986. *From Advocacy to Allocation: The Evolving American Health Care System.* New York: Free Press.

———. 1987. Correcting Misconceptions in Mental Health Policy: Strategies for Improved Care for the Seriously Mentally Ill. *The Milbank Quarterly* 65:203–230.

Mechanic, D., and L. H. Aiken. 1987. Improving the Care of Patients with Chronic Mental Illness. *New England Journal of Medicine* 317:1634–1638.

Mechanic, D., P. Cleary, and J. Greenley. 1982. Distress Syndromes, Illness Behavior, Access to Care and Medical Utilization in a Defined Population. *Medical Care* 20:361–372.

Miller, K. S. 1976. *Managing Madness: The Case against Civil Commitment.* New York: Free Press.

Myers, J. K., M. W. Weissman, G. L. Tischler, C. E. Holzer III, P. J. Leaf, H. Orvaschel, J. C. Anthony, J. H. Boyd, J. D. Burke, Jr., M. Kramer, and R. Stoltzman. 1984. Six-month Prevalence of Psychiatric Disorders in Three Communities. *Archives of General Psychiatry* 41:959–967.

National Center for Health Statistics (NCHS) (advanced data). 1978. *Office Visits To Psychiatrists: National Ambulatory Medical Care Survey, United States, 1975–76.* No. 38.

National Institute for Mental Health (NIMH). 1985. *Mental Health, United States, 1985.* Washington, D.C.: U.S. Government Printing Office.

Pasamanick, B., F. R. Scarpitti, and F. R. Dinitz. 1967. *Schizophrenics in the Community: An Experimental Study in the Prevention of Hospitalization.* New York: Appleton-Century-Crofts.

Polak, P. 1978. A Comprehensive System of Alternatives to Psychiatric Hospitalization, in L. I. Stein and M. A. Test, eds., *Alternatives to Mental Hospital Treatment.* New York: Plenum Press, pp. 115–137.

Robins, L. N. 1985. Epidemiology: Reflections on Testing the Validity of Psychiatric Interviews. *Archives of General Psychiatry* 42:918–924.

Robins, L. N., J. E. Helzer, H. Orvaschel, J. Anthony, D. Blazer, A. Burnham, and J. Burke. 1985. The Diagnostic Interview Schedule, in W. W. Eaton and L. G. Kessler, eds. *Epidemiologic Field Methods in Psychiatry.* New York: Academic Press, pp. 143–170.

Robins, L. N., J. E. Helzer, M. M. Weissman, H. Orvaschel, E. Gruenberg, J. D. Burke, Jr., and D. A. Regier. 1984. Lifetime Prevalence of Specific Psychiatric Disorders in Three Sites. *Archives of General Psychiatry* 41:949–958.

Sartorius, N., A. Jablensky, A. Korten, G. Ernberg, M. Anker, J. E. Cooper, and R. Day. 1986. Early Manifestations of First-Contact Incidence of Schizophrenia in Different Cultures. *Psychological Medicine* 16:909–928.

Scull, A. 1977. *Decarceration: Community Treatment and the Deviant.* Englewood Cliffs, N.J.: Prentice-Hall.

Segal, S. P., and U. Aviram. 1978. *The Mentally-Ill in Community-Based Sheltered Care: A Study of Community Care and Social Integration.* New York: Wiley-Interscience.

Shapiro, S., E. A. Skinner, L. G. Kessler, M. VonKorff, P. S. German, G. L. Tischler, P. J. Leaf, L. Benham, L. Cottler, and D. A. Regier. 1984. Utilization of Health and Mental Health Services: Three Epidemiological Catchment Area Sites. *Archives of General Psychiatry* 41:971–978.

Shapiro, S., E. A. Skinner, M. Kramer, D. Steinwachs, and D. A. Regier. 1985. Measuring Need for Mental Health Services in a General Population. *Medical Care* 23:1033–1043.

Shepherd, M., B. Cooper, A. C. Brown, and G.

W. Kalton. 1966. *Psychiatric Illness in General Practice*. New York: Oxford University Press.

Smith, G. R. Jr., R. A. Monson, and D. C. Ray. 1986. Psychiatric Consultation in Somatization Disorder: A Randomized Controlled Study. *New England Journal of Medicine* 314:1407–1413.

Stein, L., and L. J. Ganser. 1983. Wisconsin System for Funding Mental Health Services, in J. Talbott, ed., *New Directions for Mental Health Services: Unified Mental Health System*. San Francisco: Jossey-Bass, pp. 25–32.

Stein, L. I., and M. A. Test, eds. 1978. *Alternatives to Mental Hospital Treatment*. New York: Plenum Press.

Stein, L. I., and M. A. Test. 1980a. Alternatives to Mental Hospital Treatment I. Conceptual Model Treatment Program and Clinical Evaluation. *Archives of General Psychiatry* 37:392–397.

———. 1980b. Alternatives to Mental Hospital Treatment III. Social Cost. *Archives of General Psychiatry* 37:409–412.

Stotsky, B. A. 1970. *The Nursing Home and the Aged Psychiatric Patient*. New York: Appleton-Century-Crofts.

Strauss, J. S., and W. T. Carpenter. 1977. Prediction of Outcome in Schizophrenia: III. Five-year Outcome and Its Predictors. *Archives of General Psychiatry* 34:159–163.

Talbott, J. A. 1985. The Fate of the Public Psychiatric System. *Hospital and Community Psychiatry* 36:46–50.

Taube, C., L. Kessler, and M. Feuerberg. 1984. Utilization and Expenditures for Ambulatory Medical Care during 1980. *National Medical Care Utilization and Expenditure Survey Data Report*, No. 5. DHHS Publication No. (PHS) 84-20000.

Taube, C., E. S. Lee, and R. N. Forthofer. 1984. DRGs in Psychiatry: An Empirical Evaluation. *Medical Care* 22:597–610.

Tsuang, M. T., R. F. Woolson, and J. A. Fleming. 1979. Long-term Outcome of Major Psychoses: I. Schizophrenia and Affective Disorders Compared with Psychiatrically Symptom-free Surgical Conditions. *Archives of General Psychiatry* 36:1295–1301.

Vaughn, C. E., and J. P. Leff. 1976. The Influence of Family and Social Factors on the Course of Psychiatric Illness: A Comparison of Schizophrenic and Depressed Neurotic Patients. *British Journal of Psychiatry* 129:125–137.

Vladeck, B. 1980. *Unloving Care: The Nursing Home Tragedy*. New York: Basic Books.

Waxler, N. E. 1979. Is Outcome for Schizophrenia Better in Non-industrial Societies? The Case of Sri Lanka. *Journal of Nervous and Mental Disease* 167:144–158.

Weisbrod, B. A., M. A. Test, and L. I. Stein. 1980. Alternatives to Mental Hospital Treatment II. Economic Benefit-Cost Analysis. *Archives of General Psychiatry* 37:400–402.

Wing, J. 1978. *Reasoning About Madness*. Oxford: Oxford University Press.

Wing, J. K., and G. W. Brown. 1970. *Institutionalism and Schizophrenia: A Comparative Study of Three Mental Hospitals, 1960–1968*. Cambridge: Cambridge University Press.

World Health Organization (WHO). 1979. *Schizophrenia: An International Follow-up Study*. Geneva and New York: John Wiley.

CHAPTER
14

HEALTH PROMOTION, DISEASE PREVENTION, AND PROGRAM RETENTION

MARSHALL H. BECKER
IRWIN M. ROSENSTOCK

The explosive growth of interest in health promotion over the past decade may be accurately described as spectacular. For instance, the 1979 edition of this book contained no direct references to the topic (though some of the events contributing to the movement were chronicled). However, by 1987, health promotion and disease prevention activity had become part of the social policy of the U.S. and Canadian governments; rapidly increasing numbers of employers had begun to offer health promotion activities to some or all of their employees; and hospitals, voluntary and official health agencies, and school systems were all involved in the health promotion movement (DHHS 1984).

While the current movement is thus of recent origin, it has roots in antiquity. In Greek mythology Asclepius, god of medicine, was thought to have two daughters or maidens in attendance, Hygeia and Panakeia (Dubos 1959). For followers of Hygeia,

health was the natural order of things given to people who governed their lives wisely, and adherence to natural laws would ensure *mens sana in corpore sano* (a sound mind in a sound body). For followers of Panakeia, healing was crucial, and this concern was embodied in the search for a universal cure, or panacea. Kaplan (1985, p. 565) quotes Hippocrates (circa 400 B.C.) as advising:

Whoever wishes to investigate medicine properly should proceed thus; . . . and the mode in which the inhabitants live, and what are their pursuits, whether they are fond of drinking and eating to excess, and given to indolence, or are fond of exercise and labor, and not given to excess eating and drinking.

The Hippocratic reliance on the wisdom of the body to protect itself lay fallow for more than nineteen centuries, even with the flowering of the science of medicine that came in the middle of the nineteenth

284

century with the discovery of the germ theory of disease and, still later, with the discovery of effective drugs for the conquest of disease. As recently as 1900, Osler found it necessary to emphasize that "it is much more important to know what sort of a patient has a disease than what sort of disease a patient has" (Dubos 1959).

REBIRTH OF THE MOVEMENT

A confluence of circumstances accounts for the reawakened interest in disease prevention and health promotion that occurred around the middle of the twentieth century. Foremost among these events was a profound decline in the prevalence of serious infectious diseases and a concomitant increase in the importance of chronic diseases and such causes of death as accidents and acts of violence. The traditional model in medicine emphasizing "one disease—one cause—one preventive—one treatment" was no longer suited to dealing with these newer problems, and the philosophers of health came to understand that the most remarkable gains in life expectancy were attributable less to specific medical treatments than to preventive and health promotive measures, which included improved social conditions, sanitation, and nutrition, as well as immunizations (the "magic bullets" of prevention) (Dubos 1959; McKeown 1976; Levine, Feldman, and Elinson 1983).

A second determinant of the new focus on health promotion was the frequently observed correlation between poor health and certain behavioral practices, for example, smoking, excessive eating or drinking, and lack of exercise. A third factor was an improving level of sophistication among epidemiologists and other social scientists concerning the complex nature of causation, particularly with regard to the multiplicity of factors involved in the causation of disease.

These facts and changing philosophies underlay a newly developing approach to social policy for health protection, concentrating on the web of causation that results in excess morbidity and premature mortality and holding the conviction that central to this causal web is the very fabric of human activity—the ways in which we eat, sleep, play, relax, drink, and deal with the vicissitudes of being alive. With this new orientation, attention turned to the roles played by individual behaviors and by the structure of social and physical environments in influencing such behaviors.

THE MODERN MOVEMENT

Although there has been long-term public interest in matters relevant to health promotion (Green, Wilson, Lovato 1986), most observers mark the beginning of the modern movement in health promotion and disease prevention as social policy with the 1974 report of Marc Lalonde, Minister of National Health and Welfare for Canada. In the United States a major boost came with the publication of Healthy People, the Surgeon-General's Report on Health Promotion and Disease Prevention (DHEW 1979). Many pioneering investigators, most notably the Framingham group (Dawber 1980), Belloc and Breslow (1972), and Belloc (1973), provided much of the data base for subsequent policy formulation.

The Lalonde report introduced the concept that death and disease were caused by four contributing factors: (1) inadequacies in the health care system, (2) behavioral factors or unhealthy life-styles, (3) environmental hazards, and (4) human biological factors. The American experts represented in the Surgeon-General's report went even further, concluding that "as much as half of U.S. mortality in 1976 was due to unhealthy behavior or life-style; 20 percent to environmental factors; 20 percent to human biological factors; and only 10 percent to inadequacies in health care" (DHEW 1979, p. 9). The report highlighted the importance of interventions to deal with each of these sources of morbidity and mortality, but placed greatest emphasis on the need for life-style changes. While acknowledging that individuals do not have complete control over (or responsibility for) their own health status, the report stated that "personal health habits play critical roles in the development of many serious diseases and in injuries from violence and automobile accidents. . . . In fact, of the 10 leading causes of death in the United States . . . at least seven could be substantially reduced if persons at risk improved just five habits: diet, smoking, lack of exercise, alcohol abuse, and use of antihypertensive medication" (p. 14).

BEHAVIORAL RISKS TO HEALTH

The concept of "risk" was a natural by-product of health workers' increased sophistication about the complex nature of disease causation, and that concept has become central to planning health promotion interventions. Behavioral risk factors include personal habits capable of provoking reduced health or premature death. Some, such as smoking, increase the probability of acquiring several illnesses, whereas certain conditions, such as heart disease and cancer, are influenced by several risk factors. Risk factors often act in a synergistic fashion. For example, asbestos workers who smoke have thirty times more risk of lung cancer than their nonsmoking co-workers and ninety times more risk than people who neither smoke nor work with asbestos (DHEW 1979, p. 13). Controllability of risks lies at the heart of disease prevention and health promotion.

The reader should be wary of the unstated premise in the implied argument:

1. behavioral risk factors heighten the likelihood of premature disease or death (stated); and
2. reduction of behavioral risks will decrease likelihood of premature disease or death (unstated).

Although the stated premise is supported by substantial evidence, it is of the greatest importance, for social policy, to examine the validity of the latter (unstated) assumption, for if reduction of behavioral risk factors does not alter outcomes, there is little merit in expending public funds on those endeavors. It is informative to summarize the evidence for each premise in the argument with regard to some of the leading behavioral risk factors.

The best case can probably be made by using as illustration the harmful effects of cigarette smoking. Indeed, "cigarette smoking is clearly the largest single preventable cause of illness and premature death in the United States" (DHEW 1979, p. 121). Moreover, smoking cessation rapidly reduces the risk of death due to coronary heart disease and, more gradually, diminishes the risk of lung cancer and of mortality from other causes.

Excessive consumption of alcohol has been linked to liver cirrhosis, various cancers, spontaneous abortions, fetal alcohol syndrome, accidental deaths, and (probably) suicides and homicides (DHEW 1979). What is unclear, perhaps because of problems in quantifying the dose-response relationships, is the effectiveness of alcohol cessation or reduction in lowering the risks of those conditions. It seems likely that eliminating driving under the influence of alcohol must have beneficial effects—but would the problem drinker substitute other equally dangerous substances? While it has also been argued that many acts of violence are alcohol related, the critic must again wonder whether the frequency of such acts would be reduced by controlling the use of alcohol.

Exercise and physical fitness have been reported to increase both sense of well-being and life expectancy (DHEW 1979), but the evidence, while supportive, is far from clear, perhaps because of the difficulty of subjecting exercise programs to clinical trials. The most recent prospective surveys of Harvard alumni reported by Paffenbarger et al. (1986) reveal a significant inverse relationship between energy expenditure up to 3500 kilocalories per week and total subsequent mortality (primarily cardiovascular and respiratory). However, these studies have been criticized because their nonexperimental nature raises questions about causal inference; the authors themselves acknowledge that Harvard alumni may not be typical of the general population; and others, who accept the relationship, have questioned the extent of the protective effect of exercise on longevity. We may also question the qualitative value of each activity. For example, in letters to the editor commenting on Paffenberger's paper, Jacoby (1986, p. 399) notes that "the bad news is that although you may [by jogging] live an extra two years, those two years will be spent jogging," and Petty and Herrington (1986, p. 399–400) calculate that each individual stair step climbed increases waking life by about 4 seconds. While these replies were written with tongue in cheek, they do raise important questions about the overall societal benefit of programs to encourage more vigorous exercise, even if such programs were successful in increasing longevity.

Dietary practices have often been indicted as causal factors in premature morbidity and mortality, but much controversy is evident. The data concerning body weight provide a good example. One problem is that "ideal" weights are usually calculated from life insurance data that tend to exclude extremes. Even so, data from the much-publicized Alameda County Study indicate that the age-adjusted mortality rates for men and women are lowest for the groups whose weights are as much as 10 percent under and 30 percent over the Metropolitan Life Insurance reports of desirable mean weights; and beyond those ranges, underweight increased the likelihood of premature death even more than did overweight (Berkman and Breslow 1983).

The data on ideal blood lipid levels are at least as puzzling. Becker (1986, p. 16) has summarized some of the history of public pronouncements concerning cholesterol:

Let us take the case of the demon "cholesterol." First, it was important to avoid it. Then, a board of the National Academy of Sciences . . . took issue with recommendations urging a general reduction in eating foods with high cholesterol content, saying that the value of such action "has not been proven," and that "these recommendations . . . often lack a sound scientific foundation and some are contradictory to one another." But soon the Academy's conclusions were attacked in the N.Y. Times by the director of the Framingham Heart Study as "bad advice, misquoted data and inconsistent"—and later, a longitudinal study of 1,900 men concluded that those whose dietary intake of cholesterol was rated as "high" suffered a third more deaths from heart disease than did their lower-intake peers. . . . However, a study at Texas A & M University . . . concluded that as many as 80 percent of the population can eat cholesterol-rich foods without harm, because the body maintains a natural balance of cholesterol in the blood stream as long as the diet includes vegetables and fiber. Now a very recent study, reported in the *New England Journal of Medicine* . . . tells us that earlier advice to avoid shellfish was incorrect, and that we should be seeking out fish oils, as these oils contain fatty acids that can lower blood levels of fats and cholesterol.

Our point here is not to take a particular position in the cholesterol debate, but rather to indicate that the public has become confused, and even skeptical, about health-promotive advice.

Kaplan (1985) provides an excellent summary and critique of the evidence that behavior is related to the primary prevention of heart disease through dietary modification. He notes that dietary cholesterol may have little influence on serum cholesterol. He chronicles a history of changing professional views about the causal role of cholesterol in heart disease from a concern with total serum cholesterol to successive concerns with low-density lipoproteins, with high-density lipoproteins, with the ratio of HDL to LDL, and finally, with a re-examination of the overall relationship between cholesterol and heart disease. The conclusion reached is that, while dietary factors probably play a role in high serum cholesterol levels, which in turn cause atherosclerosis, "the proportion of variance attributable to dietary factors is probably less than is ascribed in [sic] genetic factors" (Kaplan 1985, p. 568).

Kaplan also raises an issue of extraordinary importance for social policy. In his words,

At least five studies have reported that dietary changes reduce the incidence of deaths due to heart disease. However, in each of these studies, there was an unexpected finding for total deaths; mortality averaged over all causes was not affected by the experimental dietary interventions. Reductions in deaths due to heart disease are associated with increases in deaths from other causes, in most cases cancer. (Kaplan 1985, p. 570)

Kaplan concludes that "it is somewhat unsatisfactory to leave life expectancy unaffected while influencing only the reason listed on a death certificate" (Kaplan 1985, p. 572). This state of affairs may be likened to that of rearranging the deck chairs on the Titanic.

Among the other behavioral risk factors that have been cited in the literature are maladaptive methods of coping with stress (DHEW 1979; Hamburg, Elliot, and Parron 1982; Kasl 1984) and personality factors (of which the most studied is the Type A behavior pattern) (Siegel 1984). While future research related to stress and coping may well yield important policy implications, to date there is no *consistent* evidence for the causal role of these factors in limiting either length or quality of life.

In summary, it seems reasonable to conclude that cigarette smoking and excessive drinking have substantial health effects, that the health effects of a sedentary lifestyle may be somewhat problematic, that dietary practices probably affect health (though in complex, poorly understood ways), and that personality factors have not yet been shown to influence health in any consistent way. As for the health consequences of effective interventions, smoking cessation unquestionably reduces risk of premature death and mortality, and reduction or cessation of alcohol abuse very probably confers health benefits. Concerning other often-mentioned risks associated with diet, exercise, stress, and personality, there is less certainty that interventions will have beneficial effects, in part because the relationships between each of these practices and health outcomes are not yet adequately understood. These conclusions pertain to asymptomatic persons. The roles of diet and exercise are much less ambiguous in control of certain chronic conditions, such as diabetes, hypertension, and coronary artery disease.

Many excellent reviews summarize ongoing and potential health promotion programs in health care settings, in schools, in voluntary organizations, and at the work site (Matarrazo et al. 1984; Parkinson 1982; DHHS 1984; Patterson 1986). Accordingly, it will suffice merely to note the geometric increase in activity between 1970 and 1985. These reviews make clear that there no longer can be serious questions about whether health promotion activities are effective. Reports from these settings show that behavioral risk factors can be reduced (DHHS 1984), but we are still uncertain about the degree to which such reductions protect health—nor are we certain about how to promote health efficiently (the issue of the cost-effectiveness of health promotion will be considered later).

APPROACHES TO LIFE-STYLE MODIFICATION

Locus of Responsibility

Our discussion of intervention strategies will be clarified if we deal first with the distinctions between disease prevention and health promotion. Useful definitions are provided in *Healthy People* (DHEW 1979): "Disease prevention begins with a threat to health—a disease or environmental hazard—and seeks to protect as many people as possible from the harmful consequences of that threat" (p. 119). "Health promotion begins with people who are basically healthy and seeks the development of community and individual measures which can help them to develop lifestyles that can maintain and enhance the state of well-being" (p. 119). Preventive and protective services include those that "can be delivered to people by health providers . . . and measures which can be used by governmental and other agencies, as well as by industry, to protect people from harm" (p. 81). Health promotion, on the other hand, consists of "activities which individuals and communities can use to promote healthy lifestyles" (p. 81).

Thus, preventive and protective activities include things that government and industry can do to and for people, while health promotion includes things that people and communities can do for themselves. This distinction relative to locus of responsibility is important because it implies quite different approaches to coping and helping. In recent years, we have been increasingly exhorted to take responsibility for our own health. Knowles (1977) authored the well-known statement that "over 99% of us are born healthy and made sick as a result of personal misbehavior and environmental conditions. The solution to the problems of ill-health in modern American society involves individual responsibility"

(p. 58). Two years later, Joseph Califano, then Secretary of Health, Education, and Welfare, wrote that "you the individual can do more for your own health and well-being than any doctor, any hospital, any drug, any exotic medical device" (DHEW 1979, pp. viii–ix).

How responsible are we for our own health, and how responsible should practitioners be for the health of their patients? To address these questions properly, it is useful to adopt a fresh approach that places health promotion in a new perspective and sharpens views of the proper roles of providers in working with clients. This new perspective is drawn from work on models of helping and coping with a problem (Brickman et al. 1982). In these models, two critical questions are asked about responsibility for a problem (whether it concerns health, education, or any other problem in social welfare): Who is to blame for causing the problem, and who is responsible for solving the problem? Posing these questions permits us to derive the four models shown in Figure 1. The columns reflect the issue of how to attribute blame for the problem: Is the victim himself responsible for having caused the problem, or is the cause of the problem attributed to a source outside the victim? The rows allocate responsibility for the solution to the problem: Is the victim expected to take responsibility for solving the

Responsibility for a Problem (Who Is to Blame?)

	Self	Other
Responsibility for a Solution (Who Will Control the Future?) Self	Moral Model Person Feels Lazy Person Needs Motivation	Compensatory Model Person Feels Deprived Person Needs Power (Skill)
Other	Enlightenment Model Person Feels Guilty Person Needs Discipline	Medical Model Person Feels Ill Person Needs Treatment

FIGURE 1 Four Models of Helping and Coping. (*Source:* Adapted from Philip Brickman *et al.*, 1982, Models of Helping and Coping, *American Psychology* 37(4):368–384.)

problem, or is the solution beyond the victim's capability to solve?

We are all familiar with the moral model, wherein persons are held responsible both for problems and solutions and are believed to require only the proper level of motivation. The prototypic view is "you got yourself into this—now get yourself out." Others are not obligated to help since people's problems are of their own making and they must therefore find their own solutions. In this model, substance abuse, smoking, obesity, and sedentary lifestyles are signs of weak character, and only willpower can help. This orientation often leads to blaming the victim; in its extreme form, sick people chose to be sick, rape victims chose to be raped. When victims themselves adopt this model, they come to feel guilty and to develop self-perceptions as individuals who lack moral fiber.

We now turn to the enlightenment model, so named because victims are "enlightened" as to the cause of their problems. They are themselves still seen as the cause, but they are instructed that they cannot help themselves—improvement is possible only if they submit to the discipline of authoritative agents. As was the case in the moral model, these individuals must learn that their impulses to drink, smoke, gamble, or overeat are out of control. But, unlike in the moral model, they believe that help can only come by submitting to the discipline of authority. Alcoholics Anonymous is one of the most successful examples of an enlightenment model. Alcoholics both take responsibility for their own past drinking and admit that it is beyond their power to control by themselves; they need the help of God and the community of ex-alcoholics. Note that the treatment is only effective so long as one maintains the relationship with the agents of authority.

In the medical model, people are not held responsible for the origin of their problems, nor are they expected to solve them. A typical example might be a bacterial ear infection: We would not attribute the cause to the affected patients, nor would we ordinarily expect them to recover by acts of will or by putting their faith in a higher power or in others with similar conditions. Instead, a course of antibiotics would be prescribed. The individual is not blamed for having the condition, and we expect prompt recovery if the condition is diagnosed and treated by an expert. The only responsibility of the victim or the victim's guardian is to comply with the doctor's advice; responsibility for providing the solution rests with the expert. Parsons' (1951) conceptualization of the "sick role" exemplifies this model. Note also that the medical model is not restricted to disease and the practice of medicine, but rather can include all cases where people are thought to be subject to forces beyond their control. Radical behaviorism, as espoused by Skinner, exemplifies this model: Human behavior is viewed as determined by rewards and punishments over which people have no personal control (Skinner 1976).

Finally, there is the compensatory model, so named because victims, while not blamed for causing their problems, are supposed to compensate for their handicaps by acquiring the power or skills needed to overcome these problems. Thus, individuals who smoke or overeat or abuse substances are not blamed for their problems, nor do they devote energy to searching for original causes. They are, however, expected to acquire the skills necessary to control their urges. In acquiring these skills they may enlist the aid of experts, but responsibility for the solution rests upon the person with the problem. An application of the compensatory model may be found in the often-quoted statement by Jesse Jackson: "You are not responsible for being down, but you are responsible for getting up." The critical distinction between compensatory and medical models is that in the medical model the therapist advises, "Do as I say," while in the compensatory model the therapist asks, "How can I help you?" The mutual participation model developed by

Szasz and Hollander (1956) to describe a desirable provider-client relationship reflects a compensatory model.

Let us now consider how a problem such as obesity might be viewed and treated under each set of assumptions. In the moral model, obese persons would be told (and would believe) that they have only themselves to blame for their obesity. If they wish to lose weight they must become motivated and use willpower. In the enlightenment model, obesity would be blamed on the victims, who would then be instructed that their problem can be managed only by relying for support on other victims and perhaps on some higher power, possibly for the remainder of their lives. Were they to give up that support, they would be judged likely to revert to their obese condition. In the medical model, obese individuals would not be blamed for their condition, but medical or surgical procedures would be used to control weight. Traditional (noncognitive) behavior modification techniques such as those derived from operant conditioning might also be used, all under the strict control of the therapist. In the compensatory model (as in the medical model), the behavioral causes of obesity would not be sought, but unlike the medical model, the overweight victims would now be expected to acquire skills to enable them to control their urges to overeat. The therapist here would not be in charge, but rather would serve more as an expert consultant to the client, with the client maintaining control.

How is a healthful life-style to be attained according to the precepts of each approach? In the moral model, it can only be achieved through self-determination, a personal commitment to discarding undesirable behaviors and the acquisition of desirable ones; any failure to do this is an indication of character weakness. In the enlightenment model, a healthy life-style can only be acquired by admission of personal weaknesses and, then, through continual submission to the discipline of authoritative forces. In the medical model,

the road to healthful life-styles is reliance on the expert and subsequent compliance with the professional's advice. Finally, in the compensatory model, healthful life-styles are achieved by clients' acceptance of responsibility for their own solutions and by their acquisition of requisite behavioral skills through a therapeutic alliance with a consultant. Clients adhere to goals they themselves have set using skills they have learned. A slip in the application of their skills is an occasion, not for guilt, but for finding ways of avoiding future slips.

The compensatory model is probably the approach best suited to efforts at effecting life-style modification—that is, where clients must develop new behavioral skills and relinquish old (often long-standing) habits. It is also desirable that clients be able to exhibit their new behaviors (whether alone or in a group), and learning is usually enhanced when unaccompanied by guilt or feelings of worthlessness when mistakes are made. Physicians and other health care providers who can learn to view life-style practices within the framework of a compensatory rather than a medical model will be better able to help clients to achieve their own goals, at their own pace, in their own priority order.

True patient-provider contracting (Janz, Becker, and Hartman 1984) may reflect the best use of the compensatory model. In this approach, the client and professional agree on a specific, written treatment goal (however modest) with a time limit for its accomplishment, and both sign the document. This technique is effective when properly used because the patient and provider are in a true therapeutic alliance, with both involved in goal setting and in selecting goals for which the client has a high degree of self-efficacy—that is, the conviction that he or she can successfully undertake the needed behaviors within the time limit (Bandura 1977; Strecher et al. 1986). When a client does achieve the goal, self-efficacy is enhanced, and the client is ready to contract for a newer, more difficult goal. Of course, while the compensatory model seems highly appropriate for problems of life-style modification, it is not likely to be the proper choice under all conditions or for all people. For example, it may well be that certain clients cannot accept the responsibility required in the compensatory model, preferring instead the security of the enlightenment or medical models. Individual differences and circumstances must be considered in developing any health promotion policy.

While the foregoing models of helping and coping imply desired outcomes in members of the public, they do not dictate particular approaches to achieving those outcomes. Historically, we have used educational interventions to achieve behavioral approaches. But, as Levine (1981), Syme (1986), and Syme and Guralnik (1987) point out, structural (environmental) public health approaches may be as (or more) capable of producing cost-effective behavioral and health status outcomes. Indeed, a combination of individual and structural strategies may be more effective than either alone. Such a combined approach is proposed by Levine (1981) and by the Office of Disease Prevention and Health Promotion (USDHHS 1986). A more detailed discussion of the issue of locus of intervention is presented in a subsequent section of this chapter.

PROGRAM RETENTION AND RELAPSE PREVENTION

A very promising application of the compensatory model has been made in recent years to the problem of preventing relapse among persons who have already undertaken life-style changes. Marlatt and Gordon (1985) cite extremely high rates of relapse in many behavioral treatment programs. They showed that fewer than 40 percent of the clients were still abstinent within ninety days after cessation and that less than one-third had maintained their new behaviors by twelve months.

Central to Marlatt and Gordon's model

of relapse prevention is the concept of self-efficacy mentioned earlier. According to Bandura (1977), behavior change and subsequent maintenance are a function of expectations about the *outcomes* that will result from engaging in a behavior and expectations about one's *ability* to engage in or execute that behavior. "Outcome expectations," then, consist of beliefs about whether a given behavior will lead to a given outcome, whereas "efficacy expectations" consist of beliefs about how capable one is of performing the behavior that leads to the outcome (i.e., whether one has the coping skills needed to perform the action). Thus, in order for a person to cease smoking he or she must believe that smoking cessation is likely to lead to a desired outcome (e.g., better health or lessened risk of illness) and that he or she is indeed capable of quitting smoking. Neither belief alone is sufficient to cause the behavior change.

Marlatt and Gordon believe that the chief obstacles to sustaining a new behavior are high-risk relapse situations for which the individual lacks coping skills. Such circumstances can vary widely from person to person but usually involve: (1) *intra*personal determinants, which include both negative emotional states (e.g., anger or frustration) and the desire to enhance positive emotional states; and (2) *inter*personal determinants, which include conflicts (e.g., disagreements with a spouse or with a supervisor) and social pressures (e.g., temptations at a party where others are eating, drinking, and smoking).

People encountering high-risk situations such as frustration, anger, or social pressures are in danger of returning to a former, undesirable behavior. As an example, consider a person who has recently given up drinking but is required to attend the boss's cocktail party. This circumstance may well constitute a high-risk situation, and whether the person relapses into drinking or maintains the newly acquired behavior will depend on the degree to which he or she possesses the requisite amounts of self-efficacy and needed coping skills to resist relapse (e.g., learning how to say "no" to the boss when offered a drink or, in other situations, knowing how to resolve a disagreement with a spouse or how to relax until feelings of anger subside).

If the person is able to cope, a sense of self-efficacy for the next high-risk challenge is increased. But, if the person does not perform a coping response, he or she will suffer decreased perceptions of self-efficacy and heightened feelings of helplessness and will tend to give in to temptation. While a single slip need not become full-blown relapse, it often does, because of what Marlatt and Gordon term the "abstinence violation effect." The person who has slipped once may feel guilty and also may come to see himself or herself as a failure with no willpower (the moral model again) instead of blaming the situation and resolving to try again.

The high-risk situation and the first slip are crucial points for intervention in preventing a complete relapse. People must be taught early to recognize their personal high-risk situations and to assess their self-efficacy in those situations. With this knowledge, they can then choose to avoid some risky situations (when that option is possible) and can also acquire coping skills to deal with unavoidable situations. Coping skills can be acquired through practice and rehearsal in group settings. Learning stress-reduction techniques such as relaxation or meditation may also help. All of these procedures can increase self-efficacy and, in turn, improve individuals' control over their own behavior.

The patient with a chronic disease who is trying to follow all elements of a therapeutic plan will almost surely slip from time to time and fail to comply with parts of the regimen. A lapse need not become a relapse if the patient recognizes that an occasional slip does not signify permanent failure, that environmental circumstances were at least partly responsible for the slip, and that skills can be learned to enable better coping behaviors in future high-risk situations.

Marlatt and Gordon provide research support for the relapse prevention model as applied to controlling a number of addictions, for example, alcohol abuse, smoking, and obesity. This model has considerable potential for reducing the discouragingly high rates of relapse currently noted in all life-style modification programs.

HEALTH RISK APPRAISAL

In efforts to modify risky life-styles, the use of Health Risk Appraisal (HRA), sometimes termed Health Hazard Appraisal, has grown in popularity since its formal introduction in the early 1970s (Wagner et al. 1982). In HRA, an individual's health-related behaviors and personal characteristics are compared with mortality statistics and epidemiologic data for persons of the same age and gender. From this analysis, estimates are provided of the risk of that individual's dying over some future period and of the amount of risk that could be removed by appropriate behavioral changes. The person is then informed of these risks and of the recommended behavioral changes (Wagner et al. 1982).

Given HRA's prevalence in health promotion efforts, it is surprising to discover, upon extensive literature review, that little attention has been directed toward providing a theoretical basis for this approach to modifying behavior.

Unlike many behavioral and educational interventions, HRA has not developed out of any particular educational or psychological tradition; it therefore lacks the presumption of efficacy that a close connection with a body of theory and associated empirical evidence would bring. (Beery et al. 1986, p. 36)

The logic of HRA derives from epidemiological (rather than behavioral) research, specifically the work of Dr. Lewis Robbins on data from the Framingham Heart Study. The recognition that certain characteristics and habits increased the risk of disease led to the creation of a "health-hazard chart" to help direct the *physician's* preventive efforts; only later did the intuitive notion emerge that the technique might itself be capable of motivating personal health-behavior change. However, there is as yet little consistent evidence to support the effectiveness of HRA in influencing clients' beliefs or behaviors or even in increasing their participation in health promotion programs (Schoenbach, Wagner, and Beery 1987). But, despite the current lack of proof of HRA's effectiveness, there are several theory-based reasons for continuing to explore its potential usefulness as a means of inducing desired behavioral change.

Personal Risk

The most salient psychodynamic feature of HRA is its focus on the relationship between life-style and mortality risk and on personalizing this risk by presenting individuals with data based on their *own* reports of current behaviors. Psychosocial models for explaining and predicting health-related behaviors generally view the notion of personal vulnerability to some health threat as a *sine qua non* for action. For example, Rosenstock (1966) and Becker (1974) have emphasized "perceived susceptibility," Baric (1969) discusses recognition of the "at-risk role," and Langlie (1977) uses "perceived vulnerability to a health condition." Other authors have used concepts with similar meanings.

The importance of the role played by "personal risk evaluation" has been demonstrated empirically in a considerable number of investigations summarized in a recent review on the Health Belief Model (Janz and Becker 1984). While these findings provide support for a risk-vulnerability approach, there are at least two critical differences between that approach (as conceptualized in previous research) and the HRA philosophy: the latter's emphasis on *mortality* risk and the induction of a specific *quantified* level of personal risk.

First, evoking the threat of death creates a "negative" climate for education (Hochbaum 1979), a tactic that may actually undermine other aspects of the persuasive intervention. There have been numerous reports from staff involved with HRA that the "emphasis on mortality was inappropriate to the positive messages they were trying to convey to their clients" (Beery et al. 1986, p. 38). Second, the HRA emphasis on "risk age," "achievable age," and "life expectancy" appears to stimulate the major motivational component of "fear arousal"— as in Hall and Zwemer's argument that HRA "conveys a sense of immediacy and urgency bordering on a health crisis" (1970, p. 14). Although fear appeals are sometimes effective, their influence tends to be short-lived, and fear levels that are high may actually serve to inhibit the desired behavioral outcome (Hochbaum 1979; Leventhal 1965; Leventhal, Singer, and Jones 1965). Thus, while emphasis on risk is consistent with behavior change theory, the typical HRA application may be excessive.

Efficacy of Action

Most theorists agree that there is little likelihood of a recommended health behavior being undertaken unless the individual believes such actions will prevent or reduce the threats being posed to health. Ajzen and Fishbein's (1980) model begins with "the person's beliefs that the behavior leads to certain outcomes"; Fabrega (1973) describes "assessments of treatment plans"; Kasl and Cobb (1966) list "perceived value of action"; Kosa and Robertson (1969) use "performance of actions for removing anxiety"; and one of the four major dimensions of the Health Belief Model (Rosenstock 1966; Becker 1974) is termed "perceived benefits of action." Janz and Becker (1984) found that, of nineteen studies exploring the relationship between "perceived benefits" and various preventive health behaviors, fourteen (74 percent) obtained statistically significant relationships.

The HRA strategy may act to encourage belief in the benefits of initiating or maintaining life-style modification, since it enumerates behaviors to be changed and provides science-based, quantitative data to support arguments for the efficacy of the link between altering risk factors and mortality outcomes. This approach might reasonably be expected to influence an important dimension of social learning theory mentioned earlier—outcome expectation. It is also possible that, by presenting clients with an agenda for action based on their individual current behaviors, HRA may increase efficacy expectations as well. A recent literature review (Strecher et al. 1986) has provided considerable evidence for the role of individuals' self-efficacy perceptions in predicting health-behavior change.

By quantifying the potential benefits of recommended behavioral changes, HRA also meets one of the critical requirements for a fear-arousal message to be effective—that is, it should be followed immediately by "specification of the protective response and a clear statement of its value," although HRA does *not* meet another important criterion: "exact specification of *when, where,* and *how* to take action" (Leventhal 1973, p. 573).

Knowledge Transmission

In a discussion of complex psychobehavioral factors, the critical role played by cognitive elements of the message is frequently downplayed or even overlooked. The acquisition of factual information is a necessary, albeit often insufficient, condition for reasoned action. Most theoretical formulations to explain health-related behaviors include the dimension "knowledge about disease" (Cummings, Becker, Maile 1980). HRA provides the client with several different kinds of intellectual knowledge, each having its own potential for motivation.

First, HRA presents facts about links between life-style and mortality and about the amount of relative risk the client is exposing himself or herself to through personal health habits. Second, HRA itself represents a "health education message" since it provides feedback to clients concerning their risk-factor behaviors. Thus, even when HRA is *not* accompanied by (or administered in the context of) an extensive educational program, it still assures that the client will be exposed to a basic, minimum health-promotion message. Thus, HRA overcomes a major limitation of mass-media-based health promotion messages (Hovland 1959).

Third, the necessary information for HRA is supplied by the client, assuring active involvement of the learner. The information is thus individualized, personalized, and made relevant to the participant. Fourth, by quantifying the *relative* importance of the client's risk-taking health practices, HRA allows choices among life-style modifications. In this manner, the participant is given information necessary to divide what may be a very complex set of recommendations into smaller, more-manageable (and achievable) tasks and goals—a process similar to the "graduated regimen implementation" approach supported by findings from the literature on patient compliance (Becker 1985).

Undermining the effects enumerated above are several problems.

1. Some participants will undoubtedly experience difficulty in understanding the probalistic nature of the HRA feedback or in converting such information into meaningful personal conceptualization.

2. HRA information, although personalized, has to compete for the client's attention in a media climate where people are constantly exposed to numerous messages about a large number of major and minor hazards to health.

3. The average HRA participant will probably receive a complex set of recommendations covering a variety of important, but dissimilar, behaviors. Not infrequently, HRA feedback spells out, on a single sheet of paper, advice to give up smoking, lose weight, re-

duce salt intake, increase exercise, reduce alcohol consumption, remember to take antihypertensive medications, etc., in order to add a few years to life span—and such a complex message may overwhelm the client and generate feelings of helplessness and reduced self-efficacy, which result in inaction (Leventhal 1973; Green 1978).

Needed HRA Research

A number of other factors may limit the effectiveness of HRA as it is currently utilized. These, spelled out in detail in Schoenbach et al. (1987), include questions about the truthfulness of self-report and the applicability of HRA to various population subgroups. To date, HRA seems most appropriate for white, middle-class, middle-aged persons (Fullarton 1977). Nonetheless, given its potential strengths and uses in promoting behavior change, it seems appropriate to continue research on HRA as an educational tool.

Such investigation will need to address the following questions:

1. What amounts and kinds of information are learned by individuals exposed to HRA (both absolutely and as compared with exposure to alternative health education programs)?

2. How do clients interpret the personal risks provided by their HRA feedback? Are such notions as "risk age" and "achievable age" understood? How emotionally acceptable and credible do clients find the quantification of personal risk?

3. Are individuals who participate in HRA more likely to increase their beliefs in the health benefits of life-style modifications or in their own ability to undertake them?

4. Do clients benefit from receiving a "menu" of behavioral recommendations, or do they find such a litany overwhelming?

5. What are the effects of HRA use on the organization of health-counseling efforts and on the client-practitioner interaction? How do these effects vary across different environments/settings (e.g., work place, health-care organization)?

6. What are the levels of HRA's acceptability and effectiveness in different subgroups of the population (e.g., minority groups, blue-collar workers, the young, the elderly, persons with one or more chronic illnesses?

7. For what periods of time are the different effects achieved by HRA likely to persist?

8. What is the extent of possible negative side effects of HRA (e.g., arousing maladaptive fear, reducing self-efficacy)?

The hypothesized relationships between various theories and HRA should be tested in research wherein various aspects of HRA and HRA-feedback messages are deliberately designed and manipulated in attempts to affect those factors that behavioral science theory suggests HRA already influences (e.g., messages deliberately designed to heighten self-efficacy, perceived benefits, fear arousal, source credibility, perceived risk, and so forth). We would also recommend that studies be undertaken to evaluate HRA in the context of different clusters of additional cognitive and behavioral health-promotion strategies.

LOCUS OF INTERVENTION

The foregoing material on health promotion has addressed the issue of responsibility for cause and for cure. It was directed mainly at the individual—and indeed, there is considerable evidence that such strategies are often effective (Bandura 1977; Marlatt and Gordon 1985; Matarazzo et al. 1984; DHEW 1984). However, it is also apparent that individual-level interventions do not always work, and when they do, they often are not longlasting. It is therefore at least equally important to examine possibilities for promoting health through interventions at the level of the social and physical environment (Levine 1981). Green (1984) draws a useful distinction between health education and health promotion, defining health education as "any combination of learning methods designed to facilitate voluntary adaptation of behavior conducive to health" (p. 186) and health promotion as "any combination of health education and related organizational, economic, and environmental supports for behavior conducive to health" (p. 190). Health promotion thus includes both educational and environmental interventions.

It has long been understood that the public's health is sometimes better protected by modifications of the physical environment than by direct education of individuals. We may note here the unquestioned benefits of sewage treatment, chlorination and fluoridation of public water supplies, pasteurization of milk, legal restrictions regarding disposal of hazardous wastes, restrictions on smoking in public (to protect the nonsmoker), and safety equipment requirements in automobiles. Of course, even in such cases of environmental intervention, educational interventions are always required to enlist the support of key decision makers—legislators, administrators, employers, judges, and sometimes the general public.

Health and health-relevant behaviors are also strongly influenced by the social environment. Vast changes over the past twenty years in behavior and attitudes toward smoking clearly illustrate the influence of social factors; other examples might include attitudes and behaviors concerning drinking, diet, and exercise. Social legislation impinges on the social environment and often modifies it. It would be unthinkable for the United States to abolish our Social Security retirement system. Even Medicare, only twenty years old, has so permeated and affected our notions of social justice that it has become part of the fabric of American social values. Working with the social environment provides an important locus for interventions to modify health behaviors and to promote health (Levine 1981; Syme 1986).

An interesting ongoing attempt to alter the social environment with the aim of improving health is reported by Syme (1986). His team is attempting to solve certain health problems observed among San Francisco bus drivers, including high prevalence of hypertension, musculoskeletal system problems, and diseases of the gastrointesti-nal tract. A traditional medical model approach to this problem might have focused on teaching drivers more healthful eating habits, better posture, and effective ways of coping with job stress. Syme's team, however, is also looking at the bus drivers' social environment; they have observed the "tyranny of the schedule" (Syme 1986, p. 503), in which the company sets schedules that are virtually impossible to meet. Long shifts and social isolation of the drivers have also been noted. Because of these factors, drivers tend not to go home immediately after work; instead they remain in the bus yard for several hours after work in order to wind down. By the time the drivers arrive home, it is so late that they usually go directly to bed, thus limiting interactions with spouses, children, and friends. This combination of circumstances is probably an important contributing factor in observed hostile or impatient behavior by the drivers.

Syme's research team is attempting to introduce interventions not only among the drivers but directly on those factors associated with the job. For example, if schedules were arranged to be more realistic and rest stops were located in or near central cities to permit drivers to meet other drivers from time to time, the bus company might be able to increase revenues by reducing absenteeism, accidents, and illness. Because this investigation is still in progress, its success cannot yet be evaluated. However, it is hardly debatable that working conditions can affect emotional and physical health, and therefore efforts to optimize working conditions are worthy of attention. Permanent modifications of life-style are most likely to be accomplished by strategies whose focus encompasses the physical/social environment and the individual.

EVALUATION OF HEALTH PROMOTION

The initial steps in any evaluation are specification of the problem(s) to be solved and the objective(s) to be achieved. In health promotion programs, the objectives generally relate to a group of voluntary behaviors, termed life-styles, which are believed to have an impact on health. From a "macro" or social level point of view, the health promotion movement has already enjoyed considerable success. Analyses by Green, Wilson, and Lovato (1986) of trends in smoking, in dietary practices, in exercise and fitness patterns, and in some safety practices show progressive movement in professionally recommended directions over a long period of time (although drinking patterns have not changed much over the past decade). Federal and private investment in health promotion is growing; hospitals and physician groups are adopting health promotion as an appropriate part of practice; federal, state, and municipal regulations, as well as policies of private sector organizations, have introduced restrictions on smoking, drinking, and substance abuse. Clearly, social norms of health-related behavior are changing. Green, Wilson, and Lovato (1986) present substantial evidence that such changes wrought by the health promotion movement represent a durable trend rather than a passing fad—and other analyses report considerable modifications in knowledge, beliefs, and behaviors relevant to health promotion both in communities and in health care settings (Rogers, Eaton, Bruhn 1981; DHHS 1984).

While health promotion programs at the work site would seem to provide a useful venue for controlled evaluations, most companies seem to accept the intrinsic value of the concept and usually devote their funds to programs rather than to evaluations. Nevertheless, such data as are available generally support the conclusion that work site health promotion programs do influence health behavior favorably. Data from Johnson and Johnson, Control Data Corporation, and several other companies (DHHS 1984) show that "treated" (versus control) employees have lower on-job accident rates, fewer hospital days, and

lower benefit payments. Similar effects are reported by Patterson (1986) for employees of the United Methodist Publishing House.

But, while it can scarcely be disputed that social norms for health-related behavior have been changing, there is less certainty that such changes are resulting in reduced morbidity and premature mortality. We have already commented on the difficulty of demonstrating reductions in all-cause mortality from experimental interventions aimed at reducing deaths from coronary heart disease (CHD), although CHD mortality *per se* has been substantially lowered in many such interventions (Kaplan 1985). However, a study of hypertension control through health education interventions (Morisky et al. 1983) reported significant reductions after five years both in all-cause mortality rates and in hypertension-related mortality rates as a consequence of control of hypertension through educational interventions. The Hypertension Detection and Follow-Up Program (HDFP) had also documented similar (though less dramatic) mortality differences between their stepped care and referred care randomized groups (HDFP 1979). The North Karelia study (Puska 1984) demonstrated reduced disability payments caused by cardiovascular disease in their treatment area compared with the reference (control) area or with the nation as a whole.

In considering the effectiveness of health promotion, a problem of some importance concerns the locus of evaluations. Because one cannot expect behavioral changes to affect health outcomes in the short run, it seems reasonable to focus short-term evaluations of health promotion on attitude and behavior change. The Stanford three-community study (Farquhar et al. 1977) demonstrated reduction in community risk factors through behavior change but has not yet reported changes in mortality rates. The short-term focus is endorsed by Green, Wilson, and Lovato et al. (1986). This position, however, is at variance with that of other scholars in the field.

Kaplan (1985, p. 577) believes that "health status is the only reasonable focal point for clinical health promotion activities," arguing that variables studied by health educators are important only in relation to health status. We believe this is true only under special circumstances. Some health promotional activities are indeed directed to stimulate specific behavioral change to affect health status, but their impact is not expected to be observed for many years. For example, it would be naive to believe that increasing the minimum legal drinking age from, say, 18 to 20 would have an immediate or even short-run substantial effect on the amount of alcohol consumed by 18- and 19-year-olds. We would, however, expect a gradual change in social norms to set a standard of behavior resulting in a long-term reduction in drinking rates among younger people, with health benefits accruing still further in the future.

In other cases, a health promotion intervention may not even have behavioral change as an immediate objective but rather may be directed toward increasing readiness to accept subsequent health recommendations. Roberts (1975, p. 53) has observed that "while the [mass] media may not tell us what to think, they have a significant effect on telling us what to think about." Thus, while the public may hold diverse opinions about whether smoking should be prohibited in all public places or whether drunk drivers should be jailed, they are thinking about those issues. The media (and other interventions) may therefore have more of an agenda-setting role than a persuasive role, and setting the agenda may well contribute to the ultimate persuasion process. Accordingly, while one should properly decry the paucity of well-controlled evaluations of health promotion activities, it would be equally problematic to evaluate a program before its time. Of course, the ultimate goal of all health programs is to maintain or improve health status, but not all health programs can be properly evaluated against that criterion. Recognition of this limitation has occurred in evaluations of quality of medical care, where analysts are usually limited to process, rather than outcome, evaluations.

IS PREVENTION BETTER THAN CURE?

This heading is the title of a recent provocative book by Russell (1986) that addresses costs, benefits, and effects of such preventive and curative medical interventions as vaccination (smallpox and measles), screening tests (and treatments) for hypertension and cancer, and life-style (exercise). It is important to note that the interventions described are explicitly medical—environmental interventions are not covered. Russell's work raises a number of critical questions about cost-benefit, cost-effectiveness analysis of health programs that go beyond the scope of the present chapter. However, a number of key points are reviewed here, with the discussion focusing more on cost-effectiveness than on cost-benefit analysis.

Russell's major point is that prevention is not always less expensive than providing medical care and may at times be more expensive. Preventive measures are usually directed toward large numbers of people, only some of whom would have become ill in the absence of such interventions. As a result, it may cost less to treat the few who become ill than to provide even a low-cost preventive measure to large population groups. As Russell says, "choosing investments in prevention is thus an economic choice like any other. Prevention offers good things at some additional cost" (1986, p. 112).

Thus, while cost-effectiveness analysis can provide useful information for program planning, it is restricted primarily by its value-free approach. Most people will argue that good health does have intrinsic value and is worth paying for, but we are reminded of the need to analyse what its actual costs are and to think about how much we are willing to pay for it. However, "even when prevention does not save money, it can be a worthwhile investment in better health, and this—not cost saving—is the criterion on which it should be judged" (Russell, 1986, p. 5). In a similar vein, Warner (1987) distinguishes cost-effective programs from cost-saving programs. For example, screening for and treating hypertension over a lifetime to prevent heart disease may well cost as much as bypass surgery; indeed, it may cost even more to produce the same level of quality-adjusted years of life. But when proper weight is given to the suffering of the victim of heart disease and to problems of postsurgical rehabilitation, prevention seems preferable.

While cost-effectiveness analysis provides a tool and method for systematic thinking about resource allocation, we may not yet have sufficient data or analytic techniques to permit valid conclusions. Requirements for proper application of this approach may include selecting proper discount rates, allocating valid costs to such items as time required to engage in an activity and to side effects of an activity, and assessing the "benefits" of an intervention.

CONCLUSIONS AND POLICY IMPLICATIONS

There can be no reasonable doubt that certain life-style practices influence the length and quality of life. Although additional epidemiological study is needed to specify more precisely the relationships between behavior and health, it seems entirely appropriate to allocate additional resources to the promotion of more healthful life-styles based on what is already known. Thus, at a minimum, we ought to continue efforts to eliminate smoking, to encourage moderation in drinking, and to educate for increased levels of physical activity and acceptance of "healthy" diets. As more light is thrown on the effects of stress and coping on health, additional pertinent recommendations will likely emerge. Resources should also be devoted to improving ways

of preventing relapse among those who have begun to adopt more healthful lifestyles. There is every reason to believe that widespread adoption of recommended practices for smoking, drinking, exercise, and dietary excesses would prolong lives and improve quality of living.

Because this chapter emphasizes health promotion as defined earlier, we do not address other behavioral risk factors such as noncompliance with medical regimens, though we certainly recommend that topic for inclusion on the agenda of health risks that warrant intervention. We also do not deal here with the host of environmental threats to health that are beyond the possibility of reduction through individual behavior, although these, too, are high priority items for public intervention.

As a matter of public policy, it is important to seek the most cost-effective means of controlling these health-threatening problems. This search is aided by implications of the recent monograph *Integration of Risk Factor Interventions* (DHHS 1986), which clarifies some of the key issues needing resolution before proper choices may be made. Substantial evidence supports the conclusion that a focus on fewer than ten risk factors could prevent 40 percent to 70 percent of all premature deaths, one-third of acute disability, and two-thirds of chronic disability. However, attempts to target interventions to "high-risk" subpopulations should be avoided since the population does not for the most part sort into high- and low-risk groups, and even where it does, the majority of disease (not the rate) occurs in the low-risk group. Moreover, there is no reason to believe that efforts to change norms and values underlying life-styles would be more easily accomplished in subgroups of the population than in the entire population.

Would it be better to address one risk factor at a time, or should a "menu" of alternative life-style interventions be offered? Few risk factors are present in the entire population. For example, for cardiovascular risk factors, fewer than one-third of the population are smokers, only one-quarter are hypertensive, and about half the population have serum cholesterol levels in the accepted optimal range. Yet, "more than half the population has a cardiac risk factor in the top quartile of the risk distribution" (DHHS 1986, p. 5). When one adds to these data the risk factors for other major causes of morbidity and mortality, it would appear that nearly everyone could contribute to lower morbidity and mortality rates and probably reduce the cost of health care by altering one or more behavioral risk factors. Individuals vary, however, in their preferences and self-efficacy regarding behavior change; some may wish to work on smoking rather than on diet (or before diet), others may wish to develop physical fitness first, and so on.

Based on these considerations, it would seem appropriate to develop coordinated, multiple-risk-factor national and regional programs to promote healthier life-styles concerning smoking, drinking, exercise, and diet. These programs should include both active interventions (requiring voluntary behavior change by the individual) and passive changes (which emphasize social and physical changes in the environment to alter the probability of behavior without conscious resolve by the individual). Passive interventions, including laws and economic incentives, have proven useful in lowering the incidence and prevalence of drinking, reducing alcohol-related traffic deaths, and (probably) changing attitudes and behavior concerning diet and exercise (Levine 1981; Syme 1986; DHHS 1986; Syme and Guralnik 1987). Passive intervention alone, however, will not be sufficient. At a minimum, education is required to persuade decision makers of the need for such passive interventions as legal requirements to increase automobile safety or to raise minimum drinking ages. Such education may be targeted directly at the decision-makers or at their constituents (or both). Moreover, even when laws have been passed, their effectiveness depends greatly on the willingness of the governed to be governed—on their agreement with the goals of the law. Thus, most Americans are ready to accept severe restrictions on smoking but are not yet prepared to accept legislatively enforced seat-belt use. The continuing interplay of active and passive interventions will yield better results than will reliance on either approach alone.

Still another justification for promoting active as well as passive interventions is the nearly universal acceptance in our own culture of the rights of freedom of choice and voluntariness. We hold dear peoples' rights to be let alone—to do as they wish as long as their behavior does not infringe upon our rights (including our right to health). Accordingly, we feel that individuals must be free to reject our educational efforts. There will always remain considerable numbers of individuals who are not motivated to modify their behavior and consequently will not do so—people with full knowledge of the risks associated with their particular life-styles who nonetheless *prefer* those life-styles. Our objectives should therefore be limited to encouraging people to make informed voluntary decisions.

An important caveat is the tendency of the contemporary health promotion movement to locate responsibility for the cause and the cure of health problems in the *individual*. One may speculate on the many reasons why this emphasis has come about. For example, Western ideology has always placed great value on the individual, particularly with regard to the importance of personal responsibility for one's own success or failure (and, indeed, some personal illness behaviors, such as cigarette smoking, clearly do cause illness). It also caters to our hope that we can somehow exert meaningful control over what will happen to our health and life span (Becker 1986).

A number of problems may result from such a narrow, life-style approach. First, we often ignore the more difficult, but at least equally important, influence on health of the social environment, which both creates some life-styles and inhibits the initiation or maintenance of others (Levine 1981). Second, as we indicated in discussing the moral model, it becomes easy to "blame the victim," establishing "health" as the new morality by which individual character and worth are judged and stigmatizing those who continue to engage in risky behaviors as "having no willpower" or "letting themselves go." Third, when being healthy becomes an end in itself (as opposed to a means by which other ends can be successfully accomplished), there is the danger of fostering a dehumanizing self-concern that may substitute personal health goals for more important, humane societal goals. With respect to the last point, it is useful to note Carlyon's (1984, p. 30) observations concerning the value of jogging: "I'm not sure how well it works for the unemployed, the unskilled, inner-city welfare mothers, Asian-Pacific refugees, the sick, the poor, the handicapped, and the dispossessed among us."

Proper respect must be developed for our own limitations, for no matter what technologies are developed there will always be ten leading causes of death. We will surely learn how to delay death by an average of several years, but the final result is inevitable. Health promotion efforts must therefore focus on improving the quality of life, as well as its quantity, and views of quality must be tempered by regard for the impact of these programs on others. It may be that millions of people in our society now possess a fear of obesity worse than the diseases it may cause—people who are spending hundreds of millions of dollars each year to lose weight and who are perhaps worrying or dieting themselves *into* avoidable illness. In 1985, 53 percent of *all* American women 18 years and older considered themselves overweight (compared to 37 percent of all men), and 44 percent of all women reported that they were "now trying to lose weight" while only 25% of men gave that response. (NCHS 1986, p. 3). When one considers that these are probably underestimates because they include the 75+ age

group, who are generally *not* trying to lose weight, the pervasiveness of the problem seems even greater. As someone has noted, practically every middle-class American woman feels either hungry or guilty. For all persons whose dietary practices are damaging their health, there are probably at least an equal number whose fears about diet are also damaging. While techniques of behavior modification and relapse prevention are available for the benefit of those who want them, we must guard against imposing an arbitrary set of values on those who do not. Adopting a compensatory model for guiding our interventions will help us avoid the temptation to be experts in all matters.

REFERENCES

Ajzen, Icek, and Martin, Fishbein. 1980. *Understanding Attitudes and Predicting Social Behavior.* Englewood Cliffs, N.J.: Prentice-Hall.

Bandura, Albert. 1977. Self-Efficacy: Toward a Unifying Theory of Behavioral Change. *Psychological Review* 34(2):191–215.

Baric, Leo. 1969. Recognition of the "At-Risk" Role: A Means to Influence Health Behavior. *International Journal of Health Education* 12(1):24–34.

Becker, Marshall H., ed. 1974. The Health Belief Model and Personal Health Behavior. *Health Education Monographs* 2(4):326–473.

———. 1985. Patient Adherence to Prescribed Therapies. *Medical Care* 23(5):539–555.

———. 1986. The Tyranny of Health Promotion. *Public Health Reviews* 14:15–25.

Beery, William, Victor J., Schoenbach, Edward H. Wagner, and associates. June 1986. *Health Risk Appraisal: Methods and Programs, with Annotated Bibliography.* DHHS Publication No. (PHS) 86–3396.

Belloc, Nedra B., and Lester Breslow. 1972. Relationship of Physical Health Status and Health Practices. *Preventive Medicine* 1:409–421.

Belloc, Nedra B. 1973. Relationship of Health Practices and Mortality. *Preventive Medicine* 2:67–81.

Brickman, Philip, Vita Carulli, Rabinowitz,

Jurgis Karuza, Jr., Dan Coates, Ellen Cohn, and Louise Kidder. 1982. Models of Helping and Coping. *American Psychologist* 37(4):368–384.

Carlyon, William H. 1984. Disease Prevention/Health Promotion—Bridging the Gap to Wellness. *Health Values: Achieving High Level Wellness* 8:27–30.

Cummings, K. Michael, Marshall H. Becker, and Marla Maile. 1980. Bringing the Models Together: An Empirical Approach to Combining Variables Used to Explain Health Actions. *Journal of Behavioral Medicine* 3(2): 123–145.

Dawber, Thomas R. 1980. *The Framingham Study*. Cambridge, Mass.: Harvard University Press.

Dubos, Rene. 1959. *Mirage of Health*. New York: Harper and Row.

Fabrega, Horacio. 1973. Toward a Model of Illness Behavior. *Medical Care* 11(6):470–484.

Farquhar, John W., Nathan, Maccoby, R. D. Wood, John K. Alexander, Howard Breitrose, B. W. Brown Jr., W. L. Haskell, Alfred L. McAlister, Alan J. Meyer, J. D. Nash, and M. P. Stern. 1977. Community Education for Cardiovascular Health. *Lancet*:1191–1195.

Fullarton, Jane E. 1977. Health Hazard Appraisal: Its Limitations and New Directions for Risk Assessment, in *Let's All Join the Lucky People: Proceedings of the Thirteenth Annual Meeting of the Society of Prospective Medicine*, Bethesda, Md.: Society of Prospective Medicine.

Green, Lawrence W. 1978. Determining the Impact and Effectiveness of Health Education as it Relates to Federal Policy. *Health Education Monographs* 6(1):28–66.

———. 1984. Health Education Models, in J. D. Matarazzo, Sharlene M. Weiss, J. Alan Herd, N. E. Miller, Stephen M. Weiss, eds., *Behavioral Health: A Handbook for Health Enhancement and Disease Prevention*. New York: John Wiley.

Green, Lawrence W., Alisa Wilson, and Chris Y. Lovato. 1986. What Changes Can Health Promotion Achieve and How Long Do These Changes Last? The Trade-Offs Between Expediency and Durability. *Preventive Medicine* 15:508–521.

Hall, Jack H., and Jack D. Zwemer. 1970. *Prospective Medicine*. Indianapolis: Methodist Hospital of Indiana.

Hamburg, David A., Glen R. Elliot, and Delores L. Parron. 1982. *Health and Behavior: Frontiers of Research in the Behavioral Sciences*. Washington, D.C.: National Academy Press.

Herzinger, Regina E., and David Calkins. 1986. How Companies Tackle Health Care Costs: Part III. *Harvard Business Review* January–February: 70–80.

Hochbaum, Godfrey M. 1979. An Alternative Approach to Health Education. *Health Values: Achieving High Level Wellness* 3:197–201.

Hovland, Carl I. 1959. Reconciling Conflicting Results Derived From Experimental and Survey Studies of Attitude Change. *American Psychologist* 14(1):8–17.

Hypertension Detection and Follow-up Program Cooperative Group. 1979. Five-year Findings of the Hypertension Detection and Follow-up Program, I. Reduction in Mortality of Persons With High Blood Pressure, Including Mild Hypertension. *Journal of the American Medical Association* 242:2562–2577.

Jacoby, David B. 1986. Correspondence. *New England Journal of Medicine* 315(6):399.

Janz, Nancy K., Marshall H. Becker, and Paula E. Hartman. 1984. Contingency Contracting to Enhance Patient Compliance: A Review. *Patient Education and Counseling* 5:165–178.

Kaplan, Robert M. 1985. Behavioral Epidemiology, Health Promotion and Health Services. *Medical Care* 23(5):564–583.

Kasl, Stanislav V. 1984. Stress and Health. *Annual Review of Public Health* 5:319–341.

Kasl, Stanislav V., and Sidney Cobb. 1966. Health Behavior, Illness Behavior and Sick Role Behavior. I. Health and Illness Behavior. *Archives of Environmental Health* 12(2): 246–266.

Knowles, John H. 1977. The Responsibility of the Individual, J. H. Knowles, *Doing Better and Feeling Worse: Health in the United States*. New York: Norton.

Kosa, John, and Leon S. Robertson. 1969. The Social Aspects of Health and Illness, in J. Kosa, A. Antonovsky, and I. K. Zola, eds., *Poverty and Health: A Sociological Analysis*. Cambridge, Mass.: Harvard University Press.

Lalonde, Marc. 1974. *A New Perspective on the Health of Canadians: A Working Document*. Ottawa: Government of Canada.

Langlie, Jean K. 1977. Social Networks, Health Beliefs, and Preventive Health Behavior.

Journal of Health and Social Behavior 18(3): 244–260.

Leventhal, Howard, Robert Singer, and Susan Jones. 1965. Effects of Fear and Specificity of Recommendations Upon Attitudes and Behavior. *Journal of Personality and Social Psychology* 2(1):20–29.

Leventhal, Howard. 1965. Fear Communications in the Acceptance of Preventive Health Practices. *Bulletin of the New York Academy of Science* 41(11):1144–1168.

Leventhal, Howard. 1973. Changing Attitudes and Habits to Reduce Risk Factors in Chronic Disease. *American Journal of Cardiology* 31(5):571–580.

Levine, Sol. 1981. Preventive Health Behavior, in H. Wechsler, R. W. Lamont-Havers, and G. F. Cahill Jr., eds., *The Social Context of Medical Research*. Cambridge, Mass.: Ballinger.

Levine, Sol, Jacob J. Feldman, and Jack Elinson. 1983. Does Medical Care Do Any Good? in D. Mechanic, ed., *Handbook of Health, Health Care and the Health Professions*. New York: The Free Press.

Marlatt, G. Alan, and Judith R. Gordon. 1985. *Relapse Prevention*. New York: Guilford Press.

Matarrazo, Joseph D., Sharlene M. Weiss, J. Alan Herd, Neal A. Miller, Stephen M. Weiss, eds. 1984. *Behavioral Health: A Handbook for Health Enhancement and Disease Prevention*. New York: John Wiley.

McKeown, Thomas. 1979. *The Role of Medicine: Dream, Mirage, or Nemesis?* Princeton: Princeton University Press.

Moriskey, Donald E., David M. Levine, Lawrence W. Green, Sam Shapiro, Patterson R. Russell, and Craig R. Smith. 1983. Five-Year Blood Pressure Control and Mortality Following Health Education for Hypertensive Patients. *American Journal of Public Health* 73:153–162.

National Center for Health Statistics (NCHS). 1986. Health Promotion Data for the 1990 Objectives: Estimates from the National Health Interview Survey of Health Promotion and Disease Prevention: U.S. 1985." DHHS Publication No. (PHS) 86–1250.

Paffenbarger, Ralph S., Robert T. Hyde, Alvin L. Wing, and Chung-Cheng Hsieh. 1986. Physical Activity, All Cause Mortality and Longevity of College Alumni. *New England Journal of Medicine* 314(10):605–613.

Parkinson, Rebecca S. 1982. *Managing Health Promotion in the Workplace*. Palo Alto, Calif.: Mayfield.

Parsons, Talcott. 1951. Illness and the Role of the Physician: A Sociological Perspective. *American Journal of Orthopsychiatry*, 21:452–460.

Patterson, Dave, 1986. Determining Cost Benefits of Worksite Wellness. *Business and Health*, 3:40–41

Petty, Brent G., and David M. Herrington. 1986. Correspondence. *New England Journal of Medicine* 315(6):399–400.

Puska, Pekka. 1984. Community-based Prevention of Cardiovascular Disease: The North Karelia Project, in Matarrazo et al., eds., *Behavioral Health*, op. cit., pp. 1140–1147.

Roberts, Donald F. 1975. Attitude Change Research and the Motivation of Health Practices, in A. J. Enelow, and J. B. Henderson, eds., *Applying Behavioral Science to Cardiovascular Risk*. Dallas: American Heart Association.

Rogers, Peggy Joan, Elizabeth K. Eaton, and John G. Bruhn. 1981. Is Health Promotion Effective? *Preventive Medicine* 10:324–339.

Rosenstock, Irwin M. 1966. Why People Use Health Services. *Milbank Memorial Fund Quarterly* 44:94–127.

Russell, Louise B. 1986. *Is Prevention Better Than Cure?* Washington, D.C.: The Brookings Institution.

Schoenbach, Victor J., Edward H. Wagner, and William L. Beery. 1987. Health Risk Appraisal: Review of Evidence for Effectiveness. *Health Services Research* 22:553–580.

Siegel, Judith M. 1984. Type A Behavior. *Annual Review of Public Health* 5:343–367.

Skinner, Burrhus F. 1976. *About Behaviorism*. New York: Vintage Books.

Strecher, Victor J., Brenda McEvoy DeVellis, Marshall H. Becker, and Irwin M. Rosenstock. 1986. The Role of Self-Efficacy in Achieving Health Behavior Change. *Health Education Quarterly* 13:73–91.

Syme, S. Leonard. 1986. Strategies for Health Promotion. *Preventive Medicine* 15:492–507.

Syme, S. Leonard, and Jack M. Guralnik. 1987. Epidemiology and Health Policy: Coronary Heart Disease, in S. Levine, and A. Lilienfeld, eds., *Epidemiology and Health Policy*. London: Tavistock Publications.

Szasz, Thomas S., and Marc H. Hollander, 1956. A Contribution to the Philosophy of Medicine: The Basic Models of the Doctor-Patient Relationship. *American Sociological Review* 97:585–592.

U.S. Department of Health, Education, and Welfare (DHEW). 1979. *Healthy People: The Surgeon General's Report on Health Promotion and Disease Prevention*. DHEW Publication No. 79–55071.

U.S. Department of Health and Human Services (DHHS). 1984. *Prospects for a Healthier America: Achieving the Nation's Health Promotion Objectives* Proceedings of a two-day conference sponsored by the Office of Disease Prevention and Health Promotion. Washington, D.C.: U.S. Government Printing Office.

———. 1986. *Integration of Risk Factor Interventions* Office of Disease Prevention and Health Promotion, Public Health Service: Washington, D.C.: U.S. Government Printing Office.

Wagner, Edward H., William Beery, Victor J. Schoenbach, and Robin M. Graham. 1982. An Assessment of Health Hazard/Health Risk Appraisal. *American Journal of Public Health* 72(4):347–382.

Warner, Kenneth E. 1987. Selling Health Promotion to Corporate America: Uses and Abuses of the Economic Argument *Health Education Quarterly* 14:39–55.

CHAPTER
15

SOCIAL NETWORKS AND SOCIAL SUPPORTS IN HEALTH CARE

SUSAN GORE

A theme that has captured much attention in medical sociology is the contrast between biomedical and person-centered conceptions of illness and healing (Gillick 1985; Mishler 1981; Cousins 1979; Engel 1977). Biomedical conceptions emphasize the priority of biological variables in shaping the manifestation of disease, its course, and prospects for recovery. According to Engel, the biomedical model of disease "assumes disease to be fully accounted for by deviations from the norm of measurable biological (somatic) variables. It leaves no room within its framework for the social, psycho-logical and behavioral dimension of illness" (p. 130). Consistent with this view, the biomedical perspective carries with it an emphasis on obtaining expert medical guidance and faithfully adhering to doctor's orders (Parsons and Fox 1952).

Over the past twenty-five years, behavioral scientists have worked to develop person-centered perspectives on prevention, illness, treatment, and recovery. These person-centered frameworks, while differing in analytic models and purposes, share the view that the causes, expression, and treatment of illness cannot be reduced

---

[1]Person-centered perspectives differ in focus and chosen methodology. They may emphasize personal interpretations of experience, for example, the individual's beliefs about the reasons for his bodily discomfort. Alternatively, or in addition, a person-centered approach may emphasize psychological and social psychological factors in illness causation and treatment but utilize more depersonalized, standardized measures of these variables. A number of investigators have argued that primary prevention of illness is essentially a social structural rather than a social psychological or biological problem (McKinlay 1986; Taylor 1986; Hayes-Bautista and Harveston 1977). It would be misleading to call this viewpoint person-centered because the fundamental issues are institutional. Structural and person-centered viewpoints, however, share an opposition to reducing problems of illness to the biological level (i.e., reductionism) and excluding from definitions of health and illness phenomena that cannot be so reduced (i.e., exclusionism).

to bodily phenomena.[1] Most person-centered approaches in health care are not focused on replacing biomedical understandings or professional expertise, rather they are seen as providing needed data about the patient that are usually overlooked or assumed irrelevant to the seemingly more clear-cut medical considerations (Becker 1985; Stoeckle and Barsky 1981).

Consistent with person-centered perspectives, Kessler in Chapter 4 reviewed research on social-psychological factors in illness causation. In this chapter, I will consider the importance of these factors once illness is experienced and as the individual responds to symptoms and interacts with the health care system.

The following are three interrelated areas of investigation in which the concepts of social networks and social supports have been central to demonstrating the actual clinical relevance of person-centered data:

1. the importance of psycho-social factors in affecting timing in seeking medical care and in explaining the delay, nonuse, and the inappropriate use of health services
2. the importance of maximizing the short- and long-term therapeutic impact of patient-practitioner relationships and communication
3. the importance of social-psychological influences of health care outcomes and of illness prevention and health promotion goals

After briefly introducing the concepts that have been most frequently used in the above areas of research, I will consider each of these issues in greater detail and conclude with a more explicit discussion of policy issues and summary of research needs.

PSYCHOSOCIAL FACTORS IN HEALTH CARE

Four constructs that organize our thinking in addressing each of the above issues are stressors, social networks, social supports, and psychological and behavioral predispositions. Although these same concepts also figure prominently in models of illness etiology, each takes on a different meaning in the types of investigations outlined above. For example, the concept of stress is central in research on both health care and illness causation. Stressors are generally understood as undesirable events or ongoing life circumstances that are threatening to most people and therefore elicit efforts to alleviate stressful features of the situation and the negative emotions associated with these experiences. In research on illness etiology, stressors of interest are usually undesirable, uncontrollable role-related experiences that are not associated with the individual's health status but that may bring about changes in his or her health status. Stresses of major interest include life events or conditions such as job loss, marital problems, divorce, eviction, defaulting on a loan, and other undesirable changes in the major domains of functioning for the population being studied.

Oppositely, the major stressors of interest in research on health care processes are usually medical, centering on the change or threatened change in the individual's health status. How well the individual adapts to these health challenges is the focus of study. Although health changes are set in motion by biological rather than social events, they are clearly stressors in that they are marked by anticipation of pain, impairment, and disruption of social roles. They can involve a serious diagnosis and prognosis, and this bad news is usually coupled with uncertainty, both in respect to the etiology and the course of the illness. Finally, treatment often necessitates surgery and commitment to a painful or difficult and long-term regimen.

The concept of social support has been central in research both on illness etiology and on health care. However, whereas in research on *causation* there has been an important emphasis on the preventive or "stress-buffering" role of informal supports, in *health care*—that is, in treatment and rehabilitation—the nature of patient-practitioner interaction has emerged as a significant empirical focus for the study of social support.

We can see from this consideration of the stress and support concepts that the definitions, dimensions, and measures of these important psychosocial concepts will necessarily be guided by the specific health care issues that define their relevance. In this regard, it is unfortunate that the concepts of social network and social supports are often used interchangeably. The idea of a social network has been defined with varying complexity, but basically it means that if individuals are not alone, they must have social relationships of different types (e.g., marital, familial, friendship, bureaucratic/professional) and in various numbers. These ties convey ideas and values, information or other resources, and, importantly, a sense of support and, at times, interpersonal conflict. Social network analysis calls for attention to characteristics of the ties of a reference individual. The membership of a person's social network is usually assessed by asking the individual to name the people he knows and interacts with, or who are important to him. Clearly, how the inquiry is framed will yield different numbers and types of associates. In most research on social network influences of health care, there is an interest in the following features of ties: (1) the number of ties or range of the network, which usually yields estimates of whether the person is objectively isolated or has a moderate number of ties or many; (2) the density of the network, expressed as the proportion of relationships among network members to the total number of relationships possible; (3) whether ties are familial, friendship, or of a different relational basis; and (4) characteristics of network value systems, for example, the degree to which network members are predisposed to seek medical care.

In their landmark study of social networks and mortality, Berkman and Syme (1979) constructed a measure of social net-work involvement from indicators of the type of ties maintained (familial/friendship versus formal organizational memberships) and frequency of social interaction. They found that connectedness was associated with having more healthful life-style behaviors and more utilization of preventive health services. Connectedness also independently predicted to lower mortality over the nine-year follow-up period. In sum, characteristics of social interaction are related to many dimensions of the illness experience—to changes in health status, as indicated in mortality rates; to health-related practices; and to use of health services.

Having intimate ties and extent of interaction with significant others are also used as indicators of the availability of social support, although case studies clearly illustrate the reasons why many "close" network members may be defined as unavailable for helping and will not be mobilized for help in times of need (Jacobson 1986). In a different vein, in recent studies of sex differences in social network involvement and psychological distress, Kessler and associates (Kessler, McLeod, and Wethington 1984; Kessler and McLeod 1984) have shown that women's wider range of caring relationships brings with it a type of involvement conducive to psychological distress, evidence of a different sort showing that more ties are not always better ties. In sum, although each of the network characteristics noted above may say something about the individual's potential for being supported or helped, we get only a minimal understanding of the true availability of support and of the helping transactions that are likely to take place around emergent problems from a singular focus on the structure of ties. Nor do network variables begin to suggest what constitutes effective assistance. Thus, networks are best understood to set constraints on the conditions under which social assistance or influence can occur and, as we will see, are an important source of norms influencing social behavior. While these norms or values might be understood to "support" certain behaviors or decisions, it is probably best not to confuse study of network culture and the normative regulation of social behavior with the somewhat more unique meanings tied to the social support concept.[2]

In research on social support, support is usually defined and measured with reference to the availability of types of assistance from significant others, such as informational, problem-solving, socioemotional assistance (Cohen et al. 1984), and with reference to the availability of a single important, intimate (empathetic) relationship (O'Connor and Brown 1984). However, it should be emphasized that in many cases what is important from the individual's viewpoint is his or her trust in having supporters, that is, having reliable, caring others. Although in research on the role of social supports in stress-buffering processes we tend to assume that actual helping transactions alleviate stress and directly influence distress, it may be that the perception of support is the more critical stress-mediating variable (Wethington and Kessler 1986). In any case, we see that assessing the degree of support or help received or perceived does not require a thorough understanding of network characteristics. Instead, it requires measuring the provisions that can be obtained from each or all relationships. These include intimacy, the opportunity for social participation, and the many other features of support that have been identified. Because support researchers routinely ask respondents to estimate how likely they are to receive help from persons in the general category of friends, relatives, etc., or to interact with people in these categories during a typical week, these individual level measures may be regarded as characterizing the content of the individual's social network.

Most of our analytic models of social-psychological factors in health processes include attention to stressors that set in motion "coping" processes that have consequences for health status or health behaviors. Three major means of coping with stress have been identified: (1) problem-focused coping, which aims to reverse or alter the threatening characteristics of the situation; (2) emotion-focused coping, aimed to master the feeling associated with the situation; (3) and perception-focused coping, aimed to shape the subjective meanings or understandings of threat. Until very recently, it was believed that an individual's personality and predispositional characteristics shaped his or her responses to stress. The use of social support resources was viewed as distinct from individual coping efforts; in fact, some researchers regarded social support as help that is sought after individual coping efforts have failed.

In newer formulations, support and individual coping efforts have been seen as interrelated features of a multidimensional coping process. Thoits (1984, p. 229) has probably given most thought to this matter as it features in her work to develop a more general theory of emotion-management processes: on the relationship between support and coping, she notes:

Individuals' attempts at emotion work can be supplemented and strengthened by the guiding participation of others in [coping] efforts. . . . Significant others suggest alternative techniques and/or participate directly in a person's emotion-management efforts. In other words, social support can be viewed as coping assistance—in particular, the direct application of techniques to a stressed other that one might use on oneself. . . . Recall that the coping literature points to three broad methods of adjustment: situational control, emotional control and perceptual control. These categories are quite similar to what support researchers generally have termed instrumental support, emotional support and informational support: changing the objective situation, offering reassurance of love and concern, and providing advice and personal feedback.

---

[2]Notwithstanding these distinctions, network characteristics can be regarded as good proxy variables for the availability of social support for some research purposes. The Berkman and Syme research has shown that fairly reliable indices can be constructed from minimal amounts of data.

SOCIAL NETWORKS
AND SUPPORTS
IN THE COMMUNITY
AND IN TREATMENT

I return now to the three problems in health care noted above. Figure 1 organizes our thinking about social networks and social supports in relation to these issues. There are four panels of variables representing (1) health status; (2) illness behaviors, including self-care as well as professional and lay referral; (3) treatment experiences; and (4) health behaviors affecting rehabilitative outcomes, including the maintenance of treatment regimens. Because ideas concerning social factors in health care have developed within a broader understanding of illness and treatment stages (Kasl 1985, 1986), the figure is organized to reflect the temporal as well as conceptual linkages among the three research arenas I have identified.

Our concerns begin with the experience of illness symptoms, or the presence of known risk factors. In the latter case the individual is well but at risk for illness, and he or she may engage in health promotion and illness prevention efforts. I focus attention on efforts to maintain health as well as measures taken in the face of illness because social support theory addresses issues in prevention as well as those in treatment and rehabilitation. To date, our models of illness and health behaviors (*cf.* Becker et al. 1977) do not greatly differ on the basis of a symptomatic or asymptomatic starting point.

From the presence of risks or symptoms we establish two pathways, *a* and *b*, both involving decision making around change or threatened change in health status. The first, involving few or many lay contacts, may not eventuate in seeking formal medical care. The second, pathway *b*, does. Here, in a treatment setting, we focus on

---

[3]Another important body of research on social-psychological factors in treatment deals with the preparation of patients for surgery (*cf.* Wilson 1981). Although the content of these preparations may have supportive effects, as in reducing uncertainty, they are not intended as manipulations of social support.

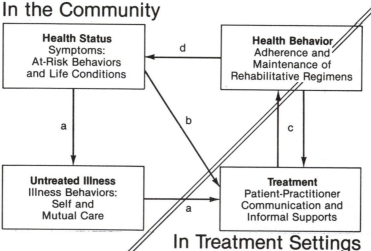

In the Community

Health Status
Symptoms:
At-Risk Behaviors
and Life Conditions

d

Health Behavior
Adherence and
Maintenance of
Rehabilitative Regimens

a

b

c

Untreated Illness
Illness Behaviors:
Self and
Mutual Care

a

Treatment
Patient-Practitioner
Communication and
Informal Supports

In Treatment Settings

FIGURE 1   Social Relational Influences in Illness Behavior and Health Care. *a,* Effects of social network structure and values on seeking care and lay referral processes; *b,* pro-medical influences and interpersonal triggers to seeking care; *c,* professional, informal supports and mutual help; *d,* outcome of care. (*Source:* Adapted from J. B. McKinlay, 1981, *Social Network Influences on Morbid Episodes and Career of Help-Seeking,* in L. Eisenberg and A. Kleinman, *The Relevance of Social Science for Medicine,* Boston: D. Reidel, p. 79.)

the nature and quality of patient-practitioner communication.[3] At this point, illness is diagnosed, and the individual is in the "sick role." This is a time of considerable stress and typically involves the greatest dependency upon health care providers.

In the final panel of variables we emphasize problems of maintaining medical and behavioral regimens as the individual begins to move away from reliance on institutional health care resources. The quality of patient-practitioner relationships remains important here, but the context is increasingly one in which biomedical interventions are few and the importance of psychosocial variables is great. At this stage the individual has been viewed in a medical sense as "on his own," relinquishing the sick role and returning to the community. But this narrow view of health care has not sufficed. With behavioral and medical regimens to maintain over lengthy periods of physical and psychological recovery—often in the context of sharply reduced hospital stays—social scientists have targeted this transition stage in health care as critical to health outcomes, quality of care, and cost-containment issues. Regarding health outcomes, the reciprocal arrows between the third and fourth panels in Figure 1 indicate the problem of repeated episodes and chronicity in illness, which in some part is due to failure in providing adequate support and guidance as the individual moves toward increasing self-care.

MODELS OF HELP-SEEKING IN THE FACE OF ILLNESS OR RISK

The first line of research identified above concerns the psychosocial factors influencing the use or nonuse of health services. Various aspects of the pre-patient world have been investigated with respect to this issue, and the concepts of stress and social networks have both been shown to be central to understanding medical help-seeking (Mechanic 1982a). First, something should be said about why this issue is important to sociologists, practitioners, and health planners. Most fundamentally, the issue ad-dresses why and when the individual comes to view himself as ill, and ill enough to warrant medical attention. The study of illness behavior, while important to scientists for understanding human decision making, has critical medical implications as well. We tend to think of illness onset as representing a sharp discontinuity from wellness, marked by physical symptoms that are visible, painful, and disruptive. We assume that bodily changes are the basic determinants of medical help-seeking and that the more severe the illness, the more quickly attention will be sought. The chronic diseases with which we are increasingly concerned, however, depart from this general model. The timing of the detection of diseases such as diabetes, heart disease, and cancer is determined by *factors outside* the disease process itself—social and psychological factors that shape the individual's response to the often subtle bodily changes that are experienced in daily living. Thus, in the face of serious illness, individuals may delay in seeking care just as they delay in paying taxes or going to the dentist. Although delay is medically advantageous in some cases, the important point is that these subjective, person-centered variables become medically highly significant. Through determining the time treatment is undertaken, they influence illness severity, treatment options, cost of care, and scientific knowledge about disease process.

Finally, in addition to the problem of delay in seeking care, practitioners are concerned with increasing health care access to "underutilizers," persons whose level of use is below that which would be expected on the basis of their health status and who suffer from preventable illnesses. Similarly, they wish to find appropriate means for treating the "worried well," those regular users of health services who feel ill but whose complaints elude diagnosis.

In sum, as Levine and Kozloff (1978) have suggested, addressing these issues of pre-patient behavior will require both clinical and scientific attention to the intermingling of two often-distinct perspectives on the nature and existence of "illness": the subjective, as seen through the eyes of the individual, and the objective, as accounted for by medical observers.

A point of departure for early sociological inquiries into the subjective perspective on medical help-seeking is the concept of illness behavior. Building on Zborowski's (1952) classic work on cultural variation in responses to pain, Mechanic and Volkart (1960) as well as Goffman (1981) described a pre-patient phase of illness behavior during which, according to Mechanic (1961, p. 189),

given symptoms may be differentially perceived, evaluated and acted (or not acted) upon by different kinds of persons. Whether by reason of earlier experiences with illness, differential training with respect to symptoms, or whatever, some persons will make light of symptoms, shrug them off, and avoid seeking medical care; others will respond to the slightest twinges of pain or discomfort by quickly seeking such medical care as is available. . . . In this sense, illness behavior even determines whether diagnosis and treatment will begin at all.

This focus on activity in the pre-patient world stands in marked contrast to earlier models of the "sick role" (Parsons and Fox 1952), which posited a fairly rigid set of expectations and obligations for both patient and practitioner once the individual and his family become dependent upon the health care system. In contrast, the study of illness behavior focuses on a stage of illness prior to the point of contact with the formal health care system, when the individual's health status is somewhat unclear and individual and social factors play a prominent role (in addition to the symptoms themselves) in determining whether and what types of help are sought.

Early research on the social network endeavored to understand how the group structure in which the individual is embedded influences health-related values and behaviors, which in turn constrain the timing and use of the formal health care system. This tradition is usually traced to Friedson's (1960) conceptualization of the culture and linkages between lay and pro-

fessional referral networks, and to Suchman's (1965) somewhat parallel cultural emphasis on social network belief systems as "scientific" and pro–medical care, or "popular" and skeptical of medical care. Anthropologists have similarly distinguished between the popular and professional health sectors (*cf.* Chrisman and Kleinman 1983, for an excellent review). What we see in this contrast between the professional and the lay systems of responding to health care needs is a recognition of two potentially competing systems of illness response. In Friedson's model this competition is classified along two variables: first, the congruity of the values of each system, and second, the number of lay consultants used in illness episodes. Where congruence is high and lay consultation limited, rapid access to formal health services is facilitated. Similarly, in Suchman's model of illness behavior, pro-medical beliefs characterize a loosely knit "cosmopolitan" structure, in contrast to the more popular (skeptical of science) beliefs evident in the more dense "parochial" networks.

Although it may appear that these generalizations on the role of the lay culture and referral system are hardly newsworthy today, there are three areas of current concern that are grounded in this tradition of research. First, in reviewing the field of social network influence of help-seeking, McKinlay (1981) has cogently argued that considerations of the network culture provide an important link between the pre-patient world and issues of treatment satisfaction and efficacy, since the pre-patient culture shapes expectations concerning diagnoses, physician behavior, and prescribed medical and behavioral regimens. McKinlay notes three ways by which network members can influence health encounters:

1. Network members can shape the nature of the encounter, that is, help members to "know the ropes" in dealing with health care organizations and providers.

2. Network members can shape expectations that clients carry into the encounter, which may be an important ingredient in eventual patient satisfaction. "What goes on during an encounter with a professional helper appears to be subsequently evaluated in discussions with network members against the common stock of knowledge of the network" (1981, p. 94)
3. Through their presence or absence, network members can influence the actual nature of the health care encounter.

McKinlay emphasizes the importance of network culture and its compatibility with the culture of medicine, including the interpersonal aspects of practice and its therapies. These cultural influences operate before, during, and after contact with the health services system. As we will see in the discussion of prevention policy issues, the network is also a critical segment of social structure as it stands between societal institutions and the individual and family, thus providing an important point of access for health-promoting interventions.

An additional significance of the lay system lies in the current emphasis on individual responsibility for health, which includes many facets of self-care and mutual care that occur prior to or instead of receiving formal health care, or when leaving a formal care system (e.g., deinstitutionalization) and in health maintenance and risk reduction programs (*cf.* Clymer, Baum, and Krantz 1984). I include self-care and mutual care in this section on the illness behaviors that precede formal treatment to acknowledge that self-care and mutual care are a major tradition in American health care (Starr 1982) and that the new cultural emphasis on prevention and cost containment is again shifting some of the burdens of health care onto the individual and community. Of course, self-care and mutual help occur at each of the three junctures illustrated in Figure 1, and these efforts may differ in origin and function at each stage. For example, individual efforts to maintain a post-hospitalization medical or behavioral regimen, as in stress-reduc-tion programs for coronary patients, involve more physician participation than other individual efforts in health promotion and risk reduction that are undertaken at an earlier asymptomatic stage. In addition, some participation in mutual help groups occurs during treatment and recovery periods to provide for the communication, support and information that patients find missing in narrow medical approaches to their problems.

In discussing nonuse of professional services a distinction must be made between nonusers who engage in self-care or mutual care and those who are unaware or unable to meet their health needs. In the former instance our models assume a level of education and awareness of opportunities for engaging in preventive and curative health behaviors, as well as for seeking formal health care. In a recent study of elderly nonusers of health services in Canada, where medical services are universally insured, Shapiro and Roos (1985) found that nonusers of ambulatory care were more likely to be single, mentally impaired, and minimally educated than those who maintained some contact with physicians. They regarded these factors as indicating a high degree of social isolation, which may function to reduce exposure to preventive health knowledge that might be obtained through either formal or informal sources. This research underscores the well-documented significance of social isolation in the etiology of illness and as a barrier to use of health services.

A final significance of the tradition of research on social network influences of illness behavior is its obvious relevance to current, more psychological models of medical decision making that emphasize the role of values and expectations regarding susceptibility to illness and the efficacy of treatment. In the popular Health Belief Model (HBM) (Rosenstock 1975) and related formulations (*cf.* Becker and Maiman 1975) the idea is that individuals will not seek health care "unless they possess minimal levels of relevant health motivation and knowledge, view themselves as potentially vulnerable and the condition as threatening, are convinced of the efficacy of intervention, and see few difficulties in undertaking the recommended health behavior" (Becker and Maiman 1983, p. 544).

Social networks and social supports are not explicitly considered in most of these models. However, the importance of the social context as a locus for transmitting beliefs about health is underscored in the recent Institute of Medicine report, *Confronting AIDS* (Institute of Medicine, National Academy of the Sciences 1987). This report's section on social science research priorities emphasizes the need to develop health education programs based on models such as the HBM and suggests that these education efforts will have to be directed at individuals within their social networks. Seeing the social network as the ultimate source of health beliefs and information and as a locus of communication and reinforcements for values and behavior is perhaps the highest priority for social network research at the present time.

In discussing the Health Belief Model, I noted that the concepts of social networks and social supports are not usually integrated into these more psychological models. Similarly, in Aday and Anderson's (1974) framework on the influences of health services utilization, social networks or supports are not easily fit into their categories of largely demographic "predisposing" variables or economic "enabling" conditions. However, the different means through which networks and supports influence use of services have been discussed on study-to-study basis. There are four basic dynamics involved:

1. Lack of adequate supports or network ties may worsen health status, therefore increasing need for services. Objective and perceived levels of morbidity are important features in most multivariate models of utilization, for example, as "need" factors in the Aday and Anderson model.
2. Social networks shape health beliefs and access to lay consultation, which intervene be-

tween symptom experience and the decision to seek formal help, as we saw in the research of Suchman and Friedson.
3. Disruptions in social networks or supports or other sources of distress "trigger" help-seeking behavior independent of changes in the nature or severity of symptoms.
4. Social networks and supports act in conjunction with stressors or other predisposing variables. Specifically, in this popular interactive framework, adequate supports are expected to offset or moderate the effects on utilization of processes such as those identified in (3).

In concluding this section, something should be said about the research pertaining to the third and fourth perspectives, since the first is covered in Chapter 4 by Kessler and Wortman, and I have adequately covered the second.

Whereas much of the research on social networks establishes how this involvement can delay the use of services, the opposite may also be the case. Zola (1973) has argued that individuals accommodate to illness symptoms over time and that changes in social conditions break this accommodation and trigger use of services. In this framework, help-seeking is a response to psychosocial events though it occurs in the presence of an ongoing physical health problem. Three of Zola's "triggers" to using services clearly involve social relational variables. The most important from the viewpoint of support processes involves the occurrence of an interpersonal crisis, such as a familial argument, which directly precedes and motivates the decision to seek help. I interpret this pattern of illness behavior within the framework developed by Tessler and Mechanic (Tessler, Mechanic, and Dimond 1976; Tessler and Mechanic 1978) on the role of psychological distress in shaping perceptions of health status and influencing utilization of services. Their multivariate analyses also support the generalization that distress influences utilization of services independently of actual levels of morbidity. Since their research shows that distress is also a significant predictor of perceived health status, the data lend further support to Mechanic's contention (1980) that distress triggers a sensitivity to bodily states and that this dispositional sensitivity mediates the relationship between distress (or crisis) and use of services.

Although study of predispositional variables is only tangentially related to the network and support concepts, a major question that has organized much of our research on social supports and networks is whether the high and often inappropriate use of services often associated with these predispositions and situational stresses can be offset by providing adequate informal supports.[4] This stress-buffering model as applied to utilization research is nicely illustrated in the work of Horowitz, Morgenstern, and Berkman (1985), who examined the influence of child's health status and parents' health beliefs, distress, stressors, and network characteristics on use of pediatric acute care services during a twelve-month period. Interestingly, in their data both large network size and geographic density of the network were associated with greater use of services, a finding interpreted to reflect the frequency of family contact with friends whose belief systems are pro-medical intervention. There was no relationship between feeling socially supported and acute episode use, suggesting no simple preventive function of emotional support. However, support did appear to play a role in a more complex set of relationships. A variable measuring the tendency to use the social network for assistance in various hypothetical situations was found to interact with and reduce the effects of a disposition to seek medical care on the use of services. Horowitz, Morgenstern, and Berkman conclude: "For low levels of propensity [to seek care] women with

many network members to call on will use more yearly acute care services. When propensity to seek care is high, however, women with many network members to call on have 1.6 fewer yearly pediatric care contacts than women with few network members to call on" (p. 954). Thus, from this data it appears that the expectation of having support or actual use of supports can counteract the effects on utilization of a high predisposition to seek medical care.

SOCIAL SUPPORTS AND COPING IN TREATMENT SETTINGS

A major force behind social scientific study of treatment issues has been the problem of promoting patient compliance with medical regimens, as well as increasing patient satisfaction with medical care. The important underlying assumption in our models of these processes and their role in promoting better treatment outcomes and ultimately reducing the cost of care is that an active patient whose needs are known and met is likely to have more favorable treatment outcomes, including greater satisfaction with care, than the patient who is less involved in the care that he or she is receiving.

In this section, I will consider research on patient-practitioner communication as well as the role of informal supports and mutual help in health care. Figure 1 depicts the individual as moving through treatment to a later period of self-care that is often identified with the processes of recovery and rehabilitation. The reciprocal arrows take into account that the individual may move back into treatment owing to, for example, the chronicity of illness or the failure to recover. Acknowledging that being under medical supervision may be a lengthy process and involve periods in which the individual is neither sick nor well, stands in sharp contrast to the conception of the illness role system in which the individual is freed from his usual role responsibilities in exchange for complete

---

[4] I am not considering the research on the cost offset of including modest psychotherapeutic interventions in general health care (*cf.* Mumford, Schlesinger, and Glass 1981), because although the principle is similar, this is largely a question of the appropriate mix and cost of formal health services.

adherence to physician authority. (Parsons and Fox 1952). In this latter prescriptive model, the family's presumed vulnerability as a support system is further rationale for reliance upon an authoritarian physician.

The fact that these assumptions about illness and the illness role system are no longer adequate for describing the variability of practitioner and patient role behavior across numerous illness and health care contexts (*cf.* Levine and Kozloff 1978, for a review of the sick role concept) emphasizes the need to develop a multifaceted understanding of treatment/recovery goals and experience. Focusing on the problem of goals, Kristeller and Rodin (1984, p. 86) have described a model of "treatment continuity" that views the multiple issues in treatment as a part of a continuous process involving three stages.

Stage 1: Compliance—the extent to which the patient initially assents to and follows the clinical prescription

Stage 2: Adherence—the extent to which the patient continues a negotiated treatment under limited supervision, in the face of conflicting demands

Stage 3: Maintenance—the extent to which the client continues health behavior without supervision, incorporating it into a general life style.

Although this is a very coherent and useful schema for understanding treatment goals, Kristeller and Rodin approach these challenges only from the viewpoint of their cognitive requirements, and the potential role for social support in information processing and in otherwise fostering these health care goals is for the reader to consider. Here we see, as mentioned earlier, the schism between research on social support and more individualistic approaches to coping with illness. However, support can be seen as facilitating coping efforts through regulating emotion; providing and structuring information and coping strategies; maintaining self-esteem, membership, and other facets of identity; and directly providing resources and help. Thus, future work can focus on integrating social sup-

port into these cognitive models of coping with illness.

In the previous discussion of social relational influences of illness behavior I emphasized the social network concept and its relevance to more current work on health motivations and values. Regarding problems in treatment, most attention has centered on the problem of what constitutes effective informal and practitioner support in the face of serious illness. (The social network concept is relevant to the extent that the mutual help group, though not a natural helping network, can be seen as a network of peer supporters.) This shift in conceptual tools—from the social network to the social support construct—reflects the very different research questions, designs, and populations that have been the basis for studying illness behavior and the use of health services, versus those used for studying the treatment context and its relationship to therapeutic outcomes.[5]

---

[5] For some time now, researchers have emphasized the benefits of situational, process-oriented studies of social support and networks for understanding how networks and supports actually function to influence health and illness behavior and health status (*cf.* Gore 1985.) Since process research requires data collections that reveal how people get from point A to point B, it is usually based on study of fairly small or homogenous samples of individuals who are more or less at point A. In the study of social support in treatment settings, this usually means initiating research at the time a diagnosis is confirmed or at some other medical turning point, for example, just after surgery. Thus, to focus on process we can engage in general discussions of the elements of effective physician-patient communication (DiNicola and DiMatteo 1984) or study the dynamics of formal and informal relationships in the face of particular illnesses at particular stages (*cf.* Wortman 1984, on the study of the cancer patient). This is not to say that social networks cannot be studied from process perspectives. For example, one important question pertaining to supports during illness is how members are mobilized to help, that is, how a network of significant others becomes a subset of actual helpers. Another critical issue calling for network study is how the illness effects a rearranging of the social network. This latter issue has been examined in studies of the mental health consequences of life transitions such as divorce and widowhood (Hirsch 1981; Wilcox 1981). An important issue in studying networks from this perspective is whether network reorganization is voluntarily or involuntarily brought about.

There are at least three excellent and recent reviews of research on support and health outcomes in serious illness (Cohen and Lazarus 1979; DiMatteo and Hays 1981; Wortman and Conway 1985), and Gottlieb (1983) has devoted an excellent volume to applications across the spectrum of physical and mental health needs. There are other reviews that focus on specific conditions (Lindsey et al. 1981, on post-mastectomy); McKinlay 1981, on bereavement; Colleetti and Brownell 1983, on obesity, smoking, and alcoholism). Levy (1983) has reviewed and critiqued the research on social support and patient compliance with medical regimens. The reader can refer to all these works for a more thorough consideration of different empirical problems and of the evidence on the effectiveness of support in improving treatment outcomes.

Most research on the role of social support in treatment has actually focused on the psychosocial aspects of recovery from coronary heart disease and cancer (*cf.* Gottlieb 1983, pp. 145–175). In addition, there have been more focused discussions of the quality of patient-practitioner communication, which is thought to influence treatment outcomes both directly and indirectly, the latter through its effect on patient compliance with medical regimens. DiNicola and DiMatteo (1984, pp. 60–61) identify two reasons why patients are noncompliant: "1. They are unable (or unwilling) to follow the specific treatment regimen that is prescribed. . .; or 2. they are rejecting the originator of the treatment recommendation (because of distrust or dislike of the practitioner)."

Communication is central to each issue. Estimates of noncompliance with medical regimens range from 15 to 94 percent; this variability is due to the complexity and length of the regimens studied rather than to unreliability in measurement. On the average, it is estimated conservatively that about 30 percent of all patients fail to take medicine or follow regimens (DiNicola and DiMatteo 1984). Other research cited by Bok (1984) suggests that over half of such patients do not understand what they are told and that their physicians are at fault. There is less empirical data to support the idea that noncompliers are rejecting their practitioners, but DiMatteo and DiNicola (1982) maintain that rejection of directives is likely to reflect degree of trust in the provider. This position is consistent with data that physicians are generally inattentive to patients' presentation of psychosocial problems, even as residents in a Family Medicine Practice program (Harrison 1979).

More germane to the social support concept is the body of research on cancer patients and their difficulty in obtaining information from physicians and nurses (Quint 1965). This research, largely on women who have developed breast cancer and experienced mastectomy, reveals that needs for information and advice can be rather specific and that the physician rather than family and friends is looked to as the source for this knowledge. The fact that types of support are not substitutable and effectively delivered by all classes of supporters, a point well documented some years ago (Weiss 1974), is one facet of a major research theme that concerns understanding when support is supportive and when support attempts fail (Wortman and Lehman 1984).

In their seminal work on interpersonal relationships and the cancer patient, Wortman and colleagues (Wortman 1984: Wortman and Dunkel-Schetter, 1979; Wortman and Conway 1985) point to the fundamental problem of social support that this illness creates: The uncertainty and fear associated with the diagnosis heighten needs for social support, while at the same time the impact of the disease on the individual's social relationships reduces the likelihood of receiving it. Patients and practitioners may disagree, for example, on what constitutes a caring relationship. Mumford, Schlesinger, and Glass (1982, p. 142) have noted that "clinicians believe that a hopeful, cooperative patient tends to have a smoother and swifter recovery than a depressed and uncooperative patient."

Notwithstanding the importance of hope and optimism, Wortman (1984) has shown that social support attempts often fail owing to misconceptions about the patient's need for significant others to create a climate (even if forced) of cheerfulness and optimism. Paralleling these findings, Thomas's (1978) research on mastectomy patients focuses on the compatibility of individual and family coping responses over ten critical phases of the diagnostic and treatment process. The data reveal that whether coping responses are congruent or conflictual usually involves the timing of each party in using denial strategies over the course of the experience. The issue of coping congruity is also prominent in research on recovery from heart disease (Stern 1978).

A different but compatible perspective is obtained when considering the giving of support in the context of a depressive illness. Reviewing the work of Coyne (1976) and Coates and Wortman (1980), Billings and Moos (1985) note how the depressed individual may increase his or her seeking of help and expressions of depression in order to elicit the support of others. Such behavior, especially in the long term, is fundamentally unattractive to significant others who offer temporary support toward controlling—but not changing—this coping style that is characteristic of the depressed individual. Because such "supportive" responses fail to provide what the depressed person seeks, the expression of distress is not alleviated, and significant others withdraw in frustration. Billings and Moos conclude that when stressors are more chronic than acute in nature, as is frequently the case in illness situations, individuals may deplete their informal resources. This scenario is another instance of social support that fails.

Moreover, studies of coping with other severe illnesses yield similar kinds of evidence of the limits of support in the context of life-threatening illness. For example, in describing the psychological situation of parents of leukemic children, Comaroff and Maguire (1986, p. 103) note that the uncertainty in the course of their child's illness led parents to search for meaning in the experiences of other families "to ease the isolation of being picked out to suffer irreversible tragedy. But when individual and collective definitions had reached relative stability, referencing [comparing notes with other parents] often declined and other sufferers were avoided as possible sources of disorienting information."

The problem of the fit between the coping style and needs of the individual with the helping strategies of significant others is also nicely illustrated in research on the effectiveness of mutual help groups in the recovery process. Recent discussions of the dimensions of social support functions have emphasized the importance of "appraisal support" (House 1981; Cohen and McKay 1984). Following the thinking of Lazarus and Folkman (1984) on the importance of the subjective meanings of stressors (i.e., stress appraisal) in determining health-related responses to these stimuli, support researchers have focused on how significant others can help in analyzing stressful situations and in redefining them as manageable and capable of mastery. This can be achieved by providing realistic information about the nature of the threat and the individual's capability for dealing with it. An important ingredient in this process of appraisal support is the status of the communicator as a "role model" who has mastered the stressor that is being confronted. In reviewing the major approaches to supportive interventions with mastectomy patients, Gottlieb (1983) accounts for some negative effects of one controlled study (Bloom, Ross, and Burnell 1978) by noting the fear-arousing potential of interventions that provide an overwhelming amount of information or disrupt coping styles based on denial. He notes that interventions that alert patients to the challenges that lie ahead might require a prior patient education component that builds patients' sense of control over their health. The next section provides further discussion of these intervention issues.

In sum, it should be emphasized that these are medically as well as socially significant experiences, since research consistently shows a relationship between the quality of interpersonal relationships and aspects of physical and social adjustment to disease (Wortman and Dunkel-Schetter 1979). Also, from a research perspective, because coping with serious illness usually involves this crisis in giving and receiving social support, it is an important empirical focus for investigating the dynamics of support. We have seen that severe illness generates needs for different types of support. This observation is in keeping with our understanding of the stress process, namely, that stressors generate a set of demands that shape coping efforts. For example, Cohen and Lazarus (1979) have noted six types of threats that illnesses impose: threats to life itself, threats to bodily integrity, threats to self-concept and future plans, threats to emotional equilibrium, threats to engaging in usual roles, and threats associated with adjustment to a new physical and social environment. Clearly, the nature of the demands imposed and the appropriate means for meeting them is variable. Researchers are increasingly attentive to these demands/resources linkages and have introduced greater specificity in models and measurement of these variables (Wheaton 1983; Cohen and McKay 1984; Thoits 1982; Gore 1981). Through study of the stresses and social situations that define a particular illness or stage in illness, we come closer to meeting the fundamental goal of research on social support in health care: to understand what provisions will be supportive to which populations and personality types under what circumstances. This research should be guided by frameworks such as the Cohen and Lazarus (1979) and Kristeller and Rodin (1984) formulations, and with attention to the subjective experiences of both the supporter and the supported.

SOCIAL SUPPORTS AND BEHAVIORAL CHANGE

Over the past ten years researchers have begun to consider how social networks help individuals to reduce risks, maintain medical and behavioral regimens, and recover from serious illness in the general absence of intensive medical supervision and in the course of daily life. In Figure 1 this phase of health activity is depicted as continuing from prior medical identification, diagnosis, and treatment, although, as discussed earlier, we recognize that prevention takes place at several points in the health care process.

In this section, I will focus on the role of social support and networks in what has been termed "self-care" and briefly consider the linkages between models of social support and the more individualistic and cognitive models of coping that have been prominent in this arena of research.

Early research on patterns of assistance during recovery from myocardial infarction (Croog, Lipson, and Levine 1972; Finlayson 1976) identified configurations of help and the role of premorbid social integration as a source of assistance and support in the later period of recovery. This research set the stage for later conceptualizations and intervention studies of how families and peers can promote adherence to medical and behavioral regimens, which is an important behavioral aspect of the recovery concept.

Levy (1983) has identified four rationale for studying social support in relation to maintaining these regimens:

1. Many health behaviors occur in the family context and are directly influenced by the behaviors of others. For example, eating behaviors are largely determined by the person who buys the food.

2. Health beliefs and motives are transmitted through socialization and modeling the behavior of others.

3. Family and friends can reinforce healthful behaviors as well as serve as resources in the development of emotional coping and self-control. (See Thoits 1984, as discussed earlier, on support as a coping resource.)

4. Social support can reduce or change the significance of environmental obstacles, thus indirectly bolstering motivation to maintain regimens through reducing adversity.

The major methodological weakness in experimental research on social support, as in all research on psychosocial interventions to improve adherence and health status, is that the content of such interventions usually includes a wide range of activities and communications. These behaviors occur to varying degrees in sessions with individuals and groups, and these variations in supportive stimuli are seldom documented (Mumford 1982). As a result, although most evaluations of psychosocial interventions to improve adherence and health status show positive effects, it is difficult to determine the specific support manipulation responsible for degrees of beneficial change associated with the social support treatments. Thus, we see in field experiments much of the same difficulty as in survey studies of support: The inclusive, often global approach to support measurement or intervention produces reasonable support effects, but the processes that account for these effects are difficult to reconstruct.

Beyond problems of design and measurement, it is important to consider the various means of social support manipulation that are the basis for intervention studies. Levy (1983) considers four such general strategies and illustrative studies. First, through home visits, health professionals or trained community members monitor some aspect of health or behavior, review the prescribed regimen, or take a more active role in educating the patient

and a single significant other. These steps represent a series of interventions of varying intensity, and may provide a mixture of education and support. For example, in a program of hypertension control, Green et al. (1979) examined the independent and combined effects of regimen review, patient participation in a support group, and education of a significant other. According to Levy (1983, p. 332), the communications with the significant others "were to identify ways patients could be assisted and reinforced in self care, to help the significant others to understand the needs for continuous adherence, and to gain a commitment from the significant other to help the patient remember to take medications and keep appointments." Largest improvements in postintervention blood pressure control were evidenced in the group receiving all three interventions, and any combination of interventions showed significant differences from the controls.

A different strategy involves training peer or family social support partners. In a major study of hypertension control interventions, Caplan et al. (1976) manipulated two support conditions: (1) meetings with a nurse who provided education, encouragement, and support for emotions; and (2) these same meetings combined with the continuous support of a partner who also attended the nurse-patient sessions. Although it was a well-designed study, Caplan reported almost 50 percent subject attrition and found no significant reductions in blood pressure associated with the intervention.

A third support intervention strategy involves what Levy (1983) calls "structured reinforcement or contracting." In experiments of this nature (*cf.* Tharp and Wetzel 1969), partners may provide monetary reinforcement for behavior change, or team members in a program of weight reduction may lose money contingent on the weight loss of the others. Levy notes that the obvious benefit of experiments of this nature is that the nature of the experimental manipulation is clear. Unfortunately, while such experiments capitalize on the presence of significant others, they define a very narrow role for the supporter.

A final intervention type involves peer support in a group setting. Here, it is important to distinguish between professionally supervised group therapy and peer-organized and patient-operated groups. In many support interventions, especially those devoted to group support for cancer patients (Cain et al. 1986; Spiegel, Bloom and Yalom, 1981) the leader is a health care practitioner. In the alternative mutual help model, the basis of membership and leadership is a shared medical condition or at-risk situation. Peer support is the basis for Alcoholics Anonymous and for various self-help weight loss groups and smoking reduction programs.

In the mental health field, the promise of informal support systems and mutual aid has been more widely discussed as a vehicle for primary prevention of the potentially adverse mental health consequences of life crises. According to Caplan (1986, p. 238–239), stressful events, so-called life crises, are "turning points of lasting significance for mental health" that present a period of danger as well as one of opportunity. The period of danger emphasizes the importance of intervening close in time to the crisis and adopting a short-term time framework. The period of opportunity "links the chance for improved mental health with the quality of the individual's immediate coping and problem-solving reactions" (Caplan 1986, p. 238). Caplan's models of emotional inoculation and preventive intervention focus on how social support techniques can encourage the types of cognitive activities that are the basis for psychological models of stress inoculation (Meichenbaum 1983) and specifically what Janis and Mann (1977) have called "vigilant coping." Although Caplan defines a role for professionals in the crisis situation, a key function is to convene individual supporters and groups or networks of supporters into a helping system. "Such help should include the essential elements for bolstering adaptive efforts (with particular reference to current level of competence) and overcoming the negative effects of stress-induced emotional arousal, cognitive erosion, and possible faltering of will to master their predicament in a reality-based way" (Caplan 1986, p. 247).

In planning interventions such as these, Gottlieb (1984) has provided insight into the functions of peer group support, a mutual help model for addressing problems that entail feelings of "undesired uniqueness." As I discussed earlier, this sense of separateness is a major defining feature in the psychology of serious illness. Paralleling the descriptive studies of cancer patients noted above, Gottlieb has identified the three coping challenges that are faced by adolescents whose parents have recently divorced or separated. The first and foremost problem is the catastrophic sense of loss and anxiety about abandonment. The second is the need to come to terms with the meaning of this experience for one's own identity and self-concept. And the third challenge concerns maintaining interactions with parents and friends. Keeping in mind these coping issues, Gottlieb effectively argues that precedence be given to what Weiss (1974) has called the "loneliness of social isolation" over the "loneliness of emotional isolation." This strategy, which contradicts the approach historically taken by the Big Brothers and Big Sisters organizations, is, according to Gottlieb, more "concerned with compensating for the loss or depletion of their peer network and fostering a sense of reliable alliance with those who were undergoing the same family crisis" (p. 424). Thus, peer support can meet the three needs identified above through the following means:

By first recognizing that other children are experiencing the same emotional turmoil, they come to see it as a natural by-product of the situation to which they have been exposed rather than as a reflection of their own emotional instability. . . . The group experience also prevents the participants from blaming themselves for being unable to effect certain changes in their family situations. . . . The support group addresses the third demand facing these children—the management of their ongoing network relationships—by directly examining ways of dealing more effectively with difficult social situations. (Gottlieb 1984, p. 424–425)

Of course, the components of intervention programs that mobilize peer support also provide the opportunity for members to find a single supportive companion. For example, in the "widow-to-widow" mutual help model (Silverman 1969; Vachon Lyall et al. 1980), each potential new member is herself contacted by another more experienced widow, and these dyadic relationships are maintained as important sources of support and resources as the small group meetings continue through time. We see here, as in the demonstrations noted earlier, that there can be more than one structure through which support is received, and there can be many different types of support available.

A final issue concerning the function social supports and social networks in prevention and maintaining long-term behavioral change is the relationship between these variables and the individual motivational, attitudinal, and decisional factors that are the basis for most social-psychological models of influencing behavior and behavior change. Leventhal (1983, p. 722) has noted that while programs to modify unhealthy behaviors have had short-term success, "none meet the acid test of producing lasting, let alone permanent, change; by three to six months after any intervention program, a substantial majority of those treated, sometimes 80%, will return to baseline values for the treated behaviors." One prominent explanation for the failure of such programs is that the unchanged social environment continues to provoke earlier habits. Psychological strategies must in turn be developed for dealing with these impediments. For example, in Janis's model of "vigilant coping," individuals must also be trained to resist the back-

sliding that results from the undermining behavior of significant others. Thus, purely psychological models of change and self-regulation under stressful circumstances can only go so far. They have been most successful in guiding interventions to improve surgical outcomes (Langer, Janis, and Wolfer 1975; Wilson 1981) because of the highly controlled nature of presurgical and postsurgical environments and the fact that only short-term health correlates have been assessed. For goals of this nature the social backdrop is not that critical.

However, since most interventions occur in the natural social environment, the role of significant others in undermining health and behavioral regimens is a critical empirical issue, one that has received some attention in general discussions of stress-buffering processes (Rook 1984; Fiore, Becker, and Coppel 1983; Eckenrode and Gore 1981). Earlier I referred to the work of Wortman and Lehman (1984) on support attempts that fail, a problem shared by professionals and friends and relatives who lack information or concern with the patient's own illness representations (Leventhal 1983). Understanding other types of undermining behavior should call attention to the special significance of social relationships among children and adolescents, two much-neglected populations in social support research. The concept of peer pressure, for example, is pivotal in most discussions of adolescent initiation of smoking, drug use, and sexual activity. These behaviors can be seen as resulting from social influence processes, which, in turn, raises questions about network structure and norms that must be addressed if these pressures are to be counteracted, neutralized, or used for health-promoting goals. According to Evans, Smith, and Raines (1984, p. 306), peer pressure to smoke must be a major target of stress inoculations since "given the strength and frequency of specific social influences to smoke experienced by adolescents, only those teenagers who are psychologically predisposed to a strong antismoking bias will be able to successfully maintain their resistance to these influences to smoke." In their model of intervention, students are familiarized with the major social influences (adult nagging, modeling, peer pressure, and cigarette advertising) of their behavior and taught how they operate. In addition, they are taught strategies for coping with this pressure. Combined with cognitive interventions that also bolster their intentions not to smoke, the hope is that students will be able to resist pressures to initiate smoking.

In sum, with the increasing emphasis on prevention, and since the major health risks for youth are associated with their own behavior in the context of social relationships, we can expect to see more applications of social support theory to health and health care problems of school-aged groups.

POLICY RELEVANCE AND CONCLUSIONS

In introducing the study of social supports in health care I suggested that individual-centered models of health and health care address limitations in strictly biomedical approaches to achieving health care goals. As Levine (1987) has noted in his review of early attempts to disseminate medical sociological knowledge of this nature, much effort was directed toward convincing physicians that our concepts and methods would facilitate their understanding of patients' motivations and behavior and thus contribute to the practice of good medicine. These "sociological overtures" were greeted with some acceptance and some skepticism.

In a brief period of time the contributions of the behavioral sciences to medicine have been more seriously sought, as evidenced in such important documents as President of Harvard University Derek Bok's 1983 report to the Harvard Trustees on the crisis in medical education (Bok 1984) and the more recent Institute of

Medicine report *Confronting AIDS* (National Academy of the Sciences 1987). This shift in the perception of valued medical sciences tools is described by Levine as the emergence of a "quality of life" criterion in health care, one which Tarlov (1983) sees as reflecting a new era of medical objectives.

The central objective in the coming era will be the maintenance or improvement of individual patient functioning in the patient's normal environment while he or she performs usual activities. The emphasis on patient functioning is partly founded on probing inquiries that ask whether the high cost of health care is yielding a proportional benefit in health. Public skepticism of the highly technical nature of medical practice and the emotional distance that has grown between the patient and the doctor as the technology has become more powerful may also contribute to a new focus on functional objectives. . . . Patients' perceptions of their health status and of their mental health bear directly on their functioning. Satisfaction with health services and reasonable expenditures for the services are also of interest. (Tarlov 1983, p. 1240)

Turning now to the specific roles of social support and social networks in policies to attain the cost and quality objectives of this new era, I return to the three arenas of research previously considered and identify some policy objectives and research needs that are informed by these research frameworks.

Coinciding with the first panel of illness behavior variables in Figure 1 and the discussion of the use and nonuse of health services, a first policy issue is the financing of appropriate forms of long-term care for the elderly. Within this general goal are efforts to contain public expenditures for nursing home care. The point of departure for considering the role of social support in long-term care is the fact that most long-term care services received by the elderly are already provided informally by family and friends. According to Lave (1985, p. 8), in an excellent review of policy options in containing the cost of long-term care, "only 5% percent of the elderly (those sixty five and older) are institutionalized, and national samples of the functionally disabled residing in the community indicate that 72% of them rely exclusively on family and friends for the long-term care assistance they need." Yet, despite this overwhelming affirmation of network sources of support in the care of the elderly, total expenditures for long term care services in 1980 were $32.3 billion, $20 billion of which was spent on nursing home care.

According to Lave, three types of policies have been proposed to encourage families to keep impaired elders at home: (1) providing direct services to the elderly in their homes, thus giving care givers instrumental support in the form of physical and emotional respite toward increasing their motivation to continue caring for their elderly family member; (2) providing cash grants to family providers; and (3) providing tax credits or deductions. Interestingly, all these means of providing aid to the supporters of the elderly are unlikely to reduce costs significantly, largely because of our current inability to target the support to those families most likely consider institutionalization. Thus, although provision of service support for care givers would seem to be an important quality-of-care component in long-term care policy, according to Lave, the lack of evidence of significant savings will slow activity on this front. Denying support to the supporters, however, may ultimately prove to be shortsighted. Many of these providers are the siblings and elder children of the very old, and the effects of unrelenting care giving on their health status may well be an unmeasured facet of the cost issue.

Fostering long-term care in the community, whether for the elderly or psychologically impaired, exemplifies the quality-of-life thrust of our current medical objectives to achieve "improved patient functioning per unit cost of services" (Tarlov 1983, p. 1240). Can our understanding of AIDS, a fundamentally different health problem, be similarly informed by attention to social supports and this quality-of-life thrust? This chapter is concerned with factors that affect the course of illness as well as with behaviors and distress in the face of risk. Thus, important problems in the study of AIDS include, but are not limited to (cf. Kaplan et al. 1987), the following: seeking and finding appropriate medical care, maintaining and mobilizing effective social support, and continuing to function in one's social roles. In part, the social support issues for an effective clinical and social response to AIDS parallel those for other life-threatening diseases, as we discussed in the case of cancer and heart disease. This is currently reflected in the proliferation of research on care-giver stress. In addition, since prevention at this time is entirely contingent upon behavioral change, all of these issues reflect the systemic goal of finding cost-effective means to improve patient and pre-patient functioning in community settings.

So, while there is no doubt that the challenge of AIDS to biomedicine is fundamentally traditional—to prevent death from infectious disease—our models of multiple etiology, emphasis on monitoring and altering the course of illness, and attention to the role of behavior in prevention, all place our responses to AIDS within the current era of medical objectives as described by Tarlov and Levine.

One critical distinction between AIDS and other illnesses lies in the threatened loss of personal and legal freedom associated with some public health measures, such as quarantine and involuntary screening, that have been discussed as potential means to control the spread of the infection. In recent reports (Institute of Medicine, National Academy of the Sciences 1986; Gostin and Curran 1987) these strategies are seen as having more dangers than benefits, and experts are instead calling for behavioral research to understand how interventions at the level of the social networks of at-risk populations can aid in prevention efforts. Such research might focus on social influence processes affecting the perception of danger, the decision to be screened for presence of the virus, exposure to educational campaigns, attitudes about medical care and health maintenance, and change of at-risk sexual practices. In respect to scientific and programmatic work of this nature, the problem of modifying attitudes and behaviors around AIDS has much in common with other major public health campaigns, such as the prevention of teenage pregnancy and teen initiation of smoking and drug use.

As noted earlier, research on the role of the support system in health and illness behaviors has not been well connected to more thoroughly developed and researched models of individual behavior such as the Health Belief Model. Perhaps the major research challenge of the immediate future—that is highlighted by the AIDS crisis but is also apparent from study of many other behavioral approaches to prevention—will be to integrate the concepts and models that focus on the interpersonal environment (and social structure) with those that deal with the individual's attitudes, values, and actions. For example, in arguing for more careful attention to theory in formulating interventions, Leventhal (1985, p. 558) has noted that most programs to alter health beliefs have rather narrowly focused on fear-arousing communications, although there is "NO necessary conceptual relationship between health belief variables and fear messages anymore than there is an immediate and logical connection between health belief variables" and many other factors. In sum, although many problems in behavioral medicine can be dealt with at the individual level in clinical settings, most in fact call attention to variables at sociological, social psychological, and psychological levels of analysis, as well as those at the biochemical level. As Leventhal notes, most problems require measures and designs that integrate these various levels.

I will now consider the health policy objectives that require modifications in the practice style of health care providers, mainly physicians, as well as changes in routine practices such as hospital discharge planning. Earlier I discussed problems in patient-practitioner communication that affect both patient satisfaction and compliance with medical regimens, two factors likely to be highly significant in mediating the relationship between quality of the patient-practitioner relationship and health status outcomes. This topic has been the subject of study for some time due to its obvious and multifaceted clinical importance, and because practitioner behavior can be a key area for intervention. In addition, these medical encounters and relationships are an empirically accessible reflection of stratification in health institutions and the larger society.

Today, with the shift toward a competitive model of achieving cost-containment goals, within a context of physician surplus, there are additional pressures on physicians to develop practice styles that promote patient participation so that ultimately patients can take an active role in managing their own health. Tarlov (1983) has argued that in the future the dominant pattern of physician employment will entail work within corporate structures that derive their income from prepaid capitation contracts. Since the mechanism for cost containment will be restraint through prepayment, along with increased out-of-pocket expenses, the incentives for both physicians and patients will be toward self-management. Moreover, Light (1986) has noted that physicians will increasingly be rewarded and retained on the basis of their ability to promote self-care and optimal functioning without underserving the client population. Since nurse midwives and nurse practitioners are less costly providers and already practice a more holistic style of health care, there will be further competition among providers, especially between established physicians and younger professionals who can demonstrate reduced costs through greater patient participation and a health-promoting practice style.

Although discussions of reform in medical education understandably emphasize improving clinical practice through greater attention to the influence of psychological and social factors in health and illness, it is less explicitly recognized that the settings in which services will be delivered will also depart from the traditional. This change is nicely reflected in the current concern with the adequacy of discharge planning for Medicare patients (Lewin, 1986). The Prospective Payment System now in place emphasizes scrutiny of the hospital sector only and encourages narrow definitions of essential procedures and a bias in favor of early discharge. In the past, when hospitals were viewed as major community resources, additional hospital days provided the time and resources to tend to extramedical factors, to promote convalescence, and assess patient resources and social supports. It may be that these assessments are no worse now than they were then, but that the tendency to discharge "sicker and quicker" has exacerbated the problems associated with the transition to nonacute care. According to Dans, Weiner, and Otter (1985, p. 1135), the major task facing us now is to reconsider the role of the hospital in the community:

It would seem advisable to step back a bit instead of aggressively applying various criteria for appropriateness of admissions and lengths of stay (criteria that have had only limited validation) in an effort to squeeze out every last nonacute day from each hospitalization. One reason is that as the proportion of a hospital stay becomes more acute there is greater likelihood of an elevated "SAG index"—i.e., a higher proportion of hospital days filled with high anxiety and low satisfaction for the patient, the physician and other providers of care. It is not clear that tomorrow's hospitals ought to be simply revolving doors for the performance of major procedures and the handling of the acute phase of serious illnesses.

Interestingly, the reality of reduced hospital stays raises questions about the appropriateness of a continued social science research emphasis on patient-practitioner communication and supportive interventions that typically take place in the hospital setting, rather than in the community. One facet of this emphasis on fostering patient functioning in daily living is the need for providers to be better informed about lay helping resources in the community and to play a more active role in helping patients make the transition to the community through linking them upon discharge to available mutual help groups. Although this is a formidable task, it is of the same order of magnitude called for in other considerations of medical education reform. For example, in presenting his agenda for changes in the Harvard Medical School, President Bok (1984, p. 11) spoke of the rapid growth of scientific knowledge that has placed heavy demands on physicians, who are faced with an expanded range of alternative diagnoses and a growing quantity of data about methods of treatment. Bok argues that physicians must begin to work with computer programs as aids in decision making and to discover methods that both improve the quality of care and are cost-effective.

This line of thinking can be extended into the realm of nontraditional care as well. For example, recognizing the mental health repercussions of physical illness, Gottlieb (1983, p. 91) has argued that providers need to be informed about the availability of self-help groups for patients with varying illnesses and disabilities in much the same manner that pharmaceutical representatives make their rounds of physician offices, but in this case to provide "explicit information about appropriate candidates for their [self help] groups, the groups' formats and helping processes, their links to professional advisers, and evidence of their benefits." Just as the information revolution will require computer support for decision making in diagnosis and treatment, proper use of community resources in prevention and aftercare will require the same approach to the vastness of the available information. Similarly, with the growing emphasis on home health care for both high- and low-technology therapies (Koren 1986), providing the means for physicians to access the information about the enormous variety and complexity of services and organizations that are available at the community level may be the only means of reversing the current lack of involvement of physicians in long-term, community-based care.

In conclusion, the emphasis on the role of social networks and social supports in health care has grown in response to new health challenges in prevention, treatment, and rehabilitation. In the earlier portions of this review I discussed three types of research that should yield important health care applications. In closing, these should be reiterated. A first priority is to study psychosocial responses to illness and the role of supports in treatment to discover the significant variables of the illness, the person, and the social context that form the basis for differentiated treatment interventions. This research goal is a significant one for health care, as well as for researchers interested in stress-buffering processes, because both practice and theory ultimately depend upon understanding the demands or stresses of illness, the coping resources required to meet these demands, and the role of social networks in providing these resources. A second research goal concerns integrating the various levels of analysis: biochemical, psychological, social psychological, and sociological. Considering just the social sciences component of this task, we have seen that psychological formulations of individual coping tend to exclude, to their detriment, the issues of social integration and help giving and receiving, as evidenced in the accumulating literature on the significance of the fit between patient's and family's coping styles. Finally, there is the problem of moving outside the clinical setting and creating the bridges between medical and lay participants in programs aimed at prevention, health maintenance, and rehabilitation.

REFERENCES

Aday, L. A., and R. Anderson. 1974. A Framework for the Study of Access to Medical Care. *Health Services Research* 9:208–220.

Becker, M. H., D. P. Hoefner, S. Kasl, T. J. Kirsch, L. Maiman, and I. Rosenstock. 1977. Selected Psychosocial Models and Correlates of Individual Health Related Behaviors. *Medical Care* 15 (5) (supp.): 27–46.

Becker, M. H., and L. A. Maiman. 1975. Socio-Behavioral Determinants of Compliance with Health and Medical Care Regimens. *Medical Care* 13:10.

———. 1983. Models of Health Related Behavior, in D. Mechanic, ed., *Handbook of Health, Health Care, and the Health Professions*. New York: Free Press, pp. 539–568.

Berkman, L. D., and S. L. Syme. 1979. Social Networks, Host Resistance and Mortality: A Nine Year Follow-Up of Alameda County Residents. *American Journal of Epidemiology* 109 (2):186–204.

Billings, A. G., and R. H. Moss. 1985. Psychosocial Stressors, Coping, and Depression, in E. E. Beckham and W. R. Leber, eds., *Handbook of Depression*. Homewood Ill: Dorsey Press, pp. 940–974.

Bloom, J. R., R. D. Ross, and G. Burnell. 1978. The Effect of Social Support in Patient Adjustment after Breast Surgery, *Patient Counseling and Health Education* 1:50–60.

Bok, D. 1984. *President's Report*. Cambridge, Mass.: Harvard University.

Cain, E., E. I. Kohorn, D. Quinlan, K. Latimer, and P. Schwartz. 1986. Psychosocial Benefits of a Cancer Support Group. *Cancer* 57 (1):183–189.

Caplan, Gerald. 1986. Recent Developments in Crisis Intervention and in the Promotion of Support Services, in M. Kessler and S. Goldston, eds., *A Decade of Progress in Primary Prevention*. Hanover, N.H.: University Press of New England. pp. 235–260.

Caplan, R. D., R. V. Harrison, R. V. Wellins, and J. R. French. 1976. *Social Support and Patient Adherence: Experimental and Survey Findings*. Ann Arbor, Mich.: Institute for Social Research.

Chrisman, N., and A. Kleinman. 1983. Popular Health Care, Social Networks, and Cultural Meanings: The Orientation of Medical Anthropology, in D. Mechanic, ed., *Handbook of Health, Health Care, and the Health Professions.* New York: Free Press, pp. 569–590.

Clymer, R., A. Baum, and D. Krantz. 1984. Preferences for Self-Care and Involvement in Health Care, in A. Baum, J. E. Singer, and S. E. Taylor, eds., *Handbook of Psychology and Health*, vol. 4. Hillsdale, N.J.: Erlbaum, pp. 149–166.

Coates, D., and C. B. Wortman. 1980. Control, Social Interaction and Depression Maintenance, in A. Baum, J. Singer, and Y. Epstein, eds., *Advances in Environmental Psychology,* vol. 2. Hillsdale, N.J.: Erlbaum.

Cohen, F., and R. F. Lazarus. 1979. Coping with the Stresses of Illness, in G. C. Stone, F. Cohen, and N. E. Adler, eds., *Health Psychology—A Handbook.* San Francisco: Jossey-Bass.

Cohen, S., and G. McKay. 1984. Social Support, Stress, and the Buffering Hypothesis: A Theoretical Analysis, in A. Baum, J. E. Singer, and S. E. Taylor, eds., *Handbook of Psychology and Health*, vol. 4. Hillsdale, N.J.: Erlbaum, pp. 253–267.

Cohen, S., R. Mermelstein, T. Kamarch, and H. Hoberman. 1984. Measuring the Functional Components of Social Support, in I. G. Sarason and B. R. Sarason, eds., *Social Support and Health.* The Hague: Martinus-Nijhoff.

Colletti, G., and K. D. Brownell. 1983. The Physical and Emotional Benefits of Social Support: Applications to Obesity, Smoking, and Alcoholism, in M. Hersen, R. M. Eisler, and P. M. Miller, eds., *Progress in Behavior Modification.* New York: Academic Press.

Comaroff, J., and P. Maguire. 1981. Ambiguity and the Search for Meaning: Childhood Leukemia in the Modern Clinical Context. *Social Science and Medicine* 15B (2):115–123.

Cousins, N. 1979. *Anatomy of an Illness as Perceived by the Patient: Reflections on Healing and Regeneration.* New York: Norton.

Coyne, J. C. 1976. Depression and the Response of Others. *Journal of Abnormal Psychology* 85:186–193.

Croog, S., A. Lipson, and S. Levine. 1972. Help Patterns in Severe Illness: The Role of Kin Network, Non-Family Resources, and Institutions. *Journal of Marriage and the Family* February: 32–40.

Dans, P. E., J. Weiner, and S. Otter. 1985. Peer Review Organizations: Promises and Potential Pitfalls. *New England Journal of Medicine* 313 (8):1131–1137.

DiMatteo, M., and R. Hays. 1981. Social Support and Serious Illness, in B. Gottlieb, ed., *Social Networks and Social Support.* Beverly Hills: Sage Publications, pp. 117–148.

DiMatteo, M. R., and D. Nicola. 1982. Practitioners, Patients, and Compliance with Medical Regimens: A Social Psychological Perspective, in A. Baum, J. E. Singer, and S. E. Taylor, eds., *Handbook of Psychology and Health*, vol. 4. Hillsdale, N.J.: Erlbaum, pp. 55–84.

Eckenrode, J., and S. Gore. 1981. Stressful Events and Social Supports: The Significance of Context, in B. H. Gottlieb, ed., *Social Networks and Social Supports.* Beverly Hills: Sage Publications, pp. 43–68.

Engel, G. 1977. The Need for a New Medical Model: A Challenge for Biomedicine. *Science* 196:129–136.

Evans, R., C. Smith, and B. Rainer. 1984. Deterring Cigarette Smoking in Adolescents: A Psychosocial-Behavioral Analysis of an Intervention Strategy, in A. Baum, S. Taylor, and J. Singer, eds., *Handbook of Psychology and Health.* Hillsdale, N.J.: Erlbaum, pp. 301–318.

Finlayson, A. 1976. Social Networks as Coping Resources: Lay Help and Consultation Patterns Used by Women in Husband's Post-Infarction Career. *Social Science and Medicine* 10:99–103.

Fiore, J., J. Becker, and D. B. Coppel. 1983. Social Network Interactions: A Buffer or a Stress. *American Journal of Community Psychology* 11 (4):423–439.

Friedson, E. 1960. Client Control and Medical Practice. *American Journal of Sociology* 65:374–382.

Gillick, M. 1985. Common Sense Models of Health and Disease. *New England Journal of Medicine* 313 (11):700–703.

Goffman, E. 1981. The Moral Career of the Mental Patient: Prepatient Phase, in G. Grusky and M. Pollner, eds., *The Sociology of Mental Illness.* New York: Holt, Rinehart, and Winston.

Gore, S. 1981. Stress—Buffering Functions of Social Supports: An Appraisal and Clarification of Research Models, in B. S. Dohrenwend and B. P. Dohrenwend, eds., *Stressful Life Events and Their Contexts.* New York:

Neale Watson Academic Publications. (Rutgers University Press ed., 1984)

———. 1985. Social Support and Styles of Coping with Stress, in S. Cohen and S. L. Syme, eds., *Social Support and Health*. Orlando, Fla.: Academic Press, pp. 263–278.

Gostin, L., and W. Curran. 1987. Legal Control Measures for AIDS: Reporting Requirements, Surveillance, Quarantine, and Regulation of Public Meeting Places. *American Journal of Public Health* 77 (2):214–218.

Gottlieb, B. H. 1983. *Social Support Strategies*. Beverly Hills: Sage Publications.

———. 1984. Theory into Practice: Issues that Surface in Planning Interventions which Mobilize Support, in I. G. Sarason and B. R. Sarason, eds., *Social Support and Health*. The Hague: Martinus-Nijhoff.

Green, L. W., M. D. Levine, J. Wolle, and S. G. Deeds. 1979. Development of Randomized Patient Education Experiments with Urban Poor Hypertensives. *Patient Counseling Health Education* 1:106–111.

Harrison, R. K. 1979. The Doctor-Patient Relationship: The Physician as a Mental Health Resource. Ph. D., Department of Psychology, State University of New York, Buffalo.

Hayes-Bautista, D., and S. Harveston. 1977. Holistic Health Care. *Social Policy* March-April (3):7–13.

Hirsch, B. 1981. Social Networks and the Coping Process: Creating Personal Communities, in B. S. Gottlieb, ed., *Social Networks and Social Supports*. Beverly Hills: Sage Publications.

Horowitz, S., H. Morgenstein, and L. Berkman. 1985. The Impact of Social Stressors and Social Networks on Pediatric Medical Care Use. *Medical Care* 23:946–960.

House, J. S. 1981. *Work, Stress, and Social Support*. Reading, Mass.: Addison-Wesley.

Institute of Medicine, National Academy of the Sciences. 1986. *Confronting Aids*. Direction for Public Health, Health Care and Research. Washington, D.C.: National Academy Press.

Jacobson, D. 1986. Types and Timing of Social Support. *Journal of Health and Social Behavior* 27:250–264.

Janis, I., and L. Mann. 1977. *Decision-Making: A Psychological Analysis of Conflict, Choice, and Commitment*. New York: Free Press.

Kaplan, H., R. J. Johnson, C. Bailely, and W. Simon. 1987. The Sociological Study of Aids: A Critical Review of the Literature and Suggested Research Agenda. *Journal of Health and Social Behavior* 28:140–157.

Kasl, S. 1985. A Discussion of the Role of Psychiatric Epidemiology. *Medical Care* 23 (5):598–606.

———. 1986. The Detection and Modification of Psychosocial and Behavioral Risk Factors, in L. Aiken and D. Mechanic, eds., *Applications of Social Science to Clinical Medicine and Health Policy*. New Brunswick, N.J.: Rutgers University Press, pp. 359–391.

Kessler, R., and J. D. McLeod. 1984. Sex Differences in Vulnerability to Undesirable Life Events. *American Sociological Review* 49:620–631.

Kessler, R., J. D. McLeod, and T. Wethington. 1984. The Costs of Caring, in I. G. Sarason and B. R. Sarason, eds., *Social Supports Theory, Research, and Applications*. The Hague: Martinus Nijhoff, pp. 491–505.

Koren, M. J. 1986. Home Care—Who Cares? *New England Journal of Medicine* 314 (14): 917–920.

Kristeller, J., and J. Rodin. 1984. A Three-Stage Model of Treatment Continuity: Compliance, Adherence, and Maintenance, in A. Baum, J. E. Singer, and S. E. Taylor, eds., *Handbook of Psychology and Health*, vol. 4. Hillsdale, N.J.: Erlbaum, pp. 85–112.

Langer, Ellen J., I. L. Janis, and J. A. Wolfer. 1975. Reduction of Psychological Stress in Surgical Patients. *Journal of Experimental Social Psychology* 11:155–165.

Lave, J. 1985. Cost Containment Policies in Long-Term Care. Inquiry. 22:7–23.

Lazarus, R., and S. Folkman. 1984. *Stress, Appraisal, and Coping*. New York: Springer.

Leventhal, H. 1983. Behavioral Medicine: Psychology in Health Care, in D. Mechanic, ed., *Handbook of Health, Health Care, and the Health Professions*. New York: Free Press.

———. 1985. The Role of Theory in the Study of Adherence to Treatment and Doctor-Patient Interactions. *Medical Care* 23 (5):556–563.

Levine, S. 1987. The Changing Terrains in Medical Sociology: Emergent Concern with Quality of Life. *Journal of Health and Social Behavior* 28:1–6.

Levine, S., and M. A. Kozloff. 1978. The Sick Role: Assessment and Overview. *Annual Review of Sociology* 4:317–344.

Levy, Rona. 1983. Social Support and Compliance: A Selective Review and Critique of Treatment Integrity and Outcome Measurement. *Social Science and Medicine* 17:1329–1338.

Lewin, L. 1986. Fixing the Flaws of Medicare Policy. *Massachusetts Medicine* September–October 1986: 30–35.

Light, D. 1986. Surplus versus Cost Containment: The Changing Context for Health Providers, in L. Aiken and D. Mechanic, eds., *Applications of Social Science to Clinical Medicine and Health Policy.* New Brunswick, N.J.: Rutgers University Press, pp. 519–542.

Lindsey, A. M., J. S. Norbeck, V. L. Carrieri, and E. Perry. 1981. Social Support and Health Outcomes in Postmastectomy Women: A Review. *Cancer Nursing.* October:377–384.

McKinlay, J. B. 1981. Social Network Influences on Morbid Episodes and Career of Help-Seeking, in L. Eisenberg and A. Kleinman, *The Relevance of Social Science for Medicine.* Boston: D. Reidel, pp. 77–107.

———. 1986. A Case for Refocussing Upstream: The Political Economy of Illness, in P. Conrand and R. Kern, eds., *The Sociology of Health and Illness.* New York: St. Martin's Press, pp. 484–498.

Mechanic, D. 1961. The Concept of Illness Behavior. *Journal of Chronic Disease* 15:189–194.

———. 1980. The Experiences and Reporting of Common Physical Complaints." *Journal of Health and Social Behavior* 21:146–155.

———. 1982a. *Symptoms, Illness Behavior, and Help-Seeking,* New York: Neale Watson Academic Publications.

———. 1982b. The Epidemiology of Illness Behavior and its Relationship to Physical and Psychological Distress, in D. Mechanic, ed., *Symptoms, Illness Behavior, and Help-Seeking.* New York: Prodist, pp. 1–24.

———. 1983. The Experience and Expression of Distress: The Study of Illness Behavior and Medical Utilization, in D. Mechanic, ed., *Handbook of Health, Health Care, and the Health Professions.* New York: Free Press, pp. 591–607.

Mechanic, D., and E. H. Volkart. 1960. Illness Behavior and Medical Diagnosis. *Journal of Health and Human Behavior* 1:86–94.

Meichenbaum, D. 1983. *Stress Reduction and Prevention.* New York: Plenum Press.

Mishler, E. 1981. The Social Construction of Illness, in E. G. Mishler, L. Amara Singhgam, S. Hauser, R. Liem, S. Osherson and N. E. Wexler, eds., *Social Contexts of Health, Illness and Patient-Care.* Cambridge: Cambridge University Press, pp. 141–161.

Mumford, E., H. Schlesinger, and G. Glass. 1981. Reducing Medical Costs through Mental Health Treatment, in A. Broskowski, E. Marks, and S. Budman, eds., *Linking Health and Mental Health.* Beverly Hills: Sage Publications, pp. 257–273.

———. 1982. The Effects of Psychological Intervention on Recovery from Surgery and Heart Attacks: An Analysis of the Literature. *American Journal of Public Health* 72 (2):141–151.

O'Connor, P., and G. W. Brown. 1984. Supportive Relationships: Fact or Fancy? *Journal of Social and Personal Relationships* 1:159–175.

Parsons, T., and R. Fox. 1952. Illness, Therapy, and the Modern Urban American Family. *Journal of Social Issues* 8 (4):31–44.

Peters-Golden, H. 1982. Breast Cancer: Varied Perceptions of Social Support in the Illness Experience. *Social Science and Medicine* 16:483–491.

Quint, J. C. 1965. Institutionalized Practice of Information Control. *Psychiatry* 28:119–132.

Rook, K. S. 1984. The Negative Side of Social Interaction: Impact on Psychological Well-Being. *Journal of Personality and Social Psychology* 46:1097–1108.

Rosenstock, I. M. 1975. Patients' Compliance with Health Regimens. *Journal of the American Medical Association* 234:402–403.

Shapiro, E., and N. Roos. 1985. Elderly Nonusers of Health Care Services. *Medical Care* 23 (3):247–257.

Silverman, P. 1969. The Widow to Widow Program: An Experiment in Preventative Intervention. *Mental Hygiene* 53:333–337.

Spiegel, D., J. Bloom, and I. Yalom. 1981. Group Support for Patients with Metastatic Cancer. *Archives of General Psychiatry* 38:527–583.

Starr, P. 1982. *The Social Transformation of American Medicine,* New York: Basic Books.

Stern, M. J. 1978. The Treatment of Post-Myocardial Infarction Depression. *Practical Cardiology* 23:35–46.

Stoeckle, J. D., and A. J. Barsky. 1981. Attributions: Uses of Social Science Knowledge in the "Doctoring" of Primary Care, in L. Eisenberg and A. Kleinman, eds., *The Relevance of Social Science for Medicine.* Boston: D. Reidel, pp. 223–240.

Suchman, E. A. 1965. Social Patterns of Illness and Health Care. *Journal of Health and Social Behavior* 6:2–16.

Tarlov, A. 1983. Shattuck Lecture—The Increasing Supply of Physicians, the Changing Structure of the Health Services System, and the Future Practice of Medicine. *New England Journal of Medicine* 308 (20):1235–1244.

Taylor, R. C. 1986. The Politics of Prevention, in P. Conrad and R. Kein, eds., *The Sociology of Health and Illness.* New York: St. Martin's Press, pp. 471–484.

Tessler, R., and D. Mechanic. 1978. Psychological Distress and Perceived Health Status. *Journal of Health and Social Behavior* 19:254–262.

Tessler, R., D. Mechanic, and M. Dimond. 1976. The Effect of Psychological Distress on Physician Utilization. *Journal of Health and Social Behavior* 17:353–363.

Tharp, R. G., and R. B. Wetzel. 1969. *Behavior Modification in the Natural Environment.* New York: Academic Press.

Thoits, P. 1982. Conceptual Methodological and Theoretical Problems in Studying Social Support as a Buffer against Life Stress. *Journal of Health and Social Behavior* 23:145–159.

———. 1984. Coping, Social Support, and Psychological Outcomes: The Central Role of Emotion, in P. Shaver, ed., *Review of Personality and Social Psychology,* vol. 5. Beverly Hills: Sage Publications, pp. 219–238.

Thomas, S. G. 1978. Breast Cancer: The Psychosocial Issues. *Cancer Nursing* 36:53–60.

Vachon, M. L. S., W. A. L. Lyall, J. Rogers, L. Freedman-Letofsky, and S. J. J. Freeman. 1980. A Controlled Study of Self-Help Intervention for Widows. *American Journal of Psychiatry* 137 (11):1380–1384.

Weiss, R. S. 1974. The Provisions of Social Relationships, in Z. Rubin, ed., *Doing Unto Others.* Englewood Cliffs, N.J.: Prentice-Hall.

Wethington, E., and R. Kessler. 1986. Perceived Support, Received Support, and Adjustment to Stressful Life Events. *Journal of Health and Social Behavior* 27:78–89.

Wheaton, B. 1983. Stress, Personal Coping Resources, and Psychiatric Symptoms: An Investigation of Interactive Models. *Journal of Health and Social Behavior* 24:208–229.

Wilcox, B. 1981. Social Support in Adjusting to Marital Disruption: A Network Analysis, in B. S. Gottlieb, ed., *Social Networks and Social Supports.* Beverly Hills: Sage, pp. 97–115.

Wilson, J. 1981. Behavioral Preparation for Surgery: Benefit or Harm. *Journal of Behavioral Medicine* 4 (1):79–101.

Wortman, C. B. 1984. Social Support and the Cancer Patient. *Cancer* 53 (10): 2339–2359.

Wortman, C. B. and T. Conway. 1985. The Role of Social Support in Adaptation and Recovery from Physical Illness, in S. Cohen and S. L. Syme, eds., *Social Support and Health.* Orlando, Fla.: Academic Press, pp. 281–302.

Wortman, C. B., and C. Dunkel-Schetter. 1979. Interpersonal Relationships and Cancer: A Theoretical Analysis. *Journal of Social Issues* 35 (1):120–155.

Wortman, C., and D. Lehman. 1984. Reactions to Victims of Life Crises: Support That Doesn't Help, in I. G. Sarason and B. R. Sarason, eds., *Social Support: Theory, Research and Application.* The Hague: Martinus Nijhoff.

Zborowski, M. 1952. Cultural Components in Response to Pain. *Journal of Social Issues* 8:16–30.

Zola, I. K. 1973. Pathways to the Doctor—From Person to Patient. *Social Science and Medicine* 7:677–689.

CHAPTER
16

HEALTH CARE IN DEVELOPING COUNTRIES

JACKOB M. NAJMAN

INTRODUCTION

For people living in the developed countries there may be a reluctance to become greatly concerned with the health and health care needs of those living in the developing countries. This reluctance reflects, in part, the current state of the North (developed countries)–South (developing countries) debate. There are however some compelling reasons for broadening our concerns.

First, the developing countries contain the bulk of the world's population, and as the demographic balance continues to shift over the next 20 years, 90 percent of the world population increase will occur in these countries (Haq 1980, p. 272). Second, with improved communication systems and consequent visibility, the international tragedy of fourteen million young children dying each year in these countries will increasingly demand an urgent and positive response. The economic support generated by publicity in Ethiopia and Sudan must not be allowed to distract attention from the many areas in no less urgent need. There are more child deaths per year in Bangladesh than Ethiopia, more in Mexico than Sudan (Grant 1987, p. 7). Third, the increased population in the developing countries means that they will command greater influence as a market for manufactured goods and a source of cheap labor. Developing countries are likely to resent their inferior economic position and, no less than the poor within the developed countries, demand a more equal economic order. Finally, the health of those living in the South provides an excellent example of the intimate association between the social, political, economic, and physical environment and health. Such an example has the capacity to influence the delivery of health care services, particularly to minority groups who experience poor health, in the developed countries.

This chapter begins with an examination

of the health problems that prevail in the developing countries. It then considers a variety of factors that have contributed to the appallingly high level of morbidity and mortality in these countries, including early European contacts, indigenous health practices, and the economic exploitation of these countries by multinational corporations. Next will be presented case studies of three developing countries (Nicaragua, Mexico, and Cuba) and a consideration of the potential for programs and initiatives that might improve the health of persons living in the developing countries. The available data suggest that substantial improvements in health in the developing countries are possible, even when economic development is limited, and that political, social, and environmental changes will be of primary importance in facilitating these improvements.

PATTERNS OF MORBIDITY AND MORTALITY IN DEVELOPING COUNTRIES

Although developing countries vary somewhat in their levels of morbidity, the general pattern is clear. High levels of poverty, illiteracy, and malnutrition produce a pattern of mineral-vitamin, protein, and calorie deficiencies (Hughes and Hunter 1970, p. 447). The dominant immediate causes of disease are acute diarrhea (Keusch and Scrimshaw 1986, p. 276), itself a consequence of a gastric infection; a variety of other infections, including measles, whooping cough, and malaria (Stock 1986, p. 696); and human parasitic infestation. They, in turn, reduce productivity, lead to apathy, and increase the need for food supplies (Hughes and Hunter 1970, p. 447).

These conditions are virtually nonexistent in the developed countries, and they can, in principle, be eliminated in the developing countries. Indeed, as the selected list of countries in Table 1 shows, there are such great differences between the developing countries in their infant mortality rates, under-5 mortality rates, and life ex-

pectancies at birth that major reductions in mortality in those countries with the highest rates could be considered a possibility.

In the countries with the worst health profiles—Afghanistan, Ethiopia, and Chad—about one in four children die before the age of 5, and life expectancies are in the late 30s and mid-40s. In contrast, in China, Sri Lanka, Guyana, Costa Rica, and Cuba, life expectancies approach or exceed 70 years of age, and less than 5 percent of children die before their fifth birthday. To understand why differences of such a magnitude persist, we begin by considering the history of early European contact with the indigenous populations of what is now the developing world.

Of course, data derived from developing countries must be interpreted with caution. Much of this data is of limited accuracy (Cumper 1984). It is not surprising that the countries with the worst health also collect inadequate statistics or, on some occasions, provide what might be deliberately erroneous statistics (Escudero 1980, p. 648). Nevertheless, the statistics in Table 1 provide a reasonable estimate of the situation that prevails in developing countries (Diaz-Briquets 1983, p. xv; Grant 1987, p. 103).

FACTORS CAUSING HIGH MORBIDITY AND MORTALITY

The high morbidity and mortality rates evident in developing countries are attributable to at least three interconnected causes. First, traditional health-related beliefs and practices have not always facilitated an adaptation to changed environmental, social, and political circumstances. Second, the early history of European contact was associated with a variety of unintended (and sometimes intended) assaults upon the health of the native populations. Third, recent activities by multinational corporations have further compromised the health of the indigenous peoples. Each of these points warrants elaboration.

Although it is impossible to obtain reliable data, there is nevertheless good reason

TABLE 1 Mortality Rates in Selected Developing Countries (1985)

	Infant Mortality (per 1,000 live births)	Under Age 5 Mortality (per 1,000 population)	Life Expectancy at Birth
Afghanistan	189	329	38
Ethiopia	152	257	41
Chad	138	232	46
Bangladesh	124	196	49
Sudan	112	187	49
Uganda	108	178	50
Pakistan	115	174	51
Zimbabwe	76	121	57
Guatemala	65	109	61
Nicaragua	69	104	62
Papua New Guinea	68	94	53
Philippines	48	78	63
Mexico	50	73	66
China	36	50	69
Sri Lanka	36	48	69
Guyana	33	41	69
Costa Rica	19	23	73
Cuba	15	19	74
United States	11	13	75

Source: James P. Grant, *The State of the World's Children*, New York: UNICEF, 1987, pp. 90–91.

to believe that native groups were relatively free of many of the conditions that are presently endemic. Thus, malnutrition was less likely to have been a problem when populations were smaller and more isolated and before cash cropping displaced traditional foods and what appeared to have been a well-rounded diet in some instances (Hughes and Hunter 1970, p. 465). Many of the now endemic infections were introduced by Europeans. This is not to imply that an idyllic life-style preceded European colonization, but rather that over a period of time cultural practices emerged that generally facilitated survival for many native groups. Thus, in one instance, the indigenous response of natives to an epidemic of sleeping sickness was to disperse to small groups of low density, so that contact with infective vectors was unlikely, an apparently effective response (Matzke 1979, p. 214).

Of course, many traditional healing practices were unlikely to have been effective. Take, for example, the belief by some groups that disease is a consequence of sorcery or the act of a reproving ancestor (Maddocks 1975, p. 28). In other instances, food taboos have limited food consumption and consequently contributed to poor nutrition (Hughes and Hunter 1970, p. 465).

In sum, indigenous health practices were a response to a pattern of disease generally associated with small, physically isolated, low-density groups. Into this environment came the European colonizers, whose motives were, understandably, self-serving.

Typically, such colonial powers would set up administrative centers in a few large cities. They would build hospitals and provide sophisticated medical services to meet their own medical needs, but they generally ignored the health needs of the indigenous peoples. A key feature of this type of administration was that it was "often organized along racially, geographically and financially discriminatory lines" (Vaughan and Walt 1984, p. 109). For what appear to be largely economic reasons, colonizing powers created infrastructures supporting more extensive communication networks (e.g., roads, trains, boats). This type of development produced important changes with many health consequences.

One consequence of the increased population mobility was the spread of communicable diseases (Maddocks 1975, p. 28; Prothero 1977, p. 259). In South Africa, for example, infections were spread along train routes by persons returning from the First World War (Hogbin 1985, p. 935). To serve these communication and transport routes, towns expanded, frequently becoming crowded, with unsanitary living conditions and many now-predictable social problems (Hughes and Hunter 1970, p. 469). In these cities were brought together people with widely different, sometimes openly conflicting, values and beliefs. Other consequences of the development of an infrastructure to support colonial exploitation included the pollution of water supplies and changes in housing and the physical landscape.

Clearly, development programs may have served to improve the economic circumstances of some, but at apparently a considerable cost. When the colonial powers finally departed, they almost invariably left behind serious health problems and a health service that was concentrated in the few urban centers where the colonial masters had lived. For example, in Kano State, Nigeria, there are 204 doctors for a population of 9.5 million. Most of the population (8.7 million persons) live outside the capital city and are served by thirty doctors; the rest of the medical practitioners are located in or around the capital (Stock 1985, p. 472). In many developing countries there are so few doctors that medical care is simply unobtainable for the bulk of the population.

As colonial powers left to be replaced by indigenous administrations (with varying levels of success), multinational corporations made renewed efforts to exploit the growing consumer market in the developing countries. There are at least three types of products of particular health significance marketed in this context: cigarettes, pharmaceuticals, and infant food formulas.

Developing countries represent a growing market for tobacco products, products that are increasingly subject to controls and restrictions in the developed countries. Cigarette consumption has increased rapidly in the developing countries, with, for example, 200 percent and 400 percent increases in Pakistan and India, respectively, between 1970 and 1980 (Yach 1986, p. 283). Over half the world's tobacco consumption now occurs in developing countries (Jacobson 1983, p. 483), where smoking appears to be more common among the poorest groups (Yach 1986, p. 284). Further, the cigarettes that are sold in these countries have up to twice the tar and nicotine content of their counterparts (with the same brand names) in the developed countries (Yach 1986, p. 285).

Perhaps of even greater concern is the extent to which tobacco, a cash crop, has displaced traditional food growing, thus contributing to the problem of malnutrition in developing countries. Three-quarters of the world's tobacco is grown in the developing countries; India, China, Malawi, Tanzania, Zimbabwe, Kenya, and Nigeria all export tobacco (Yach 1986, p. 281). Tobacco requires wood for curing, thereby leading to deforestation and the consequent destruction of natural resources (Jacobson 1983, p. 483).

Similar commercial motives are manifest when we consider the sale of pharmaceutical products in developing countries. Because most developing countries have relatively few qualified medical practitioners, pharmacies in these countries appear to serve a more central role in health care delivery. Thus, 30 to 50 percent of health care spending in developing countries is on pharmaceutical products, compared to between 5 and 16 percent in the developed countries (Taylor 1986, p. 1142).

A number of specific concerns regarding the sale of pharmaceuticals in the developing countries may be noted. First, many of these products are marketed in a manner likely to lead to their misuse. Products are represented as being effective when they are not, or safe when their dangers are well known. This practice is demonstrably unethical when it involves corporations who make contrary and conflicting claims depending upon the country being targeted for a particular product (Silverman 1976).

Second, there is evidence of the dumping of certain pharmaceutical products in developing countries that have been banned or have had restrictions placed upon their use in the United States. Chloramphenicol, an antibiotic with a high rate of serious and potentially fatal side effects, has been largely withdrawn from the U.S. market but accounts for 11 percent of all antibiotics sold in India. Perhaps most disturbing of all is the observation that Chloramphenicol is sold over-the-counter (as is Thalidomide) to this uninformed and desperately poor population (Greenhalgh 1986, p. 10).

Third, there is widespread corruption in the developing countries; multinational corporations pay substantial bribes to government officials in order to sell their products. Included are bribes to cabinet ministers for approval of unsafe products, to public servants in order to gain higher prices, to health inspectors, to customs officials, and to hospital staff. Sixteen of the top seventeen U.S. pharmaceutical companies (according to sales in 1977) have admitted to bribery and/or corrupt practices (Braithwaite 1984; 1986, p. 19).

This corruption introduces the fourth concern, namely that unnecessary products are sometimes available but necessities may be unobtainable (Ramalingaswami 1986, p. 1100). For example, Aminobrain (composed of ginseng, royal bee jelly, vitamins C and E, and iron) is marketed in the Phillipines to "increase the general intellectual capacities through improved memory and concentration," to enhance "sexual fulfillment," and to "stimulate appetites" (Silverman, Lee, and Lydecker 1982, p. 589). Although almost 50 percent of children in Zaire have intestinal parasites, six of the seven companies operating in this country do not import antiparasitic medications, presumably because it is unprofitable. It has been estimated that 95 percent of the medication budget of Zaire is spent on nonessential drugs (Glucksbert and Singer 1982, p. 385). In Kano State, Nigeria, itinerant medicine salesmen using loudspeakers travel from place to place selling products such as amphetamines, Valium, and injections (Stock 1985).

Ray Elling (1981) has coined the term "comerciogenic malnutrition" to describe situations where the health and nutritional needs of a community are undermined by commercial motives (Elling 1981, p. 30). Perhaps the best known instance of such a process is the promotion of bottle feeding and infant foods to mothers in developing countries (see Campbell 1984 for a discussion of this point). Breast feeding, especially for the first six months or so after birth, protects against infections and provides more complete nourishment than bottle feeding. Indeed, bottle-fed babies are three times as likely to die as breast-fed babies (see Grant 1987, p. 27), and infant foods spoil in the climatic conditions that prevail in developing countries. Yet some corporations have been reluctant to limit their commercial activities despite the health consequences (Elling 1981, p. 31).

In sum, developing countries have presented opportunities for commercial exploitation by multinational corporations. Perhaps it could be argued that these exploitive activities add little to the already high mortality rates in these countries. The indirect effects must, however, also be considered. These include diverting scarce resources away from more effective health care services and the promotion of practices (smoking, depletion of land that could be used to grow essential foods) that are likely to compromise the health of people living in these countries for a considerable time to come.

CASE STUDY 1—NICARAGUA

Nicaragua provides an interesting case study of the nexus between politics and health. Prior to the revolution, the country was ruled by the Somoza family, who owned some 20 percent of the arable land (Donahue 1986, p. 151). Overt oppression by the National Guard and a long history of corruption typified the Samoza administration.

One documented instance of the business practices that prevailed in Nicaragua prior to the revolution provides an indication of the health consequences of the then-existing political arrangements. Pennwalt, a U.S. company, set up its Nicaraguan plant next to Lake Managua in a subsidiary owned 48 percent by private business groups in Nicaragua and 12 percent by the ruling Somoza family (Hassan et al. 1981). An investigation of this plant after the 1979 revolution indicated that 40 tons of mercury had been dumped into Lake Managua, a source of fish for the nearby population. Furthermore, there was evidence of mercury contamination at the plant. Signs warning workers of the dangers of mercury had been left in the desk drawer of the director, and workers had apparently taken mercury home as playthings for their children. Of the 152 workers, 37 percent had central nervous system damage as a result of their exposure to mercury (Hassan et al. 1981, p. 222).

Prior to the revolution, Nicaragua had the highest infant mortality rate in Central America (Donahue 1986, p. 150), though it has been suggested that these statistics may well have understated the real situation, with many deaths remaining unreported (Escudero 1980, p. 648). Certainly there is evidence of widespread malnutrition and perhaps increasing mortality rates in the years preceding the change of government. Health care resources were restricted to

hospitals in the cities, with little being diverted to the health needs of the rural population (Escudero 1980).

The new government manifested an immediate and direct commitment to improving the health of Nicaraguans. Health was perceived as a right, with health care being seen as a service that should be accessible to all (Donahue 1986, p. 151). The new government immediately initiated a series of mass campaigns, using voluntary workers, under the direction of revolutionary committees. In 1979 there was an antipolio/antirabies campaign; in 1981 there were two campaigns to eradicate polio, and programs to improve environmental sanitation and reduce dengue fever and malaria. In order to create an infrastructure that would lead to better rural health in the longer term, literacy workers were trained and then sent to train local workers. Some 224 units were trained to provide oral rehydration therapy, largely in rural areas (Donahue 1986).

To improve the nutrition of people living in this sparsely populated country, supermarkets were nationalized and prices of basic commodities were controlled. Some private production and sale of foods was permitted (Stalker 1986). The health of people living in Nicaragua has, however, been compromised by the continuing war, a decline in GDP over the period 1978–1984, and increasing prices with decreasing real wages (Stalker 1986).

Despite the decline in the economic situation in Nicaragua, there is evidence of a dramatic improvement in health and a decline in mortality. Between 1979 and 1984, infant mortality appears to have fallen by 50 percent. Polio, diphtheria, whooping cough, and measles have been greatly reduced, if not eliminated, as causes of death (Donahue 1986, p. 153).

As Table 2 shows there has been a relatively substantial improvement in Nicaragua in the life expectancy and percent of children surviving to the age of 5 (up from 79 percent in 1960 to 90 percent in 1985), and there is reason to believe that the bulk

TABLE 2 A Comparison of Mortality Rates for Nicaragua, Mexico, and Cuba

	Nicaragua	*Mexico*	*Cuba*
Percent of children surviving to age 5 (1985/1960)	90/79	93/86	98/91
Life expectancy at birth (1985/1960)	62/47	66/57	74/64
GNP per capita (U.S. $, 1984)	860	2040	860*

*Figure for Cuba is from 1976.

Source: James P. Grant, *The State of the World's Children*, New York: UNICEF, 1987, pp. 90–102.

of this increase has occurred recently (Donahue 1986, p. 150; Escudero 1980, p. 651), despite the general poverty that still prevails in the country.

CASE STUDY 2—MEXICO

Mexico is one of the more developed of the developing countries (Horn 1985, p. 485) and one of the richest countries in Latin America (Banta 1985, p. 363). The Mexican economy is perhaps best described as state capitalism supporting both national and international investment. Much of Mexico's land and resources is foreign owned, with the United States as the dominant foreign influence (Cockcroft 1974). Mexico is ruled by an authoritarian elite via a single party state, which permits the accumulation of great wealth and the existence of massive poverty. Mexico appears to manifest the health problems of both the developing and developed countries. The major causes of death are associated with rural poverty and malnutrition—respiratory illness, gastroenteritis, and diarrhea (Horn 1985, p. 485). Poor sanitation and hygiene contribute to these disease patterns.

The health system is a reflection of the inequalities that exist in the society as a whole. The capital has a prestigious cardiac institute (Horn 1985, p. 485), and of 157 hospitals surveyed, 106 were found to have high levels of sophisticated technology available, including cardiac catheterization,

fiberoptic endoscopy, microsurgery, and computed tomography (Banta 1986, p. 363).

Overall, there is no evidence of a shortage of doctors in Mexico. There are more than 80,000 medical students in Mexico, twice the number in the United States. Indeed, Mexico trains Americans, who each year return to practice in the United States. Yet although in Mexico City there is one doctor per 400 population, in rural areas the rate declines to one doctor per 20,000 to 33,000 persons. Further, the doctors practicing in rural areas are young, inexperienced practitioners undertaking short compulsory service. They are typically middle- or upper-class youth, who are unfamiliar with the culture or the needs of the local population they have been sent to serve (Stebbins 1986, p. 139).

By contrast with the resources allocated to hospitals, the training of clinicians, and "gee whiz" technical facilities, few resources are allocated to public health. There is only one school of public health in Mexico. Although medical staff sent to isolated and rural areas are encouraged to attend to local sanitation, hygiene, and public health concerns, they lack support staff and the necessary training and time (Horn 1985; Stebbins 1986).

Table 2 shows that Mexicans have a lower life expectancy and higher child mortality rates than Cubans, yet Mexico is clearly more economically advanced. Further, between 1960 and 1985, life expectancy in Mexico increased by nine years, compared to a fifteen-year increase in Nicaragua and a ten-year increase in Cuba over the same period, the latter increase being remarkable because Cubans already had a substantially longer life expectancy. Mexico appears to demonstrate clearly the health consequences of a political and economic system that permits wide inequalities to exist within a society.

CASE STUDY 3—CUBA

The Cuban case is remarkable for a number of reasons. As Table 2 suggests, mortality rates in Cuba appear to be comparable with those in the developed countries. This observation raises the possibility that despite a country's low GNP and the limited resources that are available, there is no absolute bar to better health and lower mortality rates in the developing countries.

The changing health of Cubans has been documented by Diaz-Briquets (1983). He points out that Cubans have had relatively low mortality rates since the U.S. Army instituted public health programs after the Cuban War of Independence (1895–1898). The Cuban economy was relatively affluent prior to World War II, and there was a very high level of literacy (80 percent) by Latin American standards. Further, there was a high doctor-patient ratio prior to the revolution, with one doctor per 940 persons in 1953 (Diaz-Briquets 1983, p. 48).

Despite some conditions favorable to health in Cuba before the revolution in 1959 (sanitation programs, high literacy, adequate numbers of doctors), there was considerable inequality, with 30 to 60 percent of the population experiencing malnutrition (Benjamin and Collins 1985, p. 327). In addition, health services were concentrated in the urban centers, and rural areas were underserved.

Since the Cuban revolution, the government has initiated a range of health and welfare programs. New roads, irrigation schemes, reforestation programs, literacy programs, improved housing, a better distribution of hospital beds, improved sanitation, and the rationing of food have been directed toward improving the health of Cubans.

Programs have had both a public health and clinical care component. Women have been encouraged to give birth in public hospitals, and this education effort associated with the availability of such facilities has contributed to remarkably low infant mortality rates in Cuba. In 1983 the Cuban infant mortality rate was 16.8 deaths per 1,000 births, a rate considerably lower than the rate of 18.1 deaths per 1000 births for black Americans in 1982 (Benjamin and Collins, 1985, p. 328). While many children still contract infections and diarrhea, rapid and effective treatment means that few die from conditions that are responsible for many deaths in other developing countries.

Thus, the evidence suggests an acceleration of the mortality decline linked to structural changes in Cuban society following the revolution. This continuing decline in mortality has occurred despite a deterioration in Cuba's economic position (an absence of economic growth). This latter problem is a result of the recent difficulty of selling sugar, Cuba's major cash crop (though the USSR has compensated by providing substantial economic assistance).

SOCIOECONOMIC FACTORS INFLUENCING HEALTH IN DEVELOPING COUNTRIES

Contrasting Nicaragua, Mexico, and Cuba provides one approach to understanding the factors associated with health in the developing countries. Such a contrast is, however, inadequate if limited to three countries. The broader issue is whether economic development of itself is the limiting factor to health improvement or if other associated processes are evident. Unfortunately it is difficult to obtain all the relevant data and, as we have noted, the available data are likely to be imprecise.

TABLE 3 Correlation of Life Expectancy and Various
Social Indicators for Ninety-two[a] Selected Countries

	Males	*Females*
Population density	.25[b]	.23[b]
GNP (U.S. $)	.71[c]	.73[c]
K/cal per capita	.77[c]	.80[c]
Adult literacy	.85[c]	.85[c]
Medical team density	.76[c]	.79[c]

[a]Only countries for which complete data were available were included.

[b]$p < .01$

[c]$.01 < p < .001$

Source: World Health Organization, *Sixth Report on the World Health Situation*. Geneva: The Organization, 1980, part 1, pp. 263–267.

Table 3 shows the correlation of life expectancy and various social indicators for ninety-two selected countries (WHO 1980). Those countries for which data were missing on any one of the listed variables were excluded. It is likely that some of the remaining data is based upon estimates and approximations, but this should not provide misleading inferences when we examine aggregate measures of association for ninety-two countries. The data indicate that a country's per capita GNP is strongly correlated with life expectancy, as is average nutritional status and the ratio of health care providers to population. Of course, these figures cannot provide insights into the health impact of the unequal distribution of resources within a developing country. However, perhaps the most interesting finding is that the strongest correlation of all is with the percent of the adult population that is categorized as literate. The association between literacy and life expectancy in developing countries has been reviewed by Cochrane, Leslie, and O'Hara (1982). They suggest that each additional year of schooling is associated with a reduction of nine deaths per 1,000 population of infants and children (p. 247). The main health effect, they note, is with increased female literacy. Ramalingaswami (1986) has described this association between child health and female literacy as "crucial" to health improvements in the developing countries.

Although the explanation of this association remains somewhat speculative, increased female literacy is likely to influence the mother's choice of nutrition, health care, and physical environment. In an important sense a mother's literacy provides a base upon which other programs may be successfully mounted.

PROSPECTS FOR IMPROVED HEALTH IN THE DEVELOPING COUNTRIES

Earlier this century, Great Britain (Powles 1973; McKeown 1976), the United States (McKinlay and McKinlay 1977), and Australia (Gordon 1976) had mortality patterns not unlike those presently found in the developing countries. The rapid decline in mortality in these countries has been the subject of some speculation and is most likely attributable to improvements in sanitation, hygiene, nutrition, economic development, and, only partly, the provision of medical services.

The cases of Nicaragua, Mexico, and Cuba suggest that substantial and rapid improvements in the health and life expectancy of those living in the developing countries are also possible. The revolutions in Nicaragua and Cuba led to a restructuring of the society that resulted in greater equality of access to food, health care, higher literacy rates, and improvements in the physical environment (improved sanitary services). The absence of a similar process of societal change may explain the relatively modest improvement in life expectancy in Mexico.

These observations pose, perhaps, the most fundamental of questions for those interested in the developing countries, namely, Can there be significant improvements in health without such a restructuring of society? Is it likely that better health services could produce significant improvements in health in the absence of political and social changes within the developing countries?

THE IMPACT OF HEALTH SERVICES ON HEALTH

There is general agreement that the increased availability of sophisticated medical services is unlikely to serve the health needs of those living in the developing countries. Indeed, it is generally argued that the necessary location of these services in urban areas is counterproductive (Escudero 1980, p. 653). Thus, while Brazil boasts an average of one doctor and five hospital beds per 1,500 population, about one-third of the population has no regular health services. A study of medical equipment imported into Colombia found that 95 percent was not functioning (cited by Banta 1986, pp. 366–372). The concentration of facilities in Mexico and the consequence of this concentration have already been discussed. There would appear to be little point in advocating more sophisticated medical services as a solution to the health needs of those in the developing countries.

In the late 1970s the World Health Organization advocated a program of comprehensive primary medical care (CPMC). Such a program implies at least a partial restructuring within developing countries, with an emphasis on widespread health education, greater availability of food, improved water and sanitation, and specific maternal, child health, and immunization programs (Unger and Killingsworth 1986, p. 1002).

Services of the scale and type envisaged under the heading of CPMC would require an infrastructure that presently does not exist in many of the developing countries. If health education is to become widely available, then this presupposes that the population is literate and that there are roads and methods of transportation to connect remote areas with those who provide the services. There is also a presumption that a sufficient number of health and related workers will become available to provide the relevant services.

Because most of the developing countries have been unable or unwilling to provide the services associated with CPMC and because some more limited efforts have apparently been successful, the doctrine of selective primary medical care (SPMC) has more recently been advocated by WHO (see Unger and Killingsworth 1986 for a review of the debate between CPMC and SPMC). UNICEF in a recent report argues for the SPMC approach (Grant 1987), pointing out that about five million children a year die as a result of diarrheal disease, leading to dehydration. UNICEF suggests that 70 percent of these deaths could be prevented by the more extensive use of oral rehydration therapy. A similar case is argued on the need for widespread immunization programs, and programs encouraging breast feeding and supplementary feeding (Grant 1987, p. 27).

Those advocating SPMC argue that it is immoral and unnecessary to wait for an improvement in the economic circumstances in the developing countries. They suggest that some basic, specifically targeted programs could be immediately initiated, and these inexpensive and limited programs have the capacity to save many lives. Those opposing SPMC deny these claims and argue that the anticipated benefits are temporary and more hypothetical than real. They point out that while oral rehydration therapy may prevent child deaths, such therapy does nothing about the physical environment that led to the diarrhea, will not prevent frequent recurrences of the condition, and does not deal with the underlying malnutrition and poverty. According to these critics, more fundamental types of programs are necessary if the child is to survive episodes of diarrhea and then not succumb to subsequent infections (Unger and Killingsworth 1986, p. 1004). Given the fundamental nature of the above argument (restructuring of society and comprehensive care versus specifically targeted prevention), we consider below two experimental trial programs and a general review of ten of the better initiatives that have been tried in the developing countries.

Kasongo is a tropical rural town in Zaire with a population of 30,000 persons. Some 180,000 inhabitants live in and around the town (Kasongo Project Team 1981). There is an average annual per capita income of U.S. $200. The Kasonga project was selectively directed toward measles vaccination, a disease that principally kills young malnourished children. Following initial surveys in 1969, two adjacent areas, each with a population of 10,000 persons, were selected for the trial. The two areas were alike in all pertinent respects, including their measles mortality rates. All children in both areas under 5 years of age were visited every three months. Data on morbidity and mortality were collected at these visits. Mothers' reports of whether a child had measles or not were accepted, but the interviewer obtained this data "blind" to information about the child's vaccination status. Measles is apparently a common and easily recognized disease in the area. Vaccination was offered to all children 8 months (some 9–12 months) of age in one area, and data on survival derived for both groups up to 35 months of age. Although

there is some dispute concerning the findings of the study (see Abby et al. 1981, p. 93), both published papers agree that the group receiving the measles vaccination had lower mortality up to 35 months of age. The major reduction in mortality appears to have been between 7 and 21 months.

Another less narrowly conceived trial was undertaken in India between 1968 and 1973. This trial sought to compare the effectiveness of nutritional supplements and medical care in the treatment of diarrhea-pneumonia in the state of Punjab, some 150 miles from New Delhi (Kielmann and McCord 1978; McCord and Kielmann 1977).

The trial involved three groups of villages receiving special care and a fourth group that served as controls. Group A received nutritional education and supplements only for children and pregnant women. The mothers were encouraged to breast feed their children. Group B received medical care only, with clinic care provided for minor problems. Immunization was also provided, and there were regular medical practitioner visits. Oral rehydration therapy was readily available to treat diarrhea. Group C villages received both nutritional and medical services, and Group D villages served as controls and received no special services.

Some 1,000 infants had their growth, morbidity, and mortality levels assessed to determine the impact of the intervention. Growth was, not surprisingly, best in the areas receiving nutritional supplements. Comparing the relative contribution of nutritional supplements and medical care, the authors concluded that nutritional supplements were more effective through the first week of the baby's life, but that medical care subsequently had a greater impact on morbidity and mortality. Curiously, there was no evidence that medical care and nutritional supplements had a cumulative impact. The cost of the program was in the order of U.S. $1–$2 per capita.

Gwatkin, Wilcox, and Wray (1980) have reviewed ten experimental programs with the aim of identifying the characteristics of those that succeeded. Here it must be noted that local experimental programs will sometimes succeed because of the commitment and personal qualities of those providing the service (Vaughan and Walt 1984, p. 110). These programs could fail when implemented more generally, and thus the review of key experiments may have limited generalizability. Despite the need for caution, the Gwatkin, Wilcox, and Wray review suggests that limited (SPMC) initiatives may be successful. The more successful programs were characterized by:

1. nutritional supplements and monitoring, particularly for expectant mothers
2. maternal tetanus immunization
3. population outreach and coverage for a total target population
4. a reliance on paramedical and local health workers

The authors point out that the manner in which an initiative was implemented was of basic importance. This implies that the prior existence or subsequent creation of an organizational structure for delivering the service is perhaps as important as the service that is delivered.

Similar observations may be derived from the two trials we have considered. In the Kasonga project the health providers went into the local communities on a regular basis; they did not wait for the villagers to seek help from their usually available services. In India the providers went into the experimental program villages on a regular basis.

Thus, the available data suggest that selective primary medical care may be effective, if accompanied by a level of infrastructure development. It is clearly not sufficient to make oral rehydration therapy, immunization, or nutrition programs available. Rather, these programs need to be provided to persons in local communities who have been taught both when and how to use these services. If this assessment is correct, then the changes involved, even in SPMC, have political, social, and health implications. The provision of nutritional supplements implies a reduction in social inequalities; the provision of education implies a more literate and therefore potentially threatening (in a political sense) population. It thus follows that even the delivery of selective primary medical care services involves a level of structural change in the developing countries.

CONCLUSIONS

The developing countries contain the bulk of the world's population and, with their rapid population growth rates, a large proportion of the world's children. Death and disease rates in these countries remain extraordinarily high, with, in some instances, one-quarter of the children dying before the age of 5. It is apparent that many of the health problems that exist in these countries are a consequence of Western contact, colonial imperialism, and a continuing process of commercial exploitation.

Western nations "conquered" these countries and set up administrations that deliberately restricted economic development. Services (health, education) were available in a few urban centres, but aside from minimal infrastructures (roads, train routes) to permit the exploitation of natural resources, there was little development. At the same time, these limited infrastructures provided a conduit for many of the diseases that are now endemic. When the Western nations handed power back to indigenous administrations, they left behind the diseases they had introduced, but little else.

It may be best to proceed on the likely assumption that those Western nations that contributed to the current circumstances are unwilling to provide the economic help that the developing countries now require.

In these circumstances is it reasonable to expect an improvement in the health and well-being of those living in the developing countries?

The work of McKeown (1976), McKinlay and McKinlay (1977) and Gordon (1976) suggests that a rapid improvement in health occurred earlier this century in the now-developed countries. Comparisons within the developing countries over time (1960–1985, see Grant 1987) point to similarly dramatic improvements in some developing countries. As we have noted in the examples of Nicaragua and Cuba, these health improvements occurred despite a declining economic situation. Rapid health improvements are possible.

In the developing countries health appears to be most intimately tied to the prevailing political, social, and economic circumstances. Although various quasi-experimental studies suggest that limited, specifically targeted health initiatives have the potential to contribute to a substantial mortality decline, all these initiatives presuppose a political system responsive to local community needs. As we have noted, without increased literacy and the greater availability of basic foods, clean water, and hygienic conditions, there is little reason to expect better health in the developing countries.

For the developed countries the lessons derived from the study of developing countries are many. Health is fundamentally a consequence of the way the society is structured. Approaches to health care delivery mirror political, social, and economic forces within the society. An inappropriate emphasis on sophisticated medical technologies has the capacity to divert resources and be detrimental to the health of the community. Uncontrolled commercialism is clearly harmful to the health of the community. Finally, and more generally, health is only partly a consequence of the manner in which health services are delivered. Health is much more clearly a result of the dominant social processes and physical environment.

REFERENCES

Aaby, Peter, Jette Bukh, Ida M. Lisse, and Arjon J. Smits. 1981. Measles Vaccination and Child Mortality. *Lancet* 2 (July 11):93.

Banta, H. David. 1986. Medical Technology and Developing Countries: The Case of Brazil. *International Journal of Health Services* 16:363–373.

Benjamin, Medea, and Joseph Collins. 1985. Is Rationing Socialist? *Food Policy* 10:327–336.

Braithwaite, John. 1984. *Corporate Crime in the Pharmaceutical Industry*. London: Routledge and Kegan Paul.

———. 1986. The Corrupt Industry. *New Internationalist* November (165):19–20.

Campbell, Carolyn E. 1984. Nestle and Breast vs. Bottle Feeding: Mainstream and Marxist Perspective. *International Journal of Health Services* 14:547–567.

Cochrane, Susan H., Joanne Leslie, and Donald J. O'Hara. 1982. Parental Education and Child Health: Intracountry Evidence. *Health Policy and Education* 2:213–250.

Cockcroft, James D. 1974. Mexico, in R. H. Chilcote and J. C. Edelstein, eds., *Latin America*. New York: John Wiley, pp. 225–303.

Cumper, G. E. 1984. *Determinants of Health Levels in Developing Countries*. Letchworth, England: Research Studies Press.

Diaz-Briquets, Sergio. 1983. *The Health Revolution in Cuba*. Austin: University of Texas Press.

Donahue, John M. 1986. Planning for Primary Health Care in Nicaragua: A Study in Revolutionary Process. *Social Science and Medicine* 23:149–157.

Elling, Ray H. 1981. The Capitalist World-System and International Health. *International Journal of Health Services* 11:21–51.

Escudero, Jose C. 1980. Starting from Year One: The Politics of Health in Nicaragua. *Social Science and Medicine* 10:647–656.

Glucksberg, Harold, and Jack Singer. 1982. The Multinational Drug Companies in Zaire: The Adverse Effect on Cost and Availability of Essential Drugs. *International Journal of Health Services* 12:381–387.

Gordon, Douglas. 1976. *Health, Sickness and Society*. St. Lucia, Australia: University of Queensland Press.

Grant, James P. 1987. *The State of the World's Children.* New York: UNICEF.

Greenhalgh, Trisha. 1986. Three Times Daily— Prescription Habits in India. *New Internationalist* November (165):10–11.

Gwatkin, Davidson R., Janet R. Wilcox, and Joe D. Wray. 1980. *Can Health and Nutrition Interventions Make a Difference?* Monograph No. 13. Washington, D.C.: Overseas Development Council.

Haq, Mahbub Ul. 1980. North-South Dialogue—Is There a Future? In K. Haq, ed., *Dialogue for a New Order.* New York: Pergamon Press.

Hassan, Amin, Eliana Velasquez, R. Belmar, Molly Coye, Ernest Drucker, Phillip J. Landrigan, David Michaels, and Kevin B. Sidel. 1981. Mercury Poisoning in Nicaragua. *International Journal of Health Services.* 11:221–226.

Hogbin, Victoria. 1985. Railways, Disease and Health in South America. *Social Science and Medicine* 9:933–938.

Horn, James J. 1985. The Mexican Revolution and Health Care or the Health of the Mexican Revolution. *International Journal of Health Services.* 15:485–499.

Hughes, Charles C., and John M. Hunter. 1970. Disease and "Development" in Africa. *Social Science and Medicine* 3:443–493.

Jacobson, Bobbie. 1983. Smoking and Health: A New Generation of Campaigners. *British Medical Journal* 287:483–484

Kasongo Project Team. 1981. Influence of Measles Vaccination or Survival Pattern of 7-35-Month-Old Children in Kasongo, Zaire. *Lancet* 1:764–767.

Keusch, Gerald T., and Nevin S. Scrimshaw. 1986. Selective Primary Health Care: Strategies for Control of Disease in the Developing World. *Reviews of Infectious Diseases* 8:273–287.

Kielmann, Arnfried A., and Colin McCord. 1978. Weight-for-Age as an Index of Risk for Children. *Lancet* 1:1247–1250.

McCord, Colin, and Arnfried A. Kielmann. 1977. Home Treatment for Children Diarrhea in Punjab Villages. Journal of *Tropical Pediatrics and Environmental Child Health* 23:197–201.

McKeown, Thomas. 1976. *The Role of Medicine:*

Dream, Mirage or Nemesis. London: Nuffield Provincial Hospitals Trust.

McKinlay, John B., and Sonja McKinlay. 1977. The Questionable Contribution of Medical Measures to the Decline in Mortality in the United States in the Twentieth Century. *Milbank Memorial Fund Quarterly* Summer:405–428.

Maddocks, Ian. 1975. Medicine and Colonialism. *Australian and New Zealand Journal of Sociology* 11:27–33.

Matzke, Gordon. 1979. Settlement and Sleeping Sickness Control—A Dual Threshold Model of Colonial and Traditional Methods in East Africa. *Social Science and Medicine* 13D:209–214.

Powles, John. 1973. On the Limitations of Modern Medicine. *Science, Medicine and Man* 1:1–30.

Prothero, R. Mansell. 1977. Disease and Mobility: A Neglected Factor in Epidemiology. *International Journal of Epidemiology* 6:259–267.

Ramalingaswami, V. 1986. The Art of the Possible. *Social Science and Medicine* 22:1097–1102.

Silverman, Milton. 1986. *The Drugging of the Americas.* Berkeley: University of California Press.

Silverman, Milton, Philip R. Lee, and M. Lydecker. 1982. The Drugging of the Third World. *International Journal of Health Services* 12:585–596.

Stalker, Peter. 1986. A Journey through the New Nicaragua. *New Internationalist* February (156):7–11.

Stebbins, Kenyon R. 1986. Curative Medicine, Preventive Medicine and Health Status: The Influence of Politics on Health Status in a Rural Mexican Village. *Social Science and Medicine* 23:139–148.

Stock, Robert. 1986. "Disease and Development" or "The Underdevelopment of Health": A Critical Review of Geographical Perspectives on African Health Problems. *Social Science and Medicine* 23:689–700.

Taylor, David. 1986. The Pharmaceutical Industry and Health in the Third World. *Social Science and Medicine* 11:1141–1149.

Unger, Jean-Pierre, and James R. Killingsworth. 1986. Selective Primary Health Care: A Critical Review of Methods and Results. *Social Science and Medicine* 22:1001–1013.

Vaughan, J. Patrick, and Gill Walt. 1984. Implementing Primary Health Care: Some Problems of Creating National Programmes. *Tropical Doctor* 14:108–113.

World Health Organization (WHO). 1980. *Sixth Report on the World Health Situation*. Geneva: The Organization.

Yach, Derek. 1986. The Impact of Smoking in Developing Countries with Special Reference to Africa. *International Journal of Health Services* 16:279–292.

CHAPTER
17
THE HEALTH OF CHILDREN AND ADOLESCENTS

MARIE C. McCORMICK
J. BROOKS-GUNN

The most significant change in child health reflects the changes in causes of childhood mortality and morbidity that have occurred during this century in developed countries and are currently spreading to less developed countries. Until the early part of this century in the United States, more than 10 percent of all infants died before their first birthday, and at least an equal percentage died before their fifth. Much of this early loss of life resulted from a combination of inadequate nutrition and high levels of infectious disease, a pattern that persists in many poor countries today. In our country, the early part of the century saw an improvement in housing and sewage disposal, the use of pasteurized milk, the introduction of immunizations, and the discovery of antibiotics. Rapid declines in early mortality may be attributed to public health services against infectious disease (Shapiro, Schlesinger, and Nesbitt 1968). As the impact of acute infectious disease was controlled, childhood mortality and morbidity patterns shifted, with a resulting alteration in the need for health services. Additionally, definitions of child health care changed, with more emphasis being placed on social aspects of health.

This chapter will describe some of the newer conceptualizations of child health, highlighting important areas in the prevention and treatment of health problems. We are only providing a brief overview of a diverse and complex field—the health of children and adolescence. The issues selected for discussion are those that we believe illustrate problems of substantial concern and directions of current sociological, pediatric, and psychological research. However, by necessity, not every problem of importance is considered; our review is therefore selective and not comprehensive.

We take a life-span perspective that has emerged from the collaboration of developmental psychologists and sociologists (Baltes, Reese, and Lipsitt 1980; Brim and Kagan 1980; Featherman and Lerner

1987), generally focusing on four different life phases—pregnancy and prenatal life, infancy, childhood, and adolescence. Since health is defined in terms of functioning appropriate to one's developmental level, more attention in the field of health and social science needs to be focused on different life phases. In addition, a life-span perspective dictates that antecedents and consequences of health problems at different ages be considered. However, as will be seen in this review, across-age comparisons and long-term prospective studies of children with chronic illnesses or certain types of morbidity are rare. Finally, this perspective allows for a consideration of the sociocultural and familial factors rendering children at different ages to be at risk for health and developmental dysfunction. Although medical sociologists and pediatric psychologists study structural and more endogenous risk factors, comparisons across the first two decades of life are rare.

OVERVIEW OF THE HEALTH PROBLEMS IN INFANCY, CHILDHOOD, AND ADOLESCENCE

The Outcome of Pregnancy: Congenital Malformation and Prematurity

Despite the fact that infant and childhood mortality rates have declined markedly, infant death rates in the United States remain relatively high for a developed country. At current rates, about 1 percent of infants (10 per 1,000 live births) die before their first birthday, a death rate not exceeded in any age range until about age 65. Moreover, this death rate places the United States behind most Western European countries and some Asian ones as well (Wegman 1986). Unlike earlier parts of the decade, most of this infant loss is due to events occurring before and during pregnancy and delivery that result in death early in infancy, traditionally defined as the first month of life, or neonatal period. The major causes of neonatal mortality are congenital malformations, prematurity, or low birthweight (McCormick 1986).

Prematurity is defined as a birth before thirty-eight weeks of gestation (thirty-eight weeks since the last menstrual period); low birthweight is a birth weighing 2,500 grams (5.5 pounds) or less. Both conditions are highly correlated (i.e., a premature baby is also likely to be low birthweight) and convey much the same information that fetal growth has been inadequate. A variety of specific medical conditions, as well as maternal characteristics, are known to increase the risk of prematurity and low birthweight, but the mechanisms by which such factors alter fetal nutrition and growth and the mechanisms of labor are still being established (Institute of Medicine 1985).

Congenital malformations result from alterations of fetal development in one or more organ systems, with resulting dysfunction of varying degrees. A number of different events are known to cause congenital problems, and these include single defective genes present through inheritance or mutation, abnormal chromosomes, maternal infections in which the infecting agent crosses the placenta to infect the fetus, and maternal exposure to substances that alter fetal development (teratogens), such as radiation, alcohol, certain drugs, and other chemicals. The type of anomaly produced depends on the timing of the exposure, but, in general, most anomalies arise from events in the first three months of pregnancy (first trimester) when many women may not be aware that they are pregnant (Kalter and Warkany 1983).

Prematurity/low birthweight and congenital malformations may occur in the same infants so that there is some overlap between these two causes of mortality. In addition, they occur with comparable frequency: About 6 percent of births in the United States are low birthweight, and 1 percent very low birthweight, (1,500 grams (3.3 pounds or less). About 7 percent of births are characterized by moderate to severe anomalies, and 1–2 percent by severe malformations. However, these causes differ markedly in their contribution to perinatal mortality, with low birthweight accounting for two-thirds to three-quarters of all perinatal deaths. Moreover, low birthweight/prematurity probably reflects a limited number of mechanisms by which fetal growth and onset of labor are altered in contrast to congenital malformations, which individually may be quite rare and which in the majority of cases (60 percent) are of unknown etiology. As we will note later, these causes also differ in their potential preventability, as malformations may already be present at the onset of prenatal care whereas prematurity/low birthweight generally reflect second and third trimester events. Finally, as we also will discuss, the latter is more closely linked to socioeconomic status (McCormick 1986).

Mortality and Morbidity in Older Infants and Children

Past the first month of life, mortality decreases sharply. The mortality for the remainder of the first year (postneonatal mortality) is 3.8 per thousand live births; that for children aged 1–4 years, 51.9; and for those 5–14 years, 26.7 per 100,000 resident population. Mortality and morbidity reflect the impact of infectious conditions and injuries primarily, but neoplasms (cancer) also emerge as a cause of death in this age-range (DHHS 1986).

Of particular importance is the role of injury in mortality and morbidity past the first year of life (Alpert and Guyer 1985). For preschool children, injuries are most commonly the result of falls and exposure to household hazards. Head injuries, burns, and poisonings are common (Runyan et al. 1985). With regard to poisoning, younger children are likely to ingest aspirin, solvents, tranquilizers, and iron compounds. The incidence of hospitalizations related with poisonings is higher for blacks than for whites. Poisoning as a cause of injury for adolescents is self-inflicted (in contrast to younger children, although suicide in later childhood does occur, Trinkoff and Baker 1986).

As children grow older, other injuries reflect their broader milieu, with playground and sports injuries becoming more common. At almost all ages, motor vehicle accidents account for a substantial proportion of fatalities and hospitalizations due to trauma among children and an even greater proportion for teens (Runyan et al. 1985). These high rates are not surprising, given the relatively low use of seatbelts and child restraints. Only one-third of children under age 7 use seatbelts all or most of the time, according to the 1981 National Health Interview Survey data (Haaga 1986). Older children use them even less. Blacks and Hispanics report lower rates than whites, and more highly educated mothers report better compliance than less educated ones (Haaga 1986). Because of the relatively unpredictable nature of injury occurrence, prevention typically has focused on modifying the environment to reduce the risk of trauma when a child is exposed to a potential hazard, rather than on attempting to modify parental behavior.

One special situation for which interventions with parents are essential, however, is that of intentional injury or child abuse. The exact proportion of childhood injury that is the result of abuse is not known and is difficult to assess (Hampton and Newberger 1985). Demarcations between intentional and nonintentional injury also are not clear. However, homicide is now among the five leading causes of death in childhood and is the only leading cause of death in children to have increased in the last thirty years (Christoffel 1984). Most childhood homicides are perpetrated by parents and other relatives. Medical sociologists argue for a broader definition of child abuse to reflect the situations in which characteristics of the child, parental values, and familial stresses act to increase the risk of abuse. In part, this broad definition encourages interventions to enhance the child's environment and to alter parental behavior more generally rather than simply to prevent injury. In part, this broader definition also reflects the high mortality and morbidity rate that may occur with undetected repeated abuse for the child or perpetuation of abusive behavior across generations and associations with such structural factors as race, poverty, and education.

The role of medical personnel in the report of child abuse is critical, given that they identify over half of all cases of physical abuse (Hampton and Newberger 1985). In the National Study of the Incidence and Severity of Child Abuse and Neglect, hospital personnel were given concrete guidelines for defining child abuse. Compared to other agencies, hospitals identified children who were younger, had younger parents who were black, and who lived in urban areas, suggesting that more "middle-class" abuse cases may be underreported by the hospital personnel (Hampton and Newberger 1985).

The pattern of morbidity and mortality from infectious conditions and injuries is similar. Both types of conditions are frequent occurrences, with children experiencing four to six episodes a year. Most episodes involve minor, self-limited illnesses resulting in little if any restriction in normal activities, although they probably occasion a disproportionate amount of medical causes and purchase of medication (Fosarelli, Wilson, and DeAngelis 1987). Despite misgivings about the efficacy of medical interventions for individual episodes, the literature does suggest that access to and early contact with medical services is associated with a reduction in length of illness, reduction in symptoms, and reduction in the proportion of children progressing to more severe stages requiring hospital care (Hadley 1982; Starfield 1985). In addition, morbidity from infectious conditions and from injury are increased among poor children, as is the probability of a fatal outcome (Egbuonu and Starfield, 1982).

Morbidity and Mortality in Adolescence

Mortality rates for adolescents, like other groups, dropped from 1900 to 1960. Unlike younger and older people, however, teenage mortality rates rose over the next twenty years and in some cases are still rising (Green and Horton 1982). The leading causes of death are accidents and violence; traffic accidents, homicides, and suicides account for almost three-quarters of all teenage deaths (DHHS 1984; DHEW 1979). Social structural variables such as race and poverty, as well as gender, are associated with teenage accidents and violence: Poor males, especially those in racial minorities, are overrepresented in accidents and homicides. Neoplasms and congenital anomalies are the second and third leading causes of mortality in the teenage years.

Litt (1982) has identified several areas of teenage morbidity: (1) problems related to pubertal growth, (2) preexisting conditions that worsen during adolescence, (3) conditions associated with adult morbidity, and (4) health concerns resulting from behavioral characteristics of the age group. We would expand the list to include (5) reproductive health and (6) health concerns related to emotional well-being.

The first three are considered only briefly here. Examples include the fact that pubertal processes not only affect the reproductive system, but influence almost all organ systems. Up to 20 percent of all teenagers may have physical handicaps or growth-related problems (DHEW 1976). The leading causes are neuromuscular, musculoskeletal, and cardiovascular problems (Litt, 1982). Certain chronic disease conditions may continue and may become a particular problem for adolescents, given the cognitive, peer, and family demands occurring at this time. Finally, certain conditions associated with adult morbidity may become particularly salient during adolescence; obesity would be an example. The last three topics will be discussed in the next section.

VULNERABLE SUBGROUPS

As referred to in our brief overview of the causes of morbidity and mortality across the first twenty years of life, certain groups are more likely to be vulnerable to illness. Conditions associated with poverty cut across health category and age group. As patterns of morbidity (as well as mortality) have changed over the past century, chronic illnesses, health risk-taking behaviors, and developmental dysfunctional status play a larger role in our definitions of health and illness. And, given the disproportionate number of poor children who fall into these three groups, social structural and familial contributions to health and illness must be considered (Levine, Feldman, and Elison 1983; McKinlay and McKinlay 1986; Syme and Berkman 1986). We shall consider several conditions that are representative of health problems today, and discuss some of the social structural variables associated with them.

Children with Chronic Illness

Between 5 and 10 percent of all children have a major chronic illness. A chronic illness is defined as one that lasts more than three months and leads to a "lifestyle that must *permanently* include a regimen of frequent attention to a disorder or handicap or to a condition potentially health-damaging in a person who's otherwise in good health" (Hamburg 1982, p. 434).

Unlike the adult situation, in which two or three conditions account for the majority of those with chronic problems, childhood chronic illness is composed of a myriad of conditions, some individually quite rare. Among these conditions are hereditary metabolic and chromosomal defects, the more severe congenital mal-formations, sequelae of perinatal events such as cerebral palsy, conditions of more complex and as yet less-well-defined etiology such as asthma and diabetes mellitus, a variety of cancers, and rheumatic problems.

The management of such problems is complex, requiring multiple providers and coordination of services cutting across disciplines such as medicine, welfare, and education. Despite the heterogeneity of chronic conditions in childhood, their management presents some generic problems to parents and health care providers (Hobbs and Perrin 1985). The first of these is the preservation of normal developmental progress and psychosocial adjustment insofar as possible. To achieve this goal, those caring for such children must be sure that the child is in an educational setting that is appropriate to the cognitive and physical constraints of the condition, minimizes disruptions in activities owing to medical-care services, and fosters coping with differences in appearance because of illness. The second is the effect of maternal beliefs upon child compliance and health practices (Becker et al. 1978). The third is the effect of such illnesses on family functioning and the need for complex services, which we will discuss later. Such needs are, of course, over and above the medical needs of managing the specific problem.

Chronic illnesses are characteristic of all age groups, and the above-mentioned issues are relevant for adolescents as well as children. As Hamburg (1982) has noted, however, little research focuses on the effects of chronic diseases in adolescence despite the fact that it may present some special problems. For example, concerns with the body are heightened at the time of puberty in general (Brooks-Gunn, Petersen, and Eichorn 1985). In the chronically ill, these may be intensified, given physical signs and emotional feelings of vulnerability. Embarrassment about the body also is common during the rapid changes of puberty; examinations or visits to medical personnel may be more stressful at this time than earlier or later. Another challenge involves the renegotiation of parental relationships: Young adolescents tend to distance themselves from their parents in order to become more autonomous and to test the limits of their family's control over them (Steinberg 1981; Hill et al. 1985). Although such activities are desirable from a developmental perspective, they may cause difficulty for chronically ill adolescents who need reassurance about their illness and open lines of communication with their parents (Hamburg 1982). Additionally, compliance with medical practices may become problematic unless a supportive environment is maintained. Research is being conducted on family interventions to help parents as well as adolescents negotiate the balance between the developmental tasks of adolescents and the requirements of chronic illnesses (*cf.* Hamburg 1982).

The chronically ill adolescent also may find himself socially isolated from peers, in part because of the demands for conformity occurring at this time. The chronically ill youngster may feel "different," moving away from or actively rejecting the peer group. Additionally, the ill young person may be less socially mature, given the extent of limitations of daily activities, in particular with peers, from earlier years. Finally, parents may not encourage peer contacts as readily, fearing rejection or the inability to handle the developmental challenges associated with heterosexual behavior and peer-mediated substance use (Blum 1988).

Children with the New Morbidity

Both the acute infectious and the chronic problems of childhood reflect more classic diagnostic entities well represented in medical texts. Recognition is increasing, however, of broader dimensions of morbidity not captured in diagnostic terminology that may impair functioning within and across diagnostic categories. The phrase "the new morbidity" was coined over a decade ago in an attempt to encompass the experience of a substantial proportion of children who are unable to perform activities appropriate to their physical state as assessed by the health provider (Haggerty, Roghmann, and Pless 1975). Such dysfunctional behavior often is multicausal. It may be, for example, a reflection of parental anxiety and overprotectiveness in reaction to previous major health problems, a situation characterized as the "vulnerable child syndrome" (Green and Solnit 1964; Levy 1980). It may reflect a failure in preschool and school settings as a result of a variety of learning and behavior disorders (Levine 1982), or it may be a consequence of familial stress and social disadvantage (Johnson 1986). Although the exact proportion of children affected by such problems is imprecise, it is significant. Estimates generally range from about 15 to 20 percent of all children.

Infancy and early childhood. The expression of this new morbidity varies with the age of the child and reflects the developmental challenges being experienced. In the infancy and toddler period, the major expression is the failure of normal physical and psychosocial development. The former, often called failure-to-thrive, may result from underlying, otherwise asymptomatic illness, but more frequently it represents inadequate caloric intake, with or without emotional deprivation. Similarly, failure to attain psychosocial developmental milestones in the areas of, for example, movement and verbal skills may be the first signs of an organic problem (especially sensory or neurologic dysfunction), but more frequently reflects inappropriate parenting such that acquisition of skills is not fostered. Developmental deficiencies may be exacerbated by poor care.

In the preschool period, while developmental problems may still be encountered, behavior problems are more frequent (Hankin and Starfield 1986). To some extent, the emergence of behavior considered problematic may reflect normal development. Thus, mouthing behavior with the ingestion of nonfood items is expected of toddlers younger than age 2. However, the persistence of such behavior in older preschool children, or a large number of such maladaptive behaviors in the preschooler, places the child at future risk for problem behavior. Although the number of studies addressing this issue are relatively small, they tend to agree that about 10 percent of children have moderate to severe problems (Links 1983). Moreover, the available longitudinal work suggests that behavior problems persist and may be predictive of later delinquency and other adolescent problems (Furstenberg, Brooks-Gunn, and Morgan 1987; Stevenson, Richman, and Graham 1985).

Middle childhood. Entry into school presents a new set of challenges and in response various dysfunctions emerge, the most common of which are labeled learning disorders. A wide variety of items, diagnostic labels, and specific developmental dysfunctions have been used to characterize this problem. Levine (1982) has stressed that the specific information in processing or attention may be less important than a more general context involving the resiliency of the child in overcoming problems, the severity or multiplicity of problems, and environmental stressors and support. He further identifies difficulties in assessing the prevalence, the nature, and the outcomes of these conditions as a result of problems in instrumentation, the lack of norms for many aspects of development, the subtlety of early symptoms (e.g., such children may be classified as having behavior problems), the age of assessment, and the across-age stability of the findings. Despite these uncertainties, learning problems and related school failure are found in 5–20 percent of all children (Butler, Rosenbaum, and Palfrey 1987; Levine and Satz 1984).

Adolescence. Learning problems and related school failure, as well as behavior problems, carry through the adolescent years as indicators of the new morbidity. While there is continuity in those who exhibit school problems from the elementary school to the high school years (Furstenberg, Brooks-Gunn, and Morgan 1987; Kellam et al. 1983; Kellam et al. 1987), some children who have negotiated the early school years will exhibit problems in middle school, as the academic demands intensify and as they compete with peer group expectations, which often are not academically focused in the United States (Coleman 1961; Simmons and Blyth, 1987). For example, decreases in school grades occur during the middle school years with those children who move to the more rigorous middle school setting early, those who are going through puberty at the time of the move, and those who are experiencing simultaneous changes in family, peer, and school events being most at risk (Brooks-Gunn in press; Brooks-Gunn, Warren, and Rosso 1987; Simmons and Blyth 1987). Little is known about the long-term prognosis of these middle school adolescents whose school performance plummets or even flattens out; however, a significant proportion probably go on to have academic or behavior problems in the high school years (Simmons and Blyth 1987). More research is needed to identify those adolescents who are at risk for continued problems.

Moderate to severe behavior and emotional problems, which are seen in at least 10 percent of the school-age population and are exhibited in milder forms by an additional 15 percent of children (Achenbach and Edelbrock 1978, 1984; Links, 1983), are also characteristic of adolescents. Whether their prevalence increases depends on how behavior problems are defined.

Typically, what are termed "under control" problems manifest themselves as aggression toward others, conduct disorders, juvenile delinquency, and destruction of property. As an indication of violence, homicide is the leading cause of death in black adolescent males (Green and Horton 1982). Acting-out behavior problems, more likely to be exhibited by boys than girls, are more prevalent in adolescence than earlier; Rutter et al. (1976) found a hundredfold increase in aggression from the prepubertal to postpubertal years. The reasons for this increase are probably multidetermined (Kandel and Davies 1982, 1986). Of interest from a life-course perspective is the fact that, for boys, early behavior problems also predict later problems in adolescence (Furstenberg, Brooks-Gunn, and Morgan 1987; Kellam et al. 1987). In turn, adolescent behavior problems predict life adjustment difficulties in adulthood, as demonstrated by the elegant work of Robins (1966).

One of the most important developmental challenges to confront the adolescent is whether to engage in risk-taking activities. Many such activities revolve around cars and recreational vehicles. Motor vehicle accidents account for 37 percent of all teenage deaths, and injuries sustained during such accidents account for the largest number of hospital days even if pregnancy-related stays are included (NCHS 1983). Speeding is a factor in teenage traffic accidents more often than in traffic accidents involving adults (Brown 1979). Also, alcohol is a factor in about one-half of all motor vehicle accidents across age groups, even for teenagers who have not reached the legal drinking age (Centers for Disease Control 1984). Adolescents may be more likely to believe that they are invulnerable and to discount the consequences of risk-taking behaviors (Irwin and Millstein 1986). Risk-taking behaviors are sometimes intentionally life-threatening. The rate of completed suicides in adolescence and early adulthood has increased in the last twenty-five years, primarily because of an increase in male suicides (Deyken, Perlow, and McNamarra 1985). Repeat suicide attempts are common, suggesting that special services and training need to be implemented in hospital emergency rooms in order to reduce the number of suicides.

Experimentation with behaviors associated with acquiring adult status also is endemic during adolescence. Once termed deviant, they are now characterized as normative, given the facts that so many adolescents engage in them and that most are markers of adult status in the United States. Sexual activity, drinking, smoking, and illicit drug use are the most frequently mentioned of this class of behaviors. Trying alcohol is so common as to be a rite of passage. In a national survey of high school seniors, 93 percent had tried alcohol, and 72 percent had had a drink in the last month (Johnston, Bachman, & O'Mally 1984). Two-thirds had experimented with an illicit drug, and one-third of the seniors had tried a drug other than marijuana. The period of major risk for initiation of cigarettes, marijuana, and alcohol is prior to age 20, and for recent drugs other than cocaine prior to age 21 (Kandel and Logan 1984). After those ages, use declines dramatically.

Substance use is not limited to late adolescence, but often is initiated in the middle school years. For example, a 1982 National Institute of Drug Abuse survey provides prevalence statistics for 12- to 13-year-olds, 14- to 15-year-olds, and 16- to 17-year-olds (Shonberg 1985). Alcohol had been used by 10 percent, 23 percent, and 45 percent, respectively; marijuana by 2 percent, 8 percent, and 23 percent, respectively; and cigarettes by 3 percent, 10 percent, and 30 percent, respectively. These activities cluster together so that substance use of one kind is associated with substance use of another. Normative developmental sequences of more serious drug involvement have been documented (Donovan and Jessor 1983: Kandel 1975). Use of "harder" drugs is not due to substitution but to addition of substances. This is true across ethnic and social class groups. The progression reported by Donovan and Jessor is as follows: nonuse of alcohol or related drugs, nonproblem use of alcohol, marijuana use, problem drinking, use of pills, and use of "hard" drugs (heroin and cocaine). Of importance is the fact that problem drinking does not occur prior to any illicit drug use (i.e., marijuana).

Those who use substances are more likely to be in poor health than those who do not, even controlling for other life-style factors (Brunswick and Messeri 1986). Correlates of substance use in the teenage years include peer influence, early drug use, feelings of rejection at school and at home, and self-derogation (Kaplan, Robbins, and Martin 1983). Additionally, for a small proportion of teenagers, substance use may be associated with depression (Deyken, Levy, and Wells 1986); indeed, adolescents with depression may use drugs to "self-medicate" (Weissman 1980; Kandel 1982).

Adolescence is a time of increased risk for emotional problems, with depressive affect and suicidal ideation being of most concern from a mental health perspective. By late adolescence, up to 5 percent of young people are diagnosable with severe depression, and another 12 percent with moderate depression. Mild transient depression may appear in up to one-third of all adolescents (Petersen and Craighead 1986). In a recent study of junior high students, persistent symptoms were reported more frequently for blacks than whites. (Schoenbach et al. 1983).

The occurrence of negative life events is associated with depressive affect in adolescents (Brooks-Gunn, Warren, and Rosso 1987). Negative affect in adolescence predicts reported depression in adulthood (Kandel and Davies 1986). Additionally, self-derogation and peer rejection during early adolescence are associated with psychological distress ten years later, even controlling for intervening life events. Thus, emotional feelings (depression, self-derogation) in early adolescence may set the stage for later psychological distress. Whether such relations are specific to the early adolescent period is not known.

Early and unintended reproduction are concerns of almost all societies (Mead 1972; Paige 1983). Control of sexuality, then, is not a new issue nor a particularly

Western one. Adolescent sexuality has become a concern in our society, in part because over one million adolescents become pregnant each year and most of them did not plan to (Furstenberg and Brooks-Gunn 1986; Petersen and Brooks-Gunn in press). In a national survey, for example, less than one-fourth of the girls indicated that their pregnancy was planned, and most were upset when the pregnancy occurred (Zelnik, Kantner, and Ford 1981). It has been estimated that four in ten girls now age 14 will become pregnant in their teenage years, two out of ten girls will give birth, and three out of twenty girls will have an abortion (Guttmacher 1981).

In the last two decades the proportion of young women who have had intercourse has increased dramatically, rising by two-thirds during the 1970s. Increases were most pronounced in white girls and in younger teens, because they started from a lower baseline than blacks and older teens. By 1979, close to one-half of all teenage females were sexually active, and in certain subgroups two-thirds of all female adolescents were sexually active. These large increases have minimized earlier gender differences in sexual activity. Prior to the 1970s, teenage boys were much more likely to have had intercourse than girls; today, these differences are much less pronounced.

Most teens do not consciously plan to become sexually active, and they often do not foresee the first sexual experience. Young adolescent females are likely to be initiated into sexual activity by friends or acquaintances rather than by steady dating partners (Zelnik, Kantner, and Ford 1981). Girls are often pressured or coerced into having sex by males who are as ill-prepared as their female counterparts to assume responsibility should a pregnancy occur. The behavior of one's peers strongly influences sexual behavior; so does one's perception of the sexual experiences of peers (Furstenberg, Moore, and Petersen 1986). The rise in teenage sexuality in the last two decades may be indicative of the strength of the peer group, changing norms, societal pressures, and societal insensitivity to sexual practices. As more adolescents engage in sexual activity, it becomes less deviant (Furstenberg and Brooks-Gunn 1986). Differences in sexual norms have been postulated to account for ethnic differences in sexual activity and pregnancy rates. For example, white teenagers are more likely to engage in a predictable series of precoital behaviors prior to first intercourse than black teenagers. Black girls, who are more likely to move from necking to intercourse without intermediate steps, may be less likely to be prepared for intercourse, in the sense that there is little time to think about and obtain contraceptives (Smith and Udry 1985).

Increased sexual activity has the unwanted consequences of adolescent pregnancy and abortion, as well as sexually transmitted diseases. Teenagers account for three-quarters of all sexually transmitted diseases (DHEW 1979).

Of the 1.1 million teenage girls who become pregnant each year, about one-half deliver children (Henshaw et al. 1983). Teenage fertility rates do differ by ethnicity: Blacks have double the rate of whites; Hispanics have a rate between the two (Moore and Burt 1982). Rates of early childbearing have declined in the last twenty-five years (Moore, Simms, and Betsey 1986). However, teenage parenthood is considered a social problem for several reasons. First, the fertility rates declined more rapidly for older women than teenagers, and the proportion of teenagers in the population increased (as "baby boomers" became adolescents), leading to the relative share of births to teenagers to be higher (i.e., from 12 to 18 percent between 1955 and 1970; Baldwin 1976; Vinoskis 1981). Second, the teenager births that were out-of-wedlock has risen dramatically. Proportionally fewer teenage mothers become married, and few unmarried adolescents choose adoption as an alternative to single parenthood (Westoff, Calot, Foster

1983; Moore and Burt 1982). In a comparison study of single mothers who chose adoption and those who kept their infants, the former were younger and more likely to be white, Catholic, primiparous, and economically independent. Their pregnancies were also more likely to have been unplanned, and antenatal care was more commonly started late. However, their newborns were more healthy than the comparison group's infants, probably reflecting the lower incidence of poverty status (Yogman, Herrara, and Bloom 1983).

Possibly more relevant to concerns about teenage pregnancy are the rates of out-of-wedlock births. In part because of the changing economic opportunities for youth (Fuchs 1983), almost all teenage births to blacks are out-of-wedlock. Interestingly, blacks may have been pacesetters for the population at large, as marriage rates for white teens have been declining rapidly and out-of-wedlock births rising sharply to over 50 percent. Less information is available for Hispanics. In a recent analysis of 1982 data from the National Longitudinal Study (Darabi and Ortiz 1987), young Hispanic women of Mexican and Puerto Rican origin had similar proportions of births as did young black women. However, the marital first-birth rate for young Mexican women was twice that of the Puerto Rican women: Most Mexican and white first births occurred in the context of marriage, whereas most black and Puerto Rican births did not. Interestingly, later generations of Mexican-origin women had proportionally more premarital births than more recent immigrants, suggesting that as the traditional norms become more distant, marriage and childbearing are not as tightly linked (Bean, Curtis, and Marcum 1977). Clearly, changes in norms within and across cultural subgroups have resulted in great increases in young unmarried mothers, and differences between subgroups can be expected to decline even further.

Teenage women are less likely to receive

adequate antenatal care than older women, increasing the risk of negative health outcomes in their neonates. Additionally, the increased risk of perinatal loss and infant morbidity is seen in their latter-born as well as first-born children (Jekel et al. 1975; McCormick, Shapiro, and Starfield 1985). Teenage mothers are less likely than later childbearers to complete their education, to achieve as much work-wise, and to be married (Furstenberg, Brooks-Gunn, and Morgan 1987). Their relative disadvantage often translates into poverty status, which is associated with less adequate health care for adults and children and developmental dysfunction in children (Brooks-Gunn and Furstenberg 1986).

Antecedents of teenage motherhood have received much attention given efforts to prevent early births. Research is primarily on early births. Economically disadvantaged adolescents, given concerns about the persistence of urban poverty and use of Aid to Families with Dependent Children (Bane 1983; Moore and Burt, 1982). Girls who become pregnant are likely to be doing poorly in school, have low educational aspirations, and be sporatic contraceptive users (Furstenberg, Brooks-Gunn, and Morgan 1987). Repeat pregnancies in teenage mothers are another concern, and numerous programs have been initiated to delay second births. Increasing consistent contraceptive use has been a major thrust of many prevention programs, with some having been successful and others not (Furstenberg, Brooks-Gunn, and Morgan 1987; Klerman and Jekel 1973). Generally, family planning clinics and school-based clinics may be effective (Dryfoos 1985). A recent process study elucidates some of the factors that contribute to altering young women's health behavior. This study of client and provider attitudes and interactiveness in a large number of family planning clinics showed that the quality of interaction between family-planning clinic staff and clients influenced contraceptive use (Nathanson and Becker 1985). Additionally,

the overall attitude climate was a determining factor, over and above individual's behavior. Repeat pregnancies are as much a concern as first pregnancies, since closely spaced additional births are related to long-term welfare dependency (Furstenberg, Brooks-Gunn, and Morgan 1987). Poor academic records, lack of a job, and use of welfare seem to be predictors of first and repeated pregnancies (Koenig and Zelnick 1982; Polit and Kahn 1986).

Eating and weight problems are another set of problems that are likely to emerge in adolescence because of the convergence of physical changes and psychosocial challenges with which the individual must cope. Adolescent girls who are vulnerable either because of predisposing characteristics or the particular context in which they find themselves may respond to developmental challenges with efforts to control their weights or with overeating. Why a particular individual or a group of individuals is vulnerable to eating problems rather than to other psychosomatic syndromes or to depression is not well understood, since direct comparisons among such groups are rarely made. Typically, investigators focus on the various predisposing factors, correlates, and outcomes of various forms of adolescent psychopathology. In the case of eating disorders and depression, almost all of the research is retrospective (Attie and Brooks-Gunn, in press a, in press b). Prospective work has been done on the antecedents of adolescent conduct disorders, juvenile delinquency, and substance use (Kellam, Brown, and Fleming 1982; Robins, Davis, and Wish 1977; Robins 1966; Rutter 1979).

Anorexia nervosa is an eating disorder characterized by behavior directed toward weight loss, peculiar attitudes toward food, body-image disturbance, and an implacable refusal to maintain body weight. It occurs during adolescence, although the risk for developing an eating disorder extends well into adulthood (Pope, Hudson, and Yargelun-Todd 1984). In girls of upper-middle-class status, the incidence may be as high as 1 percent; among groups under vocational pressure to control body weight, such as ballet dancers, the problem increases severalfold, with estimates ranging from 5 to 7 percent of adolescent dancers to 30 percent of adult dancers (Garner and Garfinkel 1980; Hamilton, Brooks-Gunn, and Warren 1985). Bulimia is an eating disturbance characterized by intense concern about weight, recurrent episodes of excessive overeating accompanied by a subjective sense of loss of control, and the use of vomiting, exercise, or purgative abuse to counteract the effects of binge eating (Fairburn and Garner 1986). It occurs in about 2 to 5 percent of girls in high school and university samples (Crowther, Post, and Zaynow 1985; Katzman, Wolchik, and Braver 1984). The incidence of both anorexia nervosa and bulimia is believed to have risen over the past two decades, a period when thinness has been reified as connoting goodness and femininity and the media has portrayed these life-threatening disorders as glamorous and exciting (Attie and Brooks-Gunn in press a; Brumberg 1985). Although both have been considered a disease of the white upper middle class, the incidence is increasing in black girls, suggesting that the "their" ideal body shape is being incorporated into norms of other social class and ethnic groups (Attie and Brooks-Gunn 1987).

Obesity is a weight-related problem seen in childhood as well as adolescence. Ten to 20 percent of all children are obese, with the percentages being higher for those from lower social classes (Coates and Thoresen 1978). Overweight adolescents are highly likely to continue to be overweight as adults; the odds against an overweight adolescent becoming an average-weight adult are twenty-eight to one (Stunkard and Burt 1967). In a study from childhood to adolescence, almost one-half of the obese children remained obese, with more black than white females doing so (Freedman et al. 1987). Ethnic and social

class differences are great, with blacks and whites in lower social classes being more likely to be obese than those in higher social classes, starting in childhood and continuing through adulthood (Stunkard et al. 1986). Severe obesity may confer an increased risk for diabetes, coronary heart disease, and hypertension (although being overweight does not) (Van Itallie 1985; Bray 1985). Prejudice against and fear of being obese have led to the observation that "excessive body fat is probably the most stigmatized physical feature except skin color, but unlike skin color is thought to be under voluntary control" (Wooley and Wooley 1979, p. 69). The cultural emphasis on losing weight has led to great efforts to lose weight, even though the fact that body weight is quite heritable (Stunkard et al. 1986) may mean that obese individuals are predisposed to a higher weight and that efforts to diet may result in counter-regulatory behavior (episodes of restraining and binging to regain the set point rather than weight loss).

Because of the difficulties inherent in weight loss in adulthood, focus has been placed on treatment for children and adolescents. Efforts to alter children's weight have not been overwhelmingly successful (Coates and Thoresen 1978). Problems over and above the heritable nature of weight include compliance with reduced food intake and physician pessimism (Becker et al. 1977). Maternal attitudes about food and compliance support seem to be important determinants of compliance (Woody and Costanzo 1981). In a test of the Health Belief Model's ability to predict a mother's adherence to a diet protocol for her child, Becker et al. (1977) report that maternal health beliefs about threat of illness, beliefs about benefits of a diet, and beliefs about barriers to a diet regimen were associated with child weight loss, presumably via maternal effects to control their children's compliance (Janz and Becker 1984). This study is an excellent example of the importance of maternal beliefs in understanding child compliance to health protocols generally, as well as the usefulness of health belief models in the design of intervention programs and compliance trials.

Poor Children

As indicated in the preceding sections, poor children suffer disproportionately for most types of morbidity in infancy and childhood. Because they are more likely to be disadvantaged, black children experience much poorer health than white children, and racial disparities in child health serve as a marker for the effects of poverty (Reed 1986).

Neonatal mortality rates remain twice as high for blacks as for whites nationally. This difference can be attributed to the higher proportion of premature/low birthweight infants not to differences in malformations (Shapiro et al. 1980). Despite declines in the neonatal mortalities, the gap between black and white infants has not narrowed (Wegman 1986). The disparity in birthweight is associated with a number of factors such as an increased proportion of adolescent mothers, mothers with low educational attainment, and unmarried women (Institute of Medicine 1985). However, within more homogeneously low-income communities, such sociodemographic characteristics cease to predict risk for adverse obstetric outcome, suggesting that these factors are correlates of poverty, which may be the real risk factor (McCormick, Shapiro, and Starfield 1985). More recent attention has focused on potentially modifiable health behaviors, such as smoking, the use of alcohol and other substances, the adequacy of prenatal care, and excessive physical and emotional stress. The effect of the alteration of these factors among poor women remains to be established (Institute of Medicine 1985).

The disadvantage conferred by poverty continues through later infancy and early childhood. Postneonatal mortality is twice as high among the children of adolescent mothers than mothers of low educational attainment, and this difference is independent of birthweight disparities (Shapiro et al. 1980). Further, since deaths represent only the tip of the iceberg of morbidity, one can anticipate a substantial burden of ill health among poor children, and the evidence, albeit incomplete, supports this picture (Egbuonu and Starfield 1982; Reed 1986).

Among preschool and school-aged children, poverty appears to exacerbate the effects of the health problems noted above. For example, there is some uncertainty as to whether poor children experience higher rates of injury than more advantaged children. The mortality rates due to injury are higher, however, suggesting that either the injuries are of a more severe type or that limits in access to care may lead to worse outcomes for injuries of comparable severity. Poverty also has been shown to produce poorer outcomes for infants of low birthweight, thus placing such infants at both biologic and social risk (Escalona 1982; Ramey et al. 1978). Poor children with severe handicapping conditions have higher rates of school failure than nonpoor children, again reinforcing the notion of the cumulative effects of biologic substrate and environmental stress, a situation described as the continuum of caretaking casualty (Sameroff and Chandler 1975).

IMPLICATIONS OF CHILD AND ADOLESCENT HEALTH STATUS

The emerging picture of child and adolescent health has several implications. The first is a need for a broader definition and measurement of child health status to permit more accurate assessment of different aspects of health and evaluation of interventions designed to improve health. One major piece of work in this regard is an attempt to operationalize the World Health Organization (WHO) definition of health; Eisen and his colleagues (1980) have termed it a "state of complete physical, mental and social well-being and not just an absence of disease or infirmity." This multidimensional conceptualization of health moves from a focus on the presence or absence of symptoms due to a pathological process and/or treatment to less restrictive and more inclusive measures. The latter would include (1) limitations in activities of daily living (mobility, dressing) due to health, (2) mental health characterized as affective state (sense of well-being, depression, anxiety) and behavioral response (withdrawal, aggression), (3) social health or ability to engage in normal social activities, and (4) perceived or self-rated health and resistance to disease. This more inclusive definition is compatible with conceptualizations of health in medical sociology and developmental psychology.

While an excellent beginning, the application of such definitions to research on child health is just beginning, and some problems have been identified. First, many of the measures employed are largely modifications of adult measures, with the result that the developmental tasks of childhood and adolescence are not taken into account. Conversely, many procedures used to assess children from the developmental and educational psychology literature are not well integrated in the health field. Thus, the further definition of child health and its role in child growth and development requires multidisciplinary research.

Second, few interventions to improve health status as defined in broader terms have been developed or evaluated. Current medical approaches focus on achieving specific diagnoses amenable to surgical, pharmacological, or other types of medical interventions. The new morbidity often entails therapeutic procedures unfamiliar to most traditionally trained health providers such as counseling, behavior modification, or modification of health beliefs. Coordina-

tion of services provided in settings other than clinical ones and involving professionals other than physicians is often lacking (Task Force on Pediatric Education 1978).

In this regard, integration of medical and social science may play an important role in the provision of health care to children and adolescents and in an understanding of why health is poor in certain subgroups and how health and well-being may be enhanced. Typically, these efforts involve sociologists and psychologists. From the social scientist's perspective, one of the most relevant features of child and adolescent health is the increasing focus on prevention. Prevention efforts typically attempt to alter the health behavior of individuals via a variety of programs. Social scientists may be involved in designing, implementing, and evaluating programs with behavioral, educational, social service, management, marketing, and community outreach components. Another relevant feature of young people's health status is that many of the morbidity problems encountered are the result of behavioral and environmental factors. Social scientists study the causes and consequences of differences among individuals or groups. In the case of health, the focus may be on (1) compliance with treatment protocols and maintenance of a specific health behavior or set of behaviors, (2) life-course trajectories of chronic illness in terms of emotional well-being and limits on daily activities, (3) behavioral and environmental risk factors for a specific condition, and (4) factors related to changes in perceived health over the life course. In particular, the integration of medical and social science becomes critical when it is understood that the major mediator of child health in all social services broadly (i.e., health, welfare, and education) is the family. We will spend the remainder of this chapter on these issues. We wish to note, however, that the discussion of the family will be limited to a relatively brief examination of the effect of childhood morbidity on the family and a more lengthy consideration of the implications of changes in family structure for access to services. This disparity does not reflect negatively on the importance of family structure and changes in it, but rather reflects our decision to focus on material not covered elsewhere.

Childhood Health and the Family

As for much of child care in the United States, the responsibility for child health-related care falls to the family (which is analogous to the stress on individual responsibility in adults) (Knowles 1986; Gerson and Strauss 1975). The tasks include identifying and obtaining needed services, providing nursing and transportation, and paying for much of the care out of pocket. Thus, severe childhood illness can constitute a major stress on a family both in terms of financial resources and the time and energy required to manage it. The few studies examining this issue have found that the impact of severe illness on the family varies as a function of disease severity and some indication of family socioeconomic status (McCormick, Charney, and Stemmler 1986; Stein and Riessman 1980).

The overall financial impact in families, however, is poorly understood. For the population in general, direct costs to the family are low because the most expensive portion, hospital care, is likely to be covered by insurance, and noninsured care such as prescriptions and medical devices are required by only a minority (DHEW 1986). This relatively benign picture does not pertain, however, to families of children with major problems. One study found that about 2 percent of admissions to a neonatal intensive care unit were not covered by insurance. Even with insurance coverage, approximately 7 percent of the charges remained to be paid by the parents (McCarthy et al. 1979). Since this care may cost tens or hundreds of thousands of dollars and since the burden would fall on relatively young couples at the low end of their lifetime earning curves, it is not surprising that perinatal services are the single largest source of uncompensated care absorbed by hospitals. Others have documented substantial costs/services for other specific conditions such as cancer or spina bifida (McCormick 1986; Pendergrass, Chad, and Hartmann 1985). Few studies document less obvious costs, such as transportation costs, costs for special food and equipment, and the time devoted to obtaining services and finding therapeutic services in the home. Moreover, the focus has been on the impact of relatively severe or chronic illnesses. The impact of relatively acute, self-limited problems is only beginning to be appreciated (e.g., day-care related infections).

Parental attitude toward childhood illness and parental investment of time and resources in care are beginning to be studied. Effects of illness on the child include overprotectiveness and restriction of activities, which may hamper acquisition of appropriate developmental skills. Such restrictiveness may interact with physical limitations to further reduce childhood functioning. The investment of parental resources, both financial and emotional, in the affected child may spell relative neglect of healthy siblings and the emergence of behavior problems in these children (Breslau, Weitzman, and Messenger 1981). Whether such stresses increase the risk of marital disruption is not clear from the literature, and anecdotal evidence supports both strengthening and weakening of marital relationships within individual families in the face of childhood chronic illness. What is clear is that the burden of caring for such children falls primarily to the mother. The mothers of chronically ill children have an increased prevalence of emotional problems (Breslau, Staruch, and Mortimer 1982). In addition, the burden of child care restricts their opportunities for outside activities, including employment, resulting in lower family incomes compared to similar families without children with chronic illness (Salkever 1980). Thus, the families of children with chronic illness may have fewer resources to cope with the greater demands of their child's health problem.

To have one health problem is not to be immune to other factors affecting child health. As noted earlier, poor low birthweight children and poor children with chronic illness are more likely to experience developmental and school failure than their more advantaged peers (Escalona 1982). In addition, some studies suggest that other facets of the new morbidity, such as behavior problems and learning disorders, are more prevalent in disabled children, either as a result of physiologic problems associated with the health problem or the emotional ambience surrounding its management (Escalona 1982). The issues of the additional vulnerabilities arising from socioeconomic disadvantage or specific types of family structure and coping style are complex and are just beginning to receive attention.

In view of the stresses of caring for handicapped and severely ill children, it is not surprising that heated controversies have arisen around the decisions regarding their care, especially as technology extends the range and costs of such treatment. In the past, such decisions were often made unilaterally by health professionals or in consultation with parents. More recently, such approaches have been questioned on the basis of variable knowledge and experiences among health professionals regarding the outcomes of relatively rare conditions and the effect of acute emotional distress in the ability of young, often inexperienced parents in making such decisions. On the positive side, the opening of the debate to a broader audience has led to more rigorous examination of societal values concerning the quality of life (The Problem of Personhood 1983), institutionalization of mechanisms for assuring broader impact into such decisions (Michaels and Oliver 1986), and pressures to provide care and education in family and community settings rather than commitment to institutions (Palfrey, Mervis, and Butler 1978). On the negative side, however, young families may be subjected to acute anguish in the event that their child's care becomes the focus of public attention (Fox 1986) and that care must often be provided in the face of diminished personal and public resources, as we will see below.

Child Health, Educational, and Social Services

In our relatively brief review of child health, we have attempted to illustrate three major points: (1) the skewed distribution of morbidity and mortality such that only a minority of children experience major problems, (2) the broader functional impact of childhood morbidity, and (3) the environmental correlates of morbidity both as a mediator of severity and as a consequence of childhood illness. These themes have implications for the types of services and access to these services required to prevent childhood morbidity or to manage it if unpreventable. Included in this discussion are concerns about the efficacy of current intervention to reduce morbidity and the resources required to provide effective interventions.

Services related to pregnancy outcome. Since the late 1960s the infant mortality rate has declined rapidly from the rate in 1965 by over 50 percent. Almost all of this decrease occurred among neonatal deaths. Recent research has concluded that at most the decline seen among low birthweight/premature infants has been the result of increased survivorship through the use of neonatal intensive care (McCormick 1985). Although numerically less visible, a concomitant increase in survivorship for a variety of hereditary conditions also has occurred (Hobbs and Perrin 1985). In other words, a major factor in the decrease in neonatal mortality has been the application of "high-tech" care to increasing the survival of infants born with major health problems, not a decrease in the proportion of such infants.

Although undoubtedly effective in decreasing mortality generally, the application of such technology has raised several major concerns. Among these are the ethical issues about the value of survival in individual cases noted earlier. Decisions to withhold life-sustaining technology because the child was deemed unable to experience a meaningful existence have raised intense debate on what constitutes such existence (*The Problem of Personhood*, 1983). Intense legal and regulatory activity to protect the rights of such children, independent of parental and professional opinion, continues (Fox 1986). Equally traumatic are decisions to withdraw treatment from infants who appear not to be improving. As a result, regulations have been devised to make withholding potentially life-sustaining treatment from infants, except on a very limited basis, a reportable event under existing child abuse laws. Individual hospitals have instituted special committees to review all such decisions (Michaels and Oliver 1986).

A second issue raised by the success of neonatal intensive care is the cost. Individual hospitalizations for very tiny infants may exceed several months, resulting in bills in the hundreds of thousands of dollars. Although such enormous expenditures are rare, bills in the tens of thousands are not. These costs not only represent a considerable allocation of general societal resources but also affect many young families with inadequate or no health insurance. Because of the lack of individual resources, the costs of prenatal and neonatal services have become one of the largest components of uncompensated care (i.e., care not covered by third-party payers) reported by most hospitals, an issue of increasing salience in an era of cost containment for medical care. What is less well recognized is that discharge from the hospital does not end the expenditures for medical care, most of which are borne by the family out of its own pocket. Not only do some major problems result in large additional expenditures annually (Hobbs and

Perrin 1985), but the ability of such families to earn additional income may be reduced, as indicated earlier. These concerns are most poignant for the small number of children who survive but remain "technology-dependent," for example, those that require continued assisted ventilation with oxygen and respirators or nutritional support by vein (total parenteral alimentation). If the parents are unable to provide the considerable medical attention these infants require, longer-term institutional placement may be necessary but not available, resulting in prolonged residence in acute care hospitals at high expense.

A third issue involves variations in the quality of care among hospitals. In the early 1970s, much of intensive care was concentrated in major university hospitals because of the relative lack of skilled manpower and the rapidity of innovation. To assure access to such services, well-defined referral networks were advocated as the organizational framework for the regions surrounding these health centers (McCormick, Shapiro, and Starfield 1985). Even then, differences in outcome could be documented among units ostensibly delivering services at a similar level of intensity (Greenland, Watson, and Neutra 1981). With the expansion of training programs and the increased number of pediatricians generally, the establishment of intensive care units in community hospitals has become more widespread, a move reinforced both by institutional pride and cost-containment procedures. The extent to which this may alter the quality of care available remains to be seen.

The dilemmas of the intensive care unit have led to renewed interest in the prevention of adverse pregnancy outcome, particularly through increasing the effectiveness of reproductive care. Evidence of success in this regard is spotty. With regard to congenital malformations, success in reducing some conditions resulting from exposure to infectious agents such as rubella has been achieved, but reducing malformations caused by other intrauterine infections is proving more difficult. Avoidance of other known teratogens, such as alcohol, would also prevent some malformations. The difficulty in implementing such strategies stems from two sources. Such avoidance would have to be initiated before a conception is planned, since the teratogens often have already affected development by the time the pregnancy is confirmed. Second, as noted earlier, the causes of most malformations are not known. Thus, most approaches to the reduction of infants born with congenital malformations rely on the recognition of affected fetuses and the termination of the pregnancy before viability. Such techniques include screening parents in high-risk groups for carrier status (e.g., Tay-Sachs disease), testing maternal serum for chemicals indicative of malformation (serum alpha-fetoprotein screening), or detection of malformations on ultrasound examination for other purposes. Whether increased risk is anticipated on the basis of such examinations or on other factors such ss maternal age alone for chromosomal anomalies, the verification of the anomaly often requires examination of fetal tissues, either early in pregnancy through the technique of chorionic villus sampling or by amniocentesis, both of which carry some risk of associated abortion. However, the widespread application and acceptance of these techniques are limited by both societal and individual attitudes toward therapeutic abortion.

The prevention of low birthweight/ premature births appears more hopeful. However, as a recent Institute of Medicine report (1985) concluded, although on balance the evidence suggested a positive effect of prenatal care on birthweight, the effect is not overwhelming. Despite a relatively steady increase in the proportion of women initiating prenatal care early in pregnancy up until the early 1980s, the rate of low birthweights had declined by only a small percentage, and the proportion of very tiny infants, those weighing 1,500 grams (3.3 pounds) or less, had not changed in the same time period. Moreover, although individual programs were found to have been relatively successful in some sites, the generalizability of · these results is uncertain, as the selection factors and exact contents of the services provided often were not well described. Population-based analyses suggest that prenatal care accounted for little of the difference in birthweight among groups when other risk factors were controlled.

In defense of prenatal care, establishing its effectiveness in reducing the rate of low birthweight is fraught with difficulty. The most rigorous evidence, that derived from randomized clinical controlled trials, would be ethically impossible to obtain. In addition, prenatal care itself is not a unitary intervention but consists of several types of services, and the efficacy of each needs documentation. Besides varying among providers, the types of prenatal services required by individual women may vary according to need, further complicating the situation. Finally, those most in need of services, especially the disadvantaged who are at most risk, may have difficulty in gaining access to such services and maintaining participation in the processes of prenatal care. In sum, early initiation of prenatal care appears a necessary precondition to reducing the incidence of low birthweight, because applications of potentially useful interventions would not be possible without it. However, development of such interventions is necessary, since early care by itself is not sufficient to alter the incidence of low birthweight (Brooks-Gunn, McCormick, and Heagarty 1988).

In view of the importance of low birthweight/prematurity as a cause of neonatal mortality, research is focused on the basic mechanisms accounting for these problems and the incorporation of resulting findings into practice. The Institute of Medicine report lists several promising areas in such research, among them techniques to detect those who are at risk for premature labor and the institution of labor-inhibiting regimens. In addition, a number of research endeavors for improving access and coordination in prenatal services, especially for disadvantaged women, are highlighted in the Institute of Medicine report. The extent to which such activities may reduce levels of adverse outcome in the coming decade, however, remains to be established. Reductions in the incidence of adverse outcome will need to focus on the persistence of differential rates by ethnicity and social class. Low-income pregnant women are more likely to have low birthweight infants; therefore these are the same women who are most affected by changes in services and in economic conditions (Fisher, LoGerfo, and Daling 1985). Indeed, disadvantaged women are still less likely to receive family antenatal care: Almost two-fifths of all black women in 1983 did not receive early antenatal care, as compared to a fifth of white women (Ingram, Makuc, and Kleinman 1986). Believing that altering one's health behavior influences health outcomes may vary as a function of cultural contextual education. Ethnic or social class variations in attitudes and beliefs have not been frequently studied; one study documented differences between working-class and middle-class women's sources of information, prenatal attitudes toward childbirth, and prenatal planning, as well as their response to childbirth classes, with the working-class women being most favorable affected (Nelson 1982). Such findings suggest that more emphasis needs to be placed in the context of prenatal education, as well as on the meaning of antenatal care for different groups of women (Brooks-Gunn, Warren, and Rosso 1987). However, the question still remains as to whether changes in prenatal care will influence the incidence in low birthweight (Strobino et al. 1986).

Two nagging concerns shadow attempts to alter pregnancy outcome through the implementation of medical interventions in the prenatal and intrapartum periods. The first is financing. As with neonatal intensive care, the individual woman and her partner may be unable to provide the resources needed, particularly since obstetric care often remains an optional part of health insurance. In addition, routine obstetric care is often paid as a package (i.e., so much for the physician's fees for the prenatal care and delivery), and any referrals may result in additional costs of the patient and loss of income to the obstetrician. Obtaining adequate prenatal care for indigent women is exacerbated by the fact that many state Medicaid program fees for prenatal care are set way below general prevailing rates (although reimbursement for inpatient care at delivery may be competitive [Alan Guttmacher Institute 1987]), and public health programs may be of limited availability or attractiveness.

The second concern reflects the increase in litigation and malpractice insurance around the outcomes of pregnancy. Increasingly, any adverse outcome, no matter that it represents a chance event, may result in a malpractice suit. In an era when the desirable family size is much smaller than previously, parents' expectations are that each pregnancy result in a "perfect" child. In part, such suits may also reflect the lack of financial support for the care of handicapped children and appear as an opportunity for parents to recoup some of the costs of caring for the affected child. Another factor is the relatively extended period after the event (child's majority [age 21] plus two years) in which suits may be filed compared to other types of malpractice. Depending on one's professional affiliations, the increase in such suits also are attributed either to an excess of aggressive lawyers or to a salutatory increase in the recognition of physician error. However, malpractice concerns place restrictions on the more rigorous examination of the content and effectiveness of prenatal care because of the need to practice defensive medicine in adhering to established patterns of care and by employing unneeded testing. They also reduce access to care through the loss of practitioners willing to take on the care of high-risk, especially poor, patients.

For a small but an increasing number of conditions, screening in the neonatal period before the infant goes home for the first time has proven effective in reducing subsequent morbidity. The hallmarks of such conditions are that (1) they are detectable by the screening process before other symptoms would lead to diagnosis in a pre-symptomatic state, (2) an effective therapeutic intervention can be implemented to prevent deterioration, and (3) the disease causes severe enough consequences that screening and treatment, even of rare conditions, are outweighed by the costs of managing the conditions. Such neonatal screening activities focus on relatively rare metabolic or hereditary conditions, such as phenylketonuria (PKU), congenital hypothyroidism, and sickle-cell anemia; blood tests, state mandated and supported, are administered to newborns before the infants leave the nursery. Although the conditions are rare, their consequences are so devastating that early treatment has proven to be cost-effective by rigorous standards. Suitable screening procedures for other hereditary conditions are being implemented or developed and clearly could be less costly as the range of conditions that could be assayed with a single procedure is increased (Caravella, Clark, and Dweck 1987).

The use of neonatal screening programs raises several issues (Holtzman, Leonard, and Farfel 1981). The first relates to the nature of the reproductive counseling given to siblings and to the affected individuals themselves. The laws of genetics dictate that half of the siblings of individuals with recessive genetic disorders will be carriers, and it may not always be possible to detect the carrier state. However, this information will have been obtained at a time quite distant from that when their own reproductive decisions are being made. The type of counseling and even monitoring may be particularly important for women affected by such a disorder, since treatment may only partially correct the defect, potentially allowing any fetus that a woman carries to be exposed to harmful substances.

Second, the identification of one of these conditions may represent the commitment of the individual to a lifelong regimen, some of which—for example, the PKU diet—are restrictive and unpalatable. Financial support for such special regimens is a problem. In addition, establishing the optimal period for maintaining such regimens, with the opportunity to end or decrease the reliance on especially burdensome therapies when the risk of damage is low, remains controversial. Because of these considerations, the opportunity of achieving a more normal physiological state with the replacement of the effect of defective genes through bioengineering techniques is exciting. Recent reviews have described the substantial nature of the remaining work to be done before implementation, as well as the restricted nature of what can be achieved.

While prenatal, intrapartum, and neonatal services are being examined and improved, a major force in the reduction of adverse pregnancy outcomes is and will continue to be the prevention of pregnancies or, in the face of an early pregnancy, reduction in the number of viable births to women at high risk for adverse outcome, to carriers of hereditary problems, and to those at medical or demographic risk for premature/low birthweight births and malformations. Such approaches are particularly relevant to adolescent pregnancy. Rates of sexual activity among teens in the United States are not noticeably higher than rates in Western Europe, yet our incidence of pregnancy and childbearing exceeds the level of almost all industrialized nations (Westoff, Calot, and Foster 1983). Reproductive management may depend more on contraception than on sexuality, given the high numbers of adolescents who are engaging in sexual behavior. Mixed messages about contraception and the lack of an effective birth control delivery system have resulted in a low level of contraceptive use by the majority of teenage women. Over one-half of all teenagers do not use contraception the first time they have sexual relations, and the majority do not practice birth control regularly thereafter (Zelnick and Shah 1983). For example, most adolescents who use clinic services have been sexually active for a year or more before their initial visit (Zabin et al. 1979). Some teenagers, however, are effective contraceptive users; Zelnik and Kantner (1978) have estimated that without the practice of contraception, more than 600,000 additional pregnancies would occur each year.

The focus on adolescents has often obscured the larger problem. Controlling for socioeconomic status reduces the differential in adverse outcome between teens and older women. Alternatively, reducing the number of births to adolescent mothers would eliminate only a small, albeit important, proportion of at-risk births. In other words, the problem of adolescent pregnancy is part of the larger problem of poverty (Hayes 1987). Thus, prevention of adverse pregnancy outcomes must also address the reproductive services provided to all low-income women. However, since many of the reproductive decisions of poor women appear to occur within the context of specific relationships rather than in the context of longer-term marital and financial goals (McCormick et al. 1987), a broader array of services and approaches may be required, especially in view of the fragmentation of reproductive services currently provided low-income women (and men).

Routine medical care in infancy and childhood. Routine health care of infants and young children involves prevention of illness whenever possible, screening for presymptomatic conditions to initiate early treatment, and early diagnosis and management of morbidity to prevent more serious sequelae. Such services are usually provided in the traditional context of office-based medical professionals (usually pediatricians) and hospital and public health clinics.

The premier example of successful prevention is immunization against the common communicable diseases of childhood. Although some doubt existed that the mortality from conditions such as diphtheria was decreasing before the introduction of vaccines, unfortunate recent experience suggests that such vaccines are indeed effective, at least in controlling pertussis (whooping cough). More recent, mandated vaccines (polio, measles, mumps, rubella) were introduced in the context of large rigorous trials from which evidence of cost-effectiveness is more compelling. Either already available or nearly so are a number of new vaccines against common childhood bacterial diseases caused by such organisms as pneumococcus, hemophilus, and neisseria, which cause such serious illnesses as pneumonia and meningitis, and other viral diseases, such as chicken pox and rota virus, the latter causing a substantial proportion of the diarrheal disease in the winter. Further extension of the range of potential vaccines through modern genetic-engineering techniques likewise offers optimistic views of decreasing or eliminating much of the morbidity associated with the acute illnesses of early childhood, even in developed countries (Hinman, Bart, and Orenstein 1985).

As with pregnancy outcome, the issue of litigation has affected the use of vaccines, even those mandated by public health regulations. Recent concerns about adverse effects of vaccines, especially reactions to the pertussis component of the basic DPT shot and risk of polio in unimmunized adults exposed to young children receiving live virus vaccines, has led to a decrease in the number of pharmaceutical firms willing to produce vaccine. Indeed, the situation has become so dire that special compensation legislation was passed to assure continued production of mandated vaccines, the first such compensation legislation in the history of the United States. Whether new vaccines also will be covered by such legislation remains an unanswered question. Even with such legislation, adverse publicity has affected public acceptance of routine immunizations. In England the failure to obtain such immunizations resulted in an epidemic of pertussis before stricter compliance was enforced. Although such widespread increase in disease has not occurred in the United States, isolated instances of increases in preventable diseases have been documented in groups who for one reason or another have not received immunizations. Perhaps more widespread is the increased cost of providing immunizations because of the added cost of malpractice insurance and the alteration of immunization schedules to a more frequent and costly number of visits in the attempt to reduce the incidence of reactions.

Of equal concern is the delivery of vaccines to those who most need them, children from disadvantaged backgrounds. Assurance of immunization completion currently relies on the requirements for school entry. However, that may leave the youngest children, those most in need of protection, without adequate monitoring. Despite a variety of techniques for enhancing compliance with immunization schedules, disadvantaged children's immunizations are less likely to be complete.

The efficacy of many other preventive techniques in childhood remains less well established. Although pediatric education stresses the role of the practitioner in fostering healthful practices through counseling, little evidence supports its utility. Some studies report successful efforts to encourage preventive practices, such as the use of infant car seats (Christopherson 1982), but, in general, examinations of the effect of the current well-child schedule of visits or specific effects on development or injury prevention have revealed little relationship with practitioner activities (Hoekelman 1983; Chamberlin and Szumowski 1980; Dershewitz and Williamson 1977).

Screening for children at risk or presymptomatic for certain conditions and management for disease encompass a wide range of activities. In general, the "package" known as health care services appears to have been effective in reducing the bur-

den of morbidity. Children in the United States today experience far less morbidity than even a generation ago, and the severity of the morbidity has decreased. Although the literature is neither as strong nor as broad as desirable, it provides general support for the role of health services in bringing about these changes (Starfield 1985). For the vulnerable subgroups already mentioned, problems in identifying and obtaining needed services persist.

Despite clear evidence of increased morbidity, poor children and children with chronic illnesses may have difficulty obtaining medical services because of the organizational and financial complexities affecting child health services, perhaps even more so than services for adults. As noted earlier, children are highly dependent on their parents to pay for care, either through insurance or out of pocket. Their parents, however, belong to the age group least likely to have health insurance or much disposable income as they are just starting their careers or work for small businesses with limited fringe benefits. The major public support for child health services, Medicaid, is linked to state welfare eligibility requirements. In some states only a quarter of the children in families below the federal poverty level are covered (Blendon and Moloney 1982). Moreover, many state Medicaid programs pay providers well below their usual fees, thus discouraging acceptance of Medicaid patients (Alan Guttmacher Institute 1987). Although most units of local government (state, city, county) provide maternal and child health services in special clinics, these services tend to cover only a limited number of services (prenatal care, treatment of sexually transmitted diseases, immunizations), requiring reliance on other providers (usually hospitals) for illness-related care. National data suggest that the gap in health care use by poor and nonpoor has been essentially eliminated, but the overall national figures do not take into account the relatively increased need of poor children. After controlling for indication of morbidity, the figures reveal that poor children are still at a disadvantage in receiving needed care (Newacheck and Halfon 1986).

For children with chronic illness, financial barriers also pertain. In addition, organizational barriers may hamper even those with the resources to obtain services. Children with severe, chronic problems may require multiple services. For example, a child with juvenile rheumatoid arthritis may require the services of a pediatric rheumatologist to diagnose and treat the disease, a physical therapist to design programs to keep the joints mobile, specialized surgeons to treat severe joint problems, and other specialists, such as ophthalmologists, to monitor and treat other sequelae of the disease. In other conditions, for example, diabetes mellitus, a nutritionist may be required. Since many of these individual conditions remain relatively rare, these multidisciplinary services may be provided only in special medical centers that are inaccessible to children who live far away or are unable to pay for such services. Referral to and payment for special services may be further constrained even for middle-class families as a result of current cost-containment strategies. Many of these strategies rely on restricting payment for services to those providers practicing in specific types of supposedly less costly arrangements (e.g., health maintenance organizations or preferred provider organizations [Luft, 1985]). Rarely are the specialized centers part of such cost-saving arrangements.

Services related to child health and development. What about the children with the new morbidity? Here there is difficulty in identifying what the appropriate services might be. In part, this difficulty reflects the fact that the services may rely on techniques and approaches not traditionally considered "medical." Such techniques may involve counseling beyond that which can occur in a relatively brief office visit, education in settings outside the medical center, and regulation. Currently, the experience

with these techniques consists of relatively small experimental or demonstration programs applied to relatively small groups of single products.

An illustrative example of prevention using the new morbidity as an indicator of health is the early childhood intervention movement. An underlying goal of this movement was (and still is) to prevent or ameliorate disadvantaged children's developmental dysfunction. For example, more than 10 percent of all disadvantaged children, as compared to the population estimate of 2.5 percent, will be classified as mildly retarded during their school career (Meier 1976). Since not all disadvantaged children exhibit developmental dysfunction, what factors identify children at risk? These factors include low maternal educational attainment, poverty level incomes, parents with few job skills, familial unemployment or receipt of public assistance, minority status, English as a second language, single parents, adolescent parents, and parents or siblings with IQ scores in the mild retardation range (Begab 1981). Many of these characteristics are the same as those associated with low birthweight births.

Several strategies have been used to alter the incidence of developmental dysfunction. Some focus on remedial assistance after the child has entered the school system and is identified as dysfunctional; however, children entering special classes are not likely to emerge on a regular class track during their school years, virtually ensuring that they will be less literate than their schoolmates (Mercer 1977). Others offer services prior to the onset of school-related problems. This strategy is philosophically compatible with health-oriented approaches in that dysfunction may be prevented rather than ameliorated by altering behavior, motivation, and goals of children and their parents. Therefore, it is not surprising that early intervention programs, which historically have emphasized preventive solutions, have had close ties to the pediatric community (Brooks-Gunn and

Hearn 1982; Brooks-Gunn, McCormick, and Heagarty 1988). The designers of many of the first programs recognized the contribution of health-related problems to developmental dysfunction and provided health and nutrition services or referrals, as well as psychoeducational ones, to their children (North 1970, 1979; Zigler and Valentine, 1979).

After twenty years of intervention across many different educational approaches, early intervention has proved successful in altering children's intellectual and school functioning. Children who receive no early programming have been compared to children who attended preschool in programs that participated in a large-scale evaluation known as the Cornell Consortium of Longitudinal Studies (Darlington et al. 1980; Lazar and Darlington 1982). Children who attended the preschool programs (1) had higher intelligence scores at age 6, (2) were approximately one-half a grade ahead in mathematics ability in fourth grade, (3) benefited from the programs regardless of their initial level of functioning (i.e., not just the brighter or the less advanced children were helped), (4) were less likely to be assigned to special education classes, (5) were less likely to be held back in grade level, and (6) were less likely to drop out or to be classified as delinquents in adolescence. In addition, benefits accrue to the parents. Mothers are more likely to continue schooling and work when their children are in full-time intervention programs (Clewell, Brooks-Gunn, and Benasich in press). Often this has had the effect of allowing families to become self-sufficient; if a family moves off welfare during a child's preschool years, the chances of school failure in elementary and high school are decreased (Furstenberg, Brooks-Gunn, and Morgan 1987).

Similarly, intensive programs have been implemented to prevent smoking in school-aged children, as have programs against drinking or illicit drug use. Many of these programs have been successful, with a variety of approaches being used (Botvin, Eng, and Williams 1980; Evans and Raines 1982; Perry et al. 1980). Current research is focusing on the prevention of drinking and drug use and on specifying the program dimensions that account for the successes of the antismoking programs (Botvin 1982; Durell and Bukowski 1982; Johnson 1982; Perry and Jessor 1985). Examples of regulatory activity include changing the drinking age, requiring helmets for motorcyclists, enforcing infant car seat laws, and setting product safety standards. Such regulation has lowered morbidity associated with high-risk behavior (Litt in press; Watson, Zador, and Wilks 1981). Sometimes, however, prevention programs may have the opposite effect, as in the positive association between car accidents and driver education classes (Robertson 1980).

Several factors characterize these programs. The first is that most are multifaceted packages requiring substantial personnel and time commitments on the part of the provider. It is often impossible to disentangle the "effective elements" to design lower-cost alternatives, especially since many of these efforts have involved single sites where the personalities of both providers and participants may play significant roles. Indeed, the expense and intensity of efforts to prevent or change the sequelae of such pervasive influences as poverty may and should not be surprising. As a consequence, however, considerations of costs suggest careful targeting to those who could most benefit. The problem of targeting is illustrative of a second problem that involves limits in predicting individual outcomes. Although we are able to characterize groups at high risk, individuals within those groups may vary widely from the predicted course. In part, this reflects the insensitivity of our current measurement techniques and our lack of understanding of the effects of many of the mediations of child health and development. In part, however, the difficulty in prediction arises from the enormous resiliency and plasticity in human development that permits children to bypass and overcome major obstacles to achieve normal development. Clearly, the more these barriers are faced by the individual child, the less likely are they to achieve this success. The latter consideration raises the third major concern about existing programs in that they usually deal with children with a specific problem (e.g., poor but healthy, chronically ill but not poor, etc.). Dealing with children vulnerable on more than one basis only increases the intensity, cost, and organizational complexities of achieving maximal functioning, probably at an exponential rather than additive rate, in view of the issues noted above.

Clearly, approaches to services for the vulnerable subgroups require educational and social service programs to be integrated with pediatric services. First, age of entrance favors health care settings. Some believe that home-visitor programs are most effective when initiated prior to birth (Siegel, et al. 1980); if this is true, then antenatal clinics are a logical place to begin screening and identification procedures, as well as parenting and child-oriented services. A majority of pregnant women are already linked to prenatal care. If infancy is a point at which programming is to begin, clinical facilities such as well-baby stations in hospitals and community health centers provide access to this age group. No other social service has direct access to this population, at least in terms of identifying infants who would be most likely to benefit from early intervention. Pediatric visits present an opportunity for early identification of children who are at risk for developmental delays and other problems. Since the pediatrician is seen as a "first line of defense" for a child, links with existing intervention programs need to be developed or programs need to be included in pediatric clinical activities. Second, many community health clinics already have outreach components for the identification of individuals in need of medical services. Outreach efforts could be **expanded** to include early childhood de**velopmental** problems rather than focusing

only on health. Third, pediatricians may easily integrate psychoeducational and health information during infancy into well-baby visits, since mothers desire knowledge about physical care, emotional well-being, cognitive growth, and language development of children. Finally, several programs have been initiated that are based on intervention models and have been integrated into the health system, such as programs that serve premature and biologically at-risk infants, handicapped infants, and adolescent mothers and their infants (Baldwin and Cain 1981; Brooks-Gunn and Hearn 1982; Clewell, Brooks-Gunn, and Benasich in press).

SUMMARY

We have tried to provide an overview of infant, child, and adolescent health, focusing on those problems that represent major sources of morbidity. It is critical to consider the age of the child, given that morbidity is now defined in terms of developmental appropriateness and that the role of the family and the practitioner varies as a function of the child's developmental status. In addition, we have stressed the importance of proportionately small but highly significant vulnerable groups of children: the poor, the chronically ill, and those with the new morbidity, a dysfunction not traditionally considered in medical terms but the province of social scientists. Finally, we have attempted to illustrate the societal implications of childhood illness on two levels: (1) the family and (2) the health, educational, and social services sector.

In a chapter as brief as this, one cannot consider all relevant areas (or even most) in depth. For example, we have glossed over the efficacy of individual services and ignored some of the professional training and manpower issues inherent in a discussion of child health. Further, we have restricted our considerations solely to the United States and have not reviewed child health problems elsewhere, where they may be more serious, as in the developing countries. Finally, child health and health services are not independent of consideration of welfare, labor, and educational policies, areas too broad to be considered here.

What we have attempted to illustrate is both the good and the bad news. The good news is that American children are experiencing unparalleled good health as a result of the reduction in problems related to birth, exposure to infectious illness, and malnutrition. The bad news is that a new set of problems has emerged or, more accurately, is receiving more attention. The new morbidity may reflect the complexities and difficulties in meeting the requirements of growing up in an advanced, sophisticated culture. The ability to read fluently is not as critical to a farming economy as it is to a computer-based service economy. The other element of bad news is that not all have benefited equally from the gains in health and social services. A small proportion of children still are afflicted with serious illnesses, which effect their emotional well-being as well as their family's functioning. More importantly, poor children experience major health problems as a sequela of their poverty, and this persistence of morbidity has implications for long-term physical and mental health. Unfortunately, however, few studies have addressed the issue of continuity of health problems from childhood to adulthood.

Again, the good news is that we appear to be developing models of service delivery that alter the outcomes for these vulnerable groups. The bad news is that we have not made the financial nor organizational commitments necessary to ensure access to needed services. Additionally, study of how healthy behavior is promoted in children and their families is accorded relatively sparse funding. In the absence of an overt and inherent policy to support maternal and child health, such commitments are unlikely to emerge in view of the lack of public support for children and competition for scarce resources by more orga-

nized voting blocs, such as the elderly (Axinn and Stern 1985). The challenge in the future is to foster such a consensus.

ACKNOWLEDGMENTS

The Preparation of this chapter was supported by the W. T. Grant Foundation, the Robert Wood Johnson Foundation, the National Institutes of Health (NICHD), and the Office of Adolescent Pregnancy Problems. We wish to thank R. Deibler, L. Lissemore, and F. Kelly for their help in manuscript preparation.

REFERENCES

Achenbach, T. M., and C. S. Edelbrock. 1978. The Classification of Child Psychopathology: A Review and Analysis of Empirical Effects. *Psychological Bulletin* 85:1275–1301.

———. 1984. Psychopathology of Childhood. *Annual Review Of Psychology* 35:227–256.

Alan Guttmacher Institute. 1987. *Blessed Events and the Bottom Line.* New York: Alan Guttmacher Institute.

Alpert, J. J., and B. Guyer, eds. 1985. Injuries and Injury Prevention. *Pediatric Clinics of North America* 32:1–265.

Attie, I., and J. Brooks-Gunn. 1987. Weight-related Concerns in Women: A Response to or a Cause of Stress? In R. C. Barnett, L. Bierner, and G. K. Baruch, eds., *Gender and Stress.* New York: Free Press, pp. 218–254.

———. In press a. The Emergence of Eating Disorders and Eating Problems in Adolescence: A Developmental Perspective. *Journal of Child Psychology and Psychiatry.*

———. In press b. The Development of Eating Problems in Adolescent Girls: A Longitudinal Study. *Developmental Psychology.*

Axinn, J., and M. J. Stern. 1985. Aging and Dependency: Children and the Aged in American Social Policy. *Milbank Memorial Fund Quarterly* 63:648–670.

Baldwin, W. S. 1976. Adolescent Pregnancy and Childbearing—Growing Concerns for Americans. *Population Bulletin* 31:2. Washington, D.C.: Population Reference Bureau.

Baldwin, W., and V. Cain. 1981. The Children of Teenage Parents, in F. F. Furstenberg, Jr.,

R. Lincoln, and J. Menken, eds., *Teenage Sexuality, Pregnancy and Childbearing*. Philadelphia: University of Pennsylvania Press.

Baltes, P. B., H. W. Reese, and L. P. Lipsitt. 1980. Life-Span Developmental Psychology. *Annual Review Psychology* 31:65–110.

Bane, M. J., and D. T. Ellwood. 1983. *The Dynamics of Dependence: The Routes to Self Sufficiency*. Cambridge, Mass.: Urban Systems and Engineering.

Bean, F., R. L. Curtis, and J. P. Marcum. 1977. Familism and Marital Satisfaction among Mexican Americans. *Journal of Marriage and Family* 39:759–767.

Becker, M. H., L. A. Maiman, J. P. Kircht, D. P. Haefner, and R. H. Drachman. 1977. The Health Belief Model and Prediction of Dietary Compliance: A Field Experiment. *Journal of Health and Social Behavior* 18:348–366.

Becker, M. H., S. M. Radius, I. M. Rosenstock, R. H. Drachman, K. C. Schuberth, and K. C. Teets. 1978. Compliance with a Medical Regimen for Asthma: A Test of the Health Belief Model. *Public Health Reports* 93:268–277.

Begab, M., ed. 1981. *Psychosocial Influences and Retarded Performance: Strategies for Improving Social Competence*, vol. 2. Baltimore: University Park Press.

Blendon, R. J., and T. W. Moloney, eds. 1982. *New Approaches to the Medicaid Crisis*. New York: F and S Press.

Blum, R. W. 1988. Developing with Disabilities in Early Adolescence, in E. R. McAnarney and M. Levine, eds., *Early Adolescent Transitions*. New York: Heath Publications, pp. 177–192.

Botvin, G. J. 1982. Broadening the Focus of Smoking, Prevention Strategies, in T. J. Coates, A. C. Petersen, and C. Perry, eds., *Promoting Adolescent Health: A Dialog on Research and Practice*. New York: Academic Press, pp. 137–148.

Botvin, G. J., A. Eng, and C. L. Williams. 1980. Preventing the Onset of Cigarette Smoking through Life Skills Training. *Preventive Medicine* 9:135–143.

Bray, G. A. 1985. Complications of Obesity. *Annals of Internal Medicine* 103:1052–1062.

Breslau N., K. S. Staruch, and E. A. Mortimer. 1982. Psychological Distress in Mothers of Disabled Children. *American Journal of Diseases of Children* 136:682–686.

Breslau, N., M. Weitzman, and K. Messenger. 1981. Psychological Functioning of Siblings of Disabled Children. *Pediatrics* 67:344–353.

Brim, O. G., Jr., and J. Kagan. 1980. *Constancy and Change in Human Development*. Cambridge, Mass.: Harvard University Press.

Brooks-Gunn, J. In press. Adolescents as Children and as Parents: A Developmental Perspective, in I. E. Sigel and G. H. Brody, eds., *Family Research*, vol. 1. Hillsdale, N.J.: Erlbaum.

Brooks-Gunn, J., and F. F. Furstenberg, Jr. 1986. The Children of Adolescent Mothers: Physical, Academic and Psychological Outcomes. *Developmental Review* 6:224–251.

Brooks-Gunn, J., and R. Hearn. 1982. Early Intervention and Developmental Dysfunction. Implications for Pediatrics. *Advances in Pediatrics* 497–527.

Brooks-Gunn, J., M. C. McCormick, and M. C. Heagarty. 1988. Preventing Infant Mortality and Morbidity: Developmental Perspectives. *American Journal of Orthopsychiatry* 58(2):288–296.

Brooks-Gunn, J., A. C. Petersen, and D. Eichorn. 1985. The Study of Maturational Timing Effects in Adolescence. *Journal of Youth and Adolescence* 14:149–161.

Brooks-Gunn, J., M. P. Warren, and J. T. Rosso. In press. The Impact of Pubertal and Social Events Upon Girls' Problem Behavior. Paper presented at symposium The Development of Depressive Affect in Adolescence, *Journal of Youth and Adolescence*.

Brown, S. S. 1979. The Health Needs of Adolescents in U.S., in *Healthy People: The Surgeon General's Report on Health Promotion and Disease Prevention, Background Papers*. DHEW Publication No. (PHS) 79-55071A, pp. 333–364.

Brumberg, J. J. 1985. "Fasting Girls": Reflections on Writing the History of Anorexia Nervosa, in A. B. Smuts and J. S. Hagen, eds., *History and Research in Child Development*, Monograph of the Society for Research in Child Development 50 (serial no. 211):4–5.

Brunswick, A. F., and P. Messeri. 1986. Drugs, Lifestyle, and Health: A Longitudinal Study of Urban Black Youth. *American Journal of Public Health* 75:52–57.

Butler, J. A., S. Rosenbaum, and J. S. Palfrey. 1987. Ensuring Access to Health Care for

Children and Disabilities. *New England Journal of Medicine* 317:162–165.

Caravella, S. J., D. A. Clark, and H. S. Dweck. 1987. Health Codes for New Born Care. *Pediatrics* 80:1–5.

Centers for Disease Control. 1984. Temporal Patterns on Motor-Vehicle Related Fatalities Associated with Young Drinking Drivers, United States, 1983. *Morbidity and Mortality Weekly Report* 33:699–701.

Chamberlin, R. W., and E. Szumowski. 1980. A Follow-up Study of Parent Education in Pediatric Office Practices: Impact at Age Two. *American Journal of Public Health* 70:1180–1188.

Christoffel, K. K. 1984. Homicide in Childhood: A Public Health Problem in Need of Attention. *American Journal of Public Health* 74:68–70.

Christopherson, E. R. 1982. Incorporating Behavioral Pediatrics into Primary Care. *Pediatric Clinician of North America* 29:261–296.

Clewell, B. C., J. Brooks-Gunn, and A. A. Benasich. In press. Child-Focused Programs for Teenage Parents: Anticipated and Unanticipated Benefits. *Family Relations*.

Coates, T. J., and C. E. Thoresen. 1978. Treating Obesity in Children and Adolescents: A Review. *American Journal of Public Health* 68:143–151.

Coleman, J. S. 1961. *The Adolescent Society*. New York: Free Press.

Crowther, J. H., G. Post, and L. Zaynow. 1985. The Prevalence of Bulimia and Binge Eating in Adolescent Girls. *International Journal of Eating Disorders* 4:29–42.

Darabi, K. F., and V. Ortiz. 1987. Childbearing among Young Latino Women in the United States. *American Journal of Public Health* 77:25–28.

Darlington, R. B., J. M. Royce, A. S. Snipper, H. W. Murray, and I. Lazar. 1980. Preschool Programs and Later School Competence of Children from Low-Income Families. *Science* 208:202–204.

Dershewitz, R. A., and J. Williamson. 1977. Prevention of Childhood Household Injuries: A Controlled Clinical Trial. *American Journal of Public Health* 67:1148–1153.

Deykin, E. Y., J. C. Levy, and V. Wells. 1986. Adolescent Depression, Alcohol and Drug Abuse. *American Journal of Public Health* 76:178–182.

Deykin, E. Y., R. P. Perlow, and J. McNamarra. 1985. Non-fatal Suicidal and Life-Threatening Behavior among 13- to 17-Year Old Adolescents Seeking Emergency Medical Care. *American Journal of Public Health* 75:90–92.

Donovan, J. E., and R. Jessor. 1983. Problem Drinking and the Dimension of Involvement with Drugs: A Guttman Scalogram Analysis of Adolescent Drug Use. *American Journal of Public Health* 73:543–552.

Dryfoos, J. 1985. School-Based Health Clinics: A New Approach to Preventing Adolescent Pregnancy? *Family Planning Perspective* 17:70–75.

Durell, J., and W. Bukowski. 1982. "Issues in the Development of Effective Prevention Practices," in T. J. Coates, A. C. Petersen, and C. Perry, eds., *Promoting Adolescent Health: A Dialog on Research and Practice*. New York: Academic Press, pp. 225–253.

Egbuonu, L., and B. Starfield. 1982. Child Health and Social Status. *Pediatrics* 69:550–557.

Eisen, M., C. A. Donald, J. E. Ware, and R. H. Brook. 1980. Conceptualization and Measurement of Health for Children in the Health Insurance Study. *R-2313 HEW*. Santa Monica, Calif.: Rand Corporation.

Escalona, S. K. 1982. Babies at Double Hazard: Early Development of Infants at Biologic and Social Risk. *Pediatrics* 70:670–676.

Evans, R. I., and B. E. Raines. 1982. Control and Prevention of Smoking in Adolescents: A Psychosocial Perspective, in T. J. Coates, A. C. Petersen, and C. Perry, eds., *Promoting Adolescent Health: A Dialog on Research and Practice*. New York: Academic Press, pp. 101–136.

Fairburn, C. G., and D. M. Garner. 1986. The Diagnosis of Bulimia Nervosa. *International Journal of Eating Disorders* 5:403–420.

Featherman, D. 0., and R. M. Lerner, eds. 1983–1987. *Life-Span Development and Behavior*, vols. 6–9. Hillsdale, N.J.: Earlbaum.

Fisher, E. S., J. P. LoGerfo, and J. R. Daling. 1985. Prenatal Care and Pregnancy Outcomes during the Recession: The Washington State Experience. *American Journal of Public Health* 75:866–869.

Fosarelli, P., M. Wilson, and C. DeAngelis. 1987. Prescription Medications in Infancy and Early Childhood. *American Journal of Diseases of Childhood* 141:772–775.

Fox, D. M., ed. 1986. Special Section in the Treatment of Handicapped Newborns. *Journal of Health Politics, Policy and Law* 11:195–303.

Freedman, D. S., C. L. Shear, G. L. Burke, S. R. Srinivasan, L. S. Webber, D. W. Harsha, and G. S. Berenson. 1987. Persistence of Juvenile-Onset Obesity over Eight Years: The Bogalusa Heart Study. *American Journal of Public Health* 77:588–592.

Fuchs, V. R. 1983. *How We Live: An Economic Perspective on Americans from Birth to Death.* Cambridge, Mass.: Harvard University Press.

Furstenberg, F. F., Jr., and J. Brooks-Gunn. 1986. Teenage Childbearing: Causes, Consequences and Remedies, in L. Aiken and D. Mechanic, eds., *Applications of Social Science to Clinical and Health Policy.* New Brunswick, N.J.: Rutgers University Press, pp. 307–334.

Furstenberg, F. F., Jr., J. Brooks-Gunn, and S. P. Morgan, 1987. *Adolescent Mothers in Later Life.* New York: Cambridge University Press.

Furstenberg, F. F., Jr., K. A. Moore, and J. L. Petersen. 1986. Sex Education and Sexual Experience Among Adolescents. *American Journal of Public Health* 75:(11):1331–1332.

Garner, D. M., and P. E. Garfinkel. 1980. Sociocultural Factors in the Development of Anorexia Nervosa. *Psychological Medicine* 10:647–656.

Gerson, E. M., and A. L. Strauss. 1975. Time for Living: Problems in Chronic Illness Care. *Social Policy* 6 (November–December):12–18.

Green, L. W., and D. Horton. 1982. Adolescent Health: Issues and Challenge, in T. J. Coates, A. C. Petersen, and C. Perry, eds., *Promoting Adolescent Health: A Dialog on Research and Practice.* New York: Academic Press, pp. 23–43.

Green, M., and A. Solnit. 1964. Reactions to the Threatened Loss of a Child: A Vulnerable Child Syndrome: Pediatric Management of the Dying Child. *Pediatrics* 34:58–66.

Greenland, S., E. Watson, and R. R. Neutra, 1981. The Case-Control Method in Medical Care Evaluation. *Medical Care* 19:872–878.

Guttmacher, Alan, 1981. *Teenage Pregnancy: The Problem That Won't Go Away.* New York: Alan Guttmacher Institute.

Haaga, J. 1986. Children's Seatbelt Usage: Evidence from the National Health Interview Survey. *American Journal of Public Health* 76:1425–1427.

Hadley, J. 1982. More Medical Care! Better Health? in Economic Analysis of Mortality Rates. Washington, D.C:. The Urban Institute.

Haggerty, R. J., K. H. Roghmann, and I. B. Pless. 1975. *Child Health and the Community.* New York: John Wiley.

Hamburg, B. A. 1982. Living with Chronic Illness, in T. J. Coates, A. C. Petersen, and C. Perry, eds., *Promoting Adolescent Health: A Dialog on Research and Practice.* New York: Academic Press, pp. 431–443.

Hamilton, L. H., J. Brooks-Gunn, and M. P. Warren. 1985. Sociocultural Influences on Eating Disorders in Female Professional Dancers. *International Journal of Eating Disorders* 4:465–477.

Hampton, R. L., and E. H. Newberger. 1985. Child Abuse Incidence and Reporting by Hospitals: Significance of Severity, Class, and Race. *American Journal of Public Health* 75:56–60.

Hankin, J. R., and B. H. Starfield. 1986. Epidemiologic Perspectives on Psychosocial Problems in Children, in N. A. Krasnegor, J. D. Aresteh, and M. F. Cataldo, eds., *Child Health Behavior: A Behavioral Pediatrics Perspective.* New York: John Wiley, pp. 70–93.

Hayes, C. D., ed. 1987. *Risking the Future: Adolescent Sexuality, Pregnancy, and Childbearing.* Washington, D.C.: National Academy Press.

Henshaw, S. K., N. J. Binkin, E. Blaine, and T. C. Smith. 1983. A Portrait of American Women Who Obtain Abortions. *Family Planning Perspectives* 17:90–96.

Hill, J. P., G. N. Holmbeck, L. Marlow, T. M. Green, and M. E. Lynch. 1985. Menarcheal Status and Parent-Child Relations in Families of Seventh-Grade Girls. *Journal of Youth and Adolescence* 14:301–316.

Hinman, A. R., K. J. Bart, and W. A. Orenstein. 1985. New Vaccines. *International Journal of Epidemiology* 14:502–503.

Hobbs, N., and J. M. Perrin. 1985. *Issues in the Care of Children with Chronic Illness.* San Francisco: Jossey-Bass.

Hoekelman, R. A. 1983. Well-Child Visits Revisited. *American Journal of Diseases of Children* 137:17–20.

Holtzman, N. A., C. O. Leonard, and M. R. Farfel. 1981. Issues in Antenatal and Neonatal Screening and Surveillance for Hereditary and Congentital Disorders. *Annual Review of Public Health* 2:219–251.

Ingram, D. D., D. Makuc, and J. C. Kleinman. 1986. National and State Trends in the Use of Prenatal Care, 1970–83. *American Journal of Public Health* 76:415–423.

Institute of Medicine. 1985. *Preventing Low Birthweight*. Washington, D.C.: National Academy Press.

Irwin, C. E., and S. G. Millstein. 1986. Biopsychosocial Correlates of Risk-taking Behaviors in Adolescence: Can the Physician Intervene? *Journal of Adolescent Health Care* 7:82s–96s.

Janz, N. K., and M. H. Becker. 1984. The Health Belief Model. A Decade Later. *Health Quarterly* 11:1–7.

Jekel, J. F., J. T. Harrison, D. R. Brancroft, N. Tyler, and L. Klerman. 1975. A Comparison of the Health Index and Subsequent Babies Born to School-Age Mothers. *American Journal of Public Health* 65:370–374.

Johnson, C. A. 1982. Untested and Erroneous Assumptions Underlying Antismoking Programs, in T. J. Coates, A. C. Petersen, and C. Perry, eds., *Promoting Adolescent Health: A Dialog on Research and Practice*. New York: Academic Press, pp. 397–412.

Johnson, J. H. 1986. *Life Events as Stressors in Childhood and Adolescence*. Beverly Hills: Sage Publications.

Johnston, L. D., J. G. Bachman, P. M. O'Malley. 1984. Use of Licit and Illicit Drugs by America's High School Students, 1975–84. DHHS Publication No. 85-1394. Rockville, Md.: National Institute of Drug Abuse.

Kalter, H., and J. Warkany. 1983. Congenital Malformations: Etiologic Factors and the Role in Prevention. *New England Journal of Medicine* 308:424–431, 491–497.

Kandel, D. B. 1975. Stages in Adolescent Involvement in Drug Use. *Science* 190:912–914.

———. 1982. Epidemiologic and Psychosocial Perspectives on Adolescent Drug Use. *Journal of American Academy of Child Psychiatry* 21:328–347.

Kandel, D. B., and M. Davies. 1982. Epidemiology of Depressive Mood in Adolescents. *Archives of General Psychiatry* 39:1205–1212.

———. 1986. Adult Sequelae of Adolescent Depressive Symptoms. *Archives of General Psychiatry* 43:255–262.

Kandel, D. B., and J. A. Logan. 1984. Patterns of Drug Use from Adolescence to Young Adulthood: I. Periods of Risk for Initiation, Continued Use, and Discontinuation. *American Journal of Public Health* 74:660–666.

Kaplan, H. B., C. Robbins, and S. S. Martin. 1983. Antecedents of Psychological Distress in Young Adults: Self-Rejection, Deprivation of Social Support, and Life Events. *Journal of Health and Social Behavior* 24:230–244.

Katzman, M. A., S. A. Wolchik, and S. L. Braver. 1984. Prevalence of Frequent Binge Eating and Bulimia in a Nonclinical College Sample. *International Journal of Eating Disorders* 3:53–62.

Kellam. S. G., C. H. Brown, and J. P. Fleming. 1982. The Prevention of Teenage Substance Use: Longitudinal Research and Strategy, in T. J. Coates, A. C. Petersen, and C. Perry, eds., *Promoting Adolescent Health: A Dialog on Research and Practice*. New York: Academic Press, pp. 71–200.

Kellam, S. G., C. Brown, C. Henricks, and J. P. Fleming. 1987. Longitudinal Community Epidemiological Studies of Drug Use: Early Aggressiveness, Shyness, and Learning Problems, in L. N. Robins, ed., *Studying Drug Abuse*. New Brunswick, N.J.: Rutgers University Press, pp. 57–91.

Kellam, S. G., C. H. Brown, B. R. Rubin, and M. E. Ensminger. 1983. Paths Leading to Teenage Psychiatric Symptoms and Substance Use: Developmental Epidemiological Studies in Woodlawn, in S. B. Guze, F. J. Earls, and J. E. Barrett, eds., *Childhood Psychopathology and Development*. New York: Raven Press, pp. 17–51.

Knowles, J. H. 1986. The Responsibility of the Individual, in *The Sociology of Health and Illness: Critical Perspectives*, 2nd ed. New York: St. Martin's Press.

Klerman, L. V., and J. F. Jekel. 1973. *School-Age Mothers: Problems, Programs and Policy*. Hamden, Conn.: Linnet Books.

Koenig, M. A., and M. Zelnik. 1982. Repeat Pregnancies Among Metropolitan-Area Teenagers: 1971–1979. *Family Planning Perspective* 14:341–344.

Lazar, I., and R. Darlington. 1982. Lasting Effects of Early Education: A Report from the Consortium for Longitudinal Studies. *Monographs of the Society for Research in Child Development* 47(serial no. 195).

Levine, M. D. 1982. The High-Prevalence–Low-Severity Developmental Disorders of School Children. *Advances in Pediatrics* 29:529–554.

Levine, M. D., and P. Satz. 1984. *Middle Childhood: Development and Dysfunction.* Baltimore: University Park Press.

Levine, S., and J. J. Feldman, and J. Elinson. 1983. Does Medical Care Do Any Good? In David Mechanic, ed., *Handbook of Health, Health Care, and the Health Professions.* New York: Free Press, pp. 394–404.

Levy, J. C. 1980. Vulnerable Children: Parents Perspectives and the Use of Medical Care. *Pediatrics* 65:956–963.

Links, P. 1983. Community Surveys of the Prevalence of Childhood Psychiatric Disorders: A Review. *Child Development* 54:531–548.

Litt, I. F. 1982. Adolescent Health in the United States as We Enter the 1980's, in T. Coates, A. C. Peterson, and C. Perry, eds., *Promoting Adolescent Health. A Dialog on Research and Practice.* New York: Academic Press, pp. 45–60.

———. In press. *Adolescent Substance Abuse. The Fourteenth Ross Round Table in Critical Approaches to Common Pediatric Problems.* Columbus, Ohio: Ross Laboratories.

Luft, H. S. 1985. Competition and Regulation. *Medical Care* 23:383–400.

McCarthy, J. T., B. L. Koops, P. R. Honeyfield, and L. J. Butterfield. 1979. Who Pays the Bill for Neonatal Intensive Care? *Journal of Pediatrics* 95:755–761.

McCormick, M. C. 1985. The Contribution of Low Birthweight to Infant Mortality and Childhood Morbidity. *New England Journal of Medicine* 312:82–90.

———. 1986. Implications of Recent Changes in Infant Mortality, in L. H. Aiken and D. Mechanic, eds., *Applications of Social Science to Clinical Medicine and Health Policy.* New Brunswick, N.J.: Rutgers University Press, pp. 282–306.

McCormick, M. C., J. Brooks-Gunn, T. Shorter, J. Holmes, C. Y. Wallace, and M. Heagarty. May 9, 1985. Who Does an Outreachworker Find? Paper presented at the Ambulatory Pediatric Association meeting, Washington, D.C.

McCormick, M. C., J. Brooks-Gunn, T. Shorter, C. Y. Wallace, J. Holmes, and M. C. Heagarty. 1987. The Planning of Pregnancy among Low-Income Women in Central Harlem. *American Journal of Obstetrics and Gynecology* 156:145–149.

McCormick, M. C., E. B. Charney, and M. M. Stemmler. 1986. Assessing the Impact of a Child with Spina Bifida in the Family. *Developmental Medicine and Child Neurology* 28:53–61.

McCormick, M. C., S. Shapiro, and B. H. Starfield. 1985. The Regionalization of Perinatal Care. Summary and Evaluation of a National Demonstration Program. *Journal of the American Medical Association* 253:799–804.

McKinlay, J. B., and J. B. McKinlay. 1986. Medical Measures and the Decline of Mortality, in P. Conrad and R. Kern, eds., *The Sociology of Health and Illness. Critical Perspectives*, 2nd ed. New York: St. Martin's Press, pp. 11–23.

Mead, G. H. 1972. *Mind, Self, and Society: From the Standpoint of a Social Behaviorist.* Chicago: University of Chicago Press.

Meier, J. H. 1976. *Developmental and Learning Disabilities.* Baltimore: University Park Press.

Mercer, J. R. 1977. Cultural Diversity, Mental Retardation and Assessment: The Case for Nonlabeling, in P. Mittler, ed., *Research to Practice in Mental Retardation: Care and Intervention*, vol. 1. Baltimore: University Park Press, pp. 353–362.

Michaels, R. H., and T. K. Oliver. 1986. Human Rights Consultation: A 12-Year Experience of a Pediatric Bioethics Committee. *Pediatrics* 78:566–572.

Moore K. A., and M. R. Burt. 1982. *Private Crisis, Public Cost.* Washington, D.C.: Urban Institute.

Moore, K. A., M. C. Simms, and C. L. Betsey. 1986. *Choice and Circumstance: Racial Differences in Adolescent Sexuality and Fertility.* Draft project report. Washington, D.C.: Urban Institute.

Nathanson, C. A., and M. H. Becker. 1985. The Influence of Client-Provider Relationships on Teenage Women's Subsequent Use of Contraception. *American Journal of Public Health* 75:33–38.

National Center for Health Statistics (NCHS). September 1983. Utilization of Short-Stay Hospitals by Adolescents. United States, 1980, in *Advance Data Vital and Health Statistics.* Public Health Service Publication No. 93, pp. 1–5.

Nelson, M. K. 1982. The Effect of Childbirth Preparation on Women of Different Social

Classes. *Journal of Health and Social Behavior* 23:339–352.

Newacheck, P. W., and N. Halfon. 1986. Access to Ambulatory Care Services for Economically Disadvantaged Children. *Pediatrics* 78:813–19.

North, A. F. 1970. Project Head Start: Implications for School Health. *American Journal of Public Health* 60:698–703.

———. 1979. Health Services in Head Start, in E. Zigler and J. Valentine, eds., *Project Head Start: A Legacy of the War on Poverty.* New York: Macmillan.

Paige, K. E. 1983. A Bargaining Theory of Menarcheal Responses in Preindustrial Cultures, in J. Brooks-Gunn and A. C. Petersen, eds., *Girls at Puberty: Biological and Psychosocial Perspectives.* New York. Plenum Press, pp. 301–322.

Palfrey, J. S., R. C. Mervis, and J. A. Butler. 1978. New Directions in the Evaluation and Education of Handicapped Children. *New England Journal of Medicine* 298:819–824.

Pendergrass, T. W., R. L. Chard, and J. R. Hartmann. 1985. Leukemia, in N. Hobbs and J. M. Perrin, eds., *Issues in the Care of Children with Chronic Illness.* San Francisco: Jossey-Bass, pp. 324–343.

Perry, C. L., and R. Jessor. 1985. The Concept of Health Promotion and the Prevention of Adolescent Drug Abuse. *Health Education Quarterly* 12:169–184.

Perry, C., J. Killen, M. Telch, L. A. Slinkard, and B. G. Danaher. 1980. Modifying Smoking Behavior of Teenagers: A School-Based Intervention. *American Journal of Public Health* 70:722–725.

Petersen, A. C., and J. Brooks-Gunn. 1988. Puberty and Adolescence, in E. A. Beechman and K. Brownell, eds., *Behavioral Medicine for Women.* New York: Pergamon Press, pp. 12–27.

Petersen, A. C., and W. E. Craighead. 1986. Emotional and Personality Development in Normal Adolescents and Young Adults, in G. Klerman, ed., *Suicide and Depression among Adolescents and Young Adults.* New York: American Psychiatric Press, pp. 19–52.

Polit, D. F., and J. R. Kahn. 1986. Early Subsequent Pregnancy among Economically Disadvantaged Teenage Mothers. *American Journal of Public Health* 76:167–171.

Pope, H. G., J. I. Hudson, and D. Yurgelun-Todd. 1984. Anorexia Nervosa and Bulimia Among 300 Suburban Women Shoppers. *American Journal Of Psychology* 141:292–294.

Problem of Personhood. 1983. Biomedical, Social, Legal and Policy Views. *Milbank Memorial Fund Quarterly* 61 (special issue).

Ramey, C. T., D. J. Stedman, A. Bordens-Patterson, and W. Mengel. 1978. Predicting School Failure from Information Available at Birth. *American Journal of Mental Deficiency* 82:525–534.

Reed, W. L. 1986. Suffer the Children: Some Effects of Racism on the Health of Black Infants, in P. Conrad and R. Kerns, ed., *The Sociology of Health and Illness: Critical Perspectives,* 2nd ed. New York: St. Martin's Press, pp. 272–280.

Robertson, L. S. 1980. Crash Involvement of Teenaged Drivers When Driver Education is Eliminated from High School. *American Journal of Public Health.* 70:599–603.

Robins, L. N. 1966. *Deviant Children Grown Up: A Sociological and Psychiatric Study of Sociopathic Personality.* Baltimore: Williams and Wilkins. (Reprinted by Robert E. Krieger Publishing, Huntington, N.Y., 1974.)

Robins, L. N., D. H. Davis, and E. Wish. 1977. Detecting Predictors of Rare Events: Demographic, Family, and Personal Deviance as Predictors of Stages in the Progression Toward Narcotic Addiction, in J. S. Strauss, H. Babigian, and M. A. Roff, eds., *The Origins and Course of Psychopathology: Methods of Longitudinal Research.* New York: Plenum Press.

Runyan, C. W., J. B. Kotch, L. H. Margolis, and P. A. Buescher. 1985. Childhood Injuries in North Carolina: A Statewide Analysis of Hospitalizations and Deaths. *American Journal of Public Health* 75:1429–1432.

Rutter, M. 1979. Maternal Deprivation, 1972–1978: New Findings, New Concepts, New Approaches. *Child Development* 50:283–305.

Rutter, M., P. Graham, O. F. Chadwick, and W. Yule. 1976. Adolescent Turmoil: Fact or Fiction? *Journal of Child Psychology and Psychiatry* 17:35–36.

Salkever, D. 1980. Children's Health Problems: Implications for Parental Labor Supply and Earnings, in V. Fuchs, ed., *Economic Aspects of Health.* Chicago: University of Chicago Press, pp. 221–251.

Sameroff, A. J., and M. J. Chandler. 1975. Reproductive Risk and the Continuum of Caretaking Casualty, in F. D. Horowitz, ed., *Review of Child Development Research*, vol. 4. Chicago: University of Chicago Press, pp. 187–244.

Schoenbach, V. J., B. H. Kaplan, E. H. Wagner, R. C. Grimson, and F. T. Miller. 1983. Prevalence of Self-Reported Depressive Symptoms in Young Adolescents. *Journal of Public Health* 73:1281–1287.

Shapiro, S., M. C. McCormick, B. H. Starfield, J. P. Krischer, and D. Bross. 1980. Relevance of Correlates of Infant Deaths for Significant Morbidity at One Year of Age. *American Journal of Obstetrics and Gynecology* 136:363–373.

Shapiro, S., E. R. Schlesinger, and R. E. Nesbitt. 1968. *Infant Perinatal, Maternal and Childhood Mortality in the United States*. Cambridge, Mass.: Harvard University Press.

Shonberg, K. 1985. Perspective on the Role of the Pediatrician in the Management of Adolescent Drug Use. *Pediatrics in Review* 7:131–132.

Siegel, E., K. E. Bauman, E. S. Schaefer, M. M. Saunders, and D. D. Ingram. 1980. Hospital and Home Support During Infancy: Impact on Maternal Attachment, Child Abuse and Neglect and Health Care Utilization. *Pediatrics* 66:183–190.

Simmons, R. G., and D. A. Blyth. 1987. *Moving into Adolescence: The Impact of Pubertal Change and School Context*. New York: Aldine Press.

Smith, E. A., and J. R. Udry. 1985. Coital and Non-coital Sexual Behaviors of White and Black Adolescents. *American Journal of Public Health* 75:1200–1203.

Starfield, B. 1985. *The Effectiveness of Medical Care Validating Clinical Wisdom*. Baltimore: Johns Hopkins University Press.

Stein, R. E. K., and C. K. Riessman. 1980. The Development of an Impact on Family Scale: Preliminary Findings. *Medical Care* 18:465–472.

Steinberg, L. D. 1981. Transformation in Family Relations at Puberty. *Developmental Psychology* 17:833–840.

Stevenson, J., N. Richman, and P. Graham. 1985. Behavior Problems and Language Abilities at Three Years and Behavioral Deviance at Eight Years. *Journal of Psychology and Psychiatry* 2:215–230.

Strobino, D. M., G. A. Chase, Y. J. Kim, B. E. Crawley, J. H. Salim, and G. Baruffi. 1986. The Impact of the Mississippi Improved Child Health Project on Prenatal Care and Low Birthweight. *American Journal of Public Health* 76:274–278.

Stunkard, A. J., and V. Burt. 1967. Obesity and the Body Image: II. Age at Onset of Disturbances in the Body. *American Journal of Psychiatry* 123:1443.

Stunkard, A. J., T. I. A. Sorensen, D. Hanis, T. W. Teasdale, R. Chakraborty, W. J. Schull, and F. Schulsinger. 1986. An Adoption Study of Obesity. *New England Journal of Medicine* 314:193–198.

Syme, L. S., and L. F. Berkman. 1986. Social Class, Susceptibility and Sickness, in P. Conrad and R. Kerns, eds., *The Sociology of Health and Illness: Critical Perspectives*, 2nd ed. New York: St. Martin's Press, pp. 28–34.

Task Force on Pediatric Education. 1978. *The Future of Pediatric Education*. Evanston: American Academy of Pediatrics.

Trinkoff, A. M., and S. P. Baker. 1986. Poisoning Hospitalizations and Deaths from Solids and Liquids among Children and Teenagers. *American Journal of Public Health* 76:657–660.

U. S. Department of Health, Education and Welfare (DHEW). 1976. *Vital Health Statistics*. Data from the National Health Survey. Publication No. (HRA) 76-1639, Series 11.

———. 1979. *Healthy People: The Surgeon General's Report on Health Promotion and Disease Prevention*. Publication No. 79-55071.

U.S. Department of Health and Human Services (DHHS). 1984. *Health United States*. Publication No. 85-1232, National Center for Health Statistics.

———. 1986. *Health United States*. Publication No. (PHS) 85-1232, National Center for Health Statistics.

Van Itallie, T. B. 1985. Health Implications of Overweight and Obesity in the U.S. *Annals of Internal Medicine* 103:983–988.

Vinovskis, M. A. 1981. An "Epidemic" of Adolescent Pregnancy? Some Historical Considerations. *Journal of Family History* Summer:205–230.

Watson, G. S., P. L. Zador, and A. Wilks. 1981. Helmet Use, Helmet Use Laws and Motorcyclist Fatalities. *American Journal of Public Health* 71:297–300.

Wegman, M. E. 1986. Annual Summary of Vital Statistics—1985. *Pediatrics* 78:983–994.

Weissman, M. M., and J. K. Myers. 1980. Clinical Depression in Alcoholism. *American Journal of Psychiatry* 137:372–373.

Westoff, C. F., G. Calot, and A. D. Foster. 1983. Teenage Fertility in Developed Nations: 1971–1980. *Family Planning Perspectives* 15:105–110.

Woody, E. Z., and P. R. Costanzo. 1981. The Socialization of Obesity-Prone Behavior, in S. S. Brehm, S. M. Kassin, and F. X. Gibbons, eds., *Developmental Social Psychology: Theory and Research*. Oxford: Oxford University Press.

Wooley, O. W., and S. C. Wooley. 1979. Obesity and Women I: A Closer Look at the Facts. *Women's Studies International Quarterly* 2:69–79.

Yogman, M. W., C. Herrera, and K. Bloom. 1983. Perinatal Characteristics of Newborns Relinquished at Birth. *American Journal of Public Health* 73:1194–1196.

Zabin, L. S., L. Schwab, J. F. Kantner, and M. Zelnik. 1979. The Risk of Adolescent Pregnancy in the First Months of Intercourse. *Family Planning Perspectives* 11:215–222.

Zelnick, M., and J. F. Kantner. 1978. Contraceptive Practices and Premarital Pregnancy among Women Aged 15–19 in 1976. *Family Planning Perspectives* 10:135–142.

Zelnick, M., J. F. Kantner, and K. Ford. 1981. *Sex and Pregnancy in Adolescence*. Beverly Hills: Sage Publications.

Zelnick, M., and F. K. Shah. 1983. First Intercourse among Young Americans. *Family Planning Perspectives* 15:64–70.

Zigler, E., and J. Valentine. 1979. *Project Head Start: A Legacy of the War on Poverty*. New York: Macmillan.

CHAPTER
18

HEALTH CARE FOR ADULTS

MERWYN R. GREENLICK

INTRODUCTION

The health care of American adults has already undergone two periods of dramatic change in the twentieth century and seems to be witnessing a third.

At the turn of the century, technological advances were increasing the effectiveness of care. The widespread use of vaccination was on the horizon, and the pattern of adult diseases would soon change from predominantly contagious disease to predominantly chronic degenerative disease. Aseptic surgery had become prevalent, and the modern hospital was developing. Meanwhile, a reform of medical education had been spurred on by the Flexner Report, which exposed the dangers of the existing system of medical education (Flexner 1910). Because of these changes, far more American adults began using the professional medical care system regularly. Solo practice physicians, mostly general practitioners, delivered the services, and patients

usually paid on a fee-for-service basis, since no health insurance was available. Most care took place in the doctor's office or in the patient's home.

World War II ushered in another set of changes that would restructure the American medical care system. The concept of health insurance had already begun to spread, partly as a result of the recent economic depression. Now the price and wage stabilization program of World War II institutionalized the concept of health insurance as a benefit of employment. The war also generated major advances in medical technology, including the introduction of powerful new anti-infectives, such as the sulfa drugs, and enormously improved surgical techniques. By the end of the war the hospital had become a central clinical institution, and in the 1950s the Hill-Burton program achieved its goal of making hospital beds available for all.

The pattern for the next quarter of a century had been set. Access to health care had become a right of all citizens. Polio vaccination had apparently eliminated infectious disease as a major health concern of adult Americans, and the forefront of the medical care system's battle against disease had shifted to heart disease, stroke, and cancer. As advanced training resources expanded and the number of hospitals increased, general practice gave way to specialty care. Fee-for-service was still the predominant mode of payment, but most employed and aged adults had access to health insurance either as a benefit of employment or through the national Medicare program.

In recent years, however, this picture has begun to change, and significant developments have emerged that may establish this period as the third major transition of the century. The purpose of this chapter is to review these developments and to help the reader assess their potential impact on the care of American adults.

The developments and trends to be discussed are of two kinds: (1) changes in disease patterns and medical care technology and (2) changes in the organization and financing of health care. In the former category, two diseases will be specifically considered—cardiovascular disease and acquired immune deficiency syndrome (AIDS). These two diseases will serve as case studies to help examine the forces that are changing the face of adult medical care. In reviewing the developments in the organization and financing of health care, the discussion will focus on changes that have contributed to the increasing bureaucratization of the health care system: the growth of health maintenance organizations (HMOs); the increased supply of health professionals; the resultant shift in the social control of medicine; and changes in the health insurance industry, particularly as these changes affect adults who are uninsured or underinsured. Finally, the chapter will present a framework for analyzing health policy in light of these major changes in the health care system.

CHANGES IN MAJOR DISEASES AND IN MEDICAL TECHNOLOGY

Cardiovascular disease and AIDS have emerged as dramatic examples of the relationship between disease patterns and adult health care—the former on the positive side and the latter on the negative. Both offer important lessons in understanding and assessing recent changes in adult health care.

Cardiovascular Diseases

The battle against cardiovascular disease offers the opportunity to examine changes that can reduce the incidence and death rate from major chronic degenerative disease. These include life-style changes that have the potential for reducing risk factor profiles of American adults, as well as changes in diagnosis and treatment of disease brought about by extraordinary advances in the system's technology.

Cardiovascular diseases kill more adult Americans than all other diseases combined. One of the more striking changes in the disease pattern of American adults, however, is the significant decline in mortality rate from cardiovascular diseases in the past twenty years. The mortality rate from coronary heart disease has decreased nearly 40 percent since 1963, and the stroke death rate has decreased 55 percent during that same period (see Figure 1). Reasons for this dramatic change in death rate include widespread changes in health behavior, some changes in early disease detection, and significant changes in the technology used in the diagnosis and treatment of cardiovascular disease.

Health behavior. Significant improvements in the health behavior of American adults have reduced all three major risk factors of coronary heart disease: cigarette smoking, hypertension, and elevated blood cholesterol.

Smoking behavior, especially, has

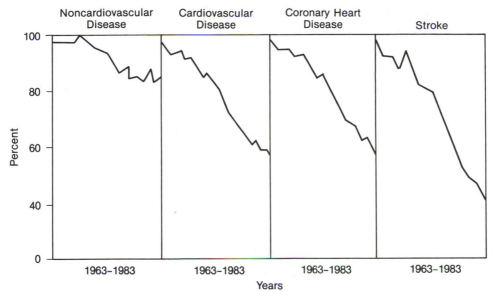

FIGURE 1 Twenty-Year Trend in Cardiovascular and Noncardiovascular Death Rates (age-adjusted) as a Percent of Rates, United States, 1963. (*Source*: National Heart, Lung, and Blood Institute (NHLBI), 1984, 12th Report of the Director, U.S. Department of Health and Human Services, Washington, D.C.: U.S. Government Printing Office, p. 6.)

changed for the better in American adults. Overall, smoking prevalence rates are at their lowest point since 1955 (USDHHS 1986, p. 179). In 1965, 43 percent of the population smoked cigarettes; by 1985 this number had dropped to 30.5 percent. The decline has been greatest for men, the group with the highest prevalence of smoking and the highest incidence of heart disease. The changes in rates since 1979 in men and women are shown in Figure 2.

Hypertension is the major risk factor for stroke. Changes in detection and treatment of hypertension have significantly influenced the death rates of cardiovascular diseases. As recently as a decade ago, less than one out of eight cases of hypertension was identified, treated, and under proper control. Today the majority of cases of hypertension are under treatment. Among the reasons for this change is the increased public awareness of the dangers of hypertension. More than 75 percent of the American population now recognize that high blood pressure causes illness, up from less than 30 percent in 1973. (See Figure 3.) Further, the results of a variety of trials of the efficacy of hypertension treatment have assured physicians of the efficacy of treating the disease. More patients are being appropriately treated for hypertension and therefore are seeing physicians more regularly.

Elevated blood cholesterol is also a heart disease and stroke risk factor that has been reduced by increased public awareness and by changes in the eating habits of American adults. These changes include reductions in the relative use of whole milk, butter, and other sources of animal fats. More Americans are aware of the need to reduce the consumption of dietary fat. As a result, the average blood cholesterol of American adults is beginning to drop (USDHHS 1986, p. 216).

Technological advances. Along with risk factor reductions, technological progress

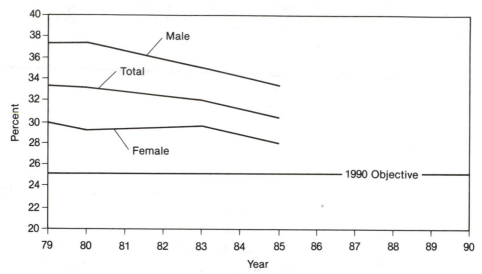

FIGURE 2 Prevalence of Smoking among Adults (percent of adults).
(*Source*: U.S. Department of Health and Human Services, 1986, *The 1990 Health Objectives for the Nation: A Midcourse Review*, Washington, D.C.: U.S. Government.Printing Office, p. 178.)

has been of major importance in the medical care of cardiovascular patients. As striking as the technological advances in this area are, they are merely examples of the variety of changes in technology through- out the medical care system. Of great importance is the increase in noninvasive diagnostic techniques. Three examples of such techniques in the cardiovascular area are echocardiography, digital subtraction

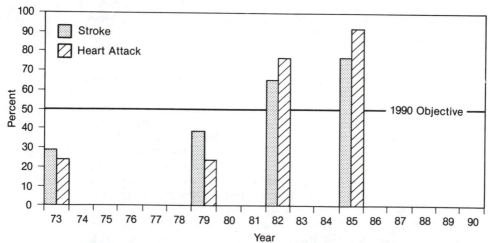

FIGURE 3 Awareness of Illnesses Caused by High Blood Pressure (percent of public aware). *(Source*: U.S. Department of Health and Human Services, 1986, *The 1990 Health Objectives for the Nation: A Midcourse Review*, Washington, D.C.: U.S. Government Printing Office, p. 20.)

angiography, and magnetic resonance imaging (MRI).

Echocardiography uses ultrasound to examine the heart. Over the past ten years, ultrasound has developed to the point where it is now a routine part of the examination of patients with suspected or known cardiovascular disease. Ultrasound technology obtains two-dimensional or moving pictures of the heart, thus making it possible to measure blood flow within the major chambers of the heart without invasive techniques and to detect leaking and narrowing cardiac valves. Further, advanced Doppler techniques now make it possible to obtain moving pictures of the blood flow within the heart.

Cardiac digital subtraction angiography involves the processing of X-ray images of the heart using digital computers. By translating pictures into numbers, digital computers enhance the use of contrast media in angiography, the process by which X-rays are taken inside the heart. The computers produce pictures that have subtracted the way the heart looked before the contrast medium was injected, allowing better pictures with a minimum of injected contrast media. This approach is useful as a diagnostic technique and can be used in conjunction with coronary angioplasty. This latter technique involves inflating and deflating balloons inside narrowed blood vessels in order to widen the vessels and improve blood flow. The use of computer-processed X-ray images of the blood vessels allows the balloons to be easily and correctly placed inside the blood vessels. This process can avoid the performance of the more dangerous and more costly coronary bypass surgery.

Magnetic resonance imaging (MRI), the newest form of imaging technology, is changing the way medical care is being provided in heart disease as well as in a variety of other diseases. It was first used about forty years ago in experiments by physicists. MRI forms images based on resonance characteristics of selected nuclei. The essential components of an MRI system are a magnet and a radio-frequency transmitter and receiver. In contrast to other whole-body imaging processes, MRI is minimally invasive and does not involve the use of ionizing radiation, as do X-ray technologies. Although a relatively new technology in its present form, MRI has extremely wide applicability in cardiovascular disease because it produces excellent three-dimensional images without the use of ionizing radiation and because it has the potential to evaluate metabolic and tissue function without the danger and expense of the more traditional techniques.

A variety of other technological innovations—including advances in transplant technology—have also affected the treatment of cardiovascular disease, the major killer of Americans.

AIDS

AIDS, first identified as a disease in 1981, presents a strikingly different picture. The disease is associated with a human retrovirus labeled HIV (previously called HTLV-III). This virus, apparently a mutation from a retrovirus found in green monkeys in Central Africa, is isolated from AIDS patients and the serum of these patients contains HIV antibodies. Approximately 30,000 cases of AIDS had been reported in the United States by December of 1986—more than twice the number reported by July of the previous year—and it is estimated that more than 500,000 people have been exposed to the disease.

AIDS is characterized by a severe depression of the body's immune system, resulting in susceptibility to many opportunistic diseases as well as to certain malignancies, such as Kaposi's sarcoma. The disease has an extremely high mortality rate, perhaps 100 percent of active cases. Originally the spread of the disease was largely confined to homosexual men, to intravenous drug users, and to people who contracted the disease through blood transfusions, particularly hemophilic patients. The disease is now generally considered to be sexually transmitted and is apparently moving into transmission through heterosexual channels. As this occurs, the disease has the potential for producing the most threatening epidemic of the twentieth century.

Although a great deal of attention has been given to research directed at producing an AIDS vaccine or discovering an effective drug to fight the disease, current American effort is also being aimed at prevention of the disease and at the organization of medical care services for AIDS patients. Prevention activities include education about the disease and about increasing the safety of sexual practices, particularly through the use of condoms. The efforts in this area appear to be making inroads, as newspapers, magazines, and even local television stations have begun to accept advertisements for condoms. Education about the danger of the disease has begun to generate significant changes in the pattern of both homosexual and heterosexual behavior.

Less success has attended the attempt to educate intravenous drug users and to provide clean needles for their use. This latter activity appears to run counter to the prejudices of mainstream America. The American blood transfusion supply, however, seems to have been protected through the use of tests to detect the presence of HIV virus in the blood.

Providing medical care for AIDS patients presents increasing challenges, some of which are common to the problem of organizing care in other fatal diseases. First of all, the cost is extremely high. Estimates of the average cost of caring for an AIDS patient from the time the disease is recognized until the patient dies range upward from $50,000 per case. And there is a growing movement to limit health insurance coverage for AIDS patients.

Hospital care, outpatient care, home care, and, generally, hospice care are required. Because the disease in new and little understood, voluntary care for the patient is difficult to find. In some cases, even professionals refuse to care for the patient. And because the public associates the disease with homosexuality and drug abuse, many patients are considered "undesirable" and made to feel guilty for acquiring the disease.

While the ultimate impact of AIDS is still unknown, the disease has already had significant and widespread effects on the way American adults view and use the health care system.

CHANGES IN THE ORGANIZATION AND FINANCING OF HEALTH CARE

Besides witnessing dramatic changes in the treatment of major diseases and the uses of medical technology, American adults have seen the health care system become increasingly bureaucratized. In one sense, this relatively recent development has had an even more profound effect than the changes described above, since it extends to virtually every adult who uses the medical care system.

For the first half of the twentieth century, medical care was dominated by the fee-for-service, solo-practice system. The physician was in control of the context and the content of care and was reimbursed directly by the patient for each item of service provided. In more recent times most patients had insurance coverage for some or all of the costs of care.

The concentration of power within the medical care system is shifting, however, with large and powerful institutions gaining dominance within the delivery system. In the early development of large concentrations of power in the field—for example, in the growth of the modern American hospital and in early prepaid group practice—individual professionals maintained very strong control over the institutions' management. This was an extension of the physician dominance exhibited in the solo-practice professional mode.

But as large organizations have begun to dominate the field, the power of individual health professionals to control these organizations has dramatically diminished. Managerial professionals have been given much more power to make decisions that influence the nature of the health care institution and, therefore, to determine the context and, to a growing extent, the content of health care. The history of the growth of health maintenance organizations (HMOs) in the United States provides an example of this phenomenon and a starting point from which to discuss the trend toward bureaucratization.

The Growth of HMOs

The history of HMOs in the United States can be divided into three phases: the movement phase, the consolidation phase, and the corporate phase. Each phase has its distinct nature and its relatively distinct time period (Greenlick, Freeborn, and Pope 1988, pp. 3–10).

The movement phase. The movement phase of HMO development began in the early 1930s, about the time of the publication of the final reports of the Committee on the Cost of Medical Care (CCMC) in the United States. One of the reports of the CCMC, the Lee-Jones study, encouraged the reorganization of the American medical care system (Lee and Jones 1933). Responding to the same problems that concerned the CCMC—mainly, the lack of physicians and the rising cost of medical care—several pioneer group practice prepayment plans were developed in the late 1930s and the 1940s. These plans had a variety of sponsors—labor unions, consumer cooperatives, industrial figures, local governments, and county medical societies—and each boasted a highly committed pioneer leader, usually a physician. These charismatic figures fostered the bureaucratization of medicine because they were able to use their personal and professional influence to attract resources and to gain physician acceptance of new practice patterns. The problems faced by these pioneer programs were enormous, but the inherent logic of the concept, and the ability

of these early programs to offer comprehensive prepaid benefits at a very reasonable price, allowed them to slowly develop an adequate membership from which to build a stable organization.

This pioneer period lasted about thirty years, until the mid-1960s. At that time there were probably fewer than four million members in HMOs in the United States (compared to more than twenty-one million by 1985), and three-quarters of these were in just two plans, Kaiser Permanente on the West Coast and HIP in New York.

The consolidation phase. Thirty-five years after the publication of the Lee-Jones study, the report of the National Advisory Commission on Health Manpower (1967) was issued. The commission reported essentially the same problems as reported earlier by the CCMC. However, it started the bandwagon of a national effort espousing the growth of HMOs as a solution to major problems of the health care system and led to the passage of the landmark HMO Act of 1973.

At the time of the passage of the HMO Act there were perhaps fifty HMO organizations in the country, with a total of about five million members. During this consolidation phase, including the remainder of the 1970s, existing HMOs grew stronger and expanded within geographic boundaries, while new programs of various types made tentative progress. Most of the HMOs of this time were organized in the nonprofit mode, but the older programs had begun to produce second-generation leadership and had developed along the lines of successful industrial organizations, particularly in the application of modern management and fiscal techniques and in the bureaucratization of the formal structure of the programs. By 1980 there were about 200 HMOs, with about eight million members.

The corporate phase. The period from about 1980 to the present can be labeled the corporate phase. It has been characterized by the entry into the HMO field of a group of large for-profit organizations. This activity has created much more rapid growth than previously because the profit-making form of organization allows significantly expanded opportunities for capital formulation, including the use of equity instruments for raising capital. There have also been significant efforts to foster both vertical and horizontal integration, using common industrial models. Giant health corporations, such as insurance companies, hospital corporations, and HMO organizations, have formed a variety of HMO chains to compete for the potential HMO business.

In 1988 the federal administration still considered stimulation of HMO growth to be a major tool in keeping the costs of medical care under control and proposed increasing use of HMOs in the areas of health care that feature government funding, particularly care of the poor and the aged. The most recent National HMO Census reported a total of 480 HMOs in operation at the end of 1985—of which 226 were less than two years old—with a total membership of more than twenty-one million (see Figures 4 and 5) (InterStudy 1986). The for-profit HMOs outnumbered the nonprofits in number of plans, but the nonprofits still had a majority of the members.

Increased Physician Supply

In the movement phase of HMO development one of the hindrances to HMO growth was the lack of physician manpower. Recruiting physicians to group and staff model HMOs was difficult, and the stiff opposition on the part of organized medicine to "closed-panel" practices placed a stumbling block in the way of managed health care systems. This was particularly true in adult medicine specialties.

American medical schools responded to the perceived major deficit in physician supply by dramatically expanding their capacities and by creating opportunities for the postgraduate education and certification of foreign medical graduates. As a result of that effort, the number of physi-

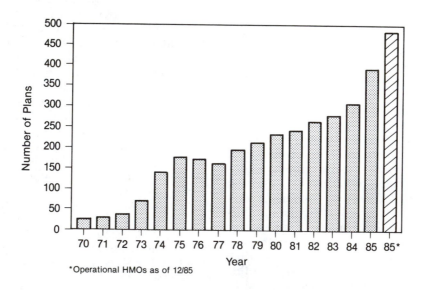

*Operational HMOs as of 12/85

FIGURE 4 Growth of Health Maintenance Organizations (June 1970–June 1985 and December 1985). *(Source:* InterStudy, 1986, *National HMO Census 1985,* Excelsior, Minn.: InterStudy, p. 2.)

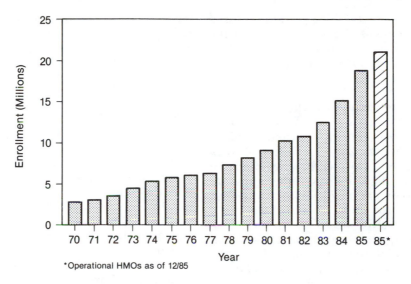

FIGURE 5 Growth of Health Maintenance Organization Enrollment (June 1970–June 1985 and December 1985). *(Source*: InterStudy, 1986, *National HMO Census 1985,* Excelsior, Minn.: InterStudy, p. 2.)

cians doubled in the United States, from a supply of 275,000 physicians in 1960 to nearly 550,000 in 1983 (see Table 1). This increase produced a change in the ratio of physicians per 100,000 people from 151 in 1960 to 228 in 1983, an increase of 50 per-

cent (U.S. Bureau of the Census 1985, p. 103, Table 162). The Department of Health and Human Services estimates that this will increase to 260 per 100,000 by the year 2000 (Iglehart 1986, p. 860). The significance of this, and other human resource trends in the health field, is reviewed by Loft and Kletke in Chapter 20. The purpose here is to comment on this trend relative to the effect of increased bureaucratization on the health care of adults.

In some ways this effect is paradoxical, since the increased physician supply has intensified the trend toward bureaucratization. As the supply of physicians increased, the traditional managed care systems began to find the recruitment of physicians much easier in most of the specialties, and plans for the expansion of existing programs and the development of new programs could proceed without concerns about the limitation of physician supply. Furthermore, the internal dominance of physicians within large health care organizations began to weaken as the supply of

TABLE 1 Physician Supply, United States, 1960 to 1983

	Number of Physicians (in thousands)	Rate per 100,000 Population*
1960	275	151
1965	305	155
1970	348	168
1975	409	187
1978	454	201
1979	472	207
1980	487	211
1981	505	217
1982	523	222
1983	542	228

*Based on Bureau of the Census resident population estimates as of July 1.
Source: Adapted from U.S. Bureau of the Census, 1985, *Statistical Abstract of the United States, 1986*, 106th ed. Washington, D.C.: U.S. Government Printing Office, p. 103, Table 161.

physicians increased. The physician dominance in hospitals began to weaken at the same time, largely through the changes in physician supply and resultant changes in the fee-for-service, solo-practice mode of medical practice.

This led to changes in how physicians within organizations assessed the appropriate balance between medical and administrative decision making. In a seminal work on this subject, Goss (1961) reviewed the mechanisms that mediated the apparent strain between the need for individual authority required for professional work and the administrative needs of an organization. Goss argued that when both supervisor and supervised are physicians, the control-oriented behavior of each is largely predetermined by established professional norms and values, to which each is equally socialized. On the other hand, physicians who become more dependent on large, complex medical care organizations and see community practice alternatives limited by increasing competition are likely to accept different authority patterns.

As the complex organizations in health care become more institutionalized, each creates a specific corporate culture that provides the structure and process required for the operation of that organization. A value system is defined, and a normative structure emerges that reflects a compromise between the professional subculture and the business culture. And in the successful organizations the culture establishes an equilibrium between the technical effectiveness of the organization, which requires meeting sets of medical goals (guarded by the professional interests), and the efficiency of the system, which requires meeting sets of economic goals (guarded by management interests).

This issue can be illustrated by some comments made by Maxicare Chairman and CEO Fred Wasserman (1986) on the takeover by Maxicare of Healthcare USA and HealthAmerica:

Well, I think the challenge is to be able to develop a corporate culture that is the same

throughout the company. . . . The cornerstone of the merger is our MIS system. That's without a doubt because once we get those plans on our MIS system, we basically have a way to work with those companies. We can put our utilization review programs in, we can put our grievance-monitoring system in and we can control other systems in a much more efficient way. (pp. 84–85)

This type of corporate jargon would probably not have been widely accepted, nor this kind of organizational concept widely implemented, had the physician glut not made community physicians more willing to be responsive to organizational demands.

The increase in supply of physicians, then, has apparently forced the community physicians to accept involvement in managed health care systems as a means of survival, perhaps causing somewhat of a decline in the measure of professional satisfaction in the American health care system. However, this same increase in the supply has also caused competitive behavior on the part of practicing physicians that could increase patients' access to and satisfaction with the medical care system. Physicians have begun to establish practices in areas that were significantly undersupplied in the past. Rural practices have begun to appear in sparsely populated places in the country, and physicians have begun to be much more willing to provide services in the inner city. These changes are mostly the result of increased competition caused by the increase in physician supply.

Shifting Control of Medicine

The nature of the medical care system involves a set of social control needs that must be met in some way for the system to function effectively. Prior to the development of HMOs and the dramatic increase in the supply of physicians, that social control was provided for within the normative structure of the culture of medicine and, therefore, within the individual socialization of the professionals in the system.

That was relatively effective, on balance, as long as the system was organized with the individual professionals in control of important decisions. When the supply of physicians increased, however, and when the system began to develop large and powerful institutions that controlled the organization and delivery of care, this locus of control began to change. Numerous social policy questions arose about the consequences of this change of control.

When the notion of medical care as a right swept Western Europe, the response was to increase the role of government in the medical care system. In the United States, however, the response was to strengthen the role of the individual physician, with the physician's internalized role structure protecting individual patients. Whenever an organization was required for solving societal problems in the health care field, the response was to increase the role of the voluntary, nonprofit form of organization. Consequently, when control of health care organizations shifted from individual physicians to professional managers, the stresses and accommodations involved were enormous.

To fully appreciate this, we must remember that the most important interaction in this social system has traditionally been that between physicians and patients. This interaction is structured in a unique way within our culture because of the functional requisites of the modern healing process. Some of the characteristics of the process are so pervasive that they have become a part of the larger American culture that determines the organization of the medical care subculture. Talcott Parsons (1951, pp. 428–479), in his classic work in the early 1950s, provided the conceptual framework for this assessment. He pointed out that the patient role is characterized by relative helplessness, a lack of technical competence, and emotional disturbance. The patient is in a particularly vulnerable situation where a high level of rational judgment is difficult.

The physician, on the other hand, works in a situation that requires the acquisition and use of a high degree of technical competence and a basic responsibility to do everything possible to forward the complete, early, and painless recovery of the patient. The physician is required to have and use a "rational orientation." Because of the nature of disease and the state of the medical sciences, the physician is faced with a difficult role set and lives in a situation of considerable uncertainty and ambivalence. The physician role that has evolved in this situation is characterized by an achievement orientation, a universalistic perspective (rather than the particularistic view of the patient), functional specificity, and affective neutrality.

This institutional pattern of medical practice serves to protect the interest of individual patients in a potentially explosive situation. The physician is given unique access to the patient's body and to the integrity of the individual. The physician has access to key confidential information about the patient and holds that information as a privileged communication. The patient is potentially exposed to physical, sexual, financial, and personal exploitation. All this is required by the nature of the healing process and is more or less freely consented to by the patient.

Up to now, the interest of the patient has been protected in our society by the professionalization of the medical practitioner. Everything in the socialization of the physician is geared to instilling the social control mechanism as an internalized component of the practicing professional. All the social control mechanisms of the profession work to create group norms to protect patients' interests and the social pressure mechanisms to enforce these norms. The system works relatively well in Western society, considering the significant pressures medical practice puts on the situation, as long as physicians are organized so that they practice alone or in small social groupings and as long as the critical decisions they make are made in an environment where the pressures are for conformity to professional norms that protect the patients.

This situation, however, is rapidly changing. Critical decisions are being made in situations where economic power is greatly concentrated and where the influence of the individual physician's professional norms is greatly weakened. More of these decisions are taking place in the context of large organizations, such as HMOs and very large hospitals, and within other kinds of organized practice settings. When this occurs, the nature of the organization becomes the controlling factor and therefore must become a unit of social analysis.

The critical decision nexus in organizations such as HMOs is the competing interest between physician concerns (for their individual patients and for their own self-interest) and the concerns of larger societal groups, such as overall HMO memberships, groups of stockholders, or the community generally. The balancing of these interests and of the relative power positions that affect decision making is most problematic. Physicians are professionally responsible to individual patients, but discharging this responsibility in an organized setting can prove difficult. Individual patient interests are not the same as the interests of the overall population.

Furthermore, physicians—individually and in groups—have a desire to maximize their own best interest. They naturally strive to enhance their own income, prestige, and working conditions. This strain becomes most apparent in organized HMO settings. Many of the critical management decisions in an HMO affect these matters. Consequently, the decision-making process tends to be implicit and circuitous, and the decisions produced are often controversial. Given this complexity, coupled with a degenerating social purpose culture, the force of public interest can easily get lost.

Changes in the Health Insurance Industry

In addition to the increased complexity and bureaucratization of the health care field, significant changes in the health insurance industry have also affected how

American adults use the health care system. Higgins and Meyers (1986) review the economic transformation of American health insurance and conclude that the power of management will grow as managers assume responsibility for both insurance products and service delivery in a variety of settings. They assert that in most metropolitan areas, physicians will be seen as replaceable and will be increasingly subordinate to management.

Higgins and Meyers point out some of the changes in the American economy that have led to particular changes in the health care system—for example, the effect of health insurance on increasing the costs of medical care to employers and to the country in general. They point to the fact that the health insurance industry's having developed largely as a passive, risk-sharing system caused much of this problem. As a result, health insurance incorporated a number of inflationary features, such as free choice of provider, cost- and charged-based reimbursement systems, fee-for-service payment, and the bias toward hospital care as opposed to ambulatory care. The high inflation and low productivity gains of the 1970s caused industry to move to such cost-saving measures as self-insurance to reduce the costs of employee benefits and thereby reduce the insurance coverage of many adults in the United States.

Other factors, however, also combined to create a situation where many adults in this country are either uninsured or underinsured. Such forces as high unemployment in the early 1980s and the movement of large segments of the work force from large industrial organizations to smaller service companies have intensified this problem. After World War II the proportion of the population with health insurance coverage increased steadily until about 1975. The trend has either flattened or declined since that period. The proportion of the population covered for hospital costs was 68.8 percent in 1960, rose to 82.1 percent by 1975, but declined to 82.0 percent in 1983. Physicians' expenses were covered for 46.7 percent of the population in 1960, 77.6 percent in 1975, and 74.5 percent in 1983 (see Table 2) (U.S. Bureau of the Census 1985, p. 102, Table 159).

Nor is the proportion without insurance evenly distributed in the population. While 15.2 percent of the total U.S. population were not covered by health insurance in 1983, 21.8 percent of the black population and 29.1 percent of the Spanish-origin population were not covered. More than 23 percent of the population aged 16–24 were without health insurance coverage, as were 18.5 percent of people 25–34 years of age (see Table 3) (U.S. Bureau of the Census 1985, p. 101, Table 157).

Significant differences also exist in the geographic distribution of insurance coverage. While only about 10 percent were uncovered in the eastern United States, more than 18 percent were without health insurance in the South and the West. A variety of studies have explored the problem in specific states. For example, a study in the Portland metropolitan area indicated that 17.5 percent of households headed by adults under age 65 did not have health insurance coverage (Center for Health Research 1986, p. 7). Nearly 36 percent of the uninsured families were headed by a woman, compared to less than 20 percent of the insured families. More than 23 percent of the uninsured families were classed as unemployed.

As could be expected, the uninsured were less likely to have received health care services. For example, more than 30 percent of the adult males and nearly 20 percent of the females in the insured households had not seen a physician for at least two years. In the uninsured households those proportions were 16 percent and 8 percent, respectively.

Similar data are available from studies of other states as well. For example, a study comparing medical care in Arizona (the last state with no Medicaid program) found that more than 32 percent of the Arizona poor had not had a physician visit in the past year, compared with about 21 percent of poor people around the country who had not had a visit within a year and 19 percent of the U.S. population who had not had a visit that year (Blendon et al. 1986).

An analysis from a Robert Wood Johnson Foundation national study provides more data on the problems of the uninsured population in the United States. According to Blendon, Altman, and Kilstein (1983), 300,000 uninsured families reported that in 1982 someone in their family was *refused* medical care for financial reasons. One million uninsured families indicated that someone in their family needed medical care but *did not receive* it for financial reasons. This and other studies report that the uninsured fall into three categories: the unemployed, families with no members in the labor force, and working people and their families. More than half are in the last group.

In a study reviewing the problem of the underinsured population, Farley (1985) estimated that in 1977 about 9 percent of the non-aged population were uninsured all of the year, 9 percent were uninsured for some of the year, and 9 percent were underinsured. This made the population that was uninsured or underinsured in 1977 a quarter of the non-aged U.S. population (Farley 1985, p. 477). It is probably higher now.

During the last national health insurance debate, around 1970, issues similar to these were advanced to prove the need for national health insurance (see Eilers and Moyerman 1971). Some felt that the issues raised at that time did not require a national health insurance plan for their solution. The problems mostly involved the organization and delivery of care, and their solution did not require such insurance (Greenlick 1971). Between that time and 1980, national health insurance discussions stopped, partly because the problems that could be solved by national health insurance were being solved by other means.

Medicare and Medicaid coverage ex-

TABLE 2 Private Health Insurance, Persons Covered for Specified Benefits, United States, 1960 to 1983

	1960	1965	1970	1975	1978	1979	1980	1981	1982	1983
Hospital expense										
Persons covered, net[1]	122.5	138.7	158.8	178.2	186.2	186.8	189.0	188.3	191.1	192.2
Percent of population covered[2]	68.8	72.4	78.7	82.1	83.2	82.5	82.5	81.4	81.7	82.0
Surgical expense										
Persons covered, net[5]	111.5	130.5	151.4	169.0	174.7	177.1	178.2	176.9	180.3	179.1
Percent of population covered[2]	62.6	68.1	75.0	77.9	78.0	78.2	77.8	76.4	77.1	76.4
Major medical expense[3]										
Persons covered, net[1]	32.6	69.7	103.5	134.1	142.7	149.9	155.3	156.0	163.1	161.5[3]
Blue Cross-Blue Shield plans	3.7	14.6	24.9	42.1	39.3	43.3	45.0	46.5	47.0[4]	44.6[4]
Physician's expense										
Persons covered, net[1]	83.2	109.6	138.7	168.3	166.8	167.2	169.5	164.1	171.6	173.1
Percent of population covered[2]	46.7	57.2	68.7	77.6	74.5	73.8	74.0	70.9	73.4	74.5

[1]Duplication among persons protected by more than one kind of insuring organization or more than one insurance policy providing the same type of coverage has been eliminated.
[2]Based on Bureau of the Census estimated civilian population as of July.
[3]Covers only persons under age 65.
[4]Estimated.
[5]Coverage provides protection against especially heavy medical bills resulting from "catastrophic" or prolonged illness and is used to supplement basic medical care insurance or as a comprehensive integrated program providing both basic and major medical protection, including charges for private duty nursing, drugs, and medical appliances.
Source: Adapted from U.S. Bureau of the Census, 1985, *Statistical Abstract of the United States, 1986*, 106th ed., Washington, D.C.: U.S. Government Printing Office, p. 102, Table 159.

TABLE 3 Health Insurance Coverage Status, by Selected Characteristics, United States, 1983

	Number (1,000)					Percent				
		Covered by private or government health insurance					Covered by private or government health insurance			
				Covered by private insurance					Covered by private insurance	
Characteristic	Total	Number	Total	Related to employment	Not covered by health insurance	Total	Number	Total	Related to employment	Not covered by health insurance
Total persons	231,209	196,177	172,674	140,372	35,032	100.0	84.8	74.7	60.7	15.2
Male	112,015	94,000	84,013	69,932	18,015	100.0	83.9	75.0	62.4	16.1
Female	119,194	102,177	88,661	70,440	17,017	100.0	85.7	74.4	59.1	14.3
White	196,823	169,308	153,629	124,696	27,514	100.0	86.0	78.1	63.4	14.0
Black	27,679	21,656	14,940	12,213	6,023	100.0	78.2	54.0	44.1	21.8
Spanish origin	13,896	9,850	7,239	6,211	4,046	100.0	70.9	52.1	44.7	29.1
Under 16 years	55,200	44,956	36,170	33,264	10,245	100.0	81.4	69.1	60.3	18.6
16–24 years	36,140	27,701	25,039	19,463	8,439	100.0	76.6	69.3	53.9	23.4
25–34 years	39,908	32,513	30,081	26,876	7,394	100.0	81.5	75.4	67.3	18.5
35–44 years	29,630	25,882	24,338	22,056	3,748	100.0	87.4	82.1	74.4	12.6
45–54 years	22,170	19,691	18,380	15,993	2,479	100.0	88.8	82.9	72.1	11.2
55–64 years	22,095	19,552	18,253	14,700	2,543	100.0	88.5	82.6	66.5	11.5
65 years and over	26,066	25,883	18,413	8,019	183	100.0	99.3	70.6	30.8	.7
Northeast	49,677	44,563	39,609	33,070	5,114	100.0	89.7	79.7	66.6	10.3
Midwest	56,628	51,516	45,860	37,009	7,112	100.0	87.9	78.2	63.1	12.1
South	79,106	64,330	56,665	45,027	14,776	100.0	81.3	71.6	56.9	18.7
West	43,798	35,769	30,540	25,265	8,029	100.0	81.7	69.7	57.7	18.3

Source: Adapted from U.S. Bureau of the Census, 1985, *Statistical Abstract of the United States, 1986,* 106th ed. Washington, D.C.: U.S. Government Printing Office, p. 101, Table 157.

panded greatly to include almost universal coverage for the aged and the poor. And organized insurance plans and health care systems such as HMOs opened to include poor and aged in their membership (Aiken and Mechanic 1986). Programs to deal with difficulties in the organization of care were proposed and implemented as a way to deal with the rising costs of the system and with some concerns over the quality of health care services. Such national programs as comprehensive health planning, peer review organizations, and the HMO Act were funded (Jonas 1977). Medicare legislation was modified to allow the inclusion of HMO risk contracts within the Medicare program (Greenlick et al. 1983), and the Medicaid programs in many states moved to risk-based insurance programs to integrate poor people into the community health care system.

This trend, however, seems to have been reversed. The market influences within the health care system have produced a variety of developments (accelerated by the influence of recent market-oriented national politics) that create significant new problems in the health care system. In addition to the issues reviewed above, it is necessary to consider the policy implications of the movement on the part of most health insurance organizations away from community-rating principles toward experience rating, and the movement of many health care organizations from the nonprofit to the for-profit mode. Both of these trends tend to create a health care culture within which management decisions are oriented toward relatively short-term market forces and away from overriding concern for larger social needs. Health care managers today refer to themselves as being market-driven; presumably, this term refers to the opposite of being value-driven. (In 1986 Congress stripped the Blue Cross plans of their tax-exempt status as a result of the apparent change in the social function of the programs.)

HEALTH POLICY ANALYSIS

Clearly, all of the developments reviewed above have serious and complex implications for analyzing health policy. While such an analysis is beyond the scope of this chapter, a word about possible approaches to health policy analysis is in order.

In the United States, the criteria most commonly used to analyze health policy issues, when any explicit criteria have been used at all, have been those that measured changes in the potential of the system to cure disease. Recently, perhaps in the last twenty years, a counterinfluence has been developing. This approach takes an equally single-minded perspective in health policy analysis, since it exclusively utilizes economic criteria. Neither of these oversimplistic approaches is sufficient for dealing with the complexities of most relevant issues.

Consequently, the reader's attention is called to an approach that was proposed several years ago for use in evaluating ambulatory care systems (Freeborn and Greenlick 1973) and that has been used for assessing various national health policy options (Greenlick and Colombo 1977). The approach requires simultaneous assessment of the effect of influences or trends on technical effectiveness, psychosocial effectiveness, and efficiency in the health care system. This method has at least two advantages. First, it provides a picture of the interrelationships of impacts among the criteria. For example, a development such as increased physician supply could be assessed as having a positive effect on one dimension and a negative effect on the other two. Secondly, this approach allows public policy decision makers to understand and make explicit the trade-offs when other parties are presenting a relatively subjective analysis or are failing to identify problems created in other dimensions of care when focusing on a single element, such as efficiency. This can move the policy debate to an explicit and, one would hope, more fruitful level.

Effectiveness (sometimes referred to as quality) requires measurement against stated goals, or possibly against generally accepted goals. This measurement has two components. The first is the measurement of technical effectiveness—that is, the extent to which the technical goals of the system are met. The second relates to measuring psychosocial effectiveness—that is, how well the psychological or social needs of the population and those who would be providers of care are met. In assessing this element it is necessary to consider patients and their satisfaction, but it is also necessary to bring questions of equity (fairness in the receipt of care) and access into this consideration. How trends affect equity will be especially relevant in considering changes in the health insurance industry.

Efficiency involves assessing costs of the total input needed to produce the required services for a population of given characteristics. In this way the costs can be assessed for the health care systems under varying conditions. In evaluating the relative efficiency of health care alternatives, the production function—the relationship between output and factor inputs—is examined, at least implicitly. An estimate of the production and cost function may permit the identification of a more efficient mix of the services and resources that are required.

The reader is invited to consider the impact of the developments reviewed in this chapter on issues of technical effectiveness, psychosocial effectiveness, and efficiency in the American health care system. The question of the effect of the growing number of adult Americans without adequate health insurance coverage can be assessed. The increasing forces that will reduce the number of people covered by health insurance through employment will need to be factored into the equation. These forces include changes in benefit packages offered by large employers, such as more self-insurance by employers and the movement to "cafeteria benefits programs" that have the effect of reducing the health insurance coverage of employees. Also to be factored into the analysis are the changes in the insurance industry that cause carriers of all kinds to move to experience rating, making it increasingly difficult for poorer risks to gain coverage.

Conditions in the economy must also be reviewed, including the frequently announced closings of so many industrial work sites, such as steel and automobile plants. These closings permanently remove large numbers of middle-aged workers from employment, thereby eliminating their access to adequate health insurance coverage. The diminished power of labor unions will also affect this analysis, because unions have been an important source for increasing the equity and coverage for health insurance. It appears that the strength of the union voice will be weakened in the coming decade.

Finally, the effect of the increasing supply of physicians on this issue can be assessed. Previous health policy debates were greatly affected by the power and influence of organized medicine. This power was based partly on the scarcity of physicians (Starr 1982) and partly on the mystique of the personal relationship between patients and physicians in the solo-practice, fee-for-service system. Both factors are disappearing. It is likely that the role, and perhaps even the position, of organized medicine will be very different in future health policy debates. The AMA has become very concerned over the growing influence of for-profit organizations in the organization and delivery of health care services. To some extent this is a conceptual reversal of the traditional support for a market-oriented health care system, but it also focuses on organized medicine's traditional concern about anything that moves toward organized, rather than solo practice, medical settings.

Since many of the issues reviewed in this chapter lead to concerns about access and equity in the adult health care system, the debate on questions of national health insurance could reignite. As growing numbers of the population lose access to the health care system, the disenfranchised group increasingly includes adults from the mainstream of society. This group has significant political power to bring to the policy debate, a different situation than when the object of concern was mostly poor people with very limited political leverage.

Further, American public policy debates are cyclical. The big debates on national health insurance happened just before and just after World War II and in the late 1960s and early 1970s. In other times more conservative forces dominated the debate. And as the pluralistic medical care system produced programs that solved the particular problems addressed in the debate, the demand for national solutions subsided. The reader should consider whether events are moving toward another such national policy debate and whether the policy analysis suggests that the specific problems emerging in the health care system serving adults will lead to increasing demands for consideration of a form of national health insurance to solve the specific deficiencies of the current system.

Even with the application of a systematic approach such as the one suggested above, the planning of health policy remains highly complex and challenging, especially when the forces involved are changing as rapidly and dramatically as they have been in recent years. Still, the future of the American health care system as it affects adults depends in great part on meeting this challenge. Technological progress will undoubtedly play an important role in that future. But decisions about the uses of technology, like those about the formulation of health policy, assume meeting an even greater challenge—the systematic and informed application of sound values.

REFERENCES

Aiken, L. H., and D. Mechanic, eds. 1986. *Applications of Social Science to Clinical Medicine and Health Policy.* New Brunswick, N.J.: Rutgers University Press.

Blendon, R. J., L. H. Aiken, H. E. Freeman, B. L. Kirkman-Liff, and J. W. Murphy. 1986. Uncompensated Care by Hospitals or Public Insurance for the Poor. *New England Journal of Medicine* 314(18):1160–1163.

Blendon, R. J., D. A. Altman, and S. M. Kilstein. 1983. Health Insurance for the Unemployed and Uninsured. *National Journal* 15(22):1146–1149.

Center for Health Research. 1986. *Health Insurance: Access and Choice—A Survey of Community Households.* Portland, Oregon: Center for Health Research, Kaiser Permanente.

Eilers, R. D., and S. S. Moyerman, eds. 1971. *National Health Insurance.* Homewood, Ill.: Richard D. Irwin.

Farley, P. J. 1985. Who Are the Underinsured? *Milbank Memorial Fund Quarterly* 63(3):476–503.

Flexner, A. 1910. *Medical Education in the United States and Canada: A Report to the Carnegie Foundation for the Advancement of Teaching* (Reprint). Washington, D.C.: Science and Health Publications.

Freeborn, D. K., and M. R. Greenlick. 1973. Evaluation of the Performance of Ambulatory Systems: Research Requirements and Opportunities. *Medical Care* 11(2) (Suppl.): 68–75.

Goss, M. E. W. 1961. Influence and Authority Among Physicians in an Outpatient Clinic. *American Sociological Review* 26(1):39–50.

Greenlick, M. R. 1971. Discussion of Ellwood Paper, in R. D. Eilers and S. S. Moyerman, eds., *National Health Insurance.* Homewood, Ill.: Richard D. Irwin.

Greenlick, M. R., and T. J. Colombo. 1977. A Framework for Assessing the Impact of Health Policy Alternatives. *Papers on the National Health Guidelines: Conditions for Change in the Health Care System.* USDHEW, PHS,

Health Resource Administration, 78-642:53–58. Washington, D.C.: U.S. Government Printing Office.

Greenlick, M. R., D. K. Freeborn, and C. R. Pope. 1988. *Health Care Research in an HMO: Two Decades of Discovery.* Baltimore: Johns Hopkins University Press.

Greenlick, M. R., S. J. Lamb, T. M. Carpenter, Jr., T. S. Fischer, S. D. Marks, and W. J. Cooper. 1983. Kaiser Permanente's Medicare Plus Project: A Successful Prospective Payment Demonstration. *Health Care Financing Review* 4(4):85–97.

Higgins, C. W., and E. D. Meyers. 1986. The Economic Transformation of American Health Insurance: Implications for the Hospital Industry. *Health Care Management Review* 11(4):21–27.

Iglehart, J. K. 1986. The Future Supply of Physicians. *New England Journal of Medicine* 314(13):860–864.

InterStudy. 1986. *National HMO Census 1985.* Excelsior, Minn.: InterStudy.

Jonas, S. 1977. *Health Care Delivery in the United States.* New York: Springer Publishing Co.

Lee. R. I., and L. W. Jones. 1933. *The Fundamentals of Good Medical Care.* Chicago: University of Chicago Press.

National Advisory Commission on Health Manpower. 1967. *Report,* vol. 1. Washington, D.C.: U.S. Government Printing Office.

National Heart, Lung, and Blood Institute (NHLBI). *12th Report of the Director.* U.S. Department of Health and Human Services. Washington, D.C.: U.S. Government Printing Office.

Parsons, T. 1951. *The Social System.* New York: Free Press.

Starr, P. 1982. *The Social Transformation of American Medicine.* New York: Basic Books.

U.S. Bureau of the Census. 1985. *Statistical Abstract of the United States, 1986,* 106th ed. Washington, D.C.: U.S. Government Printing Office.

U.S. Department of Health and Human Services (USDHHS). 1986. *The 1990 Health Objectives for the Nation: A Midcourse Review.* Washington, D.C.: U.S. Government Printing Office.

Wasserman, Fred. 1986. Interview in *Hospitals* 60(22):84–86.

CHAPTER
19
HEALTH, AGING, AND MEDICAL SOCIOLOGY

CARROLL L. ESTES
STEVEN P. WALLACE
ELIZABETH A. BINNEY

MEDICAL SOCIOLOGY AND AGING

Social gerontology and medical sociology have similar and intertwined histories. Both fields deal with topics that have attracted wide sociological interest in the past thirty years, and both are areas in which applied research is as common as theory building. Medical sociology has taken the lead in exploring major issues of importance to aging, including the organization and financing of health care, the causes and consequences of the changing patterns in the distribution of health and illness in society, the social construction of health in everyday life, and the interrelationship between health and the political-economic system. One important difference between approaches to medical sociology and to gerontology is that the former has included a focus on a powerful social *institution* (medicine), whereas the dominant focus in gerontology has been on *individuals* in later

life. The focus on older individuals in gerontology and illness in medical sociology frequently leads to an analysis of aging and health as social problems. In other societies, however, aging and health can have different meanings. In some societies aging is positively valued for the wisdom and traditions associated with advanced age, while health is defined as a spiritual rather than physiological phenomenon (Palmore 1975). In such contexts, aging is not a problem, but a valued process.

In contemporary U.S. society, old age is more commonly associated with being sick, useless, and dependent. The fact that the aging are perceived with alarm by some policymakers and social analysts (especially economists) raises the question of how aging in the United States has come to be defined as an important problem. The onset of what has come to be known as "old age" has no natural or biological marker. Physiologically, individuals have different levels of functional ability at the same chronological age (Salthouse 1982). While there are no sharp biological or chronological markers that can divide old age from other ages, age 65 is widely considered a turning point to old age, and the increasing number of people over that age are a concern in public policy.

This chapter will discuss how old age has come to be defined as a social problem, often in medical terms. We will also address some of the political and economic conditions that foster the construction of old age as a problem. Just as old age is socially constructed under specific historical conditions, the way in which health and illness are socially defined has a direct effect on one's personal experience and the society's treatment of aging. The interconnections between these social constructions are apparent in how gerontological and medical sociology theory have developed and in how social policy has been created around the elderly. To move beyond studying health and aging only as a medical or social problem, the field needs to embrace research and theory that address macrosocial issues such as the impact of social structure and institutions on aging. This includes looking at how age is used in society as a political and economic construction that benefits a limited segment of society. In medical sociology, Twaddle (1982) has called this type of focus on macro issues the "sociology of health and illness."

PARADIGMS OF AGING AND MEDICAL SOCIOLOGY

The theoretical perspective, or paradigm, that a researcher or author uses leads to the consideration of certain issues and solutions. Dominant paradigms in both medical sociology and social gerontology have traditionally reinforced a focus on medical aspects of illness and individual pathology (and the resulting social problems) of old age. The knowledge that comes from the use of these paradigms is not politically neutral (Alford and Friedland 1985). By focusing on particular elements of health and aging, those elements become the primary and legitimate target of social policy to the exclusion of other elements.

This section provides an outline of the major theories used to analyze health and aging, showing the common theoretical bonds between the study of health and aging. In subsequent sections, we will show how the foci of the dominant theories shape and are used to justify public policy and the popular ideology. The theories commonly used to understand both medicine and the aged include functionalism, interactionism, and political economy. Feminist theory is also an important but underutilized approach to understanding old age. The following discussion illuminates the underlying assumptions, basic concepts, and policy implications of the major theoretical approaches to health and aging.

Functionalism

Functionalist theory is based on an analogy between society and biological organisms. Society is generally viewed as a self-regulating system made up of functionally interdependent parts that require social consensus for optimal functioning. Functionalism analyzes how each social institution—such as medicine and the aging family—operates to benefit the society as a unit. The tendency to analyze how institutions function to maintain a stable equilibrium usually implies that the existing social order is the most desirable. In both gerontology and medical sociology, functionalists tend to take the subject matter as given, accepting the medical definition of health (Idler 1979) and the dominant definitions of aging and old age (Estes 1979) rather than seriously examining them. Individual behavior is conceptualized as bounded by roles that are generated by society. This focus draws attention to the properties of the values, attitudes, and roles of individual members of society and how they fit into society.

Parsons's (1951) influential analysis of

the sick role considers illness a social role that temporarily removes a person from full membership in society. A parallel analysis was made of aging by disengagement theory in the early 1960s. The elderly's decreasing social value and activity was seen as preparing society for the elders' death and ultimate removal from society in a functional manner (Cumming and Henry 1961). Society was conceptualized as benefiting from the withdrawal of the aged, as with the ill, from active social roles. This accords with the popular conception that aging is like (or is) an illness, undesirable and to be avoided if possible. Social control of the potential disruption of illness and old age is seen as essential to maintaining the harmonious operation (equilibrium) of society. In public policy this theory rationalizes excluding the elderly from the mainstream (e.g., retirement) while assuring that they accept this as legitimate (e.g., through medicalizing aging). It also suggests a focus on teaching the elderly how to adjust complacently to the loss of valued roles. Disengagement theory currently has little academic support, but the conceptually similar activity theory is often used. In activity theory, maintaining a large number of social roles and keeping active are the primary prescriptions for successful aging. This is similar to Parsons's sick role formulation, where it is the responsibility of ill individuals to work at regaining available productive roles that benefit society. If the elderly or the ill fail to sustain these roles, it indicates that the individual has made a poor social adjustment, or continues to be ill in a Parsonian sense (Havighurst 1963). Indicators of a poor adjustment to old age include various mental health measures of individuals, such as low morale and life satisfaction (Liang et al. 1980). This theory supports policies that provide additional social roles and activity for the elderly, such as senior centers and volunteer programs.

The life course, or human development, perspective provides a sensitivity that aging is a process rather than a static state of being. According to Neugarten (1985, pp. 296–297), "the life course approach concentrates on age-sex-related role transitions that are socially created, socially recognized and socially shared." Aging is conceptualized as a sequence of roles and age grades that an individual experiences throughout a lifetime (Lowenthal 1975), integrating experiences into a coherent whole. The age system of society broadly defines appropriate times to engage in particular roles such as marriage, parenthood, or retirement. The life course perspective proposes that individuals can continue to develop throughout life, adding a dynamic character to the consideration of aging (Rossi 1985; Sheehy 1978). The analytic focus is on continuity within lives, while allowing for individual variation. Just as medical sociology has come to recognize the lack of distinct boundaries between health and illness, the life course perspective shows that there is no firm boundary between youth and old age. Public policies based on this perspective would assist elderly individuals maintain their life patterns, whether they be high activity or low activity.

Modernization theory provides a historical aspect to functionalist theories of aging by comparing the resources the elderly command in agricultural and industrial societies (Cowgill and Holmes 1972). The elderly in modern industrial societies are analyzed as devalued and abandoned because they control few functionally necessary resources (see Rosow 1974). The problems of old age are not caused by biological decline but by the technology of the era. Modernization theory is also used to analyze differences in the health status and medical systems in different eras and nations, with technology being the primary explanatory variable (e.g. Illich 1976). This theory contributes a sensitivity that history and changing social conditions affect health and aging and suggests public policies that provide services to the elderly to compensate for their loss of social power and social support.

Age stratification theory is an influential

development in gerontology. In this theory, age involves a series of strata that are parts of the general stratification system of society (Riley 1985). Age, cohort, and period are key concepts. Age refers to the lifetime of an individual, and period refers to the historical context in which the individual lives. The aggregate of persons of similar age who pass through similar periods forms a cohort. For example, characteristics that we may attribute to the "aged" may be causally related to the fact that the elderly lived through the Depression rather than due to chronological age. The process of aging involves the movement of persons born near the same year, or cohorts, through successive social roles. Old age, in contrast, is a stratum of persons who share similar role expectations and sanctions owing to their chronological age. Age strata are divided by the attitudes, capacities, and socially sanctioned rights of the individuals in each stratum. Because society as a whole changes, the experience of aging is different for each cohort, and the composition of the age stratification system changes. Age stratification would suggest policies aimed at reducing friction or disharmony between different age strata and the orderly movement of individuals between the strata.

In general, functionalist theories see differences based on age as legitimate aspects of the social order. Old age and illness in contemporary society are problems primarily when they disrupt the smooth functioning of society as currently structured.

Interactionism

A central theme of interactionist studies is that both health and aging are highly contingent phenomena that are socially created through interaction (Rose and Peterson 1965; Gubrium 1973; Strauss 1975). Interactionist concepts give individuals an active place in the creation of society through making roles and taking part in the interactional definitions of illness and aging (Meyerhoff 1978; Becker 1980). In-

teractionist research is unique in trying to provide data on the meaning and social creation of health and of aging as *experienced* by the ill or elderly. Objective measures of "social support," for example, are not assumed to indicate the quality or importance of the relationships involved. Rather than simply counting the number of helping contacts, interactionists draw our attention to the process of engaging in social contacts and the meaning that is created during those interactions.

One area of interactionist research has challenged the view of the elderly as passive and marginal members of society. Hochschild's (1973) widely cited research on a senior housing project found an active community of elders with a distinctive subculture, role models, and mutual aid patterns. Parallel research in medical sociology has focused on provider-patient interactions, showing how the patient is an active participant in medical care rather than a passive recipient or simple consumer (Strauss et al. 1985; Murcott 1980). Research on social and cultural variations in health also frequently draws from this tradition by showing how health and illness are socially constructed (Kleinman, Eisenberg, and Good 1973).

Another interactionist theme in aging draws on Dowd's (1980) exchange theory approach to the use and control of elders' resources in interaction. Dowd conceptualizes resources broadly, including material (e.g., wealth), symbolic (e.g., beauty), and relational (e.g., friendship) resources. He theorizes that the elderly are not able to profit from interaction and therefore withdraw from exchange networks. Dowd's interactionism is most apparent in his analysis of how exchange is mediated by the participants' definitions of the situation and their strategic actions (*cf.* Goffman 1967). Dowd claims that exchange theory rounds out symbolic interactionism by analyzing power differences in relationships and draws attention to the structural conditions that limit the elderly's ability to further maximize their interactional power.

Interactionist concepts show how the elderly work to create meaningful lives and to make the most out of their situations. Researchers may need to question less often problematic individual characteristics if we conclude that elders try to act in ways advantageous to themselves and study more carefully the characteristics of the social structure that influence individual biographies and collective histories (Bastida 1984). Public policies based on interactionist analyses might focus on improving positive interpretations of old age by improving the interactional resources of the elderly or by enhancing the interactional power of the elderly and the ill.

Political Economy

The political economy analysis of both health and aging is relatively new. Political economy is ultimately concerned with the social relations of production rather than with individuals or technology as primary causal forces in society (Alford and Friedland 1985). Political economy analyses of aging have most commonly addressed how the needs of capital accumulation affect the lives of older people, such as by pushing them out of the labor force as part of the regulation of the labor force and the maximization of profits (Graebner 1980). This presents retirement as a creation of the forces of capital accumulation and the reproduction needs of the capitalist system at a social-structural level rather than as a role or life stage (Guillemard 1983). A similar focus in medical sociology examines how the organization of production for profits structures the provision of medical care (Navarro 1986; Scull 1976) and the creation of illness (Waitzkin 1983). Political economy research in aging has also increasingly focused on the state as a key structural component of advanced capitalism (Estes et al. 1984). The public policies and institutional arrangements that reinforce the dependent position of the elderly are seen as reflecting and reinforcing the prevailing class structure of society (Estes 1986). The relationship between the state and the needs of capitalism, and the structural contradictions of the state in a capitalist system, are conceptualized as visible in aging and health policies of the state (Estes et al. 1984: Brown 1979).

More than other perspectives, political economy analyses focus on social power and inequality. This alters the focus of study from how individuals or society can adapt to aging to which political and economic changes can optimize social justice and equality for all ages in society. Social policy initiatives from this perspective would call for a restructuring of the economy and political system in ways that would redress the ageism, sexism, and racism that are integral to a class society, and would suggest health care and social policy based on human needs rather than profits.

Feminist Theories

The central causal variable in feminist theory that explains social inequality based on gender is either patriarchy, capitalism, or both (Sokoloff 1980). Analyses of patriarchy show how male dominance has been practiced historically under different social and economic systems. Analyses of capitalism analyze women's work in the home as economically necessary for commodity production in a capitalist system. The focus has been on the direct contribution of unpaid, unwaged labor to the production of surplus value (profit). More recent theory has linked the analysis of capitalism with patriarchy and shown how capitalists as a class and men as a class benefit from the social relations of patriarchy and capitalism (Sokoloff 1980). Rather than conceptualizing older women as playing a complementary role in the family, feminist theory draws attention to the unequal distribution of power between men who control the political and economic sphere and women who are responsible for the home (Hartmann 1981).

In medical sociology, the state is seen as serving both the interests of capitalism and patriarchy in health policy (Petchesky 1984). Gerontology has examined how the sexual division of labor present in care-taking is reinforced by the state in a manner that benefits capitalism (Walker 1983). In both medical sociology and aging, feminist theory provides an analysis of the causes of structural inequalities between women and men as they are found in the medical system and in institutional responses to aging. Feminist theories suggest policies aimed at acknowledgment (and compensation for) unpaid labor, such as family care giving; and these theories also redress institutional and policy biases that reinforce an unequal sexual division of labor (Pascall 1986).

Each of the paradigms discussed—functionalism, interactionism, political economy, and feminist theory—draws our attention to different aspects of aging and health. Functionalism is most likely to accept the current social order and focus on how individuals can best adjust to the challenges of old age and illness. Interactionism suggests that labels like "elderly" and "sick" are variable because they are created through social interaction and should be amenable to change in a similar manner. Political economy points out how the political and economic structure of society creates pressures to create illness and aging as a devalued process in the creation of profits. Political economy theory and feminist theory are most likely to suggest changes in social institutions and the basic operation of society.

As we will show in the following discussions, the individualistic approaches to aging and health have been the dominant basis for social policy. This sets the stage for fundamental contradictions, however, since individualistic policies are incapable of dealing with concerns that are rooted in social institutions.

THE SOCIAL CONSTRUCTION OF AGING

When we talk about the "social construction" of a phenomenon we mean that both knowledge and "reality" are social products

influenced by cultural, political, and economic factors (Estes 1979). Social constructions exist within a particular context that is shaped by the way that questions are asked about society and the way that knowledge is institutionalized. The power of dominant groups in society is reflected in the knowledge and definitions that become widely shared and accepted as part of the collective stock of knowledge (Berger and Luckmann 1966). Even though knowledge is affected by social forces, most people perceive knowledge as existing independently of society.

The social construction of reality shapes attitudes toward and treatment of the elderly, as well as research and policy agendas. Gerontological paradigms need to be examined with respect to how they shape and influence (as well as how they are shaped and are influenced by) societal forces. There are two key aspects of the dominant social construction of aging that influence policy: aging as illness and aging as dependency. The following discussion shows that although these two concepts of aging do not accurately reflect social reality, the concepts do serve as political and economic tools that blame the elderly for broader social contradictions.

The first aspect of the social construction of aging concerns the construction of the aging process itself. Aging is portrayed as a biological process in which decrement, physical degeneration, and physiological decline link aging with disease. This understanding of aging and health is dominated by a biomedical paradigm that bears affinity with the individual life course perspective in social gerontology. The policy response has been to "medicalize" aging through the design and financing of a medically oriented services strategy; it has underemphasized the economic, political, and social factors that shape the experience of aging and that are associated with illness patterns at any age (Estes et al. 1984). The strength of the biomedical paradigm in aging has supported the development and dominance of an increasingly costly and profitable medical-industrial complex in control of the definitions and treatment of aging.

The second major aspect of the construction of reality concerns how aging is a dependent state. Dependency is typically treated as an individual's problem, a function of individual lifetime choices, with little attention to the social context of the "dependency." Walker (1980) challenges this perspective by noting that various institutions and policies in contemporary Western societies create a structure in which people find themselves in relations of dependency. This process of structured dependency does not occur randomly, but predictably affects specific groups of people who come to "learn helplessness" (Seligman 1975) and further perpetuate the dependency. Learned helplessness is produced by the arrangement of social institutions, not individuals. Entire groups of people are affected, such as the elderly who rely primarily on the Social Security system for their livelihood.

The association of age with both illness and dependency has a number of consequences. First, because those states labeled as illness in our society are considered "undesirable" (Conrad and Schneider 1980), aging is seen as undesirable. The result may be the stigmatization of the elderly, both by others and by themselves. Second, these constructions of aging are consistent with the adoption of expectations that may encourage elders to assume the helpless sick role, including a reduction of normal responsibilities and increased dependency on others in an imbalanced power relationship (Arluke and Peterson 1981). Third, the medicalization of aging may itself generate a self-fulfilling prophecy (Estes 1979) in which elders unwittingly participate in creating their own dependency, especially with the occurrence of losses of function or environmental control (Rodin and Langer 1980). This process, in turn, increases the propensity for utilizing medical interventions and promoting further medicalization of the aging process (Estes et al. 1984). Medicalization encourages social control through the overuse of prescription drugs for the elderly and the use of institutionalization to "treat" aging.

The social construction of aging as illness is consistent with the definition of aging as a problem. Once something has been defined as a problem—be it drug use, teen pregnancy, or old age—government resources are more likely to be committed to the issue. The association between ill health and aging has increased as the major health problem in America has shifted from infectious and acute diseases to chronic disease. This increased importance of chronic illness has shifted the burden of illness from the young to the old since the elderly are more likely to have chronic illnesses (see Table 1).

TABLE 1 Acute and Chronic Illness Rates for the Elderly, United States, 1983 (per 100/population)

	Total Population	65+
Acute Conditions		
Infective and parasitic	20.3	7.3
Upper respiratory	40.6	18.1
Digestive system	7.6	7.2
Chronic Conditions		
Heart conditions	82.8	303.0
Hypertension	121.3	387.9
Arthritis and rheumatism	131.3	471.6

Source: U.S. Bureau of the Census, 1986, *Statistical Abstract of the United States*, Washington, D.C.: U.S. Government Printing Office, Tables 164 and 166.

In 1981 the average elderly person experienced 39.9 days of activity limitation with chronic illness, about twice the level of those 45–64 years of age. Almost 10 percent of the elderly need some type of help in performing one or more basic physical activities, four times the rate of the next youngest age group (Rice 1985). Although chronic illness and disability affect all age groups, their higher prevalence among the elderly has led policymakers and others to associate aging with chronic illness, even though research is beginning to show a growing burden of chronic illness among those who are middle-aged (Rice and LaPlante 1986) and even though most elderly are healthy. Of elderly persons living in the community, two-thirds consider their health excellent, very good, or good when compared to others of their own age. Only about one-third reported their health as fair or poor, although poor elderly were more likely to report their health as fair or poor than were the nonpoor. Socioeconomic status has a significant influence on reported health status. (U.S. Senate 1986).

This construction of the elderly as sick and dependent has significant political and economic implications, including the debate about the allocation of public resources. If the elderly are conceptualized as a homogenous interest group demanding high levels of support and subsidization, they can more easily be viewed as unfairly competing with other groups, such as children. The promotion of intergenerational conflict results in fragmented policies rather than common solutions (Binney and Estes 1988). This serves to focus attention on pathology within different groups and to eliminate consideration of how the social structure may be at the base of the diverse problems groups face. While chronic illness has become the primary health issue, the medical care system remains biased toward acute care. The system is designed to treat individuals with short-term conditions that can be fully reversed. Chronic illnesses, on the other hand, are usually long-term conditions that require supportive and palliative care

and environmental modifications. Federal health policy virtually ignores these needs as it spends the majority of its "health" funds on institutional and acute care. In 1985 payers in the nation spent 10.7 percent of the gross national product ($425 billion) for medical care. The federal government paid about 40 percent of that total, and the elderly consumed about 29 percent of the total (Rice 1985). Despite the large federal role in financing health care, the elderly continue to have the highest out-of-pocket expenditures for medical care of any age group. In 1985 each person aged 65 and over paid an average of $1,660 out of their own resources for health care, about 17 percent of their income (Rice 1985). Elderly blacks paid 23 percent of their income for health care expenditures in 1981 (Estes 1985), while women and other low-income elders also consistently paid a disproportionate share of the medical cost burden compared to married couples and males.

Although the elderly have been blamed for dramatic rises in health care costs, recent data show that other factors are much more important. A Health Care Financing Administration study of 1985 national health expenditures (Waldo, Levit, and Lazenby 1986) and projections of spending to 1990 (Arnett et al. 1986) indicate that health care costs are rising as a result of rising prices in the medical care system itself (55.6 percent of increase), for example, rising hospital and physician charges; general inflation (13.6 percent of increase); and, secondarily, increased intensity of care high-tech services accounting for 22.9 percent of increase). Increased utilization of services and the much-heralded demographic imperative have contributed far less to rising health expenditures. In fact, growth of the entire population has contributed less than 8 percent to the rising cost of care, and changes in utilization have had no effect. Directly blaming the elderly for significantly higher medical expenditures would appear to illustrate one consequence of socially constructing aging as an illness. The net result is to question the

deservedness of those receiving the medical care (the aged) rather than the deservedness of those receiving payments
and making profits from providing medical
services to the aged.

It is in this environment that social policy is created and shaped, influenced by
dominant constructions of reality. Health
policy for the aged has been influenced by
the biomedical model of aging, which has
supported a medical services strategy and
conceptualized the needs of the elderly as
individual medical problems rather than as
results of societal treatment of the elderly,
inadequate income provisions, or other socially generated problems. Similarly, the
government's emphasis on providing costly
medical care rather than social support
(housing, social services, and family care al-
lowances), casts the elderly as the culprits
of the health care cost crisis. Contemporary health policies focus on attempts to
"solve" the "crisis" by addressing symptoms
rather than causes through management
strategies of either increasing competition,
regulation, or both (Estes et al 1984). Media portrayals of intergenerational conflict
and blaming the elderly for the U.S. economic crisis show how certain empirical
data can be used, and other data ignored,
in support of the definition of a crisis. National polls demonstrate that younger generations have consistently indicated the
willingness to support Social Security and
Medicare programs for their parents and
grandparents, despite their growing fears
that these programs may not financially
survive to support them in their own old
age (Harris and Associates 1984–1986).

To examine why these aspects of the
problem fail to become incorporated into
the problem definition, we must also examine the role of crisis in the construction of
social policy in health and aging.

POLICY AND SOCIAL CHANGE

Just as aging is a social construction that
has definite social consequences, the notion
of "crisis" is also a social construction. The
current crisis defined in health is the rising
cost of medical care; for aging the crisis is
defined as the demographic growth of the
elderly and the associated economic and
social burdens on society and younger generations. The definition of these trends as
causing crises has been facilitated by the
media's unquestioning dissemination of
these definitions. Alternative interpretations to crisis definitions are rarely presented by the political system, academia, or
business. Nevertheless, the recognition,
shaping, formulation, and analysis of crises
are socially produced by individuals in
dominant institutions. Empirical realities lie
at the base of the issues being constructed
as crises, but the public interpretation of
the realities are made by those who have
political and economic stakes and ultimately the power to shape the labeling of
crises and the actions that follow (Estes et
al. 1984).

Framing these constructed crises is a
very real budget deficit that looms over the
welfare state. Historically, health care policy for the elderly has developed incremen-
tally, punctuated by changes during periods when political and economic events
have led to crises being constructed. States
and localities were the first governmental
levels to assume major responsibility for
health and medical care through medical
licensure and public health actions. States
initially established medical licensing in the
1870s to limit practice to scientifically
trained practitioners. This move was in response to the medical profession's desire to
limit competition and the consequent problem that was defined of unscientifically
trained practitioners (Starr 1982).

By the turn of the century, all forty-five
states had passed modern medical practice
acts, despite the still primitive state of
"modern" medicine (Brown 1979). By 1915
public health agencies had been established
in every state and were expanding beyond
simple infectious disease control to address
such problems as water pollution, sewage
disposal, nutrition, housing, and industrial
accidents. Public health initiatives, along
with improved social and economic condi-

tions, have been credited with decreased morbidity and mortality during this period (McKeown 1979). It was during this period that "medicine" fought for the sole power to define health. The depression of the 1930s was publicly defined as a malfunctioning of an otherwise sound social and economic system. New Deal programs built on this analysis by opening the door to dramatic new federal involvement in the health and welfare of the population, while leaving the basic structures of medical and economic institutions intact. Federal policy initiatives were designed to improve the economic security of Americans against the threat of large-scale economic forces beyond the control of individuals, localities, or states. This marked the end of strictly separated responsibilities between federal, state, and local governments and the beginning of a period of shared responsibility (Lee and Benjamin 1983; Walker 1981).

The most significant piece of social legislation was the Social Security Act of 1935, which established social insurance to assure a degree of financial security in old age. America had only recently shifted to a primarily industrial form of production, and the profit imperative made many older workers redundant. Social Security helped ameliorate some of the problems of the industrial production system, while requiring recipients to have participated in that system. Other federal programs were also initiated at that time to aid the states with maternal and child health, old age assistance for the indigent, unemployment insurance, and public health. Other major programs for the elderly that would be established three decades later, including Medicare, followed the principles established in this act. The federal emphasis during the 1940s and 1950s was to solve inadequacies in medical services, housing, and other infrastructure needs through expansion along the existing model. Hospital construction soared, suburban housing and urban reconstruction expanded, and educational opportunities became more available.

By the 1960s, however, disparities between the poor and middle classes were increasingly apparent (Starr 1982). The civil rights movement grew along with discontent among the poor, who had been left behind in the postwar economic growth (Piven and Cloward 1971). This was generally defined as a problem of maldistribution that could be solved by further ameliorative programs. Great Society programs in the 1960s addressed these problems by further broadening New Deal trends and expanding the federal role in health and welfare (Lee and Benjamin 1983). The problem was defined by those in power as inadequate access to the existing system, without seriously questioning the basic soundness of the system itself. Federal medical insurance to improve access was established for the elderly and the poor through Medicare and Medicaid. The federal government also established programs to increase the number of health professionals, set up clinics in medically underserved areas, and made health screening and preventive care more available (Lee 1984). As a result, doctor visits per person per year for the poor increased 30 percent, and hospital use increased for the poor, elderly, and minorities (Rice 1985). The Older Americans Act was also established in 1965, and federal support for state and local governments and nonprofit organizations was provided for expanding health and social services for the elderly (Estes 1979).

New Federalism, beginning with the Nixon administration and continued by the Reagan administration, sought a greatly reduced federal role in the health and welfare of the population and increased responsibility for states, localities, and individuals. The problem was redefined to one of too much government since social unrest had declined while contradictions in the economy mounted (Castells 1980; O'Connor 1973). Key forces currently shaping health care policy for the elderly under New Federalism include the devolution of federal responsibility back to the states, federal budget cuts, and deregulation (Estes and Gerard 1983; Estes 1979). President Reagan has vigorously pursued policies to limit further the federal role in health and welfare through block grants, program cuts, and increased state responsibility. In its most basic form, New Federalism challenges the idea that there is any societal responsibility for meeting basic human needs in health, income, housing, or welfare (Estes and Gerard 1983).

Just as economic crisis provided the context for the New Deal, the economics of austerity have been a driving force of New Federalism. Declining federal revenues have been caused by tax cuts enacted in 1981 and by the early-1980s recession. A rapid increase in military spending and interest payments on the national debt, accompanied by reductions in domestic spending, have further constrained health and welfare policy choices (Estes 1982). While the tax burden in the United States is lower than in almost all other industrialized nations, austerity is presented as the only possible response to declining revenues (Estes 1982). The politics of austerity at the federal level continued in 1985 with the passage of the Gramm-Rudman-Hollings Balanced Budget Act, requiring that the budget be balanced over five years. In the absence of congressional budget changes to reduce the deficit, expenditure cuts were to occur automatically. In contrast to the tax surcharges used in the 1960s to compensate for deficits, this bill embodied an austerity approach to the fiscal crisis by addressing only spending. After the courts invalidated the automatic feature of the budget cuts, Congress reinstated them in a new way in 1987, demonstrating the continued dominance of New Federalism's definition of austerity.

Deregulation is a key strategy of New Federalism policy. Minimizing government influence on markets is a goal; competition and other market forces are seen as maximizing socially valued ends. This approach assumes that health can be treated as a commodity, with the consumer making fully informed rational decisions about the costs and benefits of treatments to prevent pain, illness, and death (Ricardo-Campbell 1982). The growing reliance on the market has intensified a perennial and profound health care question: Should health care be provided as a "market good," purchased as a commodity by those who can afford to pay, or should it be provided as a "merit good," available as a right or collective good, regardless of ability to pay (Estes et al. 1984)?

New Federalism, Health, and Aging

The political and economic forces that are driving New Federalism policies have several important consequences for the elderly. Federal reimbursement policies and pluralistic financing have contributed to the rising cost of medical care, the continuing medicalization of aging, the fragmentation of health care, the extremely limited availability of supportive services, and the growing privatization and commodification of health services.

Medicalization affects more than just the elderly. Medicine has become among the most powerful institutions in American society, often displacing religion and law as basis for social control and legitimacy (Conrad and Schneider 1980). Individuals lose control over aspects of their lives that are medicalized, and the genesis of problems is presented as naturally occurring and individually centered. Medicalization and the incremental nature of aging policies have led to the development of multiple overlapping services that are difficult to coordinate (Estes 1979). As reimbursement policies change, health and service organizations modify what they offer to coincide with what is reimbursable. Rather than constructing a health and service system that provides well-planned linkages between different types and levels of care, changing policies further fragment the care available. Privatization occurs when the government sheds responsibility for the provision of health services. This removes the provision of health care from the public domain and turns it into a commodity to be bought and sold like any other, with the criteria for evaluation based on economic rather than human needs and suffering. It also serves to depoliticize health services since they are easier to portray as following rational and technical rules when their link to the government is indirect.

Institutional Medical Care under New Federalism

Changes in hospital and nursing home care can be viewed as changes in aging policy. Whereas the elderly accounted for only 10 percent of the population and 15 percent of all visits to physicians in 1980, they accounted for 38 percent of all hospital days. Nursing home care is principally oriented toward the elderly; of the 1.4 million persons in nursing homes in 1980, 1.2 million were elderly (NCHS 1987). By the year 2000 the elderly are projected to account for 13.1 percent of the population, use 43 percent of all hospital days, and number over 2.1 million residents in nursing homes (Rice 1986).

Since the 1970s, the definition of medical care issues shifted such that too much rather than too little service utilization is seen as a major problem. Given the 37 million uninsured Americans and the declining proportion of poor persons who are covered by Medicaid (Sulvetta and Swartz 1986), it would appear that the 1980s "problem" definition is based on economics rather than needs. The elderly thus become viewed as a source of the problem rather than a victim of the crisis in health care. One important health care policy for the elderly introduced under the health care cost crisis has been the use of diagnosis-related groups (DRGs) to determine prospective reimbursement rates for hospitals under Medicare. Fixed-price reimbursement per diagnosis has created significant incentives for hospitals to reduce inpatient days by discharging elders "sicker and quicker." Introduced as an austerity measure to reduce federal Medicare costs, DRG reimbursement policy has indi-

rectly raised new issues of quality of care and access to medical care, both of which were major issues in the previous period (Estes 1986). The New Federalism principle is reflected in the early hospital discharge of patients to reduce federal Medicare costs, shifting care into the community, where state and local governments and individuals pay a larger share of the costs. Increasing copayments and deductibles have accompanied DRG-based reimbursement. With out-of-pocket health care costs for the elderly averaging 17 percent of their average income in 1985 (Rice 1985), states and localities are shouldering increased responsibility for expenses that the elderly (especially the poor) cannot afford. In addition, millions of days of care are shifted to the home, adding to the already significant care-giving burden of the nation's middle-aged and older women.

Although the DRG policy regulates payment by diagnosis, decisions about how to cut costs are left entirely to providers, reflecting the program's deregulatory aspect. Tax laws and deregulation have encouraged the increased entry of for-profit corporations into medical markets (including both hospital and home health care). The medical-industrial complex is uniquely positioned to take advantage of DRG-based reimbursements. Proprietary hospital chains, linked to supply companies and post-hospital care services, benefit from economies of scale, mass marketing, and the ability to cost-shift. Proprietary facilities are organized around costs, whereas public and religious facilities are traditionally organized to provide care to needy populations. Proprietary chains have pioneered new services to maximize profits, such as freestanding emergency rooms, sports medicine clinics, and drug/alcohol abuse programs, which are well reimbursed or which attract the middle class, who can pay the fees. At the same time, some public hospitals are being closed or bought by investors. As a result, while all hospitals have been earning a net profit of 15 percent under DRG reimbursements, investor-owned facilities report 21 percent higher returns than nonprofit facilities (Kusserow 1986).

By focusing on the issue of hospital costs, the major component of Medicare expenditures, DRGs perpetuate Medicare's bias toward the institutional care of the acutely ill. Innovations in medical care delivery are being driven by free market economics rather than by the needs of the elderly and others (which are often not profitable). Federal interest in developing long-term care policies to address the chronic illness of the elderly remains low because of the money, the federal responsibility, and the regulation that will be needed.

One health care proposal popular under New Federalism is the conversion of Medicare's publicly financed insurance program to a system of privately purchased (but publicly financed) commercial insurance. Insurance purchases by the elderly would be with individual vouchers in the market, consistent with the process of commodifying health. Vouchers would place health care choices in the market, where access and distribution are based on the ability to pay. Medical providers, however, increasingly need to attract profitable patients while avoiding the sickest or neediest (Relman 1980). Thus, a social good (health) becomes a private good (commodity) that is valued for its ability to create profit. With thousands of different private voucher plans, problems of public accountability and cost containment would likely grow. Proprietary chains in particular are positioned to take unique advantage of a voucher system. Hospital chains are moving to "multi clustering," where a hospital serves as the core of a regional health care network owned by one corporation. These networks can include skilled nursing facilities, home health agencies, durable medical equipment subsidiaries, and psychiatric, substance-abuse, and rehabilitation units. Although private nonprofits are also moving in this direction, they have neither the capital nor the institutional size to create

comparable competitive networks nationwide. Vouchers would benefit businesses from insurance companies to hospital corporations as new sources of profiting from the elderly are created, though the benefits that the elderly would derive are more problematic.

Long-Term Care

More important for the elderly than hospital and institutional care is the care giving that families (primarily women) provide to the ill and disabled. Over 80 percent of all supportive care provided to the disabled elderly in the community comes from their families (U.S. Senate 1986). Long-term care for the elderly, nevertheless, is also shaped by the dominance of the medical model. Given the public policies under Medicare and Medicaid, those with long-term care needs face impoverishment and institutionalization (Harrington, et al. 1985). Neither Medicare nor Medicaid adequately addresses the most needed areas of assistance for the chronically ill elderly, either in homes or in the community.

During the past thirty years, the publicly financed alternative to family support for the elderly has been the nursing home. Older persons who become ill or disabled typically turn to family and friends (Cantor 1980), who represent the best means of avoiding institutionalization: Only 8 percent of nursing home residents are married with a living spouse, while almost 50 percent have no living spouse or children. More than 80 percent of residents are (or become) poor in the nursing home, and an estimated 30 percent could be living in the community with adequate economic and social support.

Reliance on nursing homes for long-term care is a creation of social policy. The number of nursing home beds grew rapidly during the 1960s largely in response to guaranteed payment by Medicaid, doubling the proportion of the elderly in nursing homes from 2.5 to 5 percent. The majority of nursing homes are operated as profit-making enterprises, having financial incentives to admit individuals requiring less care and fewer poor persons and to provide fewer unreimbursable amenities (Vladeck 1980). A few national chains control almost one-quarter of nursing home beds. Nursing homes are a larger policy than social issue. About five percent of the elderly live in nursing homes at any one time, while about 20 percent of elderly individuals will find themselves in a nursing home at some time in their lives. Almost two-thirds of all elderly classified as "extremely impaired" and dependent on others to carry out basic activities continue to live in the community (Macken 1986).

With nursing home costs accounting for 68 percent of all Medicaid expenditures on the elderly ($10 billion in 1984 [Waldo and Lazenby 1984]), government policy initiatives are oriented to a fiscal crisis rather than a crisis in the growing institutionalized dependency of the aged or the needs of families that provide the majority of support to the elderly currently. The public policy emphasis on institutional care has resulted in other compensatory programs being designed around preventing institutionalization rather than providing care to those who could benefit from supportive care (Capitman 1986). The most important other long-term care service is home care, whose programs have been implemented primarily to reduce costs and the use of institutions. Under Medicare, home health care is medically oriented and designed to maintain a disabled or ill person in his or her home who would otherwise require institutionalization (U.S. GAO 1977). To receive home health benefits, a person must be certified by a physician as needing skilled nursing or specified therapies (Nassif 1986–1987).

Long-term care services in the United States have historically been fragmented, have failed to provide continuity of care, and have been inadequate (Cantor and Little 1985). Recent federal budget cuts have further encouraged the fragmentation of noninstitutional services. Reimbursement rate differences have encouraged home health providers to emphasize better paying medical services at the expense of lesser paying social and support services. Providers are also "unbundling" services, further fragmenting services as a strategy to optimize the number of billable services per visit (Wood and Estes 1986–1987). Other policy changes have fostered the growth of for-profit companies in the home care market. As the demand for noninstitutional care grows from $9 billion in 1985 to an estimated $16 billion in 1990 (Frost and Sullivan 1983), home health services will become an increasingly important profit source for hospitals and other companies. Proprietaries, one-third of all home health agencies in 1985, ranked first in the percent of total charges billed to Medicare (Waldo, Levit, and Lazenby 1986).

There is a growing consensus that the United States needs a long-term care policy that provides comprehensive services covering a continuum from community to institutional care; that long-term care must be integrated with other health and social services (not in an isolated separate delivery system); that incentives must be incorporated to contain costs and prevent unneeded utilization; that financing for long-term care should protect individuals from impoverishment and be accessible to those in need, regardless of age or ability to pay; and that long-term care should include preventive and restorative services. Some of these measures will require a redefinition of health and aging away from medical and dependency models and may also challenge powerful political and economic interests that profit from the current structure of health and aging policies.

CONCLUSION

We return to a theme introduced earlier in the chapter, that of the similarities and parallels in the development of the discipline of sociology, the subfield of medical sociology and the sociology of aging. Twaddle

(1982) has documented an intellectual shift from "medical sociology" to "the sociology of health." He traces and contrasts the different dimensions of work in sociology that began with study "in" medicine, trying to further clinicians' goals. The sociological emphasis then moved to a study "of" medicine, where the institution and providers became the focus of study for sociological purposes. Twaddle concludes that certain social, environmental, and behavioral factors are an increasingly important focus of sociological study in a "sociology of health." For Twaddle, the sociology of health emphasizes social science and humanism, in contrast to the biological science or psychological (role/personality) perspectives that have dominated the earlier "medical sociology."

Parallel developments can be examined to see if a shift is occurring from social gerontology to a broader field of study— the sociology of aging. The characteristics of both the earlier sociology "in" and "of" medicine have parallels in social gerontology. For example, the biological science models that influence sociological studies "in" medicine are similarly dominant in a clinical social gerontology—with parallel emphasis on the organism and physical failure and an attempt to aid practitioners service these failing bodies. Similarly, the psychological and microbehavioral models that characterize the sociology "of" medicine are repeated in social gerontology through human development, psychobehavioral, and role life-cycle studies. These studies accept the existence of a category of "aged" people as a focus of study and generally take the political and economic context as a given.

Research funding in social gerontology reinforces these two aspects. The organic/positivist dominance of the biomedical model appears in the emphasis on applied, engineering, and positivistic research supported by the Administration on Aging, the Health Care Financing Administration, and the National Center for Health Services Research. Supporting and supplement-

ing efforts of the medical profession and the medical-industrial complex in what has been termed the "aging enterprise" (Estes 1979), the research agenda has focused on research and demonstrations in economic/econometric, demographic, and behavioral medicine problems. Studies in behavioral medicine have replaced the study of social factors in relation to health. Problems are constructed with an individual etiology and treatment (often in terms of behavioral management), diverting attention from social or social structural causation or amelioration. More sociological developments were promoted first by the National Institute for Child Health and Human Development and later by the National Institute of Aging, through priorities for basic research on psychosocial, life course, and human development issues.

A small group of academics have pursued research in a "sociology of aging" that is like the sociology of health in its attention to broader social structures and social change. Begun in the late 1970s, this research looks at how age is a socially contingent phenomena that is used by different interests during social conflict and as a basis for exploitation. Twaddle (1982) describes the shift from a sociology "in" medicine to a sociology "of" medicine as broadly affecting the field. Unlike in medical sociology, there has been no clear shift from applied toward basic sociology in gerontology, but both approaches continue to operate simultaneously. We suggest that, as challenges to the established order mounted in the 1960s, developments in *both* medical sociology and social gerontology have mirrored crises in the dominant biomedical paradigm of science (germ theory) and in positivist social science and the dominant functionalist paradigm (Gouldner 1970).

The biomedicine paradigm found itself trapped by two crises. The first resulted from developments that extended the life span without resolving the problems of an increased illness burden and a shift from acute to chronic illness. The problem was, and remains, how to deal with the longevity without changing the basic premises of medicine or creating a loss of faith in the ability of biomedicine to extend a quality life span. The second crisis concerns the continued inability of the biomedical model to address macrostructural problems that are implicated in the etiology of ill health (e.g., environmental, social, economic causes). Medicine's response especially with its acute care bias, has been to focus attention on individual health behaviors and life-styles, making the individual responsible for illness. The survival of medicine in its current form depends on shifting the blame for its shortcomings and failures to those who suffer from them: the elderly, the ill, and the poor.

The social sciences have faced a similar set of crises. For example, in the 1960s and 1970s the interpretive sociologies (e.g., labeling theory and deviance) gained strength, there was a vigorous renewal of neo-Marxism, and there was the development of feminist theory, along with the "entropy of functionalism" (Gouldner 1970), which was long the dominant paradigm of the discipline. Whether caused by or simply marked by the impact of social upheaval and social movements, these developments represented a broadening and expansion of sociological theorizing to attempt to address what was perceived as the inability of the dominant paradigm to provide explanation and solution to major social problems.

The 1980s have seen the rebirth of a series of old paradigms. The social science disciplines have seen a resurgence of econometrics and microeconomics and the increased popularity of public choice–rational choice theory. The previously dominant functionalist paradigm in sociology has reemerged in the form of neofunctionalism, while dormant social Darwinian theories are renewed in sociobiology. The biomedical paradigm has gained new vigor in fields as diverse as psychiatry and the physiology of aging. This contradicts Twaddle's claim of a significant shift from

medical sociology to a sociology of health by showing that the dominant perspective in medical sociology (and the social sciences in general) and the dominant paradigm of science (biomedicine) continue to be influential and, in the final analysis, support the status quo.

The current period can be characterized by an attack on social science and humanism in the form of political conservatism and attacks on the legitimacy of social science, especially its competing theories. As a crisis response, the dominant paradigm has intensified positivism ("real science") and microanalytic approaches, simultaneously with an entropy of competing theory (especially critical and neo-Marxist theories). In aging research this has meant disincentives to develop further the sociology of aging, especially the examination of macrostructural analyses, and incentives to continue in a social gerontology that is clinical or academic with a focus on individual behavior and attitudes.

This raises a question of possible future scenarios in the development of the sociology of health and the sociology of aging. One possible response to the increased conservatism and attacks on social science in the wake of the definition of a health care economic crisis is a deepening of the trend toward theory-less empiricism and social engineering. The crisis in this scenario is defined as a *technical* problem capable of administrative correction, rather than as a political issue grounded in the contradictions of the medical system and old age policies. Coupled with demographic, econometric, and actuarial modeling, this scenario offers the potential of calculating every social policy in terms of its monetary cost-benefit and judgments of individual productive and social worth.

A second possible scenario could result if the crisis in the dominant paradigm and society allow for the further development of alternative theoretical perspectives. Potentially revolutionary developments could occur in the health social sciences if theoretical developments about the social structure are linked with micro studies, empirically substantiated in ways not previously attempted. Personal experiences and troubles concerning health and aging need to be linked with social issues of how the political and economic system fosters those problems. Only at that point could the dominant focus of sociology turn to studying health and aging rather than illness, sickness, and the problems of being old.

It would seem that medical sociology and the sociology of health and aging stand at a crossroads. Policy developments and larger structural influences on their research agendas will play a major role in the direction the fields will take.

REFERENCES

Alford, R. R., and R. Friedland. 1985. *Powers of Theory.* New York: Cambridge University Press.

Arluke, A., and J. Peterson. 1981. Accidental Medicalization of Old Age and Its Control Implications, in C. L. Fry, ed., *Dimensions: Aging, Culture, and Health.* New York: J. F. Bergin, pp. 271–284.

Arnett, R. H. III, D. R. McKusick, S. T. Sonnefeld, and C. S. Cowell. 1986. Projections of Health Care Spending to 1990. *Health Care Financing Review* 7(3):1–36.

Bastida, E. 1984. Reconstructing the Social World at 60: Older Cubans in the United States. *The Gerontologist* 24:465–470.

Becker, Gaylene. 1980. *Growing Old in Silence.* Berkeley: University of California Press.

Berger, P., and T. Luckmann. 1966. *The Social Construction of Reality.* New York: Doubleday Publishing Co.

Binney, E. A., and C. L. Estes. 1988. The Retreat of the State and Its Transfer of Responsibility: The Intergenerational War. *International Journal of Health Services* 18(1):83–96.

Brown, E. R. 1979. *Rockefeller Medicine Men.* Berkeley: University of California Press.

Cantor, Marjorie. 1980. The Informal Support System: Its Relevance in the Lives of the Elderly, in E. Borgotta and N. McCluskey, eds., *Aging and Society.* Beverly Hills, Calif.: Sage Publications, pp. 111–146.

Cantor, M., and V. Little. 1985. Aging and Social Care, in R. H. Binstock and E. Shanas, eds., *Handbook of Aging and the Social Sciences.* New York: Van Nostrand Reinhold Co., pp. 745–781.

Capitman, J. A. 1986. Community-Based Long Term Care Models, Target Groups, and Impacts on Service Use. *The Gerontologist* 26(4):389–397.

Castells, M. 1980. *The Economic Crisis and American Society.* Princeton: Princeton University Press.

Conrad, P., and J. Schneider. 1980. *Deviance and Medicalization: From Badness to Sickness.* St. Louis: C. V. Mosby Co.

Cowgill, D. O., and L. D. Holmes. 1972. *Aging and Modernization.* New York: Appleton-Century-Crofts.

Cumming, E., and W. E. Henry. 1961. *Growing Old: The Process of Disengagement.* New York: Basic Books.

Dowd, J. J. 1980. *Stratification Among the Aged.* Monterey, Calif.: Brooks/Cole Publishing Co.

Estes, C. L. 1979. *The Aging Enterprise.* San Francisco: Jossey-Bass. See especially "Decentralization and New Federalism," pp. 171–197.

———. 1982. Austerity and Aging: 1980 and Beyond. *International Journal of Health Services* 12(4):573–584.

———. 1985. The United States: Long Term Care and Federal Policy, in L. Reif and B. Trager, eds., *International Perspectives on Long Term Care.* New York: Haworth Press, pp. 315–328.

———. 1986. The Politics of Ageing in America. *Ageing and Society* 6(2):121–134.

Estes, C. L., and L. Gerard. 1983. Governmental Responsibility: Issues of Reform and Federalism, in C. L. Estes, R. J. Newcomer, and Associates, *Fiscal Austerity and Aging.* Beverly Hills, Calif.: Sage Publications, pp. 41–58.

Estes, C. L., L. E. Gerard, J. S. Zones, and J. H. Swan. 1984. *Political Economy, Health, and Aging.* Boston, MA: Little, Brown and Co.

Estes, C. L., R. J. Newcomer, and Associates. 1983. *Fiscal Austerity and Aging.* Beverly Hills, Calif.: Sage Publications.

Frost and Sullivan. 1983. *Home Healthcare Products and Services: Markets in the U.S.* New York: Frost and Sullivan.

Goffman, I. 1967. *Interaction Ritual.* Garden City, N.Y.: Anchor Books.

Gouldner, A. 1970. *The Coming Crisis of Western Sociology.* New York: Basic Books.

Graebner, W. 1980. *A History of Retirement.* New Haven, Conn.: Yale University Press.

Gubrium, J. F., ed. 1973. *The Myth of the Golden Years.* Springfield, Ill.: Charles C Thomas.

Guillemard, A. M. 1983. The Making of Old Age Policy in France, in A. M. Guillemard, ed., *Old Age and the Welfare State.* Beverly Hills, Calif.: Sage Publications, pp. 75–100.

Harrington, C., R. J. Newcomer, C. L. Estes, and Associates. 1985. *Long Term Care of the Elderly: Public Policy Issues.* Beverly Hills, Calif.: Sage Publications.

Harris, Louis, and Associates. 1984–1986. *Public Opinion Polls: Social Expenditures, 1984–1986.*

Hartmann, H. 1981. The Unhappy Marriage of Marxism and Feminism: Toward a More Progressive Union, in L. Sargent, ed., *Women and Revolution.* Boston: South End Press, pp. 1–41.

Havighurst, R. J. 1963. Successful Aging, in R. Williams, C. Tibbitts, and W. Donahue, eds, *Processes of Aging.* New York: Atherton Publishing, pp. 299–320.

Hochschild, Arlie Russell. 1973. *The Unexpected Community.* Englewood Cliffs, N.J.: Prentice-Hall.

Idler, E. L. 1979. Definitions of Health and Illness and Medical Sociology. *Social Science and Medicine* 13A:723–731.

Illich, I. 1976. *Medical Nemesis.* New York: Bantam Books.

Kleinman, Arthur, Leon Eisenberg, and Byron Good. 1973. Culture, Illness, and Care: Clinical Lessons from Anthropologic and Cross-Cultural Research. *Annals of Internal Medicine* 88(2):251–258.

Kusserow, R. 1986. *Office of Inspector General Report: Financial Impact of the Prospective Payment System on Medicare Participating Hospitals— 1984.* Washington, D.C.: U.S. Department of Health and Human Services.

Lee, P. R. 1984. Health Policy and the Health of the Public: A Two-Hundred-Year Perspective. *Mobius* 4:94–113.

Lee, P. R., and A. E. Benjamin. 1983. Intergovernmental Relations: Historical and Contemporary Perspectives, in C. L. Estes, R. J. Newcomer, and Associates, *Fiscal Austerity and*

Aging. Beverly Hills, Calif.: Sage Publications, pp. 59–81.

Liang, J., L. Dvorkin, E. Kahana, and F. Mazian. 1980. Social Integration and Morale: A Reexamination. *Journal of Gerontology* 35: 746–757.

Lowenthal, M. F. 1975. Psychosocial Variations Across the Adult Life Course: Frontiers for Research and Policy. *The Gerontologist* 15(1):6–12.

Macken, C. L. 1986. A Profile of Functionally Impaired Elderly Persons Living in the Community. *Health Care Financing Review* 7(4):33–50.

McKeown, T. 1979. *The Role of Medicine.* Princeton: Princeton University Press.

Meyerhoff, B. 1978. *Number Our Days.* New York: Simon and Schuster.

Minkler, M., and C. L. Estes, eds. 1984. *Readings in the Political Economy of Aging.* Farmingdale, N.Y.: Baywood Publishing Co.

Murcott, Anne. 1980. The Social Construction of Teenage Pregnancy. *Sociology of Health and Illness* 2(1).

Myles, J. F. 1984. *Old Age and the Welfare State.* Boston: Little, Brown and Co.

Nassif, J. Z. 1986–1987. There's Still No Place Like Home: A Primer on Home Health Care. *Generations* 11(2):5–8.

National Center for Health Statistics (NCHS). 1987. Use of Nursing Homes by the Elderly. *Advance Data from Vital and Health Statistics.* No. 135. Hyattsville, Md.: Public Health Service.

Navarro, V. 1986. *Crisis, Health and Medicine: A Social Critique.* New York: Tavistock Publications.

Neugarten, B. L. 1985. Interpretive Social Science and Research on Aging, in A. Rossi, ed., *Gender and the Life Course.* Hawthorne, N.Y.: Aldine Publishing Co., pp. 291–300.

O'Connor, J. 1973. *The Fiscal Crisis of the State.* New York: St. Martin's Press.

Palmore, E. 1975. *The Honorable Elders.* Durham, N.C.: Duke University Press.

Parsons, T. 1951. *The Social System.* New York: The Free Press.

Pascall, G. 1986. *Social Policy: A Feminist Analysis.* New York: Tavistock Publications.

Petchesky, R. P. 1984. *Abortion and Women's*

Choice: The State, Sexuality, and Reproductive Freedom. White Plains, N.Y.: Longman.

Piven, F. F., and R. A. Cloward. 1971. *Regulating the Poor.* New York: Vintage Books.

Relman, A. S. 1980. The New Medical-Industrial Complex. *New England Journal of Medicine* 303:963–970.

Ricardo-Campbell, R. 1982. *The Economics and Politics of Health.* Chapel Hill, N.C.: University of North Carolina Press.

Rice, D. P. 1985. The Medical Care System: Past Trends and Future Projections. Paper presented at the symposium Who Will Control the Practice of Medicine? New York Medical College, New York City, October 16–17.

———. 1986. The Medical Care System: Past Trends and Future Projections. *The New York Medicine Quarterly* 6(1):39–70.

Rice, D. P., and M. P. LaPlante. 1986. Chronic Illness, Disability, and Increasing Longevity. Unpublished manuscript.

Riley, M. W. 1985. Age Strata in Social Systems, in R. Binstock and E. Shanas, eds., *Handbook of Aging and the Social Sciences.* New York: Van Nostrand Reinhold, Co. pp. 369–411.

Rodin, J., and E. Langer. 1980. Aging Labels: The Decline of Control and the Fall of Self-Esteem. *Journal of Social Issues* 36:12–29.

Rose, A. M., and W. A. Peterson, eds. 1965. *Older People and Their Social World.* Philadelphia: F. A. Davis Co.

Rosow, I. 1974. *Socialization to Old Age.* Berkeley: University of California Press.

Rossi, A. S., ed. 1985. *Gender and the Life Course.* Hawthorne, N.Y.: Aldine Publishing Co.

Salthouse, Timothy A. 1982. *Adult Cognition: An Experimental Psychology of Human Aging.* New York: Springer-Verlag New York.

Scull, A. T. 1976. *Decarceration.* Englewood Cliffs, N.J.: Prentice-Hall.

Seligman, M. 1975. *Helplessness: On Depression, Development and Death.* New York: Freeman, W.H. & Co.

Sheehy, G. 1978. *Passages.* New York: Bantam Books.

Sokoloff, N. J. 1980. *Between Love and Money.* New York: Praeger Publishers.

Starr, P. 1982. *The Social Transformation of American Medicine.* New York: Basic Books.

Strauss, Anselm. 1975. *Chronic Illness and the Quality of Life.* St. Louis, Mo.: C. V. Mosby Co.

Strauss, A., S. Fagerhaugh, B. Suczek, and C. Wiener. 1985. *Social Organization of Medical Work.* Chicago: University of Chicago Press.

Sulvetta, M., and K. Swartz. 1986. *The Uninsured and Uncompensated Care: A Chartbook.* Washington, D.C.: National Health Policy Forum.

Twaddle, A. C. 1982. From Medical Sociology to the Sociology of Health: Some Changing Concerns in the Sociological Study of Sickness and Treatment, in T. Bottomore, S. Nowak, and M. Sokolowska, eds., *Sociology: The State of the Art.* Beverly Hills, Calif.: Sage Publications, pp. 323–358.

U.S. Bureau of the Census. 1986. *Statistical Abstract of the United States.* Washington, D.C.: U.S. Government Printing Office, Tables 164 and 166.

U.S. General Accounting Office (GAO). 1977. *Home Health: The Need for a National Policy to Provide for the Elderly.* Washington, D.C.: U.S. Government Printing Office.

U.S. Senate. 1986. *Developments in Aging: 1985,* volume 3. Report of the Special Committee on Aging. Washington, D.C.: U.S. Government Printing Office.

Vladeck, B. C. 1980. *Unloving Care.* New York: Basic Books.

Waitzkin, H. 1983. *The Second Sickness.* New York: The Free Press.

Waldo, D. R., and H. C. Lazenby. 1984. Demographic Characteristics and Health Care Use and Expenditures by the Aged in the United States: 1977–1984. *Health Care Financing Review.* 6:(1):1–29.

Waldo, D. R., K. R. Levit, and H. Lazenby. 1986. National Health Expenditures, 1985. *Health Care Financing Review* 8(1):1–21.

Walker, A. 1980. The Social Creation of Poverty and Dependency in Old Age. *Journal of Social Policy* 9:49–75.

———. 1983. Care for Elderly People: A Conflict Between Women and the State, in J. Finch and D. Groves, eds., *A Labour of Love: Women, Work and Caring.* Boston: Routledge and Kegan Paul, pp. 106–128.

Walker, D. B. 1981. *Toward a Functioning Federalism.* Boston: Little, Brown and Co.

Wood, J. B., and C. L. Estes. 1986–1987. Cost Containment Policies. *Generations.* 11(2):29–33.

CHAPTER
20

HUMAN RESOURCE TRENDS IN THE HEALTH FIELD

JOHN D. LOFT
PHILLIP R. KLETKE

INTRODUCTION

Trends in the number and distribution of health care professionals are best understood in the context of structural changes in the social and economic organization of health care delivery in the United States. Through the first half of this century, health care delivery was organized around the physician-patient dyad. Although researchers debated over how the two halves of this dyad interacted (see, e.g., Hendersen 1935; Parsons 1951; Freidson 1970), there was essential agreement that these were the principal actors. A patient who required medical care elected to use the services of a particular physician and paid for these services. The dominant form of medical practice was the self-employed professional. Physicians were the key deci-

The views expressed in this chapter are those of the authors and do not necessarily represent official AMA views or policy.

sion makers in the allocation of medical resources.

In the 1980s, this dyadic system is no longer a sufficient conceptual model for describing medical care delivery in the United States. Although the physician-patient relationship is still the hub of medical care, many additional actors are in the system. Rapid technological development has created a multitude of new health occupations. The rising costs of health care have spurred a variety of cost-containment strategies that place limits on the decisions of both patients and physicians. Competition in medicine, newly sanctioned by federal policy, has introduced entrepreneurial interest in medical care delivery. Large, bureaucratic organizations monitor and control the use of health resources and manage the personnel who deliver these services. The physician-patient dyad has evolved into a complex network of patients, providers, third-party insurers, government agencies, private entrepreneurs, and national corporations. Patients' decisions about physicians or other providers may be limited by their employer's health plan. Physicians' allocation of medical resources may be constrained by features of a third-party insurer or the protocol of an employer.

Organizational and technological changes have encouraged growth in the health care professions. An additional factor in this growth has been national and local health policy. Although these policies have not always been consistent, government funding of educational programs for health care professionals has been an obvious stimulant to growth.

The environment of organizational, technological, and policy change forms the backdrop of our discussion of recent trends in the health care professions. We begin with a brief discussion of recent developments in the organization of health care delivery. Next we examine how manpower policies for the health professions are formulated and provide a short history of physician manpower policy since World War II. We then discuss how these organizational and policy developments are reflected in the changing size and composition of the health care professions. The final section of the chapter looks at the various ways in which policymakers determine the adequacy of the supply of health personnel.

Changes in the Social Organization of Medicine

Bureaucratic factors have played an increasingly important role in the practice of medicine since the turn of the century. The shift in the focus of medical care delivery from solo, fee-for-service practice to larger institutions is both a cause and an effect of technological developments and managerial innovations. These changes in turn have demanded new types of health care professionals and the organizational structure necessary to coordinate their activities. Third-party payers have developed a variety of reimbursement mechanisms in attempts to achieve the often conflicting goals of broad access to health services and control over the escalating costs of providing these services.

Medical bureaucracy first developed in the context of hospital inpatient care as innovations in medical science, medical education, and public policy resulted in the development of the modern hospital. In the nineteenth century, advances in anesthetic and sterilization techniques allowed complicated surgery to be performed successfully. The identification of blood types in 1900 made transfusions safe and effective. Sophisticated medical equipment, such as the electrocardiogram (first used in 1903) and electroencephalogram (1929), were expensive and impractical for use in private offices but could be conveniently housed in hospitals. These advances also spurred diversification and specialization within the medical profession and the development of new health care professions. Hospitals developed as suitable locations where personnel, equipment, and facilities could be brought together to provide health care (Heydebrand 1973; Knowles 1965; Rakich and Darr 1983).

The Flexner Report in 1910 outlined new standards for medical education that were quickly adopted by the profession and by state licensing boards. Important for the development of hospitals was the emphasis on clinical training in the hospital. Specialization in medicine led to a proliferation of residency programs. The number of physicians in residencies doubled from 1934 to 1940 and nearly doubled again in the next five years (*Journal of the American Medical Association* 1940, 1946). The expanding requirements of medical education required hospitals to expand services and to increase numbers of staff and facilities.

The Hill-Burton Act of 1946 provided another boost to hospital development. Pointing to fears of a severe hospital shortage, the act required states to inventory facilities and identify shortage areas. Federal funds were provided to construct hospitals in the shortage areas. The Hill-Burton Act was eventually expanded to provide funding for construction of nursing homes and other long-term care facilities, as well as for the building of outpatient facilities.

Growth in the hospital sector created intense demand for personnel to staff new facilities. Federal funding was made available for educational programs in the health professions. The expansion of educational programs further contributed to the increase of the professions.

The growth and development of medical group practice is also a factor in the development of health professions. As early as 1927, the Committee on the Cost of Medical Care (CCMC) advocated group practice as an organizational form for health care delivery; the committee's final report recommended that medical services be provided by organized groups of physicians in conjunction with other health care providers (CCMC 1932). More recently, since 1969, the number of groups has increased at an average annual rate of about 6 percent, and the rate of increase accelerated to nearly 10 percent between 1980 and 1985. The average size of medical groups increased from 6.6 physicians in 1965 to 9.0 in 1985 (Havlicek 1985). The average number of allied health personnel employed per group increased from 15.2 to 23.1 during the same period. The proportion of all active nonfederal patient care physicians practicing in groups increased from less than one-sixth in 1969 to one-third in 1985. In the competitive environment of the early 1980s, and with new designs in medical equipment that produce smaller and more affordable machines, many services formerly provided in hospitals are now offered in group practices. Decentralization, in this sense, has contributed to increased demand for health care personnel in medical groups and other outpatient facilities.

A more recent development is the introduction of national corporations into health delivery (Starr 1982). The impact of corporatization on the numbers of health care professionals is unclear. To the extent that corporate medicine is an extension of bureaucratic modes of providing health services, the traditional relationships between patient and provider and among providers will certainly change as responsibilities for various aspects of health care delivery shift among providers.

Such shifts in the allocation of tasks will continue to occur in both the for-profit and nonprofit sectors of health care delivery. These shifts are an outgrowth of the bureaucratic tendency toward rationalizing activities. If medical care is broken down into functional elements, nonphysician personnel may be trained to perform many tasks in place of physicians—for example, health counseling, patient monitoring, and social services (Mechanic 1977). Data from the AMA's Socioeconomic Monitoring System (Reynolds and Abrams 1983) demonstrate a dramatic increase in the use of allied health professionals, nurses, and secretarial staff in office-based private practice. The largest absolute and percentage increases were in the allied health professions. Health economics literature points to continued increases in this area (see, e.g., Reinhardt 1975).

Complete rationalization of health services—so-called "cookbook" medicine—is unlikely to be realized. In the ideal bureaucracy, the actor has very little discretion. Decisionmaking is consolidated in higher levels of the organization, and rules are developed to increase the calculability of outcomes (Weber 1946, pp. 214–216). In medical care, however, there are many nonroutine events, and outcomes are often incalculable. Even apparently innocuous symptoms may indicate serious disease, and the costs of error may be quite high. In such a situation, the proportion of erroneous decisions may be reduced by allowing highly competent professionals a great deal of discretion in individual cases. As Scott notes: "Tasks aimed at overcoming variable resistance are usually better organized in a 'professional' manner since skilled nonroutine responses are better calculated to meet unpredictable resistance with a minimum of errors" (1966, pp. 42–43).

Medical bureaucracy is something of a mixed blessing. Certainly the development of third-party payment has increased access to medical services. Formal and informal peer review and utilization review have increased the quality of health care. The economies of scale possible in large organizations have lowered the cost of care. However, some have charged that large medical bureaucracies can fragment medical care and disperse responsibility for patients' health. Others fear constraints on physician decisionmaking may lower the quality of care. These concerns should not mask the essential fact that medical bureaucracy is here to stay.

The growth of medical bureaucracy means that the physician-patient dyad is no longer an adequate conceptual model for understanding health care delivery. While patient and physician may still constitute the first and second parties in medical care, patients now may see a number of different types of providers, including several physicians and allied health professionals. In addition to these relationships, the interests of third-party insurers have become more important in the allocation of health resources and the initiation of various cost-containment procedures. Finally, bureaucratic needs of large organizations constitute a kind of fourth party with interests in the processes and outcomes of medical decisions. As medical bureaucracies continue to grow, they will demand more personnel and different types of professionals to represent the interests of providers, insurers, and managers.

The Policy Environment

In the area of health manpower policy, the issues of quantity and quality are inextricably linked. Broadly defined, health manpower policies serve the twin functions of ensuring a supply of professionals adequate to meet the country's needs and adequately trained to provide quality health care. These policies are determined by a wide variety of actors in the public and private sectors. The policies of the various actors often reflect their conflicting goals.

In the public sector, the federal government influences the supply of health manpower by providing financial support for the training of health professionals in U.S. schools and by setting immigration laws controlling the entry of health professionals trained outside the country. State governments provide additional financial support for training of health personnel and set requirements for state licensure. All states have licensure requirements for physicians and dentists, and most require licensure for many other health professionals as well. The primary aim of licensure requirements is (at least ostensibly) to promote the quality of care by permitting health personnel to practice only if they have passed an examination or have satisfactorily completed training in approved schools or training programs.

Because health care occupations are based on highly specialized knowledge, the professions themselves play a critical role in assessing the qualifications of entrants. Professionals typically fill the majority of the positions on state licensing boards, and consequently state and national professional associations wield a strong influence over these boards. Professional organizations in the private sector are also involved in accrediting schools and educational programs in which professionals receive their training. Program accreditation is a standard explicitly recognized by state licensing boards when evaluating the training of applicants.

Finally, underpinning the policies of professional organizations and state and federal governments are the labor market aspects of the health care system. The supply and quality of health personnel are influenced by the policies of commercial organizations, which determine the economic returns associated with the various health professions. The attractiveness of the various professions is thus determined, in part, by the employment policies of HMOs and other large institutional providers; the policies of third-party payers (in both the private and public sectors) concerning the coverage and amount of payment for different types of health care; and policies of insurance companies concerning premiums for professional liability insurance.

The role of professional organizations in regulating the entry of new professionals is particularly interesting. These organizations represent the agencies best capable of assessing the quality of training. However, there is a potential conflict of interest, because judgments on quality of training indirectly affect the number of entrants to the profession and, hence, the monetary rewards associated with its practice. Consequently, the role of professions in assessing the qualifications of entrants is closely monitored by the federal and state governments.

In order to examine the relationship between policy and the supply of health manpower, we present a brief overview of changes since World War II in the manpower policies concerning a single health profession—allopathic physicians. Our discussion focuses on manpower policies of the federal government, as well as on the actions of the American Medical Association (AMA)—one of the principle actors in the private sector.

After World War II, various parts of the federal government attempted to take a more active role in promoting the health care of the American people. Evidence of these efforts can be seen in the Wagner-Murray-Dingell proposal for national health insurance, which failed to pass Congress in 1949, and in proposals to provide direct federal financial assistance to medical schools. The proposals to increase federal support for medical education were based on analyses indicating that medical schools were not producing enough physicians to meet the country's future needs. In

1948 the Ewing Report issued by the Federal Security Agency (the forerunner of the U.S. Department of Health, Education, and Welfare), projected a shortage of 42,000 physicians by 1960 (Dickenson 1949).

The AMA, which traditionally had not favored government involvement in the medical profession, opposed both the bill for national health insurance and the proposals for federal support of medical education (Campion 1984). The AMA challenged the methodology on which the Ewing report was based and rejected its conclusion of an approaching physician shortage. Furthermore, the AMA expressed concern about the effect that federal involvement might have on standards for admission to medical schools and on the integrity of academic programs. However, during this time a growing proportion of the public believed that the AMA's position was based on economic protectionism rather than a concern for academic freedom and integrity.

The concerns of a physician manpower shortage raised in the Ewing report were later echoed in two government reports— the Bayne-Jones report in 1958 and the Bane report in 1959. These two reports claimed that the United States urgently needed to increase its supply of physician manpower and recommended that the graduating class of physicians be increased in size from 7,400 to 11,000 between 1959 and 1975. The reports signaled a growing national consensus that there was in fact a physician shortage. By 1959 the AMA no longer outwardly rejected the idea of a physician shortage, and its Council on Medical Education discussed the need to expand medical education facilities. Construction funds for the enlargement of existing medical schools and the creation of new ones were provided by the Health Professions Educational Assistance Act of 1963.

The consensus that there was a physician shortage received still further support from the Coggeshall report in 1963 and the report of the National Advisory Commission on Health Manpower in 1967. Both reports recommended further expansion of medical school enrollments. These concerns were echoed by the AMA, which joined with the Association of American Medical Colleges in stating that there was an urgent need for more physicians.

Congress responded to this consensus by passing the Health Manpower Act of 1968, which provided loans and scholarships for health professionals and funds for further construction of medical schools. In 1971 Congress passed the Comprehensive Health Manpower Training Act, which provided capitation payments to medical schools as a further incentive to expand student enrollments. Meanwhile, in 1965, the Department of Labor had released a statement indicating that there was a physician shortage in the country, with the result that alien physicians wishing to immigrate to the United States were given preferred status.

In the mid-1970s the general consensus concerning the need for additional physician manpower began to change, as many people became convinced that the country was producing more physicians than needed. In 1976 the Graduate Medical Education National Advisory Committee (GMENAC) was formed by the U.S. Department of Health and Human Services. The final report of the committee, which was published in 1980, projected a surplus of 70,000 physicians in 1990 and a 145,000 surplus in 2000. In 1976, Congress passed the Health Professions Assistance Act, which stated that there was no longer a shortage of physicians and which placed restrictions on the immigration of alien foreign medical graduates into the United States. In the late 1970s the federal government stopped providing capitation payments to medical schools, thereby eliminating one incentive for large medical school enrollments.

The change in government policies concerning expanding physician supply was to some degree paralleled by a shift in AMA policy. In 1979 the AMA stated that the

physician supply should be controlled by the forces governing the marketplace, a major change from its 1967 statement that medical school enrollments should be increased. However, in response to the continued rapid growth of the physician population, the AMA revised its manpower policies once again in 1986, stating that there was currently a surplus of physicians in many areas of the United States, that the physician surplus was likely to have negative consequences on the quality and cost of health care, and that market forces could not be relied upon by themselves to assure cost-effective care.

Trends in Health Care Professionals

The health manpower legislation of the 1960s and early 1970s was quite successful in increasing the supply of personnel in virtually all of the health professions. The upper panel of Table 1 shows the growth of the various types of health personnel between 1970 and 1986. While the supply of personnel grew dramatically in all the health occupations, the percent increase was greatest for registered nurses and physicians. Osteopathic physicians had a greater percent increase than did allopathic physicians. Among the professions listed in Table 1, the smallest percent growth was for pharmacists, whose numbers increased 32.1 percent during the sixteen-year interval. However, this increase was still markedly faster than that of the general population, which increased approximately 16 percent during the same period. The lower panel of Table 1 shows that the practitioner-per-population ratio increased significantly for all the health professions. The percent increase in this ratio ranged from 13.5 percent for pharmacists to 80.6 percent for registered nurses.

Table 2 displays the annual percent growth rate of the supply of various types of health personnel during each of three periods—1970–1975, 1975–1980, and 1980–1986. The supply of registered nurses and physicians grew very rapidly

TABLE 1   Estimated Active Supply of Selected Health Personnel, 1970, 1975, 1980, and 1986

Health Occupation	Estimated Active Supply				Percent Increase, 1970–1986
	1970	*1975*	*1980*	*1986*	
Physicians	326,200	384,500	457,500	544,800	67.0
Allopathic (MD)	314,200	370,400	440,400	522,000	66.1
Osteopathic (DO)	12,000	14,000	17,140	22,800	90.0
Podiatrists	7,100	7,300	8,900	11,000	54.9
Dentists	102,220	112,020	126,240	143,000	39.9
Optometrists	18,400	19,900	22,400	24,300	32.1
Pharmacists	113,700	122,800	143,800	161,500	42.0
Registered nurses	750,000	961,000	1,272,900	1,592,600*	112.3

Health Occupation	Practitioners per 100,000 Population				Percent Increase, 1970–1984
	1970	*1975*	*1980*	*1984*	
Physicians	156.0	174.4	179.0	224.9	44.1
Allopathic (MD)	150.0	167.9	189.5	215.5	43.7
Osteopathic (DO)	6.0	6.5	7.5	9.4	56.7
Podiatrists	3.5	3.4	4.0	4.5	28.6
Dentists	49.5	51.6	55.2	58.9	19.0
Optometrists	8.9	9.2	9.8	10.1	13.5
Pharmacists	54.4	56.6	63.0	67.1	23.3
Registered Nurses	366.0	449.0	560.0	661.0	80.6

*Preliminary data

Sources: Bureau of Health Professions, *The Fifth Report to the President and Congress on the Status of Health Personnel in the United States*, DHHS Publication No. HRS–P–OD–86–1, March 1986, Table 2–1, pp. 2–6. Bureau of Health Professions, *The Sixth Report to the President and Congress on the Status of Health Professions in the United States* (forthcoming).

TABLE 2   Annual Growth Rate of Active Supply of Selected Health Personnel, 1970–1975, 1975–1980, and 1980–1986.

Health Occupation	Annual Growth Rate		
	1970– 1975	*1975– 1980*	*1980– 1986*
Physicians	3.3	3.5	3.0
Allopathic (MD)	3.3	3.5	3.0
Osteopathic (DO)	3.1	4.1	4.9
Podiatrists	0.6	4.0	3.6
Dentists	1.8	2.4	2.1
Optometrists	1.6	2.4	1.4
Pharmacists	1.6	3.2	2.0
Registered Nurses	5.1	5.8	3.8

Sources: Bureau of Health Professions, *The Fifth Report to the President and Congress on the Status of Health Personnel in the United States*, DHHS Publication No. HRS–P–OD–86–1, March 1986, Table 2–1. Bureau of Health Professions, *The Sixth Report to the President and Congress on the Status of Health Personnel in the United States* (forthcoming).

throughout the entire interval, each profession sustaining an annual increase of more than 3 percent in all three periods. In the first two periods, registered nurses increased by more than 5 percent per year, a rate that, if sustained, would result in a doubling of the population of registered nurses every fourteen years. In contrast to the rates of growth among physicians and registered nurses, those of podiatrists, dentists, optometrists, and pharmacists were somewhat erratic. These four occupations grew at a relatively slow pace during the first half of the 1970s. The percent increase for these occupations was substantially larger during the second half of the 1970s and then decreased during the first part of the 1980s.

The slower percent growth in the supply of physician personnel during the 1980s is partially due to the stabilization of school enrollments. As Table 3 indicates, first-year enrollments for all of the various health professions were much higher in 1985–1986 than in 1970–1971, more than doubling for podiatrists and increasing by more than 50 percent for physicians. However, most of the increase occurred during the 1970s and relatively little during the 1980s. The right panel of Table 3 shows

that enrollment growth was higher between 1970–1971 and 1975–1976 than after 1975–1976 for each of the health professions. The most significant declines were in the areas of podiatric medicine, where the annual percent growth rate decreased from 12.8 percent in the early 1970s to 3.1 percent in the early 1980s, and dentistry, which decreased from 4.8 percent in the early 1970s to −4.3 percent in the 1980s.

In spite of the current reductions in the rate of growth, the supply of health professionals will increase throughout the rest of this century. Table 4 indicates that in the year 2000, the Bureau of Health Professions projects nearly 700,000 physicians, a 28 percent increase over the supply in 1986. There will be 260 physicians for every 100,000 U.S. population, a substantial increase over the 1986 value. The supply of dentists will increase only 13 percent, the smallest increase of any of the professions described in Table 4.

Physician Statistics

Tables 5 through 8 display selected statistics from the AMA publication *Physician Characteristics and Distribution in the U.S.* (Roback et al. 1986 and earlier editions).

TABLE 3 First-Year Enrollments in Schools for Selected Health Occupations, Selected Academic Years 1970–1971 through 1985–1986

	First-Year Students				*Annual Growth Rate*		
Health Occupation	*1970–1971*	*1975–1976*	*1980–1981*	*1985–1986*	*1970–1971 to 1975–1976*	*1975–1976 to 1980–1981*	*1980–1981 to 1985–1986*
Medicine	11,971	16,333	18,682	18,723	6.4	2.7	0.0
Allopathic (HD)	11,348	15,295	17,186	16,963	6.2	2.4	−0.3
Osteopathic (DO)	623	1,038	1,496	1,760	10.7	7.6	3.3
Podiatric Medicine	351	641	695	811	12.8	1.6	3.1
Dentistry	4,565	5,763	6,030	4,843	4.8	0.9	−4.3
Optometry	884	1,057	1,209[1]	1,251	3.6	2.7	0.7
Pharmacy	5,864	8,710	7,511	7,084	8.2	−2.9	−1.2
Nursing (RN only)	78,524	112,174	110,201	99,300[2]	7.4	−0.4	−2.1

[1]1979–1980 data

[2]Preliminary data

Sources: Bureau of Health Professions, *The Fifth Report to the President and Congress on the Status of Health Personnel in the United States*, DHHS Publication No. HRS–P–OD–86–1, March 1986, Table 2–3, pp. 2–8. Bureau of Health Professions, *The Sixth Report to the President and Congress on the Status of Health Personnel in the United States* (forthcoming).

TABLE 4   Projected Active Supply of Selected Health Personnel, 1986, 1990, 1995, and 2000

Health Occupation	Projected Active Supply				Percent Increase, 1986–2000
	1986	*1990*	*1995*	*2000*	*1986–2000*
Physicians	544,800	587,700	645,500	696,600	27.9
Allopathic (MD)	522,000	559,500	611,100	656,100	25.7
Osteopathic (DO)	22,800	28,200	34,400	40,400	77.2
Podiatrists	11,000	12,700	15,000	17,100	55.5
Dentists	143,000	150,800	156,800	161,200	12.7
Optometrists	24,300	25,500	27,500	29,700	22.2
Pharmacists	161,500	170,800	181,200	188,200	16.5
Registered nurses	1,592,600	1,739,100	1,932,100	2,097,400	30.6

Health Occupation	Practitioners per 100,000 Population				Percent Increase, 1986–2000
	1986	*1990*	*1995*	*2000*	*1986–2000*
Physicians	224.9	235.4	248.7	259.9	15.6
Allopathic (MD)	215.5	224.1	235.5	244.9	13.6
Osteopathic (DO)	9.4	11.3	13.3	15.3	62.8
Podiatrists	4.5	5.1	5.8	6.4	42.2
Dentists	58.9	60.1	60.2	60.0	1.9
Optometrists	10.1	10.2	10.6	11.1	9.9
Pharmacists	67.1	68.1	69.6	70.0	4.3
Registered Nurses	661.0	695.0	743.0	775.0	17.2

Sources: Bureau of Health Professions, *The Fifth Report to the President and Congress on the Status of Health Personnel in the United States*, DHHS Publication No. HRS–P–OD–86–1, March 1986, Table 2–8, pp. 2–13. Bureau of Health Professions, *The Sixth Report to the President and Congress on the Status of Health Personnel in the United States* (forthcoming).

These data are derived from the AMA's Physician Masterfile, which contains professional and demographic information about all physicians in the United States. A record is initiated in the Physician Masterfile as a student enters medical school. Records are updated each year throughout the student's undergraduate and graduate medical education through contact with all U.S. medical schools and residency and fellowship programs. Graduates of foreign medical schools are added to the file as they enter residency programs or as they are licensed by state boards. Once physicians have completed medical training, their Masterfile records are monitored and updated through a variety of institutional sources as well as by the physicians themselves. These institutional sources include state licensing boards, state and county medical societies, specialty societies, and various agencies of the federal government. Physicians' addresses are monitored through AMA and other mailings. Address changes trigger the mailing of a Record of Physicians' Professional Activities (PPA) to the physician at the new address. The PPA requests information about hours spent in various activities, present employment, and specialties. The PPA Census is administered on a rotating basis to 25 percent of the physician population so that all physicians are surveyed within a four-year cycle. In addition, monthly supplemental mailings are directed to physicians who indicate address or practice changes and to other selected subpopulations.

Table 5 displays the distribution of physicians' activities for the years 1970, 1975, 1980, and 1985. Overall, the physician population has increased from 334,028 in 1970 to 552,716 in 1985, an increase of 56.5 percent in fifteen years, or about 4 percent per year. Throughout this period, about 80 percent of all physicians were involved in patient care activities, and the balance were engaged in activities such as medical teaching, administration, and re-

TABLE 5   Federal and Nonfederal Physicians by Major Professional Activity for Selected Years

Activity	1970	1975	1980	1985
Total Physicians	334,028	393,742	467,679	552,716
Patient Care	278,535	311,937	376,512	448,820
Office based	192,439	215,429	272,000	330,197
Hospital based	86,096	96,508	104,512	118,623
Residents[1]	51,228	57,802	62,042	75,411
Staff	34,868	38,706	42,470	43,212
Medical teaching	5,588	6,445	7,942	7,832
Administration	12,158	11,161	12,209	13,810
Research	11,929	7,944	15,377	23,268
Other	2,635	2,793	2,876	3,410
Not classified[2]	N.A.	26,145	20,629	13,950
Inactive	19,621	21,449	25,744	38,646
Address unknown	3,204	5,868	6,390	2,980

[1]Includes first-year and all other years of residency.

[2]Not Classified was established in 1970; however, complete data not available until 1972. Total for 1970 includes 358 "not classified" physicians.

Source: Gene Roback, Diane Mead, and Lilian Randolph, *Physician Characteristics and Distribution in the U.S.* Chicago: American Medical Association, 1986 [and earlier editions], p. 17.

search. Office-based physicians comprised about 60 percent of all patient care physicians, and hospital-based physicians, including residents, accounted for about 20 percent of all physicians.

The AMA has developed eighty-five codes for self-designations of practice specialties based on physicians' responses to the PPA. The full list of Masterfile codes for self-designated practice specialties is preprinted on the questionnaire, and physicians indicate the average number of hours spent during a typical week in those specialties to which they limit their practice. The specialty with the largest number of hours is entered on the Masterfile as the primary specialty, the specialty with the second largest number of hours is entered as the secondary specialty, and so on. The PPA questionnaire allows space for the physician to record hours worked in up to three specialties.[1]

[1]Self-designated practice specialties listed on the AMA Physician Masterfile have historically related to the record-keeping needs of the AMA and do not imply recognition or endorsement of any field of medical practice by the association. The fact that a physician chooses to designate a given specialty in AMA records does not necessarily mean that the physician has been trained or has special competence to practice in the self-designated specialty.

By contrast, American Specialty Board certification indicates that a physician has received preparation in accordance with established educational standards of one of the twenty-three member boards of the American Board of Medical Specialties (ABMS). It is not uncommon for a physician to be board certified in one field of medicine while limiting practice to another specialty. As of December 31, 1985, about 15 percent of all board-certified physicians in the United States were certified by a board other than that corresponding to their primary specialty, and about half of all physicians (48 percent) were not board certified at all. In addition to maintaining physicians' self-designated practice specialties on the AMA Physician Masterfile, the AMA collects primary specialty board certification through the ABMS.

Neither self-designated practice specialty nor certification by a member board of the ABMS should be confused with successful completion of a program or programs of accredited graduate medical education. Accreditation is the process whereby the Accreditation Council for Graduate Medical Education (ACGME) grants public recognition to a specialized program that, meets certain established educational standards as determined through initial and subsequent periodic evaluations by one of the twenty-four Residency Review Committees. The AMA collects physicians' residency training data through an annual census of all ACGME-accredited residency training programs.

TABLE 6 Five Most Popular Specialties among Physicians for Selected Years

Rank	1970	1975	1980	1985
First	General practice	Internal medicine	Internal medicine	Internal medicine
Second	Internal medicine	General practice	General surgery	Family practice
Third	General surgery	General surgery	General practice	General surgery
Fourth	Psychiatry	Psychiatry	Pediatrics	Pediatrics
Fifth	Obstetrics/ gynecology	Pediatrics	Family practice	Psychiatry

Source: Gene Roback, Diane Mead, and Lilian Randolph, *Physician Characteristics and Distribution in the U.S.*, Chicago: American Medical Association, 1986 [and earlier editions], p.19.

Table 6 shows the five most popular specialties among the total physician population for the years 1970, 1975, 1980, and 1985. The table shows a shift in most popular specialty from general practice in 1970 to internal medicine in the other three years. However, it should be noted that one reason for the apparent decline in popularity of general practice is the establishment in 1970 of family practice as a separate specialty. In 1975, 12,183 physicians were classified as family practitioners; if this figure were added to the 31,562 general practitioners listed in the 1975 column of Table 6, the combined total would rank second for the year (the same is true for subsequent years). General surgery ranked in the top five specialties for each of the years, in third place in 1970, 1975, and 1985, and in second place in 1980. Pediatrics, obstetrics/gynecology, and psychiatry have been in third, fourth, and fifth place.

Table 7 shows the number of physicians in primary care specialties, defined by the AMA as internal medicine, general practice, family practice, pediatrics, and obstetrics/gynecology. The percentage of physicians in these specialties has remained stable at around 40 percent of the physician population.

Table 8 is a profile of physicians by selected professional and demographic characteristics. The percentage of nonfederal physicians has increased slightly from 90 percent in 1970 to 96 percent in 1985. The percentage of board-certified physicians has increased from 34 percent in 1970 to 53 percent in 1985.

The percentage of physicians who are graduates of foreign medical schools has remained stable at about 20 percent of the entire physician population. However, as reported in Eiler and Loft (1986), this apparent stability masks important trends and variations within the foreign medical graduate (FMG) population. Foreign na-

TABLE 7 Federal and Nonfederal Physicians in Primary Care Specialties[1] for Selected Years

	1970	1975	1980	1985
Total physicians	334,028	393,742	467,679	552,716
Number in primary care	137,515	153,349	186,227	223,952
Percent	41.2	38.9	39.8	40.5

[1]General and family practice, internal medicine, obstetrics/gynecology, and pediatrics.

Source: Gene Roback, Diane Mead, and Lilian Randolph, *Physician Characteristics and Distribution in the U.S.*, Chicago: American Medical Association, 1986 [and earlier editions], p. 8.

TABLE 8   Federal and Nonfederal Physicians by Selected Professional and Demographic Characteristics for Selected Years

	1970	1975	1980	1985
Total Physicians	334,028	393,742	467,679	552,716
Nonfederal	301,323	359,683	443,502	528,169
Board certified	112,802	166,986	238,249	295,248
Medical school				
U.S.	270,637	306,413	362,307	424,345
Canadian	6,174	6,481	7,646	8,066
Foreign	57,217	80,848	97,726	118,875
Sex				
Female	25,401	35,636	54,284	80.725
Male	308,627	358,106	413,395	471,991
Age				
Under 35	88,413	108,393	128,506	141,622
Over 35	245,615	285,349	339,173	411,094

Source: Gene Roback, Diane Mead, and Lilian Randolph, *Physician Characteristics and Distribution in the U.S.*, Chicago: American Medical Association, 1986 [and earlier editions], p. 8, 45, 57.

tional FMGs (FNFMGs, that is, citizens of foreign countries as well as graduates of foreign medical schools) dominated the FMG cohort throughout the period 1971–1983, accounting for 65 percent of all FMGs in 1971 and 72 percent in 1983. However, the growth rate of FNFMGs declined steadily from 52 percent growth during 1971–1976, to 23 percent during 1976–1981, to 7 percent in 1981–1983. During the same twelve year period, competition for positions in U.S. medical schools plus the development of "offshore" medical schools in the Carribean encouraged U.S. citizens to seek medical degrees from foreign schools. The growth rate for U.S. citizen foreign medical graduates (USFMGs) increased from 10 percent growth during 1971–1976, to 15 percent in 1976–1981, and again 15 percent in 1981–1983. The percent of USFMGs taking degrees from Central American schools increased from 10.6 percent in 1971 to 29.3 percent in 1983. In 1971, more than three-quarters of USFMGs had graduated from European schools; in 1983, slightly more than half came from European schools, 29.3 percent graduated from Central American schools, and 12.5 percent from Asian schools.

Although the proportion of young physicians (less than 35 years of age) in the entire population has remained constant at about one-quarter during the fifteen-year period from 1970 to 1985, the sex composition of young physicians has changed, with an increase in the proportion of female physicians from 10 percent in 1970 to more than 20 percent in 1985. This has resulted in a near doubling of the proportion of female physicians in the entire physician population from 7.6 percent in 1970 to 15 percent in 1985.

Policy Formulation

As health care policymakers consider whether the supply of health care professionals in the United States is adequate to meet the country's need for health services, they find "need for health services" and "adequacy of supply" extremely complex concepts that are not easily measured by empirical analyses. Although a number of different approaches have been developed to analyze the adequacy of the health care professionals, none is completely satisfactory. Often the various methodologies do not present a consistent picture about whether there are too many or too few health care practitioners to meet the country's needs. In spite of their many shortcomings, these methodologies play a necessary role in the formulation of health manpower policy.

In this section, we divide the analyses of the supply of health personnel into five categories:

- practitioner-to-population ratios
- measures of accessibility to health care services
- professional and community satisfaction
- econometric analyses
- professional standards

The following typology is a modification of one developed by Lave et al. (1975).

Practitioner-to-population ratios. The practitioner-to-population ratio (usually expressed as the number of active practitioners in a health care profession per 100,000 population) is the most commonly used measure of the adequacy of health manpower supply. This ratio is especially useful when analyzing the relative availability of services across geographic areas or between different points in time. Its chief advantages are that it is easy to compute and has broad intuitive appeal. Also, this index has been adapted for many different types of studies, for example, analyses of individual physician specialties or of the population of a specific age group. These ratios are often used to locate shortage (or surplus) areas for various types of health care personnel.

The utility of practitioner-to-population ratios is mitigated by the fact that not all segments of the population have the same demand for health services. For example, demand for health care is influenced by age and sex distributions of the general population. Projected trends in the practitioner-to-population ratio do not take into consideration that the aging of the U.S. population will cause the demand for health care to increase faster than the growth rate of the general population. Similarly, not all members of a profession have

the same level of productivity. Simple analyses of practitioner-to-population ratios do not take into account the wide variety of factors influencing productivity, such as the changing modes of health care delivery and the impact of future technological innovations. To some extent, variation in productivity and demand can be incorporated into the study of the practitioner-to-population ratios by analyzing full-time-equivalent practitioners and making adjustments for population composition.

Table 1 shows that between 1970 and 1984 the practitioner-to-population ratio increased for all the listed health occupations, indicating a more plentiful supply of health care services. Table 4 indicates that this increase is projected to continue until the end of the century. Data from the 1983 Physician Characteristics and Distribution, sponsored by the AMA, indicate that the physician population is distributed very unevenly with respect to the general population. In 1986 the number of nonfederal physicians per 100,000 civilian population ranged from a high of 340 in Massachusetts to a low of 131 in Mississippi.[2]

Measures of accessibility. Adequacy of the supply of health personnel is sometimes related to how accessible health care is to the general public. Accessibility depends not only on the supply of health personnel but also on their geographic distribution and their availability to the public—that is, whether patients can see practitioners when and where they wish.

The relationship between supply of health personnel and access to health care is very complex, partly because geographic distribution of practitioners is much different from that of the general population.

---

[2]Note that published physician-to-population ratios may differ depending on the definition of "physician" and "population." The numerator typically can refer to either "all physicians," "all nonfederal physicians," or "all nonfederal, patient care physicians." Common denominators are "total population of the United States," "total civilian population of the United States," or population in other geographic units.

For example, in some rural areas, physicians are in short supply. In these cases, patients may not have adequate access to health care because of the long distances between their homes and physician offices. However, several studies have shown that the maldistribution of physicians has eased in recent years. A recent analysis by Newhouse et al. (1982) shows that the expanding physician supply has led many physicians to move to small towns and cities where no physician of their specialty had practiced previously. Thus, the analysis indicates that recent growth in the physician population has improved geographic accessibility of physicians in rural areas.

Access to health care is also determined by the availability of practitioners to their patients in terms of the lead time needed for an appointment, the average amount of waiting time in the office, and the amount of time practitioners spend with patients during an average patient visit. Data on physicians from the AMA's Socioeconomic Monitoring System (SMS) show that between 1982 and 1985 the average lead time needed for an appointment with a physician decreased from 6.9 to 6.2 days (Gonzalez and Emmons 1986). However, little change is seen in the SMS data for the amount of waiting time at the physician's office. Average amount of time physicians spend with patients has increased 7 percent from 1975 to 1985 (NCHS, 1982; 1985).

Professional and community satisfaction. The concerns of researchers and policymakers about the adequate supply of health personnel are also related to the perceptions of the general public. Attitudinal surveys are used to measure a population's level of satisfaction with the existing supply of health personnel. The main advantage of working with attitudinal data is that it provides the most direct information possible about the public's perceptions about whether the supply of health manpower is large enough to meet their needs. However, there are several disadvantages. Most of the public is not well informed about the supply of health personnel, and certain segments of the population may have unreasonable expectations about how many practitioners can be supported in a given community. Also, it is difficult to interpret disagreements about what level of satisfaction is necessary for the physician population to be considered adequate. Consequently, it is difficult to develop a normative standard on the adequacy of physician supply with this sort of attitudinal data.

Data from recent attitudinal surveys (Freshnock, 1984) of the general population show that in 1984 the majority of the general public (59 percent) believed there were too many doctors and 26 percent thought there were too few. Of physicians surveyed, 43 percent believed there were too many physicians in their community, and 74 percent believed there was a current or impending surplus of physicians in certain specialty areas in their community.

Econometric analyses. The methodologies described above do not take into account how market forces affect the demand for medical services and influence beliefs about whether the supply of health personnel is adequate. However, several recent studies have drawn inferences about the adequacy of physician supply by analyzing the relationship between physician supply and physician income. These studies can be divided into two groups.

Analyses of relative income compare the average annual income of physicians to the incomes of other professions. One infers that the supply of physicians is increasing relative to demand whenever the incomes of physicians decrease relative to the salaries of individuals in comparable professions.

Analyses of the rate of return to medical education consider medical education as an investment in human capital, and physician income is considered to be a return on that investment. According to these analyses, an increase in the supply of physicians relative to demand is associated with a decrease in physician income relative to the cost of a medical education.

These economic analyses focus on economic "demand" for physician services and do not take into account the "need" for services. This approach can be problematic in the area of physician manpower planning. Many people believe that society has an ethical obligation to provide health care regardless of ability to pay. The concept of demand, which embodies the ability to purchase desired services, is perceived as an inadequate guide for resource allocation because demand does not necessarily include this ethical dimension.

In a recent analysis of physician income, Burstein and Cromwell (1985) found that, between 1967 and 1980, physician income in real terms (i.e., controlling for the effect of inflation) decreased slightly at a rate of approximately 0.2 percent per year. However, this decrease was also seen in the salaries of lawyers, dentists, and college graduates. Consequently, the relative income of physicians has remained high.

Burstein and Cromwell also found that the financial rate of return for a medical education has remained consistently high in recent years, approximately the same as that for dentists and somewhat higher than that for lawyers. The rate of return for specialty training increased in recent years for internists, general surgeons, and obstetrician-gynecologists. Pediatricians, on the other hand, receive a negative rate of return for their specialty education.

Professional standards. Of the five different approaches to measuring the adequacy of physician supply, only the professional standards approach is truly normative, providing an estimate of the number of health personnel required to satisfy a population's "need" for health care. The methodology for this approach, developed by Lee and Jones in 1933 for the physician population, requires the following four pieces of information:

- estimate of how frequently each type of illness occurs in a given population;
- perceptions of a panel of experts regarding the amount and type of health services required to treat each type of illness;

- the panel's perceptions on the amount of time required to provide each type of service; and
- the panel's perceptions on the average amount of time different types of practitioners spend in patient care.

The professional standards methodology was further developed in the GMENAC study (1980) to project future requirements for physicians. The GMENAC study used an "adjusted needs"–based model to estimate these requirements. Panels of experts analyzed data on the prevalance of disease to estimate future need for health care services. These estimates were adjusted to take into account societal barriers and constraints preventing the delivery of these services, and then the "adjusted needs" for health services were allotted among physicians and other health professionals. Data on the content and productivity of physician practices were used to calculate future requirements for physicians in each specialty, and these projected requirements were then compared with the projected supply of physicians.

A major disadvantage of the professional standards approach is its requirement of large amounts of complex information. In the process of developing estimates and setting standards, it is necessary to resolve many issues in a rather arbitrary fashion. Decisions must be made on a wide variety of issues, including sometimes tacit assumptions about how the quality of care varies among different providers.

Furthermore, when the professional standards approach is used to project the need for physicians at some future date, the analyses require arbitrary assumptions about future trends in treatment regimes and the prevalence of disease. These arbitrary decisions are ultimately reflected in the projection of need.

Another difficulty with the professional standards approach is that it has traditionally been built around the concept of the epidemiological "need" for health care without proper consideration of economically determined "demand." Estimates of physician requirements based on need will be overstated if society will not finance the physician services necessary to meet those needs.

According to the GMENAC study, the United States will have a surplus of 70,000 physicians by 1990 and a surplus of 145,000 physicians in 2000. The study found that in 1990 most specialties will have an oversupply. Several specialties will be in near balance, including the primary care specialties of family practice, general internal medicine, and general pediatrics. Shortages were projected for psychiatry, physical medicine and rehabilitation, preventive medicine, and emergency medicine. The GMENAC findings proved to be very controversial. The methodology of the study was criticized for a wide variety of reasons, including inadequate data, arbitrary assumptions used to estimate need for health care, and problems in the organization of expert panels used to estimate the requirements of services. In spite of these criticisms, the GMENAC study has proved to be an important projection of physician requirements.

CONCLUSION

We have discussed broad trends in the supply of health professional in the context of health policy and the changing socioeconomic organization of health care delivery. We have also attempted to illustrate the difficulty faced by social and policy researchers in interpreting and evaluating these trends. We hope this discussion demonstrates the complexity of implementing health care policy as a result of the variety of professions involved and the interactions of organizational, technological, and policy factors.

An added complication in the implementation of health manpower policy is the length of time necessary to educate and train health professionals. A typical medical specialty requires five years of graduate medical training, after four years of medi-

cal school—a total of nine years. Thus, the results of policies designed to affect decisions of college graduates considering a career in medicine may not be felt for a decade or more. For this reason, the basic trend of growth in the health care professions is expected to continue.

The major consequence of past growth has been a new emphasis on competition in medicine. Although competition has always existed, traditional sanctions on entrepreneurial activities are giving way as economic factors favor corporate medical organizations in the delivery of health care. Cost-containment efforts initiated by the federal government and supported by various employer groups contribute to this effect by lowering demand for health care services. Corporate bureaucracies, with lower physician salaries and with a greater reliance on allied health professions, can offer services at a lower cost than traditional forms of independent professional practice. At the same time, increases in the numbers of health providers and a more intensive competitive environment are likely to make corporate forms of medical practice more attractive to physicians.

This is not to say that solo private practice will vanish. Indeed, SMS data for the ten-year period from 1975 to 1985 show only a modest drop in the proportion of physicians in solo practice (from 51 percent in 1975 to 46 percent in 1985). Nonetheless, group practice is a widely accepted form of medical practice, and the numbers of physicians in groups is expected to increase. Moreover, even solo practitioners and other self-employed physicians are likely to face some constraints in their practices because of the influence of third-party payers. Preferred provider organizations (PPOs) and independent practice associations (IPAs) provide two methods for private practitioners to compete more effectively. The American Association of PPOs reports that of 325 PPOs surveyed in 1985, 22 percent were owned by physician-hospital joint ventures and 15 percent by physicians (Richman 1986).

Such changes are likely to have a profound effect on the nature of professions and on relationships between providers and patients. The response of professionals to the growth of corporate bureaucracy and the impact of bureacratic features on provider-patient relationships both provide rich areas for future sociological analyses.

REFERENCES

Bureau of Health Professions. 1986. *Fifth Report to the President and Congress on the Status of Health Personnel in the United States.* Publication No. (HRP) 0906767, Department of Health and Human Services.

Burstein, P. L., and J. Cromwell. 1985. Relative Incomes and Rates of Return for U.S. Physicians. *Journal of Health Economics* 4:63–78.

Campion, Frank D. 1984. *The AMA and U.S. Health Policy since 1940.* Chicago: Chicago Review Press.

Committee on the Cost of Medical Care (CCMC). 1932. *Medical Care for the American People: The Final Report of the Committee on the Cost of Medical Care.* Publication No. 28. Chicago: University of Chicago Press.

Dickinson, Frank G. 1949. *An Analysis of the Ewing Report.* Bulletin 69 (August). Chicago: Bureau of Economic Research, American Medical Association.

Eiler, Mary Ann, and John D. Loft. 1986. *Foreign Medical Graduates in the United States.* Chicago: American Medical Association.

Freidson, Eliot. 1960. Client Control and Medical Practice. *American Journal of Sociology* 45 (January):374–382.

———. 1961. *Patient's View of Medical Practice.* New York: Russell Sage.

———. 1970. *Profession of Medicine: A Study of the Sociology of Applied Knowledge.* New York: Dodd, Mead, and Company.

Freshnock, L. J. 1984. *Physician and Public Attitudes on Health Care Issues.* Chicago: American Medical Association.

Gonzales, Martin L., and David W. Emmons. 1986. *Socioeconomic Characteristics of Medical Practice, 1986.* Chicago: American Medical Association.

Graduate Medical Care National Advisory Committee. (GMENAC). 1980. *Report of the Graduate Medical Educational National Advisory Committee,* vol. 1. Publication No. (HRA) 81-651, Department of Health and Human Services.

Havliçek, Penny. 1985. *Group Practice in the United States.* Chicago: American Medical Association.

Hendersen, Lawrence L. 1935. Physician and Patient as a Social System. *New England Journal of Medicine* 212:819–823.

Heydebrand, Wolf. 1973. *Hospital Bureaucracy.* New York: Dunellen.

Journal of the American Medical Association. 1940. Hospital Service in the United States 114:1171.

———. 1946. Hospital Service in the United States 130:1088.

Knowles, John H. 1965. The Teaching Hospital: Historical Perspective and a Contemporary View, in J. Knowles, ed., *Hospitals, Doctors, and the Public Interest.* Cambridge, Mass.: Harvard University Press, pp. 1–21.

Lave, Judith R., Lester B. Lave, and Samuel Leinhardt. 1975. Medical Manpower Models: Need, Demand and Supply. *Inquiry* 12:97–125.

Lee, R. I., and L. W. Jones. 1933. *The Fundamentals of Good Medical Care.* Chicago: University of Chicago Press.

Mechanic, David. 1977. The Growth of Medical Technology and Bureaucracy: Implications for Medical Care. *Milbank Memorial Fund Quarterly* 55:61–78.

National Center for Health Statistics (NCHS). 1982. *The National Ambulatory Medical Care Survey, United States, 1979 Summary.* DHHS Publication No. (PHS) 82–1727.

———. 1985. *The National Ambulatory Medical Care Survey, United States, 1985 Summary.* DHHS Publication No. (PHS) 87–1250

Newhouse, J. P., A. P. Williams, B. W. Bennet, and W. B. Schwartz. 1982. Where Have All the Doctors Gone? *Journal of the American Medical Association* 247:2392–2396.

Parsons, Talcott. 1951. *The Social System.* New York: Free Press.

Rakich, Jonathon S., and Kurt Darr. 1983. The Hospital as an Organization, in J. S. Rakich and K. Darr, eds., *Hospital Organization and Management.* New York: Spectrum Publications, pp. 17–40.

Reynolds, Roger A., and Jonathan B. Abrams. 1983. Physician Utilization of Allied Health Professionals, in J. S. Reynolds and J. B. Abrams. *Socioeconomic Characteristics of Medical Practice, 1983*. Chicago: American Medical Association.

Reinhardt, Uwe. 1975. *Physician Productivity and the Demand for Health Manpower*. Cambridge, Mass.: Ballinger.

Richman, Dan. 1986. Number of PPOs Rises at Fast Pace. *Modern Healthcare* 16 (June 6): 138–140.

Roback, Gene, Diane Mead, and Lilian Randolph. 1986. *Physician Characteristics and Distribution in the U.S.* Chicago: American Medical Association.

Scott, W. Richard. 1966. Some Implications of Organizational Theory for Research on Health Services. *Milbank Memorial Fund Quarterly* 64:35–59.

Starr, Paul. 1982. *The Social Transformation of American Medicine*. New York: Basic Books.

Stevens, Rosemary. 1971. *American Medicine and the Public Interest*. New Haven, Conn.: Yale University Press.

Weber, Max. 1946. Bureaucracy, in H. H. Gerth and C. W. Mills, eds., *From Max Weber: Essays in Sociology*. New York: Oxford University Press, pp. 196–244.

CHAPTER
21
CONTENT AND CONTEXT IN HEALTH PROFESSIONAL EDUCATION

EUGENE B. GALLAGHER
C. MAUREEN SEARLE

BACKGROUND

The education of physicians, as important a topic as any in medical sociology, remains little studied by sociologists.[1] The research by Becker et al. (1961) and by Merton, Reader, and Kendall (1957) is still the starting point. Both studies posed path-breaking questions about the making of doctors and evolved concepts such as "student culture" and "detached concern," which remain valuable in understanding professional education even *outside* the medical context. However, their continuing

appeal and influence are also due to the dearth of equivalent successors over the nearly three decades since the completion of their research. During this period several major sociological studies of medical education at the graduate level (Bosk 1979; Light 1980; Mumford 1970) have appeared, as have a larger number of studies that deal with particular aspects at the undergraduate level, such as psychological adjustment (Coombs 1978), admissions policy, and curriculum development (Haas and Shaffir 1987). But none focus broadly, as Becker and Merton did, on the four-year canvas of undergraduate education.

The fundamental pattern of medical education has remained largely unchanged since the early part of this century, when the recommendations of the Flexner Report and the philanthropies of the Rockefeller and Carnegie foundations impelled radical reform (Ludmerer 1985, Berliner 1985). Medical education is marked by a tenacious conservatism. National study

---

[1]Although most of the total manpower expansion in health care since 1950 is due to the increase in nursing and paramedical categories, physicians remain the pivotal element in medical care. We will focus primarily upon medical education, but our delineation of the academic health science center recognizes the scope of the training of nonmedical personnel. We deal explicitly with nonphysician training in a later section of this chapter.

panels, private foundations, and public agencies (whose membership has included a number of social scientists) seeking to change it, might prefer to characterize this conservatism as "perverse" rather than "tenacious."[2] However, as we shall later show, the structure of medical education is gradually yielding to pressures that emanate from changes in the financing and organization of medical practice.

Whatever the nature of its stability, medical education is not yet a well-understood phenomenon from the sociological standpoint. The Becker and Merton investigations traced general concepts such as "professionalization," which have been fruitfully used outside the domain of medical education without finally resolving their meaning within that domain. For example, whether "becoming a doctor" can be better understood as a process of adroit survival under faculty pressure—the Becker perspective—or as a process of knowledge assimilation and identification with mentors—the Merton perspective—remains a viable question. The answer to it depends on variant initial assumptions about the nature of learning and professionalization, which assumptions may color both method and empirical results. Despite the pitfalls of gathering and interpreting data on the "doctor-making" process, medical sociology needs to increase its stock of analytic concepts and empirical generalizations in this area. Further research is needed that, in the spirit of the Becker and Merton studies, focuses upon the formative attitudes, orientation, and conduct of the medical student within the system.

The medical undergraduate curriculum—that is, medical school—is the standard, historically anchored core within the sequence of educational links that constitutes the entire doctor-making process. As a four-year medial common pathway, medical school is a centerpiece that is unique in two senses. First, it is the only educational experience that all doctors have in common, not only in any given medical school but across medical schools. Before and after medical school, medical students follow curricula that are more diverse and multitracked. Second, medical school situates each student within a class that moves as a solidary cohort through the four years of the curriculum, with many implications for the forging of social ties and the early formation of professional identity. Before and after medical school, the student associates with more transient groups of fellow students whose learning motivations, tasks, and anxieties are not set in the same shared mold. Because it is a common experience, medical school training becomes for physicians a solidary platform that adds sentimental force to the legal privilege and social respect that they later enjoy during their professional practice.

The undergraduate core is preceded by a premedical phase and followed by the phase of postgraduate specialty training. Sociologists have paid more attention to the latter than the former. Specialty training is the final phase of doctor-making, from which the medical resident emerges as a qualified practitioner of specialty medicine. Given the intense American fascination with medicine—what Cluff calls a "romance" (Cluff 1986)—the preponderant focus upon soon-to-be doctors is not surprising. From the practical standpoint of improving medical service in society, residency training offers a final opportunity for intervention to correct deficiencies. The potential for effective intervention at this point may in fact be small, however, because residency training has an internal rhythm and intensity—with clinical, scientific, and professionalization aspects—

---

[2]We believe that the National Board Examination system, in effect since the 1960s, has been an important conserving as well as standardizing force in medical education; although these exams were originally intended only to provide a nationwide comparison of student knowledge, their structure and their knowledge priorities have gradually established hegemony over medical school courses and curricula. What started out as a neutral means of assessment has come to exert a strong force for maintaining the status quo.

which substantially insulates it from changes unless they emerge within the specialty field itself (Knafl and Burkett 1975; Light 1980; Scully 1980).

CURRICULUM INNOVATION: THE EXAMPLE OF TRAINING IN COMMUNICATION

Attempts to improve the doctor-making process must reckon with questions of timing and target student population. Take, for example, attempts to improve the competence and motivation of physicians to communicate with patients. One of the most widespread public complaints about medical care is "My doctor doesn't talk to me." We deal with this theme here because it has challenged the pedagogical ingenuity of many medical sociologists who have worked in medical education[3] and because it so clearly represents a basic problem in medical care.

---

[3]Variations of that complaint—"My *doctors* don't talk to me," "The doctors *here* don't talk to me," "*No one* talks to me"—draw attention to the complex structure of contemporary medical care. In both ambulatory and inpatient settings, the patient may have more than one doctor, there may be nurses, social workers, and other personnel in addition to doctors, or the patient may not know whom to ask. Problems in communication may reside in the system; they do not necessarily reflect the failings or aversions of individual physicians. Attempts to improve the communicative ability of the physician do not as a rule take into account the factor of structural complexity. They typically assume a traditional doctor-patient relationship in which the doctor's allegiance to the patient is unfettered by organizational constraints and in which the doctor has ample time to deal with the patient's questions. No account is taken of how organizational settings such as HMOs, specialty practice, or the teaching hospital affect the doctor's propensity to communicate with the patient. Such restrictive assumptions are of course made in order to give the learner a simple reality to deal with, before real-life complexity and ambiguity supervene. Similar cognitive idealizations occur in traditional medical school topics. For example, the student learns to deal with "normal" pregnancy before he deals with the complications of pregnancy; he learns the biochemistry of normal carbohydrate metabolism before he learns its role in diabetes.

With regard to target population, should all medical students receive training in communication skills, or only those who appear to need it (i.e., those who are judged likely, as physicians, to be poor communicators)? Should recognition be given to the fact that the specialty practice of many physicians no longer includes direct patient contact? Although medical school gives a generalized training that includes clinical clerkships in the main areas of specialization, no student ever becomes a "generalized physician." A sizable minority of students enter specialties such as pathology and radiology in which the physician's client is another physician instead of a patient. Dare we assume that those who lack talent or motivation for communication will benignly direct themselves into the more impersonal branches of medicine? Should training in communication be made an elective, to be sought by students who are particularly interested in it?

The logic of innovation in medical education frequently ignores such considerations. Because it identifies what are felt to be widespread faults in medical care, it urges its remedy broadside upon all doctors-to-be.

With regard to timing, there is a dilemma of too early versus too late. To expose the student to communication training before he or she deals with patients seems too early, because there has been no opportunity to try out communication techniques. But to wait until he or she sees patients seems too late, because then, even though the importance of communication can never be dismissed completely, it may take second place to the student's anxieties from dealing with the patient's medical problem. Many clinicians who acknowledge the importance of communication nevertheless believe that skill and ease in its practice are caught, not taught—acquired, that is, gradually through clinical experience rather than explicitly learned as a set of didactic techniques. Of course, such a basic personal-professional characteristic of the physician as his or her communication style is probably caught *and* taught. Some students may be so apt that no explicit training is necessary, whereas others do benefit from it; many become more competent with clinical seasoning, with or without training.

The introduction of communication training into the curriculum may in fact be as much a symbol to the doctor-to-be of the importance of the patient as a human being as it is an instrumentally effective teaching modality.[4]

Courses on communication deal with a basic process in medical care. Communication with patients is derivatively related to universal human experiences of communication. In contrast, most other recent innovations in the medical curriculum are oriented toward specialized topical content. Examples include alcoholism, biomedical

engineering, cost containment, drug abuse, emergency medicine, chronic illness, environmental health hazards, bioethics, child abuse, international health, genetic counseling, geriatrics, health care services, human sexuality, research design, medical humanities, medical jurisprudence, nutrition, occupational medicine, behavioral medicine, patient education, death and dying, and health economics (Crowley, Etzel, and Petersen 1985).

No single medical school includes all these diverse topics in its curriculum. The very fact that the bioscientific core of the medical curriculum is extensive and relatively invariant from one school to another means that the foregoing topics are not a major component within the curriculum anywhere. For the most part, these topics represent themes that arise from public concerns and dissatisfactions with medicine. Their appearance within medical education is also a consequence of the "medicalization" of social problems, and it reflects as well the attempt to adapt the semiautonomous institutional complex of medicine to the service of society (Zola 1986). Getting them into the already-crowded, resistant medical curriculum is a mark of accomplishment for the particular social groups—professionals, patient self-help organizations, public-interest associations, governmental bodies—that promote these themes. Sociologists and other social scientists working in medical education have dealt with many topics on the foregoing list, and they have had a major hand in shaping them into practical teaching formats (Lella, Gill, and McGlynn 1985; Kennedy, Pattishall, and Baldwin 1983).

The questions raised earlier about the placement of communication teaching in the curriculum apply to these topics as well. Should all students be exposed? Early or late? Should this material be taught as a distinct package, or can it be dealt with more effectively as a part of existing curricular units? Consider human sexuality. The general rationale for including it in the curriculum is (1) that future physicians

---

[4]In saying that communication training has symbolic significance, we refer to the fact that it constitutes a small part of the curriculum. It is perhaps quickly forgotten by many students, although much the same thing happens to the material in major subjects such as biochemistry and anatomy. Students are expected to pass examinations on a mass of relatively unintegrated facts, after which much of this material is forgotten, to be selectively exhumed and revivified only as it is relevant in the student's specialty training and subsequent practice. Most remains buried. Faculty psychiatrists, for example, have been known to joke, in a relaxed moment, about how much anatomy they have forgotten (and, by implication, do not need to know).

In a broad sense the undergraduate preclinical curriculum is a symbolic design that conveys to the student the idea that medicine is a scientifically grounded enterprise. As a cultural-symbolic system, medical education is a pattern of idealized meanings; yet it also deploys finite resources of time, materials, and human effort. It is difficult to maintain an awareness of the sheerly symbolic importance of a thing and at the same time to allocate to it a just share of real-world supporting resources vis-à-vis the claims of other symbols. This is the plane of consciousness on which medical school curriculum committees function; the difficulty of adjudicating among symbolic claims, especially in a milieu that values reasoned bases for decision, means that, by default, precedent and tradition almost always prevail. That is one reason why major curriculum changes occur so rarely in medical education.

can deal with patients only if they confront and understand their own sexuality; (2) that sexuality is a personality dynamic that affects the expression of illness in patients; (3) and that doctors should be well informed about sexual attitudes and practices in contemporary society. Given this, should human sexuality stand out boldly as a separate course early in the medical curriculum? The psychiatry faculty might oppose this, arguing that human sexuality should be fitted into its own psychopathology course because aberrant sexual behavior is part of the psychiatric nomenclature. The departments of pediatrics, gynecology, obstetrics, and family medicine also teach content that borders on human sexuality. The mode of incorporation of topics such as human sexuality into the curriculum usually shows that curriculum innovation is based in part upon rational pedagogical considerations and in part upon the protectiveness that departments display in guarding their teaching boundaries.

MEDICAL EDUCATION AS THE SOURCE OF FAULTS IN MEDICAL CARE

Society expects a formidable array of virtues and abilities in its doctors: technical competence, mastery of medical knowledge, sensitivity to the "whole patient," communicative ease and skill, wise judgment, compassion, and professional integrity. Medical educators clearly give the greatest emphasis to technical competence and mastery of medical knowledge. The primary purpose of medical education is to produce a knowledgeable, expert physician prepared to deal with the patient's disease on a rational scientific basis. The other "physicianly" qualities come into play primarily as the physician interacts with the patient. They are obviously important, but there is little agreement on how to develop or elicit them in physicians—or that any special effort is necessary. After all, ordi-

nary social experience goes far to endow most individuals with interpersonal sophistication and ease. Can it be relied upon, therefore, to help physicians?

Critics of medicine think not. They believe that medicine has become dehumanized, which implies a major defect in the capacity of doctors to relate to patients, and they point to medical education as constituting a major agent of that dehumanization. In this view, medical school is a systemically deforming milieu that nullifies ordinary social experience. In construing the nature of dehumanization, the role of authority comes in for special attention. Critics feel that doctors are too attached to medical authority—whether they inherently enjoy it or whether they simply believe that they must possess it. Doctors come to feel that they must exert great control in order to accomplish their work, and they seek to command great respect to maintain control and to protect themselves from criticism. This process, which is accentuated in teaching hospitals, leads doctors to become dehumanized themselves. Geiger (1975, pp. 31–32) believes that the "primacy of technical orientations, appropriately elitist behavior, and professional control" work together to create a situation in which the medical student "sees himself—not the patient—as the most important victim."

Reiser (1978) argues that a one-sided preoccupation with scientific medicine, especially with apparatus-based diagnosis, has led doctors to dismiss the patient's individuality, sentiments, and suffering as irrelevant to their work. In their analyses of clinical training, Bosk (1979) and Searle (1981) show that students become obsessed with the quality of their performance; even if everything that is done is done ultimately for the patient's benefit, a technically perfectionistic atmosphere cannot take cognizance of the patient as a sick, distressed person. This picture of medical education suggests that the social experience it provides for the students, approximating the alienating totality of a total institution in

442 Health Care Providers

the Goffman sense, will not foster social sensitivity and empathy.

Another line of criticism notes that medical aspirants form a particular stratum of the population who are, by social background and previous life experience, particularly predisposed to perform in the pressured medical school milieu. Aspiration and selection for medical school are sharply skewed in favor of white middle- and upper-class individuals. This skew has been evident for decades;, it has been intensified by the sharp decline in black students over the past decade (Lanphear 1986).

PREMEDICAL PREPARATION

The patterning of medical admissions suggests general congruence between the predisposition of the entering students and the structural demands of medical training. Recent sociological studies of the premedical education of medical students—which, for most students, immediately precedes medical school—suggest that it shapes their self-concepts and modes of learning in ways that comport with the medical education to follow (Hackman 1979; Conrad 1986).

Although the ratio of applicants to admitted students has declined in recent years, securing admission to medical school, especially to elite schools, remains fateful. Shared perceptions of this prospect generate a premed culture that is rife with rumors and tales about unscrupulous behavior of advantage-seeking students. Conrad's study, conducted on a liberal arts campus, found that despite their preoccupation with imagined "cut-throat" competitors, the premed students had positive, trusting relationships within their small supportive cliques.

The emergence of premedical education as an early shaping phase is a notable phenomenon within the long arc of medical career preparation. In the face of continuing discussion about how to shorten medi-

cal education, premedical education can only be regarded as a significant countertrend—a backing up of medical education into undergraduate college. Both the intellectual content and the emotional pressures of medical school are presaged within the premed phase. The following is a revealing recollection of the premedical atmosphere by a recent medical graduate:

In the biology laboratory Jim was again baffled by the method of examination. Microscopes were set to focus on specific structures of an animal, and students had to make immediate identifications of the structures. An alarm clock rang to tell them to move forward to another microscope and another structure. The laboratory was filled with tension and the atmosphere was sombre as students kept moving from one microscope to another. (Fredericks and Mundy 1980, p. 10)

Much of the material learned in premed physiology and in organic and biochemistry courses is repeated in medical school. Although the fast pace and demanding expectations of medical school engender in medical students an almost phobic intolerance of repetitiousness, they do not necessarily see the repetition between premed preparation and medical school material as "time-wasting." On the contrary, many welcome it; they relax in the comfort of some familiar facts, finding in them a security zone of already-known material against all the new material for which they are held accountable on examinations.

HUMANIZING MEDICINE BY BROADENING ADMISSIONS

If it is true that students arrive at medical school as the products of a grueling premedical training, then perhaps the struggle for humanized medical care is already lost. The formative pattern is already set; changes in the medical curriculum would then be largely unavailing. Perhaps, however, the culprit is not the formative effect of premedical education but rather a selective factor even prior to that, namely the characteristic attitudes and values of persons who seek to become physicians. If the prospect of a career in medicine attracts compulsive students who are receptive to the structural pressures of medical education, then would the problem be alleviated if admissions favored a different kind of student?

This idea has led to changes in admissions policy and procedure. Most medical schools now declare that they will admit students who as college undergraduates did not take the full premed major, so long as they took a minimum core (typically consisting of two courses each in physics and biology and four chemistry courses). At the extreme, some medical schools have eliminated all specific course requirements (Gruson 1987). This trend opens the way for application by students who majored in nonscientific subjects such as English, history, and philosophy. Proponents of this strategy hoped that it would remake medicine by leading to a major change in the type of student who applied and who was accepted. Most medical classes nowadays do include a few students who have come from academically offbeat domains. Their token presence proves that one need not be a "greasy grind" to get into medical school but does not, however, portend any marked shift toward a new kind of medical student.

Another proposal advanced to deal with the dehumanization problem is to rely less upon the Medical College Admissions Test (MCAT) as a criterion for admission. This test, consisting of objective questions in chemistry, biology, mathematics, and other scientific fields, is used by almost all medical schools in assessing an applicant's qualifications. The rationale for deemphasis is that many premed students become excessively preoccupied with MCAT preparation, a preoccupation that is furthered by the premed faculty, whose own performance is judged in part by the success of their students in obtaining admission to medical school. The burgeoning of propri-

etary tutorial services whose sole purpose is to increase the MCAT scores of applicants is a recent manifestation of the highly charged motivation and emotional-intellectual tension in the premed situation (Jones 1986). The premeds' narrow, highly competitive preoccupation is felt to be an early crystallization of the later depersonalized professional orientation, which ultimately neglects the patient as a person. In this rationale, the assessment of a student's qualification in non-MCAT, "non-cognitive" areas such as interpersonal acumen and empathy would help to correct the ills of medical education and medical care. This rationale recommends a more rounded selection of applicants to favor those who will function in the future as "whole doctors"—doctors who are able to deal with the needs, medical and nonmedical, of the "whole patient."

MEDICAL IDEALISM AND THE CLINICAL CONTEXT

The idea that physicians are "doing well while doing good" is a captivating formula, which, like many epigrams, captures one truth but obscures others. "Doing well" means that physicians have high material rewards and high social prestige. "Doing good" means that their goals and accomplishments in fighting disease and illness are laudatory. The linkage of "doing well" with "doing good" is a fortunate conjunction for anyone who can achieve it; few if any other occupational groups can claim to have made the linkage with both variables at such high levels. Social workers and schoolteachers might do as much or more good in the world, but they do not do as well economically. Business executives and investment bankers do well, even better than doctors, but their work has about it the taint of pecuniary self-interest; they keep the economy humming, but they are not "doing good" by directly helping their fellow humans.

Despite the tensions of medical education and medical practice, most physicians feel fulfilled in their work. A vital part of the profession's appeal is that the good that physicians do is accomplished not simply through humane intention but through scientifically grounded skills. One can, of course, point out that much of medical practice lacks scientific precision and that most physicians, even highly trained specialists, work not as research scientists but as applied scientists or technicians. Nevertheless, the physician is in the position of using systematic methods that require great judgment and skill.

Critics of medicine are prone to find pretense in the formula "doing well while doing good." One can point out the failings of medicine—unresponsiveness to individual patients, lack of decent medical care for the poor—and then question whether physicians do have an idealistic motivation.

Despite the great lacks in medical care, we believe that the idealism in medicine is not to be found in empathic outreach by the doctor to the patient, nor in the doctor's social consciousness and conscience, but instead in the doctor's assiduousness in mastering the portion of knowledge and technique relevant to his or her medical focus and then applying it to patients. It is an idealism of technical skill and judgment. The individual physician must have some minimum of empathy, but the standard by which most physicians are willing to be judged, and the core of practice that makes medicine motivationally compelling to them, is the exercise of clinical responsibility (Black 1982). Just as physicians find many of the criticisms of medicine irrelevant to their own definition of its tasks, many critics of medicine fail to appreciate the challenge that physicians find in the exercise of responsibility and judgment. Of course, much that is undesirable in medical care is also bound within this same challenge. Perhaps medical sociology should address itself to the complexity and subtlety of clinical training—trying to understand how it works—and then disentangle the "good parts" to be saved from the "bad parts" to be discarded or transformed.

With this in mind, we wish to discuss clinical training as it occurs in teaching hospitals. We will focus on the teaching hospital because it is also the context in which the training of nonmedical health providers (nurses, physical therapists, nutritionists, medical social workers, and many other categories) is conducted in relation to the work of medicine.

All teaching hospitals are organizationally affiliated with a medical school, and most of the major teaching hospitals are part of university medical centers. Although it is well known that the number of American medical schools and the annual output of medical graduates has increased markedly since 1960, a correlative fact is less widely known, namely, that the volume of medical care delivered by academic medicine in teaching hospitals is substantial. It now constitutes approximately 10 percent of the nation's aggregate medical services. Looming changes in the financing and organization of medicine will have particular significance for academic medical care and clinical teaching.

ACADEMIC HEALTH SCIENCE CENTERS AS THE CREATURE OF FEDERAL HEALTH POLICY

The classic studies of medical education focused intensively on the content and microsocial processes of medical education, but meanwhile overlooked the changes that were gradually transforming its organizational context. Medical centers, once simply medical schools attached to a hospital, have become gigantic complexes. The largest medical centers are known as academic health science centers because they have research facilities and—in addition to a medical school—schools of nursing, dentistry, pharmacy, and allied health. Categorical disease centers, most notably for cancer and heart disease, are attached to multi-building university hospitals. Another new feature of many health science centers, beginning in the early 1970s, is a Veterans Administration hospital. The rapidly developing technology of medicine caused further expansion: Buildings had to be enlarged or separately constructed for CAT (computerized axial tomography) and PET (positron emission tomography) scanners and for the NMR (nuclear magnetic resonance) imaging device. The ever-receding horizon of medical science was manifest in perpetual construction.

The size and organizational complexity of the medical center were symptoms of a fundamental restructuring in the relationship between the federal government and medical education. Beginning in the 1960s and continuing through the 1970s, the federal government subsidized medical education directly and heavily. Aid to health professions training came in the form of construction grants, student loan programs, special scholarship programs, and start-up and financial distress grants for new and existing schools, respectively.

The unprecedented investment of public moneys in health professional education was the result of a confluence of factors. By the 1960s medicine was well on its way to becoming a sophisticated technological enterprise. Because of its perceived effectiveness, it came to be regarded as essential to human existence; and the liberal political climate of the 1960s favored making health care broadly available to the public. Two major health care financing programs—Medicare for the aged and Medicaid for the poor—were enacted in 1965 and 1967, respectively.

Anticipating that the easing of financial barriers would lead to a sharp increase in demand for medical care, health economists warned that the supply of physicians would prove be inadequate. For some time the medical profession had been suspected of holding down the supply of physicians by exercising tight control over medical school enrollments. As medical school ap-

plications began to soar in the 1960s and the number of acceptances remained static, this suspicion mounted. Since the 1950s, many teaching and community hospitals had been short of resident and staff physicians. The demand for twenty-four-hour physician coverage in hospitals was met largely by foreign doctors who were allowed to enter the country on student and visitor visas and to remain indefinitely. The recruitment of foreign doctors, who lacked citizenship and professional strength, was a tactical convenience that did not, however, fully resolve the scarcity of physician coverage (Stevens and Vermeulen 1972).

To forestall a physician shortage, the federal government offered medical schools an inducement to increase their size: The Comprehensive Health Manpower Training Act of 1971 tied so-called capitation grants, which gave medical schools a flat amount for each student enrolled, to the expansion of enrollment. Because capitation replaced formula-type assistance, schools that had become dependent on the earlier type of assistance had to enlarge class size in order to get the maximum flow of dollars. At the height of federal involvement, in 1978, medical schools received an annual subsidy of $2,000 per student.

Despite the expenditure of hundreds of millions of dollars on medical education, access to health care did not materially improve. Shortages of physicians in the inner cities, in rural areas, and in primary care continued. This, of course, frustrated the federal intent to secure accessible medical care. The realization gradually dawned that, unless more stringently controlled, medicine would develop in directions contrary to federal goals.

The graduates of the medical schools in the 1960s were not in the first-contact fields of general practice and general medicine but rather the subspecialties—cardiology, oncology, nephrology, gastroenterology, rheumatology, and pulmonary medicine. The program perhaps most responsible for this proliferation of subspecialties was the National Institutes of Health (NIH) research fellowships (Petersdorf 1975). Money intended for research training of physicians was largely diverted into clinical channels: Medical residents used the fellowships simply to become trained for career practice in a subspecialty, with research in a subsidiary position.

The extraordinary growth of the health science centers signified that medical care was becoming geographically concentrated in the major metropolitan areas and fading from rural scenes. Another federal program, the National Health Planning Act of 1965, contributed to this concentration by attempting to regionalize health care and transform university hospitals into major referral centers.

The 1976 Health Professions Training Act, attached additional stipulations to the capitation grants: If schools wished to have the subsidy continue, they would have to create primary care residencies. A further requirement was that of remote-site training for medical students and residents— field clinics and periodic visits to areas low in medical resources and services.

By the late 1970s the various federal health manpower policies had had a staggering impact on medical education: The number of medical schools increased from 87 to 126 between 1963 and 1980; medical school enrollment increased from 30,000 to 64,000 from 1961 to 1980; and the number of full-time faculty rose from 11,000 in 1960 to 48,000 in 1980.

Federal policymakers were pleased with the increase in the scale of medical education. The anticipated shortage of physicians, especially primary care doctors, had been averted. By the late 1970s, however, there were signs of a sea change in federal manpower policy that would have profound implications for medical education. In 1976, Joseph Califano, then Secretary of the Department of Health, Education, and Welfare, formed an advisory panel to analyze the national physician supply (GMENAC 1980). In 1978, on the basis of its preliminary findings, this panel predicted a marked physician *oversupply* by 1990.

Health economists in this period also found that each physician trained would add some $350,000 annually to the health bill of the nation through the hospitalizations, the diagnostic tests, and other procedures he or she ordered and the medicines he or she prescribes. Each physician came to be seen as an agent of economic damage for the costs he or she incurred, instead of a source of benefit for the professional services he or she rendered. An abrupt reversal in federal support of health education ensued. Capitation grants ended, and scholarships and loans became less plentiful.

The sociological principle that organizations expand more easily than they contract after expansion held true for the medical school. Despite the alarm sounded by the federal government, medical schools could do little to slow down physician production. Federal health manpower policy had become rather like the sorcerer's apprentice: Having mobilized the medical schools, the federal government was helpless to prevent the health care system from being swamped by too many doctors.

GOAL STRAIN IN MEDICAL EDUCATION

A conventionally accepted formula holds that in medical schools and teaching hospitals an inseparable triad of activities march hand in hand—service (that is, medical care), teaching, and research. This formula, promulgated during the early 1960s when federal support of medical education and research was more plentiful, assumes that all three activities are mutually reinforcing and of equal priority in academic medicine. In the current climate of retrenchment, can the assumption of equal priority be sustained?

In particular, the concept that every medical school should emphasize research is coming under question (Petersdorf 1986). The translation of this doubt into reality means that medical research would become more concentrated in the elite universities, which have long carried out the lion's share of significant research. A subtle harbinger of the reduced research mission at many medical schools can be seen in the establishment of multiuniversity consortia that perform coordinated clinical trials and evaluations of new treatments. By making critical comparisons of treatment outcomes, such evaluations are of great value to rational medical care, but the research role of the participating institutions is confined largely to the execution of standardized protocols for selected diseases. Not only is this a mechanical form of clinical research, but adherence to the protocol on occasion overrides the clinical judgment of the responsible physicians on the scene about the treatment of particular patients, thus creating resentment on the part of the physicians.

Major changes are occurring currently in the financial support of teaching hospitals, with implications for their goal priorities. The hospitals must take into account the fact that more of their income proceeds from patient care now than formerly and that research funding is becoming scarcer. The volume of patient care has increased greatly, and the expansion of private third-party payment, along with Medicare and Medicaid, has provided a substantial flow of dollars to pay for the flow of medical care. In the late 1970s, Medicare alone accounted for 16 percent of the dollars coming into university hospitals belonging to state medical schools and 24 percent into the hospitals of private medical schools (Bergen 1977).

With research commitment in retreat and the ascendancy of service within the triad, question also arises about the place of medical education as an activity carried out within the university. The heart of medical education is generally acknowledged to be clinical teaching. As teaching hospitals have grown, however, they have become, in the words of a former medical school dean (Ebert 1977, p. 178), both "an integral part of the nation's health-care system" and "more detached . . . from the university." It seems likely that new conceptions of medical education will prevail that emphasize its service character, with greater explicitness about the fact that medical care is being provided, whether or not every patient and every procedure provide a learning opportunity for the medical student or house officer.

Faculty have become less available for teaching and research because of their greater involvement in direct patient care. To replace income lost from the cutback of research and training grants, medical schools have organized "faculty practice" plans. In a partial reversal of the long-standing trend, since the Flexner reform era, toward faculty who were full-time teachers with no private community practice, clinical faculty members are currently expected to devote considerable time to direct patient care. The patients whose fees are drawn into the faculty practice plans are mainly "private pay" (i.e., insured by Blue Cross–Blue Shield or by a commercial firm) or Medicare enrollees with supplementary insurance. They are attended by faculty only, rather than by an assortment of medical students, residents, and faculty.

FINANCIAL TENSION BETWEEN PATIENT CARE AND CLINICAL TEACHING

During the 1960s and 1970s it was considered legitimate for the medical care of patients to help pay the cost of medical education. Both private and public payers acquiesced to higher charges for patients admitted to teaching hospitals. Because patient care was the vehicle for learning medicine, one could argue that third-party payers were purchasing patient care rather than paying for education. In teaching hospitals, interns and residents delivered the bulk of the patient care services, and, unlike in community hospitals, they were available around-the-clock. This was beneficial to patients, but it was expensive.

As medical costs mounted, employers looked for ways to reduce the cost of medical coverage of their employees and were less willing to tolerate higher prices in university hospitals. Furthermore, community hospitals, corporate hospitals, and HMOs offered medical services at prices that undercut those of teaching hospitals.

When it seemed that the Medicare Trust Fund would run short of funds in the 1990s, government policymakers reassessed the part that Medicare played, indirectly but substantially, in financing graduate medical education. Although they recognized as valid the idea that Medicare should pay for the services of house officers, they recommended that the amount be reduced. In reaction, university hospital officials planned to reduce the scale of graduate medical education.

By the mid-1980s, an oversupply of physicians, combined with runaway health care costs, was forcing a contraction in health manpower production, and medical education at all levels was affected. Until 1983, however, the changes could be categorized as changes mainly of scale; increasingly after 1983 they became changes in substance. A single event seems to have caused this shift. In 1983, Congress altered the method by which Medicare reimbursed hospitals for services. Rather than paying retrospectively on the basis of costs incurred, Medicare reimbursed on a flat-rate basis according to the so-called diagnosis-related group (DRG)—that is, which one of 467 disease categories the patient's primary diagnosis fell into (Fuchs 1986). If the hospital managed to deliver care to a patient at a cost below the patient's DRG rate, it could keep the difference; if its cost exceeded the DRG rate, then it had to absorb the loss. Although the DRG method made an extra allowance in the DRG rates for teaching hospitals, Medicare reimbursement was still less than that under the earlier, retrospective cost-based system of payment.

The significance of DRGs for graduate medical education lay in their effect on the financial incentive structure. Before DRGs, Medicare passively reimbursed for everything that was done for the patient. Thus, quite apart from the clinical motive to render the best care possible, the hospital had a financial incentive to perform abundant medical tests and procedures. With DRGs, on the other hand, financial reward was inversely related to resource consumption. If physicians ordered tests too lavishly, the hospital stood to lose money.

DRGs were particularly problematic in teaching settings, where it was customary for residents to use ancillary services heavily. With faculty support, residents considered it educationally valuable to perform diagnostic procedures even if the clinical need was slight. The fact that university hospitals, as centers of technological innovation, had many diagnostic resources available made it difficult for them to narrow their choices.

Clearly, the value system of academic medicine had not promoted cost-effective medical care (Rogers 1975). Residents and interns were criticized by their peers and by faculty for failing to investigate thoroughly all possible diagnostic alternatives in a given case. Undergraduate medical students as well as house officers learned quickly that they could gain faculty approval by locating an "interesting" case—a "fascinoma"—hypothesizing unusual diagnoses, and then systematically excluding alternative possibilities. Excellence in clinical medicine was equated with diagnostic thoroughness.

As part of curbing overall resource consumption, DRGs were also intended to reduce length of hospital stay and to deemphasize hospital use. As hospitals found it difficult to deliver care within the cost constraints of the DRG rate, they began to "unbundle" the total care package. In a significant restructuring of care, hospitals contracted with community-based laboratories and radiology groups to make services available to clients on an outpatient basis. Even some categories of surgery, once unthinkable outside the hospital, have been transferred to outpatient settings. Such developments indicate that DRGs have succeeded in rationalizing medical care—that is, making the level received by the patient appropriate to his or her clinical need—more than any other mechanism had before.

In contrast to the traditional strong opposition to any infringement on "physician autonomy," the response of the medical profession to DRG-imposed cost restraints has been largely acquiescent. It would, however, be too much to claim that a cost-containment ethic has as yet penetrated the workaday attitude of the practicing physician. Likewise, academic physicians have accepted and adjusted to DRG restraints not with special enthusiasm but with the attitude that teaching and patient care will go on as best they can in the face of constraints beyond medical control. However, as we will show, we may expect to see a shift, within the arena of medical discretion, from high-cost to low-cost teaching resources.

TEACHING IMPLICATIONS OF THE SHIFT TOWARD OUTPATIENT CARE

Through their effects on the delivery of medical care in teaching hospitals, DRGs are currently challenging the time-honored assumption that excellence in clinical judgment can be bred only on the ward. The ward was typically populated by charity and, later, Medicaid patients who were assigned to a team of students in various stages of training—from third-year medical clerk to chief resident on the service. Faculty attending physicians offered supervision and guidance, but with the implicit understanding that ongoing decision making was the prerogative of house staff. Although patients often received excellent technical care, their psychosocial needs were often ignored. Sometimes those patients with major psychosocial needs or deficits were informally stigmatized as "crocks," "gorks," or "gomers" (Leiderman and Grisso 1985).

The traditional ward bias will, we believe, be replaced by a more balanced mix of ward and outpatient training experience. As new organizational forms of outpatient care multiply, physicians-in-training will have more nonhospital contexts to sample. These will include HMOs, preferred provider organizations, surgicenters, home care agencies, free-standing drop-in clinics, and multispecialty group practices.

Table 1 compares the traditional teaching ward with outpatient settings on four general characteristics of medical care and medical education.

The table suggests that the staff's greater degree of control over the patient, simply in virtue of his "being there" in a bed, is the critical element that has made the ward the traditional favored site of medical education. There, the senior medical staff could delegate its responsibility for selected patients to house staff and give them the sense of being "real doctors." The outpatient setting is, in contrast, more bureaucratic, more businesslike, and less ceremonially deferent to medical rank. The outpatient hierarchy is relatively flat. Because there is no bedside care, nurses are less in evidence. The unit of activity is the "patient visit." The disposition of patient records is a more important, exacting activity than on the ward. Everything to be done for medical care and for teaching—tests, consultations, interviews—must be precisely coordinated with the patient's scheduled presence. Although the outpatient setting can yield a high "teaching flux," greater effort to extract it is necessary than on the teaching ward.

Outpatient clinics are a venerable part of many of the distinguished older teach-

TABLE 1 Comparison of Teaching Ward and Outpatient Setting as Medical Care Locus

	Teaching Ward	*Outpatient Setting*
1. Medical control over patient	High—patient "captive" in bed	Low—patient may skip appointments, be late
2. Treatment compliance	Guaranteed by immediacy of patient	Depends on patient motivation
3. Cost	High, due to hospital per diem, occupancy, and more intensive use of hospital facilities (though constrained by DRGs)	Lower, though serial visits add to total cost per case
4. Teaching value of patient	Enhanced by traditional teaching rounds, medical hierarchy	Limited by the bureaucratic character of clinic structure

ing hospitals in the nation, but they have always been "poor relations" in the panoply of teaching units, largely because of the inherent lack of medical control over the outpatient and the medical aversion for dealing with factors beyond professional control. It is ironic that cost containment is driving medical educators for the first time to take seriously, as an educational resource, a part of the hospital that has been present for a long time. This illustrates how medical education, once impervious to outside control, is being gradually restructured through its exposure to external constraints.

INVESTOR-OWNED TEACHING HOSPITALS

Private corporations, "investor owned" and operated for the advantage of stockholders, represent another source of external influence on medical education. With the exception of Starr's work (1982), the corporate thrust and effect have been virtually unexamined by sociologists. Health care management companies and hospital chains have been purchasing and leasing university hospitals. For example, Humana Corporation acquired the University of Louisville's medical center, and Hospital Corporation of America (HCA) now owns Vanderbilt's teaching hospital. (McLean Hospital, Harvard's psychiatric hospital, resisted an attempt by HCA to buy it because

faculty feared an incompatibility between teaching and for-profit orientation.) The precarious financial circumstances of many teaching hospitals have made them vulnerable to corporate takeover. Will the "coming of the corporation" change the educational mission and training atmosphere of the teaching hospital? Despite its unique, quasi-sacred role in ministering to the human body and the human condition, medicine under corporate auspices and medicine in general are assuming a commodity character in a marketplace where sellers attempt to guarantee a need for their services and to shield themselves from competition.

New arrangements for medical coverage between individual medical school departments and investor-owned hospitals are another example of corporate penetration of medical education. The for-profit hospital facility becomes a rotation base for university-based residents, where they have access to middle-class patients. Such a rotation gives them the chance to satisfy their curiosity about practice in a for-profit facility as a source of future employment.

NONPHYSICIAN EDUCATION

The expansion and differentiation of nonphysician roles has been one of the most salient developments in modern medicine. In 1900 physicians constituted 63 percent of all health workers; by 1960, they constituted only 11 percent. The many nonphysician roles link in various ways with the physician's role; the personnel and resources devoted to their training are of considerable scope and complexity.

For illustrative purposes we will look at four such roles—the physician's assistant (PA), the nurse practitioner (NP), the renal dialysis technician (RDT), and the medical social worker (MSW). None of these roles has professional autonomy; all function under the physician's legal-administrative authority. They can be regarded as an "extra pair of hands" to carry out tasks that could conceivably be performed by doctors. Consider the MSW. Physicians have always paid some attention, albeit minimal, to the family, social, and economic circumstances of the patient. Social workers spend much of their current effort in securing medical-economic benefits for poor patients and in ensuring timely admission and discharge of patients. The presence of the social worker relieves the physician of these specific concerns, and it dilutes the physician's responsibility for communicating with the patient.

The activities of the NP and PA are roughly similar. Both perform physical examination of patients, referring difficult or ambiguous cases on to a physician. This is an activity that, unlike social work, physicians have always carried out in a full sense. The NP and PA, lesser trained and lower paid than the physician, rationalize medical care by substituting for physicians while still preserving the adequacy of medical care.

The RDT resembles the MSW in that he or she carries out a task that is only marginally performed by the doctor. He or she maintains and repairs hemodialysis apparatus for chronic renal failure patients. In the early 1960s, nephrologists, in the pioneering days of dialysis, did operate dialysis apparatus. When the RDT became available to assume a routinized "submedical" role, the physician withdrew from it. Although the current generation of ne-

phrologists well understand the biochemistry of dialysis as part of their specialized technical knowledge and could perhaps in a pinch fill in for an RDT, this does not happen in practice.

Each of these roles can be found more abundantly in teaching hospitals and academic health science centers than elsewhere. A rural nonteaching hospital would be unlikely to include an MSW on its staff, and hemodialysis is only performed in selected locations. NPs and PAs are extensively used in teaching outpatient clinics and are increasingly used in such nonteaching settings as VA hospitals and community-based HMOs.

Most NPs, PAs, MSWs, and RDTs receive their training in teaching hospitals; they are part of the complexity and diversity of such hospitals. Their training, though far less extensive than the physician's, is similar in that it starts with a didactic classroom and laboratory phase and concludes with a clinical, "hands-on" phase.

The training of nonphysicians is colored by their subordinate position in medical care. Most categories of nonphysicians (with, however, important exceptions such as pharmacists and dentists) function in response to a physician's request for their services. Many of these health workers have a strong professional aspiration to improve their status and pay. Their curricula include elements that demonstrate to the student that his or her future work role embodies physician-like intellectual mastery and clinical responsibility exceeding that of a mere technician—material, for example, on communication with patients, medical ethics, the organization of medical care, and behavioral aspects of disease (Purtilo 1973).

The tendency of nonphysician education to follow that of physicians can be seen also in its high valuation of in-hospital clinical training, despite the recent DRG-engendered push away from in-hospital care toward ambulatory modalities. The centerpiece of their clinical training remains, frequently, a lengthy "internship"—alluding to the year of hospital training that was at one time a standard requirement for physicians upon graduation from medical school.

Other examples of nonphysician education that accentuate its medical connections can be found in pharmacy and dentistry. Pharmacy education, seeking to dissociate itself from the old-fashioned corner druggist image, emphasizes "clinical pharmacy," which concerns the drug therapy of the hospitalized patient, and which, in a seeming unseating of medical authority, includes pharmacy oversight of the complex medication regime ordered by physicians for many of their inpatients. Dental education has made similar efforts to rid itself of stereotypes of the dentist as a "drill-and-fill" technician and to accent its biological and medical content. To accomplish this, it has come within recent years to emphasize oral biology in its didactics and, in its clinical teaching, the interface between dentistry and medicine in the treatment of oral cancers, facial traumata, and pain in the facial joints, as well as in the early diagnosis of AIDS.

In the heyday of federal support for medical training, most of the nonphysician categories also received federal support, but this has virtually ceased. The future need for nonphysician workers is difficult to predict, with concomitant uncertainty about their training programs. During the 1970s, organized medicine established mechanisms to supervise and certify many categories of nonphysician training. More recently it has halted the creation of new nonmedical specialties, fearing that many such workers were being trained so narrowly that further change in the delivery of medical care would be hampered.

As previously noted, some nonmedical workers perform tasks such as physical examination that doctors are also specifically trained and prepared to do. Though such "physician-extender" roles might seem as superfluous as "excessive tests" or "needless surgery," it is by no means certain that they will become less important even in an era of physician surplus. The inexorable logic of fixed-rate reimbursement, exemplified in DRGs and prospective payment, favors lower-cost over higher-cost resources. Despite their legal-administrative power, physicians may not find it easy or economically feasible to curtail the services and training of nonmedical workers. Although an underemployed physician in a crowded physician labor market might covet the chance to examine more patients, this does not mean that he or she can simply displace PAs and NPs already carrying out that function. Much depends on a close task analysis of the contribution and cost of each role and activity to the final composite "medical product." The vital nature of the RDT's activity is evident in that he or she deals with a "life-saving" machine—the dialyzer. The MSW's contribution might seem more remote; nevertheless, under an inclusive accounting of benefits over time, the MSW's contribution may prove equally great.

Much depends also on the diffusion and acceptance of the new roles beyond the academic medical centers. Thus, a medical internist who learned during his residency to work with PAs may later on wish to hire a PA in his own practice. Similarly for a dentist with a dental hygienist, or an orthopedist with a physical therapist.

Though less acclaimed than its role of innovation in medical treatment, the medical center's role in health manpower experimentation has been impressive. Medical centers have defined and trained many "allied health" (nonmedical) categories and exposed medical and allied health students reciprocally to new models of health care delivery. Given the pressures for cost containment and efficient delivery, some of the nonphysician innovations will prevail, though others may fail to take root and, in hindsight, appear to have been ill considered. To flourish outside the educational environment, the successful ones will perforce meet tests of community professional utility that differ markedly from the logic of manpower development and curriculum innovation found in medical centers.

MEDICAL EDUCATION AS A FIELD OF SOCIOLOGICAL EMPLOYMENT

Our concluding section will review the major phases of medical education and show how each phase has provided professional employment for sociologists, with the prospect of future maintenance or expansion of these opportunities.

The health sector, as a high-growth sector of the service economy, accounts for a great share of the recent total expansion of nonacademic employment for sociologists —"applied sociology." Though many applied medical sociologists are employed by government and a few in private industry, many others are employed in one or another aspect of medical education (Bloom 1986).

At the premedical level, an increasing number of premedical majors take upper-division (junior or senior) courses in medical sociology. Such courses are becoming a standard feature of undergraduate sociology curricula. Though these courses are not a fixed part of premedical requirements, premeds find that they typically purvey valuable information on the social structure of health care and social causation of disease. Sociologists have already produced textbooks and other teaching materials suitable for this purpose. In a different vein, some have, as part of their faculty roles, become advisers and counselors to premedical students.

Among the categories of nonphysician education, baccalaureate-and graduate-level nursing education has within recent years incorporated segments of sociological material—on the role and situation of the patient, sociocultural factors that affect the patient's response to treatment, and the professional structure of nursing. This material is conveyed on undergraduate campuses with nursing programs, but the greater part is taught in professional schools of nursing, where nurse-sociologists to an increasing degree constitute the relevant faculty.

Sociologists have taught in the preclinical phase of undergraduate medical education for some three decades. Indeed, this is the only level of contribution that is recognized in many discussions of sociology (or the sociobehavioral sciences more broadly) in medical education (Riska and Vinten-Johansen 1981). Sociologists have participated in teaching social epidemiology, death and dying, patient compliance, human sexuality, health care research, and many of the other topics listed in the earlier discussion of curriculum innovation. Sociologists have also contributed to medical school administration through functions such as curriculum planning, student advising, admissions policy, and public relations. Preoccupied with the press of their own affairs, medical educators and administrators are not often attuned to the distinctive contribution of sociologists *qua* sociologists, but gradually sociologists are winning more discriminating acceptance and recognition.

The most recently opened sphere of sociological endeavor is in the clinical phase of medical education. Here sociologists typically work with house staff, and the work is always under the auspices of a medical specialty. Pediatrics, internal medicine, obstetrics-gynecology, and family medicine are among the specialties that have had the greatest resort to sociology. Sociological assistance in clinical education include such areas as helping residents to learn about their interpersonal demeanor with patients; assessing resident-patient interactions that are associated with high versus low patient compliance (keeping appointments, taking medications, controlling weight); and training residents in counseling skills adapted to their particular medical specialty.

Academic physicians seem more open than formerly to new thinking and to using nonphysician teachers such as sociologists. Their traditional possessive stance toward the training of their own residents has mellowed. Though this serves to increase sociological opportunity, the mounting cost consciousness and the influence of DRGs, discussed earlier, may have a contrary, dampening effect. Our impression is that clinical training, like the rest of medical education in its simultaneous spanning of contradictory ideals, will in fact continue to reach for a more patient-oriented, sociologically informed approach even as it intensifies its technological bent. Within the total spectrum of medical education, unexploited sociological opportunity at present seems greatest in the clinical phase.

REFERENCES

Becker, Howard S., Blanche Geer, Everett C. Hughes, and Anselm L. Strauss. 1961. *Boys in White*. Chicago: University of Chicago Press.

Berger, Stanley S., Jr. 1977. The Problem of Cost, in G. E. Miller, ed. *Medical Education and the Contemporary World*. DHEW Publication No. (NIH) 7701232, pp. 119–133.

Berliner, Howard S. 1985. *A System of Scientific Medicine: The Philanthropic Foundations in the Flexner Era*. New York: Tavistock Publications.

Black, David. 1982. The Making of a Doctor. *New York Times Magazine* (Part One, May 23; Part Two, May 30).

Bloom, Samuel W. 1986. Institutional Trends in Medical Sociology. *Journal of Health and Social Behavior* 27(3):265–276.

Bosk, Charles L. 1979. *Forgive and Remember—Managing Medical Failure*. Chicago: University of Chicago Press.

Cluff, Leighton E. 1986. America's Romance with Medicine and Medical Science. *Daedalus*, Spring; 137–159.

Conrad, Peter. 1986. The Myth of Cut-Throats among Premedical Students: On the Role of Stereotypes in Justifying Failure and Success. *Journal of Health and Social Behavior*, 27:150–160.

Coombs, Robert H. 1978. *Mastering Medicine*. New York: The Free Press.

Crowley, Anne E., Sylvia Etzel, and Edward Petersen. 1985. Undergraduate Medical Education. *Journal of the American Medical Association* 254(12):1565–1572.

Ebert, Robert H. 1977. Medical Education in the United States. *Daedalus*, Winter: 171–184.

Fredericks, Marcel A., and Paul Mundy. 1980. *Making It in Med School—Biography of a Medical Student*. Chicago: Loyola University Press.

Fuchs, Victor R. 1986. *The Health Economy*. Cambridge Mass.: Harvard University Press.

Geiger, H. Jack. 1975. The Causes of Dehumanization in Health Care and Prospects for Humanization, in J. Howard and A. Strauss, eds., *Humanizing Health Care*. New York: John Wiley, pp. 11–36.

Graduate Medical Education National Advisory Committee (GMENAC) 1980. *Summary Report to the Secretary of the Department of Health and Human Services*, Vol. 1. DHHS Publication No. (HRA) 81-651, Health Resources Administration.

Gruson, Lindsey. 1987. Penn Ends Required Studies for the Premedical Student, *New York Times*, February 13, p. 10.

Haas, Jack, and William Shaffir. 1987. *Becoming Doctors: The Adoption of a Cloak of Competence*. Greenwich, Conn.: JAI Press.

Hackman, Judith D., John R. Low-Beer, Susi Wugmeister, Robert C. Wilhelm, and James E. Rosenberg. 1979. The Premed Stereotype. *Journal of Medical Education* 54:308–313.

Jones, Robert F. 1986. The Effect of Commercial Coaching Courses on Performance on the MCAT. *Journal of Medical Education* 61(4):272–284.

Kennedy, Donald A., Evan G. Pattishall, and DeWitt C. Baldwin. 1983. *Medical Education and the Behavioral Sciences*. Boulder, Colo.: Westview Press.

Knafl, Kathleen, and Gary Burkett. 1975. Professional Socialization in a Surgical Specialization: Acquiring Medical Judgment. *Social Science and Medicine* 9:397–404.

Lanphear, Joel H. 1986. Rural Medicine/Urban Responsibilities. *Journal of the American Medical Association* 256 (18):2567–2568.

Leiderman, Deborah B., and Jean-Anne Grisso. 1985. The Gomer Phenomenon. *Journal of Health and Social Behavior* 26 (3):222–232.

Lella, Joseph W., Derek G. Gill, and Thomas J. McGlynn. 1985. *Basic Curriculum Content for the Behavioral Sciences in Preclinical Medical Ed-*

ucation. McLean, Va.: Association for the Behavioral Sciences and Medical Education.

Light, Donald, Jr. 1980. *Becoming Psychiatrists.* New York: W. W. Norton.

Ludmerer, Kenneth. 1985. *Learning to Heal: The Development of American Medical Education.* New York: Basic Books.

Merton, Robert K., George G. Reader, and Patricia L. Kendall. 1957. *The Student Physician: Introductory Studies in the Sociology of Medical Education.* Cambridge, Mass.: Harvard University Press.

Mumford, Emily. 1970. *Interns—From Students to Physicians.* Cambridge, Mass.: Harvard University Press.

Petersdorf, Robert G. 1975. Medical Academe: Numbers, Distribution, Quality. *Annals of Internal Medicine* 82 (5):694–701.

———. 1986. Medical Schools and Research: Is the Tail Wagging the Dog? *Daedalus* Winter: 99–118.

Purtilo, Ruth. 1973. *The Allied Health Professional and the Patient.* Philadelphia: W. B. Saunders.

Reiser, Stanley Joel. 1978. *Medicine and the Reign of Technology.* Cambridge, England: Cambridge University Press.

Riska, Elianne, and Peter Vinten-Johansen. 1981. The Involvement of the Behavioral Sciences in American Medicine: A Historical Perspective. *International Journal of Health Services* 11 (4):583–595.

Rogers, David E. 1975. Medical Academe and the Problems of Health Care Provision. *Archives of Internal Medicine* 135:1364–1369.

Scully, Diana. 1980. *Men Who Control Women's Health: The Miseducation of Obstetrician-Gynecologists.* Boston: Houghton Mifflin.

Searle, C. Maureen. 1981. Obsessive-Compulsive Behaviour in American Medicine. *Social Science and Medicine* 15F:185–193.

Starr, Paul E. 1982. *The Social Transformation of American Medicine.* New York: Basic Books.

Stevens, Rosemary, and Joan Vermeulen. 1972. *Foreign Trained Physicians and American Medicine.* DHEW Publication No. (NIH) 73–325, Bureau of Health Manpower Education.

Zola, Irving Kenneth. 1986. Medicine as an Institution of Social Control, in P. Conrad and R. Kern, eds., *The Sociology of Health and Illness,* 2d ed. New York: St. Martin's Press, pp. 379–390.

CHAPTER 22

SOCIAL CONTROL
AND THE AMERICAN
HEALTH CARE SYSTEM

DONALD W. LIGHT

The American health care system, as one of society's largest institutions, is undergoing the most profound restructuring of this century, because purchasers of services are wresting control from providers in order to limit escalating costs.[1] Large corporations and state health programs have awakened from the habit of passively paying medical bills and are aggressively pursuing ways to stop medical costs from continuing to rise at about twice the general rate of inflation. At the federal level, Congress has responded to the imminent bankruptcy of Medicare because of escalating costs by also taking strong measures to contain expenses.

These large purchasers are buying medical services in volume at wholesale prices, a radical change from the long-held custom of individuals paying for their care retail, on a one-to-one basis. They want to know what they are getting for their money, a simple question that has threatened the autonomy of physicians and hospitals to the core, because the answer requires detailed data, close scrutiny, and ultimately outside judgment.[2]

These corporate and governmental buyers are making the same demands on Blue

---

[1]This essay is based on a policy research project to analyze the restructuring of American health care and its consequences for society. Support is gratefully acknowledged from The Twentieth Century Fund. I also wish to thank Howard Freeman, Sol Levine, Odin Anderson, Peter Conrad and Renée Fox for their suggestions and critical remarks.

[2]I do not wish to imply that corporate and organized buyers are getting everything they want. There are substantial hidden costs of getting involved in complex negotiations, running competitive benefits or delivery systems, and trying to monitor utilization. Nor are there yet well-established measures for assessing the compromises in quality that cost containment may bring. However, techniques are developing rapidly and promise to be one of the most profound consequences of the health care revolution.

Cross and the commercial insurers, transforming them from agents of providers to agents of buyers. Today, thousands of insurance agents constitute a driving force behind the American health care revolution as they compete with each other to see who can provide organized buyers with the best package of managed care, utilization review, quality control, and good service. In response, thousands of private practitioners are signing up with health maintenance organizations (HMOs), preferred provider organizations (PPOs), or other managed care arrangements for fear of being left out as these organizations take over a growing percentage of medical services.

The historic dynamics of this revolution—how the American health care system formed and the causes of upheaval—are the subject of this chapter. Although the present "system" appears to be fragmented and jerry-built—a collection of barely coordinated patches—it has in fact been meticulously designed through mechanisms of social control to maximize the legal, economic, and organizational autonomy of physicians. Central at all times is the issue of control, and sociological theories about its nature have explicitly or implicitly framed our understanding of the health care system from one period to another.[3] Ironically, sociologists present these theories in universal terms, when in fact each of them reflects the tenor of its time. Thus, despite claims to universal truth, our understanding of social control and of the American health care system keeps changing as political and social values open windows and close curtains in the chambers of our minds (See Light and Schuller 1986, Introduction).

THE NATURE OF SOCIAL CONTROL

The sociological concept of social control goes well beyond common notions of police action or governmental regulations to the question of how social life holds together at all. Sociologists fundamentally differ from economists whose ideal state would have people maximizing their self-interests in an open marketplace, because sociologists think it naive to assume that everyone's self-interests will harmonize. Therefore, social control must be part of the deep structure of any community and of each member's consciousness so that self-interests are channeled or contained (Pitts 1968; Janowitz 1978, chap. 2). What Émile Durkheim called a *conscience collective* must develop, made up of values, habits, rituals, notions of justice and fairness, patterns of sociability, deference, and sanctions in harmony with the interests of others and the community as a whole. Indeed, all the founders of sociology were concerned about the erosion of these natural forms of social control as migrants tore their social bonds and factories depersonalized the relationships that had always bound work to family and community.

Medicine men and health care have always been part of a community's infrastructure of social control. Besides trying to cure or contain the genuine disruption of social life that disease or even a broken leg can bring, they have long served to judge when someone is "really ill," what kind of illness it is, whether the person should be excused from work or other obligations, how the patient should behave, and what the family or community should do to minimize the social disruption of the disorder.

---

[3] In this essay, social control as a concept is limited to a selected sample pertinent to the macrostructure of American health care. A rich research literature has developed around dimensions of social control in the micro-interactions between doctors, patients, nurses, administrators, and other significant actors. In addition, some of the best research over the years on social control has focused on mental health and psychiatric care. Excellent analyses have been done on social control and disabilities. Thus only a fraction (but one hopes an important one) of sociological work on social control in medicine is taken up in the space of this essay.

E. A. Ross: Social Control versus Class Control

The problem of how to maintain order in a period of rapid change preoccupied the American social theorist E. A. Ross, whose landmark work *Social Control: A Survey of the Foundations of Order* (1901) was hailed by Roscoe Pound, Oliver Wendell Holmes, Jr., Theodore Roosevelt, and a wide audience of distinguished professors. *Social Control* argued that in a modern society characterized by large organizations, cities, corporations, and great differences of wealth, men "find themselves in the presence of a degree of discord, collision, and general unreliability which shuts them out of real material advantages" (p. 59). Mechanisms of social control had to be consciously constructed to restore and maintain social order, because one could no longer rely on those delicate mechanisms of sympathy, sociability, and sense of justice that had maintained order in small, stable communities. Instead, Ross concluded, society and its leaders would have to consciously develop forms of social control. Thus, the concept of social control shifted toward an emphasis on consciously formed programs and institutions for controlling deviance.

In developing this thesis, Ross devoted chapters to public opinion, beliefs, social suggestion, religion, and ceremony. These were precisely those mechanisms that had always been central to traditional social control, but now they were to be the objects of deliberate planning. In this and other ways, Ross reflected the Progressive era as a period of reform led by a class of traditional community leaders eager to restore the harmony of an earlier time by cleaning up corrupt political machines, regulating dangerous industries, busting up trusts, reducing the exploitation of workers, and regulating greedy industries that would rather poison citizens with filthy meat or dangerous drugs than lose some profit (Wiebe 1967; Rothman 1981).

At the same time, Ross gave more atten-tion than others to social power. He noted that, as social power became more concentrated, the need for more effective social control was felt more sharply, and, at the same time, social control would become more effective. However, "the more distinct, knit together, and self-conscious the influential minority, the more likely is social control to be colored with class selfishness" (p. 86). Class control, which Ross distinguished from social control, entails laws and regulations that appear to treat all parties equally yet can most benefit the dominant class (pp. 376–377). By contrast, Ross wrote that social control works best in a competitive society (pp. 393–394), presumably because countervailing forces control the excesses of each other. Otherwise, social control has a tendency to concentrate power in the hands of the controllers and evolve toward class control, a tendency that leaders of organized medicine seemed to understand well.

Physicians were part of that class of community leaders who spearheaded Progressive reforms (Cutler 1939; Weibe 1967; Berlant 1975). They sought to "clean up" the profession by strengthening licensing requirements, driving proprietary medical schools out of business, opposing commercialism in health care, isolating unlicensed practitioners, and pressing for high standards. Their conscious efforts to create mechanisms of social control echo Ross's ideas and the Progressive era (Starr 1982; Rayack 1967; Shryock 1969; Burrow 1971;, Stevens 1971; Berlant 1975; Duffy 1976; Larson 1977; Rosen 1983; Anderson 1985; Fox 1986).

What previous accounts have not realized is the degree to which the profession's drive for class control was aimed at emergent forms of corporate, competitive medicine. Seventy years before today's corporate health care revolution began, competitive health care markets were beginning to form as federal and state agencies, corporations, and fraternal associations put out bids for health care contracts. By their own account, physicians competed fiercely for the business. Differentiated markets emerged, with high volume–low price primary-care providers and low volume–high price specialists. The medical profession organized to suppress these trends and in their success shaped the American health care system to minimize cost containment, competition, and corporate services. This new history of medicine as a social institution reframes the current revolt of corporate and other organized buyers and the upheaval they are causing. First, it shows that we are witnessing not an unprecedented invasion of Huns from the corporate hills but a reemergence of institutional buyers after several decades of suppression and quiescence. Second, it shows how thoroughly the current health care system has been constructed in its culture, laws, rules, and organization to resist cost containment and price competition. Let us look at these developments more carefully.

ORGANIZING MARKETS FOR COST-EFFECTIVE CARE

During the nineteenth century, the corporate practice of medicine began in the railroad, mining, and lumber industries, where remote locations, high accident rates, and the growth of lawsuits by injured workers called for some corporate form of health care. These industries contracted for medical services on a retainer basis or on salary; some even owned hospitals and dispensaries for their workers. Some textile industries also established comprehensive medical services in mill towns. Thousands of doctors were involved in these contracts or worked on salary (Williams 1932; Selleck with Whittaker 1962).

By the end of the nineteenth century, however, more and more businesses with none of these special needs also began to contract on a competitive basis for the health care of their employees. For example, the Michigan State Medical Society reported in 1907 that many companies (of no particular size or reputation) were contracting for the health care of their employees (Langford et al. 1907). The Plate Glass Factory contracted with physicians and hospitals for all medical and surgical care of its employees and families for $1.00 a month apiece. The Michigan Alkali Company did the same but did not include family members. Several other companies had contracts for the treatment of accidents and injuries. Commercial insurance companies of the day also got involved, putting together packages of services for a flat amount per person per year (capitation) or for a discounted fee schedule. Their profits must have been enormous, since several reports allude to the "usual" 10 percent of premiums that physicians received.

More widespread than early corporate health care plans were prepaid comprehensive health care medical services offered for a flat subscription price per year to members of the fraternal orders that had proliferated rapidly during the same period. The orders of Eagles, Foresters, Moose, and Orioles, as well as other national or regional fraternal associations, offered medical care at deeply discounted prices through their local lodges (National Industrial Conference Board 1923; Ferguson 1937; Gist 1940). Various reports from Louisiana, Rhode Island, California, and New York attest to the prevalence of such plans and of "contract practice," as competitive health care was then called. "[T]he growth of contract practice has been so amazingly great during the last twenty-five years as almost to preclude belief," reported a committee of physicians in 1916. "Practically all of the large cities are fairly honeycombed with lodges, steadily increasing in number, with a constantly growing membership." (Woodruff, p. 508). Although these fraternal orders grew weak by the Depression, they have a larger theoretical importance because they embodied a model of grassroots health care that puts the members in control. Table 1 outlines the systemic dimensions of this approach, driven by member-centered values. Today

TABLE 1 Ideal Type of a Mutual Aid Health Care System

Inherent Values and Goals	To improve the health of fellow members. To promote ties and mutual support among members. To promote democratic decision making, shared responsibility To educate members and to prevent diseases. To make each member provider of care for self and others. To minimize health care costs. To be sure no major outside force (state, profession) controls the health system.
Organization	A loose federation of member groups. Administratively collegial. Egalitarian services. Emphasis on low-tech primary care and preventive programs. Strong ties to community programs (educational, occupational, social service). Organized around epidemiological patterns of illness.
Key Institutions	Mutual Benefit associations
Power	Local consumer-based control within common rules. State and profession relatively weak; facilitative role.
Finance and Cost	Members contribute to an insurance fund which contracts with physicians and facilities for service. Doctors' share of costs less than professional model.
Image of the Individual	Active, self-responsible, informed member of the group.
Division of Labor	Egalitarian. More teams and delegation. Fewer physicians and specialists

Source: Donald W. Light and Alexander Schuller, eds., 1986, *Political Values and Health Care: The German Experience*, Cambridge: MIT Press, p. 11. © 1986 by The Massachusetts Institute of Technology. All rights reserved.

there is very little evidence of member-controlled health care.

The government also became heavily involved in organized buying near the turn of the century. Most of the more comprehensive reports on contract practice describe municipal, county, and state agencies putting out for bid service contracts for the poor, for prisoners, and for civil employees. At the federal level, the armed services and Coast Guard had long contracted for medical services at wholesale prices.

Thus, one is startled to learn that what are today called health maintenance organizations (HMOs), and were more accurately called before Prepaid Group Health Plans (because they offered comprehensive health services for a prepaid flat rate per year per member) existed at the turn of the century. In addition, Preferred Provider Organizations (PPOs), in which groups of providers offer services at discount rates, were in evidence at the turn of the century.

Provider Competition

Fueling competition over contract practice and creating their own form of one-on-one competition were the multiple schools, or sects, of medicine: the eclectics, the herbalists, the naturalists, the homeopaths, the osteopaths, the chiropracters, and the allopaths (Rothstein 1972; Warner 1986). No one sect could prove itself more effective than the others, and all expanded rapidly as medical schools proliferated during the last quarter of the nineteenth century. Thus, on top of inter-sect competition, a glut of physicians added a third competitive force as doctors scrambled for patients and contracts.

Finally, a fourth form of competition arose as cities, states, and charitable organizations tried to meet the stark needs of millions of poor immigrants by offering free care (Burrow 1971). Step by step, departments of health moved from sanitation to immunization to free services at health care clinics (Starr 1982, bk. 1, chap. 5). Hospitals had always been charitable institutions, and even as they transformed themselves to attract paying patients, they continued to provide a substantial amount of free care (Davis and Warner 1918; Davis 1927; Rosner 1982; Vogel 1980). Dispensaries, or free health care clinics, proliferated as well during this early period.

The discipline of the marketplace as an agent of social control goes far beyond price in shaping the organization, quality, and professional character of services. These four sources of competition greatly distressed physicians, particularly the vast majority who belonged to the allopathic, or traditional, sect. Competitive contracting was cutting into their practices, which already faced competition from the surfeit of providers. Physicians' incomes were historically low, about $1,200 a year, the same as skilled craftsmen (Burrow 1971, p. 15). State medical societies reported that fierce competition had fostered backbiting, fee splitting, and open criticism among their members. From their point of view, no one was in control, and matters were deteriorating rapidly. But from the point of view of consumers and institutional buyers, they were exercising the control they wanted to secure adequate services at reasonable prices.

During this same period, traditional medicine finally reaped the benefits of its faith in science. A rapid succession of scientific advances ensued "like corn popping in a pan" (Stern 1945, pp. 33–34). As Bernhard Stern pointed out, the scientific advances in bacteriology, anesthetics, antisepsis, and endocrinology, as well as the development of medical instruments, powerfully affected the organization of medicine. They also were incorporated into the germ theory–magic bullet approach to illness that emphasizes control by the scientific, expert clinician. The vast majority of traditional physicians continued to practice using the crude, ineffective, and often deleterious methods they had learned at an earlier time, but a growing number of physicians traveled to Vienna, Heidelberg, Berlin, Edinburgh and other centers of medicine to gain specialized training (Stevens 1971, p. 52). The very character of hospitals changed from charitable institutions where the local poor could receive rest and nursing to professional workshops for the new medicine and businesses wooing the middle-class paying patient (Rosner 1982; Vogel 1980).

It has not been sufficiently appreciated that from the perspective of social control and consumer markets, these developments meant that differential competition was discriminating superior medical care from the mass of prescientific practice without the help of monopolistic licensing. While the average income of poorly trained physicians was being driven down, specialists were earning three to ten times as much (Stevens 1971, chap. 2; Burrow 1971; Rosen 1983)? Hospitals succeeded in attracting middle- and upper-class patients, overcoming their wariness not merely with private rooms and chefs but with what they believed to be superior medicine. The proprietary medical schools, established by physicians who used school fees to supplement income from private practice, were beginning to face competition from the serious, university-based schools, whose graduates were earning the respect of the marketplace (Billings 1903; Flexner 1911).

Thus, quality and value were being recognized on several fronts. Nevertheless, the organized profession campaigned hard for regulations, arguing that they would protect the public from inferior medicine.

THE PROFESSION TAKES CONTROL

Abraham Flexner's scathing report in 1910 against all but the most scientific, expensive, and elite medical schools is widely believed to be the key turning point in the profession's drive for social control. But a more careful examination suggests that the key event took place in 1901, the same year that E. A. Ross published his book, when the AMA reorganized into a "hierarchical democracy" in which no doctor could join unless he was a "member in good standing" of the state society and also a *bona fide* member of his county society (Starr 1982, pp. 109–110).

Other important groundwork had been laid before 1901. For example, medical societies had mounted a conscious drive in the preceding twenty years to reinstate licensure and to do so using a strategy designed to give medical societies control over licensing without appearing to do so (Berlant 1975, pp. 218–234). This drive partially succeeded, though competing sects were strong enough in a number of cases to share seats on the boards or get boards of their own. During this same period, the *Journal of the American Medical Association* (JAMA) emerged from a field of hundreds of medical journals to become the authoritative voice of traditional medicine. But it was the restructuring of the AMA, which had been ineffective for 54 years, that provided the organizational power base for taking control of health care—a testimony in itself to the power of structural forces.

The effects were immediate. By 1905, membership in several state societies increased three- to five-fold. These societies hired their own staff and began publishing their own journals. Membership in the

AMA grew from 8,401 in 1900 to 70,146 in 1910, or half the physicians in the country (Burrow 1971, p. 49). The whole structure formed a hierarchy of networks, coordinated by small groups of influentials at the center of each. These networks were used to mount campaigns against competition and corporate medicine. We shall summarize these campaigns briefly here.

Eliminating Sects and Reducing Supply

One campaign aimed to reduce the supply of physicians and eliminate competing sects. In the early 1900s, medical societies launched a campaign to eliminate dual licensing boards and to give themselves more influence on who was selected to the boards. The boards, in turn, supervised state licensing examinations, and through these the educational leaders of the societies constantly raised the standards in terms of scientific medicine, thus forcing other sects to train their students allopathically or fail the licensing exams. A related tactic was to broaden the legal definition of medicine so that all sects would be subject to the medical practice laws and then define "unprofessional behavior" in those laws by allopathic standards. By 1904, the AMA's Committee on National Legislation had lobbying organizations in every state except Nevada and Virginia, manned by 1,940 members. In many states this political machine succeeded in obtaining single boards or increasing power over composite boards (Burrow 1963, chap. 3; Burrow 1971, chap. 4).

This massive lobbying effort to squeeze out competing sects by mobilizing the power of the state was joined by the second prong of the campaign, to drive inferior medical schools out of business and once again reduce the supply of physicians (Burrow 1971, pp. 32–42). *JAMA* began collecting data on every school and every statute in 1901, and in 1904 the AMA created the Council of Medical Education. Composed of a highly talented and distinguished group of academic physicians, the Council quickly became the voice of the profession on educational matters, and that voice advocated high admission standards, long and expensive training, training in laboratories and hospitals, and demanding examinations for licensure. Working closely with JAMA, it started to publish the failure rates, by school, of graduates taking licensing examinations. The Council established forty-five committees on medical education in the states and territories to carry out its work, and it held national conferences on medical education where it propogated its ideas about model curricula. All this might be called influence or marketing. What went beyond marketing was the incorporation of the Council's model into the requirements for state boards. As Flexner himself notes, "The state boards are the instruments through which reconstruction of medical education will be largely effected" (1910, p. 167).

Another instrument of control was money from the great foundations. Indeed the need to coopt the foundations appears to have been a significant motive behind the Council's request that the Carnegie Foundation fund an "independent assessment" of medical education. Flexner's report for Carnegie and his subsequent central role at the Rockefeller foundations led these foundations to give $154 million between 1911 and 1938 to a small circle of elite schools so that they could afford to offer the extremely expensive kind of medical education that Flexner and the Council advocated. To this amount was added $600 million in other grants and matching funds from other sources (Stevens 1971; Fox 1980). Recent research shows that Flexner and the foundation staffs systematically disguised the degree to which they insisted that medical schools receiving their millions adhere to their model of medical education (Fox 1980). Thus the moneys from the great industrial monopolies of the late nineteenth century were used by leaders of the profession to create a monopoly of medical education in the early twentieth century (Berliner 1985).

This two-pronged campaign worked. The number of graduates fell from 5,440 in 1910 to 2,529 in 1922. Medical schools, which were already closing from competitive pressures before 1910, could not keep up with the rising expense of meeting standards. By 1924 there were only 80, down from 160 in 1904 (Rayack 1967, chap. 3; Burrow 1971, pp. 32–42). Six of the eight black medical schools were forced to close, and quotas on ethnic groups could be found in many places. The physician/population ratio declined sharply and did not return to its 1910 level until 1970. Those who claim that the reduced supply of physicians was simply a by-product of bringing scientific medicine ignore the repeated statements by leaders of the profession that reducing supply and raising incomes were central goals of the campaign. Between 1900 and 1928, physicians' incomes more than doubled, after accounting for inflation (Starr 1982, p. 142).

Suppressing Contract Medicine

A second, less well known, campaign which contributed to the doubling of incomes focused on suppressing contract medicine. Independent practitioners had good reason to feel threatened, because the institutions or organizations writing the contracts set the conditions under which medicine should be practiced and because the lowest bidders won contracts at cheap rates. To battle contract medicine, county and state societies took a number of actions.[4] They conducted studies and reported on the terrible conditions under which contract physicians worked. Strangely enough, however, the few times that remarks were published by physicians doing contract work, they said they liked the guaranteed income rather than having a quarter of their patients (on average) not pay their bills. They remarked on how they

[4]This section is based on numerous reports by medical societies cited in Chapter 3 of my forthcoming book on the American health care system.

learned to handle hypochondriacs and other abusers of free medical care, and they pointed out that contract medicine is an excellent way to build up a private practice. Societies were also forced to acknowledge that a sizable proportion of their members actively bid for contracts and did contract work.

To those leading this campaign, however, complicity appears to have been a good reason to redouble their efforts and save their colleagues from their own bad judgment. Some societies drew up lists of physicians known to practice contract medicine in order to embarrass them. Others drew up "honor rolls" of members who promised to swear off competitive contracts. Committee members would ferret out every recalcitrant colleague and pressure him to abandon contract practice. Some societies threatened expulsion or censure to members who did not cooperate in stamping out price-competitive contract medicine.

These pressures worked much more effectively than they had in the nineteenth century, because medical societies succeeded in getting hospitals not to grant privileges to any physician who was not a member in good standing. The hospital had established itself as the center of modern medicine and professional status so that privileges became a powerful control mechanism. Malpractice insurance and other professional needs were contingent on membership too. More broadly, the success of practice depended on good relations with one's colleagues.

Although organized medicine never eliminated competitive contracts entirely, it made rapid progress. Fraternal orders did not want to cause a row with doctors and shifted coverage to partial payments for wages lost and medical bills rather than contracted services. Reimbursement allowed doctors to set their own fees and eliminated any middlemen setting the terms of service. Several court decisions supported the profession's opposition to the corporate practice of medicine, even though its legal basis was (and is) weak. In a number of states, societies got legislation passed prohibiting the corporate practice of medicine or the practice of medicine by organizations run by nonphysicians. They got other laws passed against the organized practice of medicine for profit. Medical societies meanwhile dusted off their old fee schedules and raised their prices to a professionally respectable level.

The goal of these and other efforts to gain control over the practice of medicine has never been to eliminate competition entirely but rather to keep outsiders (i.e., consumers and buyers) from setting terms, especially price. As Max Weber (1968, p. 342) understood, guilds secure a monopoly over a domain and then let members compete freely within it. By the 1920s, the medical profession had contracts confined to the few industries that had needed them from the start, to group purchasing of services for the poor and for the military, and to a few maverick experiments on the periphery of medicine (Williams, 1932).

Creating Provider-Controlled Insurance

During the Great Depression, new forms of competitive contracts sprang up again in response to economic hardships. This time it was providers (doctors and hospitals) that used them to capture some stable portion of the market and avoid unpaid bills (Leland 1932; Williams 1932; Schwartz 1965; Stevens 1971; Rayack 1967). Again the profession and now the hospital industry faced the threat of competition pitting one provider against another.

Realizing that financial stability of some kind was needed, the American Hospital Association, and subsequently the AMA, selected one arrangement that provided stable prepayments but was not competitive and did not interfere with the practice of medicine (Rorem 1940; Reed 1947; Rayack 1967, chap. 5). That arrangement came to be called Blue Cross and Blue Shield. The AHA and the AMA even had to design a special law that would give Blue Cross and

Blue Shield legal monopolies as nonprofit community insurance organizations. Despite the prevalent view today that Blue Cross and Blue Shield arose as innocuous community insurance plans (Fein 1986), the law gave providers control of the boards and of the payment committees.

This triumph over the threat of the 1930s put in place the last piece of the profession's campaign to control the practice of medicine, a campaign that also included monopolizing access to drugs, steering public health programs away from providing free medical care, and professionalizing childbirth by discrediting midwives (Burrow 1971; Arney 1982; Caplan 1984; Starr 1982, bk. 1, chap. 5; Wertz and Wertz 1977). As E. A. Ross suggested, mechanisms of social control had been consciously constructed to address the "chaos" that corporate competition had created. These mechanisms looked more like Ross's description of class control rather than social control.

THE PROFESSIONAL MODEL OF SOCIAL CONTROL

While from one point of view the medical profession consciously set out to suppress competition and control by organized consumers, its own perspective on the matter embodied quite another paradigm, which might be called a guild or altruistic monopoly. Since the mid-nineteenth century, the AMA had built its professional model on Thomas Percival's *Medical Ethics*, written in 1803, in which trust replaces competition as the organizing principle (Berlant 1975). Rather than live by the law of the marketplace—"Let the Buyer Beware"—physicians were urged to line up to the law of professionalism—"Let the Buyer Trust." The complex, expert work of the professional, full of idiosyncratic problems and subtle decisions, can only be done in an atmosphere of trust. In this view, lay-driven competition will simply force bad decisions or cutting corners, not to men-

tion its corrosive effect on the public respect for professionals as they compete against one other in full view.

The professional model therefore prohibits advertising, because any form of advertising carries within it some public claim that other professionals are less competent. Such criticism within a profession invites control from the state or some other outside agency. Likewise, the professional model of social control contains elaborate rules for how consultations are handled so that the patient (or client) is not stolen or exposed to invidious comparisons. The profession must earn patients' trust by establishing high standards and committing itself to serving its patients. Members of the profession must pull together, be united in this philosophy.

Parsons: Legitimating the Model

By the 1920s, the professional model was well in place and became incorporated into the writings of Talcott Parsons on the medical profession. In his 1939 essay, "The Professions and Social Structure," Parsons considered the professions as occupying a uniquely central position in modern society. Because self-interest, the profit motive, and the business economy so dominate modern society, wrote Parsons, observers are likely to overlook the professions, which by contrast are based on "disinterestedness" and the heritage of medieval guilds (p. 35). Parsons noted that modern business and the professions have a number of characteristics in common: the importance of applied science, an emphasis on pursuing the most rational solution to problems, the use of functional and universalistic criteria in judging people and situations, and authority based on technical competence. But disinterestedness separates professions from business. As Parsons wrote in an essay the following year (1940), the professions put a series of limits on self-interest: no advertisements, helping clients whether they pay or not, and no price competition with other physicians (p. 63).

Parsons admired the professions as a viable alternative to the mainstream business economy based on self-interest, but he seemed completely innocent of the idea that the restraint of individual self-interest is the key to a profession's economic and legal monopoly and therefore serves the collective self-interest of its members. In fact, the medical profession drew upon the techniques of early business monopolies, which also prohibited competition within their ranks for the larger control and benefit of all.[5] Thus, Parsons did not seem aware of the depth or extent to which professional social control was a form of class control. In his writings over the next 35 years, this innocence was not lost (1975a, 1975b).

Parsons's allusion to guilds might have taken him back to Weber, who understood the dynamics of their social control more realistically. In writing about closed relationships, Weber (1968, p. 46) includes guilds as an example of a "trade economy" which pursues quality, prestige, and profit to the mutual benefit of guild members. The process begins when "jointly acting competitors now form an 'interest group' toward outsiders; there is a growing tendency to set up some kind of association with rational regulations" (p. 342). Next comes "a legal order that limits competition through formal monopolies. . . . The tendency toward the monopolization of specific, usually economic opportunities is always the driving force in such cases" (p. 342). "Full members make a vocation out of monopolizing the disposition of spiritual, intellectual, social and economic goods, duties and position" (p. 346). Requirements

are set up for admission, training and qualification to be a full member aimed at "limiting the supply of candidates for the benefices and honors of a given occupation" (p. 344). This rather fully characterizes the actions of organized medicine described above.

By uncritically accepting the forms of social control inherent in the medical profession, Parsons reflected the depth to which most Americans accepted the professional health care system characterized by physician autonomy, payments by fee, specialty care, and premium-based insurance.[6] Parsons's famous analysis (1951) of how medicine controls illness as a form of social deviance by monitoring it and by restoring people to health so that they can resume their roles in society, also reflects this acceptance. The patient is characterized as helpless, technically, incompetent, and emotionally involved, therefore needing to put himself or herself into the hands of a professional who is technically expert, functionally specific, and affectively neutral (p. 456). No attention is given to helplessness and incompetence as qualities cultivated in patients by withholding information from them that might enable patients to participate in treating their own illness (Waitzkin and Waterman 1974; Waitzkin 1983; Caplan 1981). Parsons even took the profession's point of view towards "shopping around" for doctors; he instructed the reader in the proper etiquette for seeing another doctor so that one's own doctor will not be offended (1951, p. 439).

The Professional Health Care System

The organizational and institutional implications of the professional model of so-

---

[5]Compare the techniques delineated by Jones (1921) with those described here and in Starr (1982), Rayack (1967), Berlant (1975), Fox (1980), and Burrow (1971). Parsons's noted student, Bernard Barber, reports that in lectures Parsons "referred to his Boston medical colleagues by name and most admiringly" (1985, p. 213). He greatly admired his older brother, a physician, who died prematurely. The saving grace of Barber's work, and the source of insights that transcend those of his teacher, is his concern for the *patient* (Barber 1979, 1983, 1985)

---

[6]At various points, Parsons remarks on the widespread complaints about commercialism in medicine (1939, p. 44) or on the lack of professional efforts to uphold standards of excellence (1951, pp. 463–472). But he either does not take up these matters, or he regards them as deviant rather than as indicating inadequacies in his uncritical conceptualization of the profession.

cial control are laid out in Table 2. By comparing it with Table 1, one can appreciate how societies differ in arranging resources, power, and institutions to fulfill the societal needs for health care. American medical services reflect the ideal type of a health care system shaped by professional values. The model implies that most of the dramatic developments from the 1920s to the 1980s are extensions of the structure put in place during the first two decades of this century. This interpretation provides more analytic coherence than the tendency among policy writers to see developments such as Blue Cross, Hill-Burton or Medicare/Medicaid as major turning points rather than as parts of a coherent whole.

TABLE 2 Ideal Type of a Professional Health Care System

Inherent Values and Goals	To provide the best possible clinical care to every sick patient where physicians choose to practice.
	To develop scientific medicine to its highest level.
	To protect the autonomy of physicians and keep the state or others from controlling the health care system.
	To increase the power and wealth of the profession.
	To generate enthusiasm and admiration for the medical profession.
Organization	A loose federation, administratively collegial and decentralized.
	Emphasis on acute, high-tech intervention and specialty care.
	Organized around clinical cases and doctors' preferences.
	Organized around hospitals and private offices.
	Weak ties with other social institutions.
	Services and recruitment follow the stratification of the society.
Key Institutions	Physicians' associations
	Autonomous physicians and hospitals.
	Medical schools as the wellspring of professional advance, prestige, and legitimation.
Power	Profession the sole power.
	Uses state powers to enhance its own.
	Protests state interferences.
	Protests, boycotts all competing models of care.
Finance and Cost	Private payments, by individual or through private insurance plans.
	Doctors' share of costs more than in mutual aid model.
Image of the Individual	A private individual. Chooses how to live and when to use the medical system.
Division of Labor	Hierarchical. Centered on physicians, especially specialists.

Source: Donald W. Light and Alexander Schuller, eds., 1986, *Political Values and Health Care: The German Experience*, Cambridge: MIT Press. © 1986 by The Massachusetts Institute of Technology. All rights reserved.

As the model would predict, postwar expansion centered on an immense upgrading of hospitals, heavy support of research, a further development of leading medical schools as regional centers for the best in medicine, and a rapid expansion of passive, cost-plus, provider insurance to foot the bill (Somers and Somers 1961; Fox 1986; Rayack 1967; Starr 1982). From this longer perspective, Medicare insurance for the elderly and Medicaid insurance for the poor were the offspring of Blue Cross as provider-based semi-private insurance. They picked up the two groups neglected by Blue Cross, and they extended the Blue Cross tradition of hospital-based reimbursement of whatever the doctor orders. They accelerated the professional model: specialization, hospitalization, technical services, decentralized control, and escalating expenditures.

The professional model produces unpopular side effects. With medical schools as its engine, the professionally driven health care system presses for and rewards clinical breakthroughs and specialization. The dual priorities of professional autonomy and the best clinical care lead to fragmentation and uncoordinated care. Pursuing the best clinical medicine drives up expenses and (since patients' costs are providers' income) doctors' wealth too. The system also rewards more and more procedures to a point of excess and waste. Complaints against these side effects began in the late 1950s but grew vociferous during the 1960s (Somers and Somers 1961). By the late 1960s and into the 1970s, they were joined by a national antipathy toward power, authority, and elites who were accused of accumulating wealth and power rather than serving society. In this setting, Eliot Freidson published *Professional Dominance* (1970a) and *Profession of Medicine* (1970b).

Professional Dominance as Class Control

Freidson's satirical wit had been in evidence well before these two books appeared. As early as 1960 he had wryly pointed out that the community doctor was controlled more by his patients than either the profession or Parsons wanted to admit. In his concept of professional dominance, Freidson satirized the very triumph of professional control which Parsons seemed to celebrate. The theory of professional dominance, in a sentence, holds that the organized autonomy which a skilled occupation secures in order to cope with its problematic relationships with clients is extended step by step to control work-related institutions, resources, privileges, financing, and division of labor (Freidson 1970a, chap. 4–5). Put more formally, expert authority is parlayed into bureaucratic, legal, and charismatic authority. This emphasis has led to more radical interpretations from which Freidson has distanced himself and even taken back the punch of his original theory (1986). Despite this, the concept of professional dominance has a tone of frightening inevitability: the legal core of professional autonomy leads to controlling a widening circle of people, resources, and arrangements that might otherwise impinge on the core. In contrast to Parsons's portrait of medicine as harmonious and functional, Freidson points out how the dynamics of dominance contribute to a variety of problems such as poor communication with patients and nurses and poor coordination of services.

Freidson's seminal books contained a third concept of social control, of a conscious and constructed nature like that advocated by Ross rather than a "natural" social function as depicted by Parsons, but sufficiently excessive to be socially deleterious. What strikes one about Freidson's theory is that it captured the tenor of its time: professional dominance was inevitable but offensive. According to this view, doctors have extended their institutional control over drugs, hospitals, insurance, subordinates, and health budgets; and they have produced a self-serving system that is expensive, unresponsive to patients' needs or wishes, fragmented, disinterested in prevention, and bored with chronic diseases. Not surprisingly, Freidson's ideas for reform were quite modest compared to the powerful, self-perpetuating system he had so brilliantly analyzed.

Medicalization

The theme of medicalization fits hand in hand with the professional model of social control and with professional dominance. Its proponents have described the ways in which medicine has taken over sins, crimes, and forms of deviance such as drunkenness, drug addiction, madness, hyperactivity, homosexuality, epilepsy, fatigue, and others (Scheff 1966; Zola 1972, 1975; Ehrenreich and English 1973; Illich 1976; Waitzkin and Waterman 1974; Wertz & Wertz 1977; Ruzek 1978; Oakley 1980; Conrad and Schneider 1980; Schneider and Conrad 1983; Waitzkin 1983; Oakley 1985). Ironically, medicalization stands Parsons's argument on its head: those who deviate from social roles are defined as in some way sick.

As Conrad and Schneider (1980, chaps. 2, 9, and 10) explain in some detail, medicalization is a complex societal process that goes far beyond the activities of physicians. The rise of rationalism and determinist theories of cause, the success of medicine, the institutionalization of treatment programs, and the cultural enthusiasm for medicine, are just a few of the larger societal forces contributing to medicalization (Fox 1977; Fox and Swazey 1984). Certainly schools, prisons, and other institutions of social control, as well as the public, urged medical "solutions" as much as medical entrepreneurs who saw new opportunities for programs, funds, and careers.

In addition, illness is a kind of *no-fault deviance* that fits the modern temperament better than sin and crime. Medicalization covers up the issues of distributive justice in a highly stratified society. Currently, for example, the homeless are being characterized as mentally ill when a large proportion are victims of a weak unskilled labor mar-

ket and the elimination of cheap urban housing (Snow et al. 1986; Buff, Kenny, and Light 1980). Medicalizing problems hold out the promise that the power of science—the quintessential power of modern culture—will precisely define and solve them. Other social forces contributing to the widespread support of medicalization and professional control include the deep-seated need for priest-like figures in an era when science seems to offer miracles and salvation, and the need for therapeutic paternalism by members of the weakened urban family (Parsons and Fox 1952).[7]

Medicalization also points to a problem of care becoming more technological and specialized as the profession loses sight of its purpose in society to maintain health and treat the ill, (Kennedy 1972; Carson 1975; Illich 1976; Kotelchuck 1976; Krause 1977). In the United States about 80 percent of physicians are specialists, yet 85 percent of patients' problems do not need the care of a specialist. Likewise, about 40 percent of hospital admissions are found to be unnecessary (Siu et al. 1986). It is not only critics on the left who have suggested that the American health care system is more accurately called a provider income system (Olson 1981; Meyer 1985).

UNDERSTANDING THE REVOLUTION IN BUYER CONTROL

It may be a sociological law that the prevailing sociological theory of a period tends to state in universal terms an historically situated pattern. Thus, Parsons's theory of professional disinterestedness was written in 1939, just before medicine burst into an era of big business when entrepreneurial physicians left onlookers agape with their fame, institutes, and incomes. His theory of the sick role, still considered timelessly universal in some quarters, was valid for acute

---

[7]Ironically, Parsons and Fox emphasized the very psychotherapeutic roles that doctors increasingly eschewed.

disorders yet written in 1951 at a time when chronic disorders were becoming prevalent. Freidson's theory of professional dominance was written at the end of the era it characterized and was incapable of accounting for professional decline because of its unidirectional and overdetermined character (McKinlay 1977; Coburn, Torrance, and Kaufert 1983). It took Larson (1977) and other critics to recast professional dominance in a market-sensitive way that related it to larger forces of social class and power.

If organized autonomy lies at the heart of the professional health care system, then the evidence indicates that professional autonomy leads to a medical system grossly out of line with the health needs of society. As it developed, the professionally driven health care system produced structural imbalances and excesses that resulted in the current revolution. The internal logic of a system designed to support the best possible medical care where doctors choose to practice led to maldistribution, overspecialization, worsening patient relations, millions of unnecessary procedures, the neglect of risk factors, and escalating costs that could not be stopped by a decade of regulatory measures.

Moreover, the very emphasis on technical prowess has led to health care being capitalized and externally financed. The structure of the professional health care system is an investor's dream—a high-status business with spectacular growth and limitless funds that would pay for mistakes (Light 1986). The revolt of institutional buyers (employers, government, insurers) began about 1970, took a decade to work out its strategies, and burst on the scene in the 1980s. It will take this decade to gain full momentum, and it will persist for some time unless buyers get drawn away by other priorities.

The rise, or awakening, of institutional buyers like John Deere, Chrysler, or above all Medicare has revolutionary consequences for social control and the organization of medicine (Salmon 1977, 1985;

Leyerle 1984; Califano 1986). Once again wholesale markets are being created. They force providers to organize into bargaining units so they can respond to the kinds of contracts that buyers put out for bid. Some buyers want one-stop shopping; providers form vertically integrated systems that offer everything from well-baby care to heart transplants under one management. Other buyers want specialized contracts; providers then must organize into special service corporations or lose business.

Because buyers want to know what they are getting for their money, it does not take long for them to demand detailed accounts of what services are being rendered at what cost. To most people's surprise, providers did not know what their services cost and did not even have good data on the services rendered. These data are inherently intrusive; they lead to buyer control and monitoring systems.

The battle over control of data is fierce. Even deeper, the demand for accountability is shifting from measuring inputs (supplies, equipment, facilities, and medical procedures) to outcomes (whose patients get better faster and cheaper). It is not unreasonable to predict that soon those hospitals, medical teams, or physicians whose outcomes are substandard will either lose business or be subject to retraining. Does this mean that the medical profession is becoming deprofessionalized or proletarianized, as John McKinlay and others contend (McKinlay and Arches 1985; Haug 1973, 1975)? Only if one clings to theoretical frameworks of professional control that are themselves historically situated in another time. The need for a new paradigm is clear.

Despite the revolt of buyers and the powerful controls they can exercise, this reinterpretation of the American health care system indicates the degree to which every facet of that system was designed to minimize competitive medicine and cost containment. It still is. Medical schools still train each cohort and provide leadership for the entire profession in state-of-the-art clinical medicine. The schools become large institutions rewarded by research grants to advance in clinical medicine, subspecialization, and new technology—the core values of the professional model and chief causes of escalating costs. As one might expect, the recent reports on health costs for 1980–1985 show increased intensity of care leading the way to higher costs (Anderson 1986). Hospitals, faced with fierce competition in many markets, all tend to choose the same strategy: become the premier, hi-tech medical center in their market.

Although many of the laws which organized medicine put in place to prevent competitive medicine have recently been removed or changed, in many states the corporate practice of medicine is still illegal (Rosoff 1984). The laws have just not been invoked—so far. Meanwhile the supply of physicians is growing rapidly as talented, ambitious, and debt-laden doctors begin practice each year at a rate two and a half times the rate of physicians who stop practice (Light and Widman 1986).

Most important, the public still wants the best medical care possible (Light 1986) and may sue if dissatisfied. A recent court decision also makes the third party (i.e., the buyer/insurer) liable for omitted services (*Medical Benefits* 1986a). In short, buyer control will significantly increase accountability at all levels and integrate services to reflect more fully consumers' needs, but providers still control many parts of the system, and not much money may be saved (Light 1984). So long as economic and clinical policies to contain costs fail to take into account the organizational features designed to prevent cost containment, they will not succeed.

REFERENCES

Anderson, Gerald F. 1986. National Medical Care Spending. *Health Affairs* 5(3):123–130.

Anderson, Odin W. 1985. *Health Services in the United States: A Growth Enterprise since 1985.* Ann Arbor: Health Administration Press.

Arney, William Ray. 1982. *Power and the Profession of Obstetrics.* Chicago: University of Chicago Press.

Barber, Bernard. 1979. *Informed Consent in Medical Therapy and Research.* New Brunswick, N.J.: Rutgers University Press.

———. 1983. *The Logic and Limits of Trust.* New Brunswick, N.J.: Rutgers University Press.

———. 1985. Beyond Parson's Theory of the Professions, in J. C. Alexander, ed., *Neofunctionalism: Key Issues in Sociological Theory,* Vol. 1. Beverly Hills: Sage Publications, pp. 211–224.

Berlant, Jeffrey L. 1975. *Profession and Monopoly: A Study of Medicine in the United States and Great Britain.* Berkeley: University of California Press.

Berliner, Howard S. 1985. *A System of Scientific Medicine: Philanthropic Foundations in the Flexner Era.* New York: Tavistock Publications.

Billings, Frank. 1903. Medical Education in the United States. *Science* 17 (437):761–772.

Buff, Daniel D., James F. Kenny, and Donald Light. 1980. Health Problems of Residents in Single-Room Occupancy Hotels. *New York State Journal of Medicine* 80(13):2000–2005.

Burrow, James G. 1963. *A.M.A: Voice of American Medicine.* Baltimore: Johns Hopkins University Press.

———. 1971. *Organized Medicine in the Progressive Era: The Move toward Monopoly.* Baltimore: Johns Hopkins University Press.

Califano, Joseph A., Jr. 1986. *America's Health Care Revolution: Who Lives? Who Dies? Who Pays?* New York: Random House.

Caplan, Ronald Lee. 1981. Pasturized Patients and Profits: The Changing Nature of Self-Care in American Medicine. Ph.D. diss., Department of Economics, University of Massachusetts.

Carson, Rick J. 1975. *The End of Medicine.* New York: John Wiley.

Coburn, Davis, George M. Torrance, and Joseph M. Kaufert. 1983. Medical Dominance in Canada in Historical Perspective: The Rise and Fall of Medicine? *International Journal of Health Services* 13(3):407–432.

Conrad, Peter, and Joseph W. Schneider. 1980. *Deviance and Medicalization: From Badness to Sickness.* St. Louis: C. V. Mosby.

Cutler, Lloyd N. 1939. The Legislative Monopolies Achieved by Small Business. *Yale Law Journal* 48:847–858.

Davis, Michael M., Jr. 1927. *Clinics, Hospitals and Health Centers.* New York: Harper and Brothers.

Davis, Michael M., Jr., and Andred R. Warner. 1918. *Dispensaries: Their Management and Development.* New York: Macmillan.

Duffy, John. 1976. *The Healers: The Rise of the Medical Establishment.* New York: McGraw-Hill.

Ehrenreich, Barbara, and D. English. 1973. *Complaints and Disorders: The Sexual Politics of Sickness.* Old Westbury, New York: Feminist Press.

Fein, Rashi. 1986. *Medical Care, Medical Costs.* Cambridge, Mass.: Harvard University Press.

Ferguson, Charles W. 1937. *Fifty Million Brothers: A Panorama of American Lodges and Clubs.* New York: Farrar and Rinehart.

Flexner, Abraham. 1910. *Medical Education in the United States and Canada, Bulletin No. 4.* New York: Carnegie Foundation for the Advancement of Teaching.

———. 1911. Medical Colleges. *The World's Work* 21 (April):14238–14242.

Fox, Daniel M. 1980. Abraham Flexner's Unpublished Report: Foundations and Medical Education, 1909–1928. *Bulletin of the History of Medicine* 54:475–496.

———. 1986. *Health Policies, Health Politics: The British and American Experience, 1911–1965.* Princeton: Princeton University Press.

Fox, Renée C. 1977. The Medicalization and Demedicalization of American Society, in J. H. Knowles, ed., *Doing Better and Feeling Worse.* New York: W. W. Norton, pp. 9–22.

Fox, Renée C., and Judith P. Swazey. 1984. Medical Morality Is Not Bioethics—Medical Ethics in China and the United States. *Perspective in Biology and Medicine* 27(3):336–360.

Freidson, Eliot. 1960. Client Control and Medical Practice. *American Journal of Sociology* 65:374–382.

———. 1970a. *Professional Dominance: The Social Structure of Medical Care.* New York: Atherton.

———. 1970b. *Profession of Medicine.* New York: Dodd, Mead.

———. 1986. *Professional Powers.* Chicago: University of Chicago Press.

Gist, Noel P. 1940. Secret Societies: A Cultural Study of Fraternalism in the United States. *The University of Missouri Studies* 15(4):entire issue.

Haug, Marie R. 1973. Deprofessionalization: An Alternative Hypothesis for the Future. *Sociological Review Monographs* 20:195–211.

———. 1975. The Deprofessionalization of Everyone? *Sociological Focus* 8(3):197–213.

Hofstadter, Richard. 1955. *The Age of Reform.* New York: Random House.

Illich, Ivan. 1976. *Medical Nemesis.* New York: Pantheon.

Janowitz, Morris. 1978. *The Last Half-Century.* Chicago: University of Chicago Press.

Jones, Eliot. 1921. *The Trust Problem in the United States.* New York: Macmillan.

Kennedy, Edward M. 1972. *In Critical Condition: The Crisis in America's Health Care.* New York: Simon and Schuster.

Kotelchuck, David, ed. 1976. *Prognosis Negative: Crisis in the Health Care System.* New York: Vintage.

Krause, Elliott A. 1977. *Power and Illness: The Political Sociology of Health and Health Care.* New York: Elsevier.

Langford, T. S., A. S. Kimball, H. B. Garner, E. H. Flynn. and T. E. DeGurse. 1907. Report of the Committee on Contract Practice. *Journal of the Michigan State Medical Society* 6(7):377–380.

Larson, Magali Sarfatti. 1977. *The Rise of Professionalism: A Sociological Analysis.* Berkeley: University of California Press.

Leland, R. G. 1932. *Contract Practice.* Chicago: American Medical Association.

Leyerle, Betty. 1984. *Moving and Shaking American Medicine.* Westport, Conn.: Greenwood Press.

Light, Donald W. 1984. Overstated Gains in the War on Health Costs. *The New York Times* August 6, 1984.

———. 1986. Corporate Medicine for Profit. *Scientific American* 255(6):38–45.

Light, Donald W., and Alexander Schuller, eds. 1986. *Political Values and Health Care: The German Experience.* Cambridge: MIT Press.

Light, Donald W., and Mindy Widman. 1986. Physician Growth in an Era of Cost Containment. Philadelphia: Leonard Davis Institute of Health Economics, Policy Paper No. 6.

McKinlay, John B. 1977. The Business of Good Doctoring and Doctoring as Good Business: Reflections on Freidson's View of the Medical Game. *International Journal of Health Services* 7(3):459–485.

McKinlay, John B., and Joan Arches. 1985. Towards the Proletarianization of Physicians. *International Journal of Health Services* 15(2):161–195.

Medical Benefits. 1986a. Payers Can Be Held Liable for Care Limits. October 15:3.

———. 1986b. There's Still No Cure for Exploding Health Care Costs. October 15:10.

———. 1986c. Negotiated Provider Agreements—An Emerging Force. November 15:7.

Meyer, Jack A., ed. 1985. *Incentives vs Controls in Health Policy.* Washington, D.C.: American Enterprise Institute. National Industrial Conference Board. 1923. *Experience with Mutual Benefit Associations in the United States.* New York: The Board.

Oakley, Ann. 1980. *Women Confined: Towards a Sociology of Childbirth.* New York: Schocken Books.

———. 1985. *The Captured Womb: A History of Medical Care of the Pregnant Woman.* Oxford: Basil Blackwell.

Olson, Mancur, ed. 1981. *A New Approach to the Economics of Health Care.* Washington, D.C.: American Enterprise Institute.

Parsons, Talcott. 1951. Social Structure and Dynamic Process: The Case of Modern Medical Practice, in his *The Social System.* Glencoe, Ill.: Free Press, pp. 428–479.

———. [1939] 1954. The Professions and Social Structure, in his edited volume, *Essays in Sociological Theory,* rev. ed. Glencoe, Ill.: Free Press, pp. 34–49.

———. [1940] 1954. The Motivation of Economic Activities, in his *Essays in Sociological Theory,* rev. ed. Glencoe, Ill.: Free Press, pp. 50–68.

———. 1975a. The Sick Role and the Role of the Physician Reconsidered, in his *Action Theory and the Human Condition.* New York: Free Press, pp. 17–34.

———. 1975b. Health and Disease: A Sociological and Action Perspective, in his *Action Theory and the Human Condition.* New York: [Free] Press, pp. 66–81.

Parsons, Talcott, and Renée C. Fox.

ness, Therapy and the Modern Urban American Family. *Journal of Social Issues* 8:31–44.

Pitts, Jesse R. 1968. Social Control: The Concept, in D. L. Sills, ed., *International Encyclopedia of the Social Sciences,* Vol. 14. New York: Macmillan and Free Press, pp. 381–396.

Rayack, Elton, 1967. *Professional Power and American Medicine: The Economics of the American Medical Association.* Cleveland: World Publications.

Reed, Louis. 1947. *Blue Cross and Medical Service Plans.* Washington, D.C.: Federal Security Agency.

Rorem, C. Rufus. 1940. *Non-profit Hospital Service Plans.* Chicago: Commission on Hospital Service.

Rosen, George. 1983. *The Structure of American Medical Practice 1875–1941.* Philadelphia: University of Pennsylvania Press.

Rosner, David. 1982. *A Once Charitable Enterprise: Hospitals and Health Care in Brooklyn and New York, 1885–1915.* New York: Cambridge University Press.

Rosoff, Arnold J. 1986–1987. The Business of Medicine: Problems with the Corporate Practice Doctrine. *Cumberland Law Review* 17: 485–503.

Ross, Edward A. [1901] 1969. *Social Control: A Survey of the Foundations of Order.* Reprint, with introduction. Cleveland: The Press of Case Western Reserve University.

Rothman, David J. 1981. Social Control: The Uses and Abuses of the Concept in the History of Incarceration. *Rice University Studies* 67(1):9–19.

Rothstein, William G. 1972. *American Physicians in the 19th Century: From Sects to Science.* Baltimore: Johns Hopkins University Press.

Ruzek, Sheryl B. 1978. *The Women's Health Movement: Feminist Alternatives to Medical Control.* New York: Praeger.

Salmon, J. Warren. 1977. Monopoly Capital and the Reorganization of Health Care. *Review of Radical Political Economics* 9(12):125–133.

———. 1985. Profit and Health Care: Trends in Corporatization and Proprietization. *International Journal of Health Services* 15(3):395–418.

Scheff, Thomas. 1966. *Being Mentally Ill.* Chicago: Aldine.

Schneider, Joseph, and Peter Conrad. 1983. *Having Epilepsy: The Experience and Control of*

Illness. Philadelphia: Temple University Press.

Schwartz, Jerome L. 1965. Early History of Prepaid Medical Care Plans. *Bulletin of the History of Medicine* 39:450–475.

Selleck, Henry B., with Alfred H. Whittaker. 1962. *Occupational Health in America.* Detroit: Wayne State University Press.

Shryock, Richard H. [1947]. 1969. *The Development of Modern Medicine.* New York: Hafner.

Siu, A. L., F. A. Sonnenberg, W. G. Manning, G. A. Goldberg, E. S. Bloomfield, J. P. Newhouse, and R. H. Brook. 1986. Inappropriate Use of Hospitals in a Randomized Trial of Health Insurance Plans. *New England Journal of Medicine* 315(20):1259–1266.

Snow, David A., Susan G. Baker, Leon Anderson, and Michael Martin. 1986. The Myth of Pervasive Mental Illness among the Homeless. *Social Problems* 33(5):45.

Somers, Herman Miles, and Anne Ramsay Somers. 1961. *Doctors, Patients, and Health Insurance.* Washington, D.C.: The Brookings Institution.

Starr, Paul. 1982. *The Social Transformation of American Medicine.* New York: Basic Books.

Stern, Bernhard J. 1945. *American Medical Practice in the Perspective of a Century.* New York: Commonwealth Fund.

Stevens, Rosemary. 1971. *American Medicine and the Public Interest.* New Haven: Yale University Press.

Vogel, Morris. 1980. *The Invention of the Modern Hospital.* Chicago: University of Chicago Press.

Waitzkin, Howard D. 1983. *The Second Sickness: Contradictions of Capitalist Health Care.* New York: Free Press.

Waitzkin, Howard D., and Barbara Waterman. 1974. *The Exploitation of Illness in a Capitalist Society.* Indianapolis: Bobbs-Merrill.

Warner, John Harley. 1986. *Therapeutic Perspectives: Medical Practice, Knowledge and Identity in America 1820–1885.* Cambridge, Mass.: Harvard University Press.

Weber, Max. 1968. *Economy and Society: An Outline of Interpretive Sociology,* edited by Guenther Roth and Claus Wittich. New York: Bedminster Press.

Wertz, Richard W., and Dorothy C. Wertz. 1977. *Lying-In: A History of Childbirth in America.* New York: Free Press.

Wiebe, Robert H. 1967. *The Search for Order: 1877–1920.* New York: Hill and Wang.

Williams, Pierce. 1932. *The Purchase of Medicine Care through Fixed Periodic Payments.* New York: National Bureau of Economic Research.

Woodruff, John V. 1916. Contract Practice. *New York State Journal of Medicine* 16:507–511.

Zola, Irving K. 1972. Medicine as an Institution of Social Control. *Sociological Review* 20:487–504.

———. 1975. In the Name of Health and Illness: On Some Socio-Political Consequences of Medical Influence. *Social Science and Medicine* 9:83–87.

23

HEALTH POLICY IN THE UNITED STATES: PROBLEMS AND ALTERNATIVES

HOWARD WAITZKIN

THE EVOLUTION AND FAILURE OF CURRENT POLICIES

The United States and the Republic of South Africa are the only two economically developed countries in the world without a national health policy that accepts the principle of universal entitlement to basic medical care (Roemer 1985). U.S. health services remain in a condition of chronic crisis. Despite high costs, major gaps in coverage persist. Even for the nonpoor, obtaining suitable care at a reasonable cost often is not a simple task.

Since the 1920s, proposals for a national health program (NHP) have appeared and later have faded from view (Roemer and Falk 1985; Starr 1982). Many observers believe, however, that our current situation has become intolerable, especially given our nation's wealth, and that piecemeal reforms no longer are suitable approaches to solving our fundamental problems.

A national health program that combines elements of national health insurance and a national health service is a policy that offers hope of a meaningful and lasting solution. In this chapter, I describe the major deficiencies of U.S. health care, as well as the policies proposed to deal with these problems. I show that policies other than a national health program contain crippling limitations. An NHP would help correct our present difficulties, and it would likely do so with lower costs and less restriction on doctors' and patients' freedoms than current arrangements.

Gaps in Public Coverage: A Brief History

Advocacy for a national health program in the United States dates back more than half a century. In 1926 a privately funded group, the Committee on the Costs of Medical Care (CCMC), began to consider

475

policy changes to improve the widely perceived problems of high costs and inadequate access to medical services. After deliberating for more than six years, the CCMC in 1932 published a major report that called for a comprehensive approach to the organization and funding of health services, which were to be "available to the entire population according to its needs" (see Starr 1982; Hirshfield 1970; Falk 1983; Roemer and Falk 1985). The CCMC argued that medical care should be delivered mainly by doctors organized into group practices and that funding should come from voluntary insurance plans and subsidies from local governments for low-income individuals. Because the American Medical Association (AMA) perceived a possible threat to private practice and feared government involvement, it strongly opposed the CCMC's recommendations. The CCMC's report generated so much controversy in the medical profession that the administration of President Franklin D. Roosevelt, taking office in 1932 during the Great Depression, was reluctant to pursue the issue. As a result, the CCMC's concerns and recommendations led to few actual changes in health policy.

With the initiation of the New Deal during the 1930s, many reforms in government programs won wide popular support. The Roosevelt administration expanded public employment throughout the country and enacted the public welfare provisions that led to the Social Security system. In this context, proposals for a national health program again attracted widespread attention. The Roosevelt administration proposed NHP legislation to Congress in 1938, but Congress did not act on it. During the late 1930s and early 1940s, congressional leaders held hearings and introduced legislation calling for an NHP. In particular, the Wagner-Murray-Dingell bill, first introduced in Congress during 1943, proposed a universal, compulsory, and comprehensive approach to national health insurance. While generally support-

ive, Roosevelt himself deemphasized action on this bill during World War II.

Late in 1945, President Truman's administration urged Congress to pass a comprehensive NHP that included publicly subsidized insurance providing coverage for all citizens. Although public opinion polls showed wide popular support for Truman's NHP proposal, the AMA again strongly opposed this form of government intervention and organized a national campaign against it. In this campaign, the AMA and its supporters (such as the American Hospital Association and the American Chamber of Commerce) characterized an NHP as "socialized medicine" (Starr 1982, pp. 280–286). As anticommunist sentiment increased during the Korean War and the subsequent Cold War of the 1950s, the political viability of an NHP declined. One irony of this failure was the fact that the Truman administration's approach to an NHP resembled those of several Western European countries, rather than the health systems of the Soviet Union or the Eastern European nations.

With the political upheavals of the 1960s, public sentiment again swung to support for major reforms of health policy. In particular, the civil rights movement and the widespread publicity devoted to the problem of poverty in the United States led to renewed consideration of an NHP. During the Kennedy administration and the first years of the Johnson administration, Congress considered a variety of proposals. In the context of widespread urban unrest, the Johnson administration pushed forward with its Great Society programs to create reforms in public welfare, health, and education. The health reforms passed in the mid-1960s created major changes in public funding but still fell short of a comprehensive NHP.

The enactment of Medicaid and Medicare in 1965 improved the accessibility of services for the poor and elderly, but major problems have remained. (Rogers, Blendon, and Maloney 1982; Calkins, Burns, and Delbanco 1986; Feder, Hadley, and Mullner 1984; Mundinger 1985). The provisions of Medicaid vary by state. Federal Medicaid payments go to only limited categories of the poor. Medicaid has excluded about one-third of U.S. citizens with incomes below the poverty level (Mulstein 1984). On the average, Medicare has paid approximately 44 percent of elderly people's medical expenses (Aiken and Bays 1984).

Although another cycle of interest in an NHP arose during the late 1970s (specific proposals are discussed later in this chapter), no NHP legislation has passed, and gaps in coverage have become more severe. Although Medicaid and Medicare never have covered all people in need, barriers to access have increased markedly during the 1980s. More than 35 million people in the United States are uninsured for at least part of the year (Mundinger 1985). The percentage of poor citizens covered by Medicaid has decreased from 65 percent in 1976 to 46 percent in 1984 (Blendon et al. 1986). Employed people and their dependents comprise more than three-quarters of those in the United States who are uninsured; more than half of the employed uninsured live in middle-income or high-income households (Monheit et al. 1985). The nonpoor with private insurance or Medicare face deductible provisions and limited coverage that frequently create major financial difficulties, as well as frustrating complexities in obtaining benefits (Valentine and Wilson 1985).

During the 1980s, states and counties also have reduced publicly supported services. These reductions have had detrimental effects on many patients' health (Lurie et al. 1984; Lurie et al. 1986). Statistics cannot adequately convey the wrenching emotional and physical impact of restrictive policies on the lives of patients and practitioners (Waitzkin 1984). (Table 1 presents a brief list of typical problems.) It is difficult to justify the suffering of such patients, when appropriate treatment is available

and when we live in a country with abundant economic resources.

Policies That Don't Work

Current health policies in the United States have created a patchwork of programs that leave major gaps in coverage. Policy goals are imprecisely defined, and policy implementation is often erratic and contradictory. Several unsuccessful policies illustrate this theme.

The failure of competitive strategies. During the early 1980s, competitive strategies attracted prominence in health-policy circles. A series of proposals to foster competition among providers, and thus to lower costs, gained wide attention. These strategies included Enthoven's Consumer Choice Health Plan, Stockman's health care voucher program, and various proposals calling for competition among "preferred provider organizations" (PPOs) (Enthoven 1978; Stockman 1980; Siminoff 1986).

Competitive strategies in health care now have received devastating criticism (Siminoff 1986; Ginzburg 1982, 1983). Medical services never have shown the characteristics of a competitive market. Government pays for more than 40 percent of health care. The insurance industry, pharmaceutical industry, and medical equipment manufacturers all manifest monopolistic tendencies that inhibit competition. Hospitals and physicians wield political-economic power through professional organizations that reduce the impact of competitive strategies. Physicians also affect the demand for services, through recommendations about referrals, diagnostic studies, and treatment. Analytically, the effects of competition on reduced costs are difficult to separate from other important changes, especially the general slowing of inflation, the requirement of major copayments by patients, and the impact of prepaid capitations on organizational behavior. The cost savings with current competitive strategies emerge largely from the reduc-

TABLE 1   Financial Barriers to Care at an Academic Medical Center: Selected Case Summaries, 1985–1986

U.S. citizens suffering from cutbacks and increased copayments under Medi-Cal (California's Medicaid program)	eligibility screening process because the condition was not considered an emergency.

U.S. citizens suffering from cutbacks and increased copayments under Medi-Cal (California's Medicaid program)

- A 31-year-old man with severe unilateral headaches could not afford a computerized tomographic (CT) scan of the head because his monthly deductible under Medi-Cal increased from $50 to $250. He later was brought delirious to the emergency room, where emergency CT scan revealed a brain tumor.

- A 56-year-old man with metastatic soft-tissue sarcoma could not afford follow-up visits, medications, visiting nurse, or hospice because his deductible under Medi-Cal had increased to $350 per month.

U.S. citizens facing restrictions due to policies of county-administered Medically Indigent Adult (MIA) Program

- A 63-year-old man with hypertension, renal insufficiency, and prostatic hypertrophy could not gain approval from the county's MIA program under Medi-Cal for a prostatectomy. His urinary retention and renal function have worsened, and he probably will require dialysis within one to two years.

- A 29-year-old woman presented with a breast mass. Mammography was consistent with cancer. Approval of MIA funding for outpatient biopsy was delayed for nearly one month during the

eligibility screening process because the condition was not considered an emergency.

- A 44-year-old had malignant melanoma, confirmed by limited biopsy with incomplete excision. Outpatient surgery for wider resection was delayed for three months by MIA eligibility procedures.

- A 52-year-old man developed unstable angina after a myocardial infarction. The MIA program disapproved funding for coronary angiography.

Undocumented immigrants

- A 22-year-old woman from Costa Rica, without legal documents, presented with sickle cell anemia, cardiac enlargement, and a right axillary mass. For two months, arrangements could not be made for an echocardiogram or biopsy of the mass. As a result, the patient moved to another county in California with less restrictive policies about medical care for the undocumented.

- A 31-year-old undocumented man from Mexico presented with carpal tunnel syndrome of his right hand that interfered with his work as a tailor. Acromegaly associated with a pituitary tumor was diagnosed, but radiation therapy or neurosurgery could not be arranged because of financial impediments. After waiting nearly three months, the patient was lost to follow-up when he returned to Mexico.

Source: Case Reports, 1986–1987, Department of Medicine, University of California-Irvine.

tion of comprehensive benefits, increased copayments, prospective reimbursement to providers, and similar economic measures, rather than from competition per se (Siminoff 1986).

At the practical level, competitive strategies implemented during the early 1980s have led to major dislocations and gaps in services. For example, competitive contracting and prospective reimbursement under Medi-Cal (California's Medicaid system) have worsened the financial crises of hospitals with a large proportion of indigent clients. As a result, the California legislature has enacted a series of "bail-out" measures designed to ease the economic difficulties of these institutions (Iglehart 1984, 1985). Moreover, by disrupting services, the new Medi-Cal policies have led to a measurable worsening of some patients' medical condi-

tions (Lurie et al. 1984; Lurie et al. 1986). In other states, competitive PPOs have suffered severe and unpredicted financial problems, and patients have encountered difficult barriers to access, including direct refusal of care by providers (Moore, Martin, and Richardson 1983; Freeman and Kirkman-Liff 1985; Kirkman-Liff 1985). In short, competitive strategies have exacerbated the difficulties of maldistributed and inaccessible services.

Corporate penetration of health care. Current policies encourage corporate activities in the medical field. By the mid-1970s, private insurance companies, pharmaceutical firms, and medical equipment manufacturers already had achieved lucrative positions in the medical marketplace (Ehrenreich and Ehrenreich 1970; Kotelchuck 1976; Waitzkin and Waterman 1974; Navarro 1976). In the 1980s, multinational corporations have taken over community hospitals in all regions of the country, have acquired or taken over management of many public hospitals, have bought or built teaching hospitals affiliated with medical schools, and have expanded their control of organizations providing ambulatory services (Starr 1982; Relman 1980; Gray 1983; Gray and McNerney 1986). Nationally, for-profit chains control about 15 percent of all hospitals, but in some states (e.g., California, Florida, Tennessee, and Texas) the chains operate between one-third and one-half of hospitals. Ownership of nursing homes by corporate chains has increased by more than 30 percent (Gray 1985). For-profit corporations have enrolled about 70 percent of all health maintenance organization subscribers throughout the country. Between 1981 and 1983 the number of corporate-owned home health agencies tripled, far outstripping those operated by visiting nurse associations, hospitals, skilled nursing homes, and other nonprofit agencies (Gray 1985).

Although enthusiasts perceive several economic advantages of corporate involvement in health care, the substantiation of such claims is quite limited. For example, it is argued that tough-minded managerial techniques will increase efficiency and decrease costs; however, several studies have shown that for-profit health-care organizations are no more efficient than nonprofit ones (Pattison and Katz 1983; Relman 1983; Watt et al. 1986). Similarly, research on corporate management has not supported the claim that corporate takeover can alleviate the chronic financial difficulties of hospitals serving indigent clients (Shonick and Roemer 1982). Corporations appear to offer a source of capital that is difficult to obtain from public or philanthropic sources. However, economic analysts have predicted that the financial strength of health care corporations will decline as a result of prospective reimbursement policies and other restrictions on hospitalization, prior pricing and

markup practices, and use of ancillary services (Pattison and Katz 1983; Lewin, Derzon, and Margulies 1981). Such concerns have contributed to worsened profit margins and stock market performance for several corporate chains. Some corporations have laid off staff members and have initiated rigorous productivity standards that have led to insecurity and dissatisfaction for physicians, nurses, and other employees (Waitzkin et al. 1986).

Corporate involvement in health care also has raised major ethical problems. There is growing concern that corporate strategies lead to reduced services for the poor. Although some corporations have established endowments for indigent care, the ability of such funds to assure long-term access is doubtful, especially when cutbacks occur in public-sector support (Anderson et al. 1985; Feder and Hadley 1985). Other ethical concerns have focused on physicians' conflicting loyalties to patients versus corporations (the "double agent problem"), the unwillingness of for-profit hospitals to provide unprofitable but needed services, and similar issues (Relman 1980; Gray 1983). These observations raise further doubts about the wisdom of policies that encourage corporate penetration of health care.

Public-sector programmatic cutbacks and bureaucratic expansion. The Reagan administration's policies have devastated health and welfare programs. Cutbacks have occurred in the national Medicaid program; Medicare; block grants for maternal and child health, migrant health services, community health centers, and birth control services; health planning; educational assistance for medical students and residents (affecting especially minority recruitment); the National Health Service Corps; the Indian Health Service; and the National Institute of Occupational Safety and Health. Many federally sponsored research programs also have been cut. Measures of health and well-being in the United States have either stopped improving or actually have become worse. For example, the recent halt in the rate of decline in infant mortality coincides with cutbacks in federal prenatal and perinatal programs; in several low-income urban areas, infant mortality has increased (Miller 1985). Among blacks, the maternal, postneonatal, and overall mortality rates have worsened, and a growing proportion of black women have not been able to receive adequate prenatal care (NCHS 1985; Himmelstein 1986; Children's Defense Fund 1986). These reversals in health status and health services, emerging as direct manifestations of changes in federal policies, are unique among economically developed countries.

Alongside these programmatic cutbacks, bureaucratization and regulation in the health care system have grown rapidly (Himmelstein and Woolhandler 1986; Morone and Dunham 1984). The ironic distinction between the rhetoric of reduced government versus the reality of greater government intervention, is nowhere clearer than in the Medicare diagnosis-related group (DRG) program. Intended as a cost-control device, DRGs have introduced unprecedented complexity and bureaucratic regulation. By providing reimbursement to hospitals at a fixed rate for specific diagnoses, DRGs encourage hospitals to limit the length of stay, as well as services provided during hospitalization. Hospitals have responded to DRG regulations with an expansion of their own bureaucratic staffs and data-processing operations, more intensive utilization review, and a tendency to discharge patients with unstable conditions when DRG payments are exhausted. Private hospitals admitting a small proportion of indigent patients have profited under DRGs; public and university hospitals that serve a higher percentage of indigent and multiproblem patients face an unfavorable case mix within specific DRGs and thus have fared poorly (Kotelchuck 1985; Stern and Epstein 1985). Moreover, DRGs' contribution to cost controls remains unclear, in comparison to other factors, such as reduced

inflation in the economy as a whole. Despite recent proposals for catastrophic coverage, Medicare copayments required from the elderly have continued to increase.

Some have argued that the growth of bureaucratic power has paved the way for a new national health policy that may enter, as it were, by the back door. DRGs have fundamentally modified government's role in health care. From this viewpoint, DRGs may have established the political conditions for a government-centered hospital system providing universal coverage (Morone and Dunham 1984). Although such an outcome is debatable, there is little question that federal support for health services has declined, as bureaucratic and administrative complexity has increased.

Inappropriate policy analysis in a nonrational system. While the United States continues to lack a coherent national health policy, the analysis of policy emphasizes methods that seldom affect political decision making. During the past decade, several innovative techniques have gained prominence in health policy analysis. Derived mostly from economics and management theory, these quantitative methodologies aim to clarify decisions in both policy and clinical practice. Cost-effectiveness analysis, cost-benefit analysis, clinical decision analysis, and new approaches in clinical epidemiology typify such attempts to rationalize decision making. The quantitative orientation of these methods has created an optimism that scientific transformation of health policy will lead to more rational procedures.

On a technical level, critics have raised several objections to these methods. As one example, clinical decision analysis (CDA) frequently uses practitioners' subjective assessments of probabilities to quantify decisions in clinical practice. The quantified results of CDA tend to mask the underlying subjective assumptions of the model; furthermore, the method is complex and difficult to use without computing resources and expertise (Feinstein 1977;

Harris 1981; Sox 1986). Although CDA and similar techniques can clarify certain aspects of medical practice, the optimism that these methods can solve the major problems of high costs, disorganization, and other structural irrationalities of health care is unrealistic.

Similarly, cost-effectiveness analysis (CEA) and cost-benefit analysis (CBA) depend on quantification of fundamentally subjective values. For example, these approaches frequently quantify the effects of a particular policy in terms of the financial value of additional years of life. Discounting techniques that evaluate life differently at various ages contain assumptions with dubious scientific merit (Avorn 1984). In these techniques, cost calculations usually employ the *price* of a particular technology, drug, or service, rather than the *cost* of production and distribution. Therefore, CEA and CBA usually do not examine critically the profit that derives from the gap between cost and price (Waitzkin 1982). These approaches also ignore both ethical considerations and the political process of policymaking. Economists who developed these techniques to clarify military policies at the Defense Department clearly pointed out that such "imponderable" features of policy decisions are not quantifiable (Hitch and McKean 1967). As CEA and CBA have entered the medical field, however, their inherent methodologic limitations in policy matters have not received wide attention.

Most importantly, even if these approaches involved better science, there is always a tenuous relationship between knowledge and power. The vision that scientific methods will lead to a rationally ordered society pervades the history of the natural and social sciences of the last century (Waitzkin 1968). Public policy decisions, however, emerge from a complex process in which political and economic power figures as prominently as rational knowledge, if not more so (Stockman 1986). CDA, CEA, CBA, and similar techniques do not deal adequately with such important determinants of health policy.

Rationality is only part of the process of policymaking, and probably a small part at that. Even a sound science of health policy will make only modest contributions to the construction of a rationally organized health care system (Lewis 1977).

The Results of Policies That Don't Work

Health care in the United States shows a number of important strengths. Patients with adequate insurance or personal wealth, for instance, can choose from a wide variety of high-quality medical institutions and practitioners. For such individuals, suitable care is easily accessible. Furthermore, the ability to earn substantial profit in the health sector has provided a motivation for remarkable technological achievements.

On the other hand, current policies do not adequately address basic problems of health care in the United States, and the results are very unpleasant. First, there is persistent exploitation of illness and suffering for private profit. Despite concerns about cost containment, corporate profitability in health care has encountered minimal constraints. For instance, after-tax profits for corporations with activities in health care have ranked the third highest among U.S. industrial groups (Forbes 1985). A related irony is that, despite the rhetoric of competition, health care faces increasing monopolization by a small number of large corporations and insurance companies, while smaller health care institutions have faced great difficulties in competing successfully.

Chaos, both financial and organizational, is a second major characteristic of U.S. health care. The finances of private and public insurance programs are difficult to understand for both professionals and laypersons. Gaps in insurance coverage frequently surprise even those who consider themselves well insured, and collecting benefits from insurance companies and government agencies is often very complex (Valentine and Wilson 1985). Because there is no universal entitlement to basic health care in the United States, the availability of services depends on local conditions. In some geographical regions, there is a surplus of health professionals; in others, a shortage. Access varies according to patients' personal finances, initiative, and linguistic abilities. A laissez-faire approach to planning and organization has created a situation where the world's most sophisticated medicine is available for a fortunate portion of the population, while others encounter major barriers to care.

A third feature of our current situation is callousness. Before the advent of Medicare and Medicaid, many doctors allocated some of their practice hours to patients who could not afford full fees. Municipal or county hospitals served the poor in most regions, and numerous private hospitals had charity wards (Starr 1982, pp. 180–197). The fact that charity medicine never fully met such needs was one motivation for the passage of federal programs in the 1960s. Now that devastating cutbacks have affected public programs, however, the ethic of charity no longer provides limited protection for the poor. Even when they want to care for indigent patients, practitioners frequently cannot arrange for needed hospitalization, diagnostic procedures, or treatments for uninsured or underinsured patients. The frustration of caring for the poor with inadequate public resources often leads to retreat from responsibility. Wearing blinders to the suffering in our midst then becomes a convenient defense. The resulting callousness is perhaps the most troubling feature of our present condition.

A NATIONAL HEALTH PROGRAM FOR THE UNITED STATES

A national health program (NHP), including elements of national health insurance (NHI) and a national health service (NHS), could help solve the problems that we face. NHI has waxed and waned in policy analy-

sis, and it doubtless will continue to do so. An NHS has not attracted widespread interest in the United States until recently.

Weaknesses of Prior Proposals for National Health Insurance

During the late 1970s, the U.S. Congress considered at least eighteen separate proposals for NHI. The supporters of these measures ranged across a wide political spectrum. Conservative supporters included the Nixon administration, the AMA, the American Hospital Association, and the Health Insurance Association of America. At the liberal end of the spectrum was Senator Edward Kennedy, who introduced a series of NHI proposals in collaboration with other legislators in the Senate and House of Representatives.

These NHI plans differed in important details. The conservative proposals, for example, called for major cost-sharing by patients, who would be required to pay for deductible copayments up to a specific limit each year before NHI would assume responsibility for medical bills. The liberal proposals reduced or eliminated the requirement for copayments. In addition, the conservative plans would have included participation by private insurance companies as fiscal intermediaries in distributing NHI payments from the government to physicians and hospitals. The liberal proposals called for eliminating the expensive involvement of the private insurance industry in NHI. Liberal plans for NHI also sought more extensive participation by consumers in policymaking than did the conservative proposals.

Despite wide support for NHI during the late 1970s, Congress did not enact NHI legislation. The reasons for this failure were complex. The severe economic recession of 1974, coupled with the inflationary trends that followed, meant that President Carter's administration could not advocate an approach to NHI that might increase costs. Political competition between Carter and Kennedy over the details of NHI weakened the Democratic Party's support for the measure. Liberal advocates of NHI disagreed about incorporating organizational elements of an NHS into proposals for reform. Most important, politicians and professional associations could not resolve the basic differences between the conservative and liberal approaches to NHI. When the Reagan administration took power in 1981, a policy of cutbacks in health and welfare programs eliminated the possibility that NHI could be enacted in the near future.

Within the range of NHI proposals considered during the late 1970s, several fundamental problems became clear. First, NHI would have changed payment mechanisms, not the organization of the health care system. Under these proposals, the federal government would have guaranteed payment for most health services. However, NHI would not have required that practitioners work in different ways, in different areas, or with different patients. The nature of private practice would have remained intact, and the organization of hospitals and other medical institutions would not have changed in any basic way (Waitzkin 1983, pp. 218–220).

Most plans for NHI would not have covered all needed medical services. Coinsurance provisions would have required out-of-pocket payment for some fixed percentage of health spending. Under coinsurance, as noted above, an individual or family pays the initial costs up to a specified amount before NHI takes over. For example, several NHI plans would have asked a person to pay 25 percent of all medical bills out-of-pocket, up to a maximum liability of $1,000 per year.

In most proposals, new and compulsory taxation—usually fixed payroll deductions—would have paid for NHI. The financing arrangements for NHI therefore would have been regressive; that is, low-income people would have paid a proportionately higher part of their income for health care than would the wealthy. Although various tax mechanisms could relieve the burden of health insurance for low-income patients, legislators have devoted little attention to this issue (Mitchell and Schwartz 1976).

In most NHI proposals, private insurance companies would have served as the fiscal intermediaries for NHI. They would have received compensation for distributing NHI payments from the government to health providers. Such provisions thus would have assured continued profits for the private insurance industry.

Regarding accessibility, NHI proposals contained few provisions for improving geographical maldistribution of health professionals. In some proposals fee schedules were higher for doctors who practiced in underserved areas, but such incentives could not assure that physicians actually would work in these areas (Waitzkin 1983, pp. 218–220).

Perspectives from Other Countries

A successful NHP for the United States would contain elements of both NHI and an NHS. Such an NHP would correct the weaknesses of prior NHI proposals and would achieve basic changes in the organizational structure of the health care system. The fundamental principle of the NHP would be that adequate health care is a basic human right. Thus, the NHP would strive toward equity in the availability of services, across geographical boundaries and income differentials.

Planning an NHP would require serious and open-minded consideration of NHI plans and NHSs around the world. Most countries in Western Europe and Scandinavia have initiated NHS structures, permitting private practice in addition to a strong public sector (Roemer 1985; Abel-Smith 1985; Sidel and Sidel 1983). Canada has achieved universal entitlement to health care through an NHI program that depends on private practitioners, private hospitals, and strong planning and coordinating roles for the national and provincial governments (Iglehart 1986;

Evans 1984; Detsky et al. 1986; Detsky, Stacey, and Bombardier 1983; Contandriopoulos 1986). Socialist countries in Europe, Asia, Africa, and Latin America have adopted an NHS as the basic organizational structure of the health care system, while permitting a continuing role for private practitioners (Waitzkin 1983, pp. 187–213).

NHPs vary widely in the degree to which the national government employs health professionals and owns health institutions. For example, the NHPs of Great Britain, Denmark, and the Netherlands contract with self-employed general practitioners for primary care; Canadian private practitioners receive insurance payments mainly on a fee-for-service basis; in Finland and Sweden a high proportion of practicing doctors work as salaried employees of government agencies. In Great Britain the national government owns most hospitals; regional or local governments own many hospitals in Sweden, Finland, and other Scandinavian countries; and Canada's system depends on governmental budgeting for both public and private hospitals.

The problems that have arisen in existing NHPs deserve attention (Waitzkin 1983, pp. 222–229). For example, the British NHS faces chronic financial difficulties that derive from a number of factors, including Britain's relatively lower level of national wealth, declines in industrial productivity, the severe recession of the mid-1970s, and a parallel private health care sector that consumes financial and professional resources. Rationing has affected the availability of elective surgery and technically advanced procedures like dialysis in Great Britain's NHS, although analysts have noted that Britain probably rations primary care and long-term care less than the United States; rationing has not occurred to nearly the same extent in other Western European countries, Scandinavia, or Canada (Aaron and Schwartz 1984; Miller and Miller 1986). (In Britain, despite various inconveniences, the NHS commands support from the majority of physicians and the general public.) Major bureaucratic inefficiencies have arisen in several NHSs, including the socialist systems of some Eastern European countries (Roemer 1985; Weinerman 1969). While such difficulties should be examined, the achievements of NHSs also need more attention. Throughout the world, such advantages have led to a growing trend toward the establishment of NHSs based on universal entitlement to care (Abel-Smith 1985).

The Canadian system is particularly pertinent to the United States, because of geographical proximity and cultural similarity (Iglehart 1986; Evans 1984; Detsky et al. 1986; Detsky, Stacey, and Bombardier 1983; Contandriopoulos 1986). Canada offers a combination of national and provincial insurance programs that assure universal entitlement to health care. Doctors generally receive public insurance payments through fee-for-service arrangements. Hospitals obtain public funds through prospectively negotiated contracts, eliminating the need to bill for specific services. Progressive taxation finances the Canadian system, and the private insurance industry does not play a major role in the program's administration. Most Canadian provinces have initiated policies that aim to correct remaining problems of access based on geographical maldistribution. Cost controls in Canada depend on contracted global budgeting with hospitals, limitations on reimbursements to practitioners (the latter policy remains controversial for physicians in some provinces), and markedly lower administrative expenses because of reduced eligibility, billing, and collection procedures.

Potential Problems in a U.S. National Health Program

A commonly expressed concern about an NHP focuses on costs. The costs of U.S. health care already are quite high, accounting for approximately 11 percent of the gross national product, a higher percentage than in Canada or any European country with an NHP (Iglehart 1986). It is often presumed that an NHP with expanded entitlement to services would increase U.S. health care costs substantially.

However, the presumption that an NHP would increase costs is not necessarily correct; depending on how an NHP is organized, costs might well fall to below their current level. First of all, a major savings would derive from reduced administrative overhead for complex billing operations, collection procedures, eligibility determinations, and other bureaucratic functions that no longer would be necessary. In the Canadian NHP, for instance, global budgeting for hospitals has greatly reduced such expensive administrative procedures and has contributed to substantial cost control on both the provincial and national levels (Iglehart 1986; Detsky et al. 1986). An NHP also can restrict private profit to corporations in the medical field. For example, a much smaller role for the private insurance industry has led to markedly lower costs in Canada.

Recent analyses have shown that cost savings under an NHP from reduced administrative functions and entrepreneurialism could total over $40 billion annually. Administrative cost savings would derive chiefly from reductions in insurance overhead, physicians' overhead, hospital administration, and nursing home administration; restrictions on profit would affect the private insurance industry, pharmaceutical companies, medical equipment firms, and for-profit chains (Himmelstein and Woolhandler 1986, 1987). These savings could occur even if private practice continued within the NHP, as it does in Great Britain, Canada, and many other countries, and even if physicians' incomes remained at their present levels. Several additional studies have shown that countries with publicly organized NHPs can provide universal entitlement to health care services while controlling costs far more successfully than has been possible in the United States (Navarro 1985).

A second potential problem in a federally organized NHP concerns administrative and bureaucratic responsiveness. As noted above, bureaucratic inefficiencies have plagued the NHSs in several Eastern European countries and periodically have attracted criticism in Great Britain. In the United States there is a traditional skepticism about the role of public bureaucracy; federal health care agencies have functioned less smoothly than health care professionals and the general public would like.

Although the difficulties of public bureaucracy have no simple solutions, NHPs in other countries have achieved workable arrangements that have won wide professional and popular support. Observers of the NHPs in Canada, Western Europe, and Scandinavia, for example, have noted efficient procedures and an overall reduction of administrative personnel and costs, compared to the United States. These efficiencies derive largely from the global budgeting of hospitals and elimination of unessential administrative overhead. In this country, without an NHP, cumbersome bureaucracy has fostered high costs and widespread frustration. A responsive and efficient administrative structure is one of the most important challenges in creating an NHP for the United States.

Sociocultural differences between the United States and countries with existing NHPs need consideration. European and Scandinavian countries with long histories of social welfare programs have enacted NHPs with less fanfare than might be anticipated in the United States. In Canada, a smaller population, fewer provinces, decentralized governmental practices, and traditions of cooperative interaction among government, hospitals, and the professions have aided the NHP's implementation.

On the other hand, it is inappropriate to overemphasize such sociocultural differences. The United States has implemented nationally coordinated programs that have achieved wide acceptance, including the Social Security system, protective regulation of banking and economic policy, and police and security practices. Moreover, public opinion polls consistently have shown that a majority of the U.S. population favors an NHP that assures universal entitlement to basic health care services (Navarro 1982; Shapiro and Young 1986). Such an NHP not only would protect health but also would reduce the financial insecurity that the risk of illness creates. Although an NHP would need to recognize the uniqueness of U.S. sociocultural traditions, these traditions are not insurmountable barriers to an NHP that addresses the needs of the American people.

How to deal with individual responsibility and prevention is another important challenge for an NHP. A substantial portion of the disease burden of the United States and other industrialized countries derives from self-destructive individual behaviors such as smoking, alcohol consumption, and drug abuse. An NHP would need to implement programs of prevention that encourage individuals to take responsibility for their personal health habits. Other preventive programs should address hypertension control, prenatal and perinatal care, nutrition, and occupational and environmental hazards. There is precedent for a strong emphasis on prevention in the NHPs of several Western European and Scandinavian countries. These models would be useful in planning an NHP for the United States that provides universal entitlement to needed services while promoting individual responsibility for positive health practices.

Principles and Prospects for a U.S. National Health Program

Since the mid-1970s, planners have worked with members of Congress and other prominent politicians in drafting NHP proposals that would include elements of NHI and an NHS (U.S. Congress 1985, 1986; Navarro 1986; Terris 1983). Such proposals deserve careful consideration now that other policies have failed.

Taken together, these plans include a number of basic principles for an NHP.

1. The NHP would provide for comprehensive care, including diagnostic, therapeutic, preventive, rehabilitative, environmental, and occupational health services; dental and eye care; transportation to medical facilities; social work; and counseling.

2. These services would not involve out-of-pocket payments at the "point of delivery."

3. Financing for the NHP would come from taxation of individual and corporate income, plus a tax on gifts and estates. Taxation would be progressive, with higher-income individuals and corporations paying taxes at a higher rate.

4. The NHP would reduce administrative costs and private profit in the health care system. A national commission would establish a generic formulary of approved drugs, devices, equipment, and supplies. A national trust fund would disburse payments to health facilities through global and prospective budgeting. Profit to private insurance companies and other corporations would be closely restricted.

5. Professional associations would negotiate the fee structures for health care practitioners. Financial incentives would encourage cost-control measures through health maintenance organizations, community health centers, and a plurality of practice settings.

6. To improve geographical distribution of health professionals, the NHP would provide free education and training, in return for required periods of service by medical graduates in underserved areas.

7. The NHP would initiate programs of prevention that would emphasize individual responsibility for health, risk reduction, nutrition, maternal and infant care, long-term services for the elderly, occupational and environmental health, and related health promotional interventions.

Support for an NHP in the United States is growing rapidly. For instance, the American Public Health Association (APHA) has passed several resolutions calling for an NHP; sessions concerning an NHP occur regularly at the APHA's national and regional conventions. The Coalition for a National Health System is a nationwide organization that is coordinating educational and organizing efforts throughout the country. Leaders and members of senior citizens' groups, including the Gray Panthers, the American Association of Retired Persons, and the Congress of California Seniors, have taken a very prominent role in working for an NHP.

Ballot initiatives in several states have focused on the need for an NHP. In November 1986, 67 percent of Massachusetts voters supported a proposal urging the U.S. Congress to enact an NHP that

provides high quality comprehensive personal health care including preventive, curative and occupational health services; is universal in coverage, community controlled, rationally organized, equitably financed, with no out-of-pocket charges, is sensitive to the particular health needs of all, and is efficient in containing its cost; and whose yearly expenditure does not exceed the proportion of the Gross National Product spent on health care in the immediately preceding fiscal year. (Commonwealth of Massachusetts 1985; see Danielson and Mazer 1986)

In California a ballot initiative on an NHP has been introduced in the state legislature (California Legislature 1985). Similar efforts are under way in other states to bring the option of an NHP to the voting public.

Will the medical profession continue to oppose an NHP? At the present time, dissatisfaction is rising among physicians. Practitioners face increased cost controls and bureaucratic obstacles in collecting fees. The conditions of practice have become more constrained, incomes have tended to plateau or even to decline, and individuals entering practice face financial uncertainty. More than half of all physicians now work in salaried positions, often within for-profit organizations that closely regulate productivity. Some observers have claimed that these constraints are creating a "proletarianized" medical profession (McKinlay and Arches 1985). Under these circumstances, it is important to note that

in Canada, Western Europe, and Scandinavia, despite periodic problems and reorganizations, NHPs now claim wide professional support (Abel-Smith 1985). Soon after the passage of Medicare and Medicaid, the opinions of U.S. physicians quickly reversed; by 1968 a majority of physicians favored these public programs (Colombotos and Kirchner 1986). Predictably, similar changes in professional opinion about an NHP also will occur in the United States. The seeds of these changes are evident in the AMA's proposals for a coherent national health policy (Balfe et al. 1985) and in the wide professional support for catastrophic Medicare coverage.

Strong opposition to an NHP will come from the corporations that currently benefit from the lack of an appropriate national policy: the private insurance industry, pharmaceutical and medical equipment firms, and the for-profit chains. While corporate resistance should not be underestimated, there is also potential support for an NHP from the corporate world. The costs of private-sector medicine have become a major burden to many nonmedical companies that provide health insurance as a fringe benefit to employees. Corporations that do not directly profit from health care have influenced public policy in the direction of cost containment (Triton Corporation 1986). In Western Europe and Scandinavia, corporations have come to look kindly on the cost controls and services that NHPs provide, even when corporate taxation contributes to NHP financing (Abel-Smith 1985). As the crisis of health care costs continues to affect U.S. corporations, they too may examine an NHP as a positive option.

The Time for a National Health Program Has Come

We in the United States need and deserve a national health program that protects all people who live in this country from unnecessary illness, suffering, and early death. Current health policies—

competitive strategies, corporate involvement, federal cutbacks and bureaucratic expansion, and inappropriate policy analysis—have failed. The results of these failures include continued exploitation of illness for private profit, chaotic financial and organizational arrangements, and an increasing callousness about human suffering.

An NHP is a policy that will help solve these problems. Most importantly, it will provide entitlement to health care as a basic human right. In addition to controlling health care costs, an NHP will improve the way our system is organized and will remove many of the most frustrating features of medical practice. Given the suffering in our midst, can we now aim for anything less?

ACKNOWLEDGMENTS

Work on this chapter was supported in part by grants from the National Endowment for the Humanities (FA–22922) and the Division of Medicine of the U.S. Public Health Service (PE–19154).

REFERENCES

Aaron, H. J., and W. B. Schwartz. 1984. *The Painful Prescription: Rationing Hospital Care.* Washington, D.C.: The Brookings Institution.

Abel-Smith, B. 1985. Who Is the Odd Man Out?: The Experience of Western Europe in Containing the Costs of Health Care. *Milbank Memorial Fund Quarterly* 63:1–17.

Aiken, L. H., and K. D. Bays. 1984. The Medicare Debate—Round One. *New England Journal of Medicine* 311:1196–1200.

Anderson, G. F., C. J. Schramm, C. R. Rapoza, S. C. Renn, and G. D. Pillari. 1985. Investor-Owned Chains and Teaching Hospitals: The Implications of Acquisition. *New England Journal of Medicine* 313:201–204.

Avorn, J. 1984. Benefit and Cost Analysis in Geriatric Care: Turning Age Discrimination into Health Policy. *New England Journal of Medicine* 310:1294–1301.

Balfe, B. E., J. F. Boyle, S. J. Brocki, and K. R. Lane. 1985. A Health Policy Agenda for the American People. Phase I: the Principles. *Journal of the American Medical Association* 254:2440–2448.

Blendon, R. J., L. H. Aiken, H. E. Freeman, and B. L. Kirkman-Liff. 1986. Uncompensated Care by Hospitals or Public Insurance for the Poor: Does It Make a Difference? *New England Journal of Medicine* 314:1160–1163.

California Legislature. 1985. Assembly Bill No. 1743. Sacramento: Assembly, March 7.

Calkins, D. R., L. A. Burns, and T. L. Delbanco. 1986. Ambulatory Care and the Poor: Tracing the Impact of Changes in Federal Policy. *Journal of General Internal Medicine* 1:109–115.

Children's Defense Fund. *A Children's Defense Budget: An Analysis of the FY 1987 Federal Budget and Children.* Washington, D.C.: The Fund, 1986.

Colombotos, J., and C. Kirchner. 1986. *Physicians and Social Change.* New York: Oxford University Press.

Committee on the Costs of Medical Care (CCMC). 1932. *Medical Care for the American People: the Final Report of the Committee.* Chicago: University of Chicago Press.

Commonwealth of Massachusetts. 1985. An Act Requiring a Nonbinding Question on the Ballot Regarding a National Health Program. Chapter 324, Laws of the Commonwealth, Boston.

Contandriopoulos A. P. 1986. Cost Containment through Payment Mechanisms: The Quebec Experience. *Journal of Public Health Policy* 7:224–238.

Danielson, D. A., and A. Mazer. 1986. The Massachusetts Referendum for a National Health Program. *Journal of Public Health Policy* 7:161–173.

Detsky, A. S., H. B. Abrams, L. Ladha, and S. R. Stacey. 1986. Global Budgeting and the Teaching Hospital in Ontario. *Medical Care* 24:89–94.

Detsky, A. S., S. R. Stacey, and C. Bombardier. 1983. The Effectiveness of a Regulatory Strategy in Containing Hospital Costs: The Ontario Experience, 1967–1981. *New England Journal of Medicine* 309:151–159.

Ehrenreich, B., and J. Ehrenreich, eds. 1970. *The American Health Empire*. New York: Vintage.

Enthoven, A. C. 1978. Consumer Choice Health Plan. *New England Journal of Medicine* 298:650–658, 709–720.

Evans, R. G. 1984. *Strained Mercy: The Economics of Canadian Health Care*. Toronto: Butterworths.

Falk, I. S. 1983. Some Lessons from the Fifty Years Since the CCMC Final Report. *Journal of Public Health Policy* 4:135–161.

Feder, J., and J. Hadley. 1985. The Economically Unattractive Patient: Who Cares? *Bulletin of the New York Academy of Medicine* 61:68–74.

Feder, J., J. Hadley, and R. Mullner. 1984. Falling through the Cracks: Poverty, Insurance Coverage, and Hospital Care for the Poor. *Milbank Memorial Fund Quarterly* 62:544–566.

Feinstein, A. R. 1977. The Haze of Bayes, the Aerial Palaces of Decision Analysis, and the Computerized Ouija Board. *Clinical Pharmacology and Therapeutics* 21:482–496.

Forbes. 1985. Annual Report on American Industry. January 12:260.

Freeman, H. E., and B. L. Kirkman-Liff. 1985. Health Care Under AHCCCS: An Examination of Arizona's Alternative to Medicaid. *Health Services Research* 20:245–266.

Ginzberg, E. 1982. Procompetition in Health Care: Policy or Fantasy? *Milbank Memorial Fund Quarterly* 60:386–398.

———. 1983. The Grand Illusion of Competition in Health Care. *Journal of the American Medical Association* 249:1857–1859.

Gray, B. H., ed. 1983. *The New Health Care for Profit: Doctors and Hospitals in a Competitive Environment*. Washington, D.C.: National Academy Press (Report of the Institute of Medicine, National Academy of Sciences).

Gray, B. H. 1985. Overview: Origins and Trends. The New Entrepreneurialism in Health Care. *Bulletin of the New York Academy of Medicine* 61:7–22.

Gray, B. H., and W. J. McNerney. 1986. For-Profit Enterprise in Health Care: The Institute of Medicine Study. *New England Journal of Medicine* 314:1523–1528.

Harris, J. M. 1981. The Hazards of Bedside Bayes. *Journal of the American Medical Association* 246:2602–2605.

Himmelstein, D. U. 1986. Health Care for the Poor: Recent Trends. Paper presented at the annual meeting of the American College of Physicians, San Francisco, April.

Himmelstein, D. U., and S. Woolhandler. 1986. Cost without Benefit: Administrative Waste in U.S. Health Care. *New England Journal of Medicine* 314:441–445.

———. 1987. Socialized Medicine: The Solution to the Cost Crisis in U.S. Health Care. *International Journal of Health Services* 17:339–354.

Hirshfield. D. 1970. *The Lost Reform: The Campaign for Compulsory Health Insurance in the United States from 1932 to 1943*. Cambridge, Mass.: Harvard University Press.

Hitch, C. J., and R. N. McKean. 1967. *The Economics of Defense in the Nuclear Age*. New York: Atheneum.

Iglehart, J. W. 1984. Cutting Costs of Health Care for the Poor in California: A Two-Year Follow-up. *New England Journal of Medicine* 311:745–748.

———. 1985. Medical Care of the Poor—A Growing Problem. *New England Journal of Medicine* 313:59–63.

———. 1986. Canada's Health Care System. *New England Journal of Medicine* 315:202–208, 778–784, 1623–1628.

Kirkman-Liff, B. L. 1985. Refusal of Care: Evidence from Arizona. *Health Affairs* 4:15–24.

Kotelchuck, D., ed. 1976. *Prognosis Negative: Crisis in the Health Care System*. New York: Vintage.

Kotelchuck, R. 1985. Poor Diagnosis, Poor Treatment: How the DRG System Affects Hospitals That Serve the Poor. *Health/PAC Bulletin* 16:7–13.

Lewin, L. S., R. A. Derzon, and R. Margulies. 1981. Investor-Owneds and Non-Profits Differ in Economic Performance. *Hospitals* 55:52–58.

Lewis, C. E. 1977. Health Services Research and Innovations in Health Care Delivery: Does Research Make a Difference? *New England Journal of Medicine* 297:423–427.

Lurie, N., N. B. Ward, M. F. Shapiro and R. H. Brook. 1984. Termination of Medi-Cal: Does it Affect Health? *New England Journal of Medicine* 311:480–484.

Lurie, N., N. B. Ward, M. F. Shapiro, C. Gallego, R. Vaghaiwalla and R. H. Brook. 1986. Termination of Medi-Cal Benefits: A

Follow-up Study One Year Later. *New England Journal of Medicine* 314:1266–1268.

McKinlay, J. B., and J. Arches. 1985. Towards the Proletarianization of Physicians. *International Journal of Health Services* 15:161–195.

Miller, C. A. 1985. Infant Mortality in the U.S. *Scientific American* 253:31–37.

Miller, F. H., and G. A. H. Miller. 1986. The Painful Prescription: A Procrustean Perspective. *New England Journal of Medicine* 314:1383–1386.

Mitchell, B. M., and W. B. Schwartz. 1976. Strategies for Financing National Health Insurance: Who Wins and Who Loses. *New England Journal of Medicine* 295:866–871.

Monheit, A. C., M. M. Hagan, M. L. Berk, and P. J. Farley. 1985. The Employed Uninsured and the Role of Public Policy. *Inquiry* 22:348–364.

Moore, S. H., D. P. Martin, and W. C. Richardson. 1983. Does the Primary-Care Gatekeeper Control the Costs of Health Care?: Lessons from the SAFECO Experience. *New England Journal of Medicine* 309:1400–1404.

Morone, J. A., and A. B. Dunham. 1984. Slouching toward National Health Insurance: The New Health Care Politics. *Yale Journal of Regulation* 2:263–291.

Mulstein, S. 1984. The Uninsured and the Financing of Uncompensated Care: Scope, Costs, and Policy Options. *Inquiry* 21:214–229.

Mundinger, M. O. 1985. Health Service Funding Cuts and the Declining Health of the Poor. *New England Journal of Medicine* 313:44–46.

National Center for Health Statistics (NCHS). 1985. Health—United States. DHHS Publication No. (PHS) 86–1232.

Navarro, V. 1976. *Medicine under Capitalism.* New York: Prodist.

———. 1982. Where Is the Popular Mandate? *New England Journal of Medicine* 307:1516–1518.

———. 1985. The Public/Private Mix in the Funding and Delivery of Health Services: An International Survey. *American Journal of Public Health* 75:1318–1320.

———. 1986. *The Need for a National Health Program: A Memorandum to Reverend Jesse Jackson, Rainbow Coalition.* Baltimore: Johns Hopkins University.

Pattison, R. V., and H. M. Katz. 1983. Investor-Owned Hospitals and Health-Care Costs. *New England Journal of Medicine* 309:347–353.

Relman, A. S. 1980. The New Medical-Industrial Complex. *New England Journal of Medicine* 303:963–970.

———. 1983. Investor-Owned Hospitals and Health-Care Costs. *New England Journal of Medicine* 309:370–372.

Roemer, M. I. 1985. *National Strategies for Health Care Organization.* Ann Arbor: Health Administration Press.

Roemer, M. I., and I. S. Falk. 1985. The Committee on the Costs of Medical Care and the Drive for National Health Insurance. *American Journal of Public Health* 75:841–848.

Rogers. D. E., R. J. Blendon, and T. W. Moloney. 1982. Who Needs Medicaid? *New England Journal of Medicine* 307:13–18.

Shapiro, R. Y., and J. T. Young. 1986. The Polls: Medical Care in the United States. *Public Opinion Quarterly* 50:418–428.

Shonick, W., and R. Roemer. 1982. Private Management of California County Hospitals: Expectations and Performance. *Public Affairs Report* (Bulletin of the Institute of Governmental Studies) 23:1–11.

Sidel, V. W., and R. Sidel. 1983. *A Healthy State: An International Perspective on the Crisis in United States Medical Care.* New York: Pantheon.

Siminoff, L. 1986. Competition and Primary Care in the United States: Separating Fact from Fancy. *International Journal of Health Services* 16:57–69.

Sox, H. C. 1986. Probability Theory in the Use of Diagnostic Tests: An Introduction to Critical Study of the Literature. *Annals of Internal Medicine* 104:60–66.

Starr, P. 1982. *The Social Transformation of American Medicine.* New York: Basic Books.

Stern, R. S., and A. M. Epstein. 1985. Institutional Responses to Prospective Payment Based on Diagnosis-Related Groups. *New England Journal of Medicine* 312:621–627.

Stockman, D. 1980. Can Fee for Service Private Practice Survive Competition? *Forum on Medicine* 3:21–25.

———. 1986. *Triumph of Politics.* New York: Harper and Row.

Terris, M. 1983. A Cost-Effective National Health Program. *Journal of Public Health Policy* 4:252–258.

Triton Corporation. 1986. *Best Practices of Business Coalitions and Health Planning Agencies in Controlling Health Care Costs.* U.S. Department of Health and Human Services, Office of Health Planning, Contract No. 240–85–0502. Washington, D.C.: Government Printing Office.

U.S. Congress. House. 1985. *To Establish a United States Health Service to Provide High Quality Health Care and to Overcome the Deficiencies in the Present System of Health Care Delivery.* H. R. 2049. Bill prepared by R. V. Dellums.

———. 1986. *U.S. Health: An American Health Plan.* H. R. 5070. Bill prepared by E. R. Roybal.

Valentine, R., and H. Wilson. 1985. *The Medical Mess: A Survivor's Guide to Health Care Costs and Health Insurance in the 1980's.* Murray, Ky.: MCS Publications.

Waitzkin, H. 1968. Truth's Search for Power: The Dilemmas of the Social Sciences. *Social Problems* 15:408–418.

———. 1982. Cost versus Price in Cost-Effectiveness Analysis: The Example of Cimetidine. Paper presented at the annual meeting of the American Public Health Association, Montreal.

———. 1983. *The Second Sickness: Contradictions of Capitalist Health Care.* New York: Free Press.

———. 1984. Two-Class Medicine Returns to the United States. *Lancet* 17:1144–1146.

Waitzkin, H., B. V. Akin, L. M. de la Maza, F. A. Hubbell, H. Meshkinpour, L. Rucker, and J. S. Tobis. 1986. Deciding against Corporate Management of a State-Supported Academic Medical Center. *New England Journal of Medicine* 315:1299–1304.

Waitzkin, H., and B. Waterman. 1974. *The Exploitation of Illness in Capitalist Society.* Indianapolis: Bobbs-Merrill.

Watt, J. M., R. A. Derzon, S. C. Renn, C. J. Schramm, J. S. Hahn, and G. D. Pillari. 1986. The Comparative Economic Performance of Investor-Owned Chain and Not-For-Profit Hospitals. *New England Journal of Medicine* 314:89–96.

Weinermann, R. 1969. *Social Medicine in Eastern Europe.* Cambridge, Mass.: Harvard University Press.

24

SOCIOLOGICAL PERSPECTIVES ON ETHICAL ISSUES IN MEDICAL AND HEALTH CARE

JAMES R. SORENSON
JUDITH P. SWAZEY

INTRODUCTION

Numerous indicators reflect a growing interest in ethical issues in medical and health care. For example, seldom does the popular press any longer simply report the latest biomedical development. Increasingly, media coverage includes discussion of ethical issues surrounding such developments, as has been the case with reproductive technologies such as surrogate motherhood. Moreover, professional organizations are devoting more time at their meetings and more space in their publications to discussion of ethical issues (Gottlieb, Burdine, and McLeroy 1987). As a final indicator, biomedical ethics as a discipline has expanded significantly over the past decade. A cursory review of *The Bibliography of Bioethics*, a major bibliographical resource for this field, reveals a large number of publications referenced and the scope of ethical issues covered (Walters 1975).

Against this background one might sus-

pect an equivalent development of sociological interest in biomedical ethics. This is so because many issues in biomedical ethics are sociological topics of major interest. For example, work in the area of medical care ethics, particularly work focusing on the rights and duties of medical professionals and patients, bears directly on the evolving nature of the doctor-patient relationship (Stacey 1985). Likewise, work in the ethics of human research focuses on such topics as investigator-subject relationships and the social control of science (Barber et al. 1973). Ethical analysis of medical and health care public policy has significant implication for such macrosociological issues as equality in access to care and the role of the professions in determining the availability of medical and health care services (Mechanic 1979).

A review of recent medical sociology works reveals some coverage of an array of ethical issues in medical and health care (Mechanic 1983; Susser, Watson, and Hopper 1985; Mechanic and Aiken 1986; Simmons and Canio 1979). Much of this has focused on micro-ethical issues, such as the doctor-patient relationship and treatment decisions for critically ill patients (Crane 1975). More recently there has been an extension to societally focused issues, such as the rationing of medical care (Mechanic 1979). Lesser attention has been devoted to exploring ethical issues in the interactions between institutions and professionals and to studying the dynamic relationships between the professions and society (Friedson 1970). Some sociological attention also has been given to exploring factors contributing to the rise and current interest in bioethics in our society (Fox 1974).

The purpose of this chapter is to provide an overview of developments in the field of bioethics that focus on medical and health care and public health. To provide focus we exclude issues that have as their central or sole orientation the social, psychological, or legal aspects of health and medical care. We begin with a brief discussion of bioethics, followed by a review of the bioethics movement in the United States and its major focuses. We also summarize major principles around which much of the bioethics debates concerning medical and health care have been organized.

The number of specific medical and health issues that have received ethical analysis is very large; they include such topics as death and dying, kidney dialysis, organ transplantation, clinical research, genetic counseling and screening, decisions to extend or terminate life support systems, allocation of scarce medical resources, cost containment, and ethical issues in the development of for-profit hospitals. In this overview we provide, by way of example, discussion of the evolving ethical analyses of two contemporary issues that have significant public policy components. The first focuses on the renewed interest in health promotion, particularly life-style change initiatives, and the second on the current AIDS epidemic. In reviewing these examples, we attempt to highlight major issues of concern to bioethicists. We conclude

with a brief discussion of the institutionalization of bioethics in our society and some comments on the emerging relationship between bioethics and the social sciences.

BIOETHICS

Ethics involves normative questions, reasoning, and decisions—for example, how should one act or what ought one do, both as a moral ideal and in an actual situation? Normative ethics, as a discipline, is not synonymous with law or the social sciences. Nor is ethics the same as etiquette, although codes of professional "ethics" have often confused the two (Chapman 1984).

Medical ethics, or bioethics is an area of applied ethics concerned with health and illness and health care and medical care. Ethics applied to health care and medicine has a number of roles to play and a number of limitations (Beauchamp and Childress 1983). Through the process of moral reasoning, ethical analysis can lead to the structuring of normative issues, to recognition of the moral dimensions and often conflicting values involved in given situations, and to analysis of the values that guide decisions or actions (Harron, Burnside, and Beauchamp 1983, chap. 1).

Most people involved in bioethics would agree that it is a useful but rather imprecise "diagnostic" and "prescriptive" tool when brought to bear on real-life situations. Bioethics can clarify values and provide "moral action guides" but seldom offers ready solutions to the hard choices that confront providers, patients, or policymakers. This is so, in part, because bioethics most often deals with dilemmas in which no set of moral reasons for a given view or action is obviously the correct one.

Bioethics in the United States

A question often asked about ethics, and its application to fields such as health care, is whether values are universal. Some, especially those trained in philosophy or moral theology, would answer a perhaps qualified yes. Others, especially those coming to ethics from the social sciences, would answer no, because of the belief that values are shaped strongly by culture, society, and historical periods. The view taken here is that systems of ethics and the values central to them are influenced by and hence relative to the society and culture in which they are developed.

From a sociological perspective, then, it is important to recognize that the development, content, and influence of bioethics in the United States have attributes that are characteristic of Western and, particularly, American society, in contrast to the ways that bioethics is evolving in other Western and non-Western countries. "Bioethics is not just bioethics . . . using biology and medicine as a metaphorical language and a symbolic medium, bioethics deals in public spheres and in more private domains with . . . beliefs, values, and norms that are basic to our society, its cultural tradition, and its collective conscience" (Fox and Swazey 1984, p. 338).

Although most of the issues being examined in bioethics are old ones philosophically, its emergence in the United States as an area of applied ethics dates from the 1960s. The emergence and rapid growth of bioethics occurred in response to concerns about the implications of various biomedical advances and to broader value and belief questions in American society more generally. As charted by Fox, bioethics in the United States has had a core of chief disciplinary participants; it has had a distinctive methodology and value and belief orientation; and it has gone through several phases in its brief history (Fox, in press).

Not surprisingly, the principal disciplinary shapers of bioethics have been philosophers, particularly those trained in the positivistically oriented theory and methodology of analytic philosophy. Other major disciplines represented are theology (primarily Christian), jurisprudence, medicine, biology, and, in the 1980s, economics. Sociology and other social sciences are conspic-

uously absent from this list. For reasons related to the ethos and state of both sociology and philosophy, social scientists have had at best a marginal role in the development of bioethics, and both fields have contributed to an unfortunate dichotomization of subject matter into social or ethical (Fox 1974, 1976).

In our brief review of major Western ethical theories and principles in the next section, and in the selected topics covered in this chapter, the reader will find that bioethics has developed around and focused attention on a particular cluster of values and beliefs, which are very American in character (DeCraemer 1983; Fox and Swazey 1984). The major value orientation of bioethics has involved individualism, focusing on concerns about autonomy and individual rights. A second and closely related emphasis has been on the rights and duties of persons in voluntary contractual relationships. Here, for example, the ideal informed voluntary consent agreement between researcher and subject or physician and patient epitomizes our moral and legal vision of a rational, functionally specific contractual relationship between autonomous individuals. The informed consent model also involves two other prominent values, those of veracity and of doing good or minimizing harm. Finally, the growing attention to limited medical and health care resources in the 1980s has been structured predominantly around an individualistic or individual-rights vision of the general or common good. In this framework, greater importance is attached to the value of achieving equity, rather than equality, in matters such as access to and payment for health care (Lowy 1986; President's Commission 1983a).

In a little over two decades, bioethics has gone through a number of sociologically relevant phases (Fox, in press). From the mid-1960s to the mid-1970s, one major focus of bioethical analysis was "cutting edge" developments such as applied human genetics, life support systems, and behavior control techniques. The second predominant topic was human experimentation, especially informed consent and the rights of vulnerable research subjects such as children, prisoners, and the mentally disabled.

Around the start of bioethics' second decade, in the mid-1970s, issues involving the beginning and ending of life (e.g., abortion, the handicapped neonate, treatment termination) became prominent and, through cases such as Karen Ann Quinlan and a series of "Baby Does," tightened the interface between bioethics and law. A second significant development during this period was the gradual development of bioethics in several Western European and Asian countries. Initially modeled closely on American bioethics, by the mid-1980s bioethics in other countries was taking on socially and culturally distinctive analytic frameworks.

During the 1980s the evolution of bioethics has included three particularly noteworthy developments. First, there has been a progressive "economization" of content and approaches, reflecting the growing national concern with health care costs and their "containment" and with how, especially in an era of cost containment, one can most justly distribute the various resources involved in health care (Daniels 1986; Gaylin 1984).

A second hallmark of bioethics in the 1980s has been the field's growing expansion and institutionalization. New centers for bioethics—medical ethics are springing up across the country, there are increasing numbers of academic courses and degree programs, and there has been a torrent of bioethics literature and companion bibliographies.

Third, there are signs of "incipient changes in the ēthos of bioethics," marked by "a certain amount of intellectual and moral stock-taking . . . in the bioethical community since 1980" (Fox, in press). There is a rethinking of the moral supremacy that has been given to the principle of autonomy and individual rights, which has resulted in the near neglect of values involving community and interrelatedness

(Callahan 1980, 1984; Veatch 1984). In addition, there are some calls for bioethics to become less philosophically abstract and more grounded in the substantive and experiential content of medical research, care, and policy (Clements 1985). And, finally, some prominent bioethicists are indicating that they and their colleagues need to learn to work more closely with persons in disciplines such as medicine, law, and the social sciences, as they struggle with the complex issues related to biomedical research, public and private health care, and public policy.

Ethical Theories and Principles

Moral reasoning is a process that seeks to examine the conditions under which a given ethical position, decision, or action is justified. Philosophers have distinguished four levels of "moral discourse" or reasoning (Frankena 1973).

1. *Ethical theories* are bodies of ethical principles drawn together into a system. Two of the major ethical theories in Western philosophy are *utilitarianism* and *deontology* (Beauchamp and Childress 1983, chap. 2). Utilitarianism judges the moral rightness or wrongness of an act by its nonmoral consequences. Because utilitarians think in terms of such means-to-ends moral reasoning, utilitarian ethics is especially compatible with science, medicine, and public health.

Deontology, in contrast, judges the moral correctness of a belief or act in its own right, rather than in terms of its consequences. Thus, deontologists judge rightness or wrongness before the fact (a priori), in terms of what they believe are fundamental and universally binding moral duties. Although we seldom use formal ethical labels, most of our ethical stances combine elements of deontology and utilitarianism.

2. *Ethical principles* are the main foundation of ethical theories and, in turn, serve as the foundation for ethical rules. Four major principles have been central to medi-

cal or health care ethics (Beauchamp and Childress 1983, chaps. 3–6). The principle of *autonomy* involves a moral belief in personal freedom of will or action and respect for the self-directedness of others. A corollary principle is *respect for persons*. Ethically and legally, our doctrines of informed consent and rights to refuse treatment are grounded in the principles of autonomy and respect for persons.

The principles of *beneficence* and *nonmaleficence* are major precepts in health care. Beneficence involves positive actions to do good, to remove harmful conditions, or to seek to prevent harm. Nonmaleficence, in turn, means not inflicting harm, as expressed in a central injunction of medical ethics: "First of all do no harm." "Risk-benefit" analyses as well as "due care" standards at least implicitly invoke these two ethical principles.

Justice, the fourth and perhaps most complex ethical principle, involves two major subprinciples. *Commutative justice* focuses on the rights and duties of individuals in various relationships, especially those formed by voluntary commitments and contracts as between physician-patient, teacher-student, or lawyer-client. *Distributive justice*, one of the oldest and most intractable topics in philosophy, is concerned with the proper or just distribution of social benefits and burdens under conditions of scarcity. The allocation of health care resources and cost containment, two of the major preoccupations in medical care and public policy in the 1980s, depend, in part, on varying conceptions of distributive justice.

3. *Ethical rules*, comprising the third level of moral discourse, often blend with ethical principles. Rules state that particular actions should or should not be taken because they are morally right or wrong.

4. *Ethical judgments and actions*, finally, are based on beliefs about a particular situation as well as the values brought to that situation. This is the "real world" arena of applied normative ethics, in which individuals both draw upon and generate the ethical rules and principles that form ethical theories.

BIOETHICAL ANALYSES OF HEALTH CARE ISSUES

As noted, bioethical analysis has covered a large number of specific medical and health care topics. In this overview we have chosen to present bioethical analyses and issues relating to two topics of current interest that also have major public policy implications. In this respect these examples reflect, in part, the newer thrust of bioethics into more societally focused issues and, at the same time, the more recent efforts in this literature to examine the ethical principles of individual rights in terms of some notion of distributive justice.

Historically our society has walked a narrow and winding path between valuing individual civil liberty, on the one hand, and espousing concern for the welfare of the collective on the other. Whereas individual rights seem to gain ascendancy during one period, at other times societal prerogatives seem to be emphasized. Certainly one area where the tension between civil liberties and the common good continues to manifest itself is the area of public health policy. A number of scientific, technologic, and medical developments have led to increased interest in public health problems, where the focus is less on an individual person or a patient in a medical care setting and more on the rights of individuals and the obligations of society regarding health. For example, the advent of genetic screening in the early 1970s raised a series of ethical questions about voluntary versus mandatory screening, confidentiality of results, and the right to reproduce. These issues have received considerable ethical analysis (Capron et al. 1979). Ethical debate has also arisen over recent screening programs for assaying both licit and illicit drug exposure. Another recent development, increased interest in health promotion and disease prevention and substantial financial support for such efforts by government as well as private industry, is also raising a series of ethical questions about the rights of individuals and the limits of societal responsibility. These same questions are being raised by efforts to reduce automobile-related death and injury by laws mandating seat-belt use and by legal and administrative efforts to control drinking and driving.

Health Promotion

It has become increasingly clear over the past twenty years that health is determined by numerous factors and that the role of medical care per se in affecting much premature morbidity and mortality may be significantly less than previously assumed (McKeown 1976). Scholars have critiqued the role of medical care in health promotion and have suggested that health may be more a function of biological inheritance, environmental circumstances, and, especially, personal life-style than it is of the availability and efficacy of medical care (McKinley 1979).

Along with this line of argument there has been emerging a clearer understanding of the extramedical factors that contribute to premature morbidity and mortality (Hamburg, Elliott, and Parron 1982). In particular, studies of cardiovascular disease, stroke, cancer, diabetes, and injuries have led many to suggest that if our society is serious about reducing disease, then it must get serious about promoting both environmental and individual life-style changes that are conducive to health. The renewed interest in prevention also has been fueled by rising concerns about the increasingly burdensome costs of medical or curative care and the belief that prevention could significantly reduce these costs.

There have been critics of the new prevention efforts. These critics raise a number of questions, ranging from the observation that devoting more resources to prevention could reduce the availability and quality of curative and palliative care to claims that many prevention efforts are premature, will probably be ineffective (Goodman and Goodman 1986), and may not be cost-effective (Russell 1986).

These developments have led to debate about the amount of medical versus health care that should be provided by our society, a debate that has identified numerous ethical dilemmas confronting health promotion efforts. Some of the most intensive ethical analyses and debates have focused on health promotion efforts targeting individual life-style changes.

A review of the ethical discussion of proposed life-style approaches to health promotion can be organized into three categories: (1) the adequacy of existing scientific/medical data to make public policy and recommend specific life-style changes; (2) the coerciveness of programs designed to promote health; and (3) the rights and obligations of the individual vis-à-vis the state with regard to health promotion.

Ethical Grounding for Health Promotion

Pellegrino (1981) has recommended a series of principles for developing an "ethics of prevention." Encouraged by significant advances in understanding the causes of major diseases and disabilities and concerned at the same time about the basis for launching health promotion initiatives, particularly those involving individual life-style initiatives, he argued that four principles be followed in developing health promotion programs. The first is that the causal connection between a given behavior (X) and an adverse health outcome (Y) be fully established. This means not only establishing that X is a "risk factor" for Y, but establishing that changing X will lead to a reduction in Y. Behavioral epidemiology has established risk factors for many diseases and disorders (Hamburg, Elliot, and Parron 1982). But, according to Pellegrino, for the purpose of formulating public policy, more is required. In particular what is needed is research demonstrating that in changing the risk factor there will be a net positive benefit in terms of health status. Given the multi-determined nature of most chronic diseases, accomplishing the latter is not simple. If such data are not available, we may want to share risk factor information with the public, but it is ethically unacceptable and premature to establish policy or suggest behavior change programs. At base Pellegrino is arguing from a consequentialist net benefit perspective. The issue he raises is very important for health promotion initiatives, since there are substantial variations in "expert" opinion about the evidence for, and hence questions about the ethical justification for, many lifestyle interventions.

A second principle involves the notion that, given an established causal relationship between a behavior and an adverse health outcome, establishing policy requires the availability of a reliable methodology for inducing and maintaining changes in the behavior. Otherwise, as is the case with obesity, people may move into a cycle of weight loss, weight gain, weight loss, and so forth. There is accumulating evidence that such cyclical swings, particularly with respect to weight gain and loss, may in and of themselves constitute something of a health risk and be a risk factor for eventual sustained obesity.

Pellegrino is arguing that it is unethical to expose individuals to the worry and concern about being at risk, if in fact there is no established or acceptably effective means to help the individual change. To launch programs otherwise could lead to false expectations and avoidable anxiety and to other potential types of risks.

Third, Pellegrino argues that, in developing policy, initiatives should adhere to the principle of proportionality. By this he means that increasingly coercive methods of behavior change be used in proportion to the seriousness and scope of the health problem involved. The more serious the problem and the more people affected, the greater the rationale for moving from simple educational campaigns to more sophisticated behavioral alteration methodologies and the more justified become increasingly mandatory measures.

As a fourth principle Pellegrino argues for a strong element of self-determination in health promotion programs. By this he means that before potent coercive measures are used, less coercive measures, such as educational programs, must have been tried and shown to be ineffective. He identifies a number of corollaries to this principle, including the idea that incentives be used prior to disincentives as means to regulate behavior. The major basis for the fourth principle is a strong commitment to individual autonomy and respect for the person.

In the current rush of interest in health promotion and disease prevention, health professionals are becoming increasingly cognizant of the need to consider the type of "moral grounding" or principles articulated by Pellegrino. Although there is as yet no consensus on the ethical principles to be followed, his analysis highlights some major ethical dimensions that should serve as a background for discussion of health promotion policy.

Coerciveness of Health Promotion Campaigns

With the advent of rising public and state interest in health promotion and disease prevention has come increased examination within the health professions about their role in promoting health. As an example of the seriousness with which one health promotion group is viewing this issue, the Society of Professional Health Educators devoted the spring 1987 issue of its *Health Education Quarterly* to the topic "Ethical Dilemmas in Health Promotion" (Gottlieb, Burdine, and McLeroy 1987). This group also devoted its midyear scientific conference in 1987 to the same topic.

Various authors have examined and argued for different health promotion strategies, ranging from health promotion as education, which attempts to facilitate rational, informed decisionmaking on a voluntaristic basis, to programs that use various psychological techniques to attempt to persuade individuals to adopt specific life-styles, to planned change programs using the most reliable and sophisticated behavioral change techniques available (Tones 1986). Faden and Faden (1978) have provided an informative discussion of some of the major ethical issues in health education. They argue that health promotion initiatives, and in particular health education programs, have two major ethical concerns: liberty and justice. With regard to liberty, they assert that health promotion programs should be carefully examined with reference to their degree of voluntariness. As they note, most programs are not simply informative but often involve some element of persuasion as well. They argue that programs should maintain, to the degree possible, options for voluntary behavior and personal freedom on the part of the individual.

In terms of social justice, Faden and Faden identify four justifications for state-launched health promotion initiatives: (1) government has a responsibility to protect and promote the public's health; (2) a majority of citizens may want selected health promotion programs; (3) health promotion programs, if effective, could be cost-effective; and (4) altering some behaviors can have the effect of reducing harm to others (for example, reducing drinking and driving). Faden and Faden (1978, p. 191) articulate a set of requirements that they believe need to be met to put a public health education campaign, particularly a behavioral program, above ethical suspicion:

- A program that focuses on changing individual behaviors should not lead to a reduction

in efforts to alter the sociopolitical and environmental factors contributing to the health problem;

- the program should not lead to wrongful stigmatization of individuals (blaming the victim);

- the program must be known to be cost-effective; and

- any harm or risk of harm to the individual the program carries must clearly be outweighed by the benefits

The arguments underlying these requirements reflect the ethical principles of beneficence, a respect for the person, and concern with justice and avoiding maleficence, both social and individual. Clearly, the Fadens' concern with the ethical basis for health promotion programs has much in common with Pellegrino's.

The Role of the Government and the Individual in Promoting Health

It has often been claimed that our society, as perhaps most, is more enamored with medical intervention to correct health problems than it is with preventing the health problems in the first place. This ready acceptance or desire for curative intervention rather than preventive maintenance has been fueled by a long list of biomedical and scientific breakthroughs that have contributed to the belief that, regardless of the problem, medical science can be counted on to produce a quick fix· such as a vaccine or a cure.

The recognition that an individual's behavior can contribute significantly to the risk of premature morbidity or mortality has led to numerous admonitions, on the one hand, for individuals to be more responsible for their own health (Knowles 1977), and discussions, on the other hand, of the right of the state to develop policies that coerce individuals to lead more healthy or risk-reducing lives.

In an ethical analysis of the responsibility of the state and the right of the individual concerning health, Wikler (1978) has examined three ethical justifications for state-initiated programs in health promotion that may not correspond to individual preference profiles regarding behaviors or life-styles. The first justification is based on the notion that health is a valued good. It may not be a terminal or ultimate value in most individuals' lives, but clearly many normal and routine life events cannot be experienced without a modicum of health. Accordingly, Wikler argues that state-initiated health promotion programs could be justified ethically on the basis of the principle of beneficence, or doing good. In pointing this out, Wikler also notes that health promotion programs run into problems of possible charges of paternalism: that is, forcing individuals to do something that, while it may be in the individual's long-term health interest, is something the individual may not want to do in the short run. As Wikler notes, this potential infringement on individual liberty is a major ethical dilemma in virtually any health promotion program that goes beyond the simple provision of information.

A second ethical premise examined to justify state-based health promotion initiatives rests on the argument that it is unfair for some individuals to act as they please when such action leads to significant burdens on society (Wikler 1978, p. 317). In essence, this justification argues for a fairer distribution of the burden imposed on society by illness that has a significant individual life-style component in its etiology. Programs premised on this argument can vary from those that add an extra tax, for example, on individuals who continue to engage in behaviors known to be detrimental, with tax monies going to offset the additional costs of medical care, to programs that attempt to alter high-risk behaviors by administrative regulation or law. Wikler notes many issues that make the ethical basis for such action questionable, such as the "voluntariness" of the behavior (e.g., addiction) and whether or not the avoidance of some high-risk health behaviors might lead

not only to longer life but also to significant costs to society through increased payments under the Social Security system.

A third principle Wikler identifies is that of promoting the general societal welfare (1978, p. 325). The argument here is that the state has a right to promote the general welfare, because this leads to improved societal productivity, a better economy, and so forth. The latter are goods that can benefit a majority of individuals in a society. Such benefits may be used to justify curtailment of individual life-style of those persons who engage in high-risk behaviors.

There are, Wikler notes, ethical problems with this position. An obvious one is that it is not clear why a state would focus on individual health behavior to promote general welfare when it could focus on other activities or situations to achieve the same goal. For example, the general welfare could be pursued by requiring or providing more education, leading to a more educated and a more productive labor force. At the same time, in pursuing a justification for state health promotion initiatives, it would be necessary to address the issue of why health behavior changes are usually limited to a select set of behaviors that pose a high risk for adverse health consequences (poor diet, lack of exercise) when there are societally approved behaviors that also constitute high risks for medical problems and costs (certain sports such as skydiving and automobile racing).

Wikler's analyses, along with those of Pellegrino, the Fadens, and others, provided a rich context for examining the ethical basis for state initiatives in health promotion and for claims that individuals have a right to behave as they please. Although there have been numerous calls for people to exercise more responsibility for their health, the weight of ethical analysis to date seems to place the burden of proof on the state to legitimize ethically its exercise of power and authority, more so than on individuals to justify their right to live a preferred life-style. This reflects the orientation noted above in bioethics in this country, a strong preference for defending the exercise of individual rights.

There is a corresponding preference for the less coercive health education approach to health promotion, in contrast to more coercive measures such as administrative regulations, various types of incentive and disincentive programs, and passage of laws. Nevertheless, there is a growing awareness that respect for autonomy must be viewed in light of some notion of social justice or distributive justice, a complex and difficult concept to apply in our pluralistic society.

Ethical Issues in the AIDS Crisis

Of the various topics that could be used to illustrate ethical examination of public health problems of current concern, few provide the urgency of what many view as the most significant public health problem of the current decade, the AIDS epidemic.

AIDS (acquired immune deficiency syndrome) was first clinically described in 1981 (Osburn 1986). Within three years the human immunodeficiency virus (HIV) responsible for the highly lethal disease had been identified. This development led, in turn, to the availability of screening tests to protect the blood supply as well as screen individuals for exposure to the virus and for acceptability as tissue donors (Coffin et al. 1986).

Much is presently unknown about HIV, such as the ultimate clinical significance of testing seropositive for exposure, as well as the chances of developing either an effective vaccine or a cure. What we do know about AIDS is that its health statistics are grim. At the present time, more than 50,000 cases of AIDS have been identified in the United States, and of these slightly more than half have died. It has been estimated that as many as one to one-and-a-half million Americans have been infected with HIV, and that by 1991 the cumulative total cases of AIDS in this country could reach 250,000 (Curran 1985).

The major populations at risk for HIV exposure and subsequent development of AIDS include gay or bisexual men, intravenous (IV) drug users, and gay intravenous drug users. Hemophiliacs also are at significant risk because of their need for blood products, as are infants born to IV-drug-using mothers infected with the HIV. More recently the virus has begun to spread into the heterosexual population, probably through IV drug users and bisexual males. Reliable estimates of the potential economic impact of AIDS are not available, but, given the need for often long and intensive hospitalization as the disease progresses, there seems little doubt that this epidemic could have a very pronounced economic impact (Scitovsky and Rice 1987).

Against this background there has developed increasing bioethical discussion of the AIDS epidemic. Numerous issues have surfaced in this dialogue, but most attention has focused on (1) measures to prevent the spread of the virus within high-risk populations and (2) measures to prevent the spread of the virus to low-risk populations. In the face of apparently limited scientific prospects for development soon of a vaccine or an effective cure, most efforts have focused on educational initiatives and legislative measures regarding HIV screening.

Many measures have been undertaken with respect to reducing the spread of the virus among known high-risk groups. These measures vary from educational efforts identifying "safe sex" practices for the gay community to closure of facilities such as gay bathhouses, to legislative proposals requiring HIV screening of various high-risk populations and quarantine or incarceration of individuals known to be infected with the HIV who continue practicing high-risk sex.

As the measures have moved from educational, to regulatory, to statutory, ethical discussion has increased. Regulatory and statutory initiatives pose the civil liberty of individuals against the duty of the state to protect the public health. A related ethical issue concerns whether HIV screening should be mandatory or voluntary for high-risk groups. At issue here is the right of individuals not to know their HIV status, particularly when no medical intervention or treatment would be premised on knowing one's HIV status. This right is being examined in light of the state's obligation to protect the health of the public by such screening, with the assumption that individuals would use knowledge of their HIV status to alter behavior that would put others at risk to become HIV seropositive.

The language of the evolving ethical debate concerning AIDS is replete with terms such as civil rights, paternalism, the common good, self-determination, and the right to know or not to know. Bioethicists have taken divergent positions on proposals to limit the spread of the virus within and among high-risk groups. Beauchamp (1986), for example, has argued that the major approach to limiting this epidemic within homosexual and IV-drug-using populations ought to be education, perhaps with limited regulation of places such as gay bathhouses and bars that promote high-risk sex. He expresses great concern that the ethically legitimate right of the state to protect the health of the public be clearly separated from efforts at legal moralism—forcing on a minority the morality of the majority. He senses a high risk for this occurring regarding the AIDS epidemic, because of its focus on two minorities, homosexuals and drug abusers.

In addition, Merritt (1986) has looked at the legal feasibility of various coercive measures to regulate the spread of AIDS. Clearly, the power of the state to intervene and even quarantine individuals to protect the public health is well established. Merritt identifies three judicial trends, however, that have emerged since 1940 that may make it difficult to establish potent restrictions on civil liberties in the case of AIDS. These trends are (1) the courts' increasing regard for individual liberty over the past few decades; (2) judicial recognition that the democratic process may not adequately protect the civil liberties of minority groups; and (3) what Merritt terms the

courts' "growing wariness of scientific claims," since all the evidence is not in concerning AIDS. Merritt also notes, however, that protection of the public health remains a central duty of government.

Daniel Fox (1986) has analyzed issues surrounding surveillance or case reporting for AIDS. On the one hand, for scientific and planning purposes, such information is critical. But at the same time, he notes, in contrast to case reporting for many infectious diseases, accidental disclosure of a person's HIV status could lead to stigmatization and discrimination, both socially and economically. He has identified several initiatives across the nation that have attempted to convert the modern definition of surveillance for scientific and population planning purposes to a definition that allows the isolation and regulation of HIV-seropositive carriers, a practice he considers ethically unacceptable.

Finally, Macklin (1986) has examined the AIDS epidemic in terms of the defensibility of confinement of persons known to be HIV seropositive. In general, she considers confinement on the basis of HIV-seropositive status as ethically indefensible. She argues that identification of this characteristic is not a good or reasonable predictor that the person is dangerous and may commit acts that would put others at risk to become HIV seropositive. She does argue, however, that it would be ethically defensible to incarcerate known "recalcitrants"— that is HIV-seropositive individuals who continue to practice high-risk sexual behavior. The ethical justification for this action rests on the harm they will do.

Increasing ethical attention is being given to recommendations to control the spread of the AIDS virus into low-risk populations. Much scientific and public health effort went into the development of an effective screening method and program to protect the nation's blood supply. There was some concern about confidentiality of HIV-seropositive carriers identified in this fashion, but by and large this effort met little opposition, as have efforts to control the spread of the virus by screening tissue and organ donors. More recently, measures have been proposed, or are being developed, to protect the general population. These include suggestions for mandatory premarital screening, as well as mass screening of all immigrants. At the present time such measures, while receiving some political support, have received little support from the scientific and public health communities (Darrow 1987).

The limited enthusiasm from these communities, particularly for mandatory screening, rests on several epidemiological and medical considerations, including (1) a low HIV prevalence rate in such populations, meaning a very low "yield" in terms of HIV-sero-positive cases; (2) this, in turn, would lead to a tremendous expense per positive case identified; (3) the absence of an effective therapy to treat people so identified; and (4) concern that unless such screening is also accompanied by pre- and post-screening counseling, much harm rather than good could come from such efforts.

Ethically, there would also probably be limited support for such measures. First, it could be argued that the least coercive measures, meaning in this case health education regarding risk factors and safe behavior, should be shown to be markedly ineffective before more coercive measures such as mandatory screening are adopted. Second, it could be argued that even when a person is identified as HIV seropositive, it is not clear that the person poses a real and significant danger to society. Hence, there is limited ethical justification to limit the right to immigrate and the right to be married.

By and large, ethical analyses of the current AIDS epidemic have consistently come to the conclusion that, for the present, the most ethically defensible strategy is one that relies primarily on educational efforts and voluntary use of screening options by informed people. In terms of public policy, this translates into a call for increased public health education initiatives for both high-risk groups and the general population and for making available voluntary HIV screening programs. Accumulating studies of the dominant high-risk group, practicing homosexuals, suggest that educational strategies may be having dramatic effects in terms of reducing high-risk behavior at least among some elements of this population (Martin 1987). It is less clear what is happening in IV drug using populations (Becker and Joseph 1988).

This cursory overview of the AIDS epidemic has not covered all ethical debates that have come up over the issue. For example, ethical issues have been raised concerning caring for AIDS patients and the employment and insurance rights of AIDS patients. The ethical issues discussed highlight a central public health ethical problem regarding AIDS: the civil liberties and rights of certain individuals to maintain their life-style versus the duty of the state to protect the public health. At the present time it appears that many public officials are emphasizing the obligations of the state to protect the common good, while many bioethicists are arguing strongly to protect individual liberties. Once again, the latter position reflects the strong commitment in the bioethics field to the cultural values of individual liberty, self-determination, and autonomy.

The AIDS epidemic is a very serious public health development. It came about after our society's level of bioethical sensitivity had been raised and refined by more than a decade's discussion of such issues in medicine and health care. In this respect, the development and evolution of public health policy concerning AIDS may be more ethically informed than would otherwise have been the case.

THE INSTITUTIONALIZATION OF BIOETHICS: POLICY ROLES

In its early years, bioethics by and large was a rather abstract scholarly discipline. "Hot topics" were debated in the literature and at conferences held by developing think tanks such as the Hastings Center and Kennedy Center. But the leading scholars in the new field of ethics applied to medical and health care were ambivalent about taking active advisory or decision-making roles in the "real world" arena of health care/medical care. Since the mid-1970s, however, with growing momentum, bioethics and its practitioners have become firmly entrenched and increasingly active in a wide range of policy-related arenas at the national, state, community, and institutional level.

Nationally, much like Mr. Smith of movie fame, bioethics has gone to Washington in the form of federal commissions, legislation mandating local institutional review boards (IRBs) for research involving human subjects and, more recently, animals, and a wide range of informal as well as formal advisory roles in virtually all aspects of health and medical care policy-making. Two particularly influential ethics bodies have been the National Commission for the Protection of Human Subjects of Biomedical and Behavioral Research and the President's Commission for the Study of Ethical Problems in Medicine and Biomedical and Behavioral Research. The former, appointed by the Secretary of Health, Education and Welfare, dealt primarily with issues in research on human subjects. From 1975 to 1978, it produced a series of still widely cited reports that were a basis for revisions in the federal regulations governing the protection of human subjects (National Commission 1978).

In 1978, Congress authorized a presidentially appointed advisory body, with a broader mandate to study and develop reports and recommendations on a range of the most troubling, difficult, and policy-relevent ethical and legal aspects of medicine and research. The topics dealt with by the President's Commission involved continuing issues in research on human subjects, including the adequacy of federal regulations and their implementation

through the IRB system; compensation for research-related injuries; decisions to forego life-sustaining treatment; the definition and determination of death, focusing on brain death; informed consent to medical care by competent persons; decision-making for incapacitated persons; securing access to health care; genetic screening and counseling; genetic engineering; and fraud and whistleblowing in biomedical research (President's Commission 1983).

A third ethics advisory board, appointed by and reporting to Congress, was established in 1985 and authorized through fiscal 1988. To date, however, few members have been appointed and funding has not been released, perhaps because of the committee's politically volatile mandate. Its first charge is to examine the advisability and implications of any waiver of federal protection for human fetuses in research, a task inextricably linked with such highly controversial matters as abortion, new reproductive technologies, fetal surgery, and gene therapy.

At the state, local, and institutional levels, bioethical concerns and activities involve the same types of difficult themes and concerns found in Washington. One prominent arena of bioethical influence is in the courts, where "ethicists" are frequently called as expert witnesses and where the bioethics literature is cited in cases involving matters ranging from treatment termination and surrogate parenting to malpractice. State legislatures and health planning and policy agencies, like their federal counterparts, also include so-called "bioethicists," a term we put in in quotes because of the tendency to label everyone concerned with value issues in medicine and health care an "ethicist," whether he or she is a lawyer, social or political scientist, physician, or philosopher. This labeling is at once a sign of bioethics' prominence, of society's quest for "expert" answers to moral dilemmas, and of a degree of confusion about what "bioethics" is or should be and do.

A range of institutions have also incorporated bioethics into their formal structure. Courses in bioethics abound in medical and nursing schools and in some public health programs. There are signs, however, that at least in medical schools the prominence of bioethics is rapidly being supplanted by humanities offerings designed to produce more "humane" or "humanistic" physicians, just as bioethics, in its turn, briefly reigned over social and behavioral science courses also intended to produce "better" physicians. Other institutional loci of bioethics include hospitals, with staff positions in medical ethics, institutional ethics committees, and ethics rounds and other teaching programs. Ethicists are also found in medically related corporations, such as pharmaceutical companies, and in a variety of consulting firms.

A final example of the many roles that bioethics and those concerned with ethical issues in health care are playing is the proliferation of "community bioethics" programs across the United States. Taking their lead from the Oregon Health Decisions Project that began in 1982, and with funding from sources such as the Prudential Foundation and Robert Wood Johnson Foundation, projects from Maine to Hawaii are involved in grass roots efforts to explicitly involve laypersons in the value dimensions of health care, through local and statewide forums and citizen's parliaments, surveys, newsletters, and planning and policy efforts at local, county, and state levels (Jennings 1986). These projects exemplify both the pervasiveness of so-called bioethical concerns and the growing sense that the value-laden decisions they bear on are not solely the province of "experts," be they academicians, providers, the courts, or policymakers. For, as the President's Commission emphasized in its final report, "the enormously challenging issues addressed by the Commission are not arcane. Rather, they are questions that increasingly confront all Americans, individually as participants in health care and collectively as citizens in a democracy. . . ." (President's Commission 1983, p. 3).

SUMMARY

This chapter has reviewed elements of the development of bioethics in our society, provided a description of the major ethical dimensions along which bioethical analyses of medical and health care issues are being discussed, and, by way of illustration, has discussed ethical analyses and debates concerning two contemporary health care issues, health promotion and AIDS. Clearly, we did not intend to review all contemporary work in the bioethics of medical and health care, a task that would take an entire handbook.

Without question, bioethics has become institutionalized in our society. There is evolving both a "sociology of" as well as a "sociology in" the bioethics of medical and health care. Nevertheless, it appears that sociological interest in bioethics remains limited. This is unfortunate, since, as indicated above, many of the issues of major ethical concern in medical and health care are issues of central concern to medical sociology. Moreover, bioethics as a social phenomenon itself is a topic worthy of additional sociological investigation. Particularly significant here may be cross-societal and cross-cultural comparisons of bioethics as a type of social movement or cultural change phenomenon.

The evolution of and current public policy impact of bioethics in the United States is an important social policy development, since our society is devoted to resolving difficult social issues with the help of experts and expertise. Bioethicists may not yet have the same influence as scientists or physicians, but there appears to be an increasing willingness to explore public policy issues from both the scientific-medical and the ethical points of view. This is a topic that should be of significant interest to many sociologists.

REFERENCES

Barber, Bernard, J. Lally, J. Makaruskha, and D. Sullivan. 1973. *Research on Human Subjects.* New York: Russell Sage.

Beauchamp, Daniel. 1986. Morality and the Health of the Body Politic. *Hastings Center Report.* 16:30–36.

Beauchamp, Tom L., and James E. Childress. 1983. *Principles of Biomedical Ethics.*, 2nd ed. New York: Oxford University Press.

Becker, M., and J. Joseph. 1988. AIDs and Behavioral Change to Reduce Risk: A Review. *American Journal of Public Health* 78:394–410.

Callahan, Daniel. 1980. Shattuck Lecture—Contemporary Biomedical Ethics. *The New England Journal of Medicine* 302:1228–1233.

———. 1981. Minimalist Ethics *Hastings Center Report* 11:19–25.

———. 1984. Autonomy: A Moral Good, Not a Moral Obsession. *Hastings Center Report* 14:40–42.

Capron, Alexander, Marc Lappe, Robert Murray, Tabitha Powledge, Sumner Twiss, and Daniel Bergoma, eds. 1979. *Genetic Counseling: Facts, Values, and Norms.* New York: Alan R. Liss.

Chapman, Carleton B. 1984. *Physicians, Law, and Ethics.* New York: New York University Press.

Clements, Colleen D. J. 1985. Bioethical Essentialism and Scientific Population Thinking. *Perspectives in Biology and Medicine* 28:188–207.

Coffin, J., H. Haase, J. Levy, L. Montagnier, S. Arosylan, N. Terch, H. Temin, K. Toyoshima, H. Varmus, P. Vogt, and R. Weiss. 1986. Human Immunodeficiency Viruses. *Science* 232:697–698.

Crane, Diana. 1975. *The Sanctity of Social Life: Physicians' Treatment of Critically Ill Patients.* New York: Russel Sage.

Curran, J. W. 1985. The Epidemiology and Prevention of the Acquired Immunodeficiency Syndrome. *Annual of Internal Medicine* 103:657–662.

Daniels, Norman C. 1986. Why Saying No to Patients in the United States Is So Hard. Cost Containment, Justice, and Provider Autonomy. *New England Journal of Medicine* 314:1380–1383.

Darrow, William. 1987. A Framework for Preventing AIDS. *American Journal of Public Health* 77(7):778–779.

De Craemer, Willy. 1983. A Cross-cultural Perspective on Personhood. *Milbank Memorial Fund Quarterly* 61:19–34.

Faden, R., and A. Faden. 1978. The Ethics of Health Education as Public Health Policy. *Health Education Monographs.* 6(2):180–197.

Fox, Daniel. 1986. From TB to AIDS: Value Conflicts in Reporting Disease. *Hasting Center Report* 16:11–16.

Fox, Renée C. 1974. Ethical and Existential Developments in Contemporaneous American Medicine: Their Implications for Culture and Society. *Milbank Memorial Fund Quarterly* 52:445–483.

———. 1976. Advanced Medical Technology—Social and Ethical Implications." *Annual Review of Sociology* 2:231–268.

———. In press. Sociology of Bioethics, in *The Sociology of Medicine.* Englewood Cliffs, N.J.: Prentice-Hall.

Fox, Renée C., and Judith P. Swazey. 1984. Medical Morality is Not Bioethics—Medical Ethics in China and the United States. *Perspectives in Biology and Medicine* 27 (Spring): 336–360.

Frankena, William. 1973. *Ethics*, 2nd ed. Englewood Cliffs, N.J.

Freidson, Eliot. 1970. *Profession of Medicine.* Dodd, Mead.

Gaylin, Willard. 1984. Autonomy, Paternalism, and Community. *Hastings Center Report* 14:5.

Goodman, Lenn, and Madeleine Goodman. 1986. Prevention—How Misuse of a Concept Undercuts Its Worth. *Hastings Center Report* 16:26–38.

Gottlieb, N., J. Burdine, and K. McLeroy, eds. 1987. Ethical Dilemmas in Health Promotion. *Health Education Quarterly* 14 (Spring):1–109.

Hamburg, David, Glen Elliott, and Delores Parron, eds. 1982. *Health and Behavior.* Washington, D.C.: National Academy Press.

Harron, Frank, John Burnside, and Tom Beauchamp. 1983. *Health and Human Values. A Guide to Making Your Own Decisions.* New Haven: Yale University Press.

Jennings, Bruce. 1986. Community Bioethics: Notes on a New Movement. *Foundation Reports* September-October: 18–21.

Knowles, John. 1977. The Responsibility of the

Individuals, in J. H. Knowles, ed., *Doing Better and Feeling Worse*. New York: W. W. Norton, pp. 57–80.

Lowy, Iliana. 1986. Tissue Groups and Cadaver Kidney Sharing: Socio-cultural Aspects of a Medical Controversy. *International Journal of Technology Assessment in Health Care* 2:195–218.

Macklin, Ruth. 1986. Predicting Dangerousness and the Public Health Response to AIDS. *Hasting Center Report.* 16(6):16–23.

Martin, John. 1987. The Impact of AIDS on Gay Male Sexual Behavior Patterns in New York City. *American Journal of Public Health.* 77(5):578–581.

Mechanic, D., ed. 1983. *Handbook of Health, Health Care, and the Health Professors*. New York: Free Press.

————. 1979. *Future Issues in Health Care: Social Policy and the Rationing of Medical Services.* New York: Free Press.

Mechanic, D., and L. Aiken. 1986. *Application of Social Science to Clinical Medicine and Health Policy*. New Brunswick, N.J.: Rutgers University Press.

McKeown, Thomas. 1976. *The Role of Medicine. Dream, Mirage, or Nemesis*. London: Nuffield Provincial Hospitals Trust.

McKinlay, J. B. 1979. Epidemiological and Political Determinants of Social Policies regarding The Public Health. *Social Science and Medicine.* 13A:541–558.

Merritt, Deborah. 1986. The Constitutional Balance between Health and Liberty. *Hasting Center Report* 16:2–10.

National Commission for the Protection of Human Subjects of Biomedical and Behavioral Research. 1978. *The Belmont Report.* Washington, D.C.: U.S. Department of Health, Education and Welfare.

Osborn, June. 1986. AIDS, Social Sciences and Health Education: A Personal Perspective. *Health Education Quarterly* 13(4):287–299.

Pellegrino, Edmund D. 1981. Health Promotion as Public Policy: The Need for Moral Groundings. *Preventive Medicine* 10:371–378.

President's Commission for the Study of Ethical Problems in Medicine and Biomedical and Behavioral Research. 1983a. *Securing Access to Health Care. The Ethical Implications of Differences in the Availability of Services* (vol. 1, Report; vol. 2, Appendices: Sociocultural and Philosophical studies; vol. 3, Appendices: Empirical, Legal, and Conceptual Studies). Washington, D.C.: U.S. Government Printing Office.

————. 1983b. *Summing Up. The Ethical and Legal Problems in Medicine and Biomedical and Behavioral Research*. Washington, D.C.: U.S. Government Printing Office.

Russell, Louise. 1986. *Is Prevention Better than Cure?* Washington, D.C.: The Brookings Institute.

Scitovsky, A., and P. Rice. 1987. Estimates of the Direct and Indirect Costs of Acquired Immunodeficiency Syndrome in the United States 1985, 1986, 1991. *Public Health Reports* 102:5–17.

Simmons, R., and M. DiCanio. 1979. Biology, Technology and Health, in H. Freeman, S. Levine. and L. Reeder, eds., *Handbook of Medical Sociology*, 3rd ed. Englewood Cliffs, N.J.: Prentice-Hall, pp. 150–173.

Stacey, Margaret. 1985. Medical Ethics and Medical Practice: A Social Science View. *Journal of Medicine Ethics* 11:14–18.

Susser, M., W. Watson, and K. Hopper. 1985. *Sociology in Medicine*. New York: Oxford University Press.

Tones, B. K. 1986. Health Education and the Ideology of Health Promotion: Review of Alternative Approaches. *Health Education Research* 1(1):3–12.

Veatch, Robert M. 1984. Autonomy's Temporary Triumph. *Hastings Center Report* 14:38–40.

Walters, LeRoy. 1975. *Bibliography of Bioethics*. Detroit: Gale Research Co.

Wikler, Daniel. 1978. Persuasion and Coercion for Health. *Health and Society* 56(3):303–338.

25

QUALITY OF LIFE
AND HEALTH CARE
INTERVENTIONS

SYDNEY H. CROOG
SOL LEVINE

BACKGROUND AND AIMS

In a relatively brief period, quality of life has been taking its place along with morbidity and mortality as a major criterion in evaluating health interventions (Najman and Levine 1981; Wenger et al. 1984). There are several factors that help explain the growing use of the concept of quality of life in the health field. First, since the beginning of this century chronic diseases have become increasingly prominent in Western societies, while the incidence of infectious diseases has declined (Levine, Feldman, and Elinson 1983). As larger numbers of people are living longer while burdened with chronic disease and disabling conditions, their quality of life has become increasingly important as a health care concern.

Second, there have been dramatic advances in medical technologies such as organ transplantation, artificial organs, renal dialysis, and coronary artery bypass surgery. Although these new technologies may

extend the life span, patients, their families, and health policy leaders are increasingly raising new questions about their social implications and about the quality of the life that is prolonged.

Third, we live in a period in which cost containment is becoming a prevailing concern. We are increasingly confronted as a society with the fact that our resources are finite. Accordingly, renewed attention focuses on the precise benefits that may be anticipated from the costly application of health care technology used to treat a wide range of diseases and to prolong life (Plough 1986; Thomas 1972; Evans et al. 1985). This interest includes the cost benefits of technology in terms of quality of life as well.

Fourth, increased emphasis on humanizing health care, greater participation of the patient in deciding on the course of therapy, and the growth of the self-help movement have also focused attention on quality of life. The development of alternative therapies like holistic medicine and chiropractics, criticism of the classic biomedical model within medicine, and increased concern about iatrogenic illness have led to more questioning attitudes about medical care and its effects not only on the physical condition of the patient but on larger issues of social life as well (Fuchs 1975.)

Finally, the growing attention to quality of life in health research and health care owes much to the fact that over the decades since World War II there has been more focus within the medical and dental research and clinical communities on systematic studies of behavioral factors in illness as they intersect with biological processes. These interests have led to many joint research efforts and collaborations on the topic in relation to health and disease.

Quality of life issues are not confined to exotic and dramatic deliberations at the operating table, nor are they restricted to questions of the care of the terminally ill. Instead they are manifest and pervasive in some of the most significant sectors of the health care field.

In this chapter we examine some effects of health care interventions on quality of life and, in turn, some implications of quality of life dimensions for health care research and clinical practice. We first review briefly some principal aspects of the conceptualization and measurement of the construct as they relate to health interventions. We consider quality of life issues pertaining to health interventions in five areas: medical decision making, health care technology, cost containment, recruitment of health care personnel, and consumerism and the self-help movement.

ISSUES IN ASSESSING QUALITY OF LIFE

Quality of Life: Problems in Conceptualization

In many ways quality of life has become a popular metaphor in lay parlance and in the professional literature. However, if it is to be used systematically in scientific discourse, the construct requires conceptual clarification and improvement of the methods by which it is studied.

First, the term is commonly used on two different levels. In conceptualizing quality of life, we have to separate aspects that are directly health related and may be attributable to therapeutic measures from those that are produced primarily by the basic conditions of social life. Different societies characteristically chart their progress in quality of life in terms of such areas as standard of living, satisfaction with government, forms of leisure, fear of crime, and the perceived aesthetic attractiveness of the society (OECD 1986; Gorham 1986; Cereseto and Waitzkin 1986; Lester 1985). A particular nation may assess whether it has made progress or fallen behind in each of these features. However, in general these areas of quality of life will not be appreciably affected by health or medical interventions. Pharmacological interventions, for example, may improve a person's satisfaction with his energy level but will not influence his satisfaction with the political system or his feelings about the extent of crime in his community.

A major problem in developing systematic, comparative studies of quality of life in the area of health care is the lack of agreement in regard to the nature of the core construct, "quality of life" (Levine and Croog 1984; Edlund and Tancredi 1985; Kaplan 1985; Cohen 1983; Johanna and Van Knippenberg 1985; Ware 1984). There is wide variation in the number and type of variables that have been employed in recent studies of quality of life, ranging from a few basic variables to elaborate listings (Clark and Fallowfield 1986; Spitzer et al. 1981; Guyatt, Bombardier, and Tugwell 1986; Moberg 1987). Individual constructs such as satisfaction with life, ability to function, and general health status are sometimes simply relabeled as "quality of life" (Chambers et al. 1982; Anderson, Bush, and Berry 1986; Zantra and Goodhart 1979). In some instances investigators indicate that their studies evaluate quality of life dimensions but make little attempt to specify their use of the concept and locate their measures within a conceptual framework. Hence, the reader is left to infer from the measures used that these are the relevant component elements of the construct.

An Emerging Heuristic Framework for Research and Clinical Purposes

Despite the conceptual and methodological problems that have accompanied the use of the construct, in the field of health-related research quality of life has proven useful primarily as a general rubric or framework within which relevant dimensions of life and health can be examined in research and clinical practice. One major dimension can be derived from the work of the biologist René Dubos (1982), who examined a similarly ambiguous construct, "health," and directed attention to role performance. He stressed that people are rarely completely free of disease or disability and that it is inappropriate to conceptualize health in these terms. Instead, Dubos argued, health should be understood as the ability of people to do what they want to do, to carry out the activities they want to carry out in day-to-day living. Accordingly, a major component of quality of life would be the ability of the individual to perform his or her major and desired social roles and the degree to which the individual derives satisfaction from performing these roles. Such roles would include those of spouse, parent, friend, worker, and citizen.

To illustrate, in almost all instances persons can be presumed to have higher quality of life if they are able to remain in the community with family and friends and perform the usual social roles of worker, citizen, and family member, than if they are confined to a nursing home, are unable to perform those roles, and are dissatisfied with these arrangements. Along the same vein, persons may be judged to have a higher quality of life if they are able to participate in community life and a full range of social interactions than if they are restricted involuntarily to the home environment and a narrow range of social roles.

In order to present a comprehensive profile of patients' lives which may be affected by health interventions, the measurement of quality of life generally should include four other core dimensions in addition to role performance (Levine and Croog 1984). Thus, the following five dimensions need to be assessed in varying combination or *in toto*:

1. the performance of social roles
2. the physiological state of the individual
3. the emotional status of the individual
4. the intellective or cognitive functioning of the individual
5. the sense of well-being or general satisfaction

Aside from questions about a person's ability to perform and derive satisfaction from social roles specifically, we might ask in regard to each of the other four dimensions such questions as the following:

Physiological status. To what extent is the person mobile? To what degree is the individual free from pain and physical symptoms such as weakness, dizziness, exhaustion, and sleeplessness?

Emotional status. Does the person feel anxious, jittery, or disorganized? Is there a feeling of stability and self-control?

Intellective or cognitive functioning. Is the person alert? Is the person's memory intact? Does the individual have confidence in his or her decision-making capacity? Does he or she have the ability to carry out intellective functions necessary for performance of social roles?

Sense of well-being and life satisfaction. Does the person approach each day with a sense of interest, vitality, and enthusiasm or with a feeling of dread, despair, or lethargy? How satisfied is the person with the various components of his or her life?

Applying Quality of Life Criteria: Disease Severity and Trajectory, Sociodemographic Factors, and Cultural Factors

Although the five above components underlie the assessment of an individual's quality of life, operational measures of them cannot be applied uniformly or mechanically. These components are contingent upon and modified by at least the following three considerations: the severity and course or trajectory of the illness or condition; the social and demographic characteristics of the individual; and the social context in which the individual lives.

From the standpoint of the patient's subjective experience and perception, illnesses can be characterized in terms of several possible trajectories, each of which has differing implications for evaluating quality of life. Some examples are those that have (1) progressive chronicity with long-term survival and no acute phase; (2) a clear pattern of downward course without a markedly acute phase, leading to terminal illness and death; (3) an acute phase, followed by progressive worsening, possibly continuing over a period of years; or (4) an acute phase, followed by periods of remission, and recurrence of the acute condition prior to death (Dimond 1983; Kasl 1983; Moos and Tsu 1977).

Illnesses, particularly those of chronic types, can fit the typology in a variety of ways. For example, patients with chronic conditions such as some forms of glaucoma, arthritis, or mild to moderate hypertension would fit type (1) in this categorization. Patients with AIDS are generally considered today as conspicuous examples of the type (4) category. A myocardial infarction in a middle-aged patient may be most clearly of type (2), (3), or (4). Similarly, the cancer patient with carcinoma of the colon may fit into any of the categories listed as (2), (3), or (4).

In making the evaluation of the quality of life of patients, some criteria are more salient than others, depending on such elements as the illness, sociodemograhic factors, the social context, and the point on the trajectory of the illness when measurements are made. We would thus evaluate quality of life of a patient in the terminal, debilitated stages of cancer in terms of differing criteria than that of a worker in the early stages of cancer who is at the peak of his career. Similarly, the analysis of quality of life of an elderly, homebound female heart patient must be carried out in terms of a differing framework than would be applied to the young woman with heart disease who is employed as a salesclerk. We would not expect the same band of indicators to be employed for a person with more severe impairment, such as chronic obstructive pulmonary disease. We would have less ambitious expectations of the patient's level of functioning, and hence we would use a different set of measures appropriate to his total situation (Selby et al. 1984).

Even more, if one is trying to assess the quality of life of a terminal patient, one might focus to a greater degree on more limited capacities, such as the ability of the person to recognize other individuals, to enjoy social interaction, to use the telephone, and to be alert for periods of time. One would not expect the same level of social role performance as community activities or gainful employment to enter into the quality of life assessment of the dying patient (Morris et al. 1986).

Similarly, adjustments would have to be made for patients who vary sociodemographically and culturally. For example, the meaning of work as a factor in quality of life may be evaluated differently by unskilled manual workers who do dull and repetitive jobs, as compared with those who are independent professionals who are able to control the conditions of their work. Are the quality of life measures that may be suitable for evaluating adults in New Orleans applicable automatically to residents in a small town in France? Are the quality of life assessments designed for health studies in a New York suburb suitable as well to Hispanic residents in Los Angeles? Assessment of quality of life across cultural groups or in subsegments of the society clearly requires special care to be certain the instruments developed in one context are valid in others (Patrick et al. 1985).

Investigators unfortunately have often inappropriately transferred instruments developed for subpopulations in one setting to other areas, or they have used them with other populations than for which the original instrument had been designed (Ware 1984). At the current stage of the art, such procedures seem unavoidable in many ways. However, over the long term there is a need for measures that are valid and reliable for the specific populations to be assessed.

In many circumstances, it is useful to employ generic measures that can be applied to a variety of illness conditions as well as to "normal" populations. However, depending upon the nature of the study in the health area, it will be important also to utilize disease-specific, refined measures relevant to the patient population being examined.

Other Issues in Making Assessments

Problems of validity and perspective. Over the past two decades, numerous new scales and instruments have been developed to measure quality of life in relation to health and illness (Clark and Fallowfield 1986; Wenger et al. 1984; Bergner et al. 1981; Patrick et al. 1988; Wortman and Yeaton 1985; Erickson 1984). One issue in the measurement of the construct is the lack of consistent congruence between objective and subjective measures. In evaluations of large health and social policy initiatives, quality of life is typically measured by such objective indicators as income levels, housing, sanitation facilities, or dietary intake (Campbell, Converse, and Rodgers 1976; Najman and Levine 1981). In contrast, subjective measures, such as

respondents' ratings of aspects of their lives in terms of satisfaction with income, housing, sanitation facilities, or dietary intake are used in smaller, more "clinically oriented" studies. It has been shown, however, that congruence between the two sets of measures cannot be assumed. For example, as studies by Campbell and others have noted (Campbell, Converse, and Rodgers 1976), persons with lower income may report higher levels of satisfaction in some life areas; for example, lower-income people report higher satisfaction with housing and their communities.

Another key problem in assessing quality of life is the selection of the appropriate informants. In health care the assessment of the patient, the physician, and family members on quality of life issues may differ greatly, with each applying their own standards. In the case of the hypertensive patient, for example, a study by Jachuck et al. (1982) illustrates profound differences in perception of outcomes. In an assessment of aspects of quality of life of a series of seventy-five patients, 100 percent of the physicians reported improvement in the patients, while only about half the patients themselves reported feeling improved. Moreover, only one relative-informant reported improvement in a patient, whereas the remainder reported degrees of worsening. Given such varying perspectives the issues of quality of life present complex problems in terms of conceptualization and measurement.

Measurement of quality of life. A major methodological issue in assessing quality of life in health studies is the feasibility of providing one summary assessment score for each patient. A single overall score clearly has merit for both descriptive and analytical purposes. By means of single scores, populations of patients can be characterized simply by relating the summary measures to other factors of interest (Ware 1986). Calculation of summary scores, while simplifying statistical analysis, is based on the assumption that different life areas can be meaningfully summed, with or without measures reflecting a system of weighting. Many researchers disagree, however, considering the summary score as overly simplistic for assessing a complex phenomenon for which there is no evidence of a single underlying dimension.

An alternate procedure uses a profile format to retain separate ratings for individual areas of quality of life. Such a system presents a portrait of the patient by each life area. The individual scores of patients in each area can then be compared. A disadvantage for analysis is that the individual scores give no inkling of what is going on in each of the other areas of the lives of patients. However, the profile approach is often useful in providing precise information on changes in particular aspects of quality of life in the context of a clinical trial or other health intervention. An alternative to the comparison of scores on individual areas of quality of life is the comparison of configurations of profiles or patterns of scores of patients. These configurations can serve then in a sense as summary scores for patients in making statistical comparisons in clinical trials.

QUALITY OF LIFE
AND CONTEMPORARY ISSUES
IN HEALTH CARE

Quality of Life Considerations in Medical Decision Making

Quality of life considerations increasingly are entering into medical decision making on choice of therapies, long-term medical regimens, and management of patients. As we have suggested, quality of life considerations necessarily must vary with the disease, the social characteristics of patients, and their social contexts. Some issues and dilemmas in assessing quality of life in the core of patients with serious illness are illustrated in relation to two highly prevalent diseases—hypertension and cancer.

Hypertension and Quality of Life

Hypertension is a major, widely disseminated illness in the adult population. About 25 percent of adults in the United States have a diastolic pressure of 90 mm Hg or higher (Taylor 1977). The number of hypertensive persons is about sixty million. The relatively recent development of a broad array of antihypertensive medications has opened the way to control of the disease on a mass basis. In the case of hypertension, quality of life issues have special relevance for health care of the individual patient (Lowdon and Hall 1985).

Therapeutic interventions, compliance, and quality of life. Hypertension in its mild to moderate stages is commonly experienced by patients as an asymptomatic disease. The treatment of the disease is often seen by many patients as worse than the disease itself. Patients using antihypertensive medications may experience side effects that substantially interfere with social relations, the quality of a marriage, and work performance (Curb et al. 1985; Croog et al. 1986, 1988). Feelings of lethargy and tiredness, clouded sensorium, dizziness, inability to function effectively at work because of cognitive impairment and lower energy level, emotional lability, depressed mood, sexual dysfunction including impotence, nightmares, and general feelings of malaise are among the more common symptoms. Although discomforting symptoms are not experienced by all patients, they constitute a serious medical and public health problem in the treatment of hypertensives (Bulpitt 1982).

The experiencing of side effects may contribute to inadequate adherence to the medical regimen or to total noncompliance. Indeed, some investigators have found over a 50 percent drop-out rate from the hypertensive pharmacologic regimen in the course of long-term therapy (Haynes et al. 1982). Another negative property of antihypertensive medications is their potential for discouraging persons with high blood pressure from entering therapy in the first place. Thus, knowledge of side effects among family members and acquaintances may lead persons with frank hypertension to avoid treatment. It may influence others at risk, such as those with family histories of hypertension, from seeing a physician or participating in hypertension screening programs at work or other settings. The extent to which this knowledge blocks care-seeking in the first place has been inadequately studied and is generally unknown.

Problems in doctor-patient communication. Although antihypertensive medications can have major impact on the quality of life of hypertensives, physicians are often unaware of these effects on their individual patients. In the pharmacologic treatment of this illness, problems of doctor-patient communication may play a significant role (Levine and Croog 1985). Physicians may not question the patient in sufficient depth regarding the various life areas that the drugs can affect. Further, patients may not recognize that their symptoms are related to the antihypertensive medications. For example, it is easy for the middle-aged patient experiencing fatigue, emotional lability, sexual dysfunction, or cognitive impairment to assume that the problems are related to the aging process or physical or emotional stress in the home or at work. Patients will be unable subjectively to identify other side effects, such as suppression of white blood cells, that become explicit with laboratory tests. Respiratory and other illnesses may be associated secondarily with the physiological impact of the drugs, and such illnesses will not ordinarily be brought spontaneously to the attention of the physician as medication related.

Thus, quality of life plays a major and particularly obvious role in the treatment and control of hypertension. In its mild to moderate form this disease is virtually symptomless, but the medications can produce many side effects, affecting quality of life and leading to noncompliance. These problems can perhaps best be addressed in

clinical practice if proper inquiries are made by medical personnel and treatment is adjusted accordingly and as needed.

Cancer Treatment and Quality of Life

Quality of life issues concerning the cancer patient constitute a somewhat more complex picture than in the case of the hypertensive patient. Cancer is characterized as a variety of diseases, and there is considerable variability in severity, rate of progression, areas of body affected, degree of morbidity, and effects on life span (Prout, Colton, and Smith 1987). The impact on various areas of quality of life, for example, can be relatively minor for patients with basal cell carcinoma as compared with those with cancer of the pancreas, destructive facial cancer, or advanced colon or rectal cancer. Hence, more than in the case of hypertension, the treatment of cancer raises a complex array of challenges for medical decision making.

In contrast to the pharmacologic therapy of mild to moderate hypertension, where the treatment is more subjectively noxious to the patient than the disease, the treatment of cancer in conjunction with the progressive disease itself can have consequences that are painful and costly for patients in terms of physical, psychological, and social well-being. Marshall and Graham (1986, p. 161) have described in brief, graphic terms the impact of major kinds of therapy in several key areas of quality of life. They note:

Surgery—the excising of the cancerous lesion and the removal of enough surrounding flesh to make spread of the lesion unlikely—is a crude disheartening form of therapy. It often is disfiguring: a breast cancer patient may have to live with one breast, an oral cancer patient without a lower jaw. It can be demeaning: a colon cancer patient may have to use a plastic bag attached to his or her side as a repository for feces, the prostatic cancer patient may be left impotent, and the laryngeal cancer patient, to talk, will have to swallow air and belch words or phrases.

. . . Radiation can cause severe systemic illness: anorexia, nausea, general debilitation. Moreover, an individual may be successfully treated by radiation therapy for one cancer but then later experience another caused by the therapy. . . . In spite of its significant therapeutic value, chemotherapy's severe systemic effects can devastate an individual. It is not uncommon, in fact for the course of chemotherapy to be changed because the therapy's side effects have become so severe that they are life threatening. Clearly work and other aspects of social function can be severely disrupted by such treatment.

Quality of life considerations become more complicated when they are cast against the specific data on survival rates for cancer in different sites. Survival rates for some cancers are still judged to be poor for many patients, although from the standpoint of a policymaker or epidemiologist the rates may represent substantial improvement over earlier baselines (Bailar and Smith 1986). According to data reported by Page and Asire (1985) the overall five-year survival rate for all cancer patients as of 1985 was about 48 percent. Thus, on the positive side many patients may read statistics to the effect that five-year survival rates for the period 1973-1979 were 87 percent for cancer of the uterus, 76 for skin melanoma, and 72 for breast cancer (female). On the other hand, despite the improvements in diagnosis and treatment, survival rates for cancers of the lung, stomach, pancreas, and esophagus are low (11, 13, 1, and 4 percent, respectively) (Page and Asire 1985).

In the treatment of many types of cancer, in instances where survival rates often do not differ significantly between therapies, the effects of alternate therapies on quality of life may vary profoundly (Clark and Fallowfield 1986; Schipper and Levitt 1985; Spitzer et al. 1981; Morris et al. 1986). Hence, a major issue relating to quality of life and the care of the cancer patient is the selection of the therapy, as both the short-term and long-term consequences will differ according to the choice which is made.

Who should make the choice? Using what criteria? In terms of what value system? Under what conditions should the choice be made? Decision processes are multidimensional, involving a series of actors, values, situational influences, formal and informal factors, and other elements. In the case of the selection of therapies in cancer, a major consideration for doctors, patients, and families is the need to balance considerations of potential for survival, the possible length of remission, and the impact of the therapy on quality of life.

Key factors in decisions are (1) the extent to which freedom of choice is made available to patients by their physicians and (2) the nature of the choices, that is, prediction of the anticipated effects of the method selected on quality of life. In some instances, physicians concerned primarily with the survival and physical status of patients tend to be less concerned about quality of life, since they are guided by classic and established training, values, and orientation as to what constitute the appropriate goals of medical care.

In one of the few studies of factors in physician decision making in relation to quality of life and serious illness, Pearlman and Jonsen (1985) point out that from the standpoint of the physician such decisions must be balanced not only against matters of physical survival but against a whole series of other legal and ethical questions, of which quality of life is only one consideration. Cost-benefit considerations, the patient's right to determine his own treatment, the physician's traditional responsibility to sustain life, and the patient's future social productivity are among a series of concerns that impinge on clinical decision making in addition to the patient's quality of life.

For the cancer patient, the paucity of systematic information concerning the impact of different therapies on the quality of life, both immediate and long-term, adds to the complexity of making decisions about the optimum therapy (Fayers and Jones 1983; Sugarbaker et al. 1982). However, even if good data on quality of life were available along with those on the survival and recurrence rates of different therapies, another type of issue may arise involving conflict between values and goals of the patient, the physician, the family, and other actors in the health care system. If one therapy for the cancer appears to improve survival and another affects survival minimally but improves quality of life significantly, the choice as to which one to select is a difficult one. Which set of values should be paramount? Whose judgment should prevail?

In the abstract, the answer can easily be given that the ultimate decision should be the patient's. However, we know that many influences shape the "decision" of the patient. Among the most important of these are the preferences or recommendations of the physician. In addition, social class, ethnic background, religion, psychological characteristics, relationships in the family, and many other factors may affect choices patients make when faced with questions concerning survival and quality of life. We do not as yet have adequate information with regard to factors associated with how cancer patients make their decisions in this complex matrix of influences (Pearlman and Jonsen 1985).

Decision Making: Expanding Definitions of "Patients"

The primary target person in quality of life concerns as they relate to health care is most often the patient, of course. However, for purposes of making quality of life assessments, significant others in the life of the patients should often be the focus of evaluation as well. For example, in the case of the patient with severe Alzheimer's disease, the health care concerns appropriately center first on the patient. However, in terms of quality of life problems, the family of the patient can be even more profoundly affected by Alzheimer's than the patient, who may be in a sense "lost" or impervious in the dementia of the illness.

It is estimated that for every American presently suffering some degree of dementia, there may be up to three times that number of close family members whose lives are deeply affected by the emotional, physical, social and financial burdens of caring for Alzheimer's victims. . . . The needs of an ill or frail parent with Alzheimer's disease may create or exacerbate a condition of multiple demands for their children's time, energy, money, and emotional support, resulting in increased health problems for caregivers. (Weiler 1987, p. 1157)

Given the impact of the disease of the Alzheimer's patients on their own quality of life, family members may respond with depression, resentment, frustration, and in other ways that can affect how they provide care for the patient. Thus, the impact of Alzheimer's disease on the family as well as the patient may have powerful implications for planning treatment programs and for providing continued support from family care givers (Zarit, Orr, and Zarit 1985; Gottlieb 1983).

Impingement of quality of life issues on the family are dramatically illustrated as well in the case of the dying patient. In this instance can we consider that the whole family is also the "patient" in a sense (Osterweis, Solomon, and Green 1984)? In the case of the terminal patient, studies have shown that the processes of bereavement in family members may be ongoing before death has occurred, that is, while the patient is still present to interact with the grieving person. Feelings of sorrow, hostility, and resentment toward the dying person for leaving may be present before death has occurred. If the terminal illness is one that can be interpreted as preventable—as in the case of the patient dying of lung cancer—feelings of resentment toward the patient may complicate the life of the patient's family. In the case of some family members, such as young children of the dying person, the emotional burden of the dying process may be especially hard (Levine and Scotch 1970).

In instances where a chronic or terminal illness or injury bears some stigma, such as the sequelae of suicide, AIDS, self-caused injuries from drunken driving, or use of illegal drugs, the quality of life of family members may be negatively affected both immediately and over the long term (Kane et al. 1985). Beyond the prospective physical loss of the patient, there may be problems of medical care expenses, depleted finances, loss of income from the wage earner, the need for readjustment of role relations and responsibilities, and the loss of the emotional and affectional support from the patient. Although many of these quality of life problems of the family are inherent problems of life, some of them may be profitably mediated by the physician or by administrative policies of health care organizations (Croog and Levine 1982).

If the quality of life of the family as well as the patient indeed can be defined as a legitimate object of concern, this has implications for changes in the provision of counseling and social services, the behavior of physicians and other health care personnel, and administrative policies of health care organizations. Many of the problems may be more effectively ameliorated by their interventions. Although programs and policies of many professions and organizations within the health care system are already in place and are proceeding along these lines, there is continuing controversy about their relative importance and their financial costs, given other priorities for the care of patients.

Growth of Health Care Technology and Quality of Life

As noted earlier, in many ways the diagnosis and treatment of many major illnesses and conditions are being transformed by the introduction of high technological innovations, such as lasers, nuclear imaging, organ transplantation, the CAT scan, echocardiography, microsurgery, and by the development of new drugs and treatments for some of the most resistant illnesses and chronic conditions. Some of these innovations extend life without affecting the quality of life, whereas others apper to shape quality of life without extending longevity. Hence they present an array of outcomes that have different implications for the patient and for society.

Many of these innovations have been welcomed primarily because of quality of life concerns, whereas others are objected to because these concerns appear to be violated. For example, although coronary artery bypass surgery, a prominent form of surgical intervention, has not consistently demonstrated its ability to significantly extend life, it has been credited in many studies with significantly relieving pain and enhancing quality of life (Cohen 1982; Arora, Sager, and Butler 1986; Westaby 1979). On the other hand, some respiratory and electronic devices have been able to extend life in the moribund patient but do not enhance quality of life. At the extreme end of the continuum, the artificial heart has been able to extend life for a few days or weeks, but for many persons it appears to offend definitions of what constitutes quality of life.

When the application of technology prevents premature death for a whole class of patients such as the geriatric population, then an entire set of new issues arises in regard to the effects of living with the chronic disease or condition. Not only are new financial costs entailed, but health care providers and policymakers are confronted with the immense task of addressing the health and well-being of the increasing numbers of elderly in our society (Lawrence and Gaus 1983). The problem of total costs and effects on quality of life may be presented more clearly in the case of specific illnesses and conditions, such as renal disease or heart transplants.

Renal disease offers a dramatic illustration of the intersection of technological and quality of life considerations (Plough 1986). Even more, it points out the dilemmas we encounter not only with regard to decisions made for *individual* patients but the need to weigh quality of life factors in making decisions concerning *aggregates* of patients.

The development of kidney dialysis and transplant technology now means the survival of many hundreds of thousands of patients. The additional costs to the nation because of the availability of these procedures have often been cited. Through the Medicare End-Stage Disease Program, current expenditures for care approximate $2 billion a year. Beyond issues of the costs of such substantial allocation of resources, new questions concerning quality of life come to the fore about the consequences of survival and the multiple effects of treatment programs.

Only recently has systematic research been carried out comparing the quality of life of patients receiving the four major treatments: home dialysis, in-center hemodialysis, continuous ambulatory peritoneal dialysis, and transplantation. Evans et al. (1985) have reported the highest quality of life among patients undergoing dialysis treatment at home. In this instance in which astronomical sums must be expended for the care of this aggregate of patients, the relative weight of quality of life factors remains difficult to balance against other elements of cost, feasibility, personnel costs, administrative efficiency, and other factors. In the case of renal disease and other major illnesses, furthermore, the knowledge base on quality of life effects is thin, and there is clear need for research on both the immediate and long-term effects that stem from the application of the technology.

Interactions between survival and quality of life concerns associated with new technologies are also seen in one of the more dramatic innovations, heart transplants. Among cohorts of patients who receive heart transplants a number of them do not survive the operation or the immediate recovery period. Hence, evaluations of the impact of the operation on quality of life must obviously center on the select population of survivors. Some studies have reported among survivors a high proportion who were "successfully rehabilitated" (91 percent) (Christopherson, Griepp, and Stinson 1976). These were patients carefully screened prior to surgery. The post-

surgery quality of life was tempered by the need of such patients to adhere carefully and meticulously to the medical regimen, "to master tasks of self-care that were critical to continued survival" (Christopherson, Griepp, and Stinson 1976). These included accurate and regular self-medication, avoidance of persons or situations that might be sources of infection, and adherence to restrictions on diet, weight, exercise.

Other studies have pointed to limitations on the quality of life of the heart transplant patient associated with the need of immunosuppressive therapy and its side effects, including loss of muscle strength, skin bruising, and sore knee joints (Samuelson, Hunt, and Schroeder 1984). However, pervading the lives of many of the patients was the sense of vulnerability to death, the apparent instability of their own medical condition, and the threat of infection. For some, the fact of being identified in their social relationships as a transplant patient constituted a burden. Hence, in evaluation of the effects of this technology on quality of life, it is clear that the whole array of issues involving survival, performance, and long-term social and psychological impact must be part of the assessment (Gaudiani et al. 1981).

By extending survival time of patients with critical illnesses, technological innovations are also confronting society with a host of moral and ethical issues that by now are well known in the scientific literature as well as the popular media (Brim et al. 1970; Edlund and Tancredi 1985). At the same time, these technological innovations and their pervasive effects on quality of life are encountering increasing scrutiny and skepticism from diverse quarters, including those who are sanguine about cost containment and "rational" allocation of resources. The task remains to build more precise and reliable information on the impacts that different technological innovations actually have on the quality of life of patients, as well as on that of the society as a whole (Goldman and Cook 1984).

Cost Containment in Health Care

Health care costs in the United States now approximate a half-trillion dollars per year, accounting for more than 11 percent of the gross national product (U.S. Department of Commerce 1986; Ginzberg 1987). At present there is major concern from differing perspectives about health care costs among broad segments of the population, ranging from patients, their families, and physicians to health care policymakers at the federal, state, and local levels. Also concerned are economists, politicians, hospital administrators, insurance companies, unions, and many other individuals and groups. Ways of cutting costs without compromising quality of care are under continued discussion. As Ginzberg has put it, "True cost containment depends on controlling the costs of the health care system as a whole without impairing quality" (1987, p. 1153).

In recent years many cost-control plans and programs have been devised, including formula mechanisms such as DRGs to control hospital costs and PSROs to mediate physician behavior in providing health care, the establishment of HMOs, and the application of federal and state restrictions on hospital construction and purchase of equipment. Maintaining quality of care has been a continued consideration in these efforts at cost containment, whereas less specific attention has customarily been given to the impact of cost cutting on an important aspect of quality of care—the quality of life of the patient.

From a larger policy standpoint some analysts have been increasingly employing economic cost-benefit frameworks to assess the impact of health-related government policies and technological innovations on health and life span, on monetary consequences, and on quality of life (Viscusi 1986; Zeckhauser and Shepard 1976; Rice and Cooper 1967). In considering costs and in ascribing monetary value to aspects of quality of life, the problems of assessment are obviously complex. In the case of

heart disease, for example, there are many aspects of quality of life that have different valuation to the heart patient experiencing them as compared with the family, the physician, the insurance carrier, the hospital administrator, and the finance-oriented health care planner concerned with cost containment. It is difficult to reach consensus on how to weigh the value of additional waking time for the heart patient, relief of pain for an additional hour of the day, the ability to walk up an extra flight of stairs, or working a full day with a mind unclouded by medications (Fuchs 1974). Delineating the value of different increments of improved quality of life may offend many others who feel that an "accounting" approach is demeaning, mechanistic, and a violation of human dignity.

Carrying through with cost-related quality of life concerns in health care may be accomplished through at least three different, sometimes overlapping, means. These are (1) utilization of one therapy or technology over another on the basis of both efficacy in treatment and quality of life, (2) more intensive effort by clinicians in attending to quality of life issues in the care of patients, and (3) increased use of support and paraprofessional personnel as an adjunct to the physician. In the case of the latter two strategies, the use of additional services can add to usual costs of care in major ways. For example, if physicians spend more time with patients in order to deal adequately with quality of life concerns, two costs are evident: (1) the direct cost of additional physician time, and (2) the indirect costs resulting from the fact that, in working intensively with a more limited set of patients, the physician is not applying his or her technical skills to other patients who might in other circumstances be receiving them.

If there are additional costs because of attending to quality of life, who should pay them? In the case of the private practitioner, taking more time with each individual patient may threaten loss of income. Third-party payers, for their part, may be reluctant to pay extra costs. Systematic efforts by nonphysician professionals in behalf of quality of life issues in patient care also may not garner great support if they are not adequately reimbursed.

The reorganization of medical practice in the interest of cost saving and improving efficiency may also in some instances be antithetical to quality of life concerns. In HMOs and in private hospitals, the organization of care may militate against a more traditional doctor-patient relationship and in turn may reduce attention to quality of life concerns. This, of course, may be mediated by the efforts of other health care personnel.

As we have noted earlier, an important development in recent years in the assessment of new technologies and therapies has been consideration of their impact on quality of life. Benefits in terms of both treatment efficacy and quality of life are now often balanced against the financial costs. However, in these assessments of the cost benefits of treatment, the assessments of quality of life are generally far less systematic and sophisticated than those appraising treatment efficacy. Complicating matters is the development of new alternative therapies, resulting in the prospect that the assessments become rapidly outmoded.

Costs of Alternative Therapies

As we have suggested, the high costs of coronary artery bypass surgery and the rapid proliferation of this treatment led to broad questioning about its long-term implications as a therapeutic modality. On a national level the costs have been remarkable: In 1980 costs of coronary artery surgery were estimated at approximately $2 billion, or about 1 percent of total health care expenditures (Weinstein and Stason 1982; Roe 1981). Over the past decade, studies have proliferated in order to assess the relative merit of coronary surgery over traditional medical treatment, taking into consideration survival, symptom reduction,

costs, and quality of life (Wortman and Yeaton 1985; Bass 1984; DeCaprio et al. 1980; Smith, Frye, and Piehter 1983; Jenkins 1983).

However, even as the assessment of coronary surgery is incomplete, a rival treatment of choice has appeared in the development of coronary angioplasty, the dilation of coronary arteries to relieve obstruction through a balloon device. Though the first clinical use was as recent as 1977, the diffusion of the technique has been even more rapid than in the case of bypass surgery. As Reeder (1986) reports, performance of angioplasty doubled from 32,000 in 1983 to 63,000 in 1984, whereas the number of bypass operations remained relatively stable for those two years. By 1987 it was estimated that 150,000 coronary angioplasties would be performed in the United States (Kent 1987). A major goal was symptom relief, a key criterion in the evaluation of effects of bypass surgery on quality of life.

The benefits of the one therapy over the other—in terms of cost, patient survival, the need for redoing the procedures, and quality of life—remain still to be definitively evaluated. The National Heart, Lung and Blood Institute has initiated a clinical trial to compare the two therapies. But as Kent (1987) points out, it will be many years before the results are in. In the meantime, other improved therapies are being developed, leading to the possible consequence that by the time the definitive evaluations are made, demand for the new therapies will have largely replaced need for the "old." Thus, given the complexities of assessing cost benefits of health care innovations, it is exceedingly difficult also to balance quality of life benefits against cost considerations.

The introduction of innovative medications for the treatment of hypertension also raises problems in making cost-conscious policy decisions. For example, new angiotensin converting enzyme ACE inhibitors have served to improve the quality of life for the hypertensive patient on medications (Croog et al. 1986). Such drugs have fewer negative effects on physical status, cognitive function, sexual functioning, work performance, personal energy level, and other aspects of quality of life. However, according to Stason (1987), widespread use of the ACE inhibitors or the new calcium channel blockers in the treatment of mild to moderate hypertension could add a billion dollars or more to the costs of the care of hypertensives in the United States. Stason asks, "Are the advantages of the newer, more expensive medications sufficient to warrant their higher costs—and in which patients?"

If blood pressure control is not markedly different from that for the older drugs, but quality of life is improved, the questions about whether the added costs are warranted are difficult ones from the policy standpoint. For the individual hypertensive patient, the choices may be clear, if the rewards are the avoidance of lethargy, sexual dysfunction, or impaired work performance. However, from the perspectives of national health care planners, health insurance carriers, employers, and other relevant parties, the issue may be more problematic. Here, once again, the relative value of individual patient preferences may have to be considered against the prospect of higher costs for the aggregate.

The Availability and Deployment and Training of Health Care Personnel

As policymakers focus more attention on quality of life concerns in the care of patients, the availability of resources for dealing with these concerns becomes an increasingly important matter. Two continuing problems are (1) the adequacy of the supply of personnel who can assist with quality of life aspects of health care and (2) facilitating the use of available services of such personnel by those patients who can benefit from them.

If the model of illness is expanded and if health care professionals can be expected to assume a more prominent role in ad-

dressing quality of life concerns, what implications does this have for estimates of the number of health care workers required to meet the health needs of the population? Physicians may make increasing use of social services, visiting nursing services, mental health services, support groups, and other adjunct personnel. However, even as quality of life becomes a more salient concern in health care, the availability of necessary health personnel is problematic. For example, as is well known, the role of the nurse is changing, and the recruitment of nurses for the future remains a continuing concern.

Finally, the recruitment of personnel to work with patients and families on quality of life issues may also be affected by the development of "new" forms of care. The rise of the hospice over recent years is an example (Paradis and Cummings 1986; Kane et al. 1985; Potter 1980). The programs of these institutions are oriented to quality of life, serving the needs of both patient and family and providing medical, psychological, social service, and often spiritual support. Serving as an adjunct to the traditional medical care system, they make use of traditionally trained nursing and social service personnel as well as volunteers. Fulfillment of the original humanistic goals of the hospice becomes more difficult as conflicts emerge regarding standards for quality of care, systems of funding, governmental and professional regulatory requirements, and administrative efficiency.

Channeling Patients to Appropriate Personnel

Aside from the problems of personnel supply, a pervasive issue involves the barriers to channeling patients or clients to the services of personnel from which they can benefit. Many factors can be operative. For example, bringing patients in touch with relevant service organizations and personnel—such as social services, homemakers, visiting nurses, and the hospice—is often a function of referrals by physicians. However, in many instances, patients are not informed about such services. As a result, patients and their families may have problems working through the maze of bureaucracy.

Clearly as new attention is devoted to quality of life, we can anticipate changes in demand for personnel, new ways of recruiting them, and greater focus on physician referral patterns and on ways in which patients and families may be guided to services already available.

Patient Rights, the Self-Help Movement, and the Popular Culture

The development of the patient rights movement over the past two decades, the growth of the self-help movement, and new attention to the importance of patient choice in medical decision making are having their effects as well on the quality of life of patients with serious and chronic diseases (Pancoast, Parker, and Froland 1983). In the United States, "consumerism" has assumed the dimensions of a major movement (Borman and Pasquale 1982; Katz 1981). There is increasing evidence that patients are assuming greater initiative in raising questions with their physicians and discussing matters more openly and directly than before. Many physicians in turn are also becoming more sensitive to quality of life issues in the treatment of their patients. Although both trends may still be in their early stages in some respects, the two developments appear to be converging and may lead to better communication concerning treatment, planning of regimens, and selection of medications.

These themes appear in differing degrees in relation to varying types of illness conditions. The case of hypertension perhaps represents an extreme point of the continuum in terms of the degree of attention focused by both patients themselves and their clinicians on quality of life. As Siegrist and Williams have noted (1987), until recently, quality of life considerations were judged to be important parameters in clinical decision making primarily in patients with severe chronic diseases, such as renal disease and cancer, and in persons with major physical handicaps. Over the past several decades the development of antihypertensive medications that have a widely differing spectrum of side effects has meant greater opportunities for questioning by patients and clinicians about the effects of a particular drug on quality of life (Kaplan 1983; Moser 1981; Waller 1985). Through dissemination of information in the popular media, patients now may raise questions about alternate drugs that may be more favorable to their own quality of life (*Lancet* 1986). In fact, both riding and encouraging this trend, major drug companies have recently emphasized quality of life in their advertising. Some companies through ads on television and in newspapers encourage patients and spouses to talk with their physicians about the effects of medications on quality of life.

In the case of cancer, the problem of patient choices of treatment has been a continuing theme, and the popular culture has disseminated information about a variety of alternatives. The treatment of some cancer patients has been complicated by the lure of nontraditional health practitioners and health interventions. This has been in part a reaction to observations that some traditional medical and surgical approaches are painful, do not appreciably extend survival time, and have undesirable consequences regarding quality of life (Silberfarb, Philibert, and Levine 1980). Hence, patients have sought out chiropractors, naturopaths, acupuncturists, spiritual healers, nutrition therapists, and other nonmedical practitioners.

Although they may not produce any greater rates of cure than traditional medicine, in the case of chronic diseases these alternative approaches often offer the hope of less compromise in quality of life. Often they are sought by patients after a series of negative experiences with the traditional health system. The perceived failures of the traditional health system in ways that bear on quality of life have tended to foster the use and continued viability of the less traditional health interventions.

In line with the self-help movement and consumerism trends, more cancer patients and their families may be seeking information outside the physician's office concerning the disease, therapies, survival, and quality of life. The National Cancer Institute has encouraged this trend. Recently a cancer information service has been made available on a national basis to patients and families. The data base, the Physician Data Query system, contains information on state of the art and investigational treatments (Hubbard, Henney, and DeVita 1987). Designed originally for use by physicians, it now provides the general public with information about kinds of cancer treatments and where they are available (*Hartford Courant* 1987). This information can then be discussed by patients with their doctors, helping maximize the communication process.

It would be inaccurate to portray here a massive transformation in the clinical approach to all diseases under the influence of popular culture and the patient self-help movement. Nevertheless, as we look at the "frontiers" of health care and the developing themes that will mold the future, it appears that the concerns with quality of life, as expressed through new openness between patients and physicians, may affect the planning of medical regimens, physician-patient interactions, and other aspects of health care.

CONCLUSION

The growing emphasis on quality of life as a major objective in health care poses problems and opportunities for the policymaker, the physician, the medical sociologist, and other behavioral scientists.

Policymakers will be confronted by some major areas for decision. The first pertains to the responsibility of third parties (insur-

ance carriers, government) to defray costs entailed in meeting quality of life concerns even though no improvement is anticipated in the patient's physical condition. For example, if two medications have equal impact in controlling hypertension, but the one that enhances quality of life is considerably more expensive, to what extent should the insurance carrier incur this additional cost?

For whom should inordinate efforts be expended to enhance quality of life? Should we follow the British lead in providing dialysis primarily to patients under age 60? In a similar vein, should our society pay for coronary bypass surgery for people at any age, or should there be some restriction based upon age, physical condition, and, ultimately, the presumed "social worth" of patients?

Physicians and other health care personnel will have to give increasing consideration to quality of life concerns. Indeed, in many instances quality of life considerations can be the dominant factor in decisions by patients and their families regarding therapy, even in matters involving life and death. This can range from (1) choices by the hypertensive patient to reject antihypertensive medications or not to adhere properly to a drug program to (2) the preference of the terminal patient to forgo further treatment.

As increasing emphasis is placed on quality of life as a major criterion in assessing the effectiveness and value of health interventions, the expertise of the medical sociologist and other behavioral scientists becomes increasingly relevant. Research on quality of life should include, in addition to physical functioning, at least the following dimensions: performance of social roles, emotional functioning, intellective functioning, and life satisfaction and well-being (Levine and Croog 1984). These dimensions are the special areas of expertise of the behavioral scientist. If quality of life concerns are to be met in clinical practice, research, and the formulation of health care policy, we may expect that the sociologist and other behavioral scientists will be playing significant roles.

ACKNOWLEDGMENTS

The authors are grateful to Robert Ebert, Ph.D., and Peter A. Wyman, Ph.D., for helpful editorial and substantive advice.

REFERENCES

Anderson, John P., James W. Bush, and Charles C. Berry. 1986. Classifying Function for Health Outcome and Quality-of-Life Evaluation. *Medical Care* 24:454–469.

Arora, Rohit, Jeffrey Sager, and Robert N. Butler. 1986. Therapeutic Goals: Quality and Quantity of Life. *Cardiology Clinics* 4:305–312.

Bailar, John C., III, and Elaine M. Smith. 1986. Progress Against Cancer? *New England Journal of Medicine* 314:1226–1232.

Bass, Christopher. 1984. Psychosocial Outcome after Coronary Artery By-Pass Surgery. *British Journal of Psychiatry* 145:526–532.

Bergner, Marilyn, Ruth A. Bobbitt, William B. Carter, and Betty S. Gilson. 1981. The Sickness Impact Profile: Development and Final Revision of a Health Status Measure. *Medical Care* 19:787–805.

Borman, Leonard D., and Frank L. Pasquale, eds. 1982. *Helping People to Help Themselves.* New York: Haworth Press.

Brim, Orville G., Jr., Howard E. Freeman, Sol Levine, and Norman A. Scotch. 1970. *The Dying Patient.* New York: Russell Sage.

Bulpitt, Christopher J. 1982. Quality of Life in Hypertensive Patients, in A. Amery, R. Fagard, P. Lijnen, and J. Staessen, eds., *Hypertensive Cardiovascular Disease: Pathophysiology and Treatment.* The Hague: Martinus Nijhoff, pp. 929–948.

Campbell, Angus, Philip E. Converse, and Willard L. Rodgers. 1976. *The Quality of American Life.* New York: Russell Sage.

Cereseto, Shirley, and Howard Waitzkin. 1986. Economic Development, Political Economic System, and the Physical Quality of Life. *American Journal of Public Health* 76:661–666.

Chambers, Larry W., Lorry A. MacDonald, Peter Tugwell, Watson W. Buchanan, and Gunnar Kraag. 1982. The McMaster Health Index Questionnaire as a Measure of Quality of Life for Patients with Rheumatoid Disease. *Journal of Rheumatology* 9:780–784.

Christopherson, Lois K., Randall B. Griepp, and Edward B. Stinson. 1976. Rehabilitation After Cardiac Transplantation. *Journal of the American Medical Association* 236:2082–2084.

Clark, A., and L. J. Fallowfield. 1986. Quality of Life Measurements in Patients with Malignant Disease: A Review. *Journal of the Royal Society of Medicine* 79:165–169.

Cohen, Carl. 1982. On the Quality of Life: Some Philosophical Reflections. *Circulation* 66(Supp. III):29–33.

Cohen, Cynthia B. 1983. "Quality of Life" and the Analogy with Nazis. *Journal of Medicine and Philosophy* 8:113–135.

Croog, Sydney H., and Sol Levine. 1982. *Life after a Heart Attack.* New York: Human Sciences Press.

Croog, Sydney H., Sol Levine, Abraham Sudilovsky, Robert M. Baume, and Jonathan Clive. 1988. Sexual Symptoms in Hypertensive Patients: A Clinical Trial of Antihypertensive Medications. *Achives of Internal Medicine* 148:788–794.

Croog, Sydney H., Sol Levine, Marcia A. Testa, Byron Brown, Christopher J. Bulpitt, C. David Jenkins, Gerald L. Klerman, and Gordon H. Williams. 1986. The Effects of Anti-Hypertensive Therapy on the Quality of Life. *New England Journal of Medicine* 314:1657–1664.

Curb, J. David, Nemat O. Borhani, Thomas P. Blaskowski, Neal Zimbaldi, Socrates Fotiu and Wallace Williams. 1985. Long Term Surveillance for Adverse Effects of Anti-Hypertensive Drugs. *Journal of the American Medical Association* 253:3263–3268.

DeCaprio, L. F. Rengo, N. Stampinato, P. Scarafile, L. Chiariello, P. Meccariello, and M. Romano. 1980. Exercise Tolerance as Evidence of Quality of Life in CAD Patients after Coronary Artery Bypass by Comparison with Medical Treatment. *Acta Cardiologica* 35:11–21.

Dimond, Margaret. 1983. Social Adaptation of the Chronically Ill, in D. Mechanic, ed., *Handbook of Health, Health Care, and the Health*

Professions. New York: Free Press, pp. 636–654.

Dubos, René. 1982. Interview. *Modern Maturity* August-September: 34–36.

Edlund, Matthew, and Laurence R. Tancredi. 1985. Quality of Life: An Ideological Critique. *Perspectives in Biology and Medicine* 28:591–607.

Erickson, Pennifer. 1984. Assessing Quality of Life among Persons with Cardiovascular Disease: A Supplemental Bibliography, in N.K. Wenger, M.E. Mattson, C.D. Furberg, and J. Elinson, eds., *Assessment of Quality of Life in Clinical Trials of Cardiovascular Therapies*. New York: Le Jacq., pp. 363–374.

Evans, Roger W., Diane L. Manninen, Louis P. Garrison, Jr., L. Gary Hart, Christopher R. Blagg, Robert A. Gutman, Alan R. Hull, and Edmund G. Lourie. 1985. The Quality of Life of Patients with End-Stage Renal Disease. *New England Journal of Medicine* 312:553–559.

Fayers, P. M., and D. R. Jones. 1983. Measuring and Analyzing Quality of Life in Cancer Clinical Trials: A Review. *Statistics in Medicine* 2:429–446.

Fuchs, Victor R. 1974. *Who Shall Live? Health, Economics and Social Choice*. New York: Basic Books.

Gaudiani, Vincent A., Edward B. Stenson, Edwin Alderman, Sharon A. Hunt, John S. Schroeder, Mark G. Perlroth, Charles P. Bieber, Philip E. Oyer, Bruce A. Reitz, Stuart W. Jamieson, Lois Christopherson, and Norman E. Shumway. 1981. Long-term Survival and Function after Cardiac Transplantation. *Annals of Surgery* 194:381–385.

Ginzberg, Eli. 1987. A Hard Look at Cost Containment. *New England Journal of Medicine* 316:1151–1154.

Goldman, Lee, and E. Francis Cook. 1984. The Decline in Ischemic Heart Disease Mortality Rates. An Analysis of the Comparative Effects of Medical Interventions and Changes in Lifestyle. *Annals of Internal Medicine* 101:825–836.

Gottlieb, Benjamin H. 1983. *Social Support Strategies*. Beverly Hills: Sage Publications, pp. 177–203.

Gorham, Lucy. 1986. *No Longer Leading. A Scorecard on U.S. Economic Performance and the Role of the Public Sector Compared with Japan, West Germany, and Sweden*. Washington, D.C.: Economic Policy Institute.

Guyatt, Gordon H., Claire-Bombardier, and Peter X. Tugwell. 1986. Measuring Disease-Specific Quality of Life for Clinical Trials. *Canadian Medical Association Journal* 134:889–895.

Hartford Courant. 1987. February 17, p. 33.

Haynes, R. Brian, Margaret E. Mattson, Aram V. Chobanian, Jacqueline M. Dunbar, Tilmer O. Engebretson, Thomas F. Garrity, Howard Leventhal, Robert J. Levine, and Rona Levy. 1982. Management of Patient Compliance in the Treatment of Hypertension. *Hypertension* 4:415–523.

Hubbard, Susan M., Jane E. Henney, and Vincent T. DeVita, Jr. 1987. A Computer Data Base for Information on Cancer Treatment. *New England Journal of Medicine* 316:315–318.

Jachuck, S.J., H. Brierley, S. Jachuck, and P. M. Willcox, 1982. The Effect of Hypotensive Drugs on the Quality of Life. *Journal of the Royal College of General Practitioners* 32:103–105.

Jenkins, C. David, Babette A. Stanton, Judity A. Savageau, Philip Denlinger, and Michael Klein. 1983. Coronary Artery Bypass Surgery. Physical, Psychological, Social, and Economic Outcomes Six Months Later. *Journal of the American Medical Association* 250:782–788.

Johanna, C. J. M. deHaes, and Ferdinand C. E. van Knippenberg. 1985. The Quality of Life of Cancer Patients: A Review of the Literature. *Social Science and Medicine* 20:809–817.

Kane, Robert L., Sandra J. Klein, Leslie Bernstein, Rebecca Rothenberg and Jeffrey Wales. 1985. Hospice Role in Alleviating the Emotional Stress of Terminal Patients and Their Families. *Medical Care* 23:189–197.

Kaplan, Norman M. 1983. Therapy of Mild Hypertension. *Journal of the American Medical Association* 249:365–367.

Kaplan, Robert M. 1985. Quality of Life Measurement, in P. Karoly, ed., *Measurement Strategies in Health Psychology*. New York: Wiley, pp. 115–146.

Kasl, Stanislav. 1983. Social and Psychological Factors Affecting the Course of Disease: An Epidemiological Perspective, in D. Mechanic, ed., *Handbook of Health, Health Care and the Health Professions*. New York: Free Press, pp. 683–708.

Katz, Alfred H. 1981. Self Help and Mutual Aid; An Emerging Social Movement. *Annual Review of Sociology* 7:129–155.

Kent, Kenneth M. 1987. Coronary Angioplasty. A Decade of Experience. *New England Journal of Medicine* 316:1148–1149.

Lancet. Risks of Anti-Hypertensive Therapy. *Lancet* 2 (No.8515):1075–1076.

Lawrence, Diane B., and Clifton R. Gaus, 1983. Long Term Care: Financing and Policy Issues, in D. Mechanic, ed., *Handbook of Health, Health Care and the Health Professions.* New York: Free Press, pp. 365–378.

Lester, David. 1985. The Quality of Life in Modern America and Suicide and Homicide Rates. *Journal of Social Psychology* 125:779–780.

Levine, Sol, and Sydney H. Croog. 1984. What Constitutes Quality of Life? A Conceptualization of the Dimensions of Life Quality in Healthy Populations and Patients with Cardiovascular Disease, in N. K. Wenger, M. E. Mattson, C. D. Furberg, and J. Elinson, eds., *Assessment of Quality of Life in Clinical Trials of Cardiovascular Therapies.* New York: Le Jacq., pp. 46–58.

Levine, Sol, and Sydney H. Croog. 1985. Quality of Life and the Patient's Response to Treatment. *Journal of Cardiovascular Pharmacology* 7 Supp.1:132–136.

Levine, Sol, Jacob J. Feldman, and Jack Elinson. 1983. Does Medical Care Do Any Good? in D. Mechanic, ed., *Handbook of Health, Health Care, and the Health Professions.* New York: Free Press, pp. 394–406.

Levine, Sol, and Norman A. Scotch. 1970. Dying as an Emerging Social Problem, in O. G. Brim, H. E. Freeman, S. Levine, and N. A. Scotch, eds., *The Dying Patient.* New York: Russell Sage, pp. 211–222.

Lowdon, J. Devon, and W. Dallas Hall. 1985. Quality of Life Issues in Hypertension and Behavior. *Quality of Life and Cardiovascular Care* 1:109–122.

Marshall, James, and Saxon Graham. 1986. Cancer, in L. H. Aiken and D. Mechanic, eds., *Applications of Social Science to Clinical Medicine and Health Policy.* New Brunswick, N.J.: Rutgers University Press, pp. 157–174.

Moberg, D. O., and P. M. Brusek. 1987. Spiritual Well-Being: A Neglected Subject in Quality of Life Research. *Social Indicators Research* 5:303–323.

Moos, Rudolf H., and Vivien D. Tsu. 1977. The Crisis of Physical Illness: An Overview, in R. H. Moos, ed., *Coping with Physical Illness.* New York: Plenum, pp. 3–21.

Morris, John N., Samy Suissa, Sylvia Sherwood, Susan M. Wright, and David Greer. 1986. Last Days: A Study of the Quality of Life of Terminally Ill Cancer Patients. *Journal of Chronic Diseases* 39:47–62.

Moser, Marvin. 1981. "Less Severe" Hypertension: Should it Be Treated? *American Heart Journal* 101:465–472.

Najman, Jackob M., and Sol Levine. 1981. Evaluating the Impact of Medical Care and Technologies on the Quality of Life: A Review and Critique. *Social Science and Medicine* 15F:107–115.

Organization for Economic Cooperation and Development (OECD). 1986. *Living Conditions in OECD Countries.* Paris: The Organization.

Osterweis, Marian, Fredric Solomon, and Morris Green, eds. 1984. *Bereavement, Reactions, Consequences, and Care.* Washington, D.C.: National Academy Press.

Page, Harriet S., and Ardyce J. Asire. 1985. *Cancer Rates and Risks.* NIH Publication No. 85-691, Public Health Service.

Pancoast, Diane L., and Paul Parker, and Charles Froland, eds. 1983. *Rediscovering 'Self Help.' Its Role in Social Care.* Beverly Hills: Sage Publications.

Paradis, Lenora F., and Scott B. Cummings. 1986. The Evolution of Hospice in America Toward Organizational Homogeneity. *Journal of Health and Social Behavior* 27:370–386.

Patrick, Donald L., Marion Danis, Leslie I. Southerland, and Guiyoung Hong. 1988. Quality of Life Following Intensive Care. *Journal of General Internal Medicine* 3:218–223.

Patrick, Donald L., Yoga Sittampalam, Sheena M. Somerville, William B. Carter, and Marilyn Bergner. 1985. A Cross-Cultural Comparison of Health Status Values. *American Journal of Public Health* 75:1402–1407.

Pearlman, Robert A., and Albert Jonsen. 1985. The Use of Quality-of-Life Considerations in Medical Decision Making. *Journal of the American Geriatric Society* 33:344–352.

Plough, Alonzo L. 1986. Borrowed Time, Artificial Organs and the Policy of Extending Lives. Philadelphia: Temple University Press.

Potter, John F. 1980. A Challenge for the Hospice Movement. *New England Journal of Medicine* 302:53–55.

Prout, Marianne N., Theodore Colton, and Robert A. Smith. 1987. Cancer Epidemiology and Health Policy, in S. Levine and A. Lilienfeld, eds., *Epidemiology and Health Policy.* New York: Tavistock Publications, pp. 117–156.

Reeder, Guy S. 1986. Socioeconomic Aspects, in R. E. Vlietstra and D. R. Holmes, Jr., eds., *Percutaneous Transluminal Coronary Angioplasty.* Philadelphia: F.A. Davis Co.

Rice, Dorothy, and Barbara Cooper. 1967. The Economic Value of Life. *American Journal of Public Health* 57:1954–1966.

Roe, Benson B. 1981. The UCR Boondoggle: A Death Knell for Private Practice? *New England Journal of Medicine* 305:41–45.

Samuelson, Rolf G., Sharon A. Hunt, and John S. Schroeder, 1984. Functional and Social Rehabilitation of Heart Transplant Recipients Under Age Thirty. *Scandinavian Journal of Thoracic and Cardiovascular Surgery* 18:97–103.

Schipper, H., and M. Levitt. 1985. Measuring Quality of Life: Risks and Benefits. *Cancer Treatment Reports* 69:1115–1123.

Selby, P. J., J.A. W. Chapman, J. Etazadi-Amoli, D. Dalley, and N. F. Boyd. 1984. The Development of a Method for Assessing the Quality of Life of Cancer Patients. *British Journal of Cancer* 50:13–22.

Siegrist, Johannes, and Gordon H. Williams. 1987. Introduction. *Journal of Hypertension* 5(Supp. 1):51–52.

Silberfarb, Peter M., Dawn Philibert, and Peter M. Levine. 1980. Psychosocial Aspects of Neoplastic Disease II. Affective and Cognitive Aspects of Chemotherapy in Cancer Patients. *American Journal of Psychiatry* 137:597–601.

Smith, Hugh C., Robert L. Frye, and Jeffrey M. Piehler. 1983. Does Coronary Bypass Surgery Have a Favorable Influence on the Quality of Life? *Cardiovascular Clinics* 13:253–264.

Spitzer, Walter O., Annette J. Dobson, June Hall, Esther Chesterman, John Levi, Richard Shepherd, Renaldo N. Battista, and Barry R. Catchlove. 1981. Measuring the Quality of Life of Cancer Patients. *Journal of Chronic Diseases* 34:585–597.

Stason, William B. 1987. Economics in Hypertension Management: Cost and Quality Trade-Offs. *Journal of Hypertension.* 5 (Supp.1):55–59.

Sugarbaker, Paul H., Ivan Barofsky, Steven A. Rosenberg, and Fred J. Gianola. 1982. Quality of Life Assessment of Patients in Extremity Sarcoma Clinical Trials. *Surgery* 91:17–23.

Taylor, James. 1977. The Hypertension Detection and Follow-Up Program: A Progress Report. *Circulation Research* 40(Supp. I): 1106–1109.

Thomas, Lewis. 1972. *Aspects of Biomedical Science Policy.* Washington, D.C.: Institute of Medicine.

U.S. Department of Commerce. 1986. *U.S. Industrial Outlook 1987: Health and Medical Services.* Washington, D.C.: U.S. Government Printing Office.

Viscusi, W. Kip. 1986. The Valuation of Risks to Life and Health, in J. D. Bentkover, V. T. Covello, and J. Mumpower, eds., *Benefits Assessment: The State of the Art.* Dordrecht, Netherlands: D. Reidel, pp. 193–210.

Waller, Patrick C., and Lawrence E. Ramsey. 1986. When is Drug Treatment Indicated in Mild Hypertension? *Public Health Reviews* 14:105–113.

Ware, John E., Jr. 1984. Conceptualizing Disease Impact and Treatment Outcomes. *Cancer* 53(Supp.):2316–2326.

———. 1986. The Assessment of Health Status, in L. H. Aiken and D. Mechanic, eds., *Applications of Social Science to Clinical Medicine and Health Policy.* New Brunswick, N.J.: Rutgers University Press, pp. 204–229.

Weiler, Philip G. 1987. The Public Health Impact of Alzheimer's Disease. *American Journal of Public Health* 77:1157–1158.

Weinstein, Milton C., and William B. Stason. 1982. Cost-Effectiveness of Coronary Artery Bypass Surgery. *Circulation* 66(Supp. III):56–65.

Wenger, Nanette, Margaret E. Mattson, Curt D. Furberg, and Jack Elinson, eds. 1984. *Assessment of Quality of Life in Clinical Trials of Cardiovascular Therapies.* New York: Le Jacq.

Westaby, Stephen, Ralph N. Sapsford, and Hugh Bentall. 1979. Return to Work and Quality of Life After Surgery for Coronary Artery Disease. *British Medical Journal* 2(6197):1028–1031.

Wortman, Paul M., and William H. Yeaton, 1985. Cumulating Quality of Life Results in

Controlled Trials of Coronary Artery Bypass Graft Surgery. *Controlled Clinical Trials* 6:289–305.

Zarit, Steven H., Nancy K. Orr, and Judy M. Zarit. 1985. *The Hidden Victims of Alzheimer's Disease. Families Under Stress.* New York: New York University Press.

Zautra, Alex, and Darlene Goodhart. 1979. Quality of Life Indicators: A Review of the Literature. *Community Mental Health Review* 4:1–10.

Zeckhauser, Richard, and Donald Shepard. 1976. Where Now for Saving Lives? *Law and Contemporary Problems* 40:5–45.

Contributors

LINDA H. AIKEN is Trustee Professor of Nursing and Sociology and Associate Director for Nursing Affairs of the Leonard Davis Institute of Health Economics at the University of Pennsylvania. She received her Ph.D. from the University of Texas at Austin. Aiken is the coeditor of *Applications of Social Science to Clinical Medicine and Health Policy* and *Evaluation Studies Review Annual* (Vol. 10), among others, and is the author of more than 80 papers on health policy issues.

RONALD M. ANDERSEN is Professor and Director of the Center for Health Administration Studies at the University of Chicago. His Ph.D. is from Purdue University. He is the coauthor of *Ambulatory Care and Insurance Coverage in an Era of Constraint* (1987) and has written other books and papers on health care organization and evaluation.

ROBERT BEAGLEHOLE is Associate Professor of Community Health at the Auckland University Medical School in New Zealand. Internationally respected for his contributions to the fields of cardiovascular epidemiology and medical care, his M.D. is from Auckland University.

MARSHALL H. BECKER is Professor in the Department of Health Behavior and Health Education and Associate Dean of the School of Public Health at the University of Michigan. His Ph.D. is from the University of Michigan. He is the coauthor of "Behavioral Science Perspectives on Health Hazard/Health Risk Appraisal"(*Health Services Research* 22:537–551, 1987) as well as over 100 articles on the health-related attitudes and behaviors of lay individuals and health professionals.

SUSAN E. BELL is Assistant Professor of Sociology in the Department of Sociology and Anthropology at Bowdoin College and Research Fellow in Sociology at the Laboratory in Social Psychiatry at Harvard Medical School. She received her Ph.D. from Brandeis University. She has written a number of articles about DES; medicalization; women's health; and the development, diffusion, and social impact of medical technology.

ELIZABETH A. BINNEY is a Research Associate in the Institute for Health and Aging and a doctoral candidate in the Department of Social and Behavioral Sciences of the University of California at San Francisco. She received her M.A. from Boston University. Binney is the coauthor of several articles on the political economy of health and health policy, women's issues, aging, and medical sociology.

J. BROOKS-GUNN is Senior Research Scientist at the Educational Testing Service and Clinical Associate Professor of Pediatrics at the University of Pennsylvania. She is the coauthor of *Adolescent Mothers in Later Life* and *Girls at Puberty* and has written numerous papers on childhood and adolescent health and development.

RALPH A. CATALANO is Professor of Social Ecology and Management at the University of California at Irvine. His Ph.D. is from the Maxwell School of Syracuse University. He is the author of *Health, Behavior, and the Community* and the coauthor of "Time Series Designs of Potential Interest to Epidemiologists" (*American Journal of Epidemiology* 126:724–731, 1987), and has written more than a score of publications on the health and behavioral effects of change in metropolitan economies.

SYDNEY H. CROOG is Professor of Behavioral Sciences and Community Health at the University of Connecticut Health Center in Farmington. He received his Ph.D. from Yale University. He is the coauthor, with Sol Levine, of *Life After a Heart Attack: Eight Years Later* and *The Heart Patient Recovers* and has written numerous articles on response to illness and quality of life.

GORDON H. DEFRIESE is Professor of Social Medicine and Epidemiology and Director of the

Health Services Research Center at the University of North Carolina at Chapel Hill. He received his Ph.D. from the Department of Behavioral Science at the University of Kentucky School of Medicine. His work has mainly focused on primary health care, health promotion and disease prevention, health manpower research, and health services research and program evaluation.

BRUCE P. DOHRENWEND is Chief of the Department of Social Psychiatry at the New York State Psychiatric Institute and Professor in the Department of Psychiatry and the School of Public Health at Columbia University. His Ph.D. is from Columbia University. He is the coauthor of *Social Status and Psychological Disorder* and has written several other books and a number of articles on related matters.

JO ANNE EARP is Associate Professor of Health Behavior and Health Education at the School of Public Health of the University of North Carolina at Chapel Hill. She received her Doctor of Science degree from The Johns Hopkins School of Hygiene and Public Health. A medical sociologist, Earp has published numerous articles on the influence of social factors in chronic and acute illness among children and adults. Her major research interests are social support and women's health.

CARROLL L. ESTES is Professor and Chair of the Department of Social and Behavioral Sciences and Director of the Institute for Health and Aging at the University of California at San Francisco. Her Ph.D. is from the University of California at San Diego. She is the author and coauthor of several books and numerous articles on health policy, aging, long-term care, and medical sociology, including *The Aging Enterprise, Long-Term Care of the Elderly*, and *Political Economy, Health and Aging*.

HOWARD E. FREEMAN is Professor and Chair of the Department of Sociology at the University of California at Los Angeles, where he formerly was Director of the Institute for Social Science Research. Previously, he was associated with Brandeis University, the Ford Foundation, and a number of other universities and foundations. He received his Ph.D. from New York University. Freeman evaluates health care programs and studies access to medical services.

EUGENE B. GALLAGHER is Professor in the Departments of Behavioral Science and Sociology at the University of Kentucky. His Ph.D. is from Harvard University. In addition to health professional education, his current interests focus on health services in developing societies and the psychosocial aspects of chronic renal disease.

THOMAS A. GLASS is a Doctoral Fellow with the Veterans Administration Health Services Research and Development Field Program at Duke University. He has done research on long-term care, rehabilitation from chronic illness, and the impact of social support networks on recovery from serious illness.

SUSAN GORE is Associate Professor of Sociology at the University of Massachusetts in Boston. Her Ph.D. is from the University of Pennsylvania. The author of many papers on life stress and support systems, she is currently conducting a study of adolescent stress and its mental health effects.

MERWYN R. GREENLICK is Director of the Kaiser Permanente Center for Health Research and Vice President (Research) of Kaiser Foundation Hospitals in Portland, Oregon. He has directed a number of major research and demonstration projects since founding the center in 1964, including an Office of Economic Opportunities neighborhood health center at Kaiser Permanente, a clinical center for the NIH's multiple risk factor intervention trial (MRFIT) for heart disease prevention, one of the original Medicare capitation demonstrations, and currently the Social HMO demonstration site in Portland.

HOWARD B. KAPLAN is Professor of Sociology and Marshall Endowed Professor of Liberal Arts at Texas A & M University. His Ph.D. is from New York University. He is the author of *Social Psychology of Self-Referent Behavior, Patterns of Juvenile Delinquency*, and numerous books and articles on mental illness, deviant behavior, and medical sociology. Kaplan is also the editor of *Psychosocial Stress: Trends in Theory and Research*.

RONALD C. KESSLER is Professor of Sociology and Program Director of the Institute for Social Research at the University of Michigan. His Ph.D. is from New York University. He is the coauthor of *Television and Aggression* and has written numerous papers on the social determinants of emotional disorders.

PHILLIP R. KLETKE is a Research Associate at the Center for Health Policy Research of the American Medical Association. He received his Ph.D. from the University of Chicago. He is the coauthor of *The Demographics of Physician Supply: Trends and Projections* and *Medicaid and Pediatric Primary Care* and has written other articles on physician manpower.

SOL LEVINE is Vice President for New Program Development at the Henry J. Kaiser Family Foundation. He is on leave from his position as University Professor and Professor of Sociology and Public Health at Boston University. He received his Ph.D. from New York University in 1953. Levine is the author of a large number of books and articles on such topics as social stress, psychosocial factors in coronary heart disease, and health care and quality of life.

DONALD W. LIGHT is Professor of Psychiatry at the University of Medicine and Dentistry of New Jersey and Professor of Sociology at Rutgers University. His essay here is from a forthcoming book on the American health care system that is part of a comparative historical project on the relations between profession, state, political economy, and values. The first volume in this project, *Political Values and Health Care: The German Experience*, was a joint research venture with Alexander Schuller and was published by the M.I.T. Press in 1986.

BRUCE G. LINK is Assistant Professor of Public Health (Epidemiology) at Columbia University. His Ph.D. in sociology is from Columbia University. He is the coauthor of *Mental Illness in the United States: Epidemiological Estimates* and has written a number of papers on the influence of social factors on the etiology and course of mental disorders.

JOHN D. LOFT is Assistant Director in the Division of Survey and Data Resources of the American Medical Association. His Ph.D. is from the University of Chicago. He is the coauthor of *Foreign Medical Graduates* and has written several papers and reports on the medical profession and on survey research methodology.

GEORGE L. MADDOX is Professor of Sociology and of Medical Sociology (Psychiatry) and Chair of the University Council on Aging and Human Development at Duke University. He is the editor-in-chief of *The Encyclopedia of Aging* and the author or editor of numerous books and articles on epidemiological and socioeconomic aspects of human aging.

MARIE C. MCCORMICK is Associate Professor of Pediatrics in the Department of Pediatrics of the Joint Program in Neonatology between Childrens' Hospital of Boston and Harvard Medical School. This chapter was prepared while she was a member of the Departments of Pediatrics and Medicine at the University of Pennsylvania School of Medicine. Her research focuses on the evaluation of health services for children, with a special interest in low birth-weight infants, children with chronic illnesses, and disadvantaged children.

JOHN B. MCKINLAY is Professor of Sociology and Research Professor of Medicine at Boston University and Vice President and Director of the New England Research Institute. He also holds consulting and research posts at the Beth Israel and Massachusetts General Hospitals (Harvard Medical School). His Ph.D. is from Aberdeen University in Scotland.

SONJA M. MCKINLAY is President of the New England Research Institute and Associate Professor of Community Health at Brown University. Her Ph.D. is from Aberdeen University in Scotland. She is the author of many papers on statistics and epidemiology.

DAVID MECHANIC is Director of the Institute of Health, Health Care Policy, and Aging Research at Rutgers University and University Professor and the René Dubos Professor of Behavioral Sciences. He received his Ph.D. from Stanford University. He is the author of numerous books and other publications on health policy and health services research, including *From Advocacy to Allocation: The Evolving American Health Care System* (1986); *Mental Health and Social Policy* (3rd ed., 1988); *Medical Sociology* (2nd ed., 1978); and *Future Issues in Health Care: Social Policy and the Rationing of Medical Services* (1979). Mechanic is a former member of the National Advisory Council on Aging of the NIH and Chairman of the council's Program Committee. He is a member of the Institute of Medicine of the National Academy of Sciences and former Chair of the Section on Social, Economic, and Political Sciences of the American Association for the Advancement of Science.

ROSS M. MULLNER is Associate Professor and Director of the Center for Health Services Research at the School of Public Health at the University of Illinois at Chicago. His Ph.D. is from the University of Illinois at Urbana-Champaign. He has written over 80 articles on various health care topics.

JACKOB M. NAJMAN is Senior Lecturer in the Departments of Anthropology and Sociology and Social and Preventive Medicine at the University of Queensland, Australia. He received his Ph.D. from the University of New South Wales. Najman, who has published widely in the fields of social epidemiology and medical sociology, is the coeditor of *A Sociology of Australian Society: Introductory Readings* and the forthcoming *Health and Australian Society: Some Sociological Perspectives.*

IRWIN M. ROSENSTOCK is Family Health Plan Endowed Professor and Director of the Center for Health and Behavior Studies at the California State University at Long Beach. His Ph.D. is from the University of California at Berkeley. He is the coauthor of "Comparing Social Learning Theory and the Health Belief Model" (*Advances in Health Education and Promotion* 2:245–249, 1987) and has written many articles and book chapters on health care behavior.

C. MAUREEN SEARLE is Commercial Law Legal Assistant at the San Francisco law firm of Cooley, Godward, Castro, Huddleson, and Tatum. Having received a Ph.D. from Yale University, where she specialized in medical sociology, Searle worked in health policy analysis for several years. Her foray into the legal realm was prompted by a long-held interest in the paraprofessional role and a desire to experience it herself.

JAMES R. SORENSON is Professor and Chair of the Department of Health Education and Director of the Health Promotion and Disease Prevention Program at the School of Public Health at the University of North Carolina at Chapel Hill. His Ph.D. is from Cornell University. He is the coauthor of *In Sickness and in Health* as well as *Reproductive Pasts, Reproductive Futures: Genetic Counseling and Its Effectiveness*. In addition he has published numerous articles in medical, public health, and social science journals on a variety of medical, sociological and bioethical issues.

JUDITH P. SWAZEY is president of the Acadia Institute and Adjunct Professor of Public Health (Social and Behavioral Sciences) at Boston University. She obtained her Ph.D. from Harvard University. She is the coauthor of *The Courage to Fail* and *Reproductive Pasts, Reproductive Futures: Genetic Counseling and Its Effectiveness*. She has also published numerous articles in a variety of medical and social science journals on topics in biomedical research and medical care.

HOWARD WAITZKIN is Professor of Medicine and Social Sciences and Chief, Division of General Internal Medicine and Primary Care, at the University of California, Irvine. He received his M.D. and Ph.D. in sociology from Harvard University. He is the author of *The Second Sickness: Contradictions of Capitalist Health Care* and other publications on the medical social sciences, community medicine, and cross-national health policy.

STEVEN P. WALLACE is Assistant Professor of Sociology in the Gerontology and Public Policy Administration Programs at the University of Missouri in St. Louis. He received his Ph.D. from the University of California at San Francisco. Wallace is the author or coauthor of several articles, chapters, and policy papers on aging, health policy, and minority issues.

DIANA CHAPMAN WALSH is Professor of Behavioral Sciences at the Boston University School of Public Health and Associate Director of the Boston University Health Policy Institute. Her Ph.D. is from the University Professors Program at Boston University. Walsh's publications include *Corporate Physicians: Between Medicine and Management*, an eleven-volume series on industry and health care, and over 60 journal articles and book chapters related to health and health care.

CAMILLE B. WORTMAN is Professor of Psychology and Program Director in the Institute for Social Research at the University of Michigan. Her Ph.D. is from Duke University. She is the author of *Psychology* and has published numerous articles on stress, coping, and social support.

Name Index

Subject Index